Edited with an Introduction and Commentary by

STANLEY I. KUTLER

A TOUCHSTONE BOOK

Published by Simon & Schuster

ABUSE

of

POWER

THE NEW NIXON TAPES

For Alex and Kaitlin

TOUCHSTONE
Rockefeller Center
1230 Avenue of the Americas
New York, NY 10020

First Touchstone Edition 1998

TOUCHSTONE and colophon are registered trademarks
of Simon & Schuster Inc.

Designed by Carla Bolte

Manufactured in the United States of America

10 9 8 7 6 5 4 3 2 1

The Library of Congress has cataloged the Free Press edition as follows:

Abuse of power : the new Nixon tapes / edited with an
introduction and commentary by Stanley I. Kutler.
    p. cm.
  Includes index.
   1. Watergate Affair, 1972–1974.   2. Nixon, Richard M.
(Richard Milhous), 1913– . 3. United States—Politics and
government—1969–1974.   4. Sabotage—United States—
History—20th century.   I. Kutler, Stanley I.
E860.A26 1997   97-32096
973.924'092—dc21   CIP

ISBN 0-684-84127-4
    0-684-85187-3 (Pbk)

CONTENTS

INTRODUCTION

THE TAPES OF RICHARD NIXON

xiii

PART ONE

THE PENTAGON PAPERS AND OTHER "WHITE HOUSE HORRORS"

JUNE 1971 – JUNE 1972

1

EDITORIAL NOTE

The logistics of preparing these conversations for publication have been complicated and difficult. There are no transcriptions and the tapes cannot be removed from the National Archives at this time. Professional court reporters and transcribers prepared the initial transcripts. My research assistant and I then listened to the tapes to fill in significant gaps of "unintelligibles" and to insure accuracy as far as possible. The process of deciphering the tapes is endless. Different ears pick up a once-unintelligible comment, or correct a previous understanding. Such is the nature of the material. I am aware of my responsibility for accuracy, knowing I have compiled a historical record that others will use. Some might find occasional errors in the rendering of particular words, but I am confident that there is no distortion of the thrust or intent of the passages.

I edited the conversations with an eye toward eliminating what I believe insignificant, trivial, or repetitious. I have used ellipses to telescope many conversations and often have omitted dutiful choruses of agreement by those present unless I believed them particularly important. The dialogue of innumerable uses of "right," "yeah," "okay" often has been dropped. I have retained many of Nixon's phrases to reflect his manner of speaking, such as "you get my point" and "you know what I mean." That is the authentic Nixon, I believe. The "uhs" and "ahs" usually have been eliminated, except when I think that they reflect the uncertainty in various voices, particularly Nixon's. "Unintelligible" is used when I think that something important was said, but I could not capture it. Certain bracketed identifying references come from the official logs at the National Archives of the United States.

The rendition of spoken words into written ones has been a special challenge. Others have noted that there is nothing quite like Richard Nixon in his words; to listen to him on tape gives those words an even greater human, dramatic quality. I have tried to capture those qualities as much as possible by using italics, exclamations points, and, sometimes, bracketed phrases to describe emphasis and nuance.

When the first transcripts were published nearly a quarter-century ago, few could comprehend their meaning. Conversations were cryptic and vague, and some of the material was incomprehensible because of the lack of accompanying editorial apparatus. I hope that the headnotes, the identification of the various characters, and other editorial aids in this volume will help the reader.

There are three conversations in this volume that were previously published, and are included here because of their importance: June 23, 1972 (the "smoking gun" conversation), September 15, 1972 (a meeting with John Dean that gave the lie to Nixon's later version of events), and March 21, 1973 (the "cancer on the presidency" conversation). All three conversations are newly transcribed and edited.

CAST OF CHARACTERS

Richard M. Nixon, President of the United States

Robert Abplanalp, personal friend of the President

Richard Allen, National Security Council aide

Joseph Alsop, columnist

Jack Anderson, columnist

Dwayne Andreas, businessman, contributor to both Hubert Humphrey and Nixon

Leslie Arends, Congressman (R-IL), Minority Whip

Bobby Baker, former aide to Senator Lyndon Johnson; convicted of bribery

Howard Baker, Senator (R-TN), Vice Chairman, Senate Select Committee

Dita Beard, lobbyist for ITT

Carl Bernstein, *Washington Post* reporter

William Bittman, E. Howard Hunt's lawyer

Arthur Bremer, attempted assassination of George Wallace, May 1972

Patrick Buchanan, presidential aide

Stephen Bull, presidential aide

Alexander Butterfield, presidential aide; revealed taping system

Joseph Califano, former aide to Lyndon Johnson; close ties to Alexander Haig

Dwight Chapin, presidential aide

Anna Chennault, 1968 go-between for Nixon and the South Vietnam Government

Murray Chotiner, Nixon associate and aide since 1946

George Christian, LBJ press secretary; LBJ liaison with the Nixon Administration, 1972–73

Kenneth Clawson, White House Director of Communications

Charles Colson, presidential aide

John Connally, former Democratic Texas governor and later Nixon supporter

Archibald Cox, Special Prosecutor

CREEP, Committee to Re-elect the President

Kenneth H. Dahlberg, gathered money for Dwayne Andreas

Sam Dash, Majority Counsel, Senate Select Committee

John W. Dean III, Counsel to the President

Cartha DeLoach, FBI executive

Thomas Eagleton, Senator (D-MO); temporarily vice presidential candidate, 1972

John D. Ehrlichman, Counsel to the President and Chair of the Domestic Council

Daniel Ellsberg, former National Security official; leaked the Pentagon Papers

Sam Ervin, Senator (D-NC), Chairman, Senate Select Committee

Mark Felt, FBI executive

Fred Fielding, lawyer; assistant to Dean

Dr. Lewis Fielding, Daniel Ellsberg's psychiatrist

Robert Finch, Secretary of Health, Education, and Welfare; presidential aide

Leonard Garment, Counsel to the President

David Gergen, presidential aide

Billy Graham, evangelical leader; friend of the President

Katharine Graham, Publisher, *Washington Post*

L. Patrick Gray, Acting Director and later nominee for Director of FBI

Hank Greenspun, Las Vegas newspaper editor

Edward Gurney, Senator (R-FL); member, Senate Select Committee

General Alexander M. Haig, Jr., Chief of Staff to the President, 1973–1974; Haldeman's successor

H. R. (Bob) Haldeman, Chief of Staff to the President, 1969–1973

Morton Halperin, National Security Council aide

Seymour Hersh, *New York Times* correspondent

Lawrence M. Higby, Haldeman aide

J. Edgar Hoover, Director, FBI

E. Howard Hunt, Watergate burglar; recipient of hush money

Tom Charles Huston, presidential aide; author of inter-agency plan for domestic intelligence

Herbert Kalmbach, President's personal attorney; bagman for CREEP

Henry L. Kimelman, McGovern contributor

Henry A. Kissinger, Assistant to the President for National Security Affairs

Herbert G. Klein, first Director of Communications

Richard Kleindienst, Attorney General

Joseph Kraft, columnist

Egil (Bud) Krogh, co-leader of the Plumbers

Melvin Laird, Secretary of Defense; presidential aide, 1973–1974

Hobart Lewis, Editor-in-Chief, *Reader's Digest;* friend of the President

G. Gordon Liddy, planned (poorly) Watergate break-in; hush money recipient

Clark MacGregor, Chairman of CREEP following Mitchell's resignation

James McCord, Watergate burglar; Chief of Security for CREEP

George S. McGovern, Senator [D-SD]; 1972 Democratic presidential candidate

Jeb Stuart Magruder, Deputy to John Mitchell, Committee to Re-Elect the President

Mike Mansfield, Senator (D-MT), Majority Leader

Robert Mardian, Assistant Attorney General

Louis Marx, father-in-law of Daniel Ellsberg; friend of J. Edgar Hoover

John N. Mitchell, Attorney General; Chairman, Committee to Re-Elect the President

Martha Mitchell, wife of John, blamed by Nixon for Mitchell's failure to stop the Watergate break-in

Clark Mollenhoff, presidential aide

Richard Moore, presidential aide

Edward L. Morgan, presidential aide

F. Donald Nixon, the President's brother

Lawrence O'Brien, Chairman, Democratic National Committee

Paul O'Brien, lawyer for CREEP

Robert Odle, Director of Administration, CREEP

Thomas Pappas, Greek-American businessman who provided hush money payments

Kenneth Parkinson, lawyer for CREEP

Henry Petersen, Assistant Attorney General, DOJ Criminal Division

Kevin Phillips, Republican political strategist; columnist

Herbert L. Porter, Scheduling Director, CREEP

Raymond K. Price, Nixon speechwriter

Charles G. "Bebe" Rebozo, Nixon's friend and confidant

Elliot Richardson, Secretary of Defense; Attorney General

Charles Richey, U.S. District Court Judge

Nelson A. Rockefeller, Governor of New York

William Rogers, Secretary of State

William Ruckelshaus, Acting Director FBI; Deputy Attorney General

Manolo Sanchez, Nixon's manservant

Donald E. Santarelli, Justice Department lawyer; rival of John Dean

James Schlesinger, Director, CIA

Hugh Scott, Senator (R-PA), Minority Leader

Donald Segretti, a "dirty trickster" of minor notoriety

Charles Shaffer, John Dean's lawyer

Frank Shakespeare, campaign media adviser; head of USIA

David Shapiro, lawyer for Charles Colson

George Shultz, Secretary of the Treasury

Earl Silbert, U.S. Attorney who tried and convicted the burglars

John J. Sirica, U.S. District Court Judge

Hugh Sloan, Treasurer, Finance Committee to Re-Elect the President

George Smathers, former Senator (D-FL); Nixon supporter

Maurice Stans, Chairman, Finance Committee to Re-Elect the President

Gordon Strachan, White House aide, worked for Haldeman

William Sullivan, former FBI official, critic of J. Edgar Hoover

Helen Thomas, UPI White House reporter

Fred Thompson, Minority Counsel, Senate Select Committee

William E. Timmons, White House congressional liaison

Anthony Ulasewicz, former New York City detective; bagman for cover-up

Robert Vesco, accused securities manipulator; source for illegal money for CREEP

General Vernon Walters, Deputy Director of the CIA

Gerald Warren, Deputy Press Secretary

Lowell Weicker, Senator (R-CT); member Senate Select Committee

Caspar Weinberger, Director, Office of Management and Budget

Edward Bennett Williams, lawyer for Democratic Party and the *Washington Post*

Bob Wilson, Congressman (R-CA)

John Wilson, attorney for Haldeman and Ehrlichman

Rose Mary Woods, presidential secretary

Robert U. (Bob) Woodward, *Washington Post* reporter

Charles Alan Wright, Special Counsel to the President

David Young, co-leader of the Plumbers

Ronald L. Ziegler, Press Secretary to the President

INTRODUCTION

THE TAPES OF
RICHARD NIXON

The tapes of Richard Nixon's conversations with political intimates compel our attention as do few other presidential documents. Since we first learned of their existence in July 1973, the tapes have fascinated the American public. During Nixon's Watergate crisis, the nagging question centered on what the President knew about the break-in at the Democratic National Committee headquarters in the Watergate complex in June 1972 and the subsequent cover-up of White House involvement. The revelation that he had recorded his conversations made clear that this question could be answered—if the tapes were made public.

When Richard Nixon assumed the presidency in January 1969, he ordered Lyndon B. Johnson's recording system dismantled immediately. In February 1971, however, Nixon and his Chief of Staff, H. R. Haldeman, re-installed the system with substantial improvements, including voice-activated devices. For a long while, knowledge of its existence was confined to the President, Haldeman, and a Haldeman aide, Alexander Butterfield. Three, later four, Secret Service agents who serviced the system knew about it, but apparently not the Director of the Secret Service Presidential Protective Division. The system later was expanded beyond the Oval Office to include the President's hideaway office in the Executive Office Building, Camp David, the Cabinet Room, and White House and Camp David telephones.

The Watergate story reached an entirely new level on July 16, 1973, when Butterfield acknowledged to the Senate Select Committee that "there is tape in the Oval

Office." *"Everything"* was taped, he said. "[T]he President is very history-oriented and history-conscious about the role he is going to play, and is not at all subtle about it, or about admitting it." Reaction ranged from amazement to indignation to titillation. Senator Howard Baker's query, "What did the President know, and when did he know it?" could finally, apparently, be conclusively answered. Yet the fight that ensued over access lasted far longer than anyone imagined at the time. Only now can we return to Baker's question. The answer is conclusive: the President knew virtually everything about Watergate and the imposition of a cover-up, from the beginning. The new tapes painstakingly reveal his repeated maneuvers to deny that knowledge for more than a year and, in turn, tell us much about the man. Along the way, he has given the best, most authoritative account of his involvement in Watergate we are likely to get.

When the first tapes of less than forty hours were released in April 1974, they provided a rough outline of Nixon's "abuse of power" and "obstruction of justice"— the principal charges for his proposed impeachment. The charges made his position untenable and forced his resignation in August 1974, less than two years after his magnificent re-election. The tapes mortally wounded Nixon's presidency and sent many of his associates to jail.

We knew in 1974 that Nixon's archives contained a great deal more material, and after Nixon's resignation, the remaining tapes became an important prize for the historical assessment of his administration. Nixon himself launched a twenty-year campaign, determined to impress his own interpretation on that record. He wrote numerous books and articles, made carefully staged public appearances and, in general, sought to establish himself as an "elder statesman," both in the United States and abroad.

As part of that campaign, Nixon fought ferociously to gain control over the remaining tapes. He struggled so intensely, with such determination, because of his fear that the secret tapes would cripple his hopes for historical rehabilitation. In April 1996, twenty-two years after Congress had legislated the release of the tapes of Richard Nixon's presidential conversations "at the earliest reasonable date," nineteen years after the Supreme Court had upheld that law, nine years after the National Archives completed its processing and preparations for their public release, two years after Nixon's death, and after five years of litigation and mediation, the tapes were at last liberated from their archival purgatory.

As the result of a lawsuit brought by Public Citizen and myself, a binding agreement struck with the National Archives and the Nixon Estate, which provided that over a four-year period more than 3,700 hours of Nixon presidential tapes, tapes whose release Nixon had forcefully resisted to the end of his life, would at last be available to the public. The first segment, consisting of 201 hours, released in November 1996, centers on "Watergate," and in edited form comprises the material in this volume. Conversations begin in June 1971, covering the President's reaction to the publication of the Pentagon Papers, and end in July 1973, during the height of the Senate Select Committee's hearings, when knowledge of the taping system became public. The title, *Abuse of Power,* stems from a congressional mandate. The 1974 Presidential Recordings and Materials Preservations Act required the Archivist of the

United States to "provide the public with the full truth, at the earliest reasonable date, of the abuse of governmental power popularly identified under the generic term 'Watergate.' "

The early tapes had provided a brief glimpse into the character and quality of political morality and discourse in the Nixon White House. Before their release, the President had labored desperately to delete references to Jesus Christ, and changed "Goddamn" to "damn." Nonetheless, the President's congressional allies, his friends, and friendly columnists were appalled. Senate Minority Leader Hugh Scott called them "shabby, disgusting, and immoral"; even Vice President Gerald Ford found them "a little disappointing." William Safire, a longtime Nixon aide and by then a *New York Times* columnist, thought the conversations revealed a man "guilty of conduct unbecoming a President." The Rev. Billy Graham, a faithful supporter, could not "but deplore the moral tone implied," and was dismayed that "situational ethics" had infected the White House.

The new tapes amplify the crudities of thought and language of the first group. But they also more sharply reveal a President deeply and intimately involved in sometimes criminal abuses of power, both before and after the Watergate break-in. In 1974, the President's defenders in Congress demanded "specificity"—clearly documented examples —of presidential abuse of power and obstruction of justice. Their spirited efforts for Nixon did not carry the day, but they made an enormous, momentary impression. On August 5, however, the President, complying with the Supreme Court's order in *United States v. Nixon,* released transcripts of the "smoking gun" conversations of June 23, 1972, in which he and Haldeman talked about using the CIA to thwart the FBI investigation of the Watergate break-in. That revelation dissolved the President's remaining support and made his resignation both imperative and inevitable.

These new materials provide a massive, overwhelming record of Nixon's involvement and his instigation of obstruction of justice and abuse of power. They expose a level of culpability far greater than imagined twenty-five years ago. President Nixon knew from the outset that the investigation had to be contained to protect White House secrets—or "horrors," as Attorney General John Mitchell labeled them. Accordingly, he talked for more than a year about what he had done, and continued to do, as he instigated, in effect, a cover-up of the cover-up. "Specificity" is no longer lacking.

The year of events following the Watergate break-in is at the heart of this story. Prophetically, at the outset, Nixon and Haldeman discussed their special secret—the taping system—on June 20, 1972. The President thought that it "complicates things all over." Haldeman replied: "They say it's extremely good. I haven't listened to the tapes." And Nixon quietly said: "They're kept for future purposes."

The arrest of E. Howard Hunt, a former CIA operative, following the Watergate break-in, filled Nixon with foreboding. On June 22, 1972, Haldeman told Nixon that Hunt, who had been involved in the Watergate break-in, "is in the process of disappearing." The next day, Nixon remarked that Hunt had "done a lot of things." Meanwhile, the first cover-up appears at the same time when Nixon learned of an attempt to pin it all on G. Gordon Liddy ("Is Liddy willing?" Nixon queried). A year later (April 10), Nixon worried that Hunt would expose "an earlier venture"—meaning the Plumbers and their illegal activities. Typically, such insights alternated with the President's remarks about the "comic opera" and "stupid" overtones of the caper, as he called it. Haldeman warned him of the "various lines of interlinkage in the whole damn business" (June 26, 1972), obviously referring to past White House activities that had involved such men as Hunt. But from the outset, Nixon recognized the problem of, and the difficulty of maintaining, a cover-up. On June 29, 1972, he told Haldeman, "It's a time bomb"; the next day, he said: "You can't cover this thing up, Bob." The next month (July 19), he invoked memories of the Alger Hiss case (a favorite theme): "If you cover up, you're going to get caught." That day, too, Nixon and Ehrlichman discussed whether Magruder could take responsibility. The President was now involved in the specifics of testimony (July 19: "Can't he [Magruder] state it just a little different?"). He still hoped to keep Mitchell free from blame. Yet one by one, each such firewall would be breached in the coming year. By May 29, 1973, thoroughly exasperated, Nixon would claim that the cover-up, "the whole Goddamn thing, frankly, was done because it involved Mitchell."

Nixon knew of the cover-up from the start, as we well know from the famous "smoking gun" conversations of June 23, 1972. But he kept himself informed on the subject throughout the summer. He knew, despite later protestations of his ignorance of John Dean and his role, what his young counsel had been doing. Haldeman told him on July 20, 1972: "John Dean is watching it on an almost full-time basis and reporting to Ehrlichman and me on a continuing basis. . . . There's no one else in the White House that has any knowledge of what's going on there at all." That very day, Haldeman assured Nixon that the Department of Justice investigation was going "along the channels that will not produce the kind of answers we don't want produced." On obstruction of justice, the verdict of the tapes is clear.

Nixon often expressed admiration for Dean. Less than three weeks before Dean's famous March 21, 1973, "cancer on the presidency" discussion with Nixon, the President said: "Hell, I'm convinced that Dean is a pretty good gem. . . . [H]e's awfully smart. . . . [H]e thinks things through and all that. He's not cocky" (March 2, 1973). He told Dean on March 16 that "the problem is the cover-up." Still, it was necessary because "there's a hell of a lot of other crap going to hit" (April 28, 1973). A week after the March 21 meeting, Nixon said that Dean has "been a hero." Yet by April 25, the President told Attorney General Richard Kleindienst that Dean had ordered the break-in of Daniel Ellsberg's psychiatrist's office.

Nixon always denied that he knew of "hush money" payments until Dean told him in March. But these tapes give the lie to what Nixon called a "myth." On August 1, 1972, Haldeman reported that "Hunt's happy." "At considerable cost," the President said. But hastily added: "It's worth it, . . . [t]hey have to be paid. That's all there is to that." On January 3, 1973, Haldeman told Nixon: "Liddy we're taking care of in one way. We've got to be very careful to take care of [Jeb] Magruder the right way, in the other way." After Dean left the March 21 meeting, the President told his longtime, faithful secretary Rose Mary Woods that he "may have a need for substantial cash for a personal purpose,"—a "campaign thing," he added. Again, before the

March 21 meeting, Nixon acknowledged that his good friend, prominent Republican fundraiser Thomas Pappas "has raised the money." Haldeman responded by noting Pappas's great virtue: "And he's able to deal in cash . . ." (March 2, 1973). A few days later, on March 7, Nixon personally thanked Pappas for helping out "on some of these things that . . . others are involved in."

The climax of these tapes occurs with the conversations that led to the firing of Haldeman and Ehrlichman on April 30, 1973. On March 27, Haldeman had warned Nixon: "You fire everybody now, you send them to jail." Ehrlichman, meanwhile, continued to scheme to have John Mitchell take the fall for everyone regarding the break-in, while the cover-up would remain secret (April 14, 1973). Dismissing his aides was agonizing for Nixon. But on April 12, he had set his course: "We've got to think the unthinkable sometimes." After he dismissed his aides, the President's conversations on the night of April 30 are emotional, distraught, poignant, and sprinkled with his slurred words. "I love you," he tells Haldeman. A few days earlier, he told Ziegler: "It's all over, do you know that?"

The departure of Haldeman set the stage for the emergence of General Alexander Haig as Chief of Staff. Documentation for Haig's activities is hard to come by, as most of his papers remain closed in the Library of Congress (along with Henry Kissinger's). But the new tapes reveal much about the man and his role. The conversations of May 8–9 are classic expressions of bureaucratic maneuvering, as Haig consolidated his position, established control over the President's legal defense, excluded White House counsel Leonard Garment from effective access, and eased Haldeman away from the President. For Haig, the stakes are old-fashioned: Watergate, he tells Nixon on May 11, involves "good, strong Americanism versus left-wing sabotage." He knew how to exploit Nixon's cynicism. He wanted former Supreme Court Justice Arthur Goldberg as Special Prosecutor because he "is obnoxious and doesn't wear well with the people, which would be good for our point of view" (May 12, 1973). Near the end (July 12, 1973), Haig expressed his frustration with Watergate: "It's just like Vietnam, a strange place."

Nixon's jarring language about Jews recurs throughout the tapes. "Bob, *please* get me the names of the Jews, you know, the big Jewish contributors of the Democrats. . . . Could we please investigate some of the cocksuckers?" he told Haldeman on September 13, 1971. The next year, on October 20, he criticized a reporter and an FBI executive: "[T]hey're both Jews and that has nothing to do with it, but it at least gives you a feeling of the possible motivation deep down of the liberal leftists." An anti-Semite? Perhaps; though many of his admirers quickly retort that such expressions never were "operational," that nothing resulted from them. And, it is noted, some key Administration players were Jewish. Nixon also regularly belittled Harvard men, yet he was quick to have them in his Administration. Probably, what was at work here was that corrosive cynicism that pervaded Nixon's remarks—similar to his cynical exploitation of an opponent's endorsement of school busing while his Administration compiled an enviable record on school desegregation in the South, or when he boasted to Charles Colson on June 13, 1973, that "the blacks don't like" his choice for Director of the FBI, Clarence Kelley.

Nixon reminds us of his earlier history, with references to his role in the Hiss case and the firing of Sherman Adams, Dwight Eisenhower's chief of staff. He suggested reviving the virtually moribund House Committee on Un-American Activities following the Pentagon Papers incident. The Committee, he said on July 2, 1971, could investigate a spy ring, believing it could re-create the circus atmosphere of twenty years earlier. "[W]hat a *marvelous opportunity* for the committee. . . . [Y]ou know what's going to charge up an audience. Jesus Christ, they'll be hanging from the rafters. . . . Going after all these Jews. Just find one that is a Jew, will you. . . ." Comforting old thoughts never were too far behind. On March 29, 1973, Nixon defended his use of the "Plumbers," a group engaged in illegal operations, ostensibly to thwart "leaks." "This is national security. . . . We've got all sorts of activities because we've been trying to run this town by avoiding the Jews in the government because there were very serious questions [of leaks]."

The President needed his demons, his "enemies," in more familiar White House terms. First, there was Daniel Ellsberg, who had leaked the Pentagon Papers to major newspapers. "Try him in the press," Nixon told an aide on June 30, 1971. "We want to destroy him in the press." A few days earlier, on June 24, however, Nixon expressed a sneaking admiration for Ellsberg, wanting his own "Ellsberg, an Ellsberg who's on our side; in other words, an intellectual who knows the history of the times, who knows what he's looking for." Specifically, Nixon wanted a man to study records of past presidents and foreign affairs to reveal their shortcomings and failures.

The fact that the *New York Times* published the Pentagon Papers only fueled Nixon's anger. On July 1, 1971, after the Supreme Court allowed the newspaper to continue publication, Nixon the conspiracist responded: "Do you think, for Christ sakes, that the *New York Times* is worried about all the legal niceties? Those sons of bitches are killing me. . . . We're up against an enemy, a conspiracy. They're using any means. *We are going to use any means.* Is that clear?" That same day, he attacked the media in general. "We want somebody to be a [Joseph] McCarthy. . . . Is there another [Bob] Dole?" Then: "[T]he press now is putting their right to make money, to profit, to profit from publication of stolen documents under the First Amendment and that that overrides the right of an American who is fighting for his country. . . . [G]et into some of this material. Hit it and keep hitting and ream them and [send] letters to [the] editor embarrassing, you know, Senator[s]-elect. . . . I know how this game is played."

The creation and use of the Plumbers is, of course, at the center of abuse-of-power charges against the President. Shortly after the group broke into Ellsberg's psychiatrist's office in Los Angeles, Ehrlichman told the President on September 8, 1971: "We had one more little operation. It's been aborted out in Los Angeles which, I think, is better that you don't know about. But we've got some dirty tricks underway. . . . We've planted a bunch of stuff with columnists, some of which will be given to service shortly . . . about Ellsberg's lawyer, about the Bay of Pigs." Nixon always rationalized the break-in as a justifiable "national security" operation. His aide, Charles Colson, put his own gloss on such thinking, saying, "They weren't stealing anything, . . . they had broken and entered with an intent not to steal, [only] with an intent to obtain information" (July 19, 1972).

At the end, the conversations take on a funny, sad character when, for example, the President's friend Bebe Rebozo told the President about a supportive letter from the ex-Mayor of Jersey City, then a guest of the federal government at Leavenworth (June 12, 1973). (At the end, Nixon seemed comfortable only with Rebozo, Rose Mary Woods, and possibly Press Secretary Ron Ziegler.) Or Henry Kissinger solemnly reporting to the President that he now had the support of author Norman Mailer (July 12, 1973). Nixon assured his daughter (June 19, 1973) that Dean had nothing. He merely "was the carry-outer of this thing." Finally, and fittingly, in the last conversation here, Nixon urged Kissinger to "keep on fighting."

Altogether, we have a richer, more informed portrait of the only man to have resigned the presidency. The new tapes offer the best opportunity to view the "inner man," to capture him in different facets and moods—a man alternately resourceful and inept, exhilarated and depressed, combative and passive, prosaic and articulate, repetitive and informed, self-centered and empathetic, sometimes sad yet often comical. We have no known record of such unguarded and frank talk by any other president.

These conversations provide a rare glimpse of a president uninhibited by the restraints of public appearance, and capture him in moments alone with trusted confidants. Here, we have both exceptional candor and a practiced level of deceit; the display of a constant calculus of political considerations; the exhibit of raw, human emotions; and, above all, the revelations of extraordinary, illegal, seemingly unprecedented presidential behavior and power. These tapes are the bedrock in laying bare the mind and thoughts of Richard Nixon. They constitute a record of unassailable, historical documentation he cannot escape. There is nothing quite like them.

The Nixon tapes are, however, far from the whole of the record of the Nixon presidency. The National Archives and other depositories hold countless public and private documents essential to an understanding of Nixon's administration. Memoranda between Nixon and his top aides during the first two years of his presidency are basic for understanding the nature of his presidency, as well as for extraordinary insights into his motivation and behavior. But the Nixon tapes uniquely reveal the President's voice and perspective on extraordinary events. Other presidents taped conversations, but did so selectively, at their own initiative. Those tapes often seem contrived, even staged, and have had relatively little impact in shaping our knowledge or understanding of these men. The tapes of FDR, Truman, Eisenhower, Kennedy, and Johnson offer little prospect of similar importance. The Nixon tapes, on the other hand, are central to his history and his presidency.

Richard Nixon was a very complicated man. Essentially a loner, he was at the same time the most public of public men. Few leaders have eagerly exposed themselves to such scrutiny as did Richard Nixon. His countless appearances, through almost five decades on the public stage, and numerous writings, gave him extraordinary visibility, with all the inherent advantages—and risks. Whether it was the perspiration on his upper lip that betrayed his innate uneasiness with us, the maudlin sentimentality he invoked in his "Checkers" speech, the pride he displayed at his daughter's wedding, the unbounded joy of his triumphs, and the unspeakable burden of his dramatic defeats—this man exposed his multifaceted humanity in extraordinary, vivid ways. As he left the White House in August 1974, he recalled that he had been in the highest mountains and deepest valleys; he had known triumph and failure, with all of their accompanying exhilaration and exquisite pain.

These conversations reflect Nixon's most painful, difficult political and personal moments. He occasionally reveals the true extent of his and his aides' involvement in Watergate. He knows his vulnerability, he fears exposure, and he realizes that resignation is a very real possibility for at least a year prior to that event. A man of secrets, Nixon ironically revealed more about himself than any president before or since.

The conversations between the President, his closest aides, and occasional other visitors, like other conversations, often have a prosaic quality and, at times, are terribly repetitive. No doubt, too, some were contrived, since the taping system gave Nixon and his aides a chance to speak to posterity or to "make a record" of their own. In a May 10, 1973, conversation, for example, Haldeman told the President that they never met Dean in the famous September 15, 1972, meeting, and they strain to put their own interpretation on Nixon's meeting with Dean on March 21. Yet, at other times, recorded revelations contradict their public story and offer irrefutable evidence of impeachable instances of "abuse of power" and "obstruction of justice."

Here we have essential material that adds more details, more texture, to the portrait of the nation's 37th president. Nixon's scheming, lying, and worrying about what truths might be discovered or what must be covered up, is at the heart of these tapes. Some of the "sound bites" may be misleading. They must be understood in context; we must make allowance for hyperbole and distortion, even a lack of seriousness or an occasional light moment. Was Nixon, for example, really serious about having his men burglarize Republican headquarters and blame the Democrats? More importantly, from these conversations, an ongoing narrative emerges, between Richard Nixon and his closest aides, of the Watergate crisis as viewed from their perspective. Now, from a vantage point a quarter-century later, we can watch unfold the drama that engulfed, and then destroyed, the Nixon presidency, always through the focus of the man who insured his own self-destruction.

Read as narrative, these conversations have various themes and subjects. Long before the Watergate break-in, they reveal President Nixon's insatiable desire for more information, more intelligence, about his political foes. Nixon's interest in Democratic National Chairman Lawrence O'Brien, whether it was about his income taxes or his political activities, bears some comparison to Henry II's alleged grumbling about that "accursed priest," Thomas Beckett. We learn from these tapes more about the cover-up than was revealed in the famous "smoking gun" conversations of June 23, 1972. In particular, we have a much better understanding of the need for a cover-up to protect previous illegal White House activities, most notably the work of the "Plumbers." (Nixon had created the Plumbers just after the Pentagon Papers incident. The group, ostensibly designed to stop leaks, focused instead on surreptitious attacks on White House political opponents and anti-war figures.) Even comparatively minor White House peccadilloes had to be protected. John Ehrlichman told the President on March 16, 1973, that "we're not going to get the benefit of the doubt and it's going to make for juicy reading—[that we kept] track of a United States Senator [Edward Kennedy] in his off hours for nine months." And we learn much more than ever before about the care with which the cover-up was managed for another year. These transcripts vividly instruct us in how the President and his men manipulated and fought any investigation of their wrongdoing.

Throughout these conversations, Richard Nixon repeatedly describes the Watergate break-in as "stupid" (when he wasn't excusing it as "a minuscule crime unless you get something," or saying that breaking into Democratic headquarters is "no blot on a man's record"). All the more reason, then, to consider what may be the most fundamental question of all: if the break-in was stupid, if the Nixon campaign had such loyal soldiers as the Cuban burglars, Liddy, and Hunt, who were prepared to fall on their swords for the President (while being very well-compensated for such dedication, of course), then why not sacrifice them? Whether they pled guilty or sought a trial, the affair probably would have ended with their convictions, and Watergate might well have been consigned to the ashcan of history as merely a "third-rate burglary."

The decision to cover up now seems inevitable, even logical, considering the Administration's stake in the matter. But there was more at stake than insulating the President from the "White House horrors." Nixon had carefully nourished an image through a quarter-century of public life as an upstanding law-and-order advocate. Maintaining that image required distance from what he knew of past activities, as well as what he knew of the cover-up.

While John Dean still was his loyal lieutenant for the cover-up, the President told him on March 16, 1973: "You've got always to think in terms of the presidency and the President should not appear to be hiding and not be forthcoming. Do you know what I mean? . . . The problem is the cover-up, not the facts. . . . But you cannot have the President take the rap on a cover-up." At the outset, Nixon perceptively warned Haldeman that they could not "cover this thing up, Bob"; nine months later, perception turned to pessimism as Nixon sensed the futility of maintaining the cover-up. Perhaps it was a losing game, Haldeman suggested; "that's sort of my feeling," the President replied.

By May 1973, Nixon realized his presidency had suffered a devastating blow; worse yet, he knew he might have to resign or be impeached. The facts were there, waiting only to be uncovered by proper investigative authorities. Under mounting pressure, he recognized it was only a matter of time before it all imploded. Here he was involved in an even wider cover-up, one of covering up not only the original White House connection to the Watergate break-in, but a cover-up of that cover-up. This final effort was just too much of a burden, and the Nixon presidency collapsed in August 1974.

Nixon never could publicly admit his involvement in anything illegal. Speaking of the abortive Houston Plan that would have authorized illegal break-ins for domestic counter-intelligence programs, Nixon said, "Well, then to admit that we approved . . . illegal activities. That's the problem." At another time, he admitted, "I ordered that they use any means necessary, including illegal means, to accomplish this goal" (May 16, 1973). He then hastily added: "The President of the United States can *never* admit that." Most embarrassing of all probably was the break-in of the office of Ellsberg's psychiatrist, an action Nixon and his aides insisted was dictated by "national security" considerations, when, in fact, it was designed to discredit Ellsberg (who had leaked the Pentagon Papers). Nixon knew the truth: "I believe somehow I have to avoid having the President approve the break-in of a psychiatrist's office."

Nixon's inability to confront the truth about himself was institutional, as well as personal. He always was capable of a cool assessment of presidential power and the nature of the presidency. When Nixon expressed concern for his image, he also was aware of the president's symbolic place in the popular mind as "the government." Moral legitimacy is the chief prop for that role, and Nixon realized that his actions compromised the canons of civility that sustained such legitimacy. Nixon's dark conversations with Colson, his knowledge of Hunt and the Plumbers, and his willingness to use the Internal Revenue Service as a weapon in his political shadow world—all amply documented here—undermined his own pride in the presidency, and what it should be. No wonder, then, that he had to keep the underside of his presidency from any public view or revelation.

Nixon had numerous opportunities to admit publicly his deep involvement in Watergate. Until the last few months, such action probably would have saved his presidency. Despite intense criticism of his administration, it is doubtful that until the summer of 1974 many Americans favored destroying it. But for Nixon to have confessed his sins would have required a degree of self-examination that he simply could not and would not do. The contradiction between his carefully nurtured public self-image of a law-and-order purist and the reality of his actions again was simply too much for him to bear. Of course there is a sense of the tragic to Watergate and Nixon's resignation, but what is really the stuff of drama is that Richard Nixon allowed these things to happen. The tragedy is that he knew they were wrong, as he often acknowledged in these conversations; still, he could not, or would not, prevent them.

After dismissing Haldeman and Ehrlichman on April 30, 1973, under a cloud of criminal accusations, Nixon lost his last line of defense. Despite his bravado, Nixon sensed that he now was the target. As his men left or defected, the "White House horrors" of pre-Watergate days were exposed for all to see and judge. Nixon knew the danger, and by then realized that the assault on him had the certain outcome of either executive paralysis, at best, or defeat and humiliation, at worst. What tipped the balance between the two, of course, was the revelation of the taping system. And that makes all the more compelling the old question: why didn't Nixon destroy the tapes?

Much has been made about the conflicting advice surrounding Nixon on this issue. Some of his lawyers insisted that it would be an obstruction of justice to destroy the tapes once their existence was known; on the other hand, John Connally and Nelson A. Rockefeller supposedly advised burning them. Haig reasoned that destroying the tapes would heighten suspicions of presidential guilt, and Nixon readily concurred, realizing that revelations of wrongdoing would be easier to control than the taint of having destroyed evidence. Pat Nixon reportedly could not understand why her husband did not destroy them. Nixon had told his daughter Tricia that the tapes contained nothing damaging, yet he might be impeached because of their content. "Because he has said the latter," she wrote in her diary, "knowing Daddy, the latter is the way he really feels." How odd that, for a man who adamantly insisted on controlling his papers and materials, both during his presidency and for twenty years afterward, we fail to consider Nixon's wishes on the matter.

When the Senate Select Committee and the Special Prosecutor immediately sought access to the tapes in July 1973, the likelihood of forcing the President to reveal his private conversations seemed remote, even incomprehensible. Nixon believed that the vague, but useful, defense of executive privilege provided adequate protection against any legislative or judicial demands for the tapes. Of course, as time went on, and the prospect that the tapes contained incriminating evidence loomed larger and more significant, such demands took on increased legitimacy. But at all times, Richard Nixon had to realize the value of those tapes, and it was unlikely he would destroy them.

First, the tapes had monetary value, which could only increase in time. Nixon's pursuit of his property interest in his public papers was dear to his heart and is a well-documented story. But he also has given us a better explanation of their real value to him: their usefulness in writing his own history of his presidency. Nixon believed that carefully selected excerpts from the tapes could exonerate him in the Watergate matter. After Nixon's fateful meeting on March 21 with Dean, Haldeman listened to the taped conversation on several occasions. We learn in these new tapes that the former chief of staff assured Nixon how that conversation could be interpreted in a favorable light. But beyond any specific meeting, Nixon thought his tapes would insure his control of his own history. In a tantalizing passage in his memoirs, Nixon revealed the most deep-seated of his motives. The tapes, he wrote, "were my best insurance against the unforeseeable future. I was prepared to believe that others, even people close to me, would turn against me just as Dean had done, and in that case the tapes would give me at least some protection."

In the end, instead, Nixon's tapes convicted him. He told an interviewer in 1977, "I brought myself down. I gave them a sword. And they stuck it in." Yet, he characteristically added, "And, I guess, if I'd been in their position, I'd have done the same thing." These tapes reveal anew his tragic quality of self-destruction, and they remind us all too clearly of who and what Richard Nixon was.

THE PENTAGON PAPERS AND OTHER "WHITE HOUSE HORRORS"

JUNE 1971 – JUNE 1972

The taping system was installed in the Oval Office in February 1971, and then in other parts of the White House, and the telephone system in April. We have a few "abuse of power" conversations for May, but after June, they significantly increase in number.

On Sunday morning, June 13, 1971, the *New York Times* featured front-page coverage of Tricia Nixon's Rose Garden wedding of the day before. The front page also prominently displayed a first installment of the "Pentagon Papers," a classified 7,000-page document commissioned by former Defense Secretary Robert S. McNamara. Daniel Ellsberg, a disillusioned national security intellectual and official, now a prominent antiwar activist, had leaked the papers to the newspaper. The study traced the origins and progress of the Vietnam War, and threw considerable light on the difference between public knowledge of events and the government's actual conduct of the war. By 1971, the papers offered not only historical lessons for the foreign policy and military establishments, but also political opportunities for future administrations. Melvin Laird, Nixon's Defense Secretary, told the President that 98 percent of the documents could be declassified, but the President in a note insisted that "the era of negotiations can't succeed w/o secrecy."

The Pentagon Papers involved the Kennedy and Johnson Administrations, and some Nixon aides have claimed that the President initially was inclined to let his opponents suffer embarrassment. According to this line, Henry Kissinger sparked Nixon's anger and spurred him to various repressive actions, including a court test. Nixon, however, regarded unauthorized leaks of internal government papers as a personal affront to his notions of presidential authority; as the following conversations indicate, he did not need others to prod him into lashing out at his "enemies." Leaks had upset the President quite a number of times, and have to be understood in the context of other incidents, including the Administration's so-called "tilt" to Pakistan in late 1971, information about SALT negotiations, the bombing in Cambodia, and the Paris peace talks with North Vietnam. For his efforts, Ellsberg won a featured place in Nixon's pantheon of demons, alongside such luminaries as the Kennedys and Lawrence O'Brien, as conversations over the next two years indicated.

The Pentagon Papers incident brought forth the creation of the Special Investigative Unit, more familiarly known as the "Plumbers." This group engaged in numerous illegal activities for the Administration, the most notorious being the break-in at the offices of Daniel Ellsberg's psychiatrist. Nixon and his aides to the end justified the action as a "national security" necessity when, in truth, the action was devised to secure unfavorable information about Ellsberg.

These conversations for the year preceding the Watergate break-in also include the President's ongoing concern with using the Internal Revenue Service for his political and personal purposes. Other conversations show the President's involvement in various schemes to advance his re-election bid and to undermine the candidacy of others, especially Senators Edmund Muskie and Edward Kennedy. At this time, the President already is familiar with E. Howard Hunt and John Dean, persons who will have important ties to him in the future.

June 17, 1971: The President, Haldeman, Ehrlichman, and Kissinger, 5:17–6:13 P.M., Oval Office

A few days after the publication of the Pentagon Papers, Nixon discusses how to exploit the situation for his advantage. He is interested in embarrassing the Johnson Administration on the bombing halt, for example. Here, he wants a break-in at the Brookings Institution, a centrist Washington think tank, to find classified documents that might be in the Brookings safe.

HALDEMAN: You maybe can blackmail [Lyndon B.] Johnson on this stuff [Pentagon Papers].

PRESIDENT NIXON: What?

HALDEMAN: You can blackmail Johnson on this stuff and it might be worth doing. . . . The bombing halt stuff is all in that same file or in some of the same hands. . . .

PRESIDENT NIXON: Do we have it? I've asked for it. You said you didn't have it.

HALDEMAN: We can't find it.

KISSINGER: We have nothing here, Mr. President.

PRESIDENT NIXON: Well, damnit, I asked for that because I need it.

KISSINGER: But Bob and I have been trying to put the damn thing together.

HALDEMAN: We have a basic history in constructing our own, but there is a file on it.

PRESIDENT NIXON: Where?

HALDEMAN: [Presidential aide Tom Charles] Huston swears to God there's a file on it and it's at Brookings [Institution, a centrist Washington "think tank"].

PRESIDENT NIXON: . . . Bob? Bob? Now do you remember Huston's plan [for White House–sponsored break-ins as part of domestic counter-intelligence operations]? Implement it.

KISSINGER: . . . Now Brookings has no right to have classified documents.

PRESIDENT NIXON: . . . I want it implemented. . . . Goddamnit, get in and get those files. Blow the safe and get it.

HALDEMAN: They may very well have cleaned them by now, but this thing, you need to—

KISSINGER: I wouldn't be surprised if Brookings had the files.

HALDEMAN: My point is Johnson knows that those files are around. He doesn't know for sure that we don't have them around.

June 23, 1971: The President and Haldeman, 11:39 A.M.–12:45 P.M., Oval Office

Nixon and Colson consider infiltrating one of the peace groups. Then, the President and his Chief of Staff discuss old-fashioned, but proven, fundraising methods.

SEGMENT 1

HALDEMAN: One of the best breaks is if this peace group or antiwar—can be infil-trated, can be shown to be a radical revolutionary group and they're taking stolen top secret documents and peddling them around. That shifts the whole focus of the case.

PRESIDENT NIXON: Can you get at that?

HALDEMAN: Yes, sir. We're working this—

SEGMENT 2

PRESIDENT NIXON: Oh, I've got to tell you one thing. Ambassador to Brussels, that hasn't been promised to anybody, has it?

HALDEMAN: No.

PRESIDENT NIXON: Bebe [Charles Rebozo] says Winston Guest. He's the former ambassador to Ireland with Kennedy. He says he believes—he says—

HALDEMAN: Raymond Guest.

PRESIDENT NIXON: Raymond, Ambassador Raymond Guest will give a half a mil-lion or what do you suppose he wants to hear about that? Well, anyway, I'm sure that he's talking about a quarter of a million at least because he gave 100,000 last time out in '65. . . . Now, he can be the ambassador to Brussels. Find out when [John] Eisen-hower leaves. He's fine. His wife speaks French. . . . [M]y point is that anybody that wants to be an ambassador, wants to pay at least $250,000.

HALDEMAN: I think any contributor under 100,000 we shouldn't consider for any kind of thing except just some nice—

PRESIDENT NIXON: That's right. Like, Fred Russell who was a big contributor we know. But from now, the contributors have got to be, I think [big contributors], and I'm not going to do it with, quote, *political* friends and all the rest of this crap where we've got to give them to good old Bill. . . . Now when he [Charles Bluhdorn] goes, I want him to be bled for a quarter of million, too. He's got that kind of money.

HALDEMAN: It ought to be more than that.

PRESIDENT NIXON: You're talking about 100,000. That's ridiculous. We play his games. It'll be worth a quarter of a million to just listen to him that long.

JUNE 24, 1971: THE PRESIDENT, HALDEMAN, AND ZIEGLER, 9:38–10:09 A.M., OVAL OFFICE

In the wake of the Pentagon Papers revelations, Nixon demanded that someone co-ordinate a scheme for declassifying older documents, dating back to World War II and Korea, as well as Vietnam. While he was furious about the leak of the Pentagon Papers, he plans his own leak to reveal embarrassing failures or shortcomings in foreign policies under his predecessors. He wants his own "Ellsberg who's on our side."

PRESIDENT NIXON: God, wait until these World War II things come out now we've got—I've got some more—done some more thinking on that. We've got to get a bet-ter team on it. . . .

HALDEMAN: That's right.

PRESIDENT NIXON: It will have to take about twelve guys under somebody a little bit more responsible, but he's [Tom Charles Huston] a son of a bitch. I mean, Bob, you get all this stuff. Do you realize that? We can get it all.

HALDEMAN: Yeah.

PRESIDENT NIXON: Well, we're going to expose them. God, Pearl Harbor and the Democratic party will—they'll have gone without a trace if we do this correctly. Who would you put in charge, Bob? . . .

HALDEMAN: That's what I'm trying to figure because—

PRESIDENT NIXON: You've got Colson doing too much, but he's the best. It's the Colson type of man that you need. . . . It will be very good to have somebody who knew the subject. I mean, what you really need is an Ellsberg, an Ellsberg who's on our side; in other words, an intellectual who knows the history of the times, who knows what he's looking for.

HALDEMAN: Okay. Well, then I know who to go to.

PRESIDENT NIXON: Yeah. Who would you use?

HALDEMAN: [National Security Aide Richard] Dick Allen.

PRESIDENT NIXON: That's the guy. Allen's the guy. Put him in charge of it. He's the—you've got it named. That's exactly the man I want. . . . We just desperately need, I think, we need this guy, this declassification thing.

HALDEMAN: Dick Allen is the guy to do it. He's exactly what we're talking about. Why, all the sophistication—

PRESIDENT NIXON: I want Huston in on the team.

HALDEMAN: All right.

PRESIDENT NIXON: Because Huston will know what to look for. He knows a lot about intelligence. . . .

ZIEGLER: Allen will do a good job at this.

PRESIDENT NIXON: No. This guy is—don't go back to World War II, this first. The first things I want to go back to—I want to go to the Cuban missile crisis and I want to go to the Bay of Pigs.

HALDEMAN: Well, those are the ones that are most likely to get lost the fastest. . . . World War II stuff we can always get.

PRESIDENT NIXON: People are being—probably burning stuff and hiding stuff as fast as they can. A lot of this stuff will be gone. The bombing halt story, incidentally, is run into the Ellsberg thing and I think it's now time to get that out if it's any good for us.

HALDEMAN: Okay. Well, we got, as I told you, we've got that except Huston says there's three segments yet that aren't complete, but he's got the raw material. He can complete them. . . .

JUNE 29, 1971: THE PRESIDENT AND COLSON, 2:28–2:32 P.M., WHITE HOUSE TELEPHONE

The following two conversations reveal some of the President's responses to Daniel Ellsberg, the man who leaked the Pentagon Papers, and to Nixon's enemies in the foreign-policy establishment.

PRESIDENT NIXON: If you can get him [Daniel Ellsberg] tied in with some communist groups, that would be good. Jay [Lovestone, ex-communist, then a prominent AFL-CIO official] thinks he is but, of course, that's my guess that he's in with some subversives, you know.

JUNE 30, 1971: THE PRESIDENT, MITCHELL, AND KISSINGER, 2:55–3:07 P.M., OVAL OFFICE

PRESIDENT NIXON: Well, I want to get that out. . . . Don't worry about his [Ellsberg's] trial. Just get everything out. Try him in the press. Try him in the press. Everything, John, that there is on the investigation get it out, leak it out. We want to destroy him in the press. Press. Is that clear?

JUNE 30, 1971: THE PRESIDENT, HALDEMAN, MITCHELL, KISSINGER, ZIEGLER, AND MELVIN LAIRD, 5:17–6:23 P.M., OVAL OFFICE

E. Howard Hunt, of later fame with the "Plumbers" and the Watergate break-in, was no stranger to Nixon. Here, the President wants to use Hunt's talents for breaking into the Brookings.

PRESIDENT NIXON: . . . They [the Brookings Institution] have lot of material. . . . I want Brookings, I want them just to break in and take it out. Do you understand?

HALDEMAN: Yeah. But you have to have somebody to do it.

PRESIDENT NIXON: That's what I'm talking about. Don't discuss it here. You talk to [E. Howard] Hunt. I want the break-in. Hell, they do that. You're to break into the place, rifle the files, and bring them in.

HALDEMAN: I don't have any problem with breaking in. It's a Defense Department approved security—

PRESIDENT NIXON: Just go in and take it. Go in around 8:00 or 9:00 o'clock.

HALDEMAN: Make an inspection of the safe.

PRESIDENT NIXON: That's right. You go in to inspect the safe. I mean, *clean it up.*

JUNE 30, 1971: THE PRESIDENT AND HALDEMAN, 7:22–7:27 P.M., WHITE HOUSE TELEPHONE

The President is also aware of another useful young man on his staff—John Dean.

PRESIDENT NIXON: . . . I guess we don't have anybody on our staff that's working this sort of thing except [Tom Charles] Huston; is that right?

HALDEMAN: No. [John] Dean can and his group.

PRESIDENT NIXON: Well, do they understand how we want to play the game or can you tell them?

HALDEMAN: Uh-huh.

PRESIDENT NIXON: Do they know how tough it has to be played?

HALDEMAN: Yes.

PRESIDENT NIXON: Dean, you say? . . .

JULY 1, 1971: THE PRESIDENT, HALDEMAN, AND KISSINGER, 8:45–9:52 A.M., OVAL OFFICE

Within a week after the publication of the Pentagon Papers, the President had authorized the creation of a secret, special White House investigative unit to "stop security leaks and to investigate other sensitive security matters." Thus, Nixon called into being the "Plumbers," headed by Egil Krogh and David Young, and including E. Howard Hunt and G. Gordon Liddy. For Nixon, the Plumbers was his means of matching the tactics of his enemies and the deviousness of their conspiracy against him. On July 1, Colson asked Hunt in a telephone conversation, "Should we go down the line to nail the guy [Daniel Ellsberg] cold?" Hunt replied affirmatively. Earlier that day, Nixon elaborated on his other counterattacks against leakers, drawing on his own experience in the Alger Hiss case.

SEGMENT 2

PRESIDENT NIXON: Here's what I have in mind and I've got to get [Tom Charles] Huston or somebody fast, but either Huston or somebody like Huston fast. That's why the, you know, the Dick Allen thing. I think you've got to take Dick Allen on the mountaintop and see if he wants to handle this.

HALDEMAN: Who said that he didn't?

PRESIDENT NIXON: You didn't think he was the right guy. You wanted somebody that—John [Ehrlichman] didn't, I think, or somebody because he's too—

HALDEMAN: Well, Dick doesn't think he is. . . .

PRESIDENT NIXON: . . . This is what I want. I have a project that I want somebody to take it just like I took the Hiss case, the [Elizabeth] Bentley case, and the rest. . . . And I'll tell you what. This takes—this takes 18 hours a day. It takes devotion and dedication and loyalty and diligence such as you've never seen, Bob. I've never worked as hard in my life and I'll never work as hard again because I don't have the energy. But this thing is a hell of a great opportunity because here is what it is. I don't have direct knowledge of who the Goddamn leaker is and, you see—and here's where John will recall I don't—probably we don't have to tell him.

You probably don't know what I meant when I said yesterday that we won the Hiss case in the papers. We did. I had to leak stuff all over the place. Because the Justice Department would not prosecute it. Hoover didn't even cooperate. . . . It was won in the papers. John Mitchell doesn't understand that sort of thing. He's a good lawyer. It's hard to him. John Ehrlichman will have difficulty. But what I mean is we have to develop now a program, a program for leaking out information. We're destroying these people in the papers. That's one side of it. Had a gap in the conspiracy.

The other side of it is the declassification. Declassification. And then leaking to or giving up to our friends the stories that they would like to have such as the Cuban [invasion?]. Do you know what I mean? Let's have a little fun. Let me tell you what the declassification [of other administrations' papers] in previous years that helps us. It takes the eyes off of Vietnam. It gets them thinking about the past rather than our present problems. You get the point.

HALDEMAN: Yeah. Absolutely. . . .

PRESIDENT NIXON: . . . Now, do you see what we need? I need somebody. . . . I wish you could get a personality type, oh, like [John C.] Whitaker who will work his butt off and do it honorably. I really need a son of a bitch like Huston who will work his butt off and do it dishonorably. Do you see what I mean? Who will know what he's doing and I want to know, too. And I'll direct him myself. I know how to play this game and we're going to start playing it.

SEGMENT 3

PRESIDENT NIXON: When you get to Ehrlichman now, will you please get—I want you to find me a man by noon. I won't be ready until 12:30—a recommendation of the man to work directly with me on this whole situation. Do you know what I mean? I've got to have—I've got to have one—I mean, I can't have a high minded lawyer like John Ehrlichman or, you know, Dean or somebody like that. I want somebody just as tough as I am for a change. . . . These Goddamn lawyers, you know, all fighting around about, you know—I'll never forget. They were all too worried about the [Charles] Manson case. I knew exactly what we were doing on Manson. You've got to win some things in the press.

These kids don't understand. They have no understanding of politics. They have no understanding of public relations. John Mitchell is that way. John is always worried about is it technically correct? Do you think, for Christ sakes, that the *New York Times* is worried about all the legal niceties. Those sons of bitches are killing me. I mean, thank God, I leaked to the press [during the Hiss controversy]. This is what we've got to get—I want you to shake these (unintelligible) up around here. Now you do it. Shake them up. Get them off their Goddamn dead asses and say now that isn't what you should be talking about. We're up against an enemy, a conspiracy. They're using any means. *We are going to use any means.* Is that clear?

Did they get the Brookings Institute raided last night? No. Get it done. I want it done. I want the Brookings Institute's safe *cleaned out* and have it cleaned out in a way that it makes somebody else [responsible?].

SEGMENT 6

PRESIDENT NIXON: . . . Let me show you what happened [in the Hiss case]. I know who was against it. [Tom] Clark, who literally became a judge in the Supreme Court, Tom Clark was the attorney general. He's a good man actually. He even told me that he was against it. If I were called before a grand jury in New York and told to give up the fucking papers to the grand jury, I [would have] refused. . . . I said I will not give up papers to the Department of Justice because they're out to clear Hiss. I played it in the press like a mask. I leaked out the papers. I leaked everything, I mean, everything that I could. I leaked out the testimony. I had Hiss convicted before he ever got to the grand jury. And then when the grand jury got there, the Justice Department trying desperately to clear him and couldn't do it. The grand jury indicted him and then a good Irish U.S. attorney, [Thomas] Murphy, prosecuted him.

Now, why would I do that? I did that because I knew I was fighting people who had power and who'd go—the FBI didn't even play with it. Edgar Hoover, he didn't play with him until after they got the indictment and you just read that story of the Hiss case and mine [in *Six Crises*] . . . you'll see what I mean. It's true. . . .

Now, how do you fight this [Ellsberg case]? You can't fight this with gentlemanly gloves. You appear to be. Now Ehrlichman is going to go forward on this thing [declassification project] on this same basis. . . . The second point is that beyond that, though, I am taking charge of all the rest. And I am going to have it done by somebody other than Ehrlichman.

KISSINGER: You mean, like, the Cuban missile crisis?

PRESIDENT NIXON: I mean everything. I mean, we will leak—we're going to leak out bits and pieces of—first of all, there are two different things. The conspiracy. All at once we find with regard to the conspiracy there's going to be leaked to columnists and we'll kill these sons of bitches. This [NSC official, first name unknown] Cooke, I want to get him killed. Let him get in the papers and deny it.

KISSINGER: Well, I, frankly, think he ought to be fired, Mr. President. Cooke admits now he gave it to Ellsberg, but he says Ellsberg was working for the Rand Corporation and, therefore—

PRESIDENT NIXON: And, therefore, it was not as legal.

[Withdrawn item. National Security.]

KISSINGER: Cooke admits that he gave the papers to Ellsberg and then they'll be in the Washington press. . . .

PRESIDENT NIXON: . . . [W]hy does Elliot [Richardson] sit there and defend the son of a bitch.

KISSINGER: I must say, Mr. President, it's inexcusable. He ought to be out by the end of the day today and Ellsberg—anyone who gives a paper to Ellsberg.

PRESIDENT NIXON: No. I'm not satisfied with this Cooke thing. I personally think he should be out. I will not talk to Elliot about it. Now you try to work it out any way you can. If he does not want him out, then I want you to find a way to get the story out on him. Now, do you understand what I'm talking about, Bob?

All right. Get Colson in. Get a story out and get one to a reporter who will use it. Give them the facts and we will kill him in the press. Is that clear? And I play it gloves off. Now, Goddamnit, get going on it.

JULY 1, 1971: THE PRESIDENT, HALDEMAN, COLSON, AND EHRLICHMAN, 10:28–11:49 A.M., OVAL OFFICE

On June 30, the Supreme Court ruled against the government's attempt to enjoin the publication of the Pentagon Papers. This setback further embittered Nixon and intensified Nixon's demands to pursue leaks and to embarrass the "establishment" by exposing their "secrets." He wanted, he said, "somebody to be a [Joe] McCarthy" or "another [Bob] Dole." Perhaps remembering Nixon's own history, Haldeman responded that a "sonofabitch could make himself a Senator overnight."

SEGMENT 1

PRESIDENT NIXON: What I need—I want a man in this White House staff who's full time on the two things. Why don't we just get [Tom Charles] Huston because I can't think of anybody else?

HALDEMAN: Oh, we probably can.

PRESIDENT NIXON: Is he adequate for it?

HALDEMAN: I don't know.

PRESIDENT NIXON: That's the problem. . . . I know you can. You can do it but you're only part time. Ehrlichman is half time. Colson is half time. Everybody else. I need one man directly responsible to me that can run this. I know how to—this has got to be one that's fought in the newspapers and in the paid television.

The difficulty is that all the good lawyers around here—Dick Moore, John Ehrlichman, and, of course, Mitchell even more so—they always saying, well, we've got to win the court case through the court. We're through with this sort of court case. It's our position—I don't want that fellow Ellsberg to be brought up until after the election. I mean, just let—convict the son of a bitch *in the press. That's the way it's done.* . . . Nobody ever reads any of this in my biographies. Go back and read the chapter on the Hiss case in *Six Crises* and you'll see how it was done. It wasn't done waiting for the Goddamn courts or the attorney general or the FBI. . . . We have got to get going here. . . .

HALDEMAN: It's definitely a moot position and all that. Don't you have a better chance of getting it done? If you get a creep like Huston in the woodwork or any other creep that we'd get in the woodwork here, what can he do? He can't do what you did in the Hiss case. He can't move it to the papers.

PRESIDENT NIXON: I know. I'm not even talking about moving it. Colson can move it to the papers. That doesn't bother me a bit.

HALDEMAN: Not very well.

PRESIDENT NIXON: Here's what I'm concerned about. Or he can move it to a congressman. The difficulty that I'm seeing right now is *getting the facts* to move to the papers. That has to be done by a man directed, and how do you get the facts. Who's going to break into the Brookings Institute? Who's going to go out, for example, and pull all this—the strength of this conspiracy to get this? I mean, Laird's got lots—he said there's a conspiracy. (Unintelligible.)

Who is pulling that together in one place, not with one of these Goddamn things that will come up six months from now? Who, for example, is going to be in charge of looking over the Pentagon Papers—not Pentagon Papers—but the papers on the Cuban missile crisis, on the Bay of Pigs, on World War II, and Korea? Who the hell is doing that and pulling out everything that might embarrass members of the establishment. You see? Who's going to do that. That can't be done by [Congressman] John Rousselot [R-CA]. That's got to be done by—that's what I mean, Bob. I need a man—a commander—an officer in charge here at the White House that I can call when I wake up, as I did last night, at 2:00 o'clock in the morning and I can say I want to do this, this, this and this. Get going. See my point?

And a guy, also, who will have the initiative to go out and do a few of these things. Now, we don't have the set-up at the present time. You've got—in this place—you've got at least ten magnificent soldiers and no captain. Everybody has an idea that they can send me in manual memoranda, this and that. There's no captain of them on this source. Somebody has got to pull this together. John can't do it. John Ehrlichman can't. He's got too much to do. Do you know what I mean? He's got to go back and we've decide whether we're going to pollute Lake Erie or some damn thing, or what we're going to do about the educators, what we're going to do about health, all of which are important.

But, you see, for better or worse, he could do it if he didn't have anything else to do. But I need somebody that's capable as Ehrlichman or Colson, for that matter, who *full time* will recognize that this is his job. You see, that's what we need. But all of us can put in our little ideas. You need a guy in the Congress. I agree. Rousselot will be fine. He's mean, tough, ruthless. He'll lie, do anything. That's what you need.

HALDEMAN: The other guy might be [Congressman James] McKevitt, if he will do all those things.

PRESIDENT NIXON: I'm not sure McKevitt is conservative enough. He's been a prosecutor. The question is, is he conservative?

HALDEMAN: That's the advantage of Johnnie [Rousselot]. You know he's conservative.

PRESIDENT NIXON: He's a [John] Bircher.

COLSON: Conservative.

PRESIDENT NIXON: How about that fellow [Congressman Philip] Crane [R-IL]? Can he do it? No. He's a talker. . . .

COLSON: He's not a doer. What about [Congressman John] Ashbrook [R-OH]? Is Ashbrook—

PRESIDENT NIXON: No. He's not reliable.

HALDEMAN: We trust Ashbrook. You can trust Rousselot.

PRESIDENT NIXON: Mainly, because he wants to get ahead. Well, you can use both Rousselot and the other for that matter. . . . [B]ut he [Rousselot] gets hot.

HALDEMAN: Can't really worry about that. If the guy is saying sensational enough stuff, it's trying to get stirred up in the papers. You're in the old McCarthyism business.

PRESIDENT NIXON: That's right. We want somebody to be a McCarthy. Is there a senator?

KISSINGER: . . . There's no one.

PRESIDENT NIXON: [Bob] Dole could have done it if he were still there. Is there another Dole?

COLSON: [Congressman William] Brock [R-TN] might come closest.

PRESIDENT NIXON: No. Brock is not another McCarthy.

HALDEMAN: A congressman has such a great opportunity with this.

PRESIDENT NIXON: That's right. Bob is right.

HALDEMAN: You take a pipsqueak like McKevitt or Rousselot that nobody has ever heard of, you can make—sonofabitch could make himself a Senator overnight.

PRESIDENT NIXON: . . . Well, coming back to the point, though, especially (unintelligible), I said—I said to you, Bob—I said to Bob a moment ago that at least Colson's prediction about the—last night I asked him on the phone about the progress we've had, about the coverage and so forth. I said, I wonder how (unintelligible) will play this. And I said I wanted to give the Kennedy private notes so they have to. You were right. They really gave it a hell of a (unintelligible). The networks—That's really real juicy stuff to them.

COLSON: It sure is. That's not a one-day story. That's a continuing thing. That's—

[Withdrawn item. National security.]

PRESIDENT NIXON: . . . Well, anyway I come back to the proposition that I need—do you see what I mean? I need an officer in charge and I don't what—I just want—it's actually—it could be you. It could be Colson. It could be Ehrlichman. You're the only ones in the White House staff that have the—

HALDEMAN: It could be Dick Allen.

PRESIDENT NIXON: Yes. Allen could be in it. I'm just not sure—we just don't need more for this, if Allen is willing to play, willing to do it. But another thing, it's got to be a guy, Bob—that's the other problem, and it is totally frustrating because I've got to talk to him very frankly about things that we want to do and I don't want him to make a record and go out and blast it later, well, the President ordered—do you know what I mean?

HALDEMAN: Well, that's why Huston is awful good, too.

PRESIDENT NIXON: I think Huston would die before he'd grab us.

HALDEMAN: And Huston knows more than anybody we've got around about where stuff is and what there is.

PRESIDENT NIXON: Can he get the others to get the work done? Well, he can use other help to do it.

HALDEMAN: That's the problem with Huston is—

PRESIDENT NIXON: Well, [the FBI, the CIA?] won't talk to him, probably Defense won't talk to him. There's your problem. Will they talk to Allen?

HALDEMAN: . . . I'm not so sure. He would know how to get it done. You could force it. They don't have to talk to him. If Huston—can't they do it in my name or Ehrlichman's name or Colson's name, something like that?

PRESIDENT NIXON: What I'd really like, basically, is Allen and Huston together. I'd really like the two of them to come in and then, if they would work together, and say, all right. Let's get to work here and let the two connive and screw around and just knock their brains out. But you get my point?

SEGMENT 2

PRESIDENT NIXON: In other words, our people should (unintelligible) that the press now is putting their right to make money, to profit, to profit from publication of stolen documents, that they have a constitutional right to profit—take this very carefully—from the publication of stolen documents under the First Amendment and that that overrides the right of an American who is fighting for his country. . . . John, you've got to get into some of this material. Hit it and keep hitting and ream them and [send] letters to [the] editor embarrassing, you know, Senator[s]-elect poison pen and so forth. I know how this game is played.

SEGMENT 3

PRESIDENT NIXON: Brookings has got tons of documents in safes over there. Now, we have got to start protecting the security of this government. Brookings and Rand, now Goddamnit, Haig hasn't done this—because Henry welshed on these, you know. He's a little afraid. He's got some friends at Brookings (unintelligible). But anyway, he said publicly—he told me he was for it. But he's dragging his feet or something. You've got to get this stuff from Rand and Brookings. John, you mop up. You're in charge of that. And I want it done today and I'd like a report—

SEGMENT 4

PRESIDENT NIXON: In view of this case, I want the new—look at it much deeper. I want them to give recommendations with regard to what can be done about World War II. What can be done about Korea. . . . This Goddamn thing hasn't come in here yet. Now where is the Cuban confrontation material? The Kennedy library has got it. Where is Pearl Harbor? Hyde Park has got it. Now, it's just ridiculous, John. And these are the things that will embarrass the creeps. Put it out.

SEGMENT 5

COLSON: The only thing I'm worried about with Huston is that—
PRESIDENT NIXON: He's a little difficult.
COLSON: And he picks the things that look good to him and you can't budge him if something doesn't look good to him and that's tough to get in. There's one guy on the outside that has this capacity and ideological bent who might be able to do all of this.
PRESIDENT NIXON: Who's that?
COLSON: He's a very close friend to [Senator] Jim Buckley's—

[Withdrawn item. National Security.]

He's hard as nails. He's a brilliant writer. He's written 40 books on [espionage?].
PRESIDENT NIXON: What's his name?
COLSON: His name is Howard Hunt. He's here in Washington now. He just got out of the CIA, fifty. Kind of a tiger. I don't know. You might want to—
PRESIDENT NIXON: How old is he?
COLSON: Fifty.
PRESIDENT NIXON: That's all right. He can do it. He may still have the energy.

COLSON: Ideologically, he is already convinced this is a big conspiracy.

PRESIDENT NIXON: I'd like to get Huston in and use him though. I mean, I agree Huston is difficult and this and that. But we'll order the sonofabitch to do what needs to be done. You can order him, can't you?

HALDEMAN: Not very well.

COLSON: Not very—

HALDEMAN: Huston—he really is—

PRESIDENT NIXON: All right.

HALDEMAN:—because he's great on the stuff he wants to be great on.

PRESIDENT NIXON: Arrogant little bastard.

COLSON: Well, he'd take a half an hour telling you why you shouldn't do something. It'd drive you up the wall.

PRESIDENT NIXON: All right. There must be people like that around we can get?

HALDEMAN: Dick Allen is convinced there are and that's why I would like to talk to him—

PRESIDENT NIXON: Do you know what? How about bringing [General] Vernon Walters back?

HALDEMAN: I was just thinking that myself once he mentioned the CIA because he's a spy kind of guy. . . .

PRESIDENT NIXON: I'm not sure he would play this—well, he would play this but I think he might want to—look, I don't want some guy who is going to try and second guess my judgment on this because I know more about it than any of them. I have forgotten more than anything they'll ever learn. This is a game. It's got to be played in the press. That's why Mitchell can't do this. It isn't possible for him.

HALDEMAN: It's got to be a guy you can really trust, because it's got to be—

PRESIDENT NIXON: Run from the White House without being caught. . . . The declassification is important, though. . . . But the important part about the declassification job is to get the information.

JULY 1, 1971: THE PRESIDENT AND HALDEMAN, 1:38–2:05 P.M., OVAL OFFICE

The President continues to complain about not being able to find people to dutifully carry out his orders.

HALDEMAN: . . . But I explored back with Colson, the guy he mentioned, this former CIA guy [Howard Hunt]. And I talked—I raised him with [Richard] Allen. . . . The problem there would be he's known in the intelligence establishment and you send out some waves. I said what the hell difference does that make. As soon as this guy gets started, he's going to send out waves no matter what. And he said, yeah. That's right.

PRESIDENT NIXON: But we have haven't. I still put down for consideration the possible pattern here of really putting the damn job—I just wonder if we should just put Colson in charge of it, and then putting in him—and put him in charge of the team. . . . I realize [Tom Charles] Huston is no good unless it's something that he really believes in. But couldn't you bring him in to put him in on what we've been—you did believe him, you know. And say, all right, now this is yours, Tom.

HALDEMAN: (Unintelligible) lone operator. You say, you bore in and don't come up for air until you've produced so and so.

PRESIDENT NIXON: . . . You're [Huston] going to do the declassification thing or something like the conspiracy thing.

HALDEMAN: . . . I just went through his files and he's done a damn good job on the bombing halt thing except he hasn't finished it. He didn't do the last three days. He says he's got all the stuff and he just didn't get around to doing it. Well, the son-ofabitch hasn't had nothing to do except get around to doing it.

PRESIDENT NIXON: What's the matter with him?

HALDEMAN: And I thought he had it done. He just got involved in other things, I guess.

PRESIDENT NIXON: I think we ought to get him back. I think—incidentally, I think you need more—I think you need a team. This is a big job. But you need a commander of the team and maybe—

HALDEMAN: Allen.

PRESIDENT NIXON: Maybe—incidentally, Allen should not be the commander, should he? Shouldn't Colson be? . . . He's got a lot of people working for him, hasn't he?

HALDEMAN: Yeah. And he's got good people. . . .

PRESIDENT NIXON: . . . Actually, when Mitchell leaves as Attorney General, we're going to be better off in my view. . . . John is just too damn good a lawyer, you know. He's a good strong lawyer. It just repels him to do these horrible things, but they've got to be done. We have to fight this. . . .

JULY 2, 1971: THE PRESIDENT, HALDEMAN, AND COLSON, 9:15–10:39 A.M., OVAL OFFICE

The President rails against a "conspiracy" behind the leaking of the Pentagon Papers and he talks about "repression" of antiwar people. "I'm not so interested in Ellsberg, . . ." he said, "there is a conspiracy and I've got to go after it." He wants more of a concerted effort to thwart leaks and discredit other administrations.

SEGMENT 2

PRESIDENT NIXON: . . . Now the most significant story in there, Bob, is the one that—where Ellsberg says there were a number of people that worked with him. Did you see that? I talked to [J. Edgar] Hoover last night and Hoover is not going after this case as strong as I'd like. He's talking about—I don't know. There's something dragging. There's something dragging him. He thinks that—I don't know what it is. Well, you can't tolerate it.

COLSON: It's the fear of repression.

PRESIDENT NIXON: Huh?

COLSON: The fear of repression.

HALDEMAN: Do you want him to go at it strongly?

PRESIDENT NIXON: I told him to.

HALDEMAN: Yeah. But if I call him now and say, I just wanted—

PRESIDENT NIXON: He's talking about Ellsberg and all of them are probably going to make a martyr out of him, that sort of thing.

HALDEMAN: If I call him now and just say an aside—you didn't tell me to call him. I'm telling him I just wanted him to know that in talking about this you're very concerned. You don't have the feeling the FBI is really pursuing this at a—as slow as fish.

PRESIDENT NIXON: Yeah. Particularly the conspiracy side. I want to go after everyone. I'm not so interested in Ellsberg, but we have got to go after everybody who's a member of this conspiracy. There is a conspiracy and I've got to go after it. I could tell him I've got the—tell him we've got [John] Dean on it. Now the other thing is I want you, Bob, to, somebody has got to talk to [Melvin] Laird on this. . . . This is not Ehrlichman's dish.

HALDEMAN: Well, I was just going to say you've had John on top of it.

PRESIDENT NIXON: No, no, no. John was on different people. John is . . . above some crap. Do you know what I mean? He's on the legal side. Did you see? This is the cops and robbers. There are two different things here. The main one conspiracy and then there's what do you about the *New York Times* and the case, see. John is handling that. He's totally in charge of it. Tell John that I want—that's why I say I've got to have—I simply got to have an all out, somebody in charge of this going after the conspirators. Now you've told me about the polygraph. I want that done. You've told Mitchell that? . . . Any government officials that we have doubts about. . . .

And I come back to the urgent necessity now, I think, of getting a man and maybe you've got to put—if you've got to put Colson in charge of it now, maybe you better do it. Do you understand? But get Huston back. I just think you've got to get him back on some basis and then just point in the thing where he has nothing to say about the big play. You can't put him in charge of the big play. He's too mean and so forth. But don't you think you can use him on just, say, all right. Here's your job, Tom, and point him and let him go at it or is he too difficult?

COLSON: I think he could be used on that. He's tough to work with. My only question is whether there would be people who are better.

PRESIDENT NIXON: Let me say this. Time is awasting. These people are beginning to get onto the fact that they don't want to get caught up in a conspiracy. Mitchell is—I think Mitchell's statement was good which is we're going to prosecute—got to prosecute everybody. Don't you think so?

COLSON: Excellent.

PRESIDENT NIXON: Does that bother you as being repressive?

COLSON: Oh, hell, no.

HALDEMAN: We've got to be repressive.

PRESIDENT NIXON: Well, they did that to me. . . .

HALDEMAN: Well, I think we've got—we are unduly sensitive.

PRESIDENT NIXON: I don't give a damn. . . . I told Ziegler yesterday. I said I know I'm repressive on this—

SEGMENT 3

PRESIDENT NIXON: . . . Also, I really meant it when—I want to go in and crack that [Brookings] safe. Walk in and get it. I want Brookings cut. They've got to do it. Brookings is the real enemy here. . . . Now, Laird—tell Laird—I think Laird is the one to play that game. Cut off Rand, Brookings, all outside. Oh, Council Foreign Relations. Put that one down, too. If they've got anything in the way of a secret safe and so forth, out—no more. Now the other thing—then cut the number of—as I said, let's cut the number of people who have access to top secret. . . . And a new classification to the President. I mean, the really presidential stuff. Then declassify all those things that are historically no longer injurious. . . . So then—and I really think that declassification thing is going to be a wonderful thing—don't you?

HALDEMAN: Sure.

PRESIDENT NIXON: Let the truth come out. Let them walk all around in the next stuff—Goddamn people. Just print that council directory. Goddamn [*Washington*] *Post* saying that: "Well, that's the price of the First Amendment." I hope his—his little shitass son is probably—they're draft dodgers.

COLSON: Safely tucked away in Canada . . . .

PRESIDENT NIXON: Yeah. Sure. These people from the elite don't go. . . . And they're all fucking running. . . . [Mockingly] This is about the war. What the hell are they talking about? I got no sympathy for them. The repressive position, Bob, I couldn't agree more with you. I don't buy that repression issue. They don't give a damn about this country. Fighting this. Don't you agree with me?

COLSON: Absolutely. I couldn't agree more strongly, Mr. President. I don't think that's a vote-turning issue. In fact, if it's a vote-turning issue, it turns a little bit our way, cuts a little bit our way.

PRESIDENT NIXON: Particularly if you put it in terms of the President has to think of it [in terms of national security]. The press must think of it in terms of circulation. We understand that they have to print everything. I have to look at it in terms of the life of American men and their glory. I have to protect—

HALDEMAN: . . . [I]t's the responsibility of the Executive Branch to protect the documents. . . .

PRESIDENT NIXON: Can I now go back to this point? What are we going to do about having an investigation of this conspiracy connection? Could I suggest that Chuck, maybe Ehrlichman and yourself, get Laird in? You say now, Laird, what are you going to do about this? Let's get him going on one track. And I need—he's got a whole bunch over there. Get [J. Edgar] Hoover going. I mean, deal with Hoover about the conspiracy thing, you know. The President should not be directly in this. Do you see my point? You then—you talk to Mitchell. Say I think we ought to get Hoover in it but talk to him on this conspiracy. I think we ought to get out and get some other people.

I don't need [Neil] Sheehan out of the *New York Times,* especially when I'm talking about it. First, he's guilty as hell. But you prosecute a newspaper man, you're in a difficult position. But, good God, if you go after an Ellsberg or that Cooke that's working for this Richardson, if he proves to be bad, that's for the record. I want to get one of those guys. We've got to do it.

HALDEMAN: Well, they feel there's more of them than that.

PRESIDENT NIXON: They do? Well, Ellsberg says so.

COLSON: Ellsberg admitted it. He said I'll leave to them whether they want to disclose their own names or not.

PRESIDENT NIXON: He must be a rat. What a rat. You know, the great thing about— I got to say for Hiss. He never ratted on anybody else. Never. He never ratted.

HALDEMAN: Well, Hiss was a more dedicated-type spy than Ellsberg is. Ellsberg— he's going on a totally different basis—

[Withdrawn item. Privacy.]

HALDEMAN: —totally different kind of thing. Hiss knew exactly what he was doing and why. Ellsberg probably doesn't.

COLSON: I think he's a far-out ideal—

PRESIDENT NIXON: How did he look last night? Did anybody see him?

COLSON: He was on this morning. I didn't see him. . . .

JULY 2, 1971: THE PRESIDENT, HALDEMAN, AND ROSE MARY WOODS, 12:35–12:48 P.M., OVAL OFFICE

The President's personal secretary had information for him.

WOODS: Well, we've been watching that Tony Lake [member of the NSC who resigned because of the Cambodia invasion] since he left here. I mean, did he take a lot of Xeroxes . . . .

HALDEMAN: Not very much.

WOODS: Because he's running, you know, for—

PRESIDENT NIXON: [Senator Edmund] Muskie.

WOODS: Muskie.

HALDEMAN: Not any more. He got fired.

PRESIDENT NIXON: He got fired?

WOODS: I've watched him. He's a weak character.

PRESIDENT NIXON: And [National Security Aide Morton] Halperin, also, we're watching him.

JULY 2, 1971: THE PRESIDENT, EHRLICHMAN, AND HALDEMAN, 5:49–6:20 P.M., EXECUTIVE OFFICE BUILDING

Nixon wants to revive the old House Committee on Un-American Activities, now the House Internal Security Committee, to investigate a "spy ring." "What a marvelous opportunity for the committee," he said. He also continues to press for declassification in order to leak older documents.

SEGMENT 1

EHRLICHMAN: On the conspiracy thing, if you want to run it out of here, I think we've got a couple of guys that might to able to do it.

PRESIDENT NIXON: Or should we?

EHRLICHMAN: I'm not sure we should. . . .

PRESIDENT NIXON: Well, you see, we've got Colson. You can run it out of his shop. But he's got a lot of stuff going, but I think we've got to make it—we've got to make a decision. And let me just say, you, the three of you, should—the two of you with Colson—should sit down and figure out where the hell we're going to run it. I don't know how to run it. But, Goddamnit, if you put it out in Congress—the best thing is to have it in the Congress and then us cooperate with the Congress. And the other thing, of course, is you've got to find a way to be the columnist—a paper driven. You see, the papers can start investigations. . . .

Take Laird. Now Laird—this is one place where we can take a guy who's a . . . sonofabitch and maybe Laird just might want to make a hero out of himself. I want you two to have a talk with Laird.

EHRLICHMAN: He's gone now for three weeks. . . . What about—I don't know about his, you know, talent for bird dogging? He certainly has the right instincts. . . .

HALDEMAN: I . . . like this guy [E. Howard Hunt] Colson's talking about, the former CIA guy, get him in . . . . You've got to have somebody that knows the business.

PRESIDENT NIXON: . . . If Dick Allen is around, bring him in on it, too.

HALDEMAN: Allen would like to sit on the steering committee. Allen's recommendation was . . . John and I and Dick Allen . . . be the steering committee.

PRESIDENT NIXON: Well, maybe keep Colson—Colson will run into this and some other things, too. He's awfully good at this stuff. But he's, also, been hot previously. So maybe it isn't well to have him in this one. I like [Edward] Morgan. I just think Morgan sounds good. . . .

SEGMENT 2

HALDEMAN: [Richard] Helms describes this guy [Hunt] as ruthless, quiet and careful, low profile. He gets things done. He will work well with all of us. He's very concerned about the health of the administration. His concern, he thinks, is they're out to get us and all that, but he's not a fanatic. He could be absolutely certain it'll involve secrecy. . . .

PRESIDENT NIXON: I wonder if [Senator John] Tower [R-TX] could take this and do it on the side?

HALDEMAN: Sure he could if he wanted to.

PRESIDENT NIXON: Is he too damn lazy? . . .

EHRLICHMAN: Got to have a committee.

PRESIDENT NIXON: Got to have a committee. So it's got to be somebody on that [Richard] Ichord [D-MO] committee [on Internal Security] in my opinion. . . . I think Ichord is the man. . . . Republicans have two [John] Birchers.

HALDEMAN: I got Ashbrook and Thompson. . . .

PRESIDENT NIXON: . . . I think that's the plan. Get that committee. I think that's the plan. Get somebody down there that can do it. . . . That's it. We get the witnesses and we leak the stories and—

HALDEMAN: We can help keep pushing the committee to do it especially if their counsel's a good man.

PRESIDENT NIXON: [Donald] Sanders is the name of the counsel.

HALDEMAN: Or if we could get a special counsel.

PRESIDENT NIXON: . . . Don't you see what a *marvelous opportunity* for the committee. They can really take this and go. And make speeches about the spy ring.

EHRLICHMAN: Televise their hearings.

PRESIDENT NIXON: Right. They do. Naturally, it's better than not getting any headlines. It's better than nothing. But you know what's going to charge up an audience. Jesus Christ, they'll be hanging from the rafters. . . . Going after all these Jews. Just find one that is a Jew, will you. . . .

I don't want to hear any more about it. And I didn't—I know nothing about it except on the declassification thing, we're on the right track there. [Assistant Attorney General William] Rehnquist is a bright fella. He can take charge of this thing. But on that, we've got—there is where we do really need Allen or somebody that understands the Cuban missile crisis and understands the Bay of Pigs. . . .

JULY 2, 1971: THE PRESIDENT AND WILLIAM E. TIMMONS, 6:10–6:16 P.M., WHITE HOUSE TELEPHONE

During the previous conversation, Nixon called Timmons, his congressional liaison, urging him to contact the House Internal Security Committee. "It can become a very valuable committee," the President said. Nixon apparently was inspired by his own service on the Committee more than twenty years earlier and he saw this as an opportunity for the Committee "to resuscitate itself."

PRESIDENT NIXON: Get your congressional directory out and—have you got one handy there?

TIMMONS: Yes, sir. Uh-huh.

PRESIDENT NIXON: Look at the [House Internal Security] Committee, [Richard] Ichord's committee, and give me the Republicans on it?

TIMMONS: Okay. I notice John Ashbrook is on there.

PRESIDENT NIXON: Oh, Ashbrook on it?

TIMMONS: Yeah. He's the ranking member.

PRESIDENT NIXON: He's the ranking man?

TIMMONS: Uh-huh. Roger Zion is on it.

PRESIDENT NIXON: He's all right.

TIMMONS: Fletcher Thompson of Georgia.

PRESIDENT NIXON: Fletcher Thompson.

TIMMONS: And your Congressman, John Schmitz.

PRESIDENT NIXON: Oh, boy, [John] Bircher. John Schmitz, good.

TIMMONS: They're the four.

PRESIDENT NIXON: Now who are the Democrats?

TIMMONS: It's Ichord, of course, and then Claude Pepper.

PRESIDENT NIXON: Go ahead.

TIMMONS: Ed Edwards of Louisiana.

PRESIDENT NIXON: Good.

TIMMONS: Richardson Pryor of North Carolina.

PRESIDENT NIXON: Don't know him

TIMMONS: And our friend Father Drinan of Massachusetts. [Chuckles]

PRESIDENT NIXON: Yeah. Well, now how would that committee be, do you think, to conduct an investigation of this conspiracy? Do you know what I mean?

TIMMONS: Uh-huh.

PRESIDENT NIXON: Far better than having these people indicted and so forth is really to call them before a committee and say now, look, did you do this or that or the other thing. Do you know?

TIMMONS: Yeah.

PRESIDENT NIXON: But it's going to require—what kind of a staff man do they have?

TIMMONS: They have a good guy, a Don Sanders [later a minority counsel for the Senate Watergate Committee], is—

PRESIDENT NIXON: Do you know him? Is he Counsel?

TIMMONS: I've met him. Yes. He's Chief Counsel.

PRESIDENT NIXON: Is he tough?

TIMMONS: My impression is that he is tough. We haven't dealt with that committee much because we haven't much legislation. But my impression is that he's real tough and a good man.

PRESIDENT NIXON: Do you think Ichord would be—now, he's running for governor, I understand it?

TIMMONS: Uh-huh. Uh-huh.

PRESIDENT NIXON: Don't you think he ought to be willing to take a thing like this?

TIMMONS: I would think so. It would be some headlines for him.

PRESIDENT NIXON: Headlines? Good God! It would make him a national figure. And he can have these hearings and go right after this thing.

TIMMONS: I think that—

PRESIDENT NIXON: Will Ashbrook work or is he just lazy?

TIMMONS: My impression is he's pretty lazy, frankly.

PRESIDENT NIXON: He's lazy.

TIMMONS: He hasn't done much.

PRESIDENT NIXON: Fletcher Thompson would work, wouldn't he?

TIMMONS: Fletch would be great because he wants to run for the Senate down there.

PRESIDENT NIXON: Fletcher wants to run for the Senate?

TIMMONS: Sure. He and "Bo" may square off against each other.

PRESIDENT NIXON: Is Fletcher—he and who?

TIMMONS: "Bo" Calloway. They're both—

PRESIDENT NIXON: Is Fletcher a lawyer?

TIMMONS: I don't know.

PRESIDENT NIXON: Uh-huh.

TIMMONS: I don't know. He's a businessman but—

PRESIDENT NIXON: All right. I'll have—

TIMMONS: Do you want me to set that in motion or—

PRESIDENT NIXON: Why don't you—yeah. Why don't you do a little sniffing around or something to see whether they'd like to—well, first of all, it can't be for me, of course.

TIMMONS: You're right.

PRESIDENT NIXON: But what I'm getting at is it would seem to me that this is an opportunity for the committee to resuscitate itself. You know what I mean?

TIMMONS: Uh-huh.

PRESIDENT NIXON: It can become a very valuable committee now. They call them up there.

TIMMONS: Uh-huh.

PRESIDENT NIXON: You see, we get [Morton] Halperin, [Leslie] Gelb. We have lots of names. There's a Cook over in the NSC staff. Hell, yes, we'll call them up. Give them lie-detector tests. They'd have a ball.

TIMMONS: Uh-huh.

PRESIDENT NIXON: What do you think?

TIMMONS: I think it's a great idea. I talked to Chuck Colson just briefly about this a week or so ago. I think it's tremendous. In the Senate, you know, on the government operations committee, there's a subcommittee on national security and international operations.

PRESIDENT NIXON: Who's that?

TIMMONS: It's chaired by [Senator Henry] Scoop Jackson [D-WA].

PRESIDENT NIXON: Yeah. But do you think Scoop would be willing to—

TIMMONS: I don't. I doubt it. I just don't know.

PRESIDENT NIXON: I don't think he would. I wouldn't—get—

TIMMONS: Mess around with the Senate.

PRESIDENT NIXON: Ichord's people should step in and preempt this field.

TIMMONS: Uh-huh.

PRESIDENT NIXON: Let me say this. I have told [Gerald] Ford—Ford is—and that Haldeman will call him. But I want you to call him. He's out at Burning Tree.

TIMMONS: Yeah. I've called him once out there. [*Chuckles*].

PRESIDENT NIXON: Yeah. And so in doing this, why don't you work with—you call Ford and tell him—and see whether Ford likes the idea.

TIMMONS: All right.

PRESIDENT NIXON: And then be in touch with, you know, that, well, Colson and Haldeman and Ehrlichman are all working. But over the weekend—naturally, they won't be doing anything over the weekend, but we ought to get this in motion because this could be one tremendous—you see, if this committee, they'd have the cooperation of the FBI. They can have the cooperation of Mel Laird. They can have the cooperation of everybody we can find, you see.

TIMMONS: Yeah.

PRESIDENT NIXON: And it's distinguished from how I fought the Hiss case.

TIMMONS: Sure.

PRESIDENT NIXON: They were all against me.

TIMMONS: Yeah.

PRESIDENT NIXON: So this is a different ball.

TIMMONS: Right.

PRESIDENT NIXON: And I tell you, I'd love to be on that committee now.

TIMMONS: Sure.

PRESIDENT NIXON: God darn—

TIMMONS: Those guys will just zoom right up. Well, Fletcher will just love it because he's trying to get a few headlines, too, and Schmitz will be hard on them and Zion, he's been going over to Parrish and all, off and on. He's got a real interest in this stuff and good man. And John's heart is in the right place. He's just damn lazy.

PRESIDENT NIXON: Well, he makes good speeches.

TIMMONS: Yeah.

PRESIDENT NIXON: Okay.

TIMMONS: Okay, Mr. President. 'Bye.

JULY 5, 1971: THE PRESIDENT, HALDEMAN, AND ZIEGLER, 4:28–6:15 P.M., OVAL OFFICE

Nixon complains again about leaks and unauthorized access to secret documents. He laments that as Vice President he never had a CIA briefing, and Kennedy and Johnson cut him off when they were President. "I wasn't cleared for anything. . . . I had nothing," he complained. Nixon's long-standing grievance against the CIA for having briefed Kennedy on Cuba during the 1960 campaign continues to fester.

PRESIDENT NIXON: All right. We'll give it to him. That's nothing. We're also going to give him or start giving him when we start releasing some of this stuff from World War II. I'm going to give that to the [*Chicago*] *Trib*. They deny I have that, as you know. They hated Roosevelt. . . .

HALDEMAN: Then some of the World War II. Give the *L.A. Times* some of the Kennedy stuff and see if they print it.

PRESIDENT NIXON: They won't.

HALDEMAN: They might.

PRESIDENT NIXON: I'd be surprised. They might. . . . What I'd like to do is to get into Laos. I mean, the Laotian thing, you see. . . . The '62 [Laos] Accords opens the Ho Chi Minh trail. We'll get that one mounted. Well, we can't do that for a while. Well, anyway.

HALDEMAN: Be sure and do it before you get out of the next term though so that the record is—

PRESIDENT NIXON: . . . We're going to do it before we get out of this term, boy. Don't worry. I'm not going to take any risks on that one. No risks. It's got to get out. . . . Also, I've got to have it all to take with me, whatever happens. Even the stuff we don't put out, I'm going to hand them. Gee, these guys have played a game.

You know, the thing that burns me and the reason I've bordered on hate today and the poor devil has got so much to do. But I asked him [General Alexander Haig] to have a list of outside people, nongovernment people, with clearances. . . . I said, first of all, you're going to limit every contractor to a clearance for only . . . what he needs to know with regard to that contract.

[Withdrawn item. National security.]

PRESIDENT NIXON: Then I said, now, look out. For eight years a former vice president of the United States didn't even get a CIA briefing. I wasn't cleared for anything. I was the former vice president, you know. I had nothing as the former vice president. I had nothing. And I was refused CIA briefings. I stuck that to those boys over there, you know. I knew (unintelligible) back into the CIA and both Kennedy and Johnson turned it off [access for Nixon]. I know it and they know it.

. . . I'm going to get that Council Foreign Relations. I'm going to chop those bastards off right at the neck. That's all there is to it. We've got to get—we've got to get our enemies out of the clearance business. I mean, Rand [Corporation]. That was a good move. That was welcomed, don't you agree, taking them on? Let them squeal.

HALDEMAN: The clearance thing, I'll tell you how ridiculous it is. When I was manager of the Los Angeles office of J. Walter Thompson [Advertising] Company, I had to have a clearance as did all officers for the company because we handled the advertising for Douglas Aircraft Company. It was a cleared federal contractor. The point is the stuff we dealt with was stuff that we were going to write up and put in ads and printed newspapers and magazines. We didn't deal with secret stuff. We had a stake in the offices so that maybe—a guy used to come in and inspect every once in a while, to make sure it was all locked up. There was never anything in it. . . . It was unbelievable.

PRESIDENT NIXON: It's ridiculous. Well, we're going to get this. That's the best thing we're really doing is to chop off these outside clearances and we've got a perfect excuse for it now. Perfect. Right? And, boy, just wait until those little bastards don't get their hands on this stuff any more. We're going to make it mighty tough to get stuff around—

JULY 6, 1971: THE PRESIDENT AND HALDEMAN, 9:25–9:50 P.M., OVAL OFFICE

More complaints about access to briefings. Nixon learns that Ted Kennedy is still under surveillance.

PRESIDENT NIXON: . . . As I told you yesterday, we've got to keep Vietnam as an issue and we've got to pin the whole Johnson-Kennedy papers now on these bastards on the other side. And that's why I've got to get—that's why we've got to start getting on stuff and it ruins them. You know, you were talking about we've got to be sure that we get out the papers—get out the stuff before our second term and so forth. Don't worry about that. We're going to get everything out we can now in case we lose. Do you see, Bob? . . . The reason, Bob, is that it'll all disappear forever. . . .

What the hell do you think they would be doing to us? I just can't get over the fact—I can't get over the fact that—and I'm just pissed off that we didn't think of it earlier. Here I sat for eight years [as Vice President] never getting any secrets but now we've got [McGeorge] Bundy on a secret list [for access]. [Averell] Harriman on a secret list. Now that's one thing I've got to have tomorrow. Now [Alexander] Haig I know is busy, but tell him I've to have the list of all Johnson and Kennedy Administration people who have clearances at the present time. I have to have that. Now that I've got to have. Understand? . . . Do you see what I mean? I'm going to get it. I'm going to stop them all. Don't you agree?

HALDEMAN: I sure do.

PRESIDENT NIXON: Why do we let those sons of bitches have clearances and we don't. Will you tell him?

HALDEMAN: There's no reason. They have no need to know. They're not involved with policy now.

PRESIDENT NIXON: And never will be as far as we're concerned. . . .

HALDEMAN: Even the *New York Post* in their Sunday editorial, they—

PRESIDENT NIXON: What did they say? Incredible.

HALDEMAN: Look, they turned around and took a backhand swipe at us. They said the administration should have done a better job of keeping the papers locked up. They shouldn't have let them get out.

PRESIDENT NIXON: *Now it's during our administration!* The guy carried them out before he left. But yet they say we didn't. . . .

Do you have [Senator] Kennedy—find the man, you have Kennedy.

HALDEMAN: Yeah. This morning, we made a decision to get a guy going [to follow Kennedy].

PRESIDENT NIXON: Certainly. Just one? He'll be on it full time?

JULY 20, 1971: THE PRESIDENT AND EHRLICHMAN, 11:09–11:46 A.M., OVAL OFFICE

The President gets his first report of the Plumbers' investigations of Daniel Ellsberg.

EHRLICHMAN: . . . [Egil] Krogh and his guys are going to pull together the evidence, and in two or three weeks time—

PRESIDENT NIXON: They are working on the evidence?

EHRLICHMAN: Yes, indeed. Yes, indeed. And what he's tried to do yesterday and today is get around—

PRESIDENT NIXON: How does it presently stand?

EHRLICHMAN: Well, there're a lot of leaks. There are all kinds of leaks.

PRESIDENT NIXON: Did you find anything—how did [first name unknown] Cooke come out? Did he come—

EHRLICHMAN: No. And I'm afraid Elliot [Richardson] has got some jam on his face where Cooke is concerned. Cooke spent 14 hours with Ellsberg—

JULY 27, 1971: THE PRESIDENT AND HALDEMAN, 9:03–10:25 A.M., OVAL OFFICE

Nixon renews his demand to declassify papers of his predecessors.

PRESIDENT NIXON: Another thing we should do. I had mentioned to Ehrlichman or to you—I just want to remind you again—Ehrlichman told me as I was leaving yesterday that they were going forward on getting to where GSA [General Services Administration] is going to be getting the World War II documents declassified and that's fine. But then—that's the order it ought to be done, that Korea, and the rest. But I wonder—I want to have the group in here now to get for me personally, particularly, the documents concerning the Bay of Pigs—. . . the Bay of Pigs, the U.N. confrontation, Berlin, the whole business of the Johnson and Kennedy administrations, having in mind that stuff will be burned off in the event we're not around, you see. In other words, make studies like that, Bob, like they make in the Pentagon Papers but I want to get those documents, you see. I'm supposed to have access to them, the bombing halt. Well, that's a good example of it. Now will you take the thing—

HALDEMAN: Yeah.

PRESIDENT NIXON: You tell, I guess, [Egil] Krogh is the man or somebody over there that that's an assignment that is to be given. I will expect that to be followed out so that that's in mind. I don't see it in my files or any—

AUGUST 9, 1971: THE PRESIDENT, HALDEMAN, AND KISSINGER, 8:55–10:30 A.M., OVAL OFFICE

Nixon enrolls Henry Kissinger in a scheme to get support for Eugene McCarthy to run as a fourth-party candidate.

KISSINGER: [Eugene McCarthy fundraiser] Howard Stein is coming down to have lunch with me this week.

PRESIDENT NIXON: Is he?

KISSINGER: Yeah.

PRESIDENT NIXON: New twist. Put it into him very hard about what rats and how totally irresponsible [Senator Edmund] Muskie is. You can't get away with the pettiness he's pulling, but Muskie—they both—they were total defenders of the policy that the President has been getting them out of. Now they've switched. . . . And the only man with any character on the Democratic side is [Eugene] McCarthy. Build McCarthy up. . . . Now the story, you see, is that McCarthy may go to support the party against anybody except Kennedy. I don't know. . . .

HALDEMAN: Well, he [McCarthy] also knows—you see, the only support he's really got is his own youth crusade. Teddy will knock that right out from under him.

PRESIDENT NIXON: Yeah. His youth crusade. So basically he doesn't figure he'll be around. But here's how we would like to have McCarthy in the race. You see, we need

McCarthy in the race for a purpose. On the other hand, you should say now you ought to do both. Well, we don't need his [Stein's] money. I'm just—we don't really need his money or anything. But—

HALDEMAN: His money would do us a lot more good if it goes to McCarthy.

PRESIDENT NIXON: But I think McCarthy ought to stay but he must never know that that's why we want him in.

KISSINGER: Yeah.

PRESIDENT NIXON: But I think you could build up the idea that the other charge fit. Isn't it a shame the only man—you can quote [Daniel Patrick] Moynihan—who has the intellectual capability on the Democratic side to be President is McCarthy and isn't it a shame that he really doesn't have a chance and the rest. That he has the courage, whether you agree with Nixon or whether you agree with McCarthy, they're men of character and men who stand up for what they believe in and then you go on with that. But the others are not. They're wobblers.

KISSINGER: Every now and then I have lunch with McCarthy again. He'll leak it to Mary McGrory.

HALDEMAN: But the key to McCarthy is if Stein will put up the money. McCarthy, from all that we can find out, what McCarthy is looking for is two things: one, campaign financing and the other a personal funder.

KISSINGER: Oh, really?

HALDEMAN: If Stein would give him, you know, a lead into making some money and would underwrite a campaign fund, you know, the basic start of a campaign fund, he would launch his fourth party and go. He'll go for the Democratic nomination. When he doesn't get it, he'll pull out and go for a fourth party effort.

KISSINGER: Maybe I'll just see him again.

HALDEMAN: And a fourth party effort on McCarthy would just be beautiful.

KISSINGER: I'll tell it to Howard Stein, but it also gives some plausibility. . . .

AUGUST 12, 1971: THE PRESIDENT AND COLSON, 1:01–1:30 P.M., OVAL OFFICE

Colson gives the President a warm endorsement of Howard Hunt, who, of course, was known to Nixon.

COLSON: [E. Howard Hunt is a] first-rate analyst who spent his whole life in subversive warfare. Thank God, we know they're on our side. Who has been an admirer of ours and yours since the Alger Hiss case. He's been going through this digging up names, people, incidents and events. We can build one hell of a case, and given the right forum, and the forum is the Congress. . . .

PRESIDENT NIXON: The right case, of course, is really to get our Democratic friends talking about the damn thing [Pentagon Papers] and defending and running away from it or fighting each other about it. It's their problem. It's not ours.

COLSON: I can just—

PRESIDENT NIXON: Gosh, I just—just so you have a mind about it because I briefed

Ehrlichman on it today on the investigative side. [Egil] Krogh is working on that, too. So you have in mind we need those hearings. Let's keep this—Goddamn, I want that thing inflamed. . . .

SEPTEMBER 8, 1971: THE PRESIDENT AND EHRLICHMAN, 3:36–5:10 P.M., OVAL OFFICE

On the night of September 3–4, the White House "Special Investigative Unit," led by E. Howard Hunt and G. Gordon Liddy, illegally entered the offices of Dr. Lewis Fielding, a Beverly Hills psychiatrist who numbered Daniel Ellsberg among his patients. Here, Ehrlichman tells Nixon about "one little operation," quickly adding that it "is better that you don't know about this." The two also discuss using the IRS to harass Senators Muskie and Humphrey, and Ehrlichman reports on his agents' and his own surveillance of Senator Edward Kennedy.

SEGMENT 1

PRESIDENT NIXON: Where does [Egil] Krogh stand now? He's still in charge of the—

EHRLICHMAN: He's doing the (unintelligible) the narcotics thing. But he's also spending most of his time on the Ellsberg, declassifications, and the dirty tricks business on getting stuff out. . . .

SEGMENT 2

EHRLICHMAN: We had one little operation. It's been aborted out in Los Angeles which, I think, is better that you don't know about. But we've got some dirty tricks underway. It may pay off. We've planted a bunch of stuff with columnists some of which will be given to service shortly, I think, about some of this group, about Ellsberg's lawyer, about the Bay of Pigs. Some of this stuff is going to start—is going to start surfacing.

PRESIDENT NIXON: With columnists that are somewhat respectable?

EHRLICHMAN: Yes. [Jerald] TerHorst and people like that.

PRESIDENT NIXON: Good.

EHRLICHMAN: We're running into a little problem. I've got to talk to Helms about getting some documents which the CIA have on the Bay of Pigs and things like that which they would rather not leak out. [Chuckles] It's a challenge.

PRESIDENT NIXON: It's going to be hard. They are very sensitive about that. Helms is definitely the one (unintelligible) now for CIA and the Bay of Pigs.

EHRLICHMAN: They're all new ones.

PRESIDENT NIXON: Yeah. . . . Henry [Kissinger] can sort it out because so many of the people involved are, frankly, closely associated with him.

EHRLICHMAN: Well, that's one of the things that we keep bumping into. . . .

PRESIDENT NIXON: Now, Ellsberg has been to his house and so on before. . . .

SEGMENT 3

PRESIDENT NIXON: John, but we have the power but are we using it to investigate contributors to Hubert Humphrey, contributors to Muskie, the Jews, you know, that are stealing every—. You know, they have really tried to crucify Ho[bart] Lewis, Rob[ert] Abplanalp, I mean, while we've been in office even.

EHRLICHMAN: I know.

PRESIDENT NIXON: And John Wayne, of course, and Paul Keyes. After 1964 he does one stinking commercial. . . . Made him a Goddamn martyr. What the hell are we doing?

EHRLICHMAN: I don't know.

PRESIDENT NIXON: You see, we have a new man over there. I know the other guy didn't do anything, but—

EHRLICHMAN: Oh, you mean at IRS?

PRESIDENT NIXON: Yeah. Why are—are we going after their tax returns. Do you know what I mean? . . . Do you remember in 1962? Do you remember what they [IRS] did to me in California? After those sons of bitches came out, . . . I find—finally, now they owe me more money. . . . And on the IRS, you could—are we looking into Muskie's return?

EHRLICHMAN: No, we haven't.

PRESIDENT NIXON: Hubert? Hubert's been in a lot of funny deals.

EHRLICHMAN: Yes, he has.

PRESIDENT NIXON: Teddy [Kennedy]? Who knows about the Kennedys? Shouldn't they be investigated? . . .

EHRLICHMAN: IRS-wise I don't know the answer. Teddy, we are covering—

PRESIDENT NIXON: Are you?

EHRLICHMAN:—personally, when he goes on holidays. When he stopped in Hawaii on his way back from Pakistan last Thanksgiving.

PRESIDENT NIXON: Do anything?

EHRLICHMAN: No. No. He's very clean. Very clean. Being careful now. He was in Hawaii on his own. He was staying at some guy's villa and we had a guy on him, and he was just as nice as he could be the whole time.

PRESIDENT NIXON: The thing to do is to just watch him because what happens to fellows like that who have that kind of problem is that they go for awhile and then they open out.

EHRLICHMAN: That's what I'm hoping for. . . . This time between now and the convention time may be the time (unintelligible).

PRESIDENT NIXON: You mean, that he will be under great pressure?

EHRLICHMAN: He will be under pressure, but he will also be out of the limelight somewhat. Now he was in Hawaii pretty much the entire time, with very little staff. . . . So you would expect that at a time like that you might catch him. And then he went up to Hyannis and we got an arrangement—

PRESIDENT NIXON: What's Muskie doing? What kind of a life is he living?

EHRLICHMAN: Very close group, very monkish. . . . Yeah. Big family. He's got six kids. And very ordinary type of life. So, Teddy—we were over on Martha's Vineyard last week. I had never seen that bridge before on Chappaquiddick, the Edgartown

Ferry. . . . Having seen it now, I would bet he stopped that night. I don't see why they—you know, they could build a bridge across there. It's a very short distance. . . . So it was quite interesting. I took some pictures of it. What amazed me is how short a distance it really was. But we do cover him.

PRESIDENT NIXON: He will never live that down.

EHRLICHMAN: No. I don't think he will, not that one.

PRESIDENT NIXON: I think that will be around his neck forever. Remember, his wife asked for a divorce.

EHRLICHMAN: Divorce?

PRESIDENT NIXON: Yeah. . . .

EHRLICHMAN: But this thing has a geographic identity which is interesting and they tell me that the business side apparently has tripled since this accident, people going over to look at the bridge. He's getting into the folklore. . . .

SEPTEMBER 10, 1971: THE PRESIDENT AND EHRLICHMAN, 3:03–3:51 P.M., EXECUTIVE OFFICE BUILDING

Ehrlichman proposes a break-in of the National Archives to get secret Vietnam papers of former Lyndon Johnson aides.

PRESIDENT NIXON: What about [for Defense Department official Paul] Nitze? How's he handling it?

EHRLICHMAN: He's a co-conspirator with (unintelligible).

PRESIDENT NIXON: Paul Nitze is?

EHRLICHMAN: I'm quite sure. Quite sure that he's the guy.

PRESIDENT NIXON: Damn.

EHRLICHMAN: There's a lot of hanky-panky with secret documents and on the eve of the publication of the Pentagon Papers those three guys [Nitze, Morton Halperin, Leslie Gelb] made a deposit into the National Archives under an agreement of a whole lot of papers. Now I'm going to steal those documents out of the National Archives.

PRESIDENT NIXON: You can do that, you know.

EHRLICHMAN: Photograph them and find out what the hell is there.

PRESIDENT NIXON: How do you do that?

EHRLICHMAN: Well, through [Robert] Kunzig [Administrator of GSA] I can do that. He can send the Archivist out of town for a while and we can get in there and he will photograph and he'll reseal them.

PRESIDENT NIXON: There are ways to do that?

EHRLICHMAN: Yeah. And nobody can tell we've been in there. . . .

SEPTEMBER 12, 1971: THE PRESIDENT AND EHRLICHMAN, 5:15–5:31 P.M., WHITE HOUSE TELEPHONE

This conversation concerns legal questions involving the President's Key Biscayne properties, a subject of later dispute. A brief fragment here demonstrates that John Dean was a familiar figure to him—not unknown, as Nixon contended in 1973.

PRESIDENT NIXON: The other thing that occurred to me was that it seems to me that when Dean gets the questions and this sort of business and forth on (unintelligible)—

EHRLICHMAN: Uh-huh.

PRESIDENT NIXON: Rather than just a straight stonewaller, or maybe he is doing this, what he ought to do is simply to hand them a photostat copy of the release we put out and say this was the President's position. It was fully disclosed and there has been no change.

EHRLICHMAN: Well, as a matter of fact, we have—we've reprinted that release.

PRESIDENT NIXON: Good.

EHRLICHMAN: And we keep handing it out.

PRESIDENT NIXON: Good.

EHRLICHMAN: Right along in response to the question—

PRESIDENT NIXON: And then Dean should say that is a total disclosure—

EHRLICHMAN: Uh-huh.

PRESIDENT NIXON:—and there is no change.

SEPTEMBER 13, 1971: THE PRESIDENT AND HALDEMAN, 4:36–5:05 P.M., OVAL OFFICE

Furious that his friend, Reverend Billy Graham, is being "harassed" by the IRS, Nixon orders retaliation.

PRESIDENT NIXON: . . . I'm sure of [John] Connally. But Billy Graham tells an astonishing thing. The IRS is battering the shit out of him. Some sonofabitch came to him and gave him a three-hour grilling about how much he, you know, how much his contribution is worth and he told it to Connally. Well, Connally took the name of the guy. I just got to get that nailed down to Connally when you get back. He didn't know it. Now here's the point. Bob, *please* get me the names of the Jews, you know, the big Jewish contributors of the Democrats. . . . All right. Could we please investigate some of the cocksuckers? That's all.

Now look at here. Here IRS is going after Billy Graham tooth and nail. Are they going after Eugene Carson Blake [President of the National Council of Churches, a liberal group]? I asked—you know, what I mean is, Goddamn. I don't believe—I just don't know whether we are being as rough about it. That's all. . . .

HALDEMAN: Yeah.

PRESIDENT NIXON: You call [John] Mitchell. Mitchell could get—stick his nose in the thing. . . . Say, now, Goddamnit, are we going after some of these Democrats or not? They've gone after Abplanalp. They've gone after Rebozo. They've gone after John Wayne. They're going after, you know, every one of our people. Goddamnit, they were after me. . . . Somebody told me that Muskie used Frank Sinatra's plane in California. Did you hear of that? Maybe we should investigate that?

HALDEMAN: Yeah. It, also, landed at the wrong airport. [*Chuckles*]

SEPTEMBER 14, 1971: THE PRESIDENT, HALDEMAN, AND COLSON, 12:37–1:32 P.M., OVAL OFFICE

Nixon continues to rage about the IRS and his friends. Colson then joins the conversation, offering his special contributions to White House political dirty tricks.

SEGMENT 1

HALDEMAN: We do have a system. I did some checking yesterday.

PRESIDENT NIXON: Good.

HALDEMAN: We do have a list. We do have, for instance, they've opened—and it may be interesting, as a matter of fact. On the guy that's running that Rebozo investigation, the New York IRS office has opened a check on him and think they may have something. . . .

PRESIDENT NIXON: Good. What about the rich Jews?

HALDEMAN: Well, that's—

PRESIDENT NIXON: You see, IRS is full of Jews, Bob.

HALDEMAN: Right.

PRESIDENT NIXON: That's what I think. I think that's the reason they're after Graham, is the rich Jews.

HALDEMAN: Well, the point that they took is that they've got to get the kind of guy—we're not just interested—we don't want to see the files.

PRESIDENT NIXON: We're trying to get anything on them.

HALDEMAN: But what we want to do is get a zealot who dislikes those people just as much as the zealot who dislikes Billy Graham—

PRESIDENT NIXON: Sure.

HALDEMAN:—is working on his file.

PRESIDENT NIXON: Sure.

HALDEMAN: In other words, don't just get—

PRESIDENT NIXON: Go after him like a sonofabitch.

COLSON: That's right.

HALDEMAN: And we've got—we did—

PRESIDENT NIXON: All right.

HALDEMAN: We have a go after the guy at the top who's cooperating but he's tied up with things. So they are going to be done in about anybody—just so we're reassured. . . .

SEGMENT 2

COLSON: Well, Bob Brown has some friends who are going to have signs around the Muskie rallies, [saying Carl] Stokes [the black mayor of Cleveland] for vice president. This raises the point—

HALDEMAN: I will hope the hell that Watts do go ahead with a black president candidate.

PRESIDENT NIXON: So do I.

HALDEMAN: In fact, Buchanan has come in with a suggestion that may make a lot of sense which is that—he says if we're going to spend $50 million in this campaign, then 10 percent of it, $5 million, ought to be devoted—

PRESIDENT NIXON: To the fourth party.

HALDEMAN:—to financing a black—

COLSON: Shirley Chisholm and Julian Bond.

PRESIDENT NIXON: Do you think that the blacks will vote for a black party?

HALDEMAN: Some.

COLSON: A lot of them will especially if—

HALDEMAN: Just to show that the Democratic party has no one. . . . But Pat's point is we've got to get a viable candidate—only if they get a viable candidate. If they got a Julian Bond—

PRESIDENT NIXON: Well, let me suggest this. Might—$5 million would finance Eugene McCarthy.

HALDEMAN: Well, that's—Howard Stein is working on that. There's a good story in the *U.S. News, Newsweek,* or something. Stein has outlined the McCarthy plan which is that he is not going to enter the primaries but he's going to do a major speaking tour next year will go to the convention as people—the Democratic convention as the people's candidate. If, as is expected, he's rejected by the convention, he will then go to the fourth party. The problem is that it's too late then to go to a fourth party. You have—it takes time to get a fourth party qualified. . . .

PRESIDENT NIXON: All right, Bob. Put that down for discussion—not for discussion but for action. They should finance and contribute both to McCarthy and to the black thing.

COLSON: That's a helluva lot—

PRESIDENT NIXON: We're recognizing that McCarthy—the black won't take any votes from us. Just like the damn Democrats contributed to [George] Wallace in Alabama. They did, you know. Jesus Christ, they were praying for Wallace to win that primary.

HALDEMAN: Yeah.

COLSON: That's a helluva lot better use of money than a lot of other things.

PRESIDENT NIXON: Oh, we spent—waste money on all sorts of things.

HALDEMAN: Okey-doke. What he's saying is, you know, instead of some television commercials—

PRESIDENT NIXON: Absolutely.

HALDEMAN:—we can do this.

COLSON: Or billboards.

HALDEMAN: Because we're going to need the television commercials.

SEPTEMBER 17, 1971: THE PRESIDENT AND KISSINGER, 11:29–11:41 A.M., OVAL OFFICE

Kissinger offers to help with the cynical support for Eugene McCarthy.

KISSINGER: I'm meeting with a group of Howard Stein's friends next Wednesday and I'm going to sort of speak in vague terms about the moral collapse of everybody that offers help to McCarthy and—

PRESIDENT NIXON: Yes. And that at least you got a Nixon-McCarthy, you could say, two men who disagree but their goals are the same and they have the guts to stand up and fight for it.

KISSINGER: Well, you know, McCarthy has had a deadline is (unintelligible).

PRESIDENT NIXON: But build up McCarthy. . . .

KISSINGER: Well—

PRESIDENT NIXON: Say that he's pure and Muskie with that Goddamn silly statement about a black. He's so cynical.

KISSINGER: Yeah. Well, I've been building McCarthy like crazy on the West Coast. But I'm not going to do it in New York but with Howard Stein on Wednesday.

SEPTEMBER 18, 1971: THE PRESIDENT, HALDEMAN, MITCHELL, EHRLICHMAN, AND COLSON, 12:07–2:05 P.M., OVAL OFFICE

Nixon keeps alive the controversy over the Pentagon Papers, believing it more of an embarrassment to the Democrats. "Roughest, toughest, sophisticated people have got to work on this," Nixon urged. Here, too, is the apparent origin of Colson's scheme to have Hunt forge cables by John F. Kennedy to implicate him in the assassination of South Vietnam President Diem. Ehrlichman proudly relates some of the latest feats of the Plumbers.

SEGMENT 2

PRESIDENT NIXON: Now, how this is handled—how to get that issue of the Pentagon Papers up front and center again is difficult. If it goes to the Congress, John feels that—John Ehrlichman—that we couldn't control them. In terms of leaking it into the court, it won't come out until after the election which is too late to do us any good. I mean, do you know what I mean?

If you just go through the judicial process, is it Ellsberg or [Leslie] Gelb or something else? The main thing about this is to keep it open—to keep it a running sore to allow these leaks in the columns, et cetera, et cetera, on them than to keep it to ourselves. But what I think we see at the present time is that we're at an impasse. I think a lot of work is being done. I mean, they're investigating—the FBI is investigating there and investigating here. They've done a lot of it and the rest.

But I think we may just be doing it too damn legalistically. Now, again, let's look at our opponents and at ourselves. It's in their interest—forget the Pentagon Papers and they're trying desperately to forget them—it's in our interest to have that issue front and center. In other words, you want to—there's only one weakness which we have to have in mind—showing vulnerability, and that is that Henry [Kissinger] is deeply involved not from the standpoint of criminology guilt, but from the standpoint that virtually every one of these people that are involved in stealing the papers and then publishing them were either students of his or associates of his and so forth. . . . .

MITCHELL: Are we talking about, Mr. President, of contents of the papers or the machination of just spreading them around?

PRESIDENT NIXON: Just spreading—well, the difficulty is—well, I thought so but, first—first, let me talk about a congressional hearing. The reason that we cannot allow or encourage a congressional hearing is that the congressional hearing starts down a smart concept. You will recall—I'm going to call Henry because Henry's so deeply involved and we can't allow that to happen.

MITCHELL: Well, I get back to the point. I'm not quite clear whether you're talking about the contents of the Pentagon Papers or the way they were leaked out of the government. The hearings is—

PRESIDENT NIXON: I don't give a damn about the contents or (unintelligible). I don't think people care. The main thing is to keep it stuck into the Democrats so that they squabble about it. Do you see what I mean? . . .

COLSON: The original plan with the Senate and the House is to have hearings into the origins of the Vietnam War based upon the revelations of the Pentagon Papers, the Diem coup, all the events that lead up to it, the subsequent decisions that were made, the bombing decisions, the Gulf of Tonkin. That doesn't involve—that does not involve the issue of how the papers got out of the government nor does it involve Kissinger or [Elliot] Richardson with them. . . . That nails Averill Harriman and Mc-George Bundy and a helluva lot of other guys.

EHRLICHMAN: Now, you see, when you say that then Henry says, well, wait until after we get our elections out of the way in Vietnam.

PRESIDENT NIXON: Forget it now. The elections are over. You see, that issue now—that's the reason I raise it. . . .

EHRLICHMAN: We have an ally and that is Ellsberg who still has quite a lot of visibility and who is very distressed of what's happening because they are—they are covering it up. He's going around the country on television screaming and hollering about it.

PRESIDENT NIXON: What's he distressed about?

EHRLICHMAN: That they're not opening a public scrutiny, you see. That was his great sacrifice for the nation and did it in vain. That's right. There is one way to get high visibility to the whole circumstance, again, and that would be to go after the newspapermen and that would rehash the whole First Amendment thing.

MITCHELL: You know, but that's a differential losing proposition.

EHRLICHMAN: Well, it is a very high visibility item now and it's still—we've still got that to use if you wish. The only way to really open up the contents of the Pentagon Papers themselves is with the assassination [of President Diem] and some of those really juicy things that are highly attractive and where we can give some inside information and get a controversy going. . . .

[Withdrawn item. National security.]

COLSON: That forces the hand of the people on the Hill. If you really let the whole story of the coup out, then the Republicans could say on the Hill, my God, let's get all the facts in here, you know. . . . What you really need—what are some of the underlying cables and documents that John and Egil have been studying that look pretty good around the coup period.

MITCHELL: Do you have a rundown as to which of those were in the possession of the *Times* and the *Post?*

EHRLICHMAN: Not for sure. No. . . . There's another part that we can begin to exploit that doesn't have to wait for the elections and that's the whole Bay of Pigs business and the Cuban missile crisis era and we are starting out a review of those documents to pick out the ones that should be floated out. *God, there's a ton of paper in this crazy thing.* Just the physical process of getting—but we know where it is. We have a guy in place going through everything but it's like spooning out the ocean, you know. It's a life's work. And you get 100 people who are sufficiently attuned and loyal to know what they're looking out, to go through this stuff, is nearly impossible. So, it's a monumental task to get back into this old stuff. . . .

SEGMENT 4

PRESIDENT NIXON: . . . I don't understand it. And we just don't have anybody worth a damn fighting our side of it. I have to go up to bat all the time myself.

MITCHELL: Can we get somebody that could devote full time to this project that's knowledgeable?

PRESIDENT NIXON: We have that.

EHRLICHMAN: We do have, John, and we've got Bud Krogh and Dave Young virtually full time on this with three other people.

PRESIDENT NIXON: It's just got to be an enormous job.

MITCHELL: I appreciate that.

EHRLICHMAN: But they're on salvo as far as the dirty tricks stuff from the Vietnam—

SEGMENT 5

PRESIDENT NIXON: Well, we just can't let them [Democrats] get away with this. That's the point. That is, their—it's their complicity and the Pentagon Papers are about their administration. That is why it's to our interest to put the war in their administration. Let them argue about that.

SEGMENT 6

MITCHELL: John Ehrlichman was talking about somebody that's on our side 100 percent, is knowledgeable about foreign affairs, could devote his whole time to this thing and has a little bit of dirty tricks to play.

HALDEMAN: David Young? . . .

MITCHELL: Well, Young is off the NSC staff and knows where all the bodies are buried in that group. And it is—I think as far as an understanding of what actually has gone on here, I think he's in possession of that. So we're not short in some people like that. . . .

PRESIDENT NIXON: That's right. We're going to get the facts. Well, Goddamnit, we're entitled to the facts. And, John, this is—(unintelligible) by any sonofabitch you can in there to help on it.

EHRLICHMAN: All right.

PRESIDENT NIXON: Dick Allen, Huston, anybody.

EHRLICHMAN: All right.

PRESIDENT NIXON: Roughest, toughest, sophisticated people have got to work on this. They've got to know something about it. I mean, your difficulty is—see, we're taking Krogh on it. It's awful hard to take even a fellow as capable as he is and start on this field and he won't know what he's reading. Now whatever Huston is, he's a person untrustworthy involved in many ways. But he does know what the hell he's doing.

EHRLICHMAN: That's right.

PRESIDENT NIXON: So does Dick Allen. . . . You've got to put somebody that knows what he's reading. . . .

EHRLICHMAN: That's right. . . .

PRESIDENT NIXON: Well, I could throw him into the deal, you know, because he'll have a great fellow working with him. Krogh would be excellent because he'll immediately understand the significance of things.

EHRLICHMAN: Well, we have a couple of fellows under Krogh—Liddy and Hunt—who know what they're doing and have been around. And so we could turn the media on to this . . .

SEPTEMBER 22, 1971: THE PRESIDENT AND BUCHANAN, 11:14–11:45 A.M., WHITE HOUSE TELEPHONE

Nixon and his aide/speechwriter discuss ways of embarrassing the likely Democratic presidential candidate, Senator Edmund Muskie, particularly because of his support of racial school busing. The discussion demonstrates Nixon's involvement with intricate details of political maneuvers.

BUCHANAN: Well, we've got to push Muskie's emphasis up in the headlines. . . .

PRESIDENT NIXON: That's right. That's right. Yeah. It's got to be—well, I think it's—I think it probably is going to get some play in the South now.

BUCHANAN: I think, well, that's something we could—you could really move by various statements, exaggerating his position, and then Muskie would come back sort of drawing it back and it raises—identifies him with it.

PRESIDENT NIXON: Except the thing to do really is to praise him, have some civil rights people praise him for his defense of busing.

BUCHANAN: Uh-huh.

PRESIDENT NIXON: That's the way to really get that, you know. It's much the better way than to have people attack him for it—

BUCHANAN: Uh-huh.

PRESIDENT NIXON:—is to praise him for his defense of busing. See?

BUCHANAN: Uh-huh. Uh-huh.

PRESIDENT NIXON: And I don't if you've got any people to do that or not. But I would think that would be very clever.

BUCHANAN: Uh-huh. Okay.

MAY 15, 1972: THE PRESIDENT AND COLSON, 9:23–9:24 P.M., WHITE HOUSE TELEPHONE

After Arthur Bremer shot Governor George Wallace during the 1972 presidential primaries, Nixon and Colson met to discuss possible responses.

PRESIDENT NIXON: Is he a left winger, right winger?

COLSON: Well, he's going to be a left winger by the time we get through, I think.

PRESIDENT NIXON: Good. Keep at that, keep at that.

COLSON: Yeah. I just wish that, God, that I'd thought sooner about planting a little literature out there [in Bremer's Milwaukee apartment].

PRESIDENT NIXON: [*Laughs*]

COLSON: It may be a little late, although I've got one source that maybe—

PRESIDENT NIXON: Good.

COLSON: —you could think about that. I mean, if they found it near his apartment that would be helpful.

MAY 16, 1972: THE PRESIDENT, HALDEMAN, COLSON, AND EHRLICHMAN, 8:44–9:47 A.M., OVAL OFFICE

Nixon always had ambivalent feelings about Attorney General Richard Klein-dienst. He appreciated Kleindienst's loyalty, yet he lacked respect for him. Here, Nixon makes it clear that Acting FBI Director L. Patrick Gray is to report directly to the President, not to Kleindienst.

PRESIDENT NIXON: But I mean kick the ass of the agencies. (unintelligible). You've got that for any people being an accomplice. Use it. Use Colson's outfit to snake out things. I mean, he'll do anything, I mean anything.

EHRLICHMAN: You're going to hear some squeaking about the pressure that we've put on these guys. When you see Kleindienst this morning, he may apologize to you because they didn't have their report in on time, for instance. We've got them on a very short tether. . . .

PRESIDENT NIXON: Another thing we've got to remember is that Kleindienst is, just like everybody else who goes through the horrors of investigation [for his role in ITT's alleged influence-buying earlier in 1972], he's gun-shy.

EHRLICHMAN: Very.

PRESIDENT NIXON: He's gun-shy. And he wants to prove that he's a good guy.

EHRLICHMAN: Well, I have an understanding with Kleindienst that we don't deal through him to Gray, we deal directly with Gray.

PRESIDENT NIXON: I deal directly with Gray always.

EHRLICHMAN: That is understood.

PRESIDENT NIXON: Does he not know? I told Kleindienst this in the office that day. He knows.

EHRLICHMAN: He told me that. . . .

PRESIDENT NIXON: Well, you were with me. Somebody was here when I said to Kleindienst, I said: Now, Dick, I just have one [requirement]. I do have direct relations with the [Acting FBI] Director. I told Gray that, too, and I said: "You both have to understand . . . that that's the way it's always been the case. And there are times when it's best that the Justice Department not know, we'll tell you what we think you need to know, and you've just got to understand." "I understand, I understand," [Gray said].

EHRLICHMAN: He played that back to me then.

HALDEMAN: There's no question of Dick knowing.

MAY 18, 1972: THE PRESIDENT AND HALDEMAN, 12:33–12:34 P.M., CAMP DAVID TELEPHONE

Nixon typically ordered aides to carry out some absurd order, as in the following two conversations. Usually, there is no evidence that action was taken.

PRESIDENT NIXON: I want those funds cut off for that MIT [Massachusetts Institute of Technology].

HALDEMAN: Right, I know what you mean.

PRESIDENT NIXON: You get ahold of [Budget Director Caspar] Weinberger and say I want the Goddamn funds and I want him to do it now. Get it done. Okay.

MAY 19, 1972: THE PRESIDENT AND EHRLICHMAN, 12:05–12:19 P.M., OVAL OFFICE

EHRLICHMAN: And then I just want to let you know that on MIT that Cap [Weinberger] has come up with a formula that I think does the job you want to do with a minimum amount of political damage. And so I've told him in your name to go ahead.

PRESIDENT NIXON: What do you mean, "a minimum amount of political damage?"

EHRLICHMAN: Well, in the way that it's done. I mean, the money dries up, but we don't make a big show of it. We don't let them pin it on you as retribution. And what we do is we quietly pass the word to the agency that those contracts are just not to be renewed.

PRESIDENT NIXON: It's a budget problem.

EHRLICHMAN: Yes, yes.

PRESIDENT NIXON: They say they don't have the money.

EHRLICHMAN: The other thing to do would be to send a memo around and throw it on the fire. . . .

PRESIDENT NIXON: I mean, do it.

EHRLICHMAN: Yeah, but don't get caught.

PRESIDENT NIXON: Slice them. And when they come in and whine around about that, say: "Where the hell were you when we were trying to do something about Vietnam?"

EHRLICHMAN: Okay. Well, that's where I thought you were.

JUNE 13, 1972: THE PRESIDENT AND COLSON, 4:17–5:38 P.M., EXECUTIVE OFFICE BUILDING

Nixon and Colson discuss surveillance of Nixon's Democratic opponents, including using the Secret Service.

SEGMENT 1

COLSON: Of course, I owe you an apology. I told you we had the painting I approached him on. . . .

PRESIDENT NIXON: That's Haldeman's job, as I told him.

COLSON: No. You know, I've still got a memo here that I sent over to that gathering place across the street in January telling us everything Muskie's doing. And I talked to them three weeks ago and they said they were taping everything, audio, and they were using video wherever we can. . . . And they weren't. They were just doing Humphrey in California. . . .

PRESIDENT NIXON: Particularly when we now saw that McGovern might well be nominated. Well, anyway, they've got it now? They've got it covered, have they?

COLSON: Well, they said so. . . . They haven't even been using a union. . . .

PRESIDENT NIXON: We? We have to use the union?

COLSON: That's right. You know how political this is.

PRESIDENT NIXON: Well, when did we find that out? Does that suggest an error of some sort? Goddamn it, I've used union [printers?] since I ran for the Congress and I never had any labor support . . . .

SEGMENT 2

PRESIDENT NIXON: For example, that business of the McGovern watch, it just has to be—it has to be now around the clock. . . . You never know what you're going to find.

COLSON: That's something you don't even have to—

PRESIDENT NIXON: You see, you don't—with me, hell, I've got Secret Service watching me. He does too, but, you know, there are ways that—

COLSON: Well, we've got the Secret Service. . . .

PRESIDENT NIXON: That's exactly right.

COLSON: In McGovern's case, he can go before a crowd and say one thing.

PRESIDENT NIXON: Yes.

COLSON: And the press will cover him, and he'll go before the news the next day—

PRESIDENT NIXON: You see, because he—could I just suggest this? Could we, for example, hire even like—why the hell don't we hire Dick, I don't know whether it's Dick Perlasky, or a young reporter. Could [Kenneth] Clawson find a good young reporter and say he's going to do a book. Teddy White does them . . . . And he just goes over there with his press pass. He doesn't open his mouth, but he just covers the sonofabitch like a blanket.

COLSON: I've got a good man to use for that.

PRESIDENT NIXON: I would do it.

SEGMENT 3

COLSON: I think we have to be very careful not to get caught in doing it, but I think we've got to see that it's done. And we strictly have a mechanical problem, Mr. President. . . . Under this new statute with the reporting requirements, we have got to get funded [by] the committee [CREEP]. We can't do what we used to do.

PRESIDENT NIXON: I see.

COLSON: I talked to [Robert] Ellsworth today and he will get money from Felix Rohatyn and some of the Democrats . . . .

JUNE 14, 1972: THE PRESIDENT AND HALDEMAN, 4:59–6:03 P.M., OVAL OFFICE

Maurice Stans, chief fund-raiser for the Committee to Re-elect the President (CREEP), desperately tried to nail down contributions before new reporting laws went into effect. The President was intimately involved in these dealings.

PRESIDENT NIXON: . . . I think it's very important maybe for you just to talk to Stans about . . . secret contributors. You know, I don't think the amount bothers or anything, but I think the fact that you won't reveal who the hell contributed does bother people. And I just wondered how many there are that are in that, see what I mean. First of all, I think all those that are willing haven't given 25 [thousand]—

HALDEMAN: I've already—

PRESIDENT NIXON: Told Mitchell that?

HALDEMAN: No. Had [CREEP Finance Committee Treasurer] Hugh Sloan work on it, just so they'd just do it through their office there, because that's simple. It's a damn good idea: get all the obvious names, just get them on the record, the ones that don't care.

PRESIDENT NIXON: But lean over in the direction of doing it rather than not doing it.

HALDEMAN: Right.

PRESIDENT NIXON: I would think that—

HALDEMAN: Urge everybody to—

PRESIDENT NIXON: I don't know who the hell wouldn't want to do it. I don't know who the contributors are, but all of our big ones would want to. . . .

HALDEMAN: They're all known anyway.

PRESIDENT NIXON: Right.

HALDEMAN: They're all standard Republican contributors.

PRESIDENT NIXON: And I'd put all of them in at about 25 or 20 [thousand], something like that. You're going to do that, and we would then be in a position where we say: Well, our contributors, they're all on the list. I don't know how we got on the wicket of giving out the amount. Was that necessary? . . .

HALDEMAN: Yes.

PRESIDENT NIXON: We had to reveal how much money we collected before, without any names?

HALDEMAN: That's right.

PRESIDENT NIXON: The law required that?

HALDEMAN: You had to show what money, starting on the reporting date, how much you had on hand going in. And as I said, we had substantially more than that on hand, but we got rid of it. . . . You've got to give Stans credit. It was collected over a period of three weeks.

PRESIDENT NIXON: Was it really?

HALDEMAN: The sonofabitch just got on his horse and rode, and he really worked on it and he just sucked that money in as fast as he could suck it in. . . . And you've got a hell of a time spending money as well. You've got an enormous reporting problem in spending it, including you have to show the salary you pay everybody.

PART TWO

WATERGATE:
BREAK-IN AND COVER-UP

JUNE 1972 – DECEMBER 1972

In the early morning hours of June 17, 1972, police arrested five burglars in the Democratic National Committee headquarters in the Watergate complex in Washington. Four of the burglars were Cuban; the fifth, who had been booked under an alias, was James McCord, a former CIA employee and, the FBI soon learned, Chief of Security for the Committee to Re-Elect the President (CREEP). Investigators subsequently determined that this was the second illegal entry, the first having occurred just after Memorial Day when wiretaps were installed and documents were photographed; presumably, the second entry was made to adjust the tapping equipment. E. Howard Hunt, another former CIA employee, and G. Gordon Liddy, Counsel for CREEP, who, the FBI soon learned, had done "law enforcement" work for John Ehrlichman, had observed the break-in and arrest from a nearby hotel. The FBI searched a hotel room and found evidence linking Hunt to the burglars and the White House. Hunt and Liddy were soon arrested. At the time, Charles Colson described both men as "good healthy right-wing exuberants."

White House Press Secretary Ron Ziegler refused to comment on what he called a "third-rate burglary attempt." The President described his own reaction as "cynical." Dirty tricks, he said, were familiar stuff; "I could not muster much moral outrage over a political bugging," he later wrote. Democratic National Committee Chairman

Lawrence O'Brien announced a $1 million damage suit against CREEP on June 20. By then, newspapers had mentioned Hunt's involvement and discovered his links to Colson. O'Brien charged that the case had "a clear line to the White House." Almost immediately in his White House conversations, Richard Nixon established his own rationalizations: the break-in was stupid, it may have been concocted by double agents, and breaking and entering Democratic headquarters was not really a crime.

The break-in is directly linked to President Nixon's re-election campaign. No different from other candidates, Nixon desired every possible vote. With George McGovern looming as his probable opponent, Nixon and his top advisors knew that the only question would be the size of the President's victory. Still, the White House pushed constantly for intelligence about Democratic plans and tactics. The President himself was not shy about what was needed. "We should come up with . . . imaginative dirty tricks," he told an aide. Nixon's insatiable need for "intelligence" went from Haldeman to his own man at CREEP headquarters, Deputy Campaign Director Jeb Magruder, and from Magruder to his putative superior, Campaign Manager John Mitchell. Word filtered down to Liddy, an obscure operative who had worked with the Plumbers unit. Liddy devised an overheated plan of intelligence-gathering and convention disruptions against the Democrats, which included the Watergate break-in and bugging. After initial rejection by Mitchell, Liddy got his scheme approved, and the result was high comedy that fast developed into tragedy.

No direct evidence exists demonstrating that Nixon knew the particulars of these plans; still, he constantly pressed his men for intelligence about Democratic contributors, Democratic plans for their campaign or tactics to be used against Republicans, and, a favorite Nixon object of inquiry and scrutiny, Democratic National Chairman Lawrence O'Brien. What were the Democrats doing? What did they know that might be worrisome? O'Brien's personal finances? Democratic plans regarding the Republican convention? The role of foreign money? Gordon Liddy suggested that the purpose was "to find out what O'Brien had of a derogatory nature about us, not for us to get something on him or the Democrats. In these new tapes, Haldeman offers two new, but somewhat cryptic, references to another explanation. Three days after the break-in, responding to Nixon's dismissive remark that the Democratic National Committee had nothing worth bugging, Haldeman said, "except for the financial thing." Seven months later, Haldeman said they were "looking for stuff on two things." One, he said, was "financial"; he didn't explain the second item.

Whatever the cause of the break-in, almost instantly the President and his top aides, H. R. Haldeman and John D. Ehrlichman, instituted a cover-up, and installed the young White House counsel, John Dean, as its ringmaster. These new tapes throw further light on the cover-up's motivation. On June 21, 1973, Haldeman told the President that an inquiry into Watergate would lead "to other things [and] . . . it's better to take a little heat on this than to open it up to all the others." The arrest of Howard Hunt, a man who knew many of the secrets of the "White House horrors," particularly accelerated the need for a cover-up. Nixon realized the risks. On September 11, he said: "The *cover-up* is what hurts you, not the issue. It's the cover-up that hurts." That thought recurs a number of times in Nixon's conversations; he was painfully aware of the consequences. The cover-up involved the President in fatal ventures to use the CIA to thwart the FBI, the payment of hush money to the defendants and their families, ambiguous promises of clemency, and an attempt to prevent a congressional investigation. Pressures mounted from the work of the U.S. Attorney and the grand jury, from the demands for money payments from Hunt and the burglars, and from increasingly probing media articles. In a December 11 conversation, near the end of this period, the President complained about the "aura of hanky [-panky]—worse, of corruption" that pervaded the White House. Whatever his doubts and misgivings, Nixon persisted on the course of maintaining the cover-up.

On September 15, 1972, the President and Haldeman had a lengthy conversation with John Dean, who reported on the state of the Watergate cover-up to the Commander-in-Chief. Dean promised Nixon "that fifty-four days from now [Election Day] that not a thing will come crashing down to our, our surprise." The President well knew the extent of Dean's involvement and for the next seven months, he spoke of his young aide only in the most glowing words.

Nixon celebrated his magnificent re-election in November. He swept the Electoral College, winning every state but Massachusetts and the District of Columbia; he gained 60 per cent of the popular vote, just failing to top Lyndon Johnson's 1964 margin. Later, Nixon remembered the "foreboding" that tempered his triumph and joy. He knew that Watergate's "marring effects" put a gloss on that victory—the only "sour note" of the moment. When he began his second term in January 1973, he gave his aides and Cabinet members a four-year calendar, with an inscription noting that he would serve "1,461 days—no more, no less."

June 20, 1972: The President and Haldeman, 11:26 A.M.–12:45 P.M., Executive Office Building

This is the highly publicized "18½-minute gap." Technical and scientific investigations determined that the tape had been electronically erased by unknown persons some time after Alexander P. Butterfield revealed the existence of the Nixon Administration taping system in 1973. H. R. Haldeman's diary entry for this date talks about lengthy meetings with John Ehrlichman, John Mitchell, and John Dean, which concluded that it was necessary to keep the FBI from going "beyond what's necessary in developing evidence and that we can keep a lid on that." Haldeman said that he and the President talked about "our counterattack" and "PR offensive."

June 20, 1972: The President and Haldeman, 4:35–5:25 P.M., Executive Office Building

This is the first known taped conversation on Watergate following the break-in. The President already is aware that his campaign manager, John Mitchell, had agreed to "Gemstone," an elaborate intelligence scheme that included bugging the Democratic National Committee headquarters in the Watergate complex. Nixon and Haldeman are familiar with the Cuban burglars' prior operations. They talk of the roles of James McCord and especially E. Howard Hunt. They know of Hunt's links to Colson—and hence to the White House. Throughout, Nixon has an abiding fear that Colson was involved. There is an interesting, cryptic comment that "this financial thing" may have made bugging the Democratic Committee worthwhile. Finally, the two refer to their special, shared secret: the White House taping system.

PRESIDENT NIXON: Have you gotten any further on that Mitchell operation?

HALDEMAN: No. I don't think he did [know].

PRESIDENT NIXON: I think he was surprised. . . .

HALDEMAN: . . . [T]hese guys [the burglars] apparently are a pretty competent bunch of people, and they've been doing other things very well, apparently.

PRESIDENT NIXON: Mitchell lies (unintelligible). . . . What would Mitchell's conclusion be (unintelligible), basically?

HALDEMAN: Well, I haven't talked to him since this. They have filed a suit, the Democratic committee, directly sued the Committee for Re-Election and the Republican National Committee for a million dollars, $100,000 damages and $900,000—

[Withdrawn item. Privacy.]

HALDEMAN: —they want to get to depositions.

PRESIDENT NIXON: I don't know what the law is. I mean, I don't know how long it takes.

HALDEMAN: [John] Dean said that's the kind of thing, once they file and a judge orders, sets the thing and starts the suit going and all, you could stall it for a couple of months, probably down to [the election] with technical (unintelligible) and pleadings. . . .

PRESIDENT NIXON: It's fortunately, it's fortunately a bizarre story.

HALDEMAN: Yes. . . . But its bizarreness almost helps to discredit it—

[Withdrawn item. Privacy.]

HALDEMAN: [McCord's] on a regular monthly retainer, a fee.

PRESIDENT NIXON: Does he have other clients?

HALDEMAN: And he had a regular monthly fee at the National Committee also. . . . Apparently he set up, installed some television closed circuit monitoring stuff, and then they have six guards and some supervisors. . . .

McCord, I guess, will say that he was working with the Cubans, he wanted to put this in for their own political reasons. But Hunt disappeared or is in the process of disappearing. He can undisappear if we want him to. He can disappear to a Latin American country. But at least the original thought was that that would do it, that he might want to disappear, (unintelligible) on the basis that these guys, the Cubans— see, he was in the Bay of Pigs thing. One of the Cubans, [Bernard] Barker, the guy with the American name, was his deputy in the Bay of Pigs operation and so they're kind of trying to tie it to the Cuban nationalists. . . .

PRESIDENT NIXON: We are?

HALDEMAN: Yes. Now of course they're trying to tie these guys to Colson, [and] the White House. . . . It's strange—if Colson doesn't run out, it doesn't go anywhere. The closest they come, he [Hunt] was a consultant to Colson. We have detailed somewhat the nature of his consulting fee and said it was basically (unintelligible). I don't know.

PRESIDENT NIXON: You don't know what he did? . . .

HALDEMAN: I think we all knew that there were some—

PRESIDENT NIXON: Intelligence.

HALDEMAN: —some activities, and we were getting reports, or some input anyway. But I don't think—I don't think Chuck knew specifically that this was under way. . . .

PRESIDENT NIXON: Well, if he did . . . second-guess. . . .

HALDEMAN: He seems to take all the blame himself.

PRESIDENT NIXON: Did he? Good.

HALDEMAN: He was saying this morning that it was damn stupid for him to not learn about the details and know exactly what was going on. . . . They sweep [for bugs] this office and your Oval Office twice a week. . . .

PRESIDENT NIXON: This Oval Office business [i.e., the taping system] complicates things all over.

HALDEMAN: They say it's extremely good. I haven't listened to the tapes.

PRESIDENT NIXON: They're kept for future purposes.

HALDEMAN: Nobody monitors those tapes, obviously. They are kept stacked up and locked up in a super-secure—there are only three people that know [about the system]. . . .

If they get all the circumstantial stuff tied together, maybe it's better . . . to plead guilty, saying we were spying on the Democrats. Just let the Cubans say, we, McCord . . . figured it was safe for us to use.

PRESIDENT NIXON: Well, they've got to plead guilty.

HALDEMAN: . . . [A]nd we [the Cubans] went in there to get this because we're scared to death that this crazy man's going to become President and sell the U.S. out to the communists. . . .

PRESIDENT NIXON: How was he [Hunt] directly involved?

HALDEMAN: He was across the street in the Howard Johnson Motel with a direct line of sight room, observing across the street. And that was the room in which they had the receiving equipment for the bugs.

PRESIDENT NIXON: Well, does Hunt work for us or what?

HALDEMAN: No. Oh, we don't know. I don't know. I don't know if that's one— that's something I haven't gotten an answer to, how—apparently McCord had Hunt working with him, or Hunt had McCord working with him, and with these Cubans. They're all tied together. Hunt when he ran the Bay of Pigs thing was working with this guy Barker, one of the Cubans who was arrested.

PRESIDENT NIXON: How does the press know about this?

HALDEMAN: They don't. Oh, they know Hunt's involved because they found his name in the address book of two of the Cubans, Barker's book and one of the other guy's books. He's identified as "White House." And also because one of the Cubans had a check from Hunt, a check for $690 or something like that, which Hunt had given to this Cuban to take back to Miami with him and mail. It was to pay his country club bill. . . .

PRESIDENT NIXON: Hunt?

HALDEMAN: Hunt, yes. Probably so he can pay non-resident dues at the country club or something. But anyway, they had that check, so that was another tie.

PRESIDENT NIXON: Well, in a sense, if the Cubans—the fact that Hunt's involved with the Cubans or McCord's involved with the Cubans, here are the Cuban people. . . .

PRESIDENT NIXON: My God, the committee isn't worth bugging in my opinion. That's my public line.

HALDEMAN: Except for this financial thing. They thought they had something going on that.

PRESIDENT NIXON: Yes, I suppose.

HALDEMAN: But I asked that question: If we were going to all that trouble, why in the world would we pick the Democratic National Committee to do it to? It's the least fruitful source—

JUNE 21, 1972: THE PRESIDENT, HALDEMAN, AND COLSON, 9:30–10:38 A.M., OVAL OFFICE

The cover-up takes shape. John Mitchell suggests that the FBI be "turned off." Everyone is impressed that Gordon Liddy—"apparently a little bit nuts"—would confess and take the fall for others. But E. Howard Hunt's arrest filled Nixon with foreboding: "He's done a lot of things." Nixon is a bit relieved when he hears that

Hunt has "decided he's not going to be around." The President and Haldeman nervously worry that Colson might have been involved. Nixon insists that the break-in was of no consequence: "[B]reaking and entering . . . without accomplishing it, is not a hell of a lot of crime." His rationale is a recurring theme. John Ehrlichman, Mitchell's principal White House adversary, ominously begins a nearly year-long campaign to saddle Mitchell with the blame.

SEGMENT 1

PRESIDENT NIXON: What's the dope on the Watergate incident? Anything break on that?

HALDEMAN: No. We talked about that. We don't talk about it at the staff meeting. It's very interesting because I've been prepared to cold-cock it if it comes up at the staff meeting and it hasn't even come up. . . . You know, somebody made some crack about it or something, but it didn't come up. Nobody wanted to discuss it. . . . But I talked with Mitchell afterwards.

PRESIDENT NIXON: Mitchell was at the staff meeting?

HALDEMAN: Yes.

PRESIDENT NIXON: Good, good. . . .

HALDEMAN: Yes. Doesn't say much. Well, but he does once in a while and he raises some good questions, more asking than telling. But it's very useful to have Mitchell there.

PRESIDENT NIXON: Yes.

HALDEMAN: There's nothing new. The whole question now is, Mitchell's concern is the FBI, the question of how far they're going in the process. He's concerned that, that be turned off, and then they're working on John.

PRESIDENT NIXON: My God, Ehrlichman, are you talking—it's got to be done by Ehrlichman. . . .

HALDEMAN: Well, we were told yesterday in the discussion on this that we should not go direct to the FBI. Mitchell said today that we've got to, and he asked Ehrlichman to talk to Gray. John's doing it. The question that John and I raised, both of us have been trying to think with a one step away from it and look at a strategy on creating—see whether there's something that we can do other than just sitting here and watching it drop on us bit by bit as it goes along. And there is—it's pretty tough to—

PRESIDENT NIXON: Think of anything.

HALDEMAN: —start maybe now. John [Mitchell] laid out a scenario, . . . which would involve this guy Liddy at the committee confessing and taking, moving the thing up to that level, saying: "Yeah, I did it, I did it; I hired these guys, sent them over there, because I thought it would be a good move and build me up in the operation; I'm a little guy."

PRESIDENT NIXON: Liddy?

HALDEMAN: Nobody pays any attention to him.

PRESIDENT NIXON: Who's he? He's the guy with the detective agency?

HALDEMAN: No. Liddy is the general counsel for the Re-Election Finance Committee and he is the guy who did this.

PRESIDENT NIXON: Mitchell—

HALDEMAN: I'm not sure how much—he obviously knew something. I'm not sure how much. He clearly didn't know any details.

PRESIDENT NIXON: Isn't there some way you can get a little better protection, get a little better protection for the White House on that? I think that was rather explicit. You know what I mean, the Colson thing and so forth. I mean, he's taking a bad rap there. Of course, if he's taking the rap, basically the White House is taking the rap, the White House consultant, and so forth and so on. He [E. Howard Hunt] worked for Kennedy, he worked for Johnson, now he worked for the White House. That's the whole story about him.

HALDEMAN: That he did.

PRESIDENT NIXON: Okay. Well, maybe there isn't much you can do about it. You're convinced, though, this is a situation where Colson is not involved, aren't you?

HALDEMAN: Yes. I'm completely convinced of that. As far as I can determine, it is.

PRESIDENT NIXON: I'm not concerned. . . . I just want to be sure we know what the facts are.

HALDEMAN: Well, I think that is the fact. The problem is that there are all kinds of other involvements and if they started a fishing thing on this they're going to start picking up tracks. That's what appeals to me about trying to get one jump ahead of them and hopefully cut the whole thing off and sink all of it. You see, Ehrlichman paints a rather attractive picture on that, in that that gives you the opportunity to cut off the civil suit. The civil suit is potentially the most damaging thing to us in terms of those depositions.

PRESIDENT NIXON: You mean you'd have Liddy confess and say he did it unauthorized?

HALDEMAN: Unauthorized. And then on the civil suit, we plead whatever it is and you get a, what is it, a summary judgment or something. . . . I don't know what the legal name is. But he saw that as the way to cut it off, too, and then let it go to trial on the question of damages, and that would eliminate the need for the depositions. . . .

PRESIDENT NIXON: Well, if you think that they have to [show] White House involvement (unintelligible).

HALDEMAN: Well, we're getting a bad shot to a degree because—it's 100 percent by innuendo. The only tie they've got to the White House is that this guy's name was in their books, Howard Hunt, and that Hunt used to be a consultant—

PRESIDENT NIXON: To the White House?

HALDEMAN: —to Colson at the White House.

PRESIDENT NIXON: And he worked for the CIA. He worked in the Bay of Pigs. I mean, he's done a lot of things. So I've got to guess is that, I mean, it could be isolated instances. If the man's worked for various things, he's worked for—

HALDEMAN: You've got to be careful of pushing that very hard, because he was working on a lot of stuff.

PRESIDENT NIXON: For Colson, you mean? Any classification here?

HALDEMAN: No. It was that among other things. That's what we've said.

PRESIDENT NIXON: Well, did he work on that ITT thing, too?

HALDEMAN: Yes, see, and if they track that down—

PRESIDENT NIXON: He didn't accomplish anything.

HALDEMAN: But he's the guy that went out and took—talked to [ITT lobbyist] Dita Beard in Denver.

PRESIDENT NIXON: . . . Hunt's the Dita Beard contact?

HALDEMAN: Among other things. They've used him for a lot of stuff, apparently. That's, like all these other things, it's all a fringe, bits and pieces that you don't want to [know]—that's why they have—and there's a very—I've challenged this question of Hunt disappearing and they say there is no question it's better for Hunt to disappear than for Hunt to be available, and there's no question that Hunt would be called in this. But the effectiveness of the Ehrlichman scenario or something like it is that you establish . . . the admission of guilt at a local level and get rid of it, rather than letting it imply guilt up to the highest levels, which is of course what they're trying very hard to do. By "they," [I mean] the press and the Democrats.

PRESIDENT NIXON: Well, sure it is. I understand that.

HALDEMAN: Although it's incredible, Dan Rather comes up on the news and says: Well, it's been a tough week for the presidential candidates, and we have the Republicans tarred with complicity in bugging the Democrats and McGovern in trouble with his radical views and you have Hubert in trouble because he's lost his support. He kind of socked everybody, which amazed me.

I think our people deluded themselves, and I have to a degree, in thinking this was a Washington story, that it would not be of much interest. The networks aren't going to let it be that, because they didn't have much of any interest on it. Just, there's no new news. They're investigating those Cubans. They're bound to re-run some of these strings.

PRESIDENT NIXON: Colson was telling me something about some [judgment] that [Bebe] Rebozo was involved in.

HALDEMAN: I haven't seen that.

PRESIDENT NIXON: [Columnist] Jack Anderson made some charge.

HALDEMAN: Oh, really?

PRESIDENT NIXON: . . . Jack Anderson said Rebozo was involved in it with the Cubans, one of the Cubans. I don't know.

HALDEMAN: Well, I'm sure they'll find a tie to Rebozo with the Cubans sometime.

PRESIDENT NIXON: Oh, Christ, yes. But my point is that if they get this kind of a charge—if we could get the exact charge on this and so forth, he ought to sue. You know what I mean, because he knows Goddamn well he's not involved with it. See what I mean? Jack Anderson, what they would like to do is they'd like to tie him in order to tie us into it.

HALDEMAN: Sure, sure.

PRESIDENT NIXON: Well, obviously, obviously if he has nothing whatever, had no knowledge at all. . . . So why don't you just call and ask him if he knows he's being (unintelligible).

HALDEMAN: Okay.

PRESIDENT NIXON: But find out from Colson, get the text of what Jack Anderson said on Metromedia.

HALDEMAN: Yes.

PRESIDENT NIXON: Well, it's a hard one to handle, I realize.

HALDEMAN: Unfortunately, they're inter-meshing threats. One of these guys was over at the University of Miami trying to work out housing for the Youth for Nixon group at the convention.

PRESIDENT NIXON: They're all supporters of ours.

HALDEMAN: And two of them have been principals in the Nixon stuff down there. That's why in a way—

PRESIDENT NIXON: You can't push a lot onto the Miami thing can you—I mean, the Cuban thing.

HALDEMAN: Well, yeah, you can. If you lose that—it's a pretty flimsy—

PRESIDENT NIXON: Liddy.

HALDEMAN: (unintelligible) if you bring Liddy into it. . . .

PRESIDENT NIXON: That's right.

HALDEMAN: That's one argument against it, because you could work to blame that, . . . Howard Hunt, all the other guys [that] tie to Colson.

PRESIDENT NIXON: That's right.

HALDEMAN: Except—well, no. You could imply implicitly—I was going to say, except for this security guy, what's his name, McCord?

PRESIDENT NIXON: McCord.

HALDEMAN: That he was a CIA agent for nineteen years or so.

PRESIDENT NIXON: Sure he was hired, for Christ's sakes. He was hired because of his technical equipment or his tie to the Cubans. You see what I mean?

HALDEMAN: Hunt was the tie to the Cubans.

PRESIDENT NIXON: He's the one that recruited the Cubans? An elaborate deal, wasn't it? Apparently they said or they implied that they had some plans to bug McGovern headquarters, too?

HALDEMAN: Well, I don't know. They found a plan of the—that's a pretty shady bit of journalism, incidentally, which they haven't pointed out and we shouldn't, but the committee can. They had a plan that showed the layout of the ballroom area at the Doral Hotel, which is going to be McGovern's headquarters. What the press didn't point out is the Doral Hotel is also going to be the Nixon headquarters. We had a lot of plans of the Doral Hotel all over here, because it happens to be where we're going on our room arrangements, and that's true.

PRESIDENT NIXON: I don't know who can take it on. Who's over there at the committee that can do a little slam-banging on that sort of thing? I think that you ought to chip away at things of that sort, that are so obvious.

HALDEMAN: Yeah, I think we should, and we will. I made a note on that one.

PRESIDENT NIXON: [Bob] Dole?

HALDEMAN: That's just a little—

PRESIDENT NIXON: Sure, I know, but I saw it in the paper. . . .

HALDEMAN: And they've taken a very fast chop, but I think we've got to be careful not to jump on it, a fast chop at Colson, which is going to bother him today. The *Post* runs a thing on the principals in the Democratic bugging incident, . . . biographies, a three-paragraph biography on each of the principals. The first one is Howard Hunt, they tell about him. The second is Charles Colson, and then come the five guys that were caught in the room, and then someone else—oh, the lawyer that they called in.

PRESIDENT NIXON: Liddy?

HALDEMAN: No, the lawyer that they called.

PRESIDENT NIXON: That they hired?

HALDEMAN: The counsel that they got to represent them [Douglas Caddy].

PRESIDENT NIXON: Jesus Christ, it's a rough deal on Colson, isn't it?

HALDEMAN: Yeah, it is. But we've got to be careful not to over-defend him. And Colson has to be careful not to overreact, and that's because, you know, sure he's clean on this little slice.

PRESIDENT NIXON: Yes, but he's involved in other [things].

HALDEMAN: But it leads to other things that there's just—it's better to take a little heat on this than to open it up to all the others.

PRESIDENT NIXON: The one thing they have to do is to keep it in perspective from another standpoint. I was not of the opinion that it would just be a Washington story.

HALDEMAN: I kind of was. Well, not just a Washington story.

PRESIDENT NIXON: I understand. I thought there were two, there's two different problems. Anything as bizarre as this and interesting is going to be a national story.

HALDEMAN: Yeah.

PRESIDENT NIXON: My view is, and I still hold with this view, that in terms of the re-action of people, the reaction is going to be primarily Washington and not the coun-try, because I think the country doesn't give much of a shit about it other than the ones we've already bugged. Now, somebody else, you see—now, everybody around here is all mortified by it. It's a horrible thing to rebut. And the answer of course is that most people around the country think that this is routine, that everybody's trying to bug everybody else, it's politics. That's my view. The purists probably won't agree with that, but I don't think they're going to see a great uproar in the country about the Republican committee trying to bug the Democratic headquarters.

HALDEMAN: Well, if that line of reasoning—

PRESIDENT NIXON: At least that's my view.

HALDEMAN: —then it seems to me that argues for following the Liddy scenario, saying: Sure, some little lawyer who was trying to make a name for himself did a stu-pid thing.

PRESIDENT NIXON: Is Liddy willing?

HALDEMAN: He says he is. Apparently he is a little bit nuts. I have never met him, so it's not fair to draw any judgment. But apparently he's sort of a Tom Huston type guy.

PRESIDENT NIXON: And you say [that he will] beat the bastards, right?

HALDEMAN: Well, and he sort of likes the dramatic. He's said: "If you want to put me before a firing squad and shoot me, that's fine. I'd kind of like to be like Nathan Hale."

PRESIDENT NIXON: The lawyer? Oh, I thought it was the guy that—I thought that was the fellow that runs the agency.

HALDEMAN: No. We don't know what his position is. They all seem to think he will hang tight. But you see, the beauty of the Liddy scenario is that as far as anybody under him is concerned, he's where it came from.

PRESIDENT NIXON: He ordered it.

HALDEMAN: So even if we can't count on those guys, if we admit—if Liddy admits guilt, then those guys can think any way they want and it won't matter.

PRESIDENT NIXON: Yeah.

HALDEMAN: Because it'll all tie back to Liddy and he says: Yeah, I got the money and I paid them the money and I told them to bug the place and I was going to be a hero. Then we ask for compassion: This is a poor misguided kid who read too many spy stories, a little bit nutty, and obviously we'll have to get rid of him, we made a mistake in having him in there and that's too bad.

PRESIDENT NIXON: Look, breaking and entering and so forth, without accomplishing it, is not a hell of a lot of crime. The point is that this is not—the only thing I'd say if somebody was going to ask me about, do you agree with Ziegler's cut calling it a third-rate burglary, I'd say: No, I disagree; it was a third-rate *attempted* burglary.

HALDEMAN: Yes.

PRESIDENT NIXON: That's what it was.

HALDEMAN: Yes.

PRESIDENT NIXON: And it failed. . . .

HALDEMAN: Well, they don't think they can hurt much on that. If they take a guilty plea, the lawyers all feel that they would get a fine and a suspended sentence.

PRESIDENT NIXON: Suspended sentence.

HALDEMAN: As long as they're all first offenders, which they apparently all are.

PRESIDENT NIXON: Well, who's going to talk to Mitchell today about this?

HALDEMAN: We have.

PRESIDENT NIXON: So he's thinking about the Liddy thing. My inclination is that's what you have to do. My inclination is you have to do it due to the fact that, if that's the truth, the truth you always figure may come out, and you're a hell of a lot better doing that than to build another tissue around the Goddamn thing. Let me say this. If it involved Mitchell, then I would think that you couldn't do it, just because it would destroy him.

HALDEMAN: Well, that's what bothers Ehrlichman. He's not sure it doesn't.

PRESIDENT NIXON: Doesn't involve Mitchell?

HALDEMAN: Yes. I put it almost directly to Mitchell this morning and he didn't answer, so I don't know whether it does or not.

PRESIDENT NIXON: Hell, he may have said, don't tell me about it, but you go ahead and do what you want. But that doesn't take the rap, you know.

HALDEMAN: Well, we can take care of him.

PRESIDENT NIXON: Yes. You know, I wouldn't try to shove it in Miami, but I think that you're going to have Hunt on the lam, if he is, and that's going to be quite a story. . . .

HALDEMAN: Yes, except they've got no direct tie-in from Hunt, at least up until now. . . . The problem there is, that's why it's important to get to the FBI. As of now, there's nothing that puts Hunt into the case except his name in their notebooks along with a lot of other things.

PRESIDENT NIXON: Why did the FBI put out all of that stuff? It seems to me a rather bad thing to do. I mean, when you're investigating a case you don't put out the fact that you found this bit of evidence, you found names and notebooks and the rest.

HALDEMAN: The Bureau didn't. The police did.

PRESIDENT NIXON: Oh, I see. Okay, that would add up. They're sort of stupid. Some press man gets to them.

HALDEMAN: This one, you got to figure, because of the pressure, damn near every-thing's going to get out. I'm sure that they've bought policemen and undoubtedly bought FBI agents. . . . [Joseph] Califano's got two men riding the U. S. Attorney's office.

PRESIDENT NIXON: We'd do the same thing.

HALDEMAN: Sure. Oh, hell, they're doing exactly—and the lawsuit I think, the civil suit—

PRESIDENT NIXON: Very clever.

HALDEMAN: —is a damn good move. They've got Edward Bennett Williams in to do the depositions.

PRESIDENT NIXON: How soon do they get to those?

HALDEMAN: Well, again, the lawyers think we can go for some varying things to hold that up. But the Democrats of course, Bennett Williams, is going on the basis of starting immediately. And they've made no bones about it. They've said the reason they're doing it is to get the depositions.

PRESIDENT NIXON: Ehrlichman should talk to Gray. We've got to find out what the law is on the depositions.

HALDEMAN: Yes. If they get at Colson—

PRESIDENT NIXON: . . . [T]hey'd probably try to unravel his whole relationship with Hunt.

HALDEMAN: Which he could say is irrelevant or his counsel could say is irrelevant. But that doesn't matter in a deposition. That's the problem—at least, that's what Ehrlichman and Mitchell were explaining to me. The problem with the deposition process is that you don't have the protection of a court. You don't have the judge. You can refuse to answer, but then the taker of the deposition, it's my understanding, can go to the court and get an order for you to answer. . . .

PRESIDENT NIXON: It doesn't look to me like we've got too much of a choice there. . . .

HALDEMAN: Well, Mitchell, rightly I think, is a little afraid of doing that because of Liddy's instability and the question of what exactly—he says he'll do it, but what ex-actly will he do when they turn the heat on, because obviously they'll see that as a way for us to get out of it and they aren't going to let him off any easier than they have to. They'd have to pursue that. John just developed this scenario as we were talking this morning—

PRESIDENT NIXON: Who, Ehrlichman?

HALDEMAN: Ehrlichman. And he and Mitchell and I all felt we ought not—that on first blush it looked like it had some possibilities, but we ought to work on what's wrong with it.

SEGMENT 2

PRESIDENT NIXON: [O]ur people, our people, it seems to me are not basically too discreet, you know what I mean, in the way they handle things. We know our Demo-cratic friends, Goddamn it, for years have screwed us on this sort of thing and we never—I mean, they never get caught, do they? Do you know of any times?

HALDEMAN: Oh, they do, but it doesn't—

PRESIDENT NIXON: Nobody builds it up. . . . Well, Bob, you know why.

HALDEMAN: You know, like this crappy thing, tossing Colson in today, which is—

PRESIDENT NIXON: On the basis that he's with Hunt, isn't that it? That's all?

HALDEMAN: Well, that Hunt works for him. But they spell out what he did. That's—it's just two steps removed, and to list him in the cast of characters in the robbery is just—the implication is that he was there.

SEGMENT 3

[Colson joins the President and Haldeman.]

PRESIDENT NIXON: . . . Bob was wondering what the Goddamn *Post* thinks you've been doing.

COLSON: Oh, Christ.

PRESIDENT NIXON: Incidentally, I [talked to] Bob about Rebozo. He said he didn't hear about it. I just showed him this. We have, with all of our hundreds of people around here reading things, you know—can you get a script of what the sonofabitch [Jack Anderson] said?

COLSON: Yes, sir.

PRESIDENT NIXON: Because Rebozo—

HALDEMAN: Has taken all hell.

PRESIDENT NIXON: He's been so abused. . . .

COLSON: That was the most libelous thing, to take a person [himself] who's a member of the bar and who's practiced law for ten years and put him in a lineup with a bunch of criminals.

HALDEMAN: Right.

PRESIDENT NIXON: Well, you can't libel political men.

COLSON: That's right.

PRESIDENT NIXON: So you forget it. But you can libel Rebozo. He's a banker.

COLSON: Yeah.

PRESIDENT NIXON: Goddamn it, he can sue. . . .

COLSON: You think it will go away?

HALDEMAN: That's ridiculous. Why in the world would the—

PRESIDENT NIXON: How could they let it go away?

HALDEMAN: If you were anybody at any level in the Democratic Party, would you let this go away?

PRESIDENT NIXON: Chuck, . . . they're going to make a big case out of that. . . . Well, they're getting ready to put Mitchell in a deposition.

COLSON: Well, but that can be stalled until after the election. In a civil suit? A civil suit, I don't think—I think can be dismissed. I don't believe there's a basis for an invasion of privacy. They're a public—

PRESIDENT NIXON: It's a possibility. I mean, I just hope we get a good lawyer. . . . Somebody to take on Bennett Williams, snarl at him, (unintelligible).

HALDEMAN: Warn Ehrlichman you've got to get the best guy . . .

COLSON: When I say let it go away, I'm not Pollyannish. I don't think it will necessarily blow away by itself, but I don't think we should do anything that escalates it unless—

PRESIDENT NIXON: There's a confession?

COLSON: —unless there's a clean way out of it, which I—

PRESIDENT NIXON: Well, how about the Liddy thing? Is that a clean way out of it?

COLSON: What I'm amazed at . . . is that no one, not a single reporter, has asked where Howard Hunt has been for the last three months, because they don't want to ask, because they would much rather say that he's still a consultant to the White House.

HALDEMAN: No, they have all reported that he's not.

COLSON: Yeah, but—

HALDEMAN: They all reported that he terminated on March 29.

PRESIDENT NIXON: No, the *Washington Post*—

COLSON: And every story says that he was a consultant.

PRESIDENT NIXON: No, no, no, no. In fairness, the Washington Post on its front page today in its story does not say "former consultant." He says "consultant."

HALDEMAN: That's right.

COLSON: NBC News last night—

PRESIDENT NIXON: Consultant to the White House. . . .

COLSON: Why didn't they ask where he is and what he's doing? Because they want to keep the impression that he's still here. The NBC Network News did it beautifully last night, skillfully. . . .

PRESIDENT NIXON: Well, somebody call them.

COLSON: Yes, sir, they've been called.

PRESIDENT NIXON: Did it do any good?

COLSON: I suppose they won't say that again. [*Laughter.*]

SEGMENT 4

PRESIDENT NIXON: You can talk all you want. You can get all disturbed about this, sure. But it has to be about this bugging incident and so forth and so on. I mean, taking it at its worst, all right, suppose they say, well—the only part of it that should be knocked down strongly is the White House involvement, because there is no White House involvement. That's the point, that we didn't know a Goddamn thing about it. But I guess Ziegler has done that as much as you think he can.

HALDEMAN: What they're trying to do—

COLSON: Ron did very well yesterday.

HALDEMAN: What they're trying to do with Ron, they're trying very hard to trap him into giving, a: The President is very upset about this, concerned, and then stepping in to order an investigation, and so on. And they're trying to trap him into it by saying: Well, what you're saying is the President doesn't care about this? You mean the President isn't interested? It doesn't make any difference to him? He doesn't think this is—trying to put words into it. But Ron's fully aware of what they're trying to do and he's very good at it. . . .

PRESIDENT NIXON: Goddamn it, just imagine what you'd have if you had somebody out there—just imagine what he'd be.

COLSON: Ron is—I never cease to be amazed at how adept he is at handling those guys. That's a very tough guy.

PRESIDENT NIXON: He's tough. He knows the curves and he knows what they're trying to get out and he knows what they're going to print and all the rest. He does a beautiful job. I still think, as I told Bob, that we won't get agreement from most of our White House people on this because they're so conscious about subjects. Let's see, have we had one on credibility lately? Remember, that was John Ehrlichman.

HALDEMAN: Oh, yeah. This relates to credibility.

PRESIDENT NIXON: This is a credibility issue?

COLSON: Sure. . . .

PRESIDENT NIXON: Credibility—but what I had is, I was thinking of credibility on Vietnam and that sort of thing.

HALDEMAN: No. Credibility on Vietnam has gone away.

PRESIDENT NIXON: . . . What I am saying is this, that this kind of story is going to play nationally because it's so bizarre. What I'm saying is that it's distinguished from things like ITT; it is not one that is going to get people that Goddamn excited . . . because they don't give a shit about repression and bugging and all the rest.

COLSON: I think they expect it. As I've said to you—they think that political parties do this all the time.

PRESIDENT NIXON: They do, they certainly do.

COLSON: They think that companies do this. You know, there have been marvelous stories written about industrial espionage.

PRESIDENT NIXON: Sure, sure, sure. Well, they do.

COLSON: How Ford sends agents into General Motors to get the designs. People just sort of expect this. They don't—if they were in there stealing money—

PRESIDENT NIXON: Governments do it. We all know that.

HALDEMAN: Sure.

PRESIDENT NIXON: Nevertheless, companies do it. Political parties do it. The point is that we—as I said, the main concern is to keep the White House out of it, and I think Ron's doing very well. That's probably a pretty good reason for me to do my own press thing tomorrow rather than today. . . .

SEGMENT 5

PRESIDENT NIXON: Your feeling . . . Bob, of this is we ought to put Liddy up there and tell him to take the rap, I'm sorry, and this and that, that's that? . . . See, it's the PR aspect. Remember, remember with the (unintelligible) development in ITT, it was to cut our losses and get out. Now, that's really what John Ehrlichman and Bob have been talking about, to cut our losses and get out of this damn thing.

COLSON: Well, I'd like to cut our losses and get out.

PRESIDENT NIXON: But can you think of a way?

COLSON: Well, I don't know. I don't know enough. I deliberately have not gotten that much into it because I could take an affidavit today that I know nothing about.

PRESIDENT NIXON: Good, stay out of it.

COLSON: Good position to be in.

PRESIDENT NIXON: Good idea, good idea. But given you don't know, you don't agree? What do you mean? Give us the feeling that you have about letting it ride through (unintelligible)? What do you mean, letting it go away? How can it?

COLSON: Well, I don't think it'll go away, Mr. President. I think when the grand jury convenes that there'll be stories about it. I think when they look for Hunt there'll be stories about it. I think the Democrats at the national convention will make a lot of rhetoric about it, make a lot of noise about it. My basic feeling is that it is not an issue that rubs off on you as long as the White House is out of it . . . because to most people they don't know the Committee for the Re-Election of the President or whether it's the National Committees, it's the political apparatus.

PRESIDENT NIXON: Yes.

COLSON: And I think people tend to expect this kind of thing to happen.

HALDEMAN: They're trying to do a good job on this, incidentally, over there, which is in this case when they talk about it they talk about it as the campaign committee, instead of the Committee for the Re-Election of the President. They're trying to keep the President out of it and just talk about his campaign committee, so people will think of it as—

COLSON: The TV is working right against them.

HALDEMAN: Yes.

COLSON: But they have fought hard to do that, and it's a good thing.

HALDEMAN: Obviously.

PRESIDENT NIXON: That's good, though, Bob. That's good.

COLSON: Also, using Dole as the principal spokesman is marvelous, because that looks like the Republicans National Committee, even though he—

HALDEMAN: I think [we should use] Dole to counter [Lawrence] O'Brien.

PRESIDENT NIXON: I think Dole, if I could only suggest one thing, . . . should attack O'Brien for this malicious libel by innuendo, of guilt by association on the President. In other words, don't say Colson because basically—that is what happens, you see, because the only reason they're kicking Colson is because they say White House presidential assistant Colson, see. Has that occurred to anybody? . . .

HALDEMAN: Well, that so far isn't kicking at the White House. If Dole starts defending the White House—

PRESIDENT NIXON: You don't think so?

HALDEMAN: —you're putting the White House in. . . .

PRESIDENT NIXON: He [Hunt] must be a pretty good guy, though.

COLSON: He's got one of the most interesting careers of anybody I've known. The tragedy is that the guy is a dedicated patriot, . . . *God.*

PRESIDENT NIXON: Of course. And he deliberately just decided he's not going to be around, is that right? That's what I hear.

COLSON: I don't know.

HALDEMAN: He isn't around.

COLSON: You know, he's—

PRESIDENT NIXON: Well, you know, you don't want him in here, Bob.

COLSON: He came in to me in February and he said: This is the only year I care about; the most important thing that ever happens is this man be re-elected; I just want to help. And you hate to see the poor guy get it.

PRESIDENT NIXON: Oh, well.

COLSON: It just happens. . . . Well, he's lived through this before.

PRESIDENT NIXON: What the hell, the Bay of Pigs.

COLSON: He lived in exile once before, and so forth.

HALDEMAN: He's used to this sort of stuff. . . . It's part of his life. . . .

PRESIDENT NIXON: He's written 42 novels.

COLSON: He's made a lot of money.

HALDEMAN: I must say, as inept as it certainly appears to be. . . .

COLSON: I can't believe he engineered it.

PRESIDENT NIXON: So anyway, don't let the bastards get you down, Chuck.

JUNE 21, 1972: THE PRESIDENT AND COLSON, 4:00–5:15 P.M., EXECUTIVE OFFICE BUILDING

Nixon aides, such as Haldeman and Colson, later developed a fondness for explanations that blamed the CIA for Watergate. This conversation is probably the origin of the idea, anxious as they were to "develop a theory." It probably also is the beginning of their notion that "Watergate was stupid and therefore the President could not have done it." Throughout the affair, Nixon contemptuously dismissed wiretapping as a serious issue; he insisted that he had been bugged in 1968, typically adding, "Everyone did it."

SEGMENT 1

COLSON: . . . I think that, I think that we could develop a theory as to the CIA if we wanted to. We know that he [Hunt] has all these ties with these people.

PRESIDENT NIXON: He worked with them.

COLSON: Oh, he was their boss, and they were all CIA. You take the cash, you go down to Latin America.

PRESIDENT NIXON: I'll tell you, I think that this has one plus to it, Chuck. The Cubans (unintelligible).

COLSON: Because Bebe [Rebozo] says they are. Bebe says—

PRESIDENT NIXON: I know. . . .

COLSON: We're in great shape with the Cubans, and they're proud of it. There's a lot of muscle in that gang.

PRESIDENT NIXON: (unintelligible).

COLSON: He's doing rallies. He [Bebe] wasn't getting too much. He said, first of all: Let me tell you, 99.9 percent of our people [Cubans] are for him. He said: I just talk about amnesty, bugging out of Vietnam, (unintelligible). He said: I never mention McGovern's name. But he said: Everybody gets up afterwards and says: That sonofabitch, McGovern.

PRESIDENT NIXON: They know.

COLSON: He said: I quote Radio Hanoi. . . . And he said: I just want to tell you that as far as the veterans' community, it's powerful, it's big, and the VFW is almost two million. And he said: You've got a campaign organization that will really go to town.

The second thing he said is: I hope you're not paying any attention to the bugging [Watergate] business. He said: Every place I go to small groups, I say, have you read about it? And he said a very small percentage have, and he said the reaction of those who had is that the Republicans wouldn't do that because they're in power and they would do it a hell of a lot more skillfully than that if they were doing it. He said: You're off the hook; nobody believes that you would really bungle it. . . . They're not all surprised and shocked.

PRESIDENT NIXON: I believe that—that people are all uptight about wiretapping. Let's just look at wiretapping. The country's for it. The whole country—there's a wiretap. On a thing like this, well, what the hell, you can break in, wiretap, what the hell. . . .

JUNE 22, 1972: THE PRESIDENT AND HALDEMAN, 9:40–11:25 A.M., EXECUTIVE OFFICE BUILDING

The President originates the line of "No White House involvement," which he later ascribes to John Dean. After the Democrats filed their civil suit, Nixon considered countering with libel actions. At times, he banters over what he calls the "comic opera" overtones of the affair. Haldeman considers the money found on the burglars to be untraceable, although he knows its source. In a pattern that becomes more prevalent as the scandal deepens, Nixon and aides reassure themselves that the cover-up is holding. "We're all right," "we're OK," they say. The idea of Hunt— and now, Liddy—fleeing the country continues to appeal.

SEGMENT 1

PRESIDENT NIXON: . . . The question that they'll ask [the media], was there any White House involvement, and the way that they've [his staff] prepared it sounds like a lawyer's answer (unintelligible); nothing has happened to reduce the confidence, my confidence in the White House staff. . . . I think I want to say there is no White House involvement. . . .

HALDEMAN: The only question would be whether technically that puts you in a—

PRESIDENT NIXON: Position of commenting on it?

HALDEMAN: Well, no. In a spot in the sense that—on a direct basis, White House involvement, I think you're absolutely clean. There's no question. The only—see, you could get it in the sense that Ziegler—that Hunt was involved and Hunt was a consultant to the White House.

PRESIDENT NIXON: At the time he did it?

HALDEMAN: No, no. . . . That's the only line to the White House you've got. Now, there are other people that are former White House people who could at some point become involved.

PRESIDENT NIXON: Well, maybe—

HALDEMAN: But they weren't—they aren't White House now. . . .

PRESIDENT NIXON: I'll just say: Well, Mr. Ziegler's covered that. Because he said he'd been asked whether Colson was involved in it. He was asked about Hunt and said he left the White House three months ago. He said he was asked about Colson the first day, he checked with him, he was not involved. I'll say Mr. Ziegler has covered that. . . . Then they bring up another story: President says White House not involved.

HALDEMAN: Denies White House involvement.

PRESIDENT NIXON: Denies, yes, that's right.

HALDEMAN: That's the way that—

PRESIDENT NIXON: Denies, or President concerned about this.

HALDEMAN: They're playing this thing so irresponsibly, you know. . . . They're playing it so irresponsibly in the attempt to make a White House thing out of it. The *Post* story today, which you probably saw, the headline says "White House aide disappears."

PRESIDENT NIXON: Yes.

HALDEMAN: Or "White House aide missing" or something.

PRESIDENT NIXON: Then you go into it, you have to read down ten paragraphs to find out it was a fly in the White House.

HALDEMAN: Yes. He was also a former aide to [Averill] Harriman. It doesn't say Harriman aide disappeared.

PRESIDENT NIXON: Somebody ought to call them. [L]et me say, let me say this, . . . I don't think this is the biggest story in the country some way.

HALDEMAN: It's not. . . .

PRESIDENT NIXON: Let me tell you something about this. I have a hunch that your first reaction was correct. But it's a Washington sonofabitch story.

HALDEMAN: Plus, what's happened to it is it's so fucked up that everybody's laughing about it. . . .

PRESIDENT NIXON: Now let me ask you this. I have very strong feelings with regard to the personal thing because these statements—so Rebozo ought to sue, and I'll tell you why. The reason for it, he was not involved.

HALDEMAN: No.

PRESIDENT NIXON: Huh?

HALDEMAN: No, and Anderson didn't say he was.

PRESIDENT NIXON: It doesn't make any difference.

HALDEMAN: Well, if he sues—that's gotten no play except the Anderson broadcast, and what Anderson said is true. That's the best defense against libel, and Anderson's smart enough to know that.

PRESIDENT NIXON: Bob, you could libel me and—I read that damn thing. That is libel. I could prove, I could win that case any damn day. It's an indication that Rebozo was tied up with this group that broke in, you know. I mean, conspiracy—I'm thinking also of putting them off on another trail. They sued somebody, Rebozo sues them.

HALDEMAN: Yes.

PRESIDENT NIXON: Anyway—

HALDEMAN: I'm not sure we need it now. We're in pretty good shape. Today's news is all good. In the first place, we got Judge [Charles] Richey for the civil case. The civil case is kind of worrisome.

PRESIDENT NIXON: Yes, he's a good judge.

HALDEMAN: The Democrats outsmarted themselves. They made a fatal legal error.

PRESIDENT NIXON: What's that?

HALDEMAN: They filed the suit on behalf of all Democrats, thereby disqualifying any Democratic judge from hearing it.

PRESIDENT NIXON: Ah.

HALDEMAN: So the next judge up was a Democratic judge and would have been the one assigned to the case. He had to disqualify himself on technical grounds because he's a part of the party to the pleading. Then the one up after that was Judge Richey, who has a very solid, very—

PRESIDENT NIXON: I know him.

[Withdrawn item. Privacy.]

HALDEMAN: They intend to move immediately on depositions. That was their tactic. So Edward Bennett Williams was in yesterday afternoon and stomping, banging the walls in Richey's chambers and everything, and Richey just calmly said he was busy the rest of this week, he would meet with them on Monday to discuss the question of when to decide when to start the timing on setting dates for activities on—

PRESIDENT NIXON: Another thing I think has been good, Bob—and I must say (unintelligible)—they must have gotten the word now over there to get out on our security.

HALDEMAN: Yes. . . .

PRESIDENT NIXON: Well, Bob, you know damn well that you're bugged.

HALDEMAN: We always—sure.

PRESIDENT NIXON: We sweep every hotel room. That's the other thing. I thought that the stories this morning, even in the *Post,* the idea that everybody's worried about bugging and we're doing this, and also the fact that Larry O'Brien says that [Jack] Anderson had papers from his office.

HALDEMAN: That's right.

PRESIDENT NIXON: Well now, this puts Anderson in the bugging business. . . .

HALDEMAN: And Anderson now is denying that he got the stuff from these people, but he said, of course, I got it from an inside source.

PRESIDENT NIXON: Yeah, see. Anderson—well, there's the whole thing. A Pulitzer Prize for that? You see, my point is, I just want to see that Pulitzer Prize written by one columnist.

HALDEMAN: We'll give that one—

PRESIDENT NIXON: Colson's working on that [leaking a White House story to a columnist].

HALDEMAN: Yes. We've got another thing going which has taken hold a little bit, which is we've started moving on the Hill, letting it come out from there, which is that this whole thing is a Jack Anderson thing, that Jack Anderson did it. That's what the Hill guys think, that this is—and we're trying to move that around now. We started a rumor yesterday morning and it's starting to come back already.

PRESIDENT NIXON: What?

HALDEMAN: That Jack Anderson has put all of this together, he was bugging the Democratic offices.

PRESIDENT NIXON: Oh, yes.

HALDEMAN: Because these Cubans are tied to him. These are agents he's used, and now he's trying to do a diversionary cover-up of this other thing, and all this other stuff. The great thing about this is it is so totally fucked up and so badly done that nobody believes—

PRESIDENT NIXON: That we could have done it.

HALDEMAN: That's right. . . .

PRESIDENT NIXON: Well, it sounds like a comic opera, really.

HALDEMAN: It really does. It would make a funny Goddamn movie.

PRESIDENT NIXON: I mean, you know, here's these Cubans with their accents. [*Laughing*]

HALDEMAN: Wearing these rubber gloves, standing there in their well-made, their expensive, well-made business suits, wearing rubber gloves, and put their hands up and shouting "Don't shoot" when the police come in. It really is like a comic opera. . . . Also, they have no case on Hunt.

PRESIDENT NIXON: Why?

HALDEMAN: Because there is no case on Hunt. They have not been able to make him. They can't put him into the scene at all.

PRESIDENT NIXON: We know where he was, though.

HALDEMAN: But they don't. The FBI doesn't.

PRESIDENT NIXON: That's right.

HALDEMAN: They've pursued him and been unable to tie him in at all to the case.

PRESIDENT NIXON: What about the disappearance? He'll come back?

HALDEMAN: Well, they've got no warrant for him, so they don't care whether he disappeared.

PRESIDENT NIXON: He has disappeared?

HALDEMAN: He has disappeared.

PRESIDENT NIXON: Yes, the Hunt thing is beginning to run out recently.

HALDEMAN: The legal people, the FBI, who are running the investigation, have no—there's no way to fix Hunt on the case. They have issued no warrant for him. They don't care whether he disappears or not. The only thing there is, is his name's in the phone book, in the guy's address book. But so is the hotel clerk's name.

PRESIDENT NIXON: Is Rebozo's name in anyone's address book?

HALDEMAN: No. . . . He told me he doesn't know any of these guys.

PRESIDENT NIXON: He doesn't know them?

[Withdrawn item. Privacy.]

HALDEMAN: Another good break is they can't trace the currency.

PRESIDENT NIXON: They traced it to a Miami bank.

HALDEMAN: They traced it to a Miami bank, which, that's easily done. But the bank cannot trace the thing beyond that. They're not required to and they don't maintain any record of where, who takes it when it's $100 bills. When it's bigger denominations, they have to keep a record, but with $100 bills they don't. So they don't have a record.

PRESIDENT NIXON: Because hundred dollars are so common these days? . . .

HALDEMAN: I guess. Whatever it is, they don't maintain a record. So there's no way to trace the source of the funds. Even if there were, it wouldn't be a very great problem, unless it can go two more steps, because the funds came from a money order from a South American country.

PRESIDENT NIXON: Well, that's good.

HALDEMAN: Well, but if they got to that stuff then they might be able to get to the South American country and find out where the money order came from, and that isn't good. But up to that point we're all right, and they can't even go to the next place.

PRESIDENT NIXON: So we're okay on that one. . . .

HALDEMAN: Well, the investigation is beginning to look into other Cubans and that kind of thing. These guys are allied in some other enterprises that we don't care about, and there's a lot of—that's a pretty big story, a pretty good story, as long as they don't get to—see, the thing we forget is that we know too much and therefore read too much into what we see that other people can't read into. I mean, what seems obvious to us because of what we know is not obvious to other people.

PRESIDENT NIXON: Well, the interesting thing is, Bob, is—the networks didn't play it—is that the networks main thing is that they were the (unintelligible) if they thought that they had something. But the main thing is the Cuban thing. That's a hell of a story and you say, oh shit.

HALDEMAN: Well, of course that might help us, because what the Cubans are going to say and are starting to say is that they're scared to death of McGovern.

PRESIDENT NIXON: Are they beginning—has anybody started to say that?

HALDEMAN: Yes.

PRESIDENT NIXON: Oh, good. How did you do that?

HALDEMAN: Well, they got some Cuban to put that.

PRESIDENT NIXON: Doctor somebody.

HALDEMAN: No, they're staying away from him. They don't give two shits for him.

PRESIDENT NIXON: That's right. Just so it's done, I see. . . .

HALDEMAN: So at this point it's looking pretty good. And the one thing they are thinking about doing, which we could do and it would be easy to cover it with no problem just for safety sake, is to get Liddy out of the country. I'll just have him go over to Europe and be checking on some of our financial contributions, the fundraising, the fundraising drive in Europe. . . .

PRESIDENT NIXON: You mean the idea being that they're not after him?

HALDEMAN: Not yet. But just I figure—he's moved around. They've sent him to L.A. He's had some business there. And he can as a routine matter go to Europe, and it's just as well if something does surface not to have him around or have to move him after it does. And then they can wait and see. If we want him back, it's easy to bring him back.

PRESIDENT NIXON: How the hell can you question him, unless somebody talks?

HALDEMAN: If somebody talks, which is a potential. Now, they're leaving McCord in jail to keep an eye on the other guys and maintain contact with them.

PRESIDENT NIXON: They don't want to get them out on bail?

HALDEMAN: Apparently they'd rather leave them in right now.

PRESIDENT NIXON: They probably don't mind. . . .

HALDEMAN: CBS covered it last night, NBC about a week ago, fair enough. It's a newspaper story. Scripps-Howard is quoting unnamed sources in Miami as saying they believe the five men (unintelligible) for spying on the Democrats out of fear that a Democratic President might cede Cuba to Castro. That's way ahead of where we had hoped.

PRESIDENT NIXON: Suppose the worst. . . . We just sort of say: Well, it wasn't authorized, and so forth and so on; we're going to have to tighten up on this security business.

JUNE 23, 1972: THE PRESIDENT AND HALDEMAN, 10:04–11:39 A.M., OVAL OFFICE

In three meetings on June 23, Nixon and Haldeman conduct what comes to be known as the "smoking gun" conversation. They conspire to call in CIA Director Richard Helms and his deputy, General Vernon Walters (a longtime associate of the President's), and direct them to tell FBI Acting Director Pat Gray that the Bureau's investigation impinged on CIA operations. Haldeman has some concern: "But we're relying on more and more people all the time." Haldeman also speaks of pressure on CREEP aides to produce more "information." The tape was made public on August 5, 1974—too late for consideration by the House Impeachment Inquiry, but soon enough to allow most House Republicans to abandon the President and hasten his resignation.

HALDEMAN: OK, that's fine. Now, on the investigation, you know, the Democratic break-in thing, we're back to the . . . problem area because the FBI is not under control, because Gray doesn't exactly know how to control them, and . . . their investigation is now leading into some productive areas, because they've been able to trace the money, not through the money itself, but through the bank. . . . [A]nd it goes in some directions we don't want it to go. . . . [T]here have been some things, like an informant came in off the street to the FBI in Miami, who was a photographer, or has a friend who is a photographer who developed some films through this guy [Watergate burglar Bernard] Barker, and the films had pictures of Democratic National Committee letterhead[s] . . . . Mitchell came up with yesterday, and John Dean analyzed very carefully last night and concludes—concurs—now with Mitchell's recommendation that the only way to solve this . . . is for us to have [Deputy CIA Director Vernon] Walters call Pat Gray and just say, "Stay the hell out of this . . . this is ah, business here we don't want you to go any further on it." That's not an unusual development. . . .

PRESIDENT NIXON: What about Pat Gray, you mean he doesn't want to?

HALDEMAN: Pat does want to. He doesn't know how to, and he doesn't have, he doesn't have any basis for doing it. Given this, he will then have the basis. He'll call Mark Felt in, and the two of them . . . and Mark Felt wants to cooperate because—

PRESIDENT NIXON: Yeah.

HALDEMAN: —he's ambitious.

PRESIDENT NIXON: Yeah.

HALDEMAN: He'll call him in and say, "We've got the signal from across the river to, to put the hold on this." And that will fit rather well because the FBI agents who are working the case, at this point, feel that's what it is. This is CIA.

PRESIDENT NIXON: But they've traced the money to 'em.

HALDEMAN: Well they have, they've traced to a name, but they haven't gotten to the guy yet.

PRESIDENT NIXON: Would it be somebody here?

HALDEMAN: Ken Dahlberg [who worked for prominent contributor Dwayne Andreas].

PRESIDENT NIXON: Who the hell is Ken Dahlberg?

HALDEMAN: He's, he gave $25,000 in Minnesota and the check went directly in to this, to this guy, Barker.

PRESIDENT NIXON: Maybe he's a . . . bum. He didn't get this from the committee though, from Stans?

HALDEMAN: Yeah. It is. It is. It's directly traceable and there's some more through some Texas people in—that went to the Mexican bank which they can also trace to the Mexican bank. . . . They'll get their names today. . . .

PRESIDENT NIXON: I'm just thinking if they don't cooperate, what do they say? They, they, they were approached by the Cubans? That's what Dahlberg has to say, the Texans too. Is that the idea?

HALDEMAN: Well, if they will. But then we're relying on more and more people all the time. That's the problem. And they'll stop if we could, if we take this other step.

PRESIDENT NIXON: All right. Fine.

HALDEMAN: And, and they seem to feel the thing to do is get them to stop.

PRESIDENT NIXON: Right, fine.

HALDEMAN: They say the only way to do that is from White House instructions. And it's got to be to Helms and what's his name? [Deputy CIA Director General Vernon] Walters?

PRESIDENT NIXON: Walters.

HALDEMAN: And the proposal would be that Ehrlichman and I call him.

PRESIDENT NIXON: All right, fine. . . . How do you call him in, I mean you just— well, we protected Helms from one hell of a lot of things.

HALDEMAN: That's what Ehrlichman says.

PRESIDENT NIXON: Of course, this . . . Hunt, . . . that will uncover a lot of, a lot of—you open that scab there's a hell of a lot of things in it that we just feel that this would be very detrimental to have this thing go any further. This involves these Cubans, Hunt, and a lot of hanky-panky that we have nothing to do with ourselves. What the hell, did Mitchell know about this thing to any much of a degree?

HALDEMAN: I think so. I don't think he knew the details, but I think he knew.

PRESIDENT NIXON: He didn't know how it was going to be handled though, with Dahlberg and the Texans and so forth? Well, who was the asshole that did? Is it Liddy? Is that the fellow? He must be a little nuts.

HALDEMAN: He is.

PRESIDENT NIXON: I mean he just isn't well-screwed-on is he? Isn't that the problem?

HALDEMAN: No, but he was under pressure, apparently, to get more information, and as he got more pressure, he pushed the people harder to move harder on.

PRESIDENT NIXON: Pressure from Mitchell?

HALDEMAN: Apparently. . . .

PRESIDENT NIXON: All right, fine, I understand it all. We won't second-guess Mitchell and the rest. Thank God it wasn't Colson.

HALDEMAN: The FBI interviewed Colson yesterday. They determined that would be a good thing to do. . . . An interrogation, which he did, and that, the FBI guys working the case had concluded that there are one or two possibilities: one, that this was a White House [operation], they don't think that there is anything at the Election

Committee—they think it was either a White House operation and they had some obscure reasons for it. . . . Or it was a—

PRESIDENT NIXON: Cuban thing—

HALDEMAN:—Cubans and the CIA. And after their interrogation of—

PRESIDENT NIXON: Colson.

HALDEMAN:—Colson, yesterday, they concluded it was not the White House, but are now convinced it's the CIA thing, so the CIA turnoff would—

PRESIDENT NIXON: Well, not sure of their analysis, I'm not going to get that involved. . . .

HALDEMAN: No, sir. We don't want you to.

PRESIDENT NIXON: You call them in. Good. Good deal. Play it tough. That's the way they play it and that's the way we are going to play it.

HALDEMAN: O.K. We'll do it.

PRESIDENT NIXON: Yeah, when I saw that news summary item, I of course knew it was a bunch of crap, but I thought, that, well it's good to have them off on this wild hare thing because when they start bugging us, which they have, we'll know our little boys will not know how to handle it. I hope they will though.

HALDEMAN: Good, you never know. Maybe, you think about it. . . .

PRESIDENT NIXON: When you get in these people . . . say: "Look, the problem is that this will open the whole, the whole Bay of Pigs thing, and the President just feels that"—without going into the details—don't, don't lie to them to the extent to say there is no involvement, but just say this is sort of a comedy of errors, bizarre, without getting into it. "The President's belief is that this is going to open the whole Bay of Pigs thing up again. And because these people are plugging for, for keeps, and that they should call the FBI in and say that we wish for the country, don't go any further into this case," period. . . .

JUNE 23, 1972: THE PRESIDENT AND HALDEMAN, 1:04–1:13 P.M., OVAL OFFICE

PRESIDENT NIXON: . . . Hunt . . . knows too damn much and he was involved, we have to know that. And that it gets out . . . this is all involved in the Cuban thing, that it's a fiasco, and it's going to make the FB—ah CIA—look bad, it's going to make Hunt look bad, and it's likely to blow the whole, uh, Bay of Pigs thing, which we think would be very unfortunate for the CIA and for the country at this time, and for American foreign policy, and he's just gotta tell 'em "lay off." . . .

HALDEMAN: Yeah, that's, that's the basis we'll do it on and just leave it at that.

PRESIDENT NIXON: I don't want them to get any ideas we're doing it because our concern is political.

HALDEMAN: Right

PRESIDENT NIXON: And at the same time, I wouldn't tell them it is not political. . . .

HALDEMAN: Right.

PRESIDENT NIXON: I would just say, "Look, it's because of the Hunt involvement." . . .

JUNE 23, 1972: THE PRESIDENT AND HALDEMAN, 2:20–2:45 P.M., OVAL OFFICE

HALDEMAN: Well, it's no problem. Had the . . . two of them in [Richard Helms and Vernon Walters]. . . . I didn't mention Hunt at the opening. I just said that, that, uh, this thing which we give direction to, we're gonna create some very major potential problems because they were exploring leads that led back into—to, uh, areas [that] will be harmful to the CIA, harmful to the government. . . . Walters said something—

PRESIDENT NIXON: He said—

HALDEMAN: I think Helms did, too. Helms said well, . . . Gray called and said, yesterday, and said, that he thought—

PRESIDENT NIXON: Who had, Gray?

HALDEMAN:—Gray had called Helms, which we knew, and said, "I think we've run right into the middle of a CIA covert operation."

PRESIDENT NIXON: Gray said that?

HALDEMAN: Yeah, and Helms said "nothing, nothing we've got at this point" and Gray said, "sure looks to me like that's what we did. . . . [T]his would embarrass [us] all," and that was the end of that conversation. . . . Said, well, it's probably a good thing, it tracks back to the Bay of Pigs. It tracks back to some other—if the leads run out to people who had no involvement in this except by contact or connection, but it gets to areas that are bound to be raised. . . . The whole problem of this, this fellow Hunt—so at that point Helms's kind of got the picture . . . , and he said, . . . he said, "We'll be very happy to be helpful . . . and we'll handle anything, we'll do anything you want. I would like to know the reason for being helpful." And made it clear to him he wasn't gonna get it, explicitly, but was gonna get it through generality and, so he said fine. . . . "I don't know whether we can do it"—Walters said that. [Laughs] Walters is gonna make a call to Gray. . . .

PRESIDENT NIXON: How would things work though? How would—for example, if they're desperate (unintelligible) got somebody from Miami bank to be here to count the inventory?

HALDEMAN: . . . But the point John [Ehrlichman? Dean?] made was the Bureau doesn't . . . know what they're uncovering. . . . [T]hey don't need to further . . . , as they pursue it because they're uncovering some sensitive things. . . . Sure enough, that's exactly what—but we didn't in any way say we had any political interest or concern or anything like that. One thing Helms did raise is, . . . he asked Gray why he felt they're going into a CIA thing and Gray said, "Well, because of the characters involved and the amount of money involved." . . . [T]hat probably raised Helms's suspicions. . . .

PRESIDENT NIXON: If it runs back to the bank—so, what the hell, they, who knows, maybe Dahlberg's contributed to the CIA, you know what I mean, in all seriousness. . . .

HALDEMAN: CIA gets money as we know, 'cause, I mean their money moves in a lot of different ways too. . . .

PRESIDENT NIXON: Can you imagine what Kennedy would have done with that money? . . .

JUNE 26, 1972: THE PRESIDENT AND HALDEMAN, 9:50–10:45 A.M., OVAL OFFICE

Haldeman informed Nixon that Democratic Chairman Lawrence O'Brien had publicly called for a Special Prosecutor. John Dean's role in safeguarding White House interests is first mentioned. Meanwhile, the two men savor some current political "dirty tricks."

SEGMENT 1

HALDEMAN: . . . O'Brien released yesterday a letter to you or something where he wants you to appoint a prosecutor, a special prosecutor, and all this kind of stuff.

PRESIDENT NIXON: Why? Isn't it being prosecuted?

HALDEMAN: Of course it is.

PRESIDENT NIXON: Is there any way, any way, that Ehrlichman's crowd can get these people to plead guilty and get the hell out of the case? How is it working there? I don't know what kind of jackassery is going on in the handling of it, you know, because I haven't much confidence in these lawyers. Who's watching that end of it? Is that [John] Dean?

HALDEMAN: Dean.

PRESIDENT NIXON: Mitchell?

HALDEMAN: Mitchell.

PRESIDENT NIXON: All right.

HALDEMAN: Very closely watched.

PRESIDENT NIXON: [Robert] Mardian? Okay.

HALDEMAN: Unfortunately, you know, it's one where—I have to agree with you, though it may not be that simple. It would seem to me if they plead them guilty and get them out, they've got to get them—they don't have an indictment yet.

PRESIDENT NIXON: Why not?

HALDEMAN: Well, because they keep investigating and uncovering new things. You know, hopefully we've got that turned off.

SEGMENT 2

PRESIDENT NIXON: What happened to the [Democrats'] rally? Was it the rain? They said some of the stars didn't show up.

HALDEMAN: Well, that's part of it, but that isn't all of it. It just—

PRESIDENT NIXON: Did we screw it up a little?

HALDEMAN: We tried. I don't think—I wish I could say we did. We did try to.

PRESIDENT NIXON: How? How did they try?

HALDEMAN: Well, they tried some sort of dirty stuff on some of the stars.

PRESIDENT NIXON: Calling?

HALDEMAN: (unintelligible), that they were ruining their reputation by backing this guy [McGovern]. Just calls, pen letter type things. I have a feeling that didn't do it, although maybe it did. You never know. Those people are damn sensitive to that stuff. You know, they get three letters saying you're doing wrong, they'll decide not to. It'll scare their agent. You know they'll be afraid they aren't going to get any work.

PRESIDENT NIXON: Their agents will tell them that, that's right.

JUNE 26, 1972: THE PRESIDENT AND HALDEMAN, 12:35–1:25 P.M., EXECUTIVE OFFICE BUILDING

Nixon and Haldeman prepare Mitchell's resignation as campaign chairman, hoping that will snuff out the growing scandal. Meanwhile, the White House is leaking items about Mitchell's wife, Martha, to somehow cast blame on her for Mitchell's inattentiveness. Significantly, Nixon and Haldeman both remember Hunt's and the burglars' numerous criminal involvements in behalf of the Administration— "black holes," as the President describes them—and a secret that must be kept, thus enlarging the cover-up. "There's various lines of interlinkage in the whole damn business," Haldeman says.

HALDEMAN: There's no way, unless he [John Mitchell] can put a keeper on her [Martha Mitchell] . . .

PRESIDENT NIXON: No way.

HALDEMAN: But I don't see how he could do that, because people get out.

PRESIDENT NIXON: Well, the way this is blowing now, it's getting pretty big, the story; don't you agree?

HALDEMAN: Well, yeah, if they run this stuff about throwing her on the bed and sticking a needle in her behind and that kind of stuff. . . . Someone raised the point this morning that he was concerned about, that the potential is nowhere near, but we could get to it, potential problems on the other thing, Watergate.

PRESIDENT NIXON: Right.

HALDEMAN: You could use this as a basis for Mitchell pulling out. That means we're going to have to fix nearly everything all over and at the same time start trying to put a new structure together. It isn't going to turn the other off. So Mitchell pulls out; so he's still the former Attorney General, your former campaign manager, and they're not going to let up on him just because—

PRESIDENT NIXON: This is after.

HALDEMAN: —he isn't the manager now. And then the only way you can do that is to hang him on it, say: Well, yeah, he did it, and that's why we have to get rid of him.

PRESIDENT NIXON: I can't do that. I won't do that to him. I'd rather, shit, lose the election. I really would.

HALDEMAN: You can't do that. He won't let you do that.

PRESIDENT NIXON: No.

HALDEMAN: He'll pull the plug [rather than allow you] to do that.

PRESIDENT NIXON: No, no. He was supposed to do everything he could to find out what was going on, you know what I mean? . . .

HALDEMAN: Apparently, with our limited resources in that area, they used the same people for a wide range of things. So you've got them all—you've got cross-ties in your leading people and all that. If these guys were only on this thing, you could cut them loose and sink them without a trace.

PRESIDENT NIXON: You mean they've been on ITT?

HALDEMAN: And other stuff.

PRESIDENT NIXON: Black holes? [Plumbers.]

HALDEMAN: Apparently a lot of stuff. There's stuff I don't know anything about.

PRESIDENT NIXON: Stuff we know nothing about.

HALDEMAN: But I've been told that the lines run.

PRESIDENT NIXON: Any other candidates?

HALDEMAN: Yes. Apparently this is part of the apparatus that's been used for some of these surveillance projects (unintelligible). They're tied into in some remote way the people that have been doing some of the antiwar activity and the other campaign things during the primaries. Apparently there's various lines of interlinkage in the whole damn business.

PRESIDENT NIXON: Well, we'll have to decide and so forth (unintelligible).

HALDEMAN: Doing those is no problem, but tying these people to doing those and this then is a problem. It would show that they were political operatives for the campaign.

PRESIDENT NIXON: Yes, you're right. . . .

HALDEMAN: Hunt was tied in a sense, because of these people. . . . They [the Cuban burglars] got carried away. They're emotional people who were afraid of what McGovern's going to do. Why the hell anybody would care what was happening at the Democratic Committee? There is one glimmer of hope, apparently. One of the— and a game to play; we've got to be careful, though. It might be a possibility, depending on whether it's true, is apparently in their photographs, the stuff that they were taking, they have some documents, photographs of documents that were at the Democratic Committee that were classified Defense Department documents. Now, if in fact that's true, then you've got a counter-case for Dole, that these people, (unintelligible) CIA agents or something, that something was going on. You know how it buzzed up, the Pentagon Papers and Jack Anderson and a lot of things.

PRESIDENT NIXON: (unintelligible) the Pentagon Papers. They praised all that and gave prizes for it.

HALDEMAN: Yes.

PRESIDENT NIXON: And this, when it's the other, the reverse part, now it's a horrible thing. I haven't seen anybody expressing any horror.

HALDEMAN: Yes. One of the magazines makes that point, and there was a column.

PRESIDENT NIXON: Was there?

HALDEMAN: Saying exactly that. They didn't use the Pulitzer Prize thing (unintelligible). We're trying to get someone to pick it up.

PRESIDENT NIXON: It's a double standard. Because I asked, where the hell is the horrible stuff they were running against me, you know? . . .

HALDEMAN: —you waited until you get into the campaign and then you're pulling out a device you haven't used for over a year. You're set up to do it last weekend, this week. You're not into the convention yet. You're into a big congressional mish-mosh, wrap-up. You're going to have to go into the—the debt ceiling thing is going to be a question at that point, a public question. The food price thing is bouncing around.

It isn't a major—it's featured in each of the magazines. Ehrlichman was very concerned last week that we have to start all over again on the Watergate deal this week because the magazines didn't give it the major play.

PRESIDENT NIXON: They didn't?

HALDEMAN: A couple columns.

PRESIDENT NIXON: Let me say that John on that is oversensitive anyway. Magazines have run cover stories on it. They don't make that much difference any more. Does John realize that?

HALDEMAN: No.

PRESIDENT NIXON: It's only in this town, but not in the country, Bob. The Goddamn magazines don't have the impact they used to have.

HALDEMAN: That's true.

PRESIDENT NIXON: Wouldn't you agree?

HALDEMAN: No, I would agree. You get less—it makes less difference there. But of course, it does stir up this town and it stirs up the media. They have a regenerative effect. The treatment the magazines have given it would indicate that they, that the establishment, isn't really convinced they've got something there, because they aren't—they don't go into—John pictured them as going in, you know, big charts of where they went and lurid stuff and all the history in the past of each of the guys and all that. Well, that kind of thing (unintelligible) screwed up in the past, and basically ties it to the CIA.

PRESIDENT NIXON: Our people here, most of our people, just didn't have any idea of how tough things were going to be. They've gotten—we have handled them so well and made so damn few mistakes that everybody here gets the impression that that's the way it's always supposed to be.

HALDEMAN: Well, it's kind of bothersome, though, because everything's so good and this stuff is so unnecessary, that it's just kind of ironic and frustrating to have dinner served in view over there . . . and you're stuck with the dessert. . . .

JUNE 28, 1972: THE PRESIDENT AND HALDEMAN, 11:16 A.M.–1:55 P.M., EXECUTIVE OFFICE BUILDING

Nixon raises a familiar refrain: Lyndon Johnson had bugged him during the 1968 campaign, and Nixon believes this justified the Watergate break-in. The President and Haldeman prepare for Mitchell's resignation.

PRESIDENT NIXON: Go back to Mitchell.

HALDEMAN: . . . I think also lurking down way behind there is the question of his involvement in the Watergate caper and the fact that that—

PRESIDENT NIXON: And that he does know about it?

HALDEMAN: We've got a lid on it, but it may not stay on, and his getting out might just be a good move on that, because supposedly it goes to him.

PRESIDENT NIXON: But I don't—I think, as I understand it—and I don't want to know because I've got to answer at a press conference. But as I understand it, John did not know specifically about this caper.

HALDEMAN: As I understand it, that's right.

PRESIDENT NIXON: I mean, if people down the line, Cubans and others before us, working for some asshole, and they do something stupid, we can't be responsible for that. Because . . . I was glad to see that somebody brought out, Kevin Phillips or somebody, the fact that we were tapped. You know, [Lyndon] Johnson tapped us, because he told us later.

HALDEMAN: He tapped Mrs. what's her name.

PRESIDENT NIXON: Sure, Aliyevski [?]. He knew we'd meet with her. Not we, but who was it—Rose Mary—remembers he said that he had the telephone call that was made from New Mexico, the plane?

HALDEMAN: Yes.

PRESIDENT NIXON: Of course he had her tapped, you're Goddamn right.

HALDEMAN: Well, my view would be—and John's [Mitchell] going to be back this afternoon and we'll want to talk about this. My view would be to encourage him to do it, on the basis of he's got—it's a beautiful opportunity. He'll gain great sympathy. The Martha fans will think: Isn't that a wonderful thing, that the man has given up—you know, it's kind of like the Duke of Windsor giving up the throne for the woman he loves, this sort of stuff. I mean, it has a little of that flavor to this. The poor woman hasn't been well and all and he's going to be by her side, and all of that.

PRESIDENT NIXON: And we would leak out the fact that she's not well very strongly.

HALDEMAN: Right.

PRESIDENT NIXON: We'd have to.

HALDEMAN: We're already doing that a little bit. It might not even be "leak out." He might even want to tie that right into it, just say: My wife isn't well, I've got to be with her, and that obviously is—I'm totally behind the President, but I can't, with this problem—

PRESIDENT NIXON: Have a full-time job.

HALDEMAN: That's the point, that he can say: I fully expect to help in every possible way that I can.

PRESIDENT NIXON: Incidentally, he can still do some inside jobs.

HALDEMAN: Then you use him for the kinds of things he is indispensable for, the Rockefeller—

PRESIDENT NIXON: Rockefeller.

HALDEMAN: —Reagan, Buckley, the Middlebury, putting the deal together in Missouri, and that kind of stuff he can still do without any question, but get him out of—

JUNE 29, 1972: THE PRESIDENT AND HALDEMAN, 3:20–3:50 P.M., EXECUTIVE OFFICE BUILDING

Mitchell prepares to resign, yet he resists the growing pressure to take responsibility. Liddy's resignation and willingness to accept guilt cheers the President, but Haldeman ominously warns, "It's a time bomb."

PRESIDENT NIXON: I frankly believe the remark that he [Mitchell] probably wouldn't have let this Watergate thing get out of hand.

HALDEMAN: That's quite possible.

PRESIDENT NIXON: And actually I don't think, I really don't, I really don't—I think . . . John said, well, we're trying to get information, he said, well, don't tell me anything about it. You know, that's the way you do it, thinking probably they were going to do it the way you always do, planting a person on the other side, which everybody does. But these assholes were going around bugging people or whatever it was. My view on that is that, that pretty well kills Watergate.

HALDEMAN: Which is another good—and John raised that. He said: If this thing escalates, I think it would be very good if I'm out of the place and you could say, "Well, there's an all new team over there". . . .

They fired Liddy.

PRESIDENT NIXON: Huh?

HALDEMAN: They fired Liddy, (unintelligible). . . .

PRESIDENT NIXON: On what ground did they fire him? They're going to say that he had some—in the event it comes out that he did have contact with—

HALDEMAN: Yes. They're not making any fuss about it. Nobody'll ask why they fired him unless he becomes identified. The FBI do have a line to him. They have questioned him and he didn't cooperate. He answered certain questions and then they got into other areas and he said: If you're going to get into that kind of area, then I request to have an attorney here. The FBI said: Well, if you have an attorney he'll tell you not to answer the question. Liddy said: Well then, I've got to (unintelligible). The FBI dropped it. . . .

HALDEMAN: The thing that bothers me about this thing is that it's a time bomb. They don't have to keep it alive. They can let it go under the surface. They can investigate until they get something else, and then lob it out whenever they feel like it.

PRESIDENT NIXON: Well, what do we do, then?

HALDEMAN: I don't know. I don't think there's a damn thing we can do . . . . [Mitchell can say:] "But I accept full blame for it. I was running the thing at the time and I should have known what was happening, I'm sorry I didn't."

PRESIDENT NIXON: "I didn't know it."

HALDEMAN: "I was diverted by some personal problems, which is why I've resigned from the program, because I wasn't able to spend the time and attention."

PRESIDENT NIXON: How does the resignation thing, how do you think it goes in terms of timing?

HALDEMAN: The resignation is going to be a positive story. It's going to hang it totally on [Martha?] (unintelligible).

PRESIDENT NIXON: I think he should do it. Call the press. . . .

HALDEMAN: No, sir. He should come over and talk to you first.

PRESIDENT NIXON: Do it. And then he can say, on my recommendation. . . .

JUNE 30, 1972: THE PRESIDENT AND ZIEGLER, 3:18–3:24 P.M., OVAL OFFICE

A gun and a map of the Democratic National Committee headquarters reportedly are found in Hunt's White House safe.

SEGMENT 1

ZIEGLER: You know, there's this new Hunt development, so there's sort of an agitated group out there.

PRESIDENT NIXON: What's the Hunt development? Are they tying him in now?

ZIEGLER: Well, (unintelligible) somewhere at his desk at the Executive Office Building. . . .

PRESIDENT NIXON: A gun and a map in Hunt's desk?

ZIEGLER: Right.

PRESIDENT NIXON: Map of what?

ZIEGLER: The Democratic National Headquarters.

PRESIDENT NIXON: Oh, Christ. . . .

SEGMENT 2:

ZIEGLER: . . . Well, it's a source story that appeared in the [*Washington*] *Daily News,* . . . and it said that Hunt's desk was in Colson's suite and that in that desk they found a gun and a map of the Democratic headquarters and bugging devices such as those that were found in that case. Well, so they come to me with the question, can I confirm it. I said: "Obviously, I am not going to comment on a matter that's under investigation by the Federal Bureau of Investigation. Number one, the first day that this question came to us, we made it very clear the White House has not been involved. Number two—"

PRESIDENT NIXON: This was found in his desk two months after he left the White House?

ZIEGLER: No. Well, whenever they investigated. Number two, I said, "we made clear that Mr. Colson was in no way involved."

PRESIDENT NIXON: That's right. He went out and talked to them, didn't he?

ZIEGLER: Not to the press.

PRESIDENT NIXON: Well, he was investigated, though. He had some questions?

ZIEGLER: Well, I didn't get into that. . . . Then we went through the typical Q and A thing. Finally I said: "Look, fellows; I said, I think it was most inappropriate, in the light of a source story that is not based on any official statement that has been made by the investigating authorities for you to associate in this room in the White House the name of a White House official with this particular story, particularly when we have already made very clear, the President has made it clear and I have made it clear, that there is no association whatsoever."

Now, I've talked with Dean. The FBI is going to make an official statement on this thing and Dean—

PRESIDENT NIXON: What is he going to say?

ZIEGLER: Told me that the story's inaccurate.

PRESIDENT NIXON: Inaccurate or accurate?

ZIEGLER: Inaccurate, which I did not know. At least he feels it is, which I didn't know in the briefing. But if they come out with this, it's going to undercut the—

PRESIDENT NIXON: Well, when will Dean—when will the FBI get that out?

ZIEGLER: Well, we're trying to get them to move on it right away. . . .

JUNE 30, 1972: THE PRESIDENT AND HALDEMAN, 3:28–4:22 P.M., OVAL OFFICE

The FBI continues to be an independent force in the investigation. General Vernon Walters's attempts to use his CIA position to thwart the FBI had failed, and now Nixon considers using Walters to directly confront Attorney General Kleindienst. The President understands the growing linkage: Hunt and Liddy both had worked for Egil Krogh, an Ehrlichman protégé and a co-director of the Plumbers. Meanwhile, John Dean advances the theory that the White House had been victimized by a double agent.

PRESIDENT NIXON: Well, they've reportedly found a gun in somebody's vault.

HALDEMAN: That's apparently leaked out of the Bureau, which we're—

PRESIDENT NIXON: Well, the Bureau says that's not true. . . .

HALDEMAN: The only thing that's not true is it wasn't made in Spain. They said it was a Spanish-made gun. . . .

PRESIDENT NIXON: What, you mean this guy [Hunt] has a—I thought he left two months ago.

HALDEMAN: He did, but he left his—there was a safe. He had an office over there and he left stuff in the safe. He had a safe in the office and he had stuff in the safe, and among the things in the safe were a gun and a wiretapping kit or suitcase.

PRESIDENT NIXON: What about the map of the convention?

HALDEMAN: That isn't apparently true, which is kind of interesting. There was a lot of other stuff [including Hunt's forged Kennedy cables about the Diem assassination and a psychological profile of Daniel Ellsberg], which was handled at a very supposedly high level, discreet level, with the Bureau. [Dean had turned the material over to L. Patrick Gray, who subsequently destroyed it.]

PRESIDENT NIXON: But I understood, though, that on that Bureau thing, though, that they were to watch, they were to keep up with this guy, you know what I mean?

HALDEMAN: That's what they were told. They aren't.

PRESIDENT NIXON: Huh?

HALDEMAN: They aren't. We're having problems with the Bureau. That's what we were talking about with Dean and Mitchell before our meeting with you.

PRESIDENT NIXON: I see. You mean, despite what you've told—despite [General Vernon] Walters going over there?

HALDEMAN: Gray doesn't know how to turn them off and neither does Felt[?]. They're concerned about how to do it, get the record clear, and all this sort of stuff.

PRESIDENT NIXON: Well, incidentally, there's the—

HALDEMAN: Kleindienst hasn't turned Justice off, either, which is another problem.

PRESIDENT NIXON: Huh?

HALDEMAN: The U.S. Attorney and his criminal head [Henry Petersen] are both pushing forward, and we've got to—we'll work it out. We've got to somehow get Kleindienst to tell them.

PRESIDENT NIXON: Well, I'd have Walters go see them, too. About this fellow

[Hunt]—I mean, after all, the gun and the wiretapping doesn't bother me a bit with this fellow. He's in the Cuban thing, the whole Cuban business. He's out of the country.

HALDEMAN: No.

PRESIDENT NIXON: Is he back in the country?

HALDEMAN: He never went out, but it doesn't matter. He's a—at least they say, his main stock in trade is he's a master of disguise. [*Chuckles.*] He's someplace under some disguise, although he's supposed to go abroad. . . .

PRESIDENT NIXON: It would seem to me that—was Colson aware he had stuff in his safe and all that sort of thing?

HALDEMAN: I don't think so. . . . Colson wasn't there when they opened the safe. I don't think he knows what was in it. In fact, I'm sure he doesn't. They haven't told him what was in it. . . .

PRESIDENT NIXON: They didn't find a map?

HALDEMAN: I don't think so. John Dean's the one who knows about this and he says there wasn't any. He says there was a road map, but it had nothing to do with the Democratic National Committee, and there was no map of the committee head-quarters. . . . Dean hasn't discounted the possibility that we're dealing with a double agent in this thing somewhere.

PRESIDENT NIXON: Meaning this fellow [Hunt]?

HALDEMAN: Probably not this guy. Probably one of the other guys, or several of them.

PRESIDENT NIXON: A double agent who is putting out this information, giving leads, or what?

HALDEMAN: Well, who purposely moved this thing. . . . It's still kind of hard to fig-ure the whole thing out.

PRESIDENT NIXON: Well, let me tell you, the Mitchell thing couldn't have come at a better time from our standpoint. He goes and he takes responsibility for it. He un-derstands that, doesn't he?

HALDEMAN: He mentioned that himself. He raised that. . . .

PRESIDENT NIXON: Well, I wonder then, in view of this break today, whether Mitchell going tomorrow is a good idea after all.

HALDEMAN: Yes. This thing doesn't tie back to that.

PRESIDENT NIXON: Why not?

HALDEMAN: Because it leads to the White House, not to Mitchell and the Re-Elec-tion Committee. They haven't tied Hunt to the Re-Election Committee. They're tying him to Colson.

PRESIDENT NIXON: Well, they haven't really tied Hunt to the group yet, have they?

HALDEMAN: No, except that his name was in their book.

PRESIDENT NIXON: Yes. Or Colson; does he know about all this, so he's told the story? What does he say?

HALDEMAN: I haven't talked to him, since the story—the story just came out Sat-urday night. I haven't talked to Chuck since. Knowing Chuck, I'm sure he's very dis-turbed.

PRESIDENT NIXON: Well, there's not much we can do about it, is there?

HALDEMAN: No. . . . I want him [Mitchell] to call Kleindienst and Gray in and say:

Look, this happened; I used to sit on the National Security Council. You know, this happens to lead to some lines that (unintelligible) the Watergate–National Committee caper. Your people are investigating stuff that must not be investigated. That's the signal you've gotten from the CIA. For Christ's sake, smarten up. Smarten up and turn this off. Go ahead and toss your cards to the grand jury on the open and shut case stuff, and let it go at that.

. . . McCord . . . is trying to get F. Lee Bailey to handle his case. So we may be getting into an F. Lee Bailey versus Edward Bennett Williams. . . .

[Gap of unknown length in original recording due to tape change.]

PRESIDENT NIXON: If we don't think Colson—but Colson told the Bureau he had nothing to do with Hunt, didn't he? He was questioned?

HALDEMAN: That's right.

PRESIDENT NIXON: What did he tell them?

HALDEMAN: He told them the straight truth. He has had to do with Hunt. He told them he had nothing to do with Hunt as far as this thing was concerned, that he'd worked with Hunt on totally unrelated—

PRESIDENT NIXON: Well, you know, in a sense, the fact that his gun and wiretapping equipment is still there and so forth, it would seem to me would be an indication that he's not afraid of anything. You get my point?

HALDEMAN: Yes. I can't understand why it was still there, because he came back to the office after this. I can't understand why he didn't empty his safe. A lot of this just totally passes me by. I just can't put it together and have it add up. It's just a lot of very strange things.

PRESIDENT NIXON: Well, the guy that really—the committee contact was through Liddy. What was his job?

HALDEMAN: He was the counsel for the Finance Committee, this job for Stans. That was just a cover.

PRESIDENT NIXON: And he's the guy that did this with apparently Mitchell's knowledge?

HALDEMAN: Well—

PRESIDENT NIXON: We don't know. Not this.

HALDEMAN: Not specifically this, but—

PRESIDENT NIXON: But he was getting information.

HALDEMAN: Developing intelligence and so forth.

PRESIDENT NIXON: He was off on his own, though.

HALDEMAN: And some counter-activity.

PRESIDENT NIXON: Which, as we know, is standard practice.

HALDEMAN: See, Liddy was still working for the White House, too. He worked for Bud Krogh [and the Plumbers]. So did Hunt.

PRESIDENT NIXON: Where was Krogh? What capacity?

HALDEMAN: Narcotics.

PRESIDENT NIXON: Well, there's nothing particularly wrong with that. . . .

HALDEMAN: . . . We've got a very brief announcement [of Mitchell's resignation] and then a long letter to the President.

PRESIDENT NIXON: Is the letter going to be made public?

HALDEMAN: Yes.

PRESIDENT NIXON: That's all right.

HALDEMAN: Hey, this is pretty good: "Dear Mr. President: Your words of friendship and understanding when we met today meant more to me than I can possibly convey in this letter. I have long believed and often said nothing is more important to the future of our country than your re-election as President. I had looked forward to devoting all my time and energy to that result. I have found, however, I can no longer do so on a full-time basis and still meet the one obligation which must come first (unintelligible). They [family] have patiently put up with my long absence for some four years. The moment has come when I must devote more time to them.

"Relatively few men have the privilege of serving the President of the United States. In my case, (unintelligible) the strength of your leadership. As I said today, I shall continue to work for your re-election as well as to be grateful for your unfailing friendship and confidence."

PRESIDENT NIXON: It's an excellent letter, couldn't be better. It's very subtle.

HALDEMAN: Very personal—

PRESIDENT NIXON: Very subtle.

HALDEMAN: —and all that.

PRESIDENT NIXON: Excellent.

HALDEMAN: That, you release that along with just a straight announcement: "John Mitchell announced today he's resigned as campaign director for the Committee to Re-Elect the President in order to devote more time to his wife and family. He will continue to serve the committee in an advisory capacity."

PRESIDENT NIXON: Right, that's excellent. . . .

JUNE 30, 1972: THE PRESIDENT, HALDEMAN, AND CLARK MACGREGOR, 4:30–6:19 P.M., OVAL OFFICE

Nixon and Haldeman adamantly deny any White House involvement in Watergate to Clark MacGregor, Mitchell's successor. Nixon raises a fear of double agents and expresses bewilderment about any knowledge of Hunt and Liddy—an excellent example of Nixon's ability to tailor information to suit his listener. MacGregor says very little. After he leaves, Nixon again describes breaking and entering as "a minuscule crime unless you get something." Breaking into Democratic headquarters, he adds, is "no blot on a man's record." Haldeman presses the seriousness of the Plumbers' activities, but Nixon dismisses any possibility of their being criminal. And yet, Nixon warns, "You can't cover this thing up, Bob." In Segment 3, the two men conjure detailed explanations of different aspects of the affair.

SEGMENT 1

MACGREGOR: I don't need to know anything about the past, but I need to, I guess, to know something about the future. I have said to people absolutely flat out, I've talked to Congressmen and Senators, the Committee to Re-Elect the President and the White House had absolutely nothing to do with this (unintelligible) incident.

PRESIDENT NIXON: That's what you've got, that's the line you should take. That's what Mitchell is doing. I know the White House had nothing to do with it. As far as the committee is concerned, I know Mitchell had nothing to do with it. As far as the Cubans are concerned, they certainly are Republicans; that's the problem.

HALDEMAN: There are some lines of interconnection.

PRESIDENT NIXON: And they—

HALDEMAN: That's our problem.

PRESIDENT NIXON: —they certainly were doing it to hurt McGovern and support Nixon. That's the problem and that's what Mitchell basically is concerned about. But you can be sure that, as far as Mitchell is concerned, he of course had nothing to do with it. I mean, basically the reason you can be sure, Clark, even if you figure that he was lying, which he would not do to us, is he's not a stupid man.

MACGREGOR: Oh, no.

PRESIDENT NIXON: He wouldn't do such a stupid thing. The White House thing, I mean, this fellow, what's his name, Hunt?

HALDEMAN: Hunt.

PRESIDENT NIXON: Hunt is a former CIA agent. He's a super-sleuth, et cetera, et cetera, et cetera. But he hasn't been with the White House—I mean, there's some story today that they found some gun in his safe over here or something like that, but I don't know anything about it. But he hasn't been in the White House since when?

HALDEMAN: March, I guess.

MACGREGOR: March 29th I think was the last day he was paid.

HALDEMAN: See, when he was here he worked on a totally different thing. He was in the Bay of Pigs. He was working on the declassification thing, which we had an all-out unit going on, and Hunt was working on. He knew about that stuff.

PRESIDENT NIXON: That's right.

HALDEMAN: He also, they found out when they were working with him on that, he could be very helpful on some of the narcotics stuff. . . . Now, he's also been involved, as this thing starts to develop, in other things, things we didn't know anything about. And this is what you get when you start dealing with these underground characters, as you know as a lawyer.

PRESIDENT NIXON: And I can't be sure, but I would say this. One thing I think you should know, I can't be sure that Hunt was not involved with the Cubans, because the Cubans—

HALDEMAN: They had his name in their address book. . . .

PRESIDENT NIXON: The point is he headed the Goddamn Bay of Pigs thing and these people worked with him. So I can't be sure. I don't think he is, you know what I mean. But I don't know. So that's one of the reasons why I said, all that I know is the White House had nothing to do with it. I know Colson had nothing to do with it. I know Hunt was gone, so as far as Mitchell is concerned, Mitchell is in a spot, I would have to admit, where we really don't know. You have to worry a bit about it. Mitchell is in a spot where he hasn't been watching the committee too closely and you can't be very—you can't be sure that these Cubans, who were, you know, hanging around, didn't have some contacts in that committee. I don't know who. If we did, we'd fire them.

HALDEMAN: Well, they did. The Bureau has a line into one guy at the committee named Liddy—

PRESIDENT NIXON: Liddy.

HALDEMAN: —who was working over at the Finance Committee, not at the—

PRESIDENT NIXON: For Stans.

HALDEMAN: He worked for Stans as a counsel. He is a guy that was in the White House office working with Krogh's office on the drug stuff. He knew these people. And they have some lines that tie him into some of this. In their interrogation of him, they weren't satisfied with his answers, or he said he wanted to get a lawyer and they said, well, the lawyer would tell you to shut up, and he said, well, I'll do what the lawyer says. And they said, well then, there's no point in talking to you. When the committee found that out, that that's what had happened in his interrogation, they fired him. The word that they have fired him is not out yet and we had hoped—we hope it doesn't get out. But Liddy has been released from the committee, from his post—

PRESIDENT NIXON: Let's put it this way—

HALDEMAN: He's no longer employed there.

PRESIDENT NIXON: If he was involved, and I'm not sure that he was—I mean—

HALDEMAN: That's right.

PRESIDENT NIXON: But if he was—if any of what he didn't want to talk about was his own involvement in it—

HALDEMAN: That's right. . . .

PRESIDENT NIXON: The point is, if he was involved, Clark, it was an unauthorized involvement. That's the point that you need to know. It was without—it was without the authority or without the knowledge of John Mitchell. That's the way I'd put it. As a matter of fact, this is not—this has nothing to do with John's leaving, because he has to leave for other personal reasons, but in a sense it's a good thing because at least you're in and you know very well that you had nothing to do with it. And if anything happens, I would assume John—

HALDEMAN: Yes, but I don't think—I don't know. We purposely don't know a lot of what that kind of thing was involved—

PRESIDENT NIXON: I don't want to find out.

HALDEMAN: —both on the governmental side or the committee.

PRESIDENT NIXON: To me, it's such a crude Goddamn thing. You almost think it's a bunch of double agents.

HALDEMAN: It may very well be.

PRESIDENT NIXON: Double agents, that's what I'm afraid of. It just looks to me like, almost like a fix. Doesn't it to you? How the hell—the main thing, I said, why in the name of Christ did they want to bug the National Committee? . . .

HALDEMAN: That's the overriding—

PRESIDENT NIXON: If you're going to bug, bug the McGovern committee.

HALDEMAN: Of all the things in this town to bug—

PRESIDENT NIXON: Is there anything in our Republican National Committee that anyone would want to bug? Shit.

HALDEMAN: That's the one place I couldn't care less if they bug.

PRESIDENT NIXON: When I saw that, I thought: Well, these crazy bastards. I didn't know who it was at the time, the Cuban thing, and I was surprised to find a lot of these Cuban people working around here. . . . But they're all gone now. Do we have any more of them left?

HALDEMAN: I don't think so.

PRESIDENT NIXON: Who's McCord? Is he with us?

HALDEMAN: Well, he was. He was—they hired as a security, you know, surveillance system guy, to check out their bugging. . . .

MACGREGOR: On my end of it, obviously, Mr. President, my fear is that—

PRESIDENT NIXON: He's going to get F. Lee Bailey?

HALDEMAN: He's the one that says he's going to get F. Lee Bailey.

PRESIDENT NIXON: Oh, Christ.

MACGREGOR: My fear is that the remarkable record that you've made is going to be besmirched by these extraneous things—

HALDEMAN: That's right.

MACGREGOR: —that—

PRESIDENT NIXON: Sure.

MACGREGOR: —that you have no knowledge of.

HALDEMAN: The worst thing we can do, though, the worst thing we can do is let them do exactly what they want to, which is to get us so involved in that that we don't keep shooting our guns.

PRESIDENT NIXON: Well, you're going to have this sort of thing more, I guess. People do stupid things. I mean, that long agonizing thing of ITT. We survived. It was very stupid.

HALDEMAN: We did some stupid things. . . .

MACGREGOR: Well, there are things—there are a thousand stupid things like that that don't get uncovered, that we do and that they do. It's when they get uncovered that they look so stupid.

PRESIDENT NIXON: There will be more. They're going to have a few problems, too.

MACGREGOR: I've been asking myself, Mr. President, if there's anything in my background, political or otherwise—

PRESIDENT NIXON: Forget it.

MACGREGOR: —that would redound on you.

PRESIDENT NIXON: Forget it.

MACGREGOR: I don't think that there is. . . .

PRESIDENT NIXON: Let me say this. Everybody's got something in his background, everybody.

MACGREGOR: I can't think of anything.

PRESIDENT NIXON: And if you don't have, why—

MACGREGOR: If they didn't get yours four years ago, they ain't going to get it this time, because they're a lot more confused than Hubert's people were.

PRESIDENT NIXON: We don't worry about that. But I must admit, I must say, that you're going to go in there and it'll be good that you're going in with a clean slate, and when you're asked about this, that you were confident John Mitchell had absolutely nothing to do with this, this was an activity that was unauthorized, it's a bizarre business, period. This Hunt fellow, did you ever meet Hunt? I've never seen him.

MACGREGOR: No, sir. I know nothing about him except what I've picked up.

PRESIDENT NIXON: If he had a gun. . . .

MACGREGOR: Krogh has worked with him.

PRESIDENT NIXON: But if Hunt had a gun—and what did he have, wiretapping equipment, in the safe? It would seem to me if he had any guilt about this—

HALDEMAN: He would have gotten it out.

PRESIDENT NIXON: —he'd have gotten it out. But here it is two months later, it's still in the safe. You see my point?

MACGREGOR: Well, there probably are other people around who have guns in their safes.

PRESIDENT NIXON: Isn't that bizarre—what?

MACGREGOR: I suppose there are other people around with guns in their safes.

PRESIDENT NIXON: Well, and wiretapping equipment?

MACGREGOR: Except you don't even think about it.

PRESIDENT NIXON: This guy is a wiretapper. He's been tapping for years, hasn't he?

HALDEMAN: I don't know. I don't know what he—he's a disguise type guy.

PRESIDENT NIXON: And deep cover.

HALDEMAN: He writes dirty books.

MACGREGOR: The phrase, the CIA phrase is "deep cover operative."

PRESIDENT NIXON: Deep cover. . . . Of course he was also with Kennedy and he worked for Johnson.

HALDEMAN: And he was damn helpful in uncovering some stuff we needed uncovered, which we also would just as soon not get out. Nothing wrong with it.

PRESIDENT NIXON: The main thing, frankly, that I was concerned about was Colson, because Colson did work with him on the—you know—the Pentagon Papers, whatever the hell it was they were working on. But . . . Colson has been questioned by the Bureau under oath, absolutely. So I am not concerned. That's why I said categorically the White House—and I can only say, people lie to me, but. . . .

HALDEMAN: I don't think, I honestly don't think there is any guy in the White House. I think there obviously were some contacts at the committee. There was a contact with McCord. I don't know what the hell they were, and there's nothing at any level of authority, and I don't know whether there was any contact in the effort. . . .

PRESIDENT NIXON: Why the Christ don't these guys plead guilty?

HALDEMAN: Well, I think they're going to. They waived the preliminary hearing.

PRESIDENT NIXON: They're going to? That's the new part. . . . Well, Christ, from what I've heard they're going to raise their bail and all that crap. They think it's great that they were tapping the Democrats.

SEGMENT 2

PRESIDENT NIXON: But you've got to remember this. You're going to have—you'll probably have another Watergate. Watch that. There'll be some asshole things will be done. People are going to say they can do things, steal.

HALDEMAN: Well, they're going to be desperate.

PRESIDENT NIXON: They're going to be after, for example, what about the $10 million we discussed. They were complying with the law.

MACGREGOR: Your position on that is absolutely right. It's the position that I hoped you'd take.

PRESIDENT NIXON: You know what the problem is? You know why we don't want to disclose it?

MACGREGOR: Well—

PRESIDENT NIXON: It has nothing to do with the contributors. Who are they, Clem Stone, John Mulcahy? They'll all be on the list next month. But it happens that in that Maury Stans has a number of very prominent Democrats who are playing both sides.

HALDEMAN: Well, he's got some that are only playing one side.

PRESIDENT NIXON: Well, some Democrats that are playing our side only, who don't want to get caught. That's the point, see.

HALDEMAN: Some of them we have commitments to.

PRESIDENT NIXON: We have commitments that we can't say, (unintelligible) the Democratic Party. That's what it really is. It's nothing to do with having anything to hide. There's no Mafia money or foreign money or any of that.

HALDEMAN: No problem with any of it except the Democrats? . . .

SEGMENT 3

(MacGregor leaves.)

HALDEMAN: . . . I told him about the Liddy thing because he's going to find it out right away anyway, and it was better to let him know there was a guy. What we were talking about is trying to—we're going to write a scenario—in fact, we're going to have Liddy write it—which brings all of the loose ends that might lead anywhere at all to him. . . .

PRESIDENT NIXON: What is he going to say?

HALDEMAN: He's going to say that, yes, he was doing this, he wasn't authorized. . . . He thought it was an honorable thing to do. He thought it was important. Obviously it was wrong. He didn't think he should ask for authorization because he knew it was something that he didn't want to put anybody else in a position of authorizing. How did he get the money? See, we've got that one problem, the check from [Kenneth] Dahlberg. What happened is—and that works out nicely because the check came in after the spending limit thing. So it was given to him with the instruction to return it to Dahlberg. Instead, he subverted it to this other purpose, deposited it in the bank. That explains where the money came from. That explains everything. And they're working on writing out a scenario. I think that's the answer to this, and admit that, by God, there was some campaign involvement.

PRESIDENT NIXON: But without Mitchell's knowledge.

HALDEMAN: But without Mitchell's knowledge.

PRESIDENT NIXON: Or authorization.

HALDEMAN: Or authorization.

PRESIDENT NIXON: He's fired.

HALDEMAN: And he's fired.

PRESIDENT NIXON: What does he get out of it? What's his penalty?

HALDEMAN: Not too much. They don't think it will be any big problem. Whatever it is, we'll take care of him.

PRESIDENT NIXON: Well again, if you have to. . . . I really think Mitchell is telling the truth. . . .

HALDEMAN: I can't imagine that he knew specifically that this is what they were doing. I think he said: "For God's sake, get out and get this Goddamn information; don't pussyfoot around."

PRESIDENT NIXON: How'd he [Liddy] get the check, you say?

HALDEMAN: He was processing the check. It was an illegal check. . . . [H]e was going to run it down to Mexico and put it into cash or something.

PRESIDENT NIXON: Then what did we do, return the money to the guy? What happened—

HALDEMAN: That's what they're going to say he was supposed to do.

PRESIDENT NIXON: And what—

HALDEMAN: But he didn't. He on his own initiative decided this was a good source of funds for this covert operation he was running. So he took the check, processed it through this Mexican bank, and ran it up here, which is what he did do. . . .

PRESIDENT NIXON: But the Hunt outfit was involved for other reasons?

HALDEMAN: Maybe he ties Hunt in. Maybe that's the better way. They've got to work that out. Just say he—

PRESIDENT NIXON: He found this group of people that were very amenable—

HALDEMAN: He met them over here when he was working on this other project and he used them on the side for his project.

PRESIDENT NIXON: Well, another way he could do it is to say that they came in wanting to do something. I mean, because of their concern that—

HALDEMAN: That he did funding, he shifted some money around for them.

PRESIDENT NIXON: And that he—

HALDEMAN: This sounded like a good idea to him.

PRESIDENT NIXON: It sounded like a good idea and they said: We want to do this. And he said: All right, I'll work with you. And he found the money for them, because he did work with them. But in other words, keep it, keep it—I think it's well to keep the scenario involved in the Cuban plot as much as possible. In other words, these Cubans—after all, it is to a certain extent. Why would they risk their Goddamn selves playing such a game as this?

HALDEMAN: You know who [Kenneth] Dahlberg is?

PRESIDENT NIXON: No.

HALDEMAN: He's [Dwayne] Andreas's bag man.

PRESIDENT NIXON: Oh.

HALDEMAN: So it all of a sudden starts running over to the other side, too. It's kind of intriguing.

PRESIDENT NIXON: I agree. I think the best thing to do is to cut your losses in such things, get the damn thing out. It's just one of those things and they were involved.

HALDEMAN: Otherwise they're going to keep pursuing these things that lead into the wrong directions. . . .

PRESIDENT NIXON: I don't want to get—Colson is valuable to us. I don't want to get him messed up in this damn thing.

HALDEMAN: Well, it goes beyond that, too. When he started into the other—not in this project. And he doesn't get into this project either, but you've got—Hunt's tied to Krogh, Liddy's tied to Krogh. They're all tied to Ehrlichman.

PRESIDENT NIXON: You mean they worked here?

HALDEMAN: Sure.

PRESIDENT NIXON: Well, what the hell's wrong with that?

HALDEMAN: They're tied in to Dave Young [co-head of the Plumbers]. Nothing any more than there is with Colson.

PRESIDENT NIXON: Yeah, that's what I mean. No, but not in any hanky-panky. The only thing that—you mean in the Pentagon Papers? What the hell is the matter with that?

HALDEMAN: The investigation, the process.

PRESIDENT NIXON: What?

HALDEMAN: Just the process that they used.

PRESIDENT NIXON: Well, that's perfectly all right.

SEGMENT 4

PRESIDENT NIXON: Well, when will this Liddy scenario—is Dean working on it with him?

HALDEMAN: Well, [John] Dean's working on it with Mitchell. Mitchell suggested Dean write it. I suggested let Liddy write it. Liddy knows more of the facts than anybody. Let him sit down and spend so long as it takes to spin out the whole web and see where it runs, if he's willing to take the heat, which he apparently is.

PRESIDENT NIXON: (unintelligible) get a true believer.

HALDEMAN: Yes. He says he is. He says it doesn't make any difference what they do, he will not—

PRESIDENT NIXON: And we'll give him—we'll take care of him, too. Well, it's good to have some people like that.

HALDEMAN: He may have to go to jail for a while or something, but he'll survive that.

PRESIDENT NIXON: What the hell. Worse than that, he's breaking into the Democratic Committee, Christ. That's no blot on a man's record.

HALDEMAN: Well, the embezzlement of those funds, too, and violation of the Campaign Spending Act.

PRESIDENT NIXON: That's probably a fine. . . .

HALDEMAN: Wrapping it all up into this, it doesn't make much difference. If he gets hung on it, then we'll wait a discreet interval and pardon him.

PRESIDENT NIXON: You don't want to pardon him now.

HALDEMAN: After the election.

PRESIDENT NIXON: Sure. Let me tell you something interesting. Don't be that worried about the thing and its effect on him. How much effect did Bobby Baker's thing, where he was directly involved, where he was convicted, where everybody knew that Johnson was the bag and all that sort of thing? How much did it affect him?

HALDEMAN: Probably a lot.

PRESIDENT NIXON: Bullshit. Johnson, how could he hurt when he won 61 to 39?

HALDEMAN: Oh, it didn't hurt in the election. It hurt his image.

PRESIDENT NIXON: What?

HALDEMAN: It hurt his image.

PRESIDENT NIXON: A little. . . . We're in a different area. This involves the Cam-

WATERGATE: BREAK-IN AND COVER-UP 89

paign Committee, which we don't like worth a damn. But Clark and a lot of others are terribly sensitive about this, that, and the other thing. But we don't like this.

HALDEMAN: Well, Clark's got a good right to be. If there's something there, he'd better know what he's got to cope with. . . .

PRESIDENT NIXON: Well, I'm sorry, but I guess that's the way it has to work. You can't cover this thing up, Bob. The best thing is to cut it. That's why I was hoping to get the damn guys charged. . . .

PRESIDENT NIXON: It's just such a ridiculous Goddamn thing, it really is.

JULY 1, 1972: THE PRESIDENT AND COLSON, 8:50–9:05 A.M., OVAL OFFICE

Colson praises Howard Hunt's virtues and plans some retaliatory moves, including stealing Republican Committee files and blaming Democrats. Such talk was commonplace between the two men, but apparently was of no consequence.

PRESIDENT NIXON: . . . It's interesting that the [*Washington*] *Daily News* would run with the story [about Howard Hunt's White House safe] that is so totally—I mean, it's an exaggeration. Almost, there must be somebody over there planning something like that.

COLSON: I think there is.

PRESIDENT NIXON: That can't be right. I mean, after all, the map deal. There's no map there, frankly.

COLSON: No.

PRESIDENT NIXON: Of course, the gun and the walkie-talkie, well, Christ, the guy just probably didn't put it in his briefcase. He's that kind of a guy. . . .

COLSON: He carried a gun for years. Well, he kept it—he didn't keep it in his desk. He had it locked in a safe.

[Withdrawn item. National security.]

COLSON: The tragedy of it, Mr. President, was that I never have been in his office, so I didn't know whether the story that ran in the *Daily News* was true or not, except that it said his office was in mine, which it isn't. . . . But the point is if I had known that it was untrue, I'd have had Justice deny it early in the day, rather than let it run all day. It ran all day on the wires. . . .

PRESIDENT NIXON: It was not on any of the networks?

COLSON: No, no. . . . They didn't even mention it in the *Post* this morning. . . . [Television correspondent] Howard Smith . . . said, "I still think it's a seven-day wonder."

PRESIDENT NIXON: Well, it may be, but you see, they're still investigating charges and the question is when they get finally to—they're going to find out that the money came from some Republican source, as you well know. Some Republicans felt very interested in the cause of these Cubans. I'd put in the fact that the Cubans, scared to death of McGovern, and sure, there were Republicans, there were eager beavers in the campaign committee that were—

COLSON: The Cubans, the Cubans, Mr. President, are very afraid of McGovern. You know he wrote what I would regard as a very innocuous letter about we'll treat all Latin American countries alike, and they took off on that. . . .

PRESIDENT NIXON: But my point is we know they've been trying to bug us. Everybody knows that. That's why Mitchell hired these people. What would you think? What would you think if that happened?

COLSON: I think it would be very helpful if they came in one morning and found files strewn all over the floor.

PRESIDENT NIXON: And some missing.

COLSON: Something missing. Of course, we have had some missing over here, and that was in this morning's paper.

PRESIDENT NIXON: The campaign?

COLSON: They've had several campaign files missing. Of course, we know that to be true because we went through one day trying to track something back that we were concerned about in the ITT case, and something had been taken. This goes on in every campaign.

PRESIDENT NIXON: Oh, my.

COLSON: It's just these fellows did it in a very—

PRESIDENT NIXON: Stupid way. . . . I mean, if something could be very open. But I mean demolished, do $3,000, $4,000 worth of damage, you know what I mean?

COLSON: That would have a very—that would have a very good effect.

PRESIDENT NIXON: Right during their convention.

COLSON: During theirs or during ours?

PRESIDENT NIXON: Theirs. . . .

COLSON: Then Dole is in a perfect position to say—

PRESIDENT NIXON: Sue. They could sue the committee, sue the committee. They sued him about it.

COLSON: We have that one under control. It's being postponed and we think it will be dismissed.

PRESIDENT NIXON: Well, I'd sue them. . . . There should be a rifling or missing files, something where it's really torn up, where pictures could be taken. They'll charge it's been done by the Republicans, so what the hell. We'll say: "For Christ's sake—"

COLSON: "We didn't charge that when your place got—"

PRESIDENT NIXON: That's right.

COLSON: Financial files would be the kind of thing. Financial files would be the kind of thing they would want to get their hands on. There'd be a real motive for that.

PRESIDENT NIXON: Yes, and some obvious one. You consider Hunt to be reliable, don't you?

COLSON: Always has been.

PRESIDENT NIXON: You've known him for years?

COLSON: Yes, sir. I've known him since—

PRESIDENT NIXON: How about McCord? Is he reliable?

COLSON: Never met him or know anything about him. I would doubt it, from what I have heard.

PRESIDENT NIXON: What do you think? Wasn't he in the CIA, too, with Hunt?

COLSON: Different areas, I believe.

PRESIDENT NIXON: Why do you doubt him . . . ?

COLSON: Just the way he was—

PRESIDENT NIXON: (unintelligible).

COLSON: Yes, and the money arrangements. I mean, Hunt is not—you see, Hunt in all the things he did for us never cared about the money. He just wanted to help. He's an ideologue. You read his books and all of his books have a political message, which is pretty conservative. I always trust someone whose beliefs are—

PRESIDENT NIXON: I agree.

COLSON: And not someone who's just in there for a buck.

PRESIDENT NIXON: That's right.

COLSON: Howard would die for something he believes in; he damn near did several times.

PRESIDENT NIXON: McCord you think may be—

COLSON: Just, I've never met him, but just the ring of it, the $4,000 a month contract, setting up an office.

PRESIDENT NIXON: $4,000 with whom?

COLSON: With us, with the committee, the National Committee.

PRESIDENT NIXON: To do what?

COLSON: Security.

PRESIDENT NIXON: I think that's a stupid thing to do. I don't think security is worth that much. Do you?

COLSON: Well, it is if you—it is if you do it right.

PRESIDENT NIXON: Oh, sure. The best security is for the individual himself to carry his own stuff and never have anything around.

COLSON: That's right.

PRESIDENT NIXON: I even do it here, you know. I don't leave anything around that I really, really am concerned about. I don't do it.

COLSON: No. Memos that are very sensitive, I either carry them in here and lock them up at night in a safe. I agree, I totally agree. Hunt is a fellow who I would trust. I mean, he's a true believer, a real patriot. My God, the things he's done for his country. It's just a tragedy that he gets smeared with this. Of course, the other story that a lot of people have bought is that Howard Hunt was taken out of the country by the CIA. Well, he's certainly done a lot of hot stuff. . . . Oh, Jesus. He pulled a lot of very fancy stuff in the sixties.

[Withdrawn item. National security.]

PRESIDENT NIXON: Well, I don't agree. If anything ever happens to him, be sure that he blows the whistle, the whole Bay of Pigs.

COLSON: He wrote the book.

PRESIDENT NIXON: Blow their horn.

COLSON: He tells quite a story, coming in here during that period crying and pleading with Kennedy. . . .

JULY 1, 1972: THE PRESIDENT AND COLSON, 11:28–11:36 A.M., OVAL OFFICE

Nixon continues his fascination with wiretapping—of himself and others.

PRESIDENT NIXON: . . . I don't want an impression of the big brother thing, the White House and the President ordering buggings and snooping. But Goddamn Kennedy did it all the time. Bobby Kennedy had a record number of these bugs.

COLSON: Well, you saw Kevin Phillips? Did you see Kevin Phillips's column this week?

PRESIDENT NIXON: No. What did he say?

COLSON: How they bugged [Anna] Chennault's telephones in '68.

PRESIDENT NIXON: Oh, in '68 they bugged our phones, too.

COLSON: And that this was ordered by Johnson.

PRESIDENT NIXON: That's right.

COLSON: And done through the FBI. My God, if we ever did anything like that you'd have the—

PRESIDENT NIXON: Yes. For example, why didn't we bug McGovern, because, after all, he's affecting the peace negotiations?

COLSON: Sure.

PRESIDENT NIXON: That would be exactly the same thing.

COLSON: That's right. Well, Kevin [Phillips] did—of course, no one else will pick it up. He's unfortunately considered our guy. But it's a very devastating point, that they should not be using that—

JULY 19, 1972: THE PRESIDENT AND EHRLICHMAN, 12:45–1:51 P.M., OVAL OFFICE

Ehrlichman offers an update on Watergate and suggests that Jeb Magruder "take the slide." Nixon says that he will "take care" of Magruder "afterwards." The President invokes the Alger Hiss case to warn of the dangers of lying and covering up. "If you cover up, you're going to get caught," he said. Both men warily discuss Hunt's involvement. Ehrlichman, despite later pleas of ignorance, is aware of, even actively involved with, John Dean's role in running the cover-up. The cover-up theme pervades the conversation. Ehrlichman presses for implicating Mitchell, but the President is reluctant. Ehrlichman laments the "disloyal" men in the U.S. Attorney's office and the FBI who continue to push the investigation.

SEGMENT 1

PRESIDENT NIXON: Give me an update on Watergate, where it now stands? What's the next move?

EHRLICHMAN: Well, I don't know. I talked to [John] Dean this morning and Bob talked to Mitchell. I don't know what transpired there, but he sent Dean over to talk to Mitchell, and there's something cooking this morning and I haven't been in on it.

I've had some other things going. So I don't know what the latest is. My conclusion is that from yesterday, Dean came up here planning a brief to send to you all, and my conclusion is that this little scenario that they had dreamed up that was going to preserve [Jeb] Magruder is not going to work and Magruder is probably going to have to take the slide.

PRESIDENT NIXON: How does he slide?

EHRLICHMAN: Well, he'll just have to take whatever lumps come, have to take responsibility for the thing. They're not going to be able to contrive a story that indicates that he didn't know what was going on. But I think that's what Dean's working on this morning.

PRESIDENT NIXON: Did he know?

EHRLICHMAN: Oh, yes. Oh Lord, yes. He's in it with both feet.

PRESIDENT NIXON: He can't contrive a story, then. You know, I'd like to see this thing work out, but I've been through these. The worst thing a guy can do, the worst thing—there are two things and each is bad. One is to lie and the other one is to cover up.

EHRLICHMAN: Yes.

PRESIDENT NIXON: If you cover up, you're going to get caught.

EHRLICHMAN: Yes.

PRESIDENT NIXON: And if you lie you're going to be guilty of perjury. Now, basically that was the whole story of the Hiss case.

EHRLICHMAN: Yes.

PRESIDENT NIXON: It was the story of the [Truman Administration] five percenters and the rest. It's a hell of a Goddamn thing. I hate to see it, but let me say we'll take care of Magruder immediately afterwards. . . .

EHRLICHMAN: We'll do our best to lay that foundation, but as I say, I think Bob and Dean will have a better feel for this a little later, after they've talked to Mitchell, after John's talked to Mitchell, and see where they are today. That fellow [Douglas] Caddy, the lawyer who wouldn't answer questions because it was privileged communications, refused to answer, the Judge cited him for contempt. He appealed it to the local Court of Appeals. They affirmed the trial judge and he's now down there answering questions, as far as I know.

PRESIDENT NIXON: That's probably what's breaking it up.

EHRLICHMAN: It could well be.

PRESIDENT NIXON: Who is Caddy the lawyer for?

EHRLICHMAN: Caddy is a 37-year-old lawyer who was very active in the YAFs, the very conservative Young Americans [for Freedom]—

PRESIDENT NIXON: Who does he represent?

EHRLICHMAN: He represented the five guys who got caught the night they were caught, and he was at the police station within minutes after the police brought the prisoners in there. He'd obviously been called by somebody from the outside. Well, I think what had happened is that Hunt was in the neighborhood and when he saw these guys get caught or heard it over the bug, he called Caddy and Caddy went down and tried to arrange bail and advised them not to talk and so forth. So he's been asked by the grand jury, who called you? And he's refused to answer.

PRESIDENT NIXON: That would bring Hunt into it. . . .

EHRLICHMAN: It would bring Hunt in, it would bring Liddy in. And this guy [Caddy] has an indirect connection with Colson because he is the attorney for Colson's secretary, who is in the process of getting a divorce. But that's as close as it comes to the White House.

PRESIDENT NIXON: Well, I don't think that that's a problem. . . .

EHRLICHMAN: No. No, that's not a problem. That's a sort of tangential thing. But he will not, Caddy will not disclose much beyond what was already going to be disclosed. So it isn't going to add too much to the trouble.

PRESIDENT NIXON: He could disclose that—well, the story basically is, so that Magruder, when you say take a slide, he can't plead the Fifth.

EHRLICHMAN: No, I don't think so. I don't think so. . . .

PRESIDENT NIXON: So what the hell good does he do pleading the Fifth?

EHRLICHMAN: No. I think he has to go in and say: "Well, I did this and it was a bad thing to do and I got carried away and I feel terrible about it."

PRESIDENT NIXON: Well, can't he state it just a little different? He could say he did it, but say it slightly—

EHRLICHMAN: Yes, but it isn't going to change his plea.

PRESIDENT NIXON: No, no, no. . . . What I meant is [he should say] . . . , I didn't expect to be this way, and so forth and so on. I said, "just get all the information you can. I mean, I've just got to take the responsibility for it."

EHRLICHMAN: Yes.

PRESIDENT NIXON: I think he could say that. I don't think he should—I'm thinking it would be unfortunate if he should say, I ordered wiretapping.

EHRLICHMAN: Yes.

PRESIDENT NIXON: That's a problem.

EHRLICHMAN: No, that's kept at the Liddy level if possible. But as I say, I'm operating on too little information this morning. I'll have to get updated.

PRESIDENT NIXON: What is the situation, what is the situation on [Henry] Petersen, Kleindienst, and the rest?

EHRLICHMAN: Petersen, pretty good. Kleindienst is one step removed from it. Petersen's been very good with Dean in trying to help to evaluate the thing as it goes along and in keeping Dean informed of the direction that things are going.

PRESIDENT NIXON: What the U.S. Attorney is up to, and so forth?

EHRLICHMAN: Yes. And he's managed to keep ahold of the U.S. Attorney better. It's a better situation than it was.

SEGMENT 2

PRESIDENT NIXON: . . . But the important thing is to get the Goddamn thing done.

EHRLICHMAN: Yes, yes. Well, we're urging that. We're urging that. I was all over Dean on that last night. It's never going to be any sooner. We've got to get it done as soon as possible so that people have a chance to forget.

PRESIDENT NIXON: What did he say?

EHRLICHMAN: He agrees. He agrees with that, and he says they're not dragging their feet in this by any means. He's enlisted on that.

PRESIDENT NIXON: Do you mean that the Circuit Court ordered an attorney to testify?

EHRLICHMAN: It (unintelligible) me, except that this damn circuit that we've got here, with [Judge David] Bazelon and so on, it surprises me every time they do something.

PRESIDENT NIXON: Why didn't he appeal to the Supreme Court?

EHRLICHMAN: Well, he could, I suppose. They don't have to grant certiorari. I don't know. I don't know the answer to that.

PRESIDENT NIXON: But he's now testifying?

EHRLICHMAN: My understanding is that he was going to go in this morning. Now, he may go down there and refuse and take it to the Supreme Court. I don't know. I just don't have those facts.

PRESIDENT NIXON: Just so we keep it all in one hat here, it's Dean with you, or Dean with Bob, or both?

EHRLICHMAN: Both.

PRESIDENT NIXON: Okay.

EHRLICHMAN: The two of us have been talking to him, more or less together, right along. And we've drawn on Bob's political judgment on this, which has been pretty good.

PRESIDENT NIXON: It sure is.

EHRLICHMAN: So he and I—Dean called us on the airplane and said he had to talk to us, so we stayed on the airplane after it landed and he came out, and we sat and talked for about an hour and went through all the kinds of stuff that he didn't like to talk about on the phone. He had a long meeting with Petersen yesterday.

PRESIDENT NIXON: So it really gets down to Magruder—

EHRLICHMAN: Yes, that's about right.

PRESIDENT NIXON: But what does Magruder say, basically?

EHRLICHMAN: Well, he says that he wanted to get a lot of information, that he felt he had to have information for a lot of different reasons, that they had a kind of a dirty tricks department.

PRESIDENT NIXON: The disrupting of the convention.

EHRLICHMAN: Yes.

PRESIDENT NIXON: That's a good reason.

EHRLICHMAN: Right.

PRESIDENT NIXON: We had these stories.

EHRLICHMAN: Right.

PRESIDENT NIXON: Vietnam Veterans Against the War, mention that.

EHRLICHMAN: And that he imposed on Liddy the responsibility for getting it—

PRESIDENT NIXON: Also, we had our own security to protect against this ourselves.

EHRLICHMAN: Yes, yes. The problem is that once he starts to talk I don't know how—I don't know what the scope of the, the limitations of the scope of the examination might be.

PRESIDENT NIXON: One thing of course I suppose, the main thing is whether he is the one where it stops or whether he goes to Mitchell or Haldeman.

EHRLICHMAN: That's it. And this is one of the questions that we raised with Dean last night. Dean said he didn't have any confidence really that Magruder was sufficiently tough and stable to be able to hold the line if he were pressed by adroit interrogators.

PRESIDENT NIXON: Do you think Mitchell knew?

EHRLICHMAN: Yes, I assume so. I don't know that he did. Yes, I think so.

PRESIDENT NIXON: I can't believe that.

EHRLICHMAN: Well, the proofs of this thing were around. There were transcripts of overheard conversations, for instance, and I just have a hunch that—and I don't know this. I don't know this. This may be unfair. But I just have a feeling that Mitchell in his situation saw those transcripts and had to have—

PRESIDENT NIXON: Did Bob see them?

EHRLICHMAN: No, no. And I can't find anybody in the White House, including [William] Timmons, that ever did or that ever knew about this operation. As a matter of fact, it's interesting—

PRESIDENT NIXON: I would not think that Bob would have known about it because he's too smart.

EHRLICHMAN: Bob and John Dean had a meeting with Mitchell and Magruder and some people about a different operation that was proposed, which they disapproved. And they have a right to feel, as a result of that meeting, that nothing like this was going on. But after that was disapproved, then they went ahead with this other operation without there ever being another meeting involving White House people. But the question of whether Magruder will hold and take the gaff and assume the responsibility and say Mitchell didn't know anything about this is the tough question.

PRESIDENT NIXON: Why would he (unintelligible)?

EHRLICHMAN: Well, you know that when you've got a fairly callow guy on the stand and you work on him properly, you can get him to say things that he doesn't intend to say. . . .

PRESIDENT NIXON: It's a risk, I agree. But (unintelligible) Magruder on that, just look, there's too much rides on this thing, you cannot put John Mitchell in this thing.

EHRLICHMAN: I appreciate that, and you can condition him for a thing of that kind. But I would be willing to bet you a new hat that a guy like Edward Bennett Williams could break Magruder down. . . . You'd start out with a very wide-ranging foundation, in which you would show that almost everything Magruder did he did in concert with Mitchell. . . .

[*A mock cross-examination:*] "But even notwithstanding that, Mr. Magruder, when such and such a matter came up, you didn't decide that yourself, you checked with Mr. Mitchell?"

PRESIDENT NIXON: That's right.

EHRLICHMAN: Well now, let's take this other kind of situation. "When that kind of thing came up, did you do that on your own or did you check that with Mr. Mitchell? . . . "Well, I think I did that on my own." "Well, here's a letter from your file. As a matter of fact, you wrote John Mitchell a memo about that on such a date, didn't you?" "Well, yes, I did." "And that was for the purpose of getting his approval?" "Yes." And you'd go through and you'd just tie him in a web of circumstances. Then you'd say: "Now let's go to this circumstance. Here you were going to send paid spies into the Democratic National Committee and subject your candidate to all kinds of possible exposure, and you want us to believe that you didn't check any of this with Mr. Mitchell, even though these much more minor things, and so on and so forth."

He might hang. He might hang on his denial, and again he might not, depending on how it was done. He wouldn't do it as baldly as that, but, you know, you'd nick away at the edges and you'd finally tear him down.

PRESIDENT NIXON: This is Edward Bennett Williams in the private case?

EHRLICHMAN: Yes. That's where our exposure it seems to me is even greater. . . .

PRESIDENT NIXON: The criminal case now, Magruder's side of it, what is the best tactic there? . . .

EHRLICHMAN: The best tactic if we had our way on it would be to let Liddy and Hunt go and hold it there. If Magruder is going to be involved through third party testimony and so on, then the next best tactic would be the one that's been proposed, which is to rationalize a story which doesn't lead to his conviction. That's the thing they're checking out this morning.

PRESIDENT NIXON: They didn't think they could—

EHRLICHMAN: Dean's very pessimistic and Henry Petersen's very pessimistic about that washing. There's an internal problem. He says there are disloyal guys in the U.S. Attorney's Office and in the Bureau who are just standing watching this thing and who are going to second-guess any story that you come up with.

PRESIDENT NIXON: Right.

EHRLICHMAN: So he said, whatever we come up with has got to be water-tight.

PRESIDENT NIXON: That's why the cover-up, the cover-up thing will be—I wonder, I wonder. I don't think it bothers me so much with the cover-up, John, if they had confessions and convictions of some. That's really what I think is the important thing.

EHRLICHMAN: Well, they'll have not only the five burglars, but they would have the two mystery men, Liddy and Hunt.

PRESIDENT NIXON: Both of them will confess.

EHRLICHMAN: They'll have to be convicted. I just don't see any escaping that. And that'll give—that'll give the public a lot of blood, give the Democrats a lot to chew on.

PRESIDENT NIXON: Liddy and Hunt doesn't bother me too much. . . .

EHRLICHMAN: Liddy used to be in the White House, you know, he worked here and so on, and so there's some of that.

PRESIDENT NIXON: That's right. But that's been already said.

EHRLICHMAN: If we can—if we can—I'm still hopeful that Dean and Mitchell will conclude that the Magruder scenario will work and it'll wash and that there are no extrinsic loose end facts that will impeach it, so that the disloyal guys in the U.S. Attorney's Office don't have anything to get their teeth into. . . .

PRESIDENT NIXON: Oh, yes. Then you've got cover-up and conviction.

EHRLICHMAN: Right.

PRESIDENT NIXON: Which is what happened in our investigation so far.

EHRLICHMAN: Well, Dean's been admonished not to contrive a story that's liable not to succeed. We're trying to take all the risk out of it. If there's risk that remains, he might as well just go whole-hog.

PRESIDENT NIXON: That's right. I must say that I can't see how Magruder could stand firm on Mitchell.

EHRLICHMAN: Well, he may want to. But—

PRESIDENT NIXON: He may not be tough enough.

EHRLICHMAN: He may not be tough enough. That's my theory. . . .

July 19, 1972: The President and Colson, 2:42–5:53 p.m., Executive Office Building

Both men are aware of Howard Hunt's earlier work for the White House and are concerned. Colson is full of praise for his friend, knowing that he had broken into Ellsberg's psychiatrist's office. "They weren't stealing anything," Colson rationalized the Watergate break-in. "They had broken and entered with an intent not to steal, [only] with an intent to obtain information."

PRESIDENT NIXON: What is your feeling as to what Hunt will testify to?

COLSON: . . . I think that Hunt will not think that anything he did was wrong. That's the biggest weakness of his. . . . [H]e doesn't think that trying to find communists or disruptors—he just thinks that's all [fine?]. That's the only trouble with the fellow. He's too—he's such a ideologue, he's so committed to the country.

PRESIDENT NIXON: What will he say, then?

COLSON: Well, if he's properly coached and he's got a good lawyer, I think he is one guy that I figure will take the rap, take the heat, and will not speak. See, he came to us. I have known him for a long time. He came to us and he said, "I just want to help." He was never interested in money. I don't know whether he has any. He's written a lot of books about espionage and the Cold War. . . .

He's the kind of fellow who, he's a real believer, a real believer. Bill Buckley is the godfather of his children. He . . . talked about the whimpering, simpering weaklings at the [Brown] university. He's a man of very strong feelings. . . . The place where I would worry about that is that he would say, "Well, of course I did it, (unintelligible) psychoanalyze Ellsberg because the sonofabitch, he's"—

PRESIDENT NIXON: I don't think that—

COLSON: That's the only thing I worry about.

PRESIDENT NIXON: You've got to say that's irrelevant in a criminal case.

COLSON: It clearly will be irrelevant in the civil case, because it has nothing to do with the invasion of privacy. I'm not sure in a criminal case whether it is a sign that will be relevant or not. Of course, before a grand jury there's no relevance. . . .

They weren't stealing anything. Really, they trespassed. They had broken and entered with an intent not to steal, with an intent to obtain information. You know damn well if it were an industrial espionage case they wouldn't go to jail. [We have to] push the prosecution. It's not like somebody breaking in and stealing, or to do any harm. They were unarmed. It's not the kind of case where the average judge is going to throw the book at them. . . . But I think the basic judgments on your part in cutting our losses were absolutely correct. Just, whatever it is, slice it off, get it over.

PRESIDENT NIXON: Of course, the way the Democrats have put it is this terrible web of spying that reaches into the White House, Hunt worked for the White House, Liddy worked at the White House, and Magruder worked for the White House. . . .

COLSON: This morning they dropped some charges. . . .

PRESIDENT NIXON: Some. Some of them were lies. . . .

COLSON: . . . There's no corruption in this administration. Nobody has, personally—I haven't pushed it. But you begin to get just a little bit of flavor that, oh, these fellows deal below the table, that's the kind of thing that we want to avoid.

That's something that McGovern can build on, one of the only areas he can build on. . . . There are some people who think that the . . . Cubans did this on their own.

PRESIDENT NIXON: I know. . . .

COLSON: That story in the *New York Times,* my God, it was unbelievable. Tad Szulc just nailed the Cuban community. He said they had a desperate desire to keep Mc-Govern out of the White House. . . .

JULY 20, 1972: THE PRESIDENT AND HALDEMAN, 11:52 A.M.–12:02 P.M., OVAL OFFICE

Haldeman underlines Dean's importance in running the cover-up. Nixon is concerned about the campaign money trail and where it might lead investigators.

SEGMENT 1

PRESIDENT NIXON: Any further developments on Watergate?

HALDEMAN: No.

PRESIDENT NIXON: Who testified yesterday?

HALDEMAN: Just—I haven't talked to Dean this morning. He was going to fill me in.

PRESIDENT NIXON: Who is really watching it from the White House? You? Ehrlichman?

HALDEMAN: John Dean is watching it on an almost full-time basis and reporting to Ehrlichman and me on a continuing basis.

PRESIDENT NIXON: All right.

HALDEMAN: And no one else. There's no one else in the White House that has any knowledge of what's going on there at all.

PRESIDENT NIXON: Not Colson or anybody else.

HALDEMAN: There isn't anyone else, and I think it's much better that way. In the first place, there's no need for anybody to know. There's nothing they can do about it.

PRESIDENT NIXON: That's right. It's enough for just a few of us that know to worry about it [laughter]), and don't let anybody else worry about it.

HALDEMAN: Actually, there's nothing any of us can do, either.

PRESIDENT NIXON: Except we can, of course, to a certain extent—the really key question at the moment that somehow we've got to answer is with regard to Magruder not waiting for the ax to fall and whether he—you know what I mean. The risk of us waiting it out is that he might have to be thrown out.

HALDEMAN: Let me ask Mitchell about it, because that's one thing Mitchell wants to talk about.

PRESIDENT NIXON: I just don't want that to happen. I think that Magruder, my own feeling is that his good and our good will both be served by, if he's going to get it, in other words, by his statement, whatever the hell it is—you don't know; have they called [Hugh] Sloan yet?

HALDEMAN: What they've done with Sloan, which apparently is a very good break, is granted him informal immunity, rather than—and Sloan is clean on his own involvement. But what they were going to—what they had planned to do with Sloan, because he won't perjure himself—he's clean on his own involvement, but he knows things that would have nothing to do with the Watergate caper, but there apparently are some substantial irregularities under the Campaign Spending Act which Sloan's aware of.

PRESIDENT NIXON: Christ, they should stay the hell out of that.

HALDEMAN: And some cash movements, things like that. So they've granted Sloan temporary immunity and he's going to cover what he knows about the Watergate stuff, which is nothing, and that gets him out of the thing. Now, what they had planned to do is he was going to take the Fifth. But this avoids his having to take the Fifth, which is much better because he has no guilt, where—under the Watergate thing, he has some under the other. They'd just open a new line of prosecution.

That's the one thing I wanted to raise with Dean this morning, is whether there isn't a way to give Magruder immunity and maybe get him out from under, too. I don't see why they couldn't, in a misguided part of the investigation in a sense, give Magruder immunity in order to get information on the Watergate caper people and Liddy maybe, or something like that.

PRESIDENT NIXON: He goes in and says, "I will say this, that, and the other."

HALDEMAN: Well, they apparently—that's the thing our people have been worried about, is that they'll give immunity to the wrong people and get too much of a story on it. But Magruder, Magruder, given immunity, could then go ahead and inculpate himself plus the others, but his immunity protects him from prosecution, and he seals the case on the others.

PRESIDENT NIXON: I think the way that I trust it will stand up . . . , it should be put in a way that a group of people who were hard-nosed and extreme on the Cuban communist thing, came to them and expressed their concern about McGovern and wanted to do this sort of thing, and these people said, "All right, they'll finance it." I don't know whether that'll work, or whether it was the other way around.

HALDEMAN: I'm not sure, either.

PRESIDENT NIXON: If there's some way that—

HALDEMAN: On the public side, that's sure what we want. . . .

PRESIDENT NIXON: That's what I mean, it fits in with the public image, the public story. But even if you gave Magruder immunity, I suppose you have the problem that he goes in and testifies, [it will be because] they gave him immunity. I don't know how the law works.

HALDEMAN: It saves him from going to jail.

PRESIDENT NIXON: Yes. He'd probably have to leave.

HALDEMAN: He'd still have to leave. I don't think you could keep him in the job, in any event.

PRESIDENT NIXON: He'd just leave on the basis that it's a thing that occurred while he was here.

HALDEMAN: Yes.

PRESIDENT NIXON: I think you've got a good point. If you could get—

HALDEMAN: I don't know whether they—it just occurred to me last night as I was going through the thing and this new thing with Sloan that maybe they could do the same thing with him.

PRESIDENT NIXON: Who else besides Sloan and Magruder are people [involved?]. This fellow, Martin's his name?

HALDEMAN: Bart Porter.

PRESIDENT NIXON: [*Laughs.*] Bart Porter. Did he work for Magruder?

HALDEMAN: Yes.

PRESIDENT NIXON: The question is how many people they can involve.

HALDEMAN: They're not going any further. Magruder is the last one they're going to call, apparently.

PRESIDENT NIXON: Well, it would seem it would stop someplace. I mean, Jesus Christ, you can't go through the whole Goddamn [CREEP] committee. They're not going to call Mitchell, apparently?

HALDEMAN: No. At least as of yesterday that was the word.

PRESIDENT NIXON: Okay.

SEGMENT 2

PRESIDENT NIXON: Get this Watergate thing on the way. I had a strange dream last night. It's going to be a nasty issue for a few days. I can't believe that—we're whistling in the dark, but I can't believe that they can tie the thing to me. What's your feeling?

HALDEMAN: It'll be messy. I think John's probably right. If we're going to take any time, we can't avoid getting the committee tied in somehow. It's better to get it tied in quickly and get it over with.

July 20, 1972: The President and Haldeman, 3:16–4:02 P.M., Executive Office Building

Haldeman offers a status report on the cover-up, specifically telling the President that Dean has done a good job of co-opting Assistant Attorney General of the Criminal Division, Henry Petersen. Haldeman assures Nixon that Petersen is "directing the investigation along the channels that will not produce the kind of answers we don't want produced."

HALDEMAN: It appears that there's a very good chance that Magruder will not be . . . indicted.

PRESIDENT NIXON: On what grounds?

HALDEMAN: On the grounds that there's a fine line question as to whether he made a knowledgeable decision and therefore was a part of the thing or not.

PRESIDENT NIXON: Conspiracy is a hard case to prove.

HALDEMAN: The point is his line will be that he did not know this specific action, which apparently is true, and that he had this guy Liddy and, sure, he authorized sums of money to be paid to Liddy for various . . . campaigning activities, and that he was not personally aware of this. He can say that was stupidity on my part, bad management, but it was not criminal guilt. And I was a young guy in a campaign, I didn't realize that, well, maybe we ought to check it out. And John [Ehrlichman] seems to feel that it's at least 50-50 that they'll go that way and maybe better. We'll know a lot more. He's being interrogated today by the FBI. That's the end of their interrogation. Now, it was the FBI, not the grand jury, that [Herbert L.] Porter was interrogated by yesterday. He has not been before the grand jury.

Pat Gray told John Dean today . . . that the Bureau is going to require at least another month to complete their investigation, . . . and he felt that the grand jury would probably have to have three to four months to do their work. Mitchell and Dean [believe] . . . that this thing is not going to be—the indictments are not going to be brought before the election. Mitchell argues very strongly . . . that we have a good chance of not getting the high level campaign command involved in the case and therefore we shouldn't let Magruder go out now, because his going out now would really put the focus on it. . . .

Another thing I didn't know that Mitchell told me is that John Dean . . . went in to [Henry] Petersen and laid out the whole scenario to him of what actually happened, who is involved and where it all fit. Now, on the basis of that, Petersen is working with that knowledge, directing the investigation along the channels that will not produce the kind of answers we don't want produced. Petersen also feels that the fact that there were some lines in this case that ran to the White House is very beneficial because that has slowed them down in pursuing things, because they all are of the view that they don't want to indict the White House, they only want to indict the—they want to tighten up that case on that criminal act and limit it to that to the degree that they can. . . .

[Tape malfunction.]

PRESIDENT NIXON: . . . . Apparently Mitchell says—

HALDEMAN: One of those lawyers—as I understand—Every one of them has fallen into a pattern. We've got the Ehrlichman-Mitchell controversy, where Mitchell is of the totally stonewall them, to hell with everybody; Ehrlichman's of the complete panic, cut everything off and sing.

PRESIDENT NIXON: Like Kleindienst.

HALDEMAN: Yes. And they're both wrong. Fortunately, we haven't followed either of their leads. . . .

JULY 22, 1972: THE PRESIDENT AND HALDEMAN, 3:05–4:23 P.M., CAMP DAVID

Haldeman opposes Ehrlichman's plan to pursue indictments against the burglars, preferring to let nothing happen for awhile. The cover-up progresses. Nixon and Haldeman discuss using the Secret Service to spy on McGovern. "I'm sure they've [McGovern's people] tried with us," the President says.

SEGMENT 1

PRESIDENT NIXON: Anything new on Watergate that you have? You don't know yet how Magruder will react to the problem?

HALDEMAN: The lawyer said he did extremely well, no problems. We don't have the interrogation report, but the lawyer sat in and said he did extremely well.

PRESIDENT NIXON: Is he going before the grand jury now?

HALDEMAN: Not as of yet.

PRESIDENT NIXON: What the hell is the grand jury going to do? They're going to keep, keep, keep investigating? Is that the whole point?

HALDEMAN: (unintelligible) they will.

PRESIDENT NIXON: As far as I'm concerned, that's the best of both worlds. Let it go.

HALDEMAN: Let it go until after the election.

PRESIDENT NIXON: They can.

HALDEMAN: Again, Ehrlichman urges get them indicted now and get them out. But I'm not really sure that's the best. That's the best answer if you accept as inevitable that you're going to get indictments and that you have to get them before the election. But better yet is to have nothing happen.

PRESIDENT NIXON: There is a reasonable chance that nothing happens, then just let it go. Dean is talking to whom on this?

HALDEMAN: To Ehrlichman and me on our side, to Mitchell, and the two lawyers and Petersen at Justice, and Gray at the Bureau.

PRESIDENT NIXON: (unintelligible) at the Bureau, we ought to put a Bureau man in there somewhere. . . .

HALDEMAN: Well, this guy Feldman is pushing hard. Is that his name?

PRESIDENT NIXON: [Mark] Felt.

HALDEMAN: Felt.

PRESIDENT NIXON: Yes.

HALDEMAN: Is pushing to try and be our boy, obviously.

PRESIDENT NIXON: Hoping he is our boy. You know, (unintelligible) our boy, and I'm not going to screw around on that score. But you see, if you take him out of the Bureau it's very hard for anybody to piss on him.

HALDEMAN: We ought to throw some tests at Felt. We could put some real sticky wickets to him and see how he bounces. . . .

SEGMENT 2

PRESIDENT NIXON: I don't suppose there's any way we've got any line on the McGovern camp through their Secret Service?

HALDEMAN: No, we don't.

PRESIDENT NIXON: We can obviously try.

HALDEMAN: We sure ought to try, but I don't know how to do it.

PRESIDENT NIXON: I'm sure they've tried with us.

HALDEMAN: We've got several of our—we've got some potentials. . . . To my knowledge, we're not using them, and I'm not so sure we should. If we get caught at that, that would—

PRESIDENT NIXON: Oh, no, no. I just meant if somebody volunteered information. You know, they sometimes volunteer.

HALDEMAN: Yes. Somebody might. . . .

PRESIDENT NIXON: [Tony] Ulasewicz—I've never met him.

HALDEMAN: I think he's fully capable of any of that kind of stuff.

PRESIDENT NIXON: You mean dirty tricks?

HALDEMAN: Yes. And he studied under the Kennedys.

PRESIDENT NIXON: Well, I think O'Brien is, too.

JULY 25, 1972: THE PRESIDENT, ZIEGLER, AND HALDEMAN, 11:14 A.M.–1:30 P.M., OVAL OFFICE

A cryptic conversation about available White House funds, apparently to help with "expenses." The President is amused that Hunt is exploiting Supreme Court decisions—the kind that Nixon had often attacked—to claim that his rights were in jeopardy.

SEGMENT 1

PRESIDENT NIXON: Incidentally, can I ask a question. Do we have any funds that Stans doesn't know about that's not in cash?

HALDEMAN: Well, we have cash that Stans—yes, we have some cash that Stans can't do anything about. He knows we have it.

PRESIDENT NIXON: We can handle it with a non-reporting (unintelligible), but we've got some and we may have to do something about that.

HALDEMAN: And Rose has got some cash.

PRESIDENT NIXON: Okay, good.

HALDEMAN: We don't have as much as we were going to have. We have about $300,000, but we can get anything we want. We got scared, everybody got scared, because of the (unintelligible) thing and the problem of getting ourselves tied into cash (unintelligible).

PRESIDENT NIXON: The $300,000 is left (unintelligible).

HALDEMAN: It's in our cash in boxes.

PRESIDENT NIXON: And it's part of the money Rose [Mary Woods] has?

HALDEMAN: I don't know. I think it's $300,000.

PRESIDENT NIXON: That isn't a hell of a lot. But at least that will take care of, say, Connally's expenses or something.

HALDEMAN: We can tap—we also have cash that they have that we can tap. We don't have to use only our cash. There is unreported cash over there that they'll expend at our direction.

SEGMENT 2

PRESIDENT NIXON: . . . You just don't know the potential when the grand jury finally indicts these fellows. We won't get something until next week?

HALDEMAN: Good heavens, no, it may not be this year.

PRESIDENT NIXON: How can they delay that long?

HALDEMAN: They wanted us to get a verdict early.

PRESIDENT NIXON: How is this, Bob—I don't know whether Dean knows. How does the—where did the (unintelligible) have to come from? I suppose they haven't any idea?

HALDEMAN: I didn't see the *Times* story. I haven't seen the *Times*.

PRESIDENT NIXON: The *Times* had the story.

HALDEMAN: I don't know what it says.

PRESIDENT NIXON: About fifteen telephone calls were made to the office of the counsel of the Committee to Re-Elect from [Bernard] Barker, the Miami fellow.

HALDEMAN: And they have that from?

PRESIDENT NIXON: From an investigative source.

HALDEMAN: The Bureau.

PRESIDENT NIXON: It could be the Bureau and it could be the U.S. Attorney's Office.

HALDEMAN: Yes, that's right, it could be either one. Phone records they had in both places, they have in both places, I guess.

PRESIDENT NIXON: The way to really handle that is that all of those involved (unintelligible)—understanding that the point is that I under no circumstances would suppress the investigation, but that is a violation of the defendants' rights.

HALDEMAN: Sure.

PRESIDENT NIXON: And it's a total violation, and it's a leak from a grand jury. That's the worst Goddamn thing you could do. Even in the Hiss case, when we were going through that, we never got a thing out of the grand jury until they indicted.

HALDEMAN: Hunt has come up with a rather interesting thing.

PRESIDENT NIXON: What's that?

HALDEMAN: He has told the grand jury—

PRESIDENT NIXON: Has he been before them?

HALDEMAN: No. He's been called. He's in town. I guess—no, he didn't go. But he informed them that he would—he filed a statement, I guess, with the U.S. Attorney that said, with the U.S. Attorney, that said to the grand jury, and then he—well, he challenged the grand jury. First of all, he said the grand jury must be disbanded because it's convened illegally in the sense that the publicity that's come out of it has jeopardized the defendants' rights and he as a potential defendant, as a potential—

PRESIDENT NIXON: [*Laughter.*] He's turning that damn rule of the Supreme Court on its head.

HALDEMAN: He as a potential—

PRESIDENT NIXON: Defendant.

HALDEMAN: Not defendant. There's another term.

PRESIDENT NIXON: Witness?

HALDEMAN: No, no. It had to do with that he could be subject to indictment by the grand jury as a conspirator or something under the evidence that they already had. And because of that potential that he would not—that his rights would not be properly protected if he were to be called before the jury because of the publicity and all of this. . . .

PRESIDENT NIXON: That's one way to feed on that delay. He could take that case—

HALDEMAN: That's right. And then he made some second point also. And Dean says the U.S. Attorneys and all just sat and laughed for a couple hours. They thought the guy was nuts. And then they got to thinking, well, what are they going to do about this, and then they began to realize it wasn't so funny after all. So they've now demanded that he appear, and he won't go and take the—oh, that's it. He says if he goes before the grand jury and takes the Fifth Amendment, then under long tradition it will be assumed that he is inculpated and that would jeopardize his rights and all that sort of thing, too, because of the publicity.

So he isn't going to appear. So they've now come to a thing where he has filed with his attorney a sworn statement that, if he were called before the grand jury, he would take the Fifth Amendment, and that somehow gets him off some hook or something. I don't know. They're playing some very intricate legal game that is kind of intriguing, I guess, to the guys who understand it. Hunt—as Dean said, Hunt's the only guy in the whole thing who's got the brains to—

PRESIDENT NIXON: What he's doing—

HALDEMAN: And Hunt's lawyer is—what the hell's his name? [William Bittman] He was the Deputy in the Criminal Division at Justice, and he's a very smart guy.

PRESIDENT NIXON: You see, what Hunt is doing is using all of these Goddamn permissive crap that the previous Supreme Court has given us for his purposes.

HALDEMAN: That's right.

PRESIDENT NIXON: And that's why they ought to do.

HALDEMAN: The same way that murderers and rapists get off.

PRESIDENT NIXON: Why, sure. Basically, the murderers and rapists have gotten off because of publicity, publicity, too much publicity. I'm not ready to say what the law is of this case, but they ought to use every damn thing they want to fight, twist, and turn. That's what the law is for. I never agreed with it, but now that the court has spoken that's the law of the land. And if it's good for a murderer, it's good for a wiretapper. [*Laughter.*] It's true. I have a feeling, just as I looked at the *New York Times* and it says "GOP bugging Democratic Headquarters"—I'm not sure that that is in the public mind considered to be a capital crime particularly. What do you think?

HALDEMAN: Why would the Times say "GOP bugging Democratic Headquarters"? There's no evidence of GOP bugging.

PRESIDENT NIXON: Well, that's what they called it.

HALDEMAN: Really?

PRESIDENT NIXON: Yes. That's the way the story with the headline is.

ZIEGLER: The question is it doesn't reflect here—I mean—my sense of it, it's not something that people are going to get all worked up about.

PRESIDENT NIXON: No. We'll have to just ride it, wait a little while.

JULY 26, 1972: THE PRESIDENT AND HALDEMAN, 9:02–10:40 A.M., EXECUTIVE OFFICE BUILDING

The two men discuss the news that [Senator] Thomas Eagleton [D-MO], George McGovern's vice-presidential selection, had been treated for mental illness.

HALDEMAN: If this campaign gets rough a ways down the line, we'll start putting some signs in his crowds. We'll start shouting some hecklers out, without anybody on our side (unintelligible).

PRESIDENT NIXON: The way I would put it out is not about his [Eagleton's] sanity—

HALDEMAN: His honesty.

PRESIDENT NIXON: But the lie.

HALDEMAN: Sure. Why did you lie to McGovern?

PRESIDENT NIXON: Why did you lie to McGovern?

HALDEMAN: Why did you lie to (unintelligible)?

PRESIDENT NIXON: Why did you lie to McGovern about your health?

HALDEMAN: If you lied about your health, what else are you lying about?

PRESIDENT NIXON: Why did you lie about your health? . . . They've got a big problem. They've basically got a problem.

HALDEMAN: That's right.

JULY 28, 1972: THE PRESIDENT AND HALDEMAN, 10:06–11:04 A.M., OVAL OFFICE

Haldeman reports on the progress of the Watergate investigation and definitely is optimistic. Indictments will not come down until mid-September, which means that the trial will be delayed until after the election, and that the indictments would be limited to the burglars, Hunt, and Liddy. Nixon, meanwhile, distrusts lower-echelon Department of Justice and FBI people who he believes wanted a wider investigation. "Fortunately," he tells Haldeman, "we have not tried to cover up, [we] cooperate with the investigations."

SEGMENT 1

HALDEMAN: The Watergate thing is, well—

PRESIDENT NIXON: —coming to a head—

HALDEMAN: —it's on a reasonably good track, considering. The grand jury is going through the 1701 [CREEP headquarters] people. Petersen's view to Dean is that what he expects to do—what he said to Dean once: "I think we're going to be able to finish this grand jury thing up pretty quick, and we'll bring indictments on the seven and we can probably bring them the latter part of August or wait until around mid-September."

And Dean said he got the sense that Petersen was asking for guidance as to which we wanted. But he was also telling him they were going to bring indictments on seven, and that's very good news, because that means they're indicting the Watergate five plus Hunt and Liddy and that's all.

PRESIDENT NIXON: Are they going to put out a statement about the others?

HALDEMAN: Apparently not. They'll just indict those, and what they'll do is then— our view I think is to wait, to wait, because there's a very good chance of it not going to trial until after the election. It will be called on the special calendar and the special calendar is fairly clear, so it could come up pretty soon. But even if it gets to court, there's a set of pretrial motions they've got to go through and all that stuff. So John feels that we ought to go for delay and just hope nothing happens before the election, because we're better off with that than we are—

PRESIDENT NIXON: (unintelligible).

HALDEMAN: My original feeling was get it out now, get it done in August and get it over with. But that might hit it right in the middle of the Republican convention—

PRESIDENT NIXON: No, no, no, no.

HALDEMAN: —where there's a lot of TV attention, which would be a problem, too.

SEGMENT 2

PRESIDENT NIXON: If they indict seven, we trust the ones they're thinking about are Hunt and—

HALDEMAN: They are. And that would be fine. That's almost an ideal scenario. If they would indict the seven and then not get around to the trial until after the election, we're in pretty good shape. On the civil suit, the judge took some time off. He's out of chambers. So he's coming back, and what they're going to do there is we have a motion, which they think the judge will probably uphold, to withhold any further steps on the civil suit pending the outcome of the criminal suit, that any action on the civil suit would damage or interfere with the rights of the defendants in the criminal suit or something like that. . . .

PRESIDENT NIXON: Because the criminal thing means not the indictment, it means the trial.

HALDEMAN: Right.

PRESIDENT NIXON: The trial they'll never get through before the election. The trial will never be finished by the election—well, if the people plead not guilty. If they plead guilty, it would be.

HALDEMAN: Some of them are going to go not guilty.

PRESIDENT NIXON: Hunt's going to go not guilty.

HALDEMAN: Hell, yes.

PRESIDENT NIXON: Fight it to the end.

HALDEMAN: But they've got a lot of motions they've got to go through before they get to the plea, apparently, on the trial. So it may be that by legalisms—

PRESIDENT NIXON: The problem that you've got is that some lower echelon shit-ass at the Justice Department or the FBI will try to leak out stuff about this and that and force, in some way or other, force it in another direction. Fortunately, we have not tried to cover-up, [we] cooperate with the investigations.

HALDEMAN: The record has to show us in pretty good shape.

AUGUST 1, 1972: THE PRESIDENT AND HALDEMAN, 11:03–11:58 A.M., OVAL OFFICE

Haldeman has news for the President: Democratic National Committee Chairman Lawrence O'Brien's IRS audit is proceeding, and the Department of Justice is preparing seven indictments for the Watergate break-in. Dean is successful in keeping Magruder in line; Ehrlichman instructs Kleindienst to cut off further investigations; Colson remains in the clear; and finally, Howard Hunt is receiving money. The President's questions and mood fluctuate.

SEGMENT 2

PRESIDENT NIXON: Now, with regard to O'Brien, you can of course divulge that you have had the IRS do some checking. How much did he get from [Howard] Hughes [as a consultant]? Of course, he got a hell of a lot of cash. I don't think he reported that.

HALDEMAN: $190,000—he was paid over, I think, it was a two-year period, by Howard Hughes.

PRESIDENT NIXON: My God.

HALDEMAN: Ehrlichman's got the dope on it. And we've got—that's there and the payments to Joe Napolitan.

PRESIDENT NIXON: By whom?

HALDEMAN: Hughes.

PRESIDENT NIXON: What in the hell was Hughes doing this for?

HALDEMAN: And Hubert Humphrey's son—

PRESIDENT NIXON: Leave that out.

HALDEMAN: Leave that out.

PRESIDENT NIXON: Leave that out. We don't want to hurt him.

HALDEMAN: But we bring Napolitan in because Napolitan is very much tied to Democratic politics and totally tied to O'Brien.

SEGMENT 3

PRESIDENT NIXON: Out of the Justice Department? There must be a leak over there, is that their feeling?

HALDEMAN: There was one. You know, something came out three or four weeks ago and they tracked that one down and plugged that. But apparently there's another. They've said that this is inevitable. There's too many people around, we've got people in there that are against us. They are trying to keep it all bottled up, and they've done—I must say, considering the explosive nature of what's there, they've done a pretty good job.

The scenario on that, they all seem pretty well agreed on now, is that the only danger is Magruder, who does have to go before the grand jury. But Dean has gone over and over it with him, and Jeb is going to stay with his story and stay with it solid, and they think there's no problem if he does, and he will. He will not be indicted, Magruder won't.

They will come down with seven indictments, the five plus Liddy [and Hunt], and that'll be about September 15 that they'll bring the indictments. They will then be assigned to a court and, even if it's put on a special—even if we get the worst possible judge, which hopefully we can avoid—it would then be put on special calendar, which if it is the case it would deserve special calendar treatment. If it's not put on special calendar, it won't come up for over a year. It will be put on special calendar, and special calendar is essentially cleared, so they could start moving on it fairly quickly. But they'll immediately move to motions, and Hunt has this little series of motions he's going to on all the civil liberties business—violation, publicity, pretrial stuff, and all that sort of stuff.

They feel that, in the first place, the judge can't force the lawyers to clear their own calendars, and the lawyers involved all have heavy court calendars already running through the end of the year. So they'll have to be given some time to clear their own calendars and get prepared. So John sees no possibility of the case being brought before the election.

PRESIDENT NIXON: Except the indictment—

HALDEMAN: —the indictment will be and we'll have to ride that. That'll be a very bad story, and we'll have to ride through the indictments. But we've already—Liddy's already tarnished and Hunt's already tarnished. There's no great new revelation. It'll just be a confirmation of previous stuff. It'll be bad and it'll hurt us, but not like the trial will, and Dean is not worried about that. And he also thinks that we're in good shape on holding the civil case—

PRESIDENT NIXON: Until the criminal?

HALDEMAN: —until after the criminal trial. . . . Magruder, they're pretty straight on. Magruder's scared.

PRESIDENT NIXON: Sure.

HALDEMAN: He said, might they indict—he asked Dean, he said: "Might they indict me just to get an indictment for political reasons or whatever?" Dean said, "No, the court won't do that, the jury won't do that." And Jeb said, "Well, I just want you to know, if they do, that I'm staying with my story all the way; I'll go down with it, and there's no question about that."

Dean said, "The one thing I'm worried about with you, I know you'll do that; the thing I'm worried about with you is that after you do that, if you don't get indicted, that you'll start running around blabbing about how you pulled yourself out of that. And let me explain to you that there's a five-year statute of limitations on this case and that you're subject to being hauled in any time in the next five years, and you keep your Goddamn mouth shut. Don't talk to your wife or your mother or your kids or anybody else. If you get out of this, just remember, you've got this cloud hanging over you for five years—"

PRESIDENT NIXON: That's right.

HALDEMAN: "—and you're not out until that's over. So don't have a celebration when the indictments come through and you're not on them."

PRESIDENT NIXON: He feels that they will not indict him?

HALDEMAN: That's right. They have not made a case against Magruder. A lot of lines lead to him, but they don't tie. . . .

[H]e's going to impeach [Hugh] Sloan. Sloan is the only one that leads validly to Magruder and Sloan's testimony . . . inevitably . . . leads to Magruder. But Magruder's going to say and honestly believes that Sloan pocketed some of the money. There's some discrepancy in how much money went where and Magruder's going to say he thinks Sloan pocketed it.

PRESIDENT NIXON: You don't think he did it?

HALDEMAN: No. But Magruder does, fortunately. And we're just going to leave it at that. Let him go ahead and think it, because there's no possible way he can harm Sloan. Sloan will never know what Magruder says, and Sloan's not culpable at all under this case. . . .

PRESIDENT NIXON: . . . Let's be fatalistic about the Goddamn thing.

HALDEMAN: If it blows, it blows.

PRESIDENT NIXON: If it blows, it blows, and so on. I'm not that worried about it, to be really candid with you.

HALDEMAN: It's worth a lot of work to try and keep it from blowing.

PRESIDENT NIXON: Oh, my, yes.

HALDEMAN: But if it blows we'll survive it.

PRESIDENT NIXON: After all, Mitchell's gone and . . . nobody at a higher level was involved, the White House not being involved, and all that stuff. And the Cuban crap in there. Are the Cubans going to plead not guilty?

HALDEMAN: I don't know. But everybody's satisfied. They're all out of jail, they've all been taken care of. We've done a lot of discreet checking to be sure there's no discontent in the ranks, and there isn't any.

PRESIDENT NIXON: They're all out on bail.

HALDEMAN: Hunt's happy.

PRESIDENT NIXON: At considerable cost, I guess?

HALDEMAN: Yes.

PRESIDENT NIXON: It's worth it.

HALDEMAN: It's very expensive. It's a costly—

PRESIDENT NIXON: That's what the money is for.

HALDEMAN: —exercise, but that's better spent than—

PRESIDENT NIXON: Well, . . . they have to be paid. That's all there is to that. They have to be paid, although I must say that—and I'm perhaps second-guessing people, but whoever made the decision—

HALDEMAN: Was pretty damn stupid.

PRESIDENT NIXON: —was about as stupid as I ever heard.

HALDEMAN: Whoever it is has suffered for his sins plenty.

PRESIDENT NIXON: I know. Oh, no. Never blaming. But the poor sonofabitch, what the hell, such a stupid Goddamn idea. He [Colson? Liddy?] must have got it from Hunt. It sounds like him, doesn't it? I can't think of anybody in that organization. Magruder wouldn't think of such a damn thing.

HALDEMAN: I can't conceive. I think it's Liddy. Liddy apparently is a guy that just, well, lives on this kind of stuff. He loves [it] . . . .

PRESIDENT NIXON: That's already been printed, hasn't it? And Hunt, it's been printed he's refused to talk.

HALDEMAN: I don't know where Hunt stands.

PRESIDENT NIXON: . . . I don't ever discount the kind of crap the press will put to us on a thing like this. But it does not—we have stayed completely away from it. I stayed completely away from it. MacGregor of course will take, as he should, a holier than thou attitude: "I don't know anything about it." Right?

HALDEMAN: Yes. And we've kept Colson clear.

PRESIDENT NIXON: Yes. . . . You say no cooperation from the Justice Department. I understand the FBI.

HALDEMAN: It's been very hard. Petersen has been reasonably good within—in fact, pretty I guess darn good.

PRESIDENT NIXON: That is scary.

HALDEMAN: The problem has been Kleindienst has just totally washed his hands. Now, he's come back in. Ehrlichman hauled him in yesterday and said, "This has gotten ridiculous. Now you've got everything you need. Now for God's sake turn it off, bring your indictments." He seemed to see the light. . . .

AUGUST 2, 1972: THE PRESIDENT AND HALDEMAN, 8:32–9:30 A.M., OVAL OFFICE

Haldeman now can confidently tell the President that the Department of Justice will end the investigation.

HALDEMAN: . . . Kleindienst has now ordered Gray to end the investigation. He said that they've got all they need to wrap up their case.

PRESIDENT NIXON: Do you think that's correct?

HALDEMAN: Yes.

PRESIDENT NIXON: Really, it is over. Otherwise it's a fishing expedition. We've had enough of those. The Magruder thing is the only thing that concerns me. But you know, I would think his case would be pretty good, Bob. I think he [could] say, "Look, I was in charge of the damn thing; I approved money; Liddy wanted this money and I gave it to him, but I haven't the slightest idea what the hell he's doing with it." Correct?

AUGUST 3, 1972: THE PRESIDENT, HALDEMAN, AND EHRLICHMAN, 9:44–10:40 A.M., OVAL OFFICE

Nixon continues to rage against the Internal Revenue Service, and complains that his administration is not using its power effectively. "We have all this power," he says, "and we aren't using it." Ehrlichman seconds the President, complaining that such cabinet officers as George Shultz, Melvin Laird, and Richard Kleindienst are unwilling to battle the White House's enemies. Nixon and his aides lament the "non-political" character of cabinet officers. Finally, the President calls for a direct assault on George McGovern—"kick him . . . keep whacking, whacking, and whacking."

SEGMENT 1

PRESIDENT NIXON: Here we go. What in the name of God are we doing on this one? What are we doing about the financial contributors? Now, those lists there, are we looking over McGovern's financial contributors? Are we looking over the financial contributors to the Democratic National Committee? Are we running their income tax returns? Is the Justice Department checking to see whether or not there is any antitrust suits? Do we have anything going on any of these things?

HALDEMAN: Not as far as I know.

PRESIDENT NIXON: We better forget the Goddamn campaign right this minute, not tomorrow, no. That's what concerns me. We have all this power and we aren't using it. Now, what the Christ is the matter? In other words, what I'm really saying is just that I think we've got to get it out. I'm just thinking about, for example, if there's information on Larry O'Brien. If there is, I wouldn't wait. I'd worry the sons of bitches now, because after they select somebody else it's irrelevant, even though he's still in the campaign. . . .

EHRLICHMAN: I don't know.

PRESIDENT NIXON: You've got the facts. Did they check the other side of the facts? What is being done? Who is doing this full-time? That's what I'd like to know. Who is running the IRS? Who is running over at Justice Department? What I meant is, with all the agencies of government, what in the name of God are we doing about the McGovern contributors?

EHRLICHMAN: The short answer to your question is nothing.

PRESIDENT NIXON: Well, they're doing it to us.

EHRLICHMAN: No question, no question.

PRESIDENT NIXON: And it's never happened that way before.

SEGMENT 2

PRESIDENT NIXON: What, if anything, is being done on the Democratic candidate? I mean, for example, on his income [tax], on O'Brien. Have we got anything further on that, Bob?

HALDEMAN: I don't know. Not to my knowledge. And the problem that we've had, as I understand it, going back to the '70 and '71 period when there were efforts made to do this, is—

PRESIDENT NIXON: That we get caught?

HALDEMAN: —that if we get caught, they come back with the thing of, we can't pull a file because there's got to be a reason to pull a file. And we did pull files anyway, but that gets flagged at the district office or something like that, and somebody runs out and tells—

PRESIDENT NIXON: That's IRS, okay. Is there any other agency of the government? What are the guys in the Goddamn Justice Department doing? Can we investigate people? Is there anything we can do, anything?

EHRLICHMAN: Yes. And it's kind of interesting, the problem that you have with this. I sent to the Department of Defense for McGovern's service jacket because I was curious about what his bombing experience and that kind of stuff. And I got it, but Jesus, the grief I took in getting it is unbelievable. Carl Wallace called me from [Melvin] Laird's office. Finally, the way I got it was that Dave Young went over there and he had his contacts as a result of the Ellsberg case and some other cases, and he went in and got it for me and brought it over here. But guys like Laird, like Shultz, like Kleindienst, are just touchy as hell about cooperating with us on this kind of thing.

SEGMENT 3

PRESIDENT NIXON: Well, I guess perhaps there's nothing we can do about this problem. But it's just so Goddamn frustrating—

HALDEMAN: Sure.

PRESIDENT NIXON: —to think they screwed up, and here all these people are sticking us around and we don't have anything going. I think part of the problem is maybe we are not—what is it, Bob, the Cabinet officers are afraid?

HALDEMAN: Yes. You get this playback that word's going to get out that we're doing it, and all that. John's saying we ought to move now. That's one where I would be more concerned about the potential for bad than the potential for good. I really question whether now it's worth trying to get the McGovern people. In the first place, you can't move anything fast enough to do anything anyway. I would think that we could get some people with some guts in the second term, when we don't care about the repercussions.

PRESIDENT NIXON: The trouble is, if we don't have a second term it won't do much good.

EHRLICHMAN: Yes, but doing this isn't going to get you a second term.

HALDEMAN: Why don't we—

EHRLICHMAN: I just wonder what you can do. Well, you can make them nervous, and that actually—you could put out to [columnist Victor] Reisel or somebody the Larry O'Brien–Howard Hughes tie. That'd make them nervous.

HALDEMAN: Why not put it out—no, Jack Anderson wouldn't play it anymore. [Reporter Robert] Novak?

PRESIDENT NIXON: Well, I don't know how you put it out.

HALDEMAN: I don't either. Maybe that's one [Kenneth] Clawson could peddle someplace. But we're going to get caught peddling that stuff.

PRESIDENT NIXON: Yes.

HALDEMAN: In the position we're in, we don't have the factors to work with us to do that kind of harassment that they do. We don't have the bureaucracy with us and we don't have the press with us. They do. . . .

PRESIDENT NIXON: I have a different view . . . . I totally agree with it to save the nomination. . . . Now the press does not have that knee-jerk reaction to the same extent. It is still there among many, but at the present time when a guy is under attack by this—in other words, if it were Eagleton, I'd say one thing, but here we've got McGovern. He's open, he has shown that he's more open, but he might even have feet of clay. And he is a non-sympathetic character. Under this set of circumstances, kicking around people that are around him is not going to have all that bad an effect that it once had.

The other point is that when you've got a fellow, you've got a fellow who is under attack like this, again who has fallen on his ass a few times, what you do is to kick him again. I mean, it's like Dempsey going for the kill with Firpo. I mean, you have to . . . keep whacking, whacking, and whacking.

HALDEMAN: Well, I buy that totally. I think that's right.

PRESIDENT NIXON: That's why I say on O'Brien, just to use him as an example, if you could dirty up O'Brien now I think it might be a lot better than waiting until later.

HALDEMAN: I agree on any public figure.

PRESIDENT NIXON: Huh?

HALDEMAN: I just was saying to John, I'm not so sure that I believe what I just said on the others, because you can sure put some fear into them.

PRESIDENT NIXON: That's right.

HALDEMAN: In their own minds. It worries them.

PRESIDENT NIXON: It worries us. We know that they have—we worry.

HALDEMAN: Sure.

PRESIDENT NIXON: We worry about that silly business with the ITT, which was a pure Goddamn phony. But we worried about it.

HALDEMAN: But you had half a dozen people putting full time on it for months.

PRESIDENT NIXON: For months, months. . . . These are routine investigations; their numbers came up. Well, Mr. Nixon and Senator McGovern's numbers came up, and they would press him. We don't claim it's just intentional, but his number came up, so they investigated. Did we complain? No. But they went after him.

HALDEMAN: The advantage there was nobody said anything else. The advantage here is I can guarantee you what'll happen is somebody at Internal Revenue will say: "Oh, yeah, we had a call from Chuck Colson and he said to pull the tax file on the guy."

PRESIDENT NIXON: That's true.

EHRLICHMAN: How could [George] Shultz be non-political?

PRESIDENT NIXON: It's almost impossible.

EHRLICHMAN: It cuts both ways, because if we do this the press is going to be unwilling to blame him for it. If we can cause him to do it, it would be a cover.

PRESIDENT NIXON: Everybody thinks Shultz is an honest, decent man.

HALDEMAN: Right.

EHRLICHMAN: Well, why don't I have a chat with [him]. . . .

HALDEMAN: Well, is there a way to cause him to do it externally, so that it isn't his initiative? . . . Can't we get an external tip that gives him a rationale for doing it, that he then says he orders the investigation because this information has come into his hands.

EHRLICHMAN: Well, take the O'Brien thing. . . .

HALDEMAN: It's in an IRS report, in a sensitive report. He's got every reason to move on that. . . . The reason it's sensitive is because it involves you and Humphrey.

PRESIDENT NIXON: And Don [Nixon].

HALDEMAN: Well, you because of Don. And Humphrey because Humphrey is directly involved. . . .

PRESIDENT NIXON: Which is the case with that stupid brother. . . .

EHRLICHMAN: Well, let me take that on.

HALDEMAN: And we've got Hubert Humphrey. We want to lay off on Humphrey, I think.

PRESIDENT NIXON: Well, let's see. I think so.

HALDEMAN: I think you do because I think a lot of the people that are involved with him are people who are with us. . . .

EHRLICHMAN: Well, we've got a file a foot thick on [McGovern contributor] Henry Kimelman, and this is over in the Department of Interior, where we have fewer problems. I do have some work going on that.

PRESIDENT NIXON: Scare the shit out of them. Scare the shit out of them. Now, there are some Jews with the Mafia that are involved in this all, too.

EHRLICHMAN: Well, that's—

PRESIDENT NIXON: IRS?

EHRLICHMAN: —we should go beyond anywhere on that. No, that's not IRS; that's Justice and the campaign thing. McGovern's incorporated his campaign organization. Several of the incorporators have some unpleasant affiliations. What they're trying to do there is they're afraid to let any word get out until it's done something. The corporation hasn't taken any money yet. They want to get it—they don't want to signal the fact that we're onto it until it's done something we can hang them on. Dean is on that one.

PRESIDENT NIXON: Are there any members of the Cabinet . . . as far as political?

EHRLICHMAN: Yes, but you don't have anybody with very many guts on it when it comes to is something going to bounce back on me, and with very good justification because of this jackass operation at the Watergate. They are more sensitive than they would have been before, and they would have been pretty sensitive before. But we do have a knack for doing this stuff ineptly. And the last thing we need now—that's what bothers me, is if we can't do it eptly then I think we better forego the benefits of doing it.

PRESIDENT NIXON: Well, we can do a perfectly legitimate investigation.

EHRLICHMAN: We can do things that are within legitimate parameters. . . . I don't think we'll get any indictments or stir anybody up, but it will create some fear.

HALDEMAN: We ought to move with some vengeance to destroy that stuff.

EHRLICHMAN: Damn right.

HALDEMAN: We should have done it three years ago. We partly didn't know how. Partly, when we tried we got—

PRESIDENT NIXON: Circumvented.

HALDEMAN: We sure as hell did in '70.

EHRLICHMAN: Yes, with the [Justice William O.] Douglas stuff. . . .

HALDEMAN: They've just got a hell of a lot more snakes than we do, and their snakes are a hell of a lot tougher than ours.

PRESIDENT NIXON: Vicious, brutal.

AUGUST 3, 1972: THE PRESIDENT AND HALDEMAN, 3:10–3:29 P.M., EXECUTIVE OFFICE BUILDING

Nixon finds work for Murray Chotiner, his old reliable hand at "dirty tricks," who had served in Nixon's very first campaign in 1946.

SEGMENT 1

PRESIDENT NIXON: What is your view about Chotiner and [ballot security]?

HALDEMAN: Well, he's got the goal and I think it's perfectly all right for him to stay in for the ballot security. And he's working. He's been working without big publicity and moving around and that, setting up regional ballot security programs and that sort of thing.

I think he makes a good point. We went through a whole list of things that are wrong, things that aren't being done. Most of them are in (unintelligible), and he had to sit and wallow through every ten minutes of why the Watergate thing was not well conducted. And I kept saying, "Murray, Jesus, don't even waste time talking about it; you're not going to find me defending that." He said: Well, but you shouldn't have—and I said—

PRESIDENT NIXON: Shouldn't have what?

HALDEMAN: Young guys making decisions about these things, and they don't know how to do this, and so on.

PRESIDENT NIXON: You know, I was thinking (unintelligible).

HALDEMAN: Yes.

PRESIDENT NIXON: Murray is the type that will (unintelligible).

HALDEMAN: Definitely. And about half of what Murray comes up with is totally wrong.

PRESIDENT NIXON: That's right.

HALDEMAN: I mean, really totally wrong. He just misses the point. But the area that I think he's interested in, that it seems to me is built in, has to be non-public, and where we do have a flaw and where his kind of skill is useful is in enemy intelligence.

SEGMENT 2

HALDEMAN: Anyway, we really don't, I think, have an adequate intelligence, and I do think Murray is sophisticated enough not to do the stupid things that he would get caught at. For instance, he operated that "Chapman's Friend" thing. Mitchell discounts that, but the guy did get some useful information as well as a lot of useless. But that's what you get in intelligence. Most of what you get is useless. It's worth wading through if you get one little glimmer of something that you can do something about.

Murray said flatly, "I don't want any money." He said, "To be perfectly frank, I'm doing very well financially, thanks to you people who set me up, and I'm in good shape and you owe me nothing and I want nothing financially; but I would like to repay you." He said, "The one thing I hope you understand, and I know that your candidate will, is that I care a very lot to see him re-elected." He said, "If the way I can help the most is to disappear, that's what I'll do. But I'm not sure it is. . . ."

He's right, you can't—the young guys really don't know that area. They just are a little naive. For instance, they told him to have Chapman's friend [?] get a little microphone and a tape recorder, a pocket tape recorder and microphone, so that he could record stuff when he was talking to people. Murray said, "Jesus, you know, these guys have been reading detective stories. The reason you've got this old hack reporter is so he can sit and listen and then write it up afterwards." And they wanted him to turn in the vouchers for his expenses. Murray said, "I keep the vouchers; anybody wants to audit where the money's gone, I can sit down and audit where the money's gone, what little there's been."

PRESIDENT NIXON: . . . All right, let's use him.

HALDEMAN: I think he could be helpful there, and the advantage of his doing that, it ties to ballot security in a sense, which is his cover, his front cover, and it forces anonymity and backup (unintelligible).

PRESIDENT NIXON: Another thing that's very important, too, Bob, is to be sure we keep Colson out of it totally, keep Colson totally out of it.

HALDEMAN: Murray has a great mind. He said, "Colson is probably in the same problem that I've been in," but he said, "I've got to give him credit—he's at least got a sense of humor. I saw him the other day and Colson said to me, 'I wish you'd quit using my name when you're doing all your things.'" To be perfectly frank, Murray's got better judgment than Chuck does. Murray is no good on the media side and that kind of stuff. . . . But he doesn't understand what's happening there. He's not really that much good on organization any more, because they're organizing differently.

PRESIDENT NIXON: Yes.

AUGUST 3, 1972: THE PRESIDENT AND EHRLICHMAN, 5:00–5:30 P.M., EXECUTIVE OFFICE BUILDING

Nixon now is worried about pressing O'Brien's tax matters for fear it might involve his brother, F. Donald Nixon. Nevertheless, he tells his men to push forward. George Shultz, he complains, has a "fantasy" that the IRS should not be used in a political way.

PRESIDENT NIXON: . . . And if they bring up that Goddamn Hughes loan again, we ought to break this over O'Brien's head.

EHRLICHMAN: Well, I wouldn't wait. I'd kind of like to throw a little fear. I'm going to get [George] Shultz tomorrow and sit down and I'm going to ask him to have the IRS go behind that entry in that report we got.

PRESIDENT NIXON: Right.

EHRLICHMAN: And call for those returns—a perfectly legitimate thing for him to do. We don't need to appear in it.

PRESIDENT NIXON: No. Doesn't he do it because of the Hughes thing?

EHRLICHMAN: It's under investigation.

PRESIDENT NIXON: It's under investigation why? Are we investigating Don [Nixon]?

EHRLICHMAN: No, they're investigating John Meyer, they're investigating a guy named [first name unknown] Cleveland, because Hughes bought all his mining claims out in Nevada and there was a big kickback. There was around a $9 million kickback where Hughes actually paid about $9 million more for them than they were worth.

PRESIDENT NIXON: Now, the only problem about throwing the Hughes stuff up is you wonder what the Hughes people would say about Don [Nixon].

EHRLICHMAN: Oh, I think we know pretty much everything there is to know about that.

PRESIDENT NIXON: Anyway, it's an old story.

EHRLICHMAN: That's it.

PRESIDENT NIXON: They'd have a hell of a time.

EHRLICHMAN: We're not going to publish necessarily. We just want O'Brien to quit sleeping nights.

PRESIDENT NIXON: How will he get the word?

EHRLICHMAN: He'll get the word, he's going to get an audit. They're going to pull his return, take a look. Here's a payment to [Joe] Napolitan. They call him in for an audit, they say, "What is this? Did you have anything to do with that?" And he's got to get an attorney or an accountant into it.

PRESIDENT NIXON: John, the point is, as I told you, in 1961, the first year I ever made any money, when I wrote the damn book, those sons of bitches came up and they went after it: How much did you pay for your house, and all the rest. It was horrible.

EHRLICHMAN: Sure.

PRESIDENT NIXON: And I scared the living bejeezuz out of him, because I got the guy on the phone one day and I said, "Now look, I said, you can go ahead and investigate. . . ." They cooled off Goddamn fast.

PRESIDENT NIXON: . . . That's what we're going to do, and just tell George [Shultz] he should do it.

EHRLICHMAN: I will.

PRESIDENT NIXON: George has got a fantasy. What is George's—what's he trying to do, say that you can't play politics with IRS?

EHRLICHMAN: I don't know.

PRESIDENT NIXON: Or maybe he doesn't understand (unintelligible).

EHRLICHMAN: The way it came out—it didn't come up in this setting at all. It came up, he called me because this young fellow Roger Barth is over there and we've been wanting him to be deputy general counsel of IRS because he'd be in a position to do a lot more. George called up and said, "Geez, I am really having trouble with this. My bureaucracy is really wild about this; this guy is known to be a loyalist and a hard-ass and so on, so I've had a lot of flack." I said, "George, that's the only guy we've got in the whole IRS."

PRESIDENT NIXON: Here's bureaucracy. I want to know how many of those people are . . . appointees. Aren't there several?

EHRLICHMAN: Oh, sure, at the top, six or eight guys.

PRESIDENT NIXON: Out with them, every one of those bastards, out now. I think the whole bunch goes out just because of this. Don't you agree?

EHRLICHMAN: Sure, it would be a great move. It would be a marvelous move.

PRESIDENT NIXON: . . . We'll kick their ass out of there.

EHRLICHMAN: We've got four years more.

PRESIDENT NIXON: That's right. And they can learn it. It isn't all that difficult. But out their asses go, and then investigate the bastards. They're probably on the take. . . .

AUGUST 4, 1972: THE PRESIDENT, HALDEMAN, ZIEGLER, AND EHRLICHMAN, 10:37 A.M.–1:48 P.M., OVAL OFFICE

This lengthy rambling conversation ranges from money payments to the burglars that traced back to Dwayne Andreas to the President's apparent concern for Jeb Magruder—all the while reviewing Magruder's intention to perjure himself before the grand jury.

SEGMENT 1

PRESIDENT NIXON: . . . What's the situation on that contribution? Was it before or after the 7th of April? What's the situation on that? That's the only thing that the Hughes outfit . . . .

HALDEMAN: The contribution was made before.

PRESIDENT NIXON: Right.

HALDEMAN: From [Dwayne] Andreas to [Kenneth] Dahlberg. But Dahlberg didn't go to the bank. It was a cash contribution. Dahlberg didn't go to the bank until after the 7th. He went to the bank and converted it to a cashier's check and then gave the check to Stans on the 10th. . . .

PRESIDENT NIXON: I see. So what's going to happen there? Argue about it?

HALDEMAN: I think we can work it out. . . .

SEGMENT 2

PRESIDENT NIXON: You were starting to tell me when they came in, about the Watergate thing. What did you say about that financial and so forth, how they thought they can handle that?

HALDEMAN: I'm not sure. Oh, what I started to tell you is a new development. Dwayne Andreas called Clark [MacGregor] and said, " I don't know who to talk to, so I'm going to talk to you." He said, "First of all, I was the source of the $25,000 that is now under question; I gave it to—"

PRESIDENT NIXON: Dahlberg.

HALDEMAN: —Dahlberg." He said, "I've been thinking about it and I'd be prepared to release a statement," and he read the statement to Clark. It would be to this effect, if you people want me to do it. He said, "I have to think about it; I don't know whether this is good or bad.

The statement says that: "I'm independent, have always been a political independent. I have supported candidates primarily in the Democratic Party. I've been very close particularly and provided a very major degree of support to Hubert Humphrey. However, in this election I feel and have felt very strongly that it's absolutely imperative that the President be re-elected, and I am supporting him for that reason. Consonant with that support, I made the contribution of $25,000 to the President's Re-Election Campaign prior to the reporting date, because from my position it obviously was not desirable to have my name on a campaign list because of my association, long association, with Senator Humphrey and others." So to that effect.

That may have enormous political benefit to us, not just because it cleans up this thing, which it may well do, but because it explains the $10 million. Then you say: The reason (unintelligible) we had no thought in doing that is for exactly the reason that Mr. Andreas has pointed out.

PRESIDENT NIXON: That there are a lot of Democrats.

HALDEMAN: There are a lot of others like that.

PRESIDENT NIXON: He says, I naturally, being a longtime Democrat, I did not want—when I contributed before that time—

HALDEMAN: Because the law specifically provided.

PRESIDENT NIXON: It provided that I did not have to disclose it, but now I feel I should disclose.

HALDEMAN: Because of this question that's arisen about it. And of course he could say, because Senator Humphrey is now completely out.

PRESIDENT NIXON: I think it's imperative to do that. . . .

HALDEMAN: There may be some negatives. But the problem is that it's quite likely under this GAO investigation that Andreas is going to come out anyway. If he is, we're infinitely better off to have him put out a statement before he is turned up than to let them turn him up and then have him have to explain. And then we can play back the fact that Dwayne Andreas and hundreds of other Democrats are supporting the President, as will become clear in this campaign, many of them politically, others financially, some of them openly and some of them, for their very valid reasons, not openly.

PRESIDENT NIXON: Right.

HALDEMAN: Hell, we can tie that back to Congressmen, Senators, and other Democratic officeholders, and make the point that many of them are supporting the President privately, although of course they can't publicly declare.

PRESIDENT NIXON: Well, the plan still is to go ahead with . . . an indictment [of the burglars], get the damn thing over with [by] September? . . .

HALDEMAN: And then just try to keep out these brush fires that burst up, this stupid GAO [General Accounting Office] thing. . . .

PRESIDENT NIXON: . . . I think it's been bruited about, it's called a caper, it's called all that crap. It doesn't appear to be a serious attempt or sinister, or this, that, and the other thing.

HALDEMAN: I think if it comes to its worst then we have to—if the whole thing gets out, I don't think it's all that bad.

PRESIDENT NIXON: I just don't want Magruder involved.

HALDEMAN: I just hope we can keep Magruder out. We sure as hell have got to keep Mitchell out. We can survive Magruder's involvement. We would have a real problem with Mitchell's involvement.

PRESIDENT NIXON: Oh, yes.

HALDEMAN: And I think currently we're home free on that.

PRESIDENT NIXON: Magruder hasn't testified yet?

HALDEMAN: I don't think so.

PRESIDENT NIXON: Get him out of the way.

HALDEMAN: He'll do all right on testimony. . . . It's no problem. Jeb's in and out of here.

PRESIDENT NIXON: I'd like to—I think the Andreas thing, though, is a good move. Who's going to follow up on that?

HALDEMAN: I'll talk to John again. He was going to try and figure out what negatives.

PRESIDENT NIXON: John?

HALDEMAN: Ehrlichman.

PRESIDENT NIXON: John Dean, too, I suppose.

HALDEMAN: And I've got to check with John Dean, because he needs to determine whether—. . . .

SEGMENT 6

PRESIDENT NIXON: Do you know when Magruder gets up to the grand jury?

EHRLICHMAN: No, I don't.

PRESIDENT NIXON: How will he testify?

EHRLICHMAN: That he instructed Sloan to make money available to Liddy, he did it on the basis that Liddy was engaged in making sure that there were no demonstrations at the convention, and for doing certain—

HALDEMAN: Security.

EHRLICHMAN: —yes, security and headquarters and all that sort of thing, and one thing and another; that from time to time he was vaguely aware that Sloan was making disbursements to Liddy and he assumed Liddy was doing what he was told, but that he was never given an accounting as such from Sloan.

PRESIDENT NIXON: And didn't frankly follow it up.

EHRLICHMAN: Didn't follow it up, busy with other things, and made a number of assumptions. That after this happened he discovered that Liddy had grossly exceeded the scope of his employment and—

PRESIDENT NIXON: And asked for his resignation.

EHRLICHMAN: And he was fired.

PRESIDENT NIXON: How does Sloan—

EHRLICHMAN: Sloan has been promised immunity and he has not testified yet before the grand jury. He's only—he has only talked to the U.S. Attorney and the Bureau.

PRESIDENT NIXON: Why did they [grant immunity]? . . . Why did they have to?

EHRLICHMAN: Because he said he'd take the Fifth Amendment otherwise, and they felt he was key.

HALDEMAN: He's not going to testify before the grand jury, is he? . . .

EHRLICHMAN: No, no. Well, he was there very briefly. As soon as they learned that he was going to take the Fifth, they pulled him off, they brought him in for conference with his attorney. They asked him. He said he was going to take the Fifth because of technical violations of the Campaign Spending Act or the Campaign Financing Act. So they granted him immunity, and then they've been interrogating him in the office. They've not taken him back. . . .

PRESIDENT NIXON: Is he going to say that he was aware of all of this, et cetera?

EHRLICHMAN: No. He's going to say that he was told by Magruder to—

PRESIDENT NIXON: So he puts the whole thing on Liddy.

EHRLICHMAN: —give Liddy the money and he did.

PRESIDENT NIXON: He was just a conduit.

EHRLICHMAN: And what he did in keeping unreported cash and handing it out and so on is a violation. There isn't any question about that. Maury Stans's face is very long because some of this obviously comes back to him, because Sloan couldn't possibly have done all the things that it's clear he did without Maury having some knowledge of it.

PRESIDENT NIXON: Is Maury involved?

EHRLICHMAN: Well, he undoubtedly had some knowledge of the fact there was a lot of cash.

HALDEMAN: Maury didn't have any knowledge—I would be very surprised if Maury had any knowledge of what was being done with the cash.

EHRLICHMAN: Oh, I agree with that totally. I'm talking about these technical violations of the Campaign Spending Act.

HALDEMAN: Maury had full knowledge of that, I'm sure. He knew there was cash there and he knew that they were using it for intelligence and dirty tricks business. He knew that Liddy was the guy that was doing that, and he knew that it was X amounts of money. Maury doesn't let money go out without knowing about it.

SEGMENT 7

PRESIDENT NIXON: . . . Are they going to call Maury?

HALDEMAN: No, they're not. We've made sure they're not. They did and we stopped it. I woodshedded Kleindienst.

PRESIDENT NIXON: On what basis?

HALDEMAN: That it's very embarrassing to you, that this guy's [Stans] not just some bohunk off the street, he's a former Cabinet officer, he'd be subject to all kinds of notoriety, he hasn't any way of protecting himself against the inferences, and that it just would raise hell with the campaign and it just couldn't happen.

PRESIDENT NIXON: Well, I certainly hope he has the same view with regard to Mitchell.

HALDEMAN: That's right, that's right, absolutely. And in fairness to Kleindienst, this took place while he was out of town, by one of his guys, who exercised some bad judgment. . . . [Maury will] handle himself very well, I'm sure. At the same time, he is quite long in the mouth about the whole chilling effect this has on his ability to raise money. . . .

HALDEMAN: The best guess now is that nobody's going to get indicted except the burglars and Liddy and Hunt.

PRESIDENT NIXON: And Hunt fights like hell.

HALDEMAN: Well, they all plead not guilty and there are no trials until after the election.

EHRLICHMAN: All the burglars plead not guilty?

HALDEMAN: The burglars are all going to plead not guilty. . . . I can't imagine. I cannot imagine, but that's what they're going to do. [Laughter]

EHRLICHMAN: Make them prove it.

AUGUST 7, 1972: THE PRESIDENT AND EHRLICHMAN, 11:24 A.M.–1:18 P.M., OVAL OFFICE

The progress of the O'Brien audit; the President provides news about former LBJ aide Bobby Baker's allegations against prominent Democrats, including Lyndon Johnson; and when Ehrlichman proposes a policy decision on pending railroad legislation, Nixon immediately measures the political repercussions.

EHRLICHMAN: Remember we talked about Larry O'Brien and the IRS and so on. I did some checking. It seems that Larry O'Brien was already invited in for an audit just last week, and he failed to show up. So [George] Shultz wanted some guidance as to how to play this. I said, "Okay, invite him one more time, this week before Wednesday, while the National Committee is meeting. If he doesn't show up, then subpoena him."

PRESIDENT NIXON: Yes, sir, absolutely.

EHRLICHMAN: So Wednesday we'll know.

PRESIDENT NIXON: What do you do, if you know—as I understand it, he can send his lawyer in, can't he?

EHRLICHMAN: He can send his lawyer or his accountant, yes. But I think they've got him. They may have him, and it's this. This fellow [Joe] Napolitan has already been audited and he has testified, or he's reported, that the Hughes money that he got was split three ways. . . .

PRESIDENT NIXON: The problem we have with the Hughes thing is twofold. One, it allows them to re-open the Don [Nixon] thing.

EHRLICHMAN: Yes.

PRESIDENT NIXON: That was a long time ago.

EHRLICHMAN: Yes.

PRESIDENT NIXON: Now, you don't have anything on the Hughes thing, just to be sure? Because I assume that, if you've been watching Don, Don hasn't taken any more money from them.

EHRLICHMAN: Not that I know of, and none that shows up in this thing.

PRESIDENT NIXON: Good. . . Now, very interesting. Rose [Mary Woods] . . . said she'd had a call from Bobby Baker at 7:30. That was at the time Muskie was expected to be the nominee. Baker said, told her: "I must talk to somebody, and I'll talk to Bebe or I'll talk to you." He said: "These people are really awful. I have the goods on them, particularly on Muskie." And so Rose called. So I instructed Bebe to call back. . . . Bobby Baker got on the phone and he said, "This McGovern, I hate the son ofabitch." He says, "He's a disaster for the country." And he says, "I'll do anything to help." He said, "I've got some information that involves Muskie, and I've got some also that involves O'Brien, because after Muskie turned him down he later thought he would certainly take O'Brien."

EHRLICHMAN: Exactly.

PRESIDENT NIXON: And he said, " When can I see you?" So Bebe, with very good judgment, said, "Well, look, I'm going back to Florida. If you want to talk to me, we can meet down there any time." So I told Bebe to follow through at the earliest, with the idea of getting the information on both Muskie and O'Brien and also, I said, on any other Senator, except those maybe like [former Senator George] Smathers. Now, we may have one here, because Bobby Baker, the major one that he has information on will never come to trial—[Lyndon] Johnson.

EHRLICHMAN: Sure.

PRESIDENT NIXON: Because Bobby was thick with him and he never went to the can without talking to him. On the other hand, he was a bag man, and they were really bag men. He was about ten times the bag man that that poor fellow we had, Dave Johnson [?], was. Bobby was just about—

EHRLICHMAN: less able.

PRESIDENT NIXON: . . . My view is, let's see what Bebe finds out, if it's just hearsay or whatever it is. My view is if it's on Ed Muskie we tear him to pieces.

EHRLICHMAN: And particularly O'Brien.

PRESIDENT NIXON: Right, if it's O'Brien. But if it's Muskie, let's face it, let's see what that tarnished image was.

EHRLICHMAN: Yes.

PRESIDENT NIXON: And . . . you just might find one of those other white knights, like [Senator Gaylord] Nelson [D-WI]. . . .

EHRLICHMAN: . . . Speaking of Smathers, we've got this railroad bailout bill.

PRESIDENT NIXON: Mitchell has already talked about that. He doesn't think it's very wise.

EHRLICHMAN: I talked to him just now upstairs. I think his concern is we're not getting enough for it.

PRESIDENT NIXON: If it's going to hurt us with the Teamsters, I would not.

EHRLICHMAN: No, it won't. They're for it.

PRESIDENT NIXON: They are?

EHRLICHMAN: Yes, sir. The Teamsters, the truckers, the surface carriers.

PRESIDENT NIXON: They're all for it?

EHRLICHMAN: The water carriers.

PRESIDENT NIXON: Where the hell did he get the information and the idea that they were against it?

EHRLICHMAN: Well, he didn't know and he assumed that they would be against it because it was favorable to the railroads.

PRESIDENT NIXON: I see.

EHRLICHMAN: But Smathers has covered his flanks pretty well and he's got these people. As a matter of fact, the truckers will put in money and they will give us field men. The Teamsters are definitely for it. Colson has checked. So what we've got is an interesting lineup, and we've got an offer of money and this field help that Smathers is coming across, which is sort of a fringe benefit, in return for withdrawing our objection to a bill that may not pass anyway.

Now, that looks like we've got things all our own way. The negatives are that, on the merits, we tried to get some reforms in the transportation industry. If we withdraw our objection to this bill now, the reforms are probably dead in the water. Our one chance of getting certain kinds of deregulation, more competition in the industry and so on, would be for us to continue to object to it, to make sure that the bill didn't go anyplace this year, to re-introduce it next year with our reforms attached to it and try and get it through over a period of four years.

PRESIDENT NIXON: [It will] look like a payoff to Smathers. He talks a lot.

EHRLICHMAN: Then I would have to say yes. He will undoubtedly peddle his services to other people by saying, "Look, this thing was cracked in the White House; I have access to the President; I had a three-year contract with the railroads; I pulled this thing off; I got the administration to back off its objections and demand for reforms; I'm a helluva guy." And he'd be entitled to say that, because that's in effect what he'd be doing.

PRESIDENT NIXON: It isn't worth it. . . .

EHRLICHMAN: That's the amount of money that the railroads—half a million dollars is what the railroads have offered us, plus the truckers offering us a couple hundred thousand dollars and field men. And that's the quid pro quo.

PRESIDENT NIXON: What's the explanation for our abandoning our transportation policy?

EHRLICHMAN: Well—

PRESIDENT NIXON: We couldn't get it through the Congress. . . .

EHRLICHMAN: [Transportation Secretary John] Volpe rationalizes it. He says we are getting some reforms in the bill. We've got a very sick railroad industry. We have to take what we can get now and then fight vigorously for the reforms in the new Congress. Volpe's strongly in favor of this thing on the merits. He thinks we've gotten a modicum of reform and that we ought to go for it. But he made the case on the merits. At the same time, Smathers undoubtedly will be arguing that it was a perfect lobbying job and that he pulled it off and the merits didn't have much to do with it.

PRESIDENT NIXON: Well, who are the people that are going to blow the whistle? [House Commerce Committee Chairman Harley O.] Staggers?

EHRLICHMAN: Yes.

PRESIDENT NIXON: Won't he raise hell with us about our big change?

EHRLICHMAN: I don't think he will raise hell with us. He will raise hell with the railroads. Staggers has frustrated Smathers in this thing from the beginning, and Smathers is frank to say that he may not be able to get it through.

PRESIDENT NIXON: I don't think it has enough negatives to be bothered. You've got to remember that you can't deliver Smathers, you can't deliver the money. . . . The question is, I suppose, does it look like we're doing something for big business, because that's another thing?

EHRLICHMAN: Yes, it does. It will be seen as a railroad bailout.

PRESIDENT NIXON: How about the railroad unions?

EHRLICHMAN: Well, they'd kind of like to see the railroads get this, because it'll make a fatter contract for them next year. But to the outsider, it'll look like a $900 million gain for the railroads in terms of guaranteed loans and so forth. . . . [T]he railroad presidents [have] been in and they put on their presentations and lobbied us hard. They say that Southern Pacific and Union Pacific are all right, but that the rest of the railroads are in big trouble, and that they need—

PRESIDENT NIXON: Help.

EHRLICHMAN: The main thing, it's just basically digging up the money and the workers.

PRESIDENT NIXON: It's a losing proposition.

EHRLICHMAN: Well, it certainly isn't a winner. It doesn't do you any good to go out and say, I've saved the railroads. Nobody gives a damn about the railroads . . . . , and so on. On the other side, McGovern ought to be saying: The poor people can't get anything to eat, but the railroad's getting $9 billion.

PRESIDENT NIXON: I just don't see any reason to buy the problem of giving something to big business at this point. Just stay away from it. . . .

AUGUST 9, 1972: THE PRESIDENT, DICTATING, 10:19 A.M.–1:47 P.M., CAMP DAVID

Nixon is on one of his periodic anti-*Washington Post* crusades. Ironically, the *Post* supported most of Nixon's policies, and did not make an endorsement in the 1972 presidential election.

PRESIDENT NIXON: This is a memorandum for Ehrlichman. Apparently Joe Alsop has told Kay Graham—Joe Alsop says that Kay Graham's anti-RN attitude is exacerbated by the fact that she believes we are going to lift the TV licenses on some of her stations in the event that we succeed in the election. . . . You can point out that this administration has an impeccable record over the past three and a half years of never interfering with TV licenses, even though (unintelligible) stations on the other side, as far as (unintelligible) stations are concerned. The story came from Alsop. It is possible that you should use him as the conduit, but handle it any way you like.

For your confidential information, [we will take care of] this whole matter of licenses after the election. [Let me know] what recommendations you have. Have this handled by one of your associates very discreetly. Don't talk to anyone else about it.

AUGUST 11, 1972: THE PRESIDENT, HALDEMAN, AND EHRLICHMAN, 10:00–10:15 A.M., OVAL OFFICE

Nixon discusses plans for his second-term Cabinet, and ones for McGovern contributors, as well.

SEGMENT 2

PRESIDENT NIXON: What I wanted to tell you was this, that my view as to how to handle the whole thing here after the elections is I want everybody who has worked this investigation, have (unintelligible) pick out anyone, Petersen or maybe one other that has played our game, and everybody else is fired.

EHRLICHMAN: Yes.

PRESIDENT NIXON: You see what I mean?

EHRLICHMAN: Right.

PRESIDENT NIXON: . . . [F]ind anybody who contributed to the McGovern campaign, [like] Max Palevsky.

EHRLICHMAN: Good.

HALDEMAN: All we need is one.

EHRLICHMAN: Kimelman has had—

HALDEMAN: One big contribution they didn't report and we've got it made.

PRESIDENT NIXON: We've got to get this now. Don't leave it.

EHRLICHMAN: I understand. I'll just find out what the source is.

PRESIDENT NIXON: If it's possible. You've got to find out. You've got to find out, and you follow up on it.

EHRLICHMAN: All right.

PRESIDENT NIXON: Not yesterday, but by tomorrow.

EHRLICHMAN: I understand, I understand.

PRESIDENT NIXON: Give them a call.

EHRLICHMAN: Okay. Kimelman has had—well, he's in a cute position. He doesn't pay income tax in the United States.

PRESIDENT NIXON: Where does he—

EHRLICHMAN: Virgin Islands. So he's been audited the last two years by IRS agents acting for the Virgin Islands, and he's clean according to them.

PRESIDENT NIXON: What about the Interior Department? What about the Justice Department?

EHRLICHMAN: I've got the Justice Department file coming over for Gray. . . .

AUGUST 13, 1972: THE PRESIDENT AND EHRLICHMAN, 9:53–10:02 A.M., CAMP DAVID

The President urges his staff to go after McGovern's supporters. Ehrlichman agrees, adding: "Process them."

PRESIDENT NIXON: What else is new?

EHRLICHMAN: Well, not a whole lot. Got through the [Henry L.] Kimelman file last night.

PRESIDENT NIXON: Nothing in it you think we can use?

EHRLICHMAN: Well, I don't know. I don't know. There may be. An awful lot of McGovern's people were involved in this Virgin Islands scandal.

PRESIDENT NIXON: Were they?

EHRLICHMAN: It's [former Interior Secretary Stewart] Udall and a fellow named [Lawrence] Halprin and Kimelman and Kimelman's father-in-law, a fellow named [Sidney] Kessler ["Kessel"].

PRESIDENT NIXON: What kind of scandal is it?

EHRLICHMAN: Well, it's a deal where Stewart Udall, several months before he left as Secretary of the Interior, formed a partnership with these people and one of them was given a $550,000 contract to do some work in the Virgin Islands.

PRESIDENT NIXON: Well, I've got a good idea. Isn't it about time we called on [reporter] Clark Mollenhoff to do something and give him the whole file.

EHRLICHMAN: Well, I think he could make something out of this.

PRESIDENT NIXON: That's what I mean.

EHRLICHMAN: Yes.

PRESIDENT NIXON: And let him go out and say—

EHRLICHMAN: One thing I want to cover, I want to talk to Kleindienst about why the Justice Department never prosecuted.

PRESIDENT NIXON: Well, hell. You mean while we were in?

EHRLICHMAN: Well, yes.

PRESIDENT NIXON: Well, you know damn well why. Mitchell and the rest—

EHRLICHMAN: But that's an angle, you see, that's available to Mollenhoff, and I want to find out what the answer to that is.

PRESIDENT NIXON: The answer is because we didn't want to be political. But now we want to be political [*laughter*], I suppose, I don't know.

EHRLICHMAN: I don't either. I want to check it, and I'll talk to Dick [Kleindienst] today and see what he says about it.

PRESIDENT NIXON: Now, the other thing that occurred to me that I want you to do, I don't really—I don't know. I suppose we could have Haldeman do it, but I think he's—but remember I've indicated that we should take all the major McGovern supporters and/or financial contributors—I mean the 50 G's and above or something like that—and—

EHRLICHMAN: Process them.

PRESIDENT NIXON: Exactly, and see who they are. Look, they go after everything from [Joe] Mulcahy to Rebozo—

EHRLICHMAN: Yes.

PRESIDENT NIXON: —to [his friend, Bob] Abplanalp. You know what I mean, every one of ours.

EHRLICHMAN: Right.

PRESIDENT NIXON: Now, my point is who are McGovern's friends, who are his major supporters? Are they bad guys, good guys? Now, we've gone—the only thing I think has been done is Jerry Rubin. [*Laughter.*] No, there must be others.

EHRLICHMAN: Right. . . . It shouldn't be that hard to put a catalogue together of a few donors.

PRESIDENT NIXON: Have you done anything on that? Well, could you put—could you put a very, very smart team of about three guys on it?

EHRLICHMAN: Sure. . . .

PRESIDENT NIXON: Because you know, everybody has got somebody in there who's a bad apple.

EHRLICHMAN: Right, right. You know, this is the kind of thing Murray's [Chotiner] awfully good at.

PRESIDENT NIXON: All right, all right. That's very good. Why don't you give him that to do, and then he says: I need this file, this file, and this file.

EHRLICHMAN: Yes, yes.

PRESIDENT NIXON: Give him a couple of young guys to work with him on it.

EHRLICHMAN: Yes.

PRESIDENT NIXON: But I think it's a nice project.

EHRLICHMAN: Do you think Murray would be all right for that?

PRESIDENT NIXON: Sure, sure, provided he doesn't do anything public.

EHRLICHMAN: Right. This would be research. . . .

PRESIDENT NIXON: And Murray could say: "I want to look over all these people; who are the bad ones?" Provided he isn't—I don't want him to be soft on the Jews. That's one problem. But he won't, I don't think.

EHRLICHMAN: I don't think Murray will. . . .

PRESIDENT NIXON: I told Haldeman. Maybe ask him what he's done on that.

EHRLICHMAN: All right, I will.

PRESIDENT NIXON: I said I want to know what—I want a list of all their contributors and supporters and I want some investigations made. . . .

AUGUST 14, 1972: THE PRESIDENT, HALDEMAN, MITCHELL, AND MACGREGOR, 9:55–10:42 A.M., OVAL OFFICE

The President believes Watergate still is a PR matter, and can be confined to the burglars, Hunt, and Liddy.

PRESIDENT NIXON: . . . The important thing to consider is the real decision you have to face up to as to whether or not to wait for whether the federal grand jury indicts or whether you prepare the stage for it. The weakness, I see, in the present situation—and of course it's a bad situation to begin with, very embarrassing, and so forth and so on. The weakness I see at the present time is that we have people on the outside saying, well, they need special investigators and oh, let's have a special prosecutor, and all that sort of thing. Look what they did at the time of the Bobby Baker fiasco. Was there any suggestion of special prosecutors then?

HALDEMAN: I'm sure there was, Mr. President. I'm sure there was.

PRESIDENT NIXON: The main point that I make is this. I think that the case has got to be made that the Re-Election Committee, John, with total cooperation and support by us, has conducted its own investigation and is conducting its own investigation of this matter. I think that's very important that they know. I think that the other way, to get in the position of saying, well, that's a matter for the courts and it's all hands off and we don't give a shit—well, everybody knows that the people from the Re-Election Committee are involved at a lower level. . . .

Then, having in mind the fact that the grand jury indicts, we get indictments on people who obviously have gotten caught with their hands in the cookie jar and does not indict others like Magruder, Sloan, and so forth, there will be immediately an outcry for: "What are the facts with regard to the others? What are they covering up?" . . .

So the choices it seems to me are very, very limited. The choice is either to go down that sort of fall, and then have a hell of a bitch, then have an investigation demanded by everybody and everything else. Or, having in mind that this has nothing to do with law, forget the law, I mean except the poor guys that are going to go to jail and be fined, but that this has to do with public relations. Then the line would be to get something out in our own way prior to the time the grand jury indicts.

That's about the only thing I can suggest. I say this based on long experience that I had in an entirely different thing, doing investigations, 500 or 600 cases and all the rest. We never waited until the courts acted. We as a committee always put out our version before the courts. So we won the fucking public relations matter, we didn't give a Goddamn what happened in the court.

Well, as it turned out we won in the courts, too, but it wouldn't have made any difference if we had [not] won the case beforehand. In this instance we are simply trying to avoid a loss, to cut a loss. It might be—I think it might be that you can absolve . . . all the top officials of the Re-Election Committee . . . .

MITCHELL: I think you've put it in exactly the right posture as to how to get the minimum impact out of it. I think we have to be very careful to know what the facts are going to be and what's going to come out of that grand jury. . . .

PRESIDENT NIXON: That's why, Bob, you should have Dean head off that meeting.

MACGREGOR: He's good.

PRESIDENT NIXON: Yes. Now, the point is that if you're reasonably sure of what the facts are—is Magruder going forward tomorrow?

HALDEMAN: Yes.

MACGREGOR: It's anticipated he'll be in tomorrow and Wednesday.

PRESIDENT NIXON: Well, his questions will indicate to me to a certain extent what's going to come out.

MACGREGOR: Well, at least the grand jury proceedings will be controlled in the Justice Department. They're not going to go off on their own over at the U. S. Attorney's

Office. And that's where we've got to know what they're going to recommend to the grand jury. And once we know that, then you can set the timing of the indictments and the timing of your statement.

PRESIDENT NIXON: Right, unless the grand jury runs away. You don't think it will?

MACGREGOR: I don't believe it will.

PRESIDENT NIXON: Well, it seems to me that if you can lay that down, nail that down, that a procedure whereby Clark would do this—in other words, I look at that, I think it's very important to let them know that we have been investigating and not sitting on our ass.

MACGREGOR: Well, this has been stated. . . .

PRESIDENT NIXON: It's been stated and they have constantly said that the White House and the rest are completely oblivious to this.

MACGREGOR: Well, they even went further than that in the Goddamn Time magazine article, in which they inferred that there was a blockage at the Committee and the White House. That was last week's *Time*.

PRESIDENT NIXON: Yes, that's right. They said that we were . . . not cooperating, obstructing. But anyway, the point is that you want to be sure you handle this in a way that you don't get marred by it, because that'll hurt the campaign, too. The way I have in mind was to say Mitchell had hired this high-powered firm of investigators, . . . and so forth and so on, because we want to know on our own. These grand jury proceedings take a long time. We want to know what the facts are. You expect a report from your committee, say, before the end of the month—I mean, your firm—and then you will act based on that report. By that time there'll be nobody to act against, because Liddy's gone.

HALDEMAN: Right.

PRESIDENT NIXON: McCord is gone.

HALDEMAN: Sloan is gone.

PRESIDENT NIXON: Well, his involvement is only technical. What do you think? You have any other ideas? . . . [J]ust you cut the losses on the damn thing. . . .

AUGUST 19, 1972: THE PRESIDENT AND HALDEMAN, 3:23–3:26 P.M., CAMP DAVID TELEPHONE

Nixon is pleased with O'Brien's tax audit and annoyed that O'Brien wants an extension because of the election. "That's a lot of nerve, to say to put it off until after the election," Nixon says.

HALDEMAN: I got the report on the O'Brien audit. John said he'd forgotten to tell me about it and I'd forgotten to ask him this morning. But O'Brien showed up yesterday as instructed, with his son and with all their records, and he asked that his case be postponed until after the election and they declined. They said, no, that they had to pursue it right away. . . . And he's quite shook up about the whole thing. A cursory examination . . . would indicate that, if everything that he says is true, he is clear. But he's left all the records there and they're starting through them. And our guy, Roger

Barth, will be going through them also. So we've got his files and now we can do some exploring.

PRESIDENT NIXON: But it looks as if you say it's—

HALDEMAN: On the basis of what he says, if what he says is true. But this is true of almost anybody when they come in. He's not going to come in and say, I've not paid my taxes. He's going to say I have it all covered.

PRESIDENT NIXON: At least we've got a guy working on it like Barth that's not going to give it a cursory examination.

HALDEMAN: That's right. It will be very thoroughly examined on the merits, and also for the political interest of anything else that might be in there. See, that was the other thing. We wanted to rummage through the records . . . .

PRESIDENT NIXON: That's a lot of nerve, to say to put it off until after the election.

HALDEMAN: Yes.

SEPTEMBER 7, 1972: THE PRESIDENT, HALDEMAN, AND EHRLICHMAN, 10:32–10:40 A.M., OVAL OFFICE

Senator Edward M. Kennedy requests Secret Service protection. The White House agrees but wants to be certain that the Service will report to the President's staff on Kennedy's activities. "A candidate requires total coverage," Nixon says.

SEGMENT 2

PRESIDENT NIXON: . . . You understand what I'm talking about? You have anybody in the Secret Service that can you get to, do you have anybody that you can rely on?

HALDEMAN: Yes. We got several.

PRESIDENT NIXON: Plant one. Plant two guys on him [Edward M. Kennedy]. This will be very useful.

HALDEMAN: What I was going to suggest is give orders to the detail that they are never at any hour of the day or night to let him out of their sight.

PRESIDENT NIXON: That's right. Never. Right. A candidate requires total coverage.

EHRLICHMAN: That's it. Absolutely. That's the way to do it. I'm not going to have George [Shultz] do it. He screwed up the O'Brien thing.

PRESIDENT NIXON: Got any more reports on that?

EHRLICHMAN: It's a dry hole [income tax audit]. I talked to [Roger] Barth privately, and he says it's a dry hole. And we'll do it the other way. We'll do it the other way.

PRESIDENT NIXON: But on this one, George [Shultz] will raise this Kennedy thing with him. Why don't you just tell him that we'll extend the coverage, but that you want Bob to handle the details?

EHRLICHMAN: Yes. All right. Fine. I'll understand.

HALDEMAN: Sure. Sure. Alex [Butterfield] handles the details.

PRESIDENT NIXON: Alex handles the details. . . .

SEPTEMBER 7, 1972: THE PRESIDENT, HALDEMAN, AND BUTTERFIELD, 5:44–6:15 P.M., OVAL OFFICE

The conversation continues about Kennedy's Secret Service protection, now joined by Alexander Butterfield.

SEGMENT 1

PRESIDENT NIXON: Now, the other thing that I want understood, have you covered the business on the Kennedy coverage? What man? Have you assigned a man to him?

HALDEMAN: Yeah. It's all in here, sir.

BUTTERFIELD: It's going to be in full force.

HALDEMAN: Don't put a big detail on him.

PRESIDENT NIXON: A big detail. Correct. Right. One that can cover him round the clock, every place he goes.

BUTTERFIELD: Everybody gets it. [*Laughter.*] That too.

PRESIDENT NIXON: Right. He has got to have the same coverage that we give the others because we are concerned about security and we will not assume the responsibility—

HALDEMAN: [Kennedy friend] Amanda Burden can't be trusted. She's not—I don't know what she might do.

PRESIDENT NIXON: I want it to be damn clear that he requested it, he requested it, because of threats, that sonofabitch, I want to make sure that he is followed.

HALDEMAN: Sure.

BUTTERFIELD: Yes.

SEGMENT 2

PRESIDENT NIXON: Just might get lucky and catch this sonofabitch and grill him for '76. He doesn't really know what he is getting into. We are going to cover him. He is not going to take no for an answer. Kennedys are arrogant as hell with these Secret Service. He can't say no. I said fine, he should pick the details.

HALDEMAN: Then you go on the basis that, what, Kennedy may throw it out?

PRESIDENT NIXON: That's fine. That's going to be fine. . . .

SEPTEMBER 8, 1972: THE PRESIDENT AND HALDEMAN, 9:28–10:20 A.M., OVAL OFFICE

Nixon is anxious to establish some distance between Colson and the White House. He and Haldeman talk about setting up Colson as a leader of the Washington legal establishment. "[G]ive Chuck access to the IRS stuff . . . the FBI stuff. You let him go ruthless until you kill these people," the President comments. Nixon also has post-election plans for a renewed assault on the media.

SEGMENT 5

PRESIDENT NIXON: I want to get a list, on whether [Bryce] Harlow is objective enough to do this, but I want it done. I want a list. We are getting a list of people that—

HALDEMAN: Colson's office can do that.

PRESIDENT NIXON: Colson's office. Colson's office. Of the Washington Democratic lawyers, and lobbyist types, so that we can cut them out forever. We really sucked the asses out of them last November. . . . We sort of needed some of them. But there are ways that we can do it, and you can—look—this fella who owns the Redskins [Edward Bennett Williams], he has always wanted to do something, he has always had his Goddamn hands out. You just cut him off at the hip pockets early, never desire to see such a sonofabitch, you see my point? Or his agent, or his partner, or his wife. See what I mean? And let's build up some of our own lawyers, you know, that are—are our type lawyers from the start. [Democratic lawyer Clark] Clifford, for example, it's ridiculous that he's still (unintelligible).

HALDEMAN: I've been thinking about this. This is an assignment that's dangerous in a sense, but I think it's worth doing. That after the election, you got to do it in some very careful way, but it would be worthwhile . . . to give Colson the responsibility for building a Nixon–Washington establishment.

PRESIDENT NIXON: Exactly.

HALDEMAN: And for killing the opposition.

PRESIDENT NIXON: Exactly. Right.

HALDEMAN: He is the one guy who knows enough and is ruthless enough to do that. It might be—it might be because [Murray] Chotiner doesn't know—

PRESIDENT NIXON: And (unintelligible) Chotiner, maybe he is not—Judaism. It's Jew—

HALDEMAN: Chotiner can't do it because Chotiner doesn't know the track record.

PRESIDENT NIXON: And Chotiner's too—well, frankly, he's not some. . . .

HALDEMAN: He can be taken by some of the—

PRESIDENT NIXON: Yep. It's the Jew business.

HALDEMAN: . . . Chuck, he would be—he would be ideal to take that kind of thing on.

PRESIDENT NIXON: Killer instinct.

HALDEMAN: To take that kind of thing on—that Chuck could do after the election, that he can't do now. See, after the long haul, and it would be good for him, see because he wants to stay in Washington, and it's the only way he can build himself up for the rest of his life.

PRESIDENT NIXON: We are going to do it?

HALDEMAN: Yes.

PRESIDENT NIXON: For example, the other thing is—

HALDEMAN: The thing, you give Chuck access to the IRS stuff. You give Chuck access to the FBI stuff. You let him go ruthless until you kill these people.

SEGMENT 6

PRESIDENT NIXON: What I was going to say is if we could get a situation worked out where we can take on getting [Herbert] Klein, I want to get on him, the price of the people, *Washington Post* members, and individual reporters, you understand, this business ought to be just upon us. You can't take Ziegler, for example, but we have got to have money, you know what I mean. Remember which ones were against us.

HALDEMAN: Yep.

PRESIDENT NIXON: I want a study made that I want you to undertake, and don't write a memorandum on this. I think you better get ahold of [White House aides] Mort Allin or [Pat] Buchanan, or both. I want to pick the twenty most vicious Washington reporters and most vicious and influential Washington reporters and television people, and the title of this little memorandum would be "Things That We'd Like To Forget They Said."

Now, here's what I want. I don't want anything said about me so much, . . . but I'm more interested in predictions they have made with regard . . . to Nixon–McGovern . , . I want to write a piece here . . . and just kill the sons of bitches. Now, who can you—can you please follow up on this?

HALDEMAN: *Yes, sir!*

PRESIDENT NIXON: Who will you give it to?

HALDEMAN: Pat [Buchanan].

PRESIDENT NIXON: And then have Pat have a story run. It's an interesting commentary. . . .

HALDEMAN: . . . I see Chuck as a monumental asset because then you don't have to be afraid of Chuck. We still do a little bit now—but afterwards—and you got the personal motivation, because this is a guy who wants to stay in Washington, and can build himself into a damn good position as the kingpin of the power structure.

PRESIDENT NIXON: That's right.

HALDEMAN: And then when all the rest of the people leave, Chuck will be here to get that gain for years ahead.

PRESIDENT NIXON: Marvelous.

SEPTEMBER 8, 1972: THE PRESIDENT AND EHRLICHMAN, 12:22–1:05 P.M., OVAL OFFICE

The President is briefed on the Larry O'Brien tax investigation, Bobby Baker's latest information, and the vulnerabilities of McGovern's campaign manager, Gary Hart. Nixon downplays Watergate and belittles those in his administration who are worried about events.

SEGMENT 1

EHRLICHMAN: I got the Larry O'Brien numbers, and they are quite interesting. This guy has a hell of an income. In '69, he got $43,500 roughly from Hughes, but he had adjusted gross income of $173,800. That's deducted. But he got a lot of that from the stock brokerage firm he was with. Seventy-five, he got $28,000 speaking fees, he got $6,000 in interest and dividends, and he got a fee from something called Ducor Industries. I have to find out about that. The next year, he then nearly doubled his income, he was at—$218,280, $100[,000] roughly was from Hughes, $36,000 from this Ducor, and some other lobbying fees, PR fees, but he paid tax on all of that. So it is a dry hole from that standpoint. . . .

Now, the [Gary] Hart thing, the Hart thing has some problems. Apparently, this is known in Democratic circles.

PRESIDENT NIXON: Oh, forget it.

EHRLICHMAN: So it's not going to be a surprise to anybody.

PRESIDENT NIXON: I think it's good to get it out, what do you think?

EHRLICHMAN: Oh, I think. Hank [Greenspun, Las Vegas newsman], ran a bannered story on it. But as far as planting it with Hart, and hoping that Hart will cause a revolution—

PRESIDENT NIXON: My feeling is that it's just a good way to blunt it advance their attack on Don [Nixon, Nixon's brother, similarly involved with Howard Hughes]. It isn't good. Let's attack him first, and let him squeal about what happened to Don fifteen years ago.

EHRLICHMAN: Right. Absolutely.

SEGMENT 2

PRESIDENT NIXON: What is the situation with regard to, or are you aware of, Herb Kalmbach's contacts, or Bobby Baker?

EHRLICHMAN: Well, I haven't heard from Herb since he's been back here. He's got here this week.

PRESIDENT NIXON: Press him hard.

EHRLICHMAN: I will.

PRESIDENT NIXON: Get everything you possibly can. Any little crumb or lead involving anyone. I don't care. O'Brien, another Senator. Anything that falls Democrat, Goddamn it, put it—

EHRLICHMAN: Okay. Well, I have a call out for Herb. . . .

PRESIDENT NIXON: I put it on the basis that I do not want any political prosecutions to backfire, this and that and the other thing. Kleindienst's office never comes up with any left winger—they don't have any Goddamn people that are right for us. . . .

SEGMENT 3

PRESIDENT NIXON: . . . There is one thing to be said, an interesting thing, I'd . . . rather have him [Lawrence O'Brien] talking about this [Watergate] than the fact that we are the party of the rich and the fact that the prices are high. Talk about both. But the public can only—talk about one story at a time. This [Watergate] story is not helpful, but it is not one that—that the average guy—whether or not the Republicans fuck the Democrats, doesn't mean a Goddamn thing. It means something to the elections, it means something to people that is about refreshing credibility and all that bullshit. But that average guy, he's interested in a job, and he is interested in war and peace, and defense and patriotism. And that's a little bit on the social side.

EHRLICHMAN: Mm-hmn. And I don't think it rubs off on you, even the negative aspects.

PRESIDENT NIXON: Well, I didn't figure—well, I don't think people believe basically in terms of their—they wouldn't be so stupid. [*laughter*]

EHRLICHMAN: That's right. Yes, sir, yes. And—

PRESIDENT NIXON: There isn't a Goddamn thing you can ask about this.

EHRLICHMAN: It gives us a chance to make that kind of a point. It was a dumb deal. Nobody in government involved.

PRESIDENT NIXON: That's right. Overzealous, jerks.

EHRLICHMAN: Yes. Hart played that yesterday, very well.

SEGMENT 4

EHRLICHMAN: And so hopefully, we can talk to them in terms of taxes and several others, and say here's how you turn this, here's how you turn Watergate. Never defend in an answer. [Commerce Secretary Peter] Peterson, for instance, always denying, always justifying, instead of turning. Yes.

PRESIDENT NIXON: It's a mindset.

EHRLICHMAN: Yes. They don't have a mindset.

PRESIDENT NIXON: They are worried. They are the ones who call Stan, "Gee you gotta get out!" We find that our businessmen are the ones that are most worried about Watergate. Our labor guys don't give one shit. Believe me. . . . I never had one of the labor guys mention Watergate. They talk about the flag and the country. And I say this Communist sonofabitch [McGovern], I mean, you got all these horrible people around. People around the government [*laughter*]—

EHRLICHMAN: That's right.

PRESIDENT NIXON: —people around the government—Watergate. Why Watergate really is directed to people around Nixon. Let's talk about the people who run the government. That's a . . . theme. Who are they? Who is [McGovern contributor Henry] Kimelman? *Who is Kimelman?*

EHRLICHMAN: [Joseph] Alsop whacked Kimelman good and hard this time. . . . He said there are enormous discrepancies in McGovern's money. Kimelman has been saying this and this. But we know from the facts that he is getting gifts from— what's this left-wing Harvard professor, [first name unknown] Pomerantz, or whatever his name is, whatever.

PRESIDENT NIXON: Pomerantz?

EHRLICHMAN: I forget his name. It's a left-wing professor.

PRESIDENT NIXON: Heard a lot about him.

EHRLICHMAN: He's got a lot of good facts in there. I think Henry Kimelman has got a lot of explaining to do when he gets home. And so it sucks.

SEPTEMBER 11, 1972: THE PRESIDENT AND COLSON, 12:40–1:45 P.M., EXECUTIVE OFFICE BUILDING

In one of Nixon's periodic pep talks, he invokes Harry Truman and Alger Hiss and the dangers of a cover-up.

SEGMENT 1

PRESIDENT NIXON: . . . I just think that you can't—I just think that you can't be in a position of . . . looking like you're scared. On Watergate, for example, . . . [Clark] MacGregor . . . said flatly that we will cooperate fully, and that anybody who stalls or refuses to cooperate will be discharged immediately. . . .

In '48, for example, the Hiss investigation and the Chambers-Hiss confrontation, this whole attack, took place before the '48 election. And Truman just said "It's a red herring," and won the election. Dewey, however, did not use the issue. But neverthe-less, he won the election. How did Truman handle it? *Didn't answer at all.* He said it's all a red herring. . . . The *cover-up* is what hurts you, not the issue. It's the cover-up that hurts. . . .

SEPTEMBER 11, 1972: THE PRESIDENT, HALDEMAN, AND COLSON, 3:15–6:11 P.M., EXECUTIVE OFFICE BUILDING

Haldeman projects a perverse theory that Watergate is a plus because Democratic charges of involvement by higher-ups have fallen flat. "Don't even worry about it," Nixon says regarding the pending indictments. Nixon, meanwhile, relishes some gossip by Bobby Baker involving Teddy Kennedy. Haldeman proposes a Warren-type Commission to determine whether the Department of Justice investigation has been "exhaustive and thorough."

SEGMENT 1

PRESIDENT NIXON: What do they anticipate on the Watergate? What comes next?

HALDEMAN: They still anticipate the indictments on Friday the 15th, that area, or early next week. . . .

PRESIDENT NIXON: Do they know who's going to be indicted?

HALDEMAN: Yes. The five plus—

PRESIDENT NIXON: Plus the two?

HALDEMAN: Yes, that's all. The plan still is to follow, ride with the indictments with a MacGregor statement. . . .

HALDEMAN: . . . But you know, there's a perverse theory that we talked through this morning. . . . [W]e might be better off with the Watergate story. It isn't doing us any harm.

PRESIDENT NIXON: Yes, not much. What I mean is the harm that's done when re-porters are in a hurry too much. . . .

HALDEMAN: That's right, but the difference also is that the indictments will be less than we anticipated, rather than more. The indictments don't—see, they've all said all along, if the indictments or the guilt reaches into the upper levels of the commit-tee or in the White House, then there's a problem. . . .

PRESIDENT NIXON: . . . [Bobby] Baker knows a hell of a lot more than he's talking about. We don't care who it's on. It can be on Teddy, it can be on anybody, but just get it. I prefer it be Teddy. Is the Teddy story being properly kicked around about the woman [Amanda Burden] on the boat and so forth.

COLSON: The *Boston Globe* ran a little tiny thing like that, cited that, and their lead was "Wire services refuse to carry story," one paragraph or so. So that nobody can say they didn't print the story.

PRESIDENT NIXON: We'll nail the Goddamn thing. . . .

COLSON: Teddy's campaigning with McGovern these three days.

PRESIDENT NIXON: And you got a sign out? A man out?

COLSON: And somebody got a sign that says: "Who's Amanda [Burden] sailing with while you're out here?"

SEGMENT 2

PRESIDENT NIXON: See, the point about that is that they're going to say—a lot of people may feel, well, this is just a huge prank and so forth and nothing's going to happen. But when they indict them, well, they're guilty. See, that's the point.

HALDEMAN: Yes, but look at the level they're indicting. The Democrats have been running around saying that you were the one that ordered it, that Chuck Colson was over there manning the bugging phones, and the implication is that all the high level people were in this. Then what the indictments say—and indeed that's why I think we need the MacGregor statement, (unintelligible) which doesn't just say we completed our investigation and this is all, but he goes on the attack and he demands an apology and a retraction of all the crap they've been shoveling out and an apology to the innocent people. . . .

PRESIDENT NIXON: The lawsuit doesn't bother me a bit. . . . The indictments are one thing. Don't even worry about it.

HALDEMAN: This time I think everybody figures, they know there was a break-in, they know there are guilty parties. I don't think the indictments are going to have the impact. . . .

Yet another ploy that we haven't perfected yet, but you might go off your chair [*laughter*]; you won't like it. I'm not sure it's so bad even with all the complications, which is that we announce with the delivery of the indictments that we're now instructing the Justice Department and requesting all other Departments to turn over to [*laughter*] . . . .

COLSON: To the CIA?

HALDEMAN: No. No, to a blue-ribbon commission, all of the facts in this case, as has been suggested, to review the question of whether a proper and thorough investigation has been conducted, to be chaired by—we would request the commission be chaired by Earl Warren, staffed or backed up by [former Solicitor General J.] Lee Rankin and [former Justice] Tom Clark.

Now, those folks are judicious enough that they would not want a criminal case pending, saying the [commission?] could be prejudicial. What they would say is that they had reviewed the investigative procedures followed by the FBI and the Department of Justice and found that they were exhaustive and thorough; we are sure that the investigation has been so complete that the record on its face will show that it is. Now, what you're doing is taking the issue away from McGovern, because he has said he wants Warren and Rankin appointed to conduct an independent inquiry. You say, fine. Or a special prosecutor. We wouldn't ever do that.

COLSON: This isn't a special prosecutor. This is to review the evidence of the prosecutor that's been working.

HALDEMAN: What this is an independent judgment that the investigation was adequate and thorough, and that's all they're to be charged with. . . .

COLSON: They probably would decline to serve.

HALDEMAN: Well, if they decline to serve, the basis for their declining to serve is that this is a normal criminal case, a case pursued in the normal course, and they don't believe it's proper for them to look over the shoulder of the President.

COLSON: You could have the Attorney General set this up.

PRESIDENT NIXON: I don't think I should do this.

COLSON: No, no. Kleindienst. . . . He says I believe this is the most thorough investigation since the assassination of John Kennedy, and . . .

HALDEMAN: I would be happy to turn this over to a panel of Chief Justice Warren, Justice Clark.

PRESIDENT NIXON: Well, you can pick up old [former Justice Stanley] Reed. Pick him up, too. All former Justices of the Supreme Court. That's all right.

HALDEMAN: I put Rankin and Warren in as Republicans, and Fortas and Clark in as Democrats. You have a bipartisan commission. Obviously, Warren chairs it, Chief Justice. . . .

PRESIDENT NIXON: Is there any standing group that we could turn it over to?

COLSON: That you wouldn't give it to the Goddamn Bar Association.

PRESIDENT NIXON: Yea, well, I'm just thinking if the Judicial—

COLSON: The Judicial Conference?

PRESIDENT NIXON: . . . I mean if you name a group, you got to ask them to serve. I'd like you to really look at that. Take them all, take them months to find out what the hell the story is [laughter].

COLSON: Especially those guys. They're too old to get around, I'm afraid [laughter]. . . . Warren would love to serve because he'd love to be back in the limelight. He did the Warren Committee. . . . It sure as hell shows that we have nothing to hide. If we are willing and if we throw in a Democrat like Fortas.

HALDEMAN: We just started this morning. We're not convinced we're on the right track . . . .

SEPTEMBER 12, 1972: THE PRESIDENT, HALDEMAN, AND COLSON, 11:07 A.M.–12:00 P.M., OVAL OFFICE

The discussion continues about a Warren Commission to look at Watergate. They float the idea of using former U.S. Supreme Court Justice Abe Fortas—whom the Nixon Administration forced from the bench for ethical improprieties.

PRESIDENT NIXON: The agreement you should not announce before getting them to agree to do it.

COLSON: You have to offer—you have to ask Warren if he will do it.

HALDEMAN: You ought to be able to, in case you have to.

COLSON: Oh hell, they'd read about it.

PRESIDENT NIXON: They'd read it in the paper, they'd ask what the hell

COLSON: We are being used.

HALDEMAN: [*Laughter.*] You ought to be able to say, I asked Chief Justice Warren to do it, and he said no.

COLSON: Yes.

PRESIDENT NIXON: He should.

HALDEMAN: But fortunately, Justice Fortas, somebody would agree to do it.

PRESIDENT NIXON: Fortas is a Johnson man.

COLSON: Oh hell, Fortas is—

PRESIDENT NIXON: (unintelligible) I don't think Fortas is on—

COLSON: McGovern's side?

PRESIDENT NIXON: No. No. He is very much on our side.

COLSON: He was the biggest supporter, advisor, Lyndon Johnson had.

HALDEMAN: He was deeply grateful (unintelligible). We got a couple of other things. I said—did he say anything about the government by any chance? . . . . I don't know if Fortas is good. Fortas is true. You got a crooked judge.

PRESIDENT NIXON: I'll tell you why he would be good. He is a Jew (unintelligible) and he's got business to do with the government.

HALDEMAN: We can do it that way. There is no question. I'm just saying whether he will be good in the public mind. The reason he is not Chief Justice—

PRESIDENT NIXON: Oh, he would be great in the public mind, because he is a Jew, and also because he is a martyr.

COLSON: People would think that we screwed him and this is his opportunity to get even with us. That's turning it over to a guy who has every motive to embarrass you, the opportunity to look at it. You are going to the extreme.

PRESIDENT NIXON: Okay.

SEPTEMBER 13, 1972: THE PRESIDENT AND HALDEMAN, 11:40 A.M.–1:12 P.M., CAMP DAVID

The two discuss Democratic campaign law violations and note Kleindienst's support for a Warren-type Commission to review the Watergate affair.

SEGMENT 1

PRESIDENT NIXON: And the analysis of the McGovern funds, that's being done by [Murray] Chotiner?

HALDEMAN: Yes. Well, he's analyzing the people, is that what you mean, the sources?

PRESIDENT NIXON: Doesn't he have something on contributors?

HALDEMAN: Yes, those are out.

PRESIDENT NIXON: I noticed the story in the [*Washington*] *Post* this morning talking about three big Nixon contributors, none of whom I know.

HALDEMAN: It's interesting because one of them, the McDonald's hamburger guy—the guy named McDonald from McDonald hamburgers is a big McGovern contributor.

PRESIDENT NIXON: Maybe that was just the way that it was placed?

HALDEMAN: Sure.

PRESIDENT NIXON: Democratic violations are minor.

HALDEMAN: Well, they are.

PRESIDENT NIXON: *So are ours.*

HALDEMAN: So are ours.

PRESIDENT NIXON: What the hell.

HALDEMAN: Well, except the GAO [General Accounting Office] report, ours—there's more questions in ours than there is on theirs. But I don't think—you know, that's a fine line. I think we've got that confused, and if we're arguing about whose is the worst violation we're in pretty good shape.

PRESIDENT NIXON: Well, you're satisfied with the Chotiner operation, that's all I want to know. Keep going after it adequately, and it's well enough staffed. Is Ehrlichman following through on the IRS?

HALDEMAN: Yes.

PRESIDENT NIXON: I just want to know. Okay.

HALDEMAN: No, I'm not fully satisfied with the Chotiner operation. I think we can do more there. We can talk about that.

PRESIDENT NIXON: We might put a younger guy in there.

HALDEMAN: Well, I was thinking about, you know, maybe we ought to move a Dave Young, a guy that's a little, that's straight and younger, in with Chotiner, because Dave knows where all the bodies are now.

PRESIDENT NIXON: Yes.

SEGMENT 2

HALDEMAN: What it would be good to talk about with that group is this idea of the [Warren-type] commission, or whatever it is, to review the Watergate, unless you just don't want to get into that at all, the reason being, I talked to Kleindienst and he just burst out laughing. And I said, "What's so funny?" He said, "That's been my idea for three weeks, but John Mitchell pisses on me every time I start to raise it. He thinks—he won't even listen to me." And he said, "I didn't have a commission in mind; what I had in mind was one man, and the one man I had in mind was—

PRESIDENT NIXON: Earl Warren?

HALDEMAN: No, Clark, Tom Clark. He said, "My thought was, rather than getting a commission and getting all, wallowing around and having to have a staff and everything, if you just ask Tom Clark as an individual, without setting up the apparatus, to review this stuff. . . ."

PRESIDENT NIXON: It would be a lot better if Mitchell was on this, since Mitchell is somewhat—

HALDEMAN: I think Mitchell has kind of swung over to this thing, anyway.

PRESIDENT NIXON: The commission? . . .

SEPTEMBER 14, 1972: THE PRESIDENT, NELSON ROCKEFELLER, AND EHRLICHMAN, 10:03–11:01 A.M., OVAL OFFICE

Nixon looks for support from Nelson Rockefeller and the party's wing of moderates. Rockefeller, however, is wary.

PRESIDENT NIXON: Nelson, let me fill you in. You should know these things. This record, this distressing Watergate thing, as you probably know, as you have been told today, is one of those Goddamn things that a bunch of kids (unintelligible). Here's what happened.

ROCKEFELLER: Maybe I'm better off not to know, Mr. President. Because I was asked on television yesterday whether or not I had been told not to talk, and I said look, I never talked to anybody.

PRESIDENT NIXON: Well, they are going to indict tomorrow.

EHRLICHMAN: It's iffy. That's preliminary—

PRESIDENT NIXON: Let me just say, let me just say, you can speak with great confidence on the fact that no one in a high place had a damn thing. . . . If we did, we wouldn't have been so stupid. Why are you going to attack the national committee?

EHRLICHMAN: That's of course what everybody else wonders. But still it was done.

PRESIDENT NIXON: The indictments will come down and they will involve all those lawyers. I don't want you to feel that Maury Stans—Maury Stans is *impeccable,* or John Mitchell—John Mitchell is too bright. Chuck would do it. He would not do it dumb.

ROCKEFELLER: I just don't know.

PRESIDENT NIXON: Don't worry about it.

ROCKEFELLER: But I am. I don't honestly think—

PRESIDENT NIXON: It doesn't affect a man's life, the cost of living, transportation.

ROCKEFELLER: I think they are cynical about all this stuff. They know it's going on all the time.

SEPTEMBER 14, 1972: THE PRESIDENT AND COLSON, 2:50–3:41 P.M., EXECUTIVE OFFICE BUILDING

The two men discuss plans for retaliation against the *Washington Post*.

PRESIDENT NIXON: What are you going to do about the *Washington Post?*

COLSON: Well, I don't know what we can do, but we can't do a thing before the election, you know we'll get no breaks. . . . [T]he White House has got to do something. We'll just put it in the deep freeze. What do you think?

PRESIDENT NIXON: I don't know what you can do, Chuck.

COLSON: I'd love to take them on, but is there a way you can do it?

PRESIDENT NIXON: Well, you buy the stock for sale.

COLSON: Well, they've got two classes of stock. Seventy percent of the voting powers are in stock she [Katharine Graham, principal owner] alone holds, but there is a way to get at it.

PRESIDENT NIXON: Screw around with her television license?

COLSON: Oh, yes.

PRESIDENT NIXON: How?

COLSON: Just not renew it.

PRESIDENT NIXON: Is there a way we can do that?

COLSON: Yes, sir. It has to come up for renewal every three years.

PRESIDENT NIXON: When does it come up?

COLSON: I don't know.

PRESIDENT NIXON: I hope to Christ it comes up this year.

COLSON: The sooner the quicker.

PRESIDENT NIXON: Then how would we do that?

COLSON: You put a group together with blacks in it, (unintelligible), as a way to get at her.

PRESIDENT NIXON: They shouldn't have the power. . . .

SEPTEMBER 15, 1972: THE PRESIDENT AND HALDEMAN, 9:12–9:58 A.M., OVAL OFFICE

Indictments are handed down for Watergate break-in. Nixon believes he will benefit from the Cubans' militant anti-communism in contrast to McGovern's perceived left-wing softness.

SEGMENT 1

PRESIDENT NIXON: Is the line pretty well set now on, when asked about Watergate, as to what everybody says and does, to stonewall? You were telling us whatever came in about these Cubans. I saw that news summary and I thought I'd die. It's so funny.

HALDEMAN: It really was. . . . [S]imple-minded, totally sincere, Cuban type. And they said, God, you can't not believe it. What they say, they mean what they're saying. They're not covering up anything. They're working. They've seen communism. They know what it is and they're worried about it infiltrating into this country. They were so rough that John Chancellor at the end of the thing had to say, "Well, I'm sure McGovern will have an answer to this, or something." And he was right to say it, because it was a direct—as far as the viewers [were] concerned, it was a direct challenge to McGovern: "The Democratic Committee is being used by the communists."

PRESIDENT NIXON: Which they are. Interesting.

SEGMENT 2

HALDEMAN: . . . To the people who saw it, it had to be pretty telling, because it was one guy after another, independently. And then this guy [Cuban burglar Bernard] Barker, he turned it—they said, "Why won't you tell who the people are behind this, and all?" And he turned it the other way and he said, "I don't see myself in the role of an informer." And then he turned and [said] he was worried about the communist conspiracy.

PRESIDENT NIXON: That's a good line. That's a good line. That can hurt these bastards, if they get a little of that out.

HALDEMAN: Well, it sure as hell got them on TV last night.

PRESIDENT NIXON: Was that NBC or any of the other networks?

HALDEMAN: NBC and ABC. CBS had a little of it, but not—they didn't have this devastating series of interviews. They had Barker.

PRESIDENT NIXON: But they sound very believable, the Cubans, don't they?

HALDEMAN: Oh, yeah, *totally believable.* I think they really believe it. I mean, that was their motivation.

PRESIDENT NIXON: They hate the sonofabitch.

HALDEMAN: They're afraid of McGovern. They're afraid he'll sell out to the Communists, which he will.

PRESIDENT NIXON: That's right. You know, I think we ought to—and I noticed McGovern's lawyer did it, too.

HALDEMAN: Our lawyer.

PRESIDENT NIXON: Huh?

HALDEMAN: [Henry] Rothblatt.

PRESIDENT NIXON: Sorry, our lawyer and Barker's lawyer, just knocked the shit out of him.

HALDEMAN: But he explains it, see. They get kind of tangled up and then he explains what that means. But it's clear what they mean when they say it, too. It's like Manolo [Sanchez, Nixon's manservant], they have that kind of intensity, and the accent. They're worried, sincere, and emotional. They're not talking—that's no slick cover-up and there's no way that anybody who sees it thinks that it is.

PRESIDENT NIXON: That's very good.

HALDEMAN: And Barker, whoever it was, the guy that had the *Times* interview, made that point, that these people aren't motivated by money.

SEPTEMBER 15, 1972: THE PRESIDENT, HALDEMAN, AND ZIEGLER, 3:15–4:49 P.M., OVAL OFFICE

Nixon praises John Dean a few hours before a lengthy meeting with him to receive a report on the cover-up. The President was familiar with Dean and his work, contrary to his later claims.

PRESIDENT NIXON: . . . Dean has been a real strong man in this, hasn't he?

HALDEMAN: Yes, yes. He's very good at—

PRESIDENT NIXON: He's strong.

HALDEMAN: It's been interesting to watch. He's very low key and cool about things.

PRESIDENT NIXON: He doesn't get all excited.

HALDEMAN: He's good at keeping other people calmed down, which has been probably the most key thing of all, keeping the Hugh Sloans and the Maury Stans and the [Robert] Mardians has been a big cross.

PRESIDENT NIXON: I thought we were going to get Mardian out in the field somewhere. Dry him up.

HALDEMAN: Well, we did for a while.

PRESIDENT NIXON: But then he came back.

HALDEMAN: Tiptoed back in. They've got him out in the mainstream of things. He's not been any real problem for the last month or so. . . .

SEPTEMBER 15, 1972: THE PRESIDENT, DEAN, AND HALDEMAN, 5:27–6:17 P.M., OVAL OFFICE

This fateful meeting gives the lie to Nixon's later claims that he never met John Dean until late February 1973. Dean, the cover-up's chief field officer, reports to the man on top. Seven indictments had been handed down earlier in the day. Dean promises the President a clear path, at least through the November election. He talks about his effort to quash the proceedings of Wright Patman's House Bank and Currency Committee investigation, which looked very promising. From then on, the talk is a general, familiar one of the President's advocacy of war upon his enemies. This tape was used in the 1974 criminal trial of Nixon's top aides.

PRESIDENT NIXON: Well, you had quite a day today, didn't you? You got Watergate on the way, huh?

DEAN: Quite a three months.

HALDEMAN: How did it all end up?

DEAN: Uh, I think we can say "well," at this point. The, the press is playing it just as we expect.

HALDEMAN: Whitewash?

DEAN: No, not yet; the, the story right now—

PRESIDENT NIXON: It's a big story. . . .

HALDEMAN: Five indicted—

DEAN: Plus . . . two White House aides.

HALDEMAN: Plus, the White House former guy [Hunt] and all that. That's good. That, that takes the edge off whitewash really—which—that was the thing Mitchell kept saying that . . . to those in the country, Liddy and, and Hunt are big men.

DEAN: That's right.

PRESIDENT NIXON: Yeah, they're White House aides.

DEAN: That's right. . . .

PRESIDENT NIXON: We couldn't do that (unintelligible) just remember all the trouble they gave us on this. We'll have a chance to get back at them one day. How are you doing on your other investigations? . . .

HALDEMAN: What's happened on the bug?

PRESIDENT NIXON: . . . [O]n the what?

HALDEMAN: The bug.

DEAN: The second bug. There was another bug found in the phone of, uh, the first—

PRESIDENT NIXON: You don't think it was one left over from the previous job?

DEAN: . . . The Bureau [FBI] has checked and rechecked . . . and it was not there in the instrument.

PRESIDENT NIXON: What the hell do you think is involved? What's your guess?

DEAN: I think the DNC [Democratic National Committee] did it, quite clearly.

PRESIDENT NIXON: You think they did it?

DEAN: Uh, huh.

PRESIDENT NIXON: Deliberately? . . . Well, what in the name of Christ did they think that anybody was—they really want to believe that we planted that?

HALDEMAN: Did they get anything on the fingerprints?

DEAN: No latents at all . . . . So, so, [Acting FBI Director L. Patrick] Gray is pissed now and his people are pissed off. So they're moving in because their reputation's on the line. That's, uh, I think that's a good development.

PRESIDENT NIXON: I think that's a good development because it makes it look so Goddamned phony, doesn't it? The whole—

DEAN: Absolutely.

PRESIDENT NIXON: Or am I wrong?

DEAN: No, no sir. It, it—

PRESIDENT NIXON: —looks silly. . . .

DEAN: The resources that have been put against this whole investigation to date are really incredible. It's truly a . . . larger investigation than was conducted against— the after inquiry of the JFK assassination.

PRESIDENT NIXON: Oh.

DEAN: And good statistics supporting that. Kleindienst is going to have a—

HALDEMAN: Isn't that ridiculous though?

DEAN: What is?

HALDEMAN: This silly-ass damn thing.

PRESIDENT NIXON: Yeah.

HALDEMAN: That kind of resources against—

PRESIDENT NIXON: Yeah, for Christ's sake. . . .

HALDEMAN: Who the hell cares?

PRESIDENT NIXON: Goldwater put it in context, he said "Well, for Christ's sake, everybody bugs everybody else." We know that.

DEAN: That was, that was priceless.

HALDEMAN: Yeah. I bugged—

PRESIDENT NIXON: Well, it's true. It happens to be totally true. . . . We were bugged in '68 on the plane and bugged in '62, even running for *Governor.* Goddamnedest thing you ever saw.

DEAN: It was a shame that evidence of the fact that happened in '68 was never preserved around. I understand that only the former Director had that information.

HALDEMAN: No, that's not true.

DEAN: There was direct evidence of it?

PRESIDENT NIXON: Yeah.

HALDEMAN: There's others who have that information.

PRESIDENT NIXON: Others know it.

DEAN: [Former FBI Executive Cartha] DeLoach?

PRESIDENT NIXON: DeLoach, right.

HALDEMAN: I've got some stuff on it, too, in the bombing halt study. 'Cause it's all—that's why, the, the stuff I've got we don't—

PRESIDENT NIXON: The difficulty with using it, of course, is that, it reflects on Johnson.

DEAN: Right.

PRESIDENT NIXON: He ordered it. If it weren't for that, I'd use it. Is there any way we could use it without reflecting on Johnson? How—now, could we say, could we say that the Democratic National Committee did it? No, the FBI did the bugging though.

HALDEMAN: That's the problem.

DEAN: Is it going to reflect on Johnson or Humphrey?

HALDEMAN: Johnson. Humphrey didn't do it.

DEAN: Humphrey didn't do it?

PRESIDENT NIXON: Oh, hell no.

HALDEMAN: He was bugging Humphrey, too [laughs].

PRESIDENT NIXON: Perhaps the Bureau ought to go over—[noise]

HALDEMAN: The Bureau ought to go into Edward Bennett Williams and let's start questioning that sonofabitch. Keep him tied up for a couple of weeks. . . .

DEAN: Another interesting thing that's developed is, regarding the private litigation we've got is the [Maurice] Stans libel action was assigned to Judge [Charles] Richey.

PRESIDENT NIXON: Oh, Christ.

DEAN: Well, now, that's good and bad. Uh, Judge Richey is not known to be one of the intellects on the bench. That's conceded by many that he is . . . .

PRESIDENT NIXON: (Unintelligible) in his own stupid way he's sort of, uh . . . .

DEAN: Three months ago I would have had trouble predicting where we'd be today. I think that I can say that fifty-four days [Election Day] from now that not a thing will come crashing down to our, our surprise.

PRESIDENT NIXON: Say what?

DEAN: Nothing is going to come crashing down to our surprise, either—

PRESIDENT NIXON: Well, the whole thing is a can of worms, as you know. A lot of this stuff went on. . . . [B]ut the way you, you've handled it, it seems to me, has been very skillful, because you—putting your fingers in the dikes every time that leaks have sprung there. . . . The Grand Jury is dismissed now?

DEAN: That is correct. They'll, they will have completed and they will let them go, so there will be no continued investigation prompted by the Grand Jury's inquiry. The, uh, GAO [General Accounting Office] report that was referred over to Justice is on a shelf right now because they have hundreds of violations. They've got violations of McGovern's; they've got violations of Humphrey's; they've got Jackson violations, and several hundred congressional violations. They don't want to start prosecuting one any more than they want the other. So that's, uh—

PRESIDENT NIXON: They damn well not prosecute us unless they prosecute all the others. . . .

What about, uh, uh, watching the McGovern contributors and all that sort of thing?

DEAN: We've got a, we've got a hawk's eye on that.

PRESIDENT NIXON: Yeah.

DEAN: And, uh, he is, he is not in full compliance.

PRESIDENT NIXON: He isn't?

DEAN: No . . . .

PRESIDENT NIXON: They should just, just behave and, and, recognize this—this is, again, this is war. We're getting a few short and it'll be over, and we'll give them a few shots and it'll be over. Don't worry. I wouldn't want to be on the other side right now. Would you? I wouldn't want to be in Edward Bennett Williams's position after this election.

DEAN: No. No.

PRESIDENT NIXON: None of these bastards—

DEAN: He, uh, he's done some rather unethical things that have come to light already, which in—again, [Judge] Richey has brought to our attention.

PRESIDENT NIXON: Yeah.

DEAN: He went down—

HALDEMAN: Keep a log on all that.

DEAN: Oh, we are, indeed. Yeah. . . .

HALDEMAN: Because afterwards that's the guy,

PRESIDENT NIXON: We're going after him.

HALDEMAN: That's the guy we've got to ruin. . . .

PRESIDENT NIXON: You want to remember, too, he's an attorney for the *Washington Post.*

DEAN: I'm well aware of that.

PRESIDENT NIXON: I think we are going to fix the sonofabitch. Believe me. We are going to. We've got to, because he's a bad man.

DEAN: Absolutely.

PRESIDENT NIXON: He misbehaved very badly in the Hoffa matter. Our—some pretty bad conduct, there, too, but go ahead.

DEAN: Well, that's, uh, along that line, uh, one of the things I've tried to do, is just keep notes on a lot of the people who are emerging as—

PRESIDENT NIXON: That's right.

DEAN:—as less than our friends.

PRESIDENT NIXON: Great.

DEAN: Because this is going to be over some day and they're—we shouldn't forget the way that some of them (unintelligible)—

PRESIDENT NIXON: I want the most, I want the most comprehensive notes on all of those that have tried to do us in. Because they didn't have to do it.

DEAN: That's right.

PRESIDENT NIXON: They didn't have to do it. I mean, if . . . they had a very close election everybody on the other side would understand this game. But now [they] are doing this quite deliberately and they are asking for it and they are going to get it. And this, this—we, we have not used the power in this first four years, as you know.

DEAN: That's true.

PRESIDENT NIXON: We have never used it. We haven't used the Bureau and we haven't used the Justice Department, but things are going to change now. And they're going to change, and, and they're going to get it right—

DEAN: That's an exciting prospect.

PRESIDENT NIXON: It's got to be done. It's the only thing to do.

HALDEMAN: We've got to.

PRESIDENT NIXON: Oh, oh, well, we've just been, we've been just Goddamn fools. For us to come into this election campaign and not do anything with regard to the Democratic Senators who are running, and so forth. They're, they're crooks, they've been stealing, they've been taking (unintelligible). That's ridiculous. Absolutely ridiculous. It's not going, going to be that way any more . . . .

DEAN: I, I suppose the other area we are going to see some publicity on in the coming weeks because, uh, I think after the, now that the indictments are down, there's going to be a cresting on that. The whitewash charge of course, but I think we can handle that while the civil case is in abeyance. But [Congressman Wright] Patman's hearings, his Banking and Currency Committee, and we've got to—whether we will be successful or not in turning that off, I don't know. We've got a plan whereby [Henry] Rothblatt and [William] Bittman, who are counsel for the five men who were, or actually a total of seven, that were indicted today, are going to go up and visit every member and say, "If you commence hearings you are going to jeopardize the civil rights of these individuals in the worst way, and they'll never get a fair trial," and the like, and try to talk to members on, on that level. Uh—

PRESIDENT NIXON: Why not ask that they request to be heard by, by the Committee and explain it publicly?

DEAN: Publicly, they've planned that. What they're going to say is, "If you do commence with these hearings, we plan to publicly come up and say what you're doing to the rights of individuals." Something to that effect . . . .

PRESIDENT NIXON: How about trying to get the criminal cases, criminal charges dismissed on the grounds that there, well, you know—

HALDEMAN: The civil rights type stuff.

DEAN: Civil rights—well, that, we're working again, we've got somebody approaching the ACLU for these guys, and have them go up and exert some pressure because we just don't want Stans up there in front of the cameras with Patman and Patman asking all these questions. It's just going to be the whole thing, the press going over and over and over again. One suggestion was that [John] Connally is, is close to Patman and probably if anybody could talk turkey with Patman, Connally might be able to. Now I don't know if that's a good idea or not. I don't think he— don't know if he can. Jerry Ford is not really taking an active interest in this matter that, that is developing, so Stans can go see Jerry Ford and try to brief him and explain to him the problems he's got. And then the other thing we are going to do is we're looking at all the campaign reports of every member of that Committee because we are convinced that none of them have probably totally complied with the law either.

And if they want to get into it, if they want to play rough, some day we better say, "Well, gentlemen, we think we ought to call to your attention that you haven't complied with A, B, C, D, E, and F, and we're not going to hold that a secret if you start talking campaign violations here."

PRESIDENT NIXON: Uh, what about Ford? Do you think so? Do you think he can do anything with Patman? Connally can't be sent up there.

HALDEMAN: No. . . .

DEAN: That would be very helpful, to get our minority side at least together on the thing.

PRESIDENT NIXON: Jerry's really got to lead on this. He's got to really lead.

HALDEMAN: Jerry should, damn it. This is exactly the thing he was talking about, that the reason they are staying in is so that they can—

PRESIDENT NIXON: That's right.

HALDEMAN:—run investigations.

PRESIDENT NIXON: Well, the point is that they ought to raise hell about this, uh, this—these hearings are jeopardizing the—I don't know that . . . the counsel calling on the members of the Committee will do much good. I was, I—it may be all right but—I was thinking that they really ought to blunderbuss it in the public arena. You know what I mean, publicize.

DEAN: Right.

HALDEMAN: Good.

DEAN: Right.

PRESIDENT NIXON: That's what this is, public relations. . . .

HALDEMAN: . . . It has been kept away from the White House almost completely and from the President totally. The only tie to the White House has been the Colson effort they keep trying to haul in. . . .

DEAN: The two former White House people, low level, indicted, one consultant and one member of the Domestic Council staff. That's not very much of a tie.

HALDEMAN: No.

PRESIDENT NIXON: Well, their names have been already mentioned. . . . You, know, they've already been convicted in the press. . . . Goddamn it, if they'd been Communists you'd have the *Washington Post* and the *New York Times* raising hell about their civil rights.

DEAN: That's right.

PRESIDENT NIXON: Or [Charles] Manson. . . .

DEAN: . . . [I]t'd be just, you know, just a tragedy to let Patman have a field day up there.

PRESIDENT NIXON: What's the first move? When does he call his wit—witnesses?

DEAN: Well, he, he has not even gotten the vote of his Committee; he hasn't convened his Committee yet on whether he can call hearings. That's why, come Monday morning, these attorneys are going to arrive on the doorstep of the Chairman and try to tell him what he's doing if he proceeds. One of the members, Garry Brown [R-MI] wrote Kleindienst a letter saying, "If the Chairman holds Committee hearings on this, isn't this going to jeopardize your criminal case?"

PRESIDENT NIXON: Brown's a smart fellow. He's from, he's from Michigan—

DEAN: That's right.

PRESIDENT NIXON:—and some tie into Ford. He's very, he's a very smart fellow. Good.

DEAN: Good lawyer and he's being helpful. He is anxious to help.

PRESIDENT NIXON: Right, just tell him that, tell, tell, tell Ehrlichman to get Brown in and Ford in and then they can all work out something, but they ought to get off their asses and push it. No use to let Patman have a free ride here. . . .

SEPTEMBER 16, 1972: THE PRESIDENT AND ROBERT FINCH, 11:26–11:48 A.M., OVAL OFFICE

Nixon learns of a second telephone tap planted in Watergate. He tells former Cabinet member, now White House aide, Robert Finch that he hopes the Democrats themselves had installed it or, better yet, his people "could find a woman" to blame.

PRESIDENT NIXON: How about you? Are you going to finesse Watergate all right?

FINCH: I just say we're going to get the FBI report in, that if action is required it'll be taken.

PRESIDENT NIXON: Well, they're going to indict today, I understand. You know, the committee [CREEP] is saying they found another bug. Christ, I beg this is one they [Democrats] planted themselves.

FINCH: I think they must have. Christ, they'll do anything to keep the story alive. I wish we could prove it.

PRESIDENT NIXON: Wouldn't it be great if you could find a woman—well, it's too much (unintelligible).

SEPTEMBER 20, 1972: THE PRESIDENT AND COLSON, 8:03–8:30 A.M., WHITE HOUSE TELEPHONE

Nixon and Colson discuss McGovern's campaign woes and their own plans to further disrupt the Democrats' campaign.

COLSON: Of course, he [McGovern] had one hell of a bad day, Mr. President.

PRESIDENT NIXON: Today?

COLSON: Yes, sir. He got confronted in an assembly line.

PRESIDENT NIXON: What happened?

COLSON: Oh, God. It was three minutes of CBS tonight, the finest television commercial I have ever seen in my life. We couldn't buy it if we tried.

PRESIDENT NIXON: Really?

COLSON: Yes, sir. He was walking through an assembly plant—

PRESIDENT NIXON: Why did they have him doing that, the stupid assholes?

COLSON: Well, but every place he goes—

PRESIDENT NIXON: He's a candidate for President.

COLSON: That's right. And [Vice Presidential candidate Sargent] Shriver is getting the same treatment.

PRESIDENT NIXON: So what happened?

COLSON: This is one aspect of our campaign operation that's working very effectively. I noticed one of the wires tonight said that we were responsible for that. They didn't say that on TV. He went through the plant and as they stopped—

PRESIDENT NIXON: What kind of plant was it?

COLSON: Let's see. The Formica plant in Columbus.

PRESIDENT NIXON: Oh, that was last night, I think. But anyway, that doesn't make any difference. A plant. What happened?

COLSON: Western Electric plant, Columbus, Ohio. And an employee shouted at him and said, "Why are you going to give amnesty to these traitors?" And McGovern stopped and started to debate with him, and he said—well, there's several accounts on the wires. They're all different. I guess he had several confrontations in the plant.

One of the best ones, he said, "Why are you giving amnesty to traitors?" And then he [McGovern] got very angry and apparently he stopped and said, "There is nothing I wouldn't do if it would get those prisoners out one day earlier," McGovern said. [First name unknown] Grover asked if that wasn't negotiating from weakness and would hurt U.S. prestige. He said, "I'm not trying to save face." Then he said that you—he said Nixon's engaging in slow surrender.

PRESIDENT NIXON: Oh, Christ.

COLSON: And these people said, "Well, you're giving up the country, you're surrendering, and let's bomb hell out of them." And McGovern said, "Bomb hell out of people, why?" And the employee said, "Right, we should bomb hell out of them a lot more and get our boys home." He said, "Well, listen; do you think that's going to get the prisoners out?" Employee: "Yes, I do, that's right; Nixon wants to show them we have a power over here and we're not just a flunky second-rate country."

Then the man went on and was interviewed and said Nixon was right the way he was handling Vietnam, that McGovern was wrong, that it was a surrender. Oh, God, he just cut the hell out of him. And apparently it was quite—I've got four pages of wire service story. The press had picked it up and carried it very extensively. Unfortunately, CBS was the only network that got it. We checked this afternoon.

PRESIDENT NIXON: That's all right.

COLSON: But that's damn good coverage, extensive.

PRESIDENT NIXON: Just on that issue, that's what I want. I want a little on that issue. . . .

COLSON: But he's [McGovern] crazy to be walking through these plants, and he's going to get it every place he goes. He's got a little thing that he'll encounter in Detroit this week. Shriver has been getting it everywhere.

PRESIDENT NIXON: The same thing?

COLSON: Yes, the same thing. Detroit, he's going to run into a little busing squabble when he goes in there tomorrow night.

SEPTEMBER 24, 1972: THE PRESIDENT AND HALDEMAN, 3:30–4:46 P.M., CAMP DAVID

More discussion of campaign tactics, including turning anti-Nixon demonstrations to the President's advantage.

SEGMENT 1

HALDEMAN: And we have a problem in California in the demonstrator thing which makes it very difficult. We were going to build a crowd in San Francisco at the hotel when we arrived. We can't do it, and I've been going over that today, the problem being that there's a major demonstration planned and it's a violent demonstration. They plan to try—they plan to try to forcibly prohibit the people from getting to the luncheon, and then they plan to forcibly prohibit you from getting to the luncheon and to stone your car and a lot of stuff.

PRESIDENT NIXON: Who are these people?

HALDEMAN: It's the super-Yippie types.

PRESIDENT NIXON: Are we going to hang McGovern on it?

HALDEMAN: We already have. Did you hear what happened?

PRESIDENT NIXON: About the thing in Los Angeles?

HALDEMAN: See, that sets the groundwork.

PRESIDENT NIXON: But you don't understand. I didn't see it, though, in the press.

HALDEMAN: It was in the paper. There was a box in the paper that reported it, just as a straight wire story, that they had ordered them to stop using the phones. Well, that's fine. It was on the radio heavily yesterday—

PRESIDENT NIXON: Was it?

HALDEMAN: On the newscasts, yes.

PRESIDENT NIXON: Well, let me say, don't track the crowds where there are going to be demonstrations.

HALDEMAN: We're not, we're not.

PRESIDENT NIXON: I think I should just go right in there and get the Secret Service to—

HALDEMAN: What we're doing instead is we're playing the threat game there and the Yippie game. We're saying that there have been threats, and the San Francisco police are fully cooperative. They're very rough police anyway.

PRESIDENT NIXON: Are they?

HALDEMAN: And you can't fool with them. . . .

PRESIDENT NIXON: Will the Mayor back you? . . .

HALDEMAN: The Mayor will on this one. And the police, what they have decreed is that there is to be nobody allowed within a block of the hotel because of this demonstration threat. Dave Packard is very strong on not trying to turn any of our crowd out. What I am trying to do is that we've got it set for all these events we're going to have a group of young people in the next room. It'll be the Youth for Nixon types, that'll be allowed in to the dinners.

PRESIDENT NIXON: I noticed you had a couple hundred in the yard, right?

HALDEMAN: And there would be the same thing in L.A. and the same thing in San

Francisco. Now, what we'll do is those kids will have tickets, so they'll get through the police line and into the hotel. And just before you arrive, we'll run them out to the front of the hotel, and they can whoop it up when you pull up. And a few hundred at the hotel entrance, wildly enthusiastic, are going to look and sound as good as if we had had a big rally there. We can't stage a people thing.

PRESIDENT NIXON: Good.

SEGMENT 2

PRESIDENT NIXON: . . . Where do they get these Yippies, Bob? They're the same group that hit us in Santa Fe, isn't it, the same kind?

HALDEMAN: Yeah, same kind of people. They're violent. They're based in San Francisco.

PRESIDENT NIXON: Are they students?

HALDEMAN: Mostly non-students. They work the students. They use the students. They foment the students.

PRESIDENT NIXON: I mean, are they dopies?

HALDEMAN: They were. I don't know if they still are or not. They probably are—I imagine they are. They're on that dope culture probably the same way.

PRESIDENT NIXON: Okay. They turned them out. What do you think McGovern's let them do it for?

HALDEMAN: I'm not so sure he has any control.

PRESIDENT NIXON: Why, they're his. I think he's got control.

HALDEMAN: Maybe just to disrupt you, just so you don't get a free ride.

PRESIDENT NIXON: Why didn't they do it in Texas? Unbelievable.

HALDEMAN: That totally baffled me, why they didn't have the Mexicans, because there, hell, you could buy a batch of demonstrators.

SEPTEMBER 29, 1972: THE PRESIDENT, COLSON, AND HALDEMAN, 12:17–2:03 P.M., OVAL OFFICE

Nixon hears reports about radical McGovern demonstrators and savors how this works to the Democrats' disadvantage.

PRESIDENT NIXON: Well, they burned down your headquarters in Phoenix last night.

COLSON: Oh, really?

PRESIDENT NIXON: Burned it down.

COLSON: Do we know who did it?

HALDEMAN: Not yet.

PRESIDENT NIXON: Nobody got hurt. Good. . . . It's getting rough.

COLSON: It was destroyed by arson.

PRESIDENT NIXON: I know you don't want to—we talked about not exploiting, but there certainly is an indication with the press, at least that I saw this summer, that the McGovern people were responsible for those demonstrators.

COLSON: You got it in ahead of time.

HALDEMAN: And we pushed maybe too much, and that's Chuck's analysis and I agree, that we—

PRESIDENT NIXON: Can't push it.

HALDEMAN: Well, we did push it, and we didn't get it even with pushing it.

PRESIDENT NIXON: They [the media] don't want to use it.

COLSON: They won't use it.

HALDEMAN: They won't use it, and the closest we've come to is they start playing it back the other way.

COLSON: They make more news, unfortunately, but the media, this is one area that they're going to screw us on. They made more news out of the fact that we were exploiting it than the fact itself.

PRESIDENT NIXON: What do you want to do, just let them have it? . . . Dick Moore went out and looked them over and he said: Hell, that wasn't an anti-war rally. He said he saw the signs: ITT, Watergate. . . .

HALDEMAN: It was a McGovern rally. It was an anti-Nixon rally, not an anti-war rally at all. But combined with the pictures, it would be good. Combined with it are these Communists. Remember I told you, I've got pictures of the Communists. I mean, they really were Communists, big red banners lettered in yellow, just like in China, cloth banners that they hold up, huge banners, that said: "Communism must win in Southeast Asia." That's one of them.

COLSON: Was that at this one?

HALDEMAN: At the Century Plaza. And they had another big thing saying "All workers unite for socialism." It looked the same as with Mao.

PRESIDENT NIXON: I would think that [Los Angeles television newscaster] George Putnam would put that on his show.

HALDEMAN: He might very well have done so. . . .

PRESIDENT NIXON: I think the McGovern people are radical. They're going to get Goddamn extreme right now.

COLSON: I don't know. I'm sure some of them are.

HALDEMAN: But a lot of it is the frustration—the kids, most of the demonstrators at the Century Plaza were not radical, were not extreme; typical kids out for a thing, like most of the demonstrators here, even in the hard days.

PRESIDENT NIXON: And very small crowds. . . .

OCTOBER 7, 1972: THE PRESIDENT AND COLSON, 12:33–1:00 P.M., CAMP DAVID TELEPHONE

A "dirty trick": manipulating poll data to "sandbag" the McGovern campaign

COLSON: Well, we did a little dirty trick this morning.

PRESIDENT NIXON: Of course, everybody should say, "We expect the Harris Poll to show a 10-point closing." Is that what you did?

COLSON: No. What we did is we had someone from the *Chicago Tribune Syndicate* phone Gary Hart and tell him that the spread is going to be 19 points and it's great news for McGovern because he's gaining rapidly. I hope that he will go out and have a press conference and talk about the closing of the polls just before the damn thing hits Monday showing— [*laughter*]

PRESIDENT NIXON: 27 [points].

COLSON: It'll sandbag him. Jesus, it'll sandbag him.

PRESIDENT NIXON: Sandbag them always, that's right.

OCTOBER 13, 1972: THE PRESIDENT AND COLSON, 7:26–7:28 P.M., WHITE HOUSE TELEPHONE

Nixon listens to reports of violence by McGovern supporters and considers how to use this for his own media advantage.

COLSON: And we're continuing to get out the stories of what they've done to us. I've now just gone through it, just finished going through it. We've got some good white papers on what they've done to our headquarters. God, I didn't realize they'd done so much. Now that you see it all written out, truly they've raised a lot of hell with us—Molotov cocktail at the door of one of our headquarters in California. A number of threats, a number of phone threats have got in, a couple of headquarters burned. And of course, we know organizing the anti-war demonstrators.

PRESIDENT NIXON: Sure, sure.

COLSON: People marching throughout state headquarters in Boston.

PRESIDENT NIXON: Did they do that?

COLSON: Yes, sir. We put that down. Arlington, Massachusetts, they broke our storefront operation apart. So we've got all of these and we'll put it out.

PRESIDENT NIXON: They're engaging in violence.

COLSON: Oh, yes. That's the point that I want to get Dole and MacGregor Monday to make as an answer to this fellow, that, Goddamn it, you know, they can accuse us of pranks and they're not true, that's one thing; but my God, these are violent activities.

PRESIDENT NIXON: And the thing is for Dole and MacGregor to attack the press on this.

COLSON: I think they have to.

PRESIDENT NIXON: They have to attack the press for its double standard.

COLSON: Yes, I think it's the only way.

PRESIDENT NIXON: And by making it an all-out assault on the press for their double standard and the rest and say, now, come on, you're going to report this campaign, let's report what's happening. . . .

COLSON: Yes. I think we could say that the press seems to have become obsessed with what would normally be regarded as gossip column humor. And my God, there are serious things going on in this campaign that aren't being reported.

PRESIDENT NIXON: Right.

COLSON: Just go through this whole litany. I think we can make some points on it. Maybe that's just what will be needed.

OCTOBER 15, 1972: THE PRESIDENT AND HALDEMAN, 9:16–10:55 A.M., CAMP DAVID

Nixon and Haldeman note how events connect. They discuss media revelations of Donald Segretti's campaign "dirty tricks," his links to White House aide Dwight Chapin, and Segretti's receipt of money from Herbert Kalmbach, the White House bagman, usually identified as the President's personal attorney. "[A]ll these little strings," Haldeman notes, "one leads to another." Nixon typically complains that he is a victim of a media double standard.

PRESIDENT NIXON: One thing we did do I think rather cleverly was to review O'Brien's income tax returns. I think that's why he's so Goddamn silent.

HALDEMAN: That's right.

PRESIDENT NIXON: And we followed up.

HALDEMAN: O'Brien is very interesting. Since he's been in there, there may have been a couple of squeaks out of him and that's all. . . .

PRESIDENT NIXON: What is the situation on [Donald] Segretti? I think that's really a shocking Goddamn story on [Dwight] Chapin this morning.

HALDEMAN: Yes.

PRESIDENT NIXON: All hearsay, but hearsay or not. Segretti went to school with Chapin?

HALDEMAN: Yes.

PRESIDENT NIXON: Segretti, what is he, rabid? What, did he get mad about something?

HALDEMAN: No. . . .

PRESIDENT NIXON: Well, for Christ sakes, that's where the problem is. Remember, I told you all the time the kids around our shop talk too much.

HALDEMAN: They just don't—the people in our shop didn't talk at all.

PRESIDENT NIXON: Well, Segretti was in our shop.

HALDEMAN: Not really.

PRESIDENT NIXON: Okay.

HALDEMAN: He was a guy they had working out as a solo lone operator.

PRESIDENT NIXON: Remember I told you, Bob, after the '68 campaign, it's like [campaign aides Leonard] Garment and [Frank] Shakespeare talking to that asshole that wrote the book [Joe McGinness, *The Selling of the President*] on the other thing. They asked somebody—you've got to check the loyalty of people before you ever confide on confidential matters. . . .

HALDEMAN: Segretti, just so you know, is incommunicado, but he calls John Dean from a public phone and calls onto a line that's not traceable or whatever here, every day around noon. So that there's no way we can reach Segretti, but we can get him every day. And he can be—he'll do anything. I'm told he was supposedly the ideal guy for this kind of thing. He had just gotten out of the Army and he was a guy that loves this sort of college prank politics. Chapin had known him in campus politics at SC [University of Southern California] and so did [Gordon] Strachan. He was a fraternity brother of Strachan's, but not of Chapin's. So they recruited him. . . .

PRESIDENT NIXON: What does [Herbert] Kalmbach say? Is he tied there as attorney for the President? How does he handle it? . . .

HALDEMAN: . . . That was why we got the guy, this man we got, because he was one to take outside, get him paid outside, and get him completely away from the place, that could be trusted. And he was trusted and he worked fine. He was doing—there was another problem in there, and this may have some bearing. Liddy was setting up the same kind of operation at 1701 [Re-election Committee headquarters]. This guy was not working with them. He was working as a total independent operator.

PRESIDENT NIXON: Just for that—

HALDEMAN: Moving on his own.

PRESIDENT NIXON: I think you better . . . get the story ready on Kalmbach as to what funds he was using. . . .

HALDEMAN: He crossed wires somewhere with Liddy's people and Liddy was rather vicious and informed somebody—I remember the time with John Dean or somebody. He said, "There's some guy out in the field sabotaging what we're doing, and my people are going to kill him. So if there's any way that he's our guy, you better find out because he's going to be in serious jeopardy."

PRESIDENT NIXON: You mean Segretti is different, working a different field than Liddy?

HALDEMAN: Well, he was. So then Dean or somebody checked it out and found out he was working as our guy, and they did tell Liddy that and I think that Segretti started working with Liddy. They screwed up some things in the primaries. The other thing on this is Colson didn't even know it was being done and he was doing some of his own separate [things].

PRESIDENT NIXON: That's good. . . .

HALDEMAN: Unfortunately, it kind of all came together, and Liddy—that's what we've been concerned about, is all these little strings that we have. One leads to another. . . .

PRESIDENT NIXON: You see, Bob, I thought of the charge (unintelligible), but we've tried that and they are not going to buy it. There's a double standard, so I just think we've got to sort of brazen it through. They're not going to be likely to raise any big fuss on the other side about this. I wish it were otherwise.

HALDEMAN: I'm afraid you're right.

PRESIDENT NIXON: If there were any fairness in the press, it would be different, Bob. But it isn't going to be that way.

HALDEMAN: Well, the problem is that the press that would be fair with it don't do anything with the story at all. . . .

PRESIDENT NIXON: I've always felt that the leak is at the FBI.

HALDEMAN: We've talked to—Ehrlichman's talked to Gray, and Gray now I think—I shouldn't say this because I'm not sure. It's my understanding that Gray has submitted to Ehrlichman that he now believes that it's an FBI leak. That's an internal process there. . . .

PRESIDENT NIXON: Meanwhile, Kalmbach—what's he have to say?

HALDEMAN: Kalmbach doesn't have to say a Goddamn thing.

PRESIDENT NIXON: No, no, no, no. I know that. I'm not concerned about his saying. It's a question whether what he says is—if the lawyer for the President is involved in putting up the money, that's a bad story.

HALDEMAN: Right.

PRESIDENT NIXON: Pretty Goddamn close. That was my concern, Bob. If, however, a fundraiser for the President's Committee to Re-Elect or something was doing it, that's not as bad a story. . . .

HALDEMAN: I think they have a statement from Kalmbach. I don't know if he's tied into this (unintelligible).

PRESIDENT NIXON: . . . You understand—

HALDEMAN: —the precise nature of Kalmbach's role is.

PRESIDENT NIXON: Right.

HALDEMAN: Kalmbach's statement.

PRESIDENT NIXON: Yes, that's the most important thing.

OCTOBER 16, 1972: THE PRESIDENT AND HALDEMAN, 8:50–9:20 A.M., OVAL OFFICE

The two men periodically had conversations that seem to have been contrived and staged for taping to reiterate what they did or did not know. In this exchange, Nixon goes to elaborate lengths to disassociate himself from recently revealed campaign dirty tricks and the Watergate break-in. He interrogates Haldeman as if he is conducting his own investigation, and Haldeman dutifully denies any White House involvement. For Nixon, rough campaign tactics fall within the bounds of American politics' "little games," he calls it—yet he realizes that the Watergate incident posed more serious problems.

SEGMENT 1

PRESIDENT NIXON: What is the present analysis of it? I know of course the main problem is to give Ziegler a position on how to talk before he goes out, so that he's positioned as to what he should say. But what is the present analysis?

HALDEMAN: Well, the present basic strategy is Ziegler is going to go out with a very strong personal reaction of indignance and disgust, really.

PRESIDENT NIXON: Let me ask. Let me say a couple, three things that occurred to me as I read, as I deliberately thought, I better read these for a change. The main thing they are trying to do is to try to tie it to me personally; and second, to indicate that I was not telling the truth. You may not have gotten this, when I said that nobody in the White House was in it.

HALDEMAN: Correct, right. The way to have to do that is to link the spaghetti [Segretti] thing with the Watergate.

PRESIDENT NIXON: Which they're trying to do, correct? Now, let me ask a question. Are they linked?

HALDEMAN: No.

PRESIDENT NIXON: Under no circumstances? Nobody here knew about it?

HALDEMAN: No.

PRESIDENT NIXON: Because I don't want to have any Goddamn lying.

HALDEMAN: On the Watergate, no.

PRESIDENT NIXON: Okay.

HALDEMAN: And they are not linked, except in the sense that Howard Hunt—

PRESIDENT NIXON: Worked on both.

HALDEMAN: —worked on both, I guess, because he apparently was in contact with Segretti.

PRESIDENT NIXON: I just want to know whether Chapin or you guys were involved in Watergate.

HALDEMAN: No, sir.

PRESIDENT NIXON: That's the important thing.

HALDEMAN: Chapin hasn't been linked. Chapin has been linked to Segretti.

PRESIDENT NIXON: No Watergate, fine. Nobody here's on the Watergate?

HALDEMAN: No.

PRESIDENT NIXON: Well, everyone is assuming that it was basically the Committee.

HALDEMAN: That's for sure.

PRESIDENT NIXON: I just don't want Ziegler to lie about this. I don't want anybody to lie about Watergate, you know what I mean?

HALDEMAN: Right.

PRESIDENT NIXON: If we are, we've got to admit it, you know what I mean, because I have said it and I'm out there on a limb. That's the only thing I'm concerned about. Now, I don't care about the little games. I mean, that's their job. I mean, they've got to play the games and so forth. Now, are we absolutely clear on that, Bob?

HALDEMAN: Yes.

PRESIDENT NIXON: Nobody is on Watergate. Chapin, what will he say? He'll say a person that's not in the Watergate. Then what is he going to say about the others? He'll say—this is hearsay. What's he going to say about Kalmbach. How does he handle that? . . .

HALDEMAN: Oh, it's clear this *Time* stuff comes out, has to come out of Justice or the FBI. It's a different story.

PRESIDENT NIXON: How did they get it? All right.

HALDEMAN: The Kalmbach involvement is another . . . way to try to tie it to you, too. But Kalmbach also has nothing to do with the Watergate, as I understand it. . . . [T]he whole line of the press taking this on—

PRESIDENT NIXON: Guilt by association.

HALDEMAN: Guilt by association.

PRESIDENT NIXON: They went to the same college, right, and (unintelligible), University of Southern California. I just wanted to remind you that she [Pat Nixon] is also a graduate of the University of Southern California, and so is O. J. Simpson, (unintelligible). Now, the second line. What are they going to say again? The main thing, you have to live with it now, Bob. That's the main thing. So tell them the truth, don't tell any more than you need to, but tell exactly what you need to.

HALDEMAN: Well, I'm not going to tell anything, because the White House should not bargain. The plan is to straight-arm all the questions. There's no intention of answering anything, of getting to the merits or identification of any of these people. It's to get to: What the hell is the press doing, building its case on this thing?

He's [Ziegler] going to be very outraged about this whole thing. Then he'll be asked, is the President outraged, and he's going to say, I'm not going to characterize the President's position; I'm speaking for myself on this. But I can tell you that the President doesn't concern himself with press matters; that's my job. The President's concerned about the issues in this election, and in that regard it's very disturbing to see the issues being ignored while this obsession—

PRESIDENT NIXON: I would say, not ignored, but evaded. Evaded, not ignored, because the opposition obviously feels it doesn't have a good case on the issues, the opposition press, put it that way, put it that way. The opposition media feels it doesn't have a good case in the media, so they're talking about, so they're trying to make up a phony case.

HALDEMAN: Then we were just talking to MacGregor about the idea of MacGregor going out and pulling out all the stops on the double standard, and where are the front page stories about the rash of burnings of Republican headquarters, breaking in, and all the other side of the story.

PRESIDENT NIXON: The attacks.

HALDEMAN: The attacks, the mobilization of demonstrators, the obscenity shouters, and the attempts to shout down the President at rallies. . . . The shouting of obscenities at his family.

PRESIDENT NIXON: The first lady and members of his family. . . .

HALDEMAN: But you put it in a different term. You say: You [the media] get very upset about some young guy who is out sending pizzas to somebody's fundraising dinner, and then you can turn attention to that and say, well, we love pizzas at our fundraising dinners, for the Italians. But you get all excited about that, but nobody seems to be concerned about the—

PRESIDENT NIXON: What kind of tactics are we really talking about here? I don't really have any ideas about it. I never heard that any of this was particularly effective.

HALDEMAN: Apparently there was in the primaries, but Ehrlichman has turned that and will stay with that line, too, that it's hard to believe that you could pin, when you have Hubert Humphrey, Ed Muskie, and George McGovern running very hard against the others—

PRESIDENT NIXON: And Henry Jackson.

HALDEMAN: —it's hard to believe that we would be very much concerned with one or the other. There's other people with far stronger motives. . . . Oh, they get into the disruption of rallies, the planting of people in headquarters of one candidate to spy and report to another candidate, the diversion of crowds, the disruption of meetings, by telling people the meeting's been canceled or the candidate isn't going to come. . . .

PRESIDENT NIXON: And as a matter of fact, and also, let the record show that the President has spoken out strongly and issued instructions to all of his people against violence, disruption of rallies, heckling, et cetera, across the country. And you will note that there has not been any. You see my point? The opposition has been absolutely mum. It has failed to call off. You see what I mean? As a matter of fact, on the other side, the President's attitude has been indicated that he has given orders that are being carried out: no disruption.

You understand what I mean? No disruption, no violence, no heckling of the candidates. I know it's hard to handle, but I think it's really very important to have in mind the fact that we cannot be in the position of condoning what was done.

HALDEMAN: No.

PRESIDENT NIXON: Because people think it's worse than it was, and that's the whole point. Now, it wasn't. The whole point is, the second point is, of course, you cannot—you've got to separate it from Watergate and point out that there is huge investigation here and all these people have given statements—well—

HALDEMAN: That's the area he's going to get into, too.

PRESIDENT NIXON: He is?

HALDEMAN: Well, the point that—

PRESIDENT NIXON: And what is he going to say about this? Was the President aware of this kind of activity? What's he going to say?

HALDEMAN: Certainly not.

PRESIDENT NIXON: Right. Does he approve of this kind of activity?

HALDEMAN: Certainly not.

PRESIDENT NIXON: What about the funds for it? What's he going to say?

HALDEMAN: See, he's going to take this attack and he's going to say: I'm not going to get into all these things. You can report that I have denied—refused to answer twenty-nine times, if you want to. You can report this. But I want to say this, and go back the other way. The idea is to hit this hard today by Ziegler here and by MacGregor outside, and then not to say anything, say we've covered that, now let's turn to the issues. . . .

PRESIDENT NIXON: We're running a high road campaign. There's been no name-calling. We're hard-hitting on the issues. And we're up against the dirtiest, libelous, most libelous, slanderous, attack on the President in the history of American politics, and the press is strangely silent on it, most especially the Eastern establishment press. The Eastern establishment, you've got that? . . . . The Eastern establishment press is strangely silent. It's the *Post,* it's the *Times,* it's the *New York Times.* That's the Eastern establishment press, and the *St. Louis Post-Dispatch,* right? There is no more Eastern establishment press than that. That's it, the Eastern establishment press. It's totally on an adverse course.

OCTOBER 16, 1972: THE PRESIDENT, HALDEMAN, AND EHRLICHMAN, 11:44 A.M.–12:45 P.M., OVAL OFFICE

Segretti's story, according to him, had been given to the *Post* by an attorney he had consulted. This prompted Nixon to push a pet idea of filing a libel suit as a tactical matter. When he started law practice in New York, he argued the famous case of *Time v. Hill* (1966) before the Supreme Court. He advanced remarkable notions of privacy. He eventually lost and inevitably viewed the case as another setback to him from the media. Here, Nixon also talks about a successful 1962 campaign-practices lawsuit filed against him and Haldeman following the California gubernatorial election.

EHRLICHMAN: Dean had a talk with Segretti this morning. Segretti feels he's been jobbed. He didn't talk to this guy except as an attorney, he says. He went to him for legal help. Well hell, that's grounds for disbarment, for the guy to disclose the confidence of the conversation. . . .

PRESIDENT NIXON: Can I suggest, doesn't anybody go for my idea of somebody suing the *Washington Post?* Do you see the reason?

HALDEMAN: I hadn't heard that.

PRESIDENT NIXON: Well, I've suggested it to several people. Nobody seems to understand it. They all bring up the fact that there can be no political libel since [*New York Times v.*] *Sullivan.* Good God, I tried *Hill v. Kahn* [sic]. I know that. Even when they're not public—even when they become public figures against their will. But the public doesn't know that.

HALDEMAN: That's right.

PRESIDENT NIXON: They remember TR [Theodore Roosevelt] got a twenty-five cents judgment, you know. They remember Bill Lamb got $25,000 from *Time* magazine once. Goddamn it, sue them for a million dollars. Somebody should sue the bastards. It's a hell of a good story. Do we have anybody that would want to sue them? Who is it—could Segretti sue them?

HALDEMAN: Yes.

PRESIDENT NIXON: Has he been libeled?

EHRLICHMAN: I'm not sure. I'm not sure. There certainly is a lot of innuendo.

PRESIDENT NIXON: He's been charged, he's been charged with being in the Watergate, which of course is—

HALDEMAN: No, but he's been linked, he's been linked to a lot of things by innuendo that he couldn't possibly have done.

PRESIDENT NIXON: Now, I mean—

HALDEMAN: He's not a public figure.

PRESIDENT NIXON: Yes, he is.

HALDEMAN: Just by—

PRESIDENT NIXON: That's what *Hill v. Time* was all about. In *Hill v. Time,* what happened was that the Hills were the subject of a famous movie where a group of escaped convicts—

HALDEMAN: Yes, hostages, sure.

PRESIDENT NIXON: . . . *Time* magazine came in, *Life* went in, and got the story after it was made into a movie and . . . showed obscenities and that the girl had been raped, and so forth and so on. That did not happen. So Hill brought suit against them for making his family—

HALDEMAN: Celebrated.

PRESIDENT NIXON: And Hill lost on the ground that—it was basically a five-and-a-half to four-and-a-half decision, but he lost, in which we got, strangely enough, Tom Clark, Earl Warren, and Fortas, and half of the other, the guy that's—not [Hugo] Black, the other one—[John Marshall] Harlan, and lost the others. But my point is that they held in *Hill* that anybody . . . becomes a public figure by reason of being the subject of a public event. . . . John, there is no libel any more. The Goddamn press can do anything. Now, it's wrong. I'd like to see Segretti sue the sons of bitches. The question is if he sues now, would he be deposed before the election?

HALDEMAN: Probably.

PRESIDENT NIXON: Do you want that?

EHRLICHMAN: . . . Let Segretti sue the *Post* and then give an interview to the [*Washington*] *Star.*

PRESIDENT NIXON: Right, give a statement to the *Star*. But you see, my point about the suit is that I know he'll lose it, but good God, in the public mind it creates an impression that they lied. . . . Right, Bob? You see the point?

HALDEMAN: Yes.

PRESIDENT NIXON: Sue the sons of bitches.

HALDEMAN: If they go in on a—how fast can they get a plea of whatever, *nolo contendere* or something—I mean, the opposite.

EHRLICHMAN: You mean a summary judgment? Oh, it'll take 15 days. They have to serve a notice.

PRESIDENT NIXON: And you have arguments.

EHRLICHMAN: I would say a minimum of 45 days.

PRESIDENT NIXON: They couldn't get it before the election?

EHRLICHMAN: I don't see how. . . .

PRESIDENT NIXON: All you've got to do is to sue them and then drop the case. Do you remember in '62? . . . . the little asshole sued us during the campaign and then dropped the case the day after the election. [Nixon lost the case.]

OCTOBER 17, 1972: THE PRESIDENT, JOHN CONNALLY, AND HALDEMAN, 3:03–4:07 P.M., OVAL OFFICE

In August, Nixon had disavowed any intention of participating in fund-raising. But in the following meeting with John Connally, he talks a great deal about it. Connally, who had left the Democratic Party to support Nixon, was vital for fund-raising among disgruntled Democrats, and the President treated him respectfully. Nixon also informs Connally about Howard Hunt's other activities and LBJ's 1968 wiretapping.

SEGMENT 1

PRESIDENT NIXON: What was the proposition? Did you talk to John [Mulcahy, a contributor] about my idea of showing this to ten potential contributors and letting them put up 100 G's each in the budget?

CONNALLY: No, but I think we ought to.

PRESIDENT NIXON: That's always a tremendous scheme. You know from your campaigns, big contributors like, rather than just giving it to the general fund, like to—

CONNALLY: Have something specific.

PRESIDENT NIXON: Exactly.

HALDEMAN: That's the program. If you got your top ten money guys in (unintelligible), Democrat money guys—

PRESIDENT NIXON: Do they have to be Democrats? . . . .

HALDEMAN: He can put up half a million. We have them sit there and when it's over you say, "Gentlemen, if we're going to get this program across like it's got to go, we need a million dollars and we need it this afternoon. There's ten of you here. You've each got to give us 100,000 yourselves or get us 100,000 immediately." I guarantee you, all ten of them will pledge $100,000. Then you do the same thing in Chicago for another million, and you've got your two million.

PRESIDENT NIXON: Let's pick your names. Just a few of your people and maybe one from Texas, your good people there. But I think Mulcahy . . . will come down to this one. I'll tell you what—

HALDEMAN: Mulcahy will give you the million dollars. The problem with him is he'd—

PRESIDENT NIXON: He'd want to give it all. But nevertheless—

HALDEMAN: That's okay. Get him in.

PRESIDENT NIXON: Another one is—

HALDEMAN: It's the way to solve this whole problem of Democrats for Nixon funding, and get over all of it in one jump, and then forget about it. You said you were going to try to raise some money.

CONNALLY: Well, I'm probably going to get [Teamsters President] Frank Fitzsimmons. We ought to get some of his money in.

PRESIDENT NIXON: There, there, that's right. It's about time. How about the milk money? Have we taken that?

CONNALLY: Yes, we've taken it. We've taken a hell of a lot of milk money. We ought to get the truckers. They're trying to get together a half million.

PRESIDENT NIXON: Now we're talking. What about that?

HALDEMAN: Get them to a separate meeting from these others. . . .

PRESIDENT NIXON: It would be great to have Fitzsimmons sitting in on a thing like that with these guys.

CONNALLY: Dwayne [Andreas]. [Meshulam] Riklis [?] has already sent in his fifty thousand—no, he hasn't yet.

HALDEMAN: This is a way to get another fifty.

CONNALLY: All right, get Riklis down here. And Arthur Cohen. Arthur's already sent in his fifty.

PRESIDENT NIXON: Who's interested?

CONNALLY: I just had [Wall Street speculator Daniel K.] Ludwig in.

PRESIDENT NIXON: Ludwig? Has he ever contributed?

CONNALLY: Not to this point.

PRESIDENT NIXON: He's never contributed anything to my memory.

CONNALLY: No, well, he—I don't know.

HALDEMAN: He did exactly this, I remember, in '68. We took him into the studio, ran a special showing of the film and everything.

PRESIDENT NIXON: He didn't give a thing. . . .

HALDEMAN: I think with this he might.

CONNALLY: No, he's not talking to us. He is a strange, strange fellow. All sorts of things. Anyway—

PRESIDENT NIXON: I'll tell you what to do. Ask Tom Watt for the rest of the names. He knows the guys at this point that he's talked to over these months that would open up.

CONNALLY: See, I don't know who's contributed. I don't keep up with it, because, see, I hit some of these people and I don't know who's given. Leon Hess I understand after a dinner in New York contributed another 100,000, which makes him $250,000. John Loeb sent in, he sent in fifteen. I understand after the dinner up there he sent in another fifty.

PRESIDENT NIXON: Loeb? Loeb would like this. He's interested in foreign policy.

CONNALLY: His son-in-law sent in fifty, but he sent it to the committee.

PRESIDENT NIXON: Incidentally, your Jewish contributors will be big on this.

CONNALLY: Oh, yes, sure.

HALDEMAN: Well, it isn't fine and dandy, because we are much better off getting the money into the Democrats for Nixon, see, as a gift, so that it can then be spent under the Democrats for Nixon and get this thing we were talking about last week, because—

CONNALLY: Because we ought to go by now, because we're well over $2 million now being spent.

HALDEMAN: Really?

CONNALLY: Yes, 2.4 million.

PRESIDENT NIXON: Great.

HALDEMAN: Including this thing?

CONNALLY: Yes.

SEGMENT 2

HALDEMAN: . . . This Howard Hunt that was in the Watergate thing, and clearly was, was before that at the White House working on Pentagon Papers stuff.

PRESIDENT NIXON: And drugs.

HALDEMAN: And drugs. And it involved some damn sensitive stuff.

PRESIDENT NIXON: Very good.

HALDEMAN: Very damn sensitive stuff, and he was using these Cubans, I think.

PRESIDENT NIXON: That's right.

HALDEMAN: For bugging.

PRESIDENT NIXON: Trying to find out—he was working the Pentagon Papers, trying to make sure it was Ellsberg. He found out about his girlfriend. He's the guy that got—

HALDEMAN: Of course, the tragedy of what's happened is, by trying to do it all right we've succeeded in totalling fucking it up.

PRESIDENT NIXON: The main point is, it's three weeks before the election. The next point is that in terms of this you've got to—I don't like to see us having to talk on it, and so forth. We have other things to talk about. But you've got to keep it away from this office. You've got to first [because] it's absolutely true; and secondly, you have to condemn it. Now, as a matter of fact, when you condemn it you've got to be damn sure that you know what you're condemning. I don't need you to condemn the legitimate activities of following the other people.

CONNALLY: No, no. All you condemn is—

PRESIDENT NIXON: Is the illegal.

CONNALLY: —is the illegal, electronic surveillance, that's right. That's against the law.

PRESIDENT NIXON: So that's what we're talking about. The other thing—but on other things—

CONNALLY: The point is, I would admit that. I'd have Clark MacGregor or Bob Dole, I'd say—sure, what the fuck's wrong with this? Sure, Segretti, we hired him. You bet we hired him, and we hired him to go and case the rallies of all these people—

PRESIDENT NIXON: See how they operate.

CONNALLY: —see what was going on, see what was acting, see how they were operating against each other.

HALDEMAN: But we've been accused—Muskie came out with a big long list of all the things that happened to him and he said he might sue us. They decided not to. Well, we found out why he decided not to. That whole business, like the pizzas at his party and all that stuff, which was really pretty funny . . . .

PRESIDENT NIXON: Incidentally, you know the situation with regard to our own. I told you about it. . . . That's all it was. We are never, we are never going to put that out, you know.

CONNALLY: Well, this morning—

PRESIDENT NIXON: There's no reason to embarrass you. But I think that you will know what the situation is. Edgar Hoover told Mitchell that our plane was bugged for the last two weeks of the campaign. Now, the reason for bugging it, Johnson had it bugged. He ordered it bugged. And so was Humphrey's, I think. I'm not sure about Humphrey's. I know about ours. But the reason he says he had it bugged is because he was talking about—he had his Vietnam plans in there and he had to have information as to what we were going to say about Vietnam. But the plane was bugged, John, and that whole—

HALDEMAN: Two weeks.

PRESIDENT NIXON: —by J. Edgar Hoover, and Johnson knew every conversation. And you know where it was bugged? In my compartment. So every conversation I had, for two weeks Johnson had it. Now, we're not happy with it. We're not going to say anything. It would look like hell.

HALDEMAN: I don't know what the pressure is.

CONNALLY: They asked me at the press conference this morning if this went on during the Johnson administration. I said, "I don't know; I wasn't part of the Johnson administration; I was in Texas, being Governor of Texas." But I said, "I would not want to give that or any other administration in my lifetime any seal of purity."

HALDEMAN: They all laughed. . . .

CONNALLY: Incidentally, one thought. I had lunch with [potential contributors] Del Webb and Ludwig today at lunch.

PRESIDENT NIXON: Ludwig was there, too?

CONNALLY: Well, he's an old tough bastard.

PRESIDENT NIXON: He's always whining. He's only got $2 billion and he wants three.

CONNALLY: Yeah, he was whining at something. And I said, "What the hell have they done to you?" He was whining, oh God, about the administration.

PRESIDENT NIXON: Herb Brownell's his lawyer.

CONNALLY: Yes, Herb Brownell is his lawyer. . . . I said, "Well, Mr. Ludwig, . . . I thought you all were rolling in money." And I said, "No, we don't make any money.

. . . We're a million and a half short, and I said the committee's in bad shape now because of just fellows like you, that think everybody is loaded. We're not loaded." But I said, "I'm not going to ask you to contribute money. Hell, if you don't want to contribute, that's fine; I don't want you to do something you don't want to do. You'll be unhappy . . . if you can't do it in good grace, if you can't do it enthusiastically. . . ."

PRESIDENT NIXON: What I would have, Bob, is I'd have ten people, each of whom would not be embarrassed if somebody got up and said, I'm going to put up one hundred [thousand]. Now, I know Mulcahy will start, of course, and he will start it too high, and that'll embarrass the others. But I'd have Mulcahy there and have him—Mulcahy actually will put up—he's not rich compared with—he's only, Mulcahy's only worth $75 or $80 million, but he's willing to give ten. It's amazing. You know him?

CONNALLY: No, I don't.

PRESIDENT NIXON: The most amazing, lovable Irishman.

OCTOBER 18, 1972: THE PRESIDENT, HALDEMAN, AND EHRLICHMAN, 4:08–5:46 P.M., OVAL OFFICE

Nixon establishes that Dwight Chapin was not that close to him. Here again, Nixon complains about a "double standard" that applauded the theft of the Pentagon Papers while condemning the Watergate break-in.

HALDEMAN: I had a vicious thing today Chapin struck me with. They say their big front-page lead is that some twenty-eight phone calls were made by Segretti to the White House, Chapin, or Howard Hunt. They don't break it down, so it might have been one call to Chapin, one to the White House, and twenty-five to Hunt, which is probably what it was. . . . [J]ust tons of innuendo, implication, and they get away with it and it doesn't bother them a bit.

EHRLICHMAN: Yes, that's the thing that amazes me.

HALDEMAN: And they're so Goddamn moralistic about it.

PRESIDENT NIXON: There's no mistaking it. I mean, they won Pulitzer Prizes for the thieves who took the stuff out of Kissinger's office, for those who got the Pentagon Papers. Now what the hell is the difference? . . .

EHRLICHMAN: This is dishonesty in the thing. The *Post* editorial this morning said, "Well, Daniel Ellsberg isn't a government employee."

HALDEMAN: He wasn't working for the Committee to Re-Elect the President.

EHRLICHMAN: That's the distinction. Yes. That's awful. [laughter]

PRESIDENT NIXON: But Hunt was a former government employee.

EHRLICHMAN: Yes, but they were equating Chapin and Ellsberg. . . .

PRESIDENT NIXON: What do they think Chapin did?

HALDEMAN: They're trying to get Chapin tapping. . . . They're getting closer every day. They're going to have Chapin running wiretaps right into his office in the White House with an indirect line to your phone before they're through.

PRESIDENT NIXON: Is that right?

HALDEMAN: That's what they're doing by insinuation.

EHRLICHMAN: They've got Chapin built up to the station of the secretary of the National Security Council now. He's making all the key decisions. . . .

PRESIDENT NIXON: You mean he's in the President's office?

EHRLICHMAN: Yes.

PRESIDENT NIXON: He sees him every day?

EHRLICHMAN: Whenever he feels like it.

HALDEMAN: One of the very few members of the White House staff who sees you all of the time. Has he been in this office in the last year? I doubt if I've ever seen him.

PRESIDENT NIXON: No.

HALDEMAN: But he was in here once, but I think it was over a year ago.

PRESIDENT NIXON: He was in this office I think once, but only once over the four years that I recall.

HALDEMAN: That's right.

PRESIDENT NIXON: That doesn't mean that he isn't very important.

HALDEMAN: Yes, but the point is he doesn't see you every day, or even every month.

PRESIDENT NIXON: There are a lot of people I don't see in this office that are very important. Sure he's important. You're getting a bad rap. . . .

OCTOBER 19, 1972: THE PRESIDENT AND HALDEMAN, 1:48–4:09 P.M., EXECUTIVE OFFICE BUILDING

Haldeman informs the President that Mark Felt, Number Two in the FBI hierarchy, is the source of leaks. Haldeman refuses to tell the President the source of his information.

SEGMENT 1

PRESIDENT NIXON: Well, if they've got a leak down at the FBI, why the hell can't Gray tell us what the hell is left? You know what I mean? . . .

HALDEMAN: We know what's left, and we know what's leaked and we know who leaked it.

PRESIDENT NIXON: Somebody in the FBI?

HALDEMAN: Yes, sir.

PRESIDENT NIXON: How'd you find out?

HALDEMAN: Through a full circle through the—

PRESIDENT NIXON: Department?

HALDEMAN: . . . The FBI doesn't know. Gray doesn't know, and it's pretty high up.

PRESIDENT NIXON: Somebody next to Gray?

HALDEMAN: Mark Felt.

PRESIDENT NIXON: Now why the hell would he do that?

HALDEMAN: You can't say anything about this, because it will screw up our source, and there's a real concern. Mitchell is the only one that knows this and he feels very strongly that we better not do anything because—

PRESIDENT NIXON: Do anything? Never.

HALDEMAN: If we move on him, he'll go out and unload everything. He knows everything that's to be known in the FBI. He has access to absolutely everything.

Ehrlichman doesn't know this yet. I just got this information. I'm just going to tell Ehrlichman without telling him the source.

PRESIDENT NIXON: Don't tell him the source.

HALDEMAN: I'm not going to. But I'll tell him the fact and suggest that he, without saying that we know that, tell Pat Gray that he doesn't know anything about this, but he knows that Pat must not have confidence in Mark Felt any more, because I think Pat ought to know about it. . . .

PRESIDENT NIXON: What would you do with Felt?

HALDEMAN: Well, I asked Dean.

PRESIDENT NIXON: What the hell would he do?

HALDEMAN: He says you can't prosecute him, that he hasn't committed any crime. . . . Dean's concerned if you let him know now he'll go out and go on network television.

PRESIDENT NIXON: You know what I'd do with him, the bastard? Well, that's all I want to hear about it.

HALDEMAN: I think he wants to be in the top spot.

PRESIDENT NIXON: That's a hell of a way for him to get to the top.

HALDEMAN: . . . You can figure a lot of—maybe he thought—first of all, he has to figure that if you stay in as President there's a possibility or probability that Gray will stay on. If McGovern comes in, then you know Gray's going to be out. . . .

PRESIDENT NIXON: Is he a Catholic? . . .

HALDEMAN: (unintelligible) Jewish.

PRESIDENT NIXON: Christ, put a Jew in there?

HALDEMAN: Well, that could explain it, too.

SEGMENT 2

PRESIDENT NIXON: What's the conveyor belt for Felt?

HALDEMAN: The *Post.*

PRESIDENT NIXON: How did we stumble on (unintelligible)?

HALDEMAN: Through an official in a publication who knows where a reporter in the publication is getting his stuff. In other words, we learned it from the reporter.

PRESIDENT NIXON: Why is he telling us?

HALDEMAN: Because he has stronger ties here than he does to the publication.

PRESIDENT NIXON: [*Time* correspondent Jerrold L.] Schecter?

HALDEMAN: No. It's a legal guy.

PRESIDENT NIXON: The *Post?*

HALDEMAN: A legal guy.

PRESIDENT NIXON: Great.

HALDEMAN: And actually, I believe he's a former Justice Department man or a former FBI man.

PRESIDENT NIXON: Who made the contact?

HALDEMAN: He made the contact here, with a guy at the Justice Department.

PRESIDENT NIXON: Why did he do it?

HALDEMAN: Because he knows what the problem is. He is deeply concerned about it. He is a former FBI man. He knows that the FBI is leaking to a reporter in his publication. . . . So he has told the guy at Justice, who he knows, what the route is. He said, "I think you ought to know this; I don't know what you can do about it." The guy at Justice told John Dean. He has not told anybody else, including Kleindienst or Pat Gray, because he's afraid that either of them might react in such a way as to do more harm than good.

PRESIDENT NIXON: So say nothing. . . .

OCTOBER 20, 1972: THE PRESIDENT AND HALDEMAN, 10:36–10:56 A.M., EXECUTIVE OFFICE BUILDING

Nixon is alarmed by Mark Felt's close ties to Ehrlichman, probably because of Plumbers' operations that Ehrlichman directed. The President fears Felt might leak this information.

PRESIDENT NIXON: I had some more thoughts about the FBI, about that person [Felt]. Are you sure? . . . Now, the other thing that concerns me is Haldeman's relationship with this—I mean, Ehrlichman's relationship to this fellow. He says that this fellow has handled a lot of problems for him. I don't know what they are, but you check with him to find out. I think you better tell him what the situation is. But also, he's got to see what kind of games this fellow—what he knew. . . . But I think Ehrlichman said that he is the man.

HALDEMAN: I did not know Ehrlichman has been involved in a lot of things with the FBI. . . .

PRESIDENT NIXON: He's his contact. That's the thing I'm concerned with. Under the circumstances, you'll have to—

HALDEMAN: I've got to talk to him. . . .

PRESIDENT NIXON: . . . Who is checking this for you? Is it John Dean? Is he the fellow who's on top of this? . . .

HALDEMAN: Dean's view is that . . . Felt is working on the basis that he is not known to be doing this and is not going to get caught. Then you get to the question of what his motive could be, and that's a hard one.

PRESIDENT NIXON: It could be the Jewish thing. I don't know. It's always a possibility.

HALDEMAN: The *Time* reporter—I can't remember his name, but it wasn't what struck me as a Jewish name.

PRESIDENT NIXON: You can't tell that way.

HALDEMAN: That's right.

PRESIDENT NIXON: But what the hell. And incidentally, suppose they're both Jews and that has nothing to do with it, but it at least gives you a feeling of the possible motivation deep down of the liberal leftists.

OCTOBER 25, 1972: THE PRESIDENT AND COLSON, 12:29–1:10 P.M., EXECUTIVE OFFICE BUILDING

Nixon and Colson again raise plans to attack the *Washington Post* after the election.

PRESIDENT NIXON: We're going to screw them [the *Post*] another way. They don't really realize how rough I can play. I've been such a nice guy around here a lot of times, and I always play (unintelligible) on a hard-hitting basis. But when I start, I will kill them. There's no question about it.

They should give some thought to taking on the guy that went into Cambodia and Laos, ran the Cambodian bombing campaign. What the hell do they think they're doing in there? They know I'm not going to destroy them on this or do anything against free speech, but it's going to be fair speech. . . .

COLSON: I'll tell you exactly what they think. They'll attack the hell out of us.

PRESIDENT NIXON: And then afterwards, be nicey-nice.

COLSON: They will come to us and say, " Well now, look,—

PRESIDENT NIXON: . . . we're here in this town together, we want to get along, we'll be fair."

COLSON: "We'll write very helpful editorials for you." . . . [Kenneth] Clawson said, "Use it. We'll wipe up the floor with them." . . . I'm dead serious. . . . They really, they have an influence like that is [just excessive?].

PRESIDENT NIXON: They've got a radio and television station, WTOP, a CBS outlet.

COLSON: Yes, sir, plus they have Miami.

PRESIDENT NIXON: They should never have gotten that.

COLSON: They have a lot of real estate as well. . . .

PRESIDENT NIXON: Did you find out when they come up?

COLSON: Well, they have to in the next term . . . .

PRESIDENT NIXON: Check that out and find out . . . .

OCTOBER 27, 1972: THE PRESIDENT AND KISSINGER, 9:10–9:50 A.M., EXECUTIVE OFFICE BUILDING

The *Washington Post*'s revelations of Haldeman's $350,000 secret fund, ostensibly for campaign purposes, again angers Nixon. The President tells Kissinger how he has been a victim of political dirty tricks, including those by Kissinger's former patron, Nelson A. Rockefeller.

SEGMENT 3

PRESIDENT NIXON: . . . [P]lay with the *New York Times*. Play it with them, that's fair. But—

KISSINGER: I don't talk to the *Washington Post*.

PRESIDENT NIXON: You must not, for a reason. Basically, Haldeman would never say it, but he's been deeply hurt personally. They've lied on the poor sonofabitch and he's an honest man, and there's nothing to do with all this shit.

KISSINGER: He's an honest, honorable man and, look, I don't know what the facts are about the funds, but they were private funds.

PRESIDENT NIXON: They should be.

KISSINGER: They should be . . . .

PRESIDENT NIXON: Don't you think the Rockefeller people did this when they were running against me?

KISSINGER: No question.

PRESIDENT NIXON: Hah!

KISSINGER: Sure.

PRESIDENT NIXON: They went to the rallies, they sent out the wrong information, they filed false (unintelligible).

KISSINGER: I've been told, I've been told by a Rockefeller associate, in fact that he does it in New York now.

PRESIDENT NIXON: Hah. It's common practice, but we didn't—Watergate of course was not our . . . . Listen, I, we, frankly haven't done any tapping. The tappings that were done in Watergate were these *assholes* that worked over—that had these hard-line former CIA people. But why they were tapping the Goddamn Democratic Committee proves that we didn't do it, because as a professional the Democratic Committee didn't know anything.

KISSINGER: Exactly. Larry O'Brien didn't know anything.

PRESIDENT NIXON: If you were tapping anything, you would tap Humphrey or Muskie or something.

KISSINGER: The stupidity of the operation (unintelligible).

PRESIDENT NIXON: Sure.

NOVEMBER 1, 1972: THE PRESIDENT AND EHRLICHMAN, 2:10–2:51 P.M. EXECUTIVE OFFICE BUILDING

As the election approaches, the President is increasingly buoyant. Again, he plans his revenge on the *Washington Post*. The newspaper virtually ceases its Watergate stories as the election nears, perhaps explaining Nixon's confidence that he could dismiss the subject.

SEGMENT 4

PRESIDENT NIXON: And now they're [the *Washington Post*] finished.

EHRLICHMAN: Believe me, I would be very disappointed to see us now forgive and forget.

PRESIDENT NIXON: There ain't going to be no forgetting, and there'll be Goddamn little forgiving, except they're going to know (unintelligible). They're off the guest list, they don't come to the Christmas party.

EHRLICHMAN: That to my way of thinking would be not nearly as important as coming down the pike—there will be our main chance. There will be a license application—

PRESIDENT NIXON: Oh, I know. I know that, sure.

EHRLICHMAN: But I would love to see you fire the silver bullets.

PRESIDENT NIXON: How can I?

EHRLICHMAN: Well, your day will come. . . .

PRESIDENT NIXON: But John, how do you fire a silver bullet at the *Post* without them saying you're taking the FCC and trying to get after somebody?

EHRLICHMAN: I think you could get away with it. This is what the President wants, [FCC Chairman] Dean [Burch], and you have them do it, and send him back over there to do it. I think he'd do it if we get some more appointments on that Commission. Pretty soon [FCC Commissioner Nicholas] Johnson goes off. . . . We'll get some team players.

SEGMENT 5

PRESIDENT NIXON: . . . I don't know where Mitchell was. He may have. It's hard to believe . . . . If he did, he's stupid. . . . Because . . . it seems that he did hire some people, and I think these guys were off on a Goddamn escapade, because the main point is what in the name of Christ did they think they were going to accomplish by bugging the National Committee of the Democratic Party? . . . I think that's to me embarrassing because it was so dumb, and that these people—that's why all these people were shucked off immediately. Tying it to us is an insult to our intelligence, that's what I would say.

EHRLICHMAN: We don't mind being called crooks, but not stupid crooks.

PRESIDENT NIXON: That's right.

EHRLICHMAN: [*Laughter.*]

PRESIDENT NIXON: We know we'll never convince them on our morality, but do they think we're that dumb?

NOVEMBER 3, 1972: THE PRESIDENT AND HALDEMAN, 10:46–10:54 A.M., OVAL OFFICE

This is a rather cryptic exchange involving Lyndon Johnson's bugging of Nixon in 1968. Apparently, the two men have an agreement of mutual convenience: Johnson acknowledges his wiretapping of Nixon, Nixon makes no public complaints, and LBJ recognizes that Nixon did no wrong.

HALDEMAN: I talked to [former Johnson press secretary] George [Christian]. He talked to President Johnson again this morning. Johnson had his staff working all night reviewing his files and everything. Last night Johnson had said to George, you know, they're going to deny this, and all. This morning Johnson—first of all, after reviewing the files, he's not going to say anything. He was going to deny it. Now he's not going to. He's just going to slough it off.

PRESIDENT NIXON: Good.

(Withdrawn item. National security.)

HALDEMAN: . . . Johnson told George, "I have no idea whether that was right or not." He said, "I did call Nixon [in 1968] and go through the problem with him, and we agreed to have [Senator Everett] Dirksen . . . get it straightened out, and Dirksen met with [South Vietnam Ambassador Nguyen Van Bui] Diem on November 9 and went through all that, smoothed it all over. . . .

PRESIDENT NIXON: You're citing Johnson?

HALDEMAN: Johnson said that he decided at the time to interpret this as something foolish that someone did without Nixon's knowledge, and that he and Nixon agreed to do nothing to slow the talks down, and we should look at the way he handled it in his books. That's his position, which was that Nixon cooperated fully in proceeding with the peace talks and all that stuff. Then he said to Christian, he said—here's the lead-in line. He said, "It is conceivable that somebody here may have asked the FBI to follow on up this." See, last night he said it was absolutely not true. And he said, "So maybe it's possible that Hoover did tell the President that he was asked to do this."

Christian then said, "You better handle the thing straight. . . . That is true, Hoover did tell the President that; you should know that." And he said Johnson wasn't surprised and didn't try to deny that at all. . . . Now it's clear, Johnson knows the position we're in; he knows that you know that Hoover did the bugging and that we did nothing about it. Johnson was very grateful for that. . . . Christian also went into great detail with him about our concern about the FBI leak and our concern that, if we try to move on this story or anything like this, it could be a trap. In other words, the FBI may be prepared to leak on this.

PRESIDENT NIXON: That's right.

HALDEMAN: Johnson understood that immediately. He didn't have to spell that out at all.

PRESIDENT NIXON: Good.

NOVEMBER 13, 1972: THE PRESIDENT AND HALDEMAN, 3:08–3:55 P.M., CAMP DAVID

In his post-election euphoria, Nixon plans to attack numerous enemies to deflect the Watergate story. Here he discusses Colson's work on tax-exempt foundations.

PRESIDENT NIXON: . . . What would he [Colson] do with the foundations? What would he do there?

HALDEMAN: He may start investigations on the abuse of their tax-exempt privileges and status.

PRESIDENT NIXON: Well, I'm going to go—of course, we've got to go after Common Cause.

HALDEMAN: Common Cause? Ford Foundation is worse, because Ford Foundation funds Common Cause.

PRESIDENT NIXON: That's right.

HALDEMAN: That's where the money is. Rip in there, scare the shit out of them. You know how we get scared when they say they're going to investigate the Watergate. Well, let them sit around, like we did for months on end on ITT and the Watergate. Let them and their Goddamn PR people and lawyers sit around in their board rooms shaking and trembling and wondering what [the] IRS is doing.

PRESIDENT NIXON: Like CBS will sit around and worry and so forth.

HALDEMAN: That's right.

PRESIDENT NIXON: That's why you go after Mrs. Graham and all those people, right down the line.

HALDEMAN: Forget how much that worries people when they start getting into all that stuff.

PRESIDENT NIXON: Just let them be worried.

NOVEMBER 24, 1972: THE PRESIDENT AND HALDEMAN, 11:49 A.M.–12:47 P.M., OVAL OFFICE

Nixon returns to favorite themes: Watergate is a PR matter, to be fought in the arena of public opinion; the presidency is not involved; and the presidency must be protected.

PRESIDENT NIXON: Did Mitchell have any other gems of wisdom?

HALDEMAN: No. He said they were looking good, hanging in.

PRESIDENT NIXON: Did you sit and talk to him about . . . the Watergate and so forth. Why the hell don't you get Mitchell and John Ehrlichman, you, and Dean and sit down and thrash the damn thing out?

HALDEMAN: Dean and I are going to do that right now. Let us do it one round first before we get into that.

PRESIDENT NIXON: Here's what I would like to do with it, in re the Dean conversation. I think what needs to be done—and I know everybody says we've got to protect this one and then the other one. The main thing you've got to protect is the presidency, and on that we need a simple, clear statement and we need it early, which simply says again what we've already said by the Dean report to the President:

"Pursuant to your request, I have checked with regard to the so-called Watergate episode and I have found that there is no present member of the White House staff who had knowledge of or was involved in the, dah-dah-dah, Watergate matter." You see, I have said that publicly. I want him [Dean] to say it again. Then . . . if he can, he ought to use the opportunity to clear Stans and Mitchell—you know what I mean, just say that they were not involved. . . .

Now, with regard to the Segretti thing, you should say that maybe that statement has to come a little later. But it should be one, you've got all the business about, as John says, letting it all hang out. That's fine, some sort of piece. But in the end, there may not be that flat categorical statement, and I think it's got to come from Dean, that I have conducted an investigation pursuant to your direction, and I have found that. And then he just takes everything, he names names. The implications, for example, he should pick them up: that Mr. Haldeman was involved—untrue; that Mr. Colson was involved—untrue; that as far as Mr. Chapin was concerned, he recommended and so forth, but did not have knowledge, or whatever you want to say.

I think that kind of a statement is needed from the standpoint of the presidency. Now, I don't want to do anything that will harm other individuals if we can avoid it. But you see, unless you get the very simple statement of that sort out, that's the kind of thing, you see, that we stand on. Ziegler says, there is the statement and we stand on it. Now, John Ehrlichman's view probably will be, and Dean's as a lawyer, well, let it all come out and it will be clear that the President was not involved. That won't do it. This is a public relations exercise as much as anything else. Dean has got to report that, pursuant to my direction, he has conducted a thoroughgoing investigation of this and has found that, and so forth. You see what I mean? . . .

NOVEMBER 28, 1972: THE PRESIDENT AND HALDEMAN, 12:14–1:50 P.M., CAMP DAVID

Nixon confidently predicts that L. Patrick Gray will have no problems in his confirmation hearings. After much hesitation, he had decided to nominate Gray as FBI Director. Nixon and Haldeman exchange lavish praise for John Dean's work in handling the cover-up.

SEGMENT 1

PRESIDENT NIXON: Come to think of it, you know, if they did ask Pat Gray in his confirmation about Watergate, what the hell. He's going to be asked about it some time. He'll say, "Yes, sir, I conducted an investigation into this, that, and the other thing, and the administration totally cooperated, and these are the people that were involved. Was the Attorney General involved? No. Was [Stans?]? No." What does he say about the finances? "I can't comment upon that because that's in trial at the present time."

SEGMENT 2

HALDEMAN: . . . [Haldeman aide Gordon] Strachan we've moved over and it's done, we've moved over to USIA, the counsel's office there. So he's out of the White House, in another job, the assignment here is finished and he moved on to something else.

PRESIDENT NIXON: That'll be a good job, too.

HALDEMAN: It's a good job. No announcement, no problems for him. He is apparently the one guy that is a problem on testimony in what he knows. But Dean says he's the one guy he's the least worried about on testimony; he's absolutely solid. He said the important thing is to keep him in the government, keep him where he doesn't feel that he's been cut off at all, and just let him roll. So that's what they've done. Dean did all of this. Dean's doing a hell of a good job. He's a damn good lawyer.

PRESIDENT NIXON: Oh, boy.

HALDEMAN: Thank God we've got him there.

PRESIDENT NIXON: I never thought he was up to that.

HALDEMAN: You wouldn't quite move him up. Dean has stepped up. He's a hell of a lot better person than anybody over at Justice. He's taken a much rougher time of it.

PRESIDENT NIXON: Poor John. . . . I'm a little bit concerned about this thing with Segretti coming out in *Newsday*.

HALDEMAN: No. I've gone through the thing with him and it's got to be a—

PRESIDENT NIXON: —a statement by Dean.

HALDEMAN: —the Dean report.

PRESIDENT NIXON: To the President.

HALDEMAN: That says, oh, he was involved, or somebody was, but only in this extent.

PRESIDENT NIXON: That's right.

HALDEMAN: And it had no bearing on it, and so on.

PRESIDENT NIXON: Yes. You can hit Watergate square on the nose. . . .

NOVEMBER 29, 1972: THE PRESIDENT AND HALDEMAN, 8:40–10:10 A.M., CAMP DAVID

The two men are optimistic that the Watergate story has run its course, with apparently little interest in Congress for pursuing any investigation.

HALDEMAN: . . . There is no hearing, there may not be any hearing, it now looks like.

PRESIDENT NIXON: Why?

HALDEMAN: Congress may drop the whole thing.

PRESIDENT NIXON: Why?

HALDEMAN: Because it doesn't go anywhere.

PRESIDENT NIXON: Well, who's got to whom? Has Mitchell finally got off his Goddamn fat ass and gotten to [Senator James] Eastland [D-MS]? No.

HALDEMAN: Well, yes, he has, but I don't think that's what's doing it. I think what's doing it is [Senator Edward] Kennedy's found it isn't going anywhere. I think it's being dropped on the merits, not on anybody getting to anybody.

PRESIDENT NIXON: Well, it's sour grapes, frankly.

HALDEMAN: It doesn't matter who gets to whom. If the Kennedy clique think they've got something, they're going to go with it. If they don't think they've got something, they aren't.

PRESIDENT NIXON: What about, fellows, our own friends like [Senators] Glenn Beall [R-MD] and [Charles] Mathias [R-MD], who are calling for investigations, and [Charles] Percy [R-IL]?

HALDEMAN: Again, if it doesn't go anywhere, they're not—of course, the other thing is it may be to our interest to have it investigated and not go anywhere.

PRESIDENT NIXON: No, the best thing to our interest is to have Dean write out that nice little statement so that I can mail it to all my friends.

HALDEMAN: Yes, yes.

PRESIDENT NIXON: Believe me, I know Ehrlichman hasn't understood this. Nobody's understood it. You do. Bob, I've got to have a little statement, and I can say, "All right, that is the statement, that covers it." You see the point?

HALDEMAN: Yes.

DECEMBER 11, 1972: THE PRESIDENT, HALDEMAN, AND EHRLICHMAN, 11:07 A.M.–12:25 P.M., OVAL OFFICE

This is an extraordinary conversation. The President and Haldeman discuss the death of Howard Hunt's wife, Dorothy, in a plane crash in Chicago. She was found carrying more than $10,000 in cash and had taken out $225,000 in flight insurance without a stipulated beneficiary. They worry that the money might be traced to White House campaign funds, for in all probability, it was "hush money." The FBI and the National Transportation Safety Board investigated the crash for possible sabotage—a sign of the times. They talk about legal strategy for securing acquittals for Hunt and Liddy. At the end of Segment 2, the President blurts out a remarkably confused statement on his responsibility. Some of his earlier optimism is gone and the President and his men are torn between a legal strategy and a PR focus. Finally, at the end of Segment 3, Nixon irrevocably sets himself down the path of placing the blame for Watergate on John Mitchell.

SEGMENT 1

PRESIDENT NIXON: Do they have any reading yet from the traceability of that $10,000 bag?

HALDEMAN: No. Dean spent most of the weekend on that, he said. She was going out to—apparently she [Dorothy Hunt, wife of Howard Hunt] and her family have some investments in Howard Johnson restaurants around out there. She was going out with the money for their investment. It was a business thing. They have a pattern of dealing in cash. That's the way the family has moved it. When they carry stuff out, they carry it in cash. The bills are still in the hands of the Chicago police, to be turned over to Hunt apparently today, because it's obviously his money and it will be returned to him. So until then, John doesn't know whether it's traceable money or not and he's not particularly concerned about it. He doesn't think it is.

PRESIDENT NIXON: I guess on re-escalating it—

HALDEMAN: Well, I don't know.

PRESIDENT NIXON: There's the point. There's no reason to escalate from the standpoint of the staff, that's for sure.

HALDEMAN: Well, the PR types argue that we should—

PRESIDENT NIXON: The real problem I suppose that we have here is whether or not you have the whole administration, the President and so forth, sort of an aura of hanky [-panky]—worse, of corruption—that's the way they want to call it—when I refuse to answer any questions. The idea is to clear it up. You've got to understand, that's the point. I don't give a damn what they think, nothing is said. If something could just be said, so that I could simply point to something in the record—

HALDEMAN: Right.

PRESIDENT NIXON: —you know that I am not dodging questions. You see what I mean? I don't want to get anybody else in trouble. If there is something to be said that they've got to watch that point very, very carefully about how the office functions and the people around the President.

HALDEMAN: That's the whole view they're taking. The problem that concerns them is exactly that, that if you take—if you reopen it, you raise . . . raise more questions than you answer, and you bring the thing back up to a level of public attention. And it's a really strategic question, not a tactical one. It's whether you close it off better from the President by opening it one more time and trying to box it, or by letting time fade it away. The latter is in a sense sort of unsatisfactory because it never answers it, but the other question may be more unsatisfactory because it doesn't answer enough to clean it up, either. In other words, a halfhearted attempt to clean it up may be worse than no attempt, in that it re-raises it again. Now, it's going to re-raise public attention when you get to the criminal trial and the Watergate comes up.

The thing that bothers me still is that the Segretti thing and the other stuff like that tends to be tied to the Watergate, and it doesn't have anything to do with the Watergate. Somehow you need to separate those. But then you get into, when it's separated, where you go on Watergate. As far as you can go on that is to say nobody presently in the White House staff had any involvement. You've already said that and reconfirmed it. But nobody's asking whether anybody did at this point. You still get, it isn't the White House staff; it's the President's former Attorney General, the President's former Secretary of Commerce. Where did the money come from? Who allocated the money?

PRESIDENT NIXON: . . . They have Chapin, they have you, and naturally Colson, and tangentially Ehrlichman. And those are just bad raps; that's what I don't like. . . . I mean, it's there. It's there. If you read Buchanan's stuff—and I always read it with a jaundiced eye, I can assure you in all honesty—if you read it, though, that's what they're implying when they say the President ought to do some housekeeping, and so on and so on.

SEGMENT 2

PRESIDENT NIXON: . . . You know, they've got a little problem with this fellow Hunt. I don't think they can try him for a while.

EHRLICHMAN: Well, that's the other development. He's moving this morning for a severance, or whatever the legal term is. See, as of now he and Liddy are charged together. He's moving to separate himself from Liddy. And that works out rather neatly, because the whole case that they've got, the prosecution's interest is in keeping them together because the whole case they've got is against Hunt. They can make a case on Hunt. They have a very tough time on the evidence making a case against Liddy, except by tying him to Hunt.

If they separate the cases and try them separately, Liddy's case will collapse, which is very much to our interest of course, and Hunt's case, he's going on the basis he's got a ten-year-old daughter and a lot of problems with his wife getting killed. So there's still a lot of legal remedies they're playing with, but none of those get to the key point. Those get to avoiding it getting worse, but they don't get to the point you raise of how do you separate this from the White House and the President.

PRESIDENT NIXON: Just say, [defiantly] "The President approved the Goddamn bugging of the National Committee, which I approved—I didn't disapprove of." I mean, it should be said.

SEGMENT 3

HALDEMAN: Do you want to cover the Watergate thing with John?

PRESIDENT NIXON: Yes, yes. Understandably, all the lawyers say there's nothing that we can say. The problem that I have with the whole thing is that some time before the Inauguration, before I go out and face the press, something has to be said. . . .

And the idea that, well, anything we say will open the door. We've got to remember the aura surrounding it that I'm trying to hide something. Remember I said that's the one thing we couldn't have. And that I'm trying to protect somebody, hiding and protection. . . .

EHRLICHMAN: Well, it's going to hurt. There's no two ways about that, because what you'll have to say is that you had a couple young fellows around here who recruited the guy.

PRESIDENT NIXON: You're talking about Segretti?

EHRLICHMAN: Segretti and so on. The Watergate thing, I don't think there's anything to add to what you've already said.

HALDEMAN: You might re-say it. . . .

EHRLICHMAN: That nobody in the government did this thing.

HALDEMAN: The White House.

PRESIDENT NIXON: . . . [W]hat do you mean, Watergate, White House? Nobody currently, nobody in government.

HALDEMAN: Currently employed in the government. Say "currently employed."

PRESIDENT NIXON: *Ever* involved in government.

HALDEMAN: *No, sir!*

EHRLICHMAN: Now, you have Liddy and Hunt, who were at one time employed.

PRESIDENT NIXON: But while they were doing it even, while they were doing it.

EHRLICHMAN: That's right. Then employed, I could say.

PRESIDENT NIXON: No one who is an employee of the White House, who is an employee of the White House.

EHRLICHMAN: Either at the time of the incident or since.

PRESIDENT NIXON: Or since. That's what I mean.

EHRLICHMAN: Yes.

PRESIDENT NIXON: And that we've conducted a thorough investigation and that was the case; that as far as the remainder, the trial and so forth, it would not be proper to comment upon it, it would be grounds for a mistrial and so forth.

EHRLICHMAN: . . . Do you want to get into the question of campaign finances or the conduct of the business of the Re-Election Committee? That seems to me to be gratuitous. I don't know why you would reach out for that, because that begins to open the doors, doors, doors, doors, and doors.

PRESIDENT NIXON: We're not going to get into that. . . . What do we say about Magruder?

EHRLICHMAN: Well, one of them's left. Strachan's left.

PRESIDENT NIXON: Yes, but not the government. He left the White House.

EHRLICHMAN: He left the White House. He's in the government. . . .

PRESIDENT NIXON: Well, what would you say, that he's been reprimanded?

EHRLICHMAN: You could say that you discussed it with him, that you felt there was questionable judgment involved, and even though the opposition pulled stuff like that, that that didn't mean that it was right to do, but nevertheless on balance he'd been a loyal, faithful, hardworking guy who contributed a great deal to his country and the government.

PRESIDENT NIXON: And he had nothing to do with Watergate.

EHRLICHMAN: And there is absolutely no connection with Watergate, and there's no wrongdoing of a criminal or other nature involved, and you thought that a strong reprimand was sufficient. Now, that—

PRESIDENT NIXON: That's one point of view.

EHRLICHMAN: That's one point of view. The other point of view is, of course, that the second administration should start without a taint, without an inference of impropriety, and that dig it out root and branch, and you start as clean as possible.

PRESIDENT NIXON: Then you've got to get rid of Strachan, don't you?

EHRLICHMAN: I think so. He was more deeply involved, probably, and if there is grounds for letting Chapin go I think—

PRESIDENT NIXON: What I mean is, if you've got to get it out root and branch, you can't have anybody in government, government or the White House.

EHRLICHMAN: I think that would have to follow. But he's out of the White House.

HALDEMAN: To a minor extent he should go, and Clawson should go also, and Colson, who's gone.

EHRLICHMAN: Yes. I think that's where all that leads. . . .

PRESIDENT NIXON: I made the point, which nobody around here wants me to make, of course, because it happens to be true, and second because it puts responsibility on others. Basically, the point is I didn't take over the Goddamn campaign, as you may recall, until after the convention. I didn't pay attention enough to this campaign. I wasn't following the primaries all that closely.

HALDEMAN: No, sir.

PRESIDENT NIXON: And it's really true, Bob. It's sort of building the Nixon myth that I run all my campaigns. In this instance, I mean, let's face it, we all know who the hell should have handled this. Goddamn it, it was Mitchell, and he wasn't handling it. . . .

MacGregor is my appointment. When I took over the campaign I put MacGregor in and that was that. From that time on, all this crap stopped. And then go on to make a positive point, that throughout the campaign from the time that the President—from that time on—

HALDEMAN: The reason that that shouldn't be said is nobody in the world would believe that there is a crack of daylight between you and Mitchell.

PRESIDENT NIXON: Yes, that's right.

HALDEMAN: Now, there's a way to do this, and that I think has to wait until you write your book maybe. That is to dump Mitchell on this thing and say he's the [culprit?].

PRESIDENT NIXON: I would dump him; it would kill him financially. John Mitchell has a serious problem with his wife. He was unable to watch the campaign and as a result underlings did things without his knowledge.

HALDEMAN: That really dumps on Magruder.

EHRLICHMAN: There are no good choices. There are no good choices once you start down that road.

PRESIDENT NIXON: If you start down that road. . . . Somebody did it.

HALDEMAN: Once you dump on somebody down the road, that guy is at least potentially capable of defending himself. Each of those guys—the problem you're dealing with here is you're dealing, not with the Howard Hunts who are not honorable people, but you're dealing with the Magruders and Chapins, who were doing what they thought was right.

EHRLICHMAN: The minute you dump on Mitchell indirectly by saying he didn't have a chance to watch the underlings, the underlings are going to produce their diaries and show that Mitchell was in eighteen meetings where this was discussed, ratified, approved, authorized, financed.

PRESIDENT NIXON: Was he?

EHRLICHMAN: I gather so.

PRESIDENT NIXON: Well, Mitchell then did it. . . .

DECEMBER 13, 1972: THE PRESIDENT, HALDEMAN, AND EHRLICHMAN, 5:00–6:09 P.M., OVAL OFFICE

The President and his men have second thoughts about Pat Gray. The FBI Acting Director, in fact, suspects a White House cover-up. The news is taken rather calmly in the Oval Office.

EHRLICHMAN: See, my confidence in Gray was badly shaken in this whole Watergate episode.

PRESIDENT NIXON: Why?

EHRLICHMAN: Just because he was not—he was not tracking.

HALDEMAN: He was not tracking the investigation.

EHRLICHMAN: That's right.

HALDEMAN: He didn't tell us the truth about what he was doing. He didn't level with Dean all the way through.

EHRLICHMAN: And he was spending an awful lot of time in Connecticut, which really bothered me.

HALDEMAN: He didn't stay on top of it.

PRESIDENT NIXON: What the hell was he doing in Connecticut?

EHRLICHMAN: That's where he lives.

HALDEMAN: He may have been sick.

EHRLICHMAN: Well, it may be.

HALDEMAN: We don't know.

EHRLICHMAN: I don't know.

PRESIDENT NIXON: But Gray had the idea—now, in fairness to him, you see, the problem we've got, too, in the Watergate—and Gray had the idea, which of course permeates a lot of the people who don't know very much here because of the fact that everybody had to really protect Mitchell, that the White House staff was really involved in this Goddamn thing and that the White House staff was trying to keep him from getting at it. You remember, he made a telephone call to me about it.

HALDEMAN: He thought we were covering up.

PRESIDENT NIXON: That's right, that's right.

HALDEMAN: Dick [Vernon] Walters did, too, and we moved on (unintelligible)—

PRESIDENT NIXON: So you see, that's the thing—but that was untrue, you know. He knows that. I think Gray's got to know that it's untrue. Maybe he doesn't. Maybe he thinks the White House ordered the whole Goddamn thing.

EHRLICHMAN: If he doesn't know that, then that's another reason why my confidence in him is shaken. So—

PRESIDENT NIXON: You wonder, for example, what you're going to do about those top FBI people. . . . You've got to get all of them out.

EHRLICHMAN: That's right.

PRESIDENT NIXON: In fact, you can't move on one or he'll go out and yack around. That's probably all we have anyway. I don't know what you can do.

EHRLICHMAN: It's got to be a total thing. There isn't any question about it.

PART THREE

WATERGATE:
THE UNRAVELING OF
THE COVER-UP

JANUARY 1973 – APRIL 1973

The first month of the new year ended with the convictions of Howard Hunt, Gordon Liddy, James McCord, and the Cuban burglars, Bernard Barker, Virgilio Gonzales, Eugenio Martinez, and Frank Sturgis. Judge Sirica deferred sentencing until March, apparently to give the accused some time to consider cooperating with the government and perhaps implicating "higher-ups." Choosing his words carefully, Sirica said, "I am still not satisfied that all the pertinent facts that might be available—I say might be available—have been produced before an American jury." He expressed hope that an anticipated Senate hearing might "get to the bottom of what happened in this case." What the White House had hoped would be the end of the case was only the beginning.

Throughout these months, the President was an active participant in maintaining the cover-up. He thanked Thomas Pappas, a man who had provided a significant amount of money for the defendants. He kept tabs on the prospective fates of various other players in the events, including John Mitchell, Jeb Magruder, and Hugh Sloan. He realized the vulnerabilities of his nominee for the FBI Directorship,

L. Patrick Gray—and how Gray's past action might expose the White House role in Watergate and the cover-up.

The prospect of Senate hearings became reality in this period. Senator Sam Ervin (D-NC), with the active help of Senate Majority Leader Mike Mansfield (D-MT), gained unanimous backing for a resolution authorizing a Senate Select Committee to conduct hearings on "campaign finances." The unanimity was transparent as Republicans doggedly fought for an investigation to look at presidential campaigns in 1964 and 1968 as well, and to have a committee evenly divided along partisan lines. Both efforts failed, and preparations promptly began for public hearings beginning in May.

The possibility of an Administration-inspired cover-up gained important public recognition when McCord sent Judge Sirica a letter just prior to sentencing in March. Realizing the possibility of a severe sentence, McCord told Sirica of pressure to maintain silence, that perjury had occurred during the trial, and that he wanted an opportunity to speak to the judge—all this, he said, was "in the interest of restoring faith in the criminal justice system, . . . [and to] be of help to you in meting out justice in this case." Judge Sirica handed down his version of justice on the 23rd, sentencing Liddy to prison for six to twenty years, thirty-five years for Hunt, and forty years for the Cubans, plus fines. Sirica made clear that the sentences were designed to force cooperation from the defendants.

Meanwhile, the Administration had two notable disasters, both of which threatened exposure of the cover-up. First, L. Patrick Gray's nomination to be Director of the FBI ran afoul of vigorous congressional criticism, particularly because of his dealings with John Dean. This resulted in mounting demands that Dean appear before the Senate Judiciary Committee, then considering Gray's nomination. Second, the Plumbers' break-in of Daniel Ellsberg's psychiatrist's office became public knowledge, and the Department of Justice had to disclose the information to the trial judge. Charles Colson feared that the judge's requests for affidavits from Hunt and himself "would disclose [the] White House role and RMN's role." The trail of "White House horrors" began to unfold.

Just two days before McCord's letter to Sirica, John Dean had his famous meeting with the President in which he informed Nixon that there was a "cancer on the presidency." Dean worried that the cover-up, with its hush-money payments, could not be maintained. This news, coupled with Sirica's action, galvanized the President into personal command of the White House's defenses. When Dean understood that the President would retain and protect Haldeman and Ehrlichman—because of their special knowledge of Watergate and other "White House horrors"—Dean turned to a criminal lawyer for his own defense. The irony then was that Dean, who aided in the cover-up but sought to end it, would be castigated by the President and his men as the perpetrator of that cover-up and also had been deeply complicit in the original crime. Still, the day after meeting with Dean, the President and Haldeman agreed to pay more "hush money" and continue the cover-up. Much of the material in these conversations, from the end of March until July, centers on Dean's villainy and culpability. He is at the center of the President's attention—and concern.

Dean's cooperation, first with the prosecutors, and then with the Senate Select Committee, brought mounting exposure and pressure on Haldeman and Ehrlichman. Haldeman told Nixon in late March that if he fired everybody, "you send them to jail." The President, as indicated in these conversations, eventually had no choice but to cut his advisors loose and force their resignations. The beleaguered president was painfully aware that with their departure, he would lose his last line of defense. The last days of April revealed a President profoundly affected by the rush of events, despondent and depressed, and painfully aware that his presidency probably was fatally wounded.

January 1, 1973: The President and Colson, 9:40–10:40 a.m., Oval Office

Nixon and Colson decide to check Henry Kissinger's telephone logs, hoping to catch him leaking to the media. They also propose a new line of assault against the *Washington Post*. With the Paris peace talks approaching a climax, the unspoken rivalry between Nixon and Kissinger for prominence is highlighted at this time, according to Haldeman's diaries.

SEGMENT 1

COLSON: We're having a log now on all of his [Kissinger's] calls. We'll know from now on. We won't be able to—

PRESIDENT NIXON: You can't get the others? You can't check that?

COLSON: Well, we've asked. We've asked for—just one person at a low level has been asking whether there were any calls incoming or outgoing to [*New York Times* writer James] Reston.

PRESIDENT NIXON: There were not?

COLSON: There were none but they could ask.

[Withdrawn item. Privacy.]

COLSON: He had to have talked to him, or he had to have talked to [*New York Times* writer Max] Frankel, who talked to him.

PRESIDENT NIXON: There is another possibility, that he could have called Frankel. . . . Frankel is not writing. . . . [H]e's gone upstairs. But Henry is compulsive on Frankel. He's Jewish.

COLSON: Frankel, he's the Sunday editor. This was the Sunday edition, so he could well have—

PRESIDENT NIXON: The *Times* works that way.

MR. COLSON: That's right.

PRESIDENT NIXON: They pass it around.

COLSON: I thought of that last night.

PRESIDENT NIXON: You should check the Frankel calls.

COLSON: Mr. President, I just thought of that. I thought of it last night.

PRESIDENT NIXON: Henry—the *New York Times,* see if he talked to Frankel.

SEGMENT 2

COLSON: That Miami TV station challenge will be filed, although I've had several talks with [first name unknown] Sloan [an investor] and [Paul] McCray. He won't be in it initially, which is good. That's a real long shot. That's more of a harassment. The *Washington Post* is very clever. They put that station together and ran it for three years, and they hired twenty-eight Spanish-speaking and they hired blacks and they did all the things the law requires.

PRESIDENT NIXON: What the hell can you take them on?

COLSON: Well, you take them on basically not investing the profits of the station in the community and taking them back here to Washington.

PRESIDENT NIXON: Oh.

COLSON: So the new group will promise to reinvest all of the profits for five years in the community, et cetera, et cetera.

PRESIDENT NIXON: That's good.

COLSON: Enough to tie it up in court, that's all. But the real place where the *Post* can be taken is in some stockholder litigation. I'm convinced that this gal [Katharine Graham] is vulnerable.

PRESIDENT NIXON: What about [Edward] Bennett Williams? That's one of the [IRS] files which should be pulled.

COLSON: Should be.

PRESIDENT NIXON: One of the quickest. What do you think? I'll bet you he hasn't had an audit. What do you think?

COLSON: I'll bet anything he has not.

PRESIDENT NIXON: That's my point.

JANUARY 2, 1973: THE PRESIDENT AND COLSON, 4:51–6:09 P.M., OVAL OFFICE

Colson brags about the quality and discreetness of his covert political operations, contrasting them to Watergate. He is anxious to undermine those directly responsible for Watergate.

SEGMENT 1

COLSON: The wires are carrying a story that the "group headed by President Nixon's chief Florida fund-raiser announced Tuesday it will file a rival application for the operating license of television station WJFC, which is now held by a subsidiary of the Washington Post Company."

PRESIDENT NIXON: Isn't that too bad.

COLSON: Isn't that something, a group of concerned citizens. That's Jacksonville. They're going to have quite a contest. . . . But that will fix the *Post* . . . .

PRESIDENT NIXON: Our people can afford it?

COLSON: Yes sir.

PRESIDENT NIXON: Is it worth, is it really worth our paying all that kind of money? No.

COLSON: No. Well, I've told them this and I've told them what their chances are. Their chances are good initially. They lose in the Court of Appeals, this terrible Court of Appeals that we have. That is one—they have a very slim chance, except if the whole community gets behind the idea of reinvesting the profits. That might have some appeal. But these people want to go ahead even knowing the odds against them.

PRESIDENT NIXON: Why do they want to?

COLSON: I think they want to raise hell with the *Post*. . . .

PRESIDENT NIXON: *Good!*

COLSON: And they're going to do some minimum effort kind of stuff, but it puts the burden on the *Post* to defend themselves. The *Post* will spend a fortune on this. Meanwhile, while that's going on, you take them on a couple of other fronts.

PRESIDENT NIXON: I hope you can get that stockholder thing going.

COLSON: Oh, I can get that. That's one of the great virtues of having [lawyers David] Shapiro and [Sidney] Dickstein.

SEGMENT 2

PRESIDENT NIXON: Let's face it. The only thing in my view, the main thing that was unfortunate from the standpoint of the presidency on the Watergate was the Segretti business, and Haldeman slipped a bit in here, . . . he shouldn't have had, say Chapin, working on the damn thing. My point is that's *too Goddamn close.* You know what I mean? That kind of operation should be on the outside.

COLSON: Three steps removed. And we know that.

PRESIDENT NIXON: We know that. You see, the point is by having Chapin in we had a White House man, a White House man, directly involved in a political operation, Chuck. You get the point? Don't you agree?

COLSON: Oh, absolutely. I totally agree. . . .

PRESIDENT NIXON: But basically, on these other things, on these attacks, I think for example you can—a bunch of this op-ed stuff and all that other stuff, I think that's got to be done from outside. . . . I don't know how you're going to do that from the outside. You can't do it at your law firm. How will you do it?

COLSON: Well, we have a small group . . . that will be at the PR focus.

PRESIDENT NIXON: Really?

COLSON: Oh, yes, Bob knows about this.

PRESIDENT NIXON: Great! Well, that's why I was wondering. How do we get stuff to that group. [William J.] Baroody will call you?

COLSON: Baroody will call me or he will start working directly with them. . . .

PRESIDENT NIXON: I don't want Baroody caught. I don't want the White House caught and I don't want stories charging the White House that he's a White House man, that Baroody is now working with a group to do this or that or the other. You see my point? . . .

COLSON: The only thing is this—I did a hell of lot of thing on the outside . . . and you never read about it. The things you read about were the things I didn't do [*laughter*], Watergate and Segretti. I had nothing to do with it. . . .

PRESIDENT NIXON: I see your point, by yourself. I just want it done. You know, let's do it.

COLSON: Oh, it'll be done.

PRESIDENT NIXON: [George] Bush will never do it. He'll do positive things, but that's all.

COLSON: But the key to it, if I may say so, is to be damn sure that the things you do are done in such a way that they don't bounce back. In other words, the Watergate was—whoever finally approved that, and I don't know who it was and I don't want to know, was just plain stupid, Mr. President. I would never—if I'd have known of that then, I would have fallen down in the doorway to block somebody from doing it, because it was inevitable you get caught. You can't put five men into that Goddamn building without getting caught. And no matter how much you protest, in a campaign you're going to get hurt. You could have ten people between us and the Watergate and we'll get blamed.

PRESIDENT NIXON: Sure.

COLSON: The mistake of the Watergate was whoever said do it. That was the mistake. No way we could do that without getting exposure. Segretti, in a way the same thing. The only way you can handle Segretti is somebody far removed from us sets it up, and that you can do. That person just came in too close. But my God.

PRESIDENT NIXON: Particularly with Segretti and the committee. It was a mistake to have it financed out of . . . [Herbert] Kalmbach. It was very close to me.

COLSON: Which was unnecessary . . . . You see, I did things out of Boston, we did some blackmail and you say, my God. I'll go to my grave before I ever disclose it, but we did a hell of a lot of things and never got caught. The things that blew up and became newsworthy were the things that we just did because they were stupid to do.

PRESIDENT NIXON: Our Democratic friends did a hell of a lot of things, too, and never got caught.

COLSON: Oh, sure.

PRESIDENT NIXON: Because they're used to it. But our people were too Goddamn naive, in my opinion, amateurish.

COLSON: Well, you had one of the men who was in line at your Christmas tree lighting reception who ran 15 or 20 black projects in Boston, and that'll never be traced. No way. And I could under oath say I didn't know how it happened. And that's the way to do it.

SEGMENT 3

COLSON: There was another case in point. We had a mass of letter-writing campaigns of Catholic parents, who were given mimeographed letters that went out a week before the election, two weeks before the election. And they would copy those letters and send them to their congressman, and the letter said, you know, next session I want your pledge that you will support President Nixon's tax credit. And those were sent to the schools and every parent would sit down and write the damn thing. You talk about being blazoned in their mind. And we checked the Hill. In New Jersey they were absolutely inundated and I really believe, 62 percent in New Jersey, we had to do damn well with the Catholics, had to with the Catholics. But that kind of stuff we never even talked about.

So it can be done. Just, as I told Ehrlichman, the key is just don't let people, don't let people inside authorize stupid things. Take time to do them right.

JANUARY 3, 1973: THE PRESIDENT AND HALDEMAN, 11:30 A.M.–1:00 P.M., OVAL OFFICE

The President's chief aide is similarly anxious to cast blame and undermine others. He tells Nixon that Colson knew about Watergate, a question that had constantly preyed on Nixon's mind for the previous six months. Jeb Magruder is a subject of concern. "Liddy we're taking care of in one way," Haldeman says. "We've got to be

WATERGATE: THE UNRAVELING OF THE COVER-UP 195

very careful to take care of Magruder the right way, in the other way." More importantly, Haldeman underlines the dangers of campaign treasurer Hugh W. Sloan, Jr.
revealing money disbursements from the Republican campaign, money that eventually bought silence from Hunt. Nixon wanted to know: "What are we doing to
take care of him?" Again, high praise for John Dean: "He's in it, in a sense, himself,
because of what he's trying to do," Haldeman notes.

HALDEMAN: I found out some things that John [Ehrlichman] thinks were, even
though he's [Colson] going to be missed, there was more to his involvement in some
of this stuff than I realized.

PRESIDENT NIXON: Really?

HALDEMAN: Yes.

PRESIDENT NIXON: Which part?

HALDEMAN: Watergate.

PRESIDENT NIXON: Colson? Does he know?

HALDEMAN: I think he knows.

PRESIDENT NIXON: Does he know you know?

HALDEMAN: I don't think he knows I know.

PRESIDENT NIXON: What do you mean, through Hunt or what?

HALDEMAN: Yes, through Hunt and Liddy. And if Liddy decides to pull the cord,
Colson could be in some real soup. Liddy can do it under oath and then Colson is in
a position of having perjured himself. See, Colson and Mitchell have both perjured
themselves under oath already . . . .

PRESIDENT NIXON: You mean Colson was aware of the Watergate bugging? That's
hard for me to believe.

HALDEMAN: Not only was aware of it, but was pushing very hard for results, and
very specifically that.

PRESIDENT NIXON: Who was he pushing?

HALDEMAN: Magruder and Liddy. And that's why we've got to be awful careful to
take—Liddy we're taking care of in one way. We've got to be very careful to take care
of Magruder the right way, in the other way.

PRESIDENT NIXON: How can you do that?

HALDEMAN: I don't know. But I'm going to make sure he has the feeling that
he's—John Dean's been doing a superb job of just patting on him, covering all facets.

PRESIDENT NIXON: What about Magruder? What does he need, a job of some sort,
or what?

HALDEMAN: Well, either a job or ample recognition so he can go out into something outside. And he doesn't know what he wants to do. He doesn't know what he
should do. . . . But the main thing is he's got to feel in his own mind and in his own
heart, really, that he's—

PRESIDENT NIXON: That we're going to back him up.

HALDEMAN: That we're on his side. And I've told him that. I've told him solidly—

PRESIDENT NIXON: He's working on the Inauguration, isn't he?

HALDEMAN: Oh, yes. He's the director of the inaugural and is doing all the running
of that thing. So that gives him an ongoing base through the [January] 20th.

PRESIDENT NIXON: Does Mitchell know that Colson was involved, and does Colson know that Mitchell was involved?

HALDEMAN: I think the answer is yes to both of those, although I'm sure Colson assumes that Mitchell is involved if he doesn't know it directly as a fact. And I'm not positive if Mitchell knows that Colson was involved. See, Mitchell's involvement was early and then he backed out. Again, it's a question—

PRESIDENT NIXON: I can see Mitchell, but I can't see Colson getting into the Democratic office.

HALDEMAN: The stupidity.

PRESIDENT NIXON: What the Christ was he looking for?

HALDEMAN: They were looking for stuff on two things. One, on financial.

PRESIDENT NIXON: Yes.

HALDEMAN: And the other on stuff that they thought they had on what they were going to do at Miami to screw us up, because apparently—a Democratic plot. And they thought they had it uncovered. Colson was salivating with glee at the thought of what he might be able to do with it. And they were very reluctant, the investigator types were reluctant, to go in there. They were put under tremendous pressure that they had to get that stuff. None of this—I don't know any of this firsthand. I can't prove any of it, and I don't want to know it. As I pointed out, if I ever get called in I'll be ignorant, which I am.

But Hunt also knows. See, if Hunt decided to talk he could really screw Colson. But apparently there's no real danger of that. There doesn't appear to be any great danger of Liddy flipping, and I think we're okay on Magruder. The other one that's a problem is Sloan, and he doesn't know enough, apparently, to matter, although he suspects a lot, and if they start him wandering along his suspicions he could make a lot of news, if not any illegal.

PRESIDENT NIXON: What are we doing to take care of him?

HALDEMAN: Well, they're trying to keep him taken care of.

PRESIDENT NIXON: Has he got a job?

HALDEMAN: Yes.

PRESIDENT NIXON: What is Magruder going to do?

HALDEMAN: Give John Dean a lot of credit for being a damn effective operator in this one, without bothering anybody with the details, just sort of living with it hour by hour. He's got an interest in that. He's in it, in a sense, himself because of what he's trying to do.

PRESIDENT NIXON: What about Magruder? What can we do there?

HALDEMAN: Who?

PRESIDENT NIXON: Magruder.

HALDEMAN: Well, he's intrigued with the Bicentennial Commission and that is something we could give him without any problem. He'd be perfectly adequate to handle, not as the president, but as—

PRESIDENT NIXON: Executive director or something.

HALDEMAN: The problem with it is it's a politically visible spot and I'm not sure it's something you want to—

PRESIDENT NIXON: No, no.

HALDEMAN: —get him into.

PRESIDENT NIXON: I wouldn't put him in—

HALDEMAN: He doesn't want anything and wouldn't consider anything until after the trial and the thing is all over with. He doesn't even want to be thought of during that.

PRESIDENT NIXON: What's the present plan for the trial?

HALDEMAN: I'm not sure what the dates are.

PRESIDENT NIXON: Do we know whether they're going to plead guilty or go to trial or what?

HALDEMAN: They're apparently going to plead guilty, but they're still playing with their maneuvers, you know, their civil rights and all that sort of stuff.

PRESIDENT NIXON: What's that?

HALDEMAN: They're still playing with their civil rights maneuvers and all that sort of stuff.

PRESIDENT NIXON: All in all, it's better for them to plead guilty, frankly.

HALDEMAN: I would think so.

PRESIDENT NIXON: And then the Congress goes after it, I guess, persecuting, you know, men who have paid the price.

HALDEMAN: There's apparently some question as to what the Congress is going to do still. Indications are that the Kennedy staff have faded away in their activity.

PRESIDENT NIXON: That's on Segretti.

HALDEMAN: They may have turned it over to either Jackson or Ervin, if either one is going to pick it up.

JANUARY 8, 1973: THE PRESIDENT, HALDEMAN, AND EHRLICHMAN, 11:31 A.M.–1:28 P.M., OVAL OFFICE

The President's men brief him on the forthcoming burglars' trial and report on Lyndon B. Johnson's wiretaps during the 1968 campaign. Nixon believes he can use information of LBJ's activities to gain Johnson's and Hubert Humphrey's support in quashing further Watergate inquiries.

SEGMENT 2

HALDEMAN: Well, the way it appears now is that Hunt is going to take a guilty plea on three counts, and he'll do it after [U. S. Attorney Earl] Silbert's opening statement and the jury is empaneled and sequestered. They will ask him, presumably, whether there were any higher-ups involved after he takes his guilty plea, and he'll say no, and he'll go to jail. The rest apparently will go to trial. The attorney for the Cubans, this guy [Henry] Rothblatt, is a super guy who wants to—I mean a zealot who wants to play the game with them. Liddy is not going to go guilty. He's going to go for an innocent plea, go to trial on the basis of [looking] for an error. He thinks he can screw something up somewhere, that they'll screw something up somewhere and [he will] get off. They all will sit—none of them will testify.

PRESIDENT NIXON: But they'll have to testify.

HALDEMAN: And none of them will take the stand, except McCord, who does intend to take the stand, but McCord has no firsthand knowledge of any involvement of other people; therefore, Dean's not too worried about his taking the stand. All of the Cubans and Liddy, if convicted—which presumably they will be—and, if immunized after conviction by the Congress in order to take them up there for stuff, will sit mute and will take contempt of Congress charges—

PRESIDENT NIXON: And spend another year in jail.

HALDEMAN: Rather than testify before Congress. At least that's their present position.

PRESIDENT NIXON: Can the Congress bring them up and immunize them? Can the court immunize them?

EHRLICHMAN: Grand jury.

PRESIDENT NIXON: What?

EHRLICHMAN: A grand jury proceeding. The court immunizes them. And the procedure would be after they are sentenced to bring them back in—the grand jury or the Congress, either one.

HALDEMAN: But they intend—the Cubans intend not to talk, and it's not clear what the defense is going to be with the Cubans at this point. The one thing Dean raises in the congressional thing is whether we have in any way any hard evidence that the plane [in the 1968 campaign] was bugged. The reason he asked is that he sent me a strategy on the Hill of going for an attempt to force the Congress to investigate hanky-panky in both '68 and '72, rather than letting them just go do an investigation of '72 activities. And he can intercede, but we can also start moving on individual Senators and some of the problems they wouldn't like known as to what they've done and not done, but also the question of whether—see, that plane bug thing was logged out. Who had the story? Somebody had it—the [*Washington*] *Star* had the story.

PRESIDENT NIXON: Johnson admitted it, I understand.

HALDEMAN: Well, sort of.

PRESIDENT NIXON: Did you talk to him?

HALDEMAN: No, George Christian did. He finally admitted it to George. But the question is whether there will be hard evidence on it. The only input we have on it is J. Edgar Hoover, who is dead, I presume.

EHRLICHMAN: Well, [Cartha] DeLoach is around. He's never admitted it, to my knowledge.

HALDEMAN: Was DeLoach the one who did it?

EHRLICHMAN: Yep. Johnson called DeLoach and had him do it.

HALDEMAN: Well, maybe you do have hard evidence. . . .

PRESIDENT NIXON: Well, we have nothing now as far as Johnson is concerned, and we have nothing to worry about. Johnson did not support us . . . , and at the present time I wouldn't [give] any damn, I'd play that right up to the hilt. What does it do to the Bureau? It's a nasty story. It's just too damn bad. *They should not have bugged the candidate's plane!*

SEGMENT 3

PRESIDENT NIXON: Well, getting back to the bugging . . . . It's a hell of a reflection on Johnson. You don't really have to have hard evidence, Bob. You're not trying to take this to court. All you have to do is to have it out, just put it out as authority, and the press will write the Goddamn story, and the *Star* will run it now.

EHRLICHMAN: I think in the congressional context you have to be in a position to go to somebody like Hubert Humphrey and say Senator, there are very strong reasons why this whole inquiry is not a good idea, and here's a statement that I'll show you by a fellow who was in the Bureau at the time, and I think you'll see the implications.

PRESIDENT NIXON: Well, why don't you get hold of Mitchell and see what he can give you? I assume Mitchell has been told.

HALDEMAN: I had a call in to him.

PRESIDENT NIXON: Mitchell has said, Bob, he has said candidly that J. Edgar Hoover told him. I don't know how it came up that we found out about her [the wiretapping of Anna Chennault, who was a go-between for Nixon and the South Vietnam government], why Hoover would ever have told her, or did we suspect?

EHRLICHMAN: Well, I think it was in that whole period of time involving bugging and the question of authorization of bugging and all that. You remember there was a lot of controversy at one point.

HALDEMAN: And Hoover was ingratiating himself with you and was always running around about how Johnson had the White House telephone lines all monitored and all that stuff, telling you what you ought to watch out for and what he was up to.

PRESIDENT NIXON: Yeah. He said don't make calls on your White House phones, I know. Well, why don't you get at it tentatively? . . .

EHRLICHMAN: Well, let's find out if Mitchell has anything hard. He may have squirreled away some files or something. If he didn't, then I don't see any reason why we shouldn't go to DeLoach and just say we've got this—

PRESIDENT NIXON: Does he still work for [Donald] Kendall [of Pepsico]?

EHRLICHMAN: Sure. . . .

PRESIDENT NIXON: And then go to DeLoach and DeLoach's got to come clean on it. We'll go to Kendall and Kendall puts the arm on him and says he's got to go ahead and say it. He was ordered to do it and he did have the President's plane bugged. . . . The reason for it, of course, was in order to get information [on] Vietnam . . . .

HALDEMAN: Well, we could start pushing on the other bugging that Johnson did, because he did a hell of a lot of his own staff and everything else. You know, you could—

PRESIDENT NIXON: Try and find the witnesses.

HALDEMAN: I was going to say one of the witnesses in the Watergate case is going to be a kid who Hunt recruited who was in the Muskie headquarters and then in the McGovern headquarters—

PRESIDENT NIXON: Worked for Hunt?

HALDEMAN: Worked for Hunt, was paid $3,500, and finally broke off with Hunt because he refused to bug Gary Hart's telephone over at McGovern headquarters. That's going to reopen and reinsulate this whole political sabotage business, I would guess, and that will come fairly early in the trial, I would think, because that's part of the conspiracy. . . .

PRESIDENT NIXON: . . . [A]nd it will come down to this—he was in the headquarters of one, the headquarters of another. *That,* believe me, doesn't bother me too much. Good God, there are people planted in headquarters all the time.

EHRLICHMAN: The posture of this is that some people don't know. It isn't commonly understood out around the country that this is done or has been done in prior years.

PRESIDENT NIXON: We know it was.

EHRLICHMAN: That's right, sure.

PRESIDENT NIXON: Well, let me say we have to use the material on the Johnson thing, and if Mitchell doesn't have the hard evidence, we just put it out. We'll float it out there . . . for now.

HALDEMAN: . . . Johnson . . . admitted it to George [Christian], admits to the discussion, which George found very enlightening, because Johnson had never admitted it to him before.

PRESIDENT NIXON: Well, this is one of those things we have to [exploit?]. . . .

JANUARY 8, 1973: THE PRESIDENT AND HALDEMAN, 5:49–6:09 P.M., OVAL OFFICE

The two men discuss exploiting the 1968 bugging incident with Johnson and Humphrey.

HALDEMAN: On the other thing, he [John Mitchell] said that the information came directly from Hoover.

PRESIDENT NIXON: He did?

HALDEMAN: Yes. And he said that DeLoach was involved, and he's trying to reach DeLoach now to get—you know, refurbish his own mind on the circumstances . . . .

PRESIDENT NIXON: Who was DeLoach supposed to have told? I thought DeLoach was supposed to have told somebody.

HALDEMAN: Hoover told Mitchell, apparently. I said did the information come from DeLoach or from Hoover, and he said, no, it came directly from Hoover. I thought Hoover had told you.

PRESIDENT NIXON: He may have, but I can't say anything about it. Do you see what I mean? You've gotta have somebody out there that will say something, and it's got to be somebody other than Mitchell. That's why DeLoach is so key to this thing, and whether a guy like that'll speak up, I just don't know. Otherwise, Bob, Mitchell will—it looks like a self-serving statement if he goes in and says that Edgar Hoover said that, and so what's Johnson going to say?

HALDEMAN: Johnson's got—he may try and lie . . . , but he's got a problem because he knows he's lying.

PRESIDENT NIXON: It's a messy business.

HALDEMAN: It's not only Johnson that was lying, but George Christian and John Connally and a few others know he's lying.

PRESIDENT NIXON: Does Connally know?

HALDEMAN: Well, you told Connally. . . . And I think Connally surely knows about Christian's conversation with Johnson, which confirmed it.

PRESIDENT NIXON: Even based on this, even this much information, we can still play the game. . . . I would have [Dwayne] Andreas go see Hubert Humphrey. I think you've got to get Mitchell into the show, and Andreas has got to talk to Hubert and say now this is the situation, the finances, and the rest of the situation, what the hell do you want to do, kill Johnson?

HALDEMAN: Well, it'll hurt Hubert, too.

PRESIDENT NIXON: Well, Goddamnit, Bob, every person in his right mind—who is not in his right mind is going to think Hubert knew too, isn't he?

HALDEMAN: Of course. I'm convinced Hubert will realize that.

PRESIDENT NIXON: That's right. Hubert will deny it, and nobody will believe him. Hell, Johnson was for Hubert. Andreas to Hubert I think is the way it's got to be played. So if you'll follow through rigorously on that.

JANUARY 9, 1973: THE PRESIDENT AND HALDEMAN, 9:42–10:02 A.M., OVAL OFFICE

Egil Krogh, an Ehrlichman protégé and a rising young White House staffer, closely allied to Ehrlichman, was co-director of the Plumbers, but apparently Haldeman, who knew of his activities, confidently believes that Krogh could keep vital secrets.

HALDEMAN: . . . If we're going to have anybody getting hurt on Watergate, Krogh's the guy to be hurt. In the first place, he doesn't know diddly-shit, nothing about Watergate, had nothing to do with it, and the other operation, the leak coverage thing he was involved in, he can handle without batting an eye. He would be ideal, and he goes up [to the grand jury?] Thursday.

PRESIDENT NIXON: He makes a hell of an impression.

JANUARY 10, 1973: THE PRESIDENT, HALDEMAN, AND ROSE MARY WOODS, 9:56 A.M.–1:20 P.M., OVAL OFFICE

Nixon admits that an earlier FBI check on reporter Daniel Schorr was not for a background inquiry for a job.

PRESIDENT NIXON: As a matter of fact, you're quite aware of the fact that when we were looking into him [Schorr]—and we were looking into him—it was not for a job.

HALDEMAN: That's right.

PRESIDENT NIXON: Actually, we were looking into him, Rose, because of national security.

JANUARY 10, 1973: THE PRESIDENT AND HALDEMAN, 1:20–2:24 P.M., OVAL OFFICE

Nixon orders Haldeman to check Henry Kissinger's telephone logs, insisting Haldeman not "do anything that's going to look like we're spying."

PRESIDENT NIXON: There's only one thing I want, and this is to be done with the security people. I want Henry's phones logged. Now, can you do that. Will the telephone company do that without—I mean, the point is, we've got to look in terms of leaks.

HALDEMAN: You mean bugged?

PRESIDENT NIXON: Oh, God, no. I don't care what he's saying. I just want to know who he talks to. But to me it's really valuable to know if he talked to [columnist Joseph] Kraft two days before Kraft came up with the piece, as you know.

HALDEMAN: I don't know if we can do that. I'll find that out.

PRESIDENT NIXON: Well, the White House switchboard, we certainly can know who he calls at the White House.

HALDEMAN: We can know who he calls out, yeah. We can at least know the number he calls.

PRESIDENT NIXON: Any calls he asks the White House operator to get, we can have all that.

HALDEMAN: He probably doesn't ask the operator to get it. He has his secretary call for him. And then incoming calls, the operators, the White House operator doesn't ask who's calling. If they call in and say Dr. Kissinger, and they give him the office, and his office sees who's calling. . . . I'm sure we can do it.

PRESIDENT NIXON: Don't do anything that's going to look like we're spying.

JANUARY 11, 1973: THE PRESIDENT AND HALDEMAN, 10:20–11:03 A.M., OVAL OFFICE

Haldeman informs Nixon that former FBI executive Cartha DeLoach will share his knowledge of LBJ's bugging orders. The President decides to ratchet up the pressure on Johnson. But Nixon miscalculates. According to Haldeman's diary, LBJ said he would counter by revealing Nixon's back-channel dealings with the South Vietnam government to delay the peace talks. Furthermore, by January 1973, Johnson's influence is negligible in national affairs and particularly in his party; finally, Johnson dies on January 22.

SEGMENT 1

PRESIDENT NIXON: Have you had any further development, Bob, with regard to the bugging at—I mean in regard to Mitchell and his talks with DeLoach? If he had?

HALDEMAN: Yes.

PRESIDENT NIXON: Did he see DeLoach?

HALDEMAN: Yes. He talked to DeLoach.

PRESIDENT NIXON: DeLoach denies?

HALDEMAN: No. DeLoach says it's true and that he has hard—he thinks—he has some hard evidence or some specifics that will lock the thing up.

PRESIDENT NIXON: Will he say so?

HALDEMAN: I don't know whether he'll say so, but he'll give us the information so that we can say so, and that's all we need.

PRESIDENT NIXON: Well, what I want is this from DeLoach. We know he knows who is in charge of that, probably still in the Bureau, a bugger. Do you know what I mean? The point on that is that Gray gives him a lie detector test, calls him in, or asks him—do you see what I mean . . . ? That's what I'd like to do. I'd like to get it so it's nailed down in terms of evidence, rather than that DeLoach told Mitchell or that Hoover, a dead man, told Mitchell, because Johnson will lie about this, if necessary, if we have to use it. My only view is that I would not want to use this story at all. This is something that I would use only for purposes of—

HALDEMAN: Dean's idea also goes the other way, which we may want to figure out a way to play around with, which is to use it on Johnson, because a lot of the problem we're dealing with on the Hill stuff, and all you get [Joseph] Califano and some of those people into, and if Johnson turns them off, it could turn them the other way. In other words—

PRESIDENT NIXON: Why doesn't somebody go down and tell Johnson?

HALDEMAN: Well, here's the other side of it. The *Star* is back on the story again.

PRESIDENT NIXON: Yeah.

HALDEMAN: See, the *Star* had it during the campaign. They're back on it also.

PRESIDENT NIXON: On the Johnson bugging?

HALDEMAN: Mm-hmm. And that'll stir Johnson up, and that gives us a way to get back to Johnson on the basis that, you know, we've got to get this turned off, because it's going to bounce back to the other story and we can't hold them—and scare him. And at his stage and with his attitude right now, he's strutting around like crazy.

PRESIDENT NIXON: I know.

HALDEMAN: He may decide to get word out to his troops and, if he did, that could be very helpful.

PRESIDENT NIXON: Could Connally go to him? Who's the best? Who could talk to Johnson about this? Mitchell?

HALDEMAN: George Christian. [Then working on behalf of Democrats for Nixon, while maintaining ties to LBJ.]. . . .

PRESIDENT NIXON: Call George in and say—

HALDEMAN: George knows the whole story, so you're not letting any new—

PRESIDENT NIXON: Well, at least it can be done. . . and done now. . . . [Have] Johnson start to use some of it. He could use it not only to Califano, but possibly even to Humphrey. How do we know the *Star* is back on the story?

HALDEMAN: They contacted DeLoach. . . . What I've got is from John Dean.

PRESIDENT NIXON: And DeLoach says it was true and he has hard evidence; is that correct?

HALDEMAN: Yeah. I've got a call in to Mitchell now. I think he's meeting with

DeLoach now, as a matter of fact. He said he'd have to call me back. I called him a half an hour ago.

PRESIDENT NIXON: The story has been a great problem. Don't you think so?

SEGMENT 2

PRESIDENT NIXON: . . . Well, get Christian in, would you, today, like today, or whenever you can, or tomorrow and say that they're on this damn story again and are on DeLoach, and he's to go tell Johnson that we're trying to keep an eye on it. We'll do our best, but he'd better get ahold of Califano and Humphrey and anybody else he knows and tell them to pipe down on this thing. . . . [W]e will use it without question, Bob, if it comes to nut time. Do you agree?

HALDEMAN: Sure.

FEBRUARY 3, 1973: THE PRESIDENT AND COLSON, 11:05 A.M.–12:08 P.M., OVAL OFFICE

On January 30, after a sixteen-day trial, the Watergate jury convicted Gordon Liddy and James McCord on eight counts. Howard Hunt had pled guilty to six counts on January 11. He told reporters that the evidence was "substantially" correct, and no "higher-ups" were involved in a wider conspiracy. Four days later, the Cuban burglars also pled guilty. Judge John Sirica ordered all seven held until a bond hearing. Sirica, a loyal Republican, baffled the President by his conduct. In this conversation, Nixon tells Colson he wants to counterattack in every way possible, using every bit of leverage possible against various senators to persuade them to call off proposed hearings.

SEGMENT 1

PRESIDENT NIXON: Let me spend a minute on the Watergate and so forth. What the hell is the strategy going to be here now? We don't—we just have to—all we are doing is just sort of letting them, you, here is the judge, and saying this . . . his Goddamn conduct is shocking. As a judge.

COLSON: Is it?

PRESIDENT NIXON: He's not being a judge. I suppose on the other side. What is he buying for? Is he young enough to look for an appointment [to the Supreme Court] with the Democrats for the next four years?

COLSON: No. No. Sirica is a tough, hard-boiled, law-and-order judge. Who—

PRESIDENT NIXON: I'm not blaming you. I'm just wondering why he is going far beyond. I'm just wondering.

COLSON: No. No. He is a Republican. I know him pretty well. I have been with him at various events—social events. Very decent guy, dedicated to you and to Eisenhower. I can't understand what he's doing. He's been ill. The only thing I can figure is that he—this case just got under his craw for some reason, and he is a hot-headed Italian, and he blew on it. He has handled himself terribly. Awfully, refusing to accept the plea, and of course, the odd thing about it is that the U.S. Attorney [Earl Silbert], who has been prosecuting this case is not our guy. I would imagine he is a Democrat. He has been there since 1964 in the U.S. Attorney's office, but I think Sirica figures he is doing what he has been—being told to do.

PRESIDENT NIXON: . . . [I]s he trying to get the Senate to conduct the big investigation? Thank God it's Ervin . . . . At least, he is now going to be hoisted on his own petard, because he is the great constitutionalist, and talk about hearsay and all the rest. If I were on the Committee, I'd tear the hell out of him.

COLSON: I don't know that Ervin has decided what to do. I have talked to him once. He is very, very reasonable. He says, you know, this fight over separation of powers has gone on for 200 years. It'll go on for 200 more years. He says it's just one of those things that the Congress and the executive are always going to be debating.

PRESIDENT NIXON: Getting back to this. What's he going to do? I know [Senator Henry] Jackson [D-WA] said he'd take it because maybe his own campaign was involved. He thinks we were spying on him.

COLSON: No. I think Jackson knows that we were feeding him a lot of stuff in the campaign, . . . we were arranging for stuff to be fed to him. I think he wants to stay out of it.

PRESIDENT NIXON: Well, more than anything, what, if anything, is being done, or can be done to counterattack, etc.? Are any of the charges against our Democrat friends being investigated, have they been? Will they be?

COLSON: Yes. . . .

PRESIDENT NIXON: Well, let me suggest another thing, this [recently convicted Senator Daniel] Brewster thing, according to Bobby Baker, he says runs a hell of a lot deeper and runs to a number of Democratic senators. . . . What are we doing about having an investigation, calling in the Speaker, putting him under oath, FBI, and saying what other senators, going right down the list? What are we doing about that?

COLSON: That's a good point. I don't know what we're doing. . . .

PRESIDENT NIXON: And you should get over to Kleindienst and say, after all, Brewster has made a very serious charge on television this morning. . . . This charge must now be investigated. . . . [F]irst, the FBI can conduct an investigation, before they conduct the Goddamn grand jury. I just think they're making Brewster guilty. I really do.

COLSON: I know they are.

PRESIDENT NIXON: [T]he Senate is full of people who take money. Christ, I was one of the few that didn't take anything.

COLSON: On both sides of the aisle.

PRESIDENT NIXON: I don't give a shit if he was a Republican. I really don't.

COLSON: This one's got [Senators Vance] Hartke, Russell B. Long, [Joseph] Montoya [D-NM]. . . .

PRESIDENT NIXON: Get at Hartke, that would be great. I mean call him in. I mean, they are going to talk about this separation of powers. The FBI should get right into this thing, and let it be known. For God's Christ, why doesn't somebody get into this thing?

SEGMENT 2

PRESIDENT NIXON: Can we get in this investigation by Ervin, can we get one of our senators to take this whole record and say, "I demand all this be investigated"? . . .

COLSON: I think your idea, Mr. President, on the Brewster thing, is marvelous. Because I've always felt when push came to shove, that Ervin would not go ahead with those hearings, because people would have been quite satisfied with throwing stones. Ervin I'm sure is clean as a whistle. There is damn few of his colleagues who don't have a skeleton—

PRESIDENT NIXON: But the point is, how do we get those colleagues so they will tell Ervin to lay off. I don't know what the Christ is the matter around here, Chuck, that this has really got to be pushed. I mean, I don't want you to be in a position where you are just the bad guy pushing. Haldeman, I think, is too busy on his stuff. Somebody has got to get out at it. Dean is a gunfighter.

COLSON: Dean is good. Ehrlichman has been sort of in charge of this. But maybe get John Dean more deeply into it. John is good.

PRESIDENT NIXON: Ehrlichman has certainly to be aware of this. I think we ought to conduct a hell of an investigation of these people and see where the chips fly and if, for example, they find that even Hugh Scott is involved, Goddamn Hugh Scott is involved, right?

COLSON: They may find [the late Senator Everett] Dirksen [R-IL] is involved. Dirksen.

PRESIDENT NIXON: *Oh Christ,* Dirksen had a black box. Jesus. Everybody is counterattacking, do you know what I mean? But, let's get at it. You are going to spend five years in jail, the fall guy for the whole thing. Damn it all to hell. Let's stick around, get him, Bobby Baker. Rose, for example, I got her working on that . . . .

What do you think, we can't let Mitchell get involved. It just can't be done. We have to protect him. Of course, we have also got to be sure that Haldeman's not involved, we've got to be sure they don't piss around on you, or Ehrlichman, anybody. But the point is that sure, this, I think this activity . . . it was perfectly legitimate to have it for the purpose of counter-espionage, spying. I don't think the country is all that stirred up about that—what do you think?

COLSON: No. Oh, God, no the country is bored with it. We get less than 1 percent who ever mention Watergate. The Watergate issue has *never* been a public issue. It's a Washington issue. It's a way to get at us. It's the way Democrats think they can use to embarrass us, and keep us on the defensive, and keep us worried, and keep us from doing other things. That's why they have kept it alive. I don't think it's worth a damn in the country. . . .

PRESIDENT NIXON: That's right . . . . Well. My whole point here is this, and don't take this now as a directive to go out and raise hell with Ehrlichman, Dean . . . that they are not here today. But I think it's a good thing to discuss quietly with Dean; let it come from him. And the rest, you already thought of what you are going to do in the Brewster case, and do it. Then you thought what you were going to do about all this, dredge up every damn violation they've got, and do it, and insist on it. You have a Senator that will raise every one of these things in that committee. I think they have got to realize what we are going to raise. We have got to fight it, and damn it, we want to do this.

COLSON: . . . [I]n defense of Dean, . . . he has done a spectacularly good job.

PRESIDENT NIXON: When is he [Sirica] going to sentence?

COLSON: Well, I would think he would sentence any time. All he has to do is get the pre-sentencing report. I don't know whether the mistrial appeal gets heard before he sentences or not—the counsels for Liddy and McCord. I have never seen a better case for a mistrial. Of course, all that will do is get a new judge and a new trial. . . .

PRESIDENT NIXON: The grand jury will be reconvened?

COLSON: Yes, sir.

PRESIDENT NIXON: Are they going to call [Hugh] Sloan in again?

COLSON: Well, I don't know about Sloan. They will call in the seven defendants because now they have no Fifth Amendment protection. In other words, they are out of jeopardy. They have already been sentenced. . . .

FEBRUARY 6, 1973: THE PRESIDENT, EHRLICHMAN, AND HALDEMAN, 9:20–9:34 A.M., OVAL OFFICE

Although Lyndon Johnson is dead, Nixon persists in believing he can use the 1968 bugging incidents to forestall any Watergate inquiries. Despite growing pressure from the Senate, Nixon remains defiant.

EHRLICHMAN: There is one other thing. That's this Ervin special committee inquiring into Watergate. . . . Well, the feeling is we ought to use every effort to throw sand in their eyes to frustrate the damn thing to get it amended to [cover] other political campaigns, to get into John Kennedy's political campaign, and so on and so forth. There are a whole bunch of options. We have got a working group working on it.

PRESIDENT NIXON: You may have to use, for instance, throw in the Johnson wiretap.

EHRLICHMAN: Well, yes, if they brought—the way they drafted the resolution is very narrow. It applies only to this campaign, and only to certain specified charges. . . .

PRESIDENT NIXON: So maybe we should just level with the Republicans.

EHRLICHMAN: Yes. It's going to be rough as hell. So, we will get our heads together.

PRESIDENT NIXON: I don't see how the Senate can destroy us. . . .

FEBRUARY 6, 1973: THE PRESIDENT AND HALDEMAN, 12:51–1:23 P.M., OVAL OFFICE

As the Senate prepares to authorize a Select Committee, Haldeman discusses Republican strategy for gaining parity on the committee. Again, the two consider an alternative to Pat Gray for the FBI post.

PRESIDENT NIXON: Let me ask you another thing about it, Bob. Did (unintelligible) Mitchell [know]?

HALDEMAN: Yeah.

PRESIDENT NIXON: Mitchell's got to get—he's got to get a greater interest in this himself, I think.

HALDEMAN: I think he is. He came down to the meeting this morning.

PRESIDENT NIXON: It's going to be right on his back and I don't know who else's. . . . Well, now, what about the Johnson wiretap, for example?

HALDEMAN: We're playing that out today.

PRESIDENT NIXON: How about having that played to our friend Andreas?

HALDEMAN: They did. Andreas took it to Hubert, and Hubert took it to Ervin, and Ervin was totally unimpressed, couldn't care less. Hubert was a little concerned about it, but Ervin not at all. Ervin—these guys who were doing the analysis here, that Ervin is not the great constitutional authority he sets himself up to be. He is nothing but—

PRESIDENT NIXON: A partisan Democrat.

HALDEMAN: Well, a partisan Democrat and very anxious to get publicity. He loves, and he's finally come into the limelight. Some staff member has made a crack that was quoted this morning that you should see the number of speaking invitations he's getting. We've waited thirty years for this. But anyway, he's playing this role of above and beyond.

PRESIDENT NIXON: So all this business about we thought that maybe he wouldn't go forward is wrong. He's going to seek to squeeze every bit of publicity out of it as he can. . . . What of the expanding investigation? . . .

HALDEMAN: Well, [Republicans offered] amendments today on the charge to the committee, and they're working in a meeting right now at the Policy Committee. . . . Bryce [Harlow] comes up with a good talking point here, as we start into the Senate thing, which is that this is a dire threat to the two-party system, because for the first time in our history we have one of the political parties using the machinery of government to investigate the other political party. He's trying to get them stirred up. It isn't going to make any difference, and he doesn't have any illusions that it will. He's just trying to make a case that this is totally a partisan thing.

Now the committee that they are setting up under their bill is three Democrats and two Republicans. They're going to make a pitch to make it three Democrats and three Republicans on the basis that the Senate Ethics Committee is also that way in order to be bipartisan, and that this must be bipartisan; therefore, it's got to have three of each party. Then they're going to go for an executive session on the vote of three members, in the hopes that—if they can get those two, then we're in awfully good shape compared to where we will probably be, which is—because we probably won't get them—is open hearings with only two Republicans, so we have no control.

PRESIDENT NIXON: And we don't know who the hell the Republicans are. Who appoints them?

HALDEMAN: The Majority Leader—Minority Leader. . . .

PRESIDENT NIXON: And we'll get a couple sons of bitches on our side.

HALDEMAN: Well, the recommendations are, if it's two, is that it's [Senators

William] Brock—excuse me, that it's [Robert] Griffin and [John] Tower, Griffin to nitpick the legal stuff and Tower to play the political, and, if it's three, to add Brock to it.

PRESIDENT NIXON: Right. Good. Good.

HALDEMAN: That's what they're going to push for on membership.

PRESIDENT NIXON: It seems to me that the Johnson wiretap thing has got to be blown. I would wait a while.

HALDEMAN: Well, they're going to rumor it this afternoon and going to use that on the floor as a basis, and they're also getting Goldwater to cut loose this afternoon on his, "what the hell, I wired—I bugged my opponents and they bugged me and it's always done." And they're going to make some allusions to some probable Kennedy wiretapping in 1960, or surveillance of your campaign activities. . . .

PRESIDENT NIXON: It's all such a bunch of Goddamn dirty shit. . . . Has anybody followed up on my suggestion that the FBI immediately, because what Senator [Daniel] Brewster [D-MD, who eventually was convicted for corruption charges] said. . . . It's such an obvious thing that it should have been done maybe like last week. Remember when Brewster said there might be members of the Senate involved in this, and everybody knows that . . . ? I would call him. But, Goddamnit, the FBI can investigate on that.

What is the present thinking, Bob, with regard to the FBI? Do we go with Gray?

HALDEMAN: There was one other guy they were running a final check on, and then they were going to come back.

PRESIDENT NIXON: I saw one that I didn't like, some guy that graduated from Harvard and is now a criminologist in Chicago—wrong signal [Orlando Wilson?].

HALDEMAN: That one is out. There was another one that—well, you've got that other guy that Ehrlichman rules out because he didn't graduate from Harvard but looks like he did.

PRESIDENT NIXON: Yeah, and you've got Ruckelshaus.

HALDEMAN: And Ruckelshaus.

FEBRUARY 7, 1973: THE PRESIDENT, HALDEMAN, EHRLICHMAN, AND ZIEGLER, 10:25 A.M.–12:21 P.M., OVAL OFFICE

The Senate votes unanimously to authorize the Select Committee late in the day on February 7. Republican attempts to broaden the Committee's scope of inquiry to include past campaigns and to secure equal representation fail, and they have no choice but to support the investigation. Earlier that day, Nixon and his men discuss prospects for delaying the hearings. They recognize the widening scope of the affair. Here, they begin to develop and support the legal theory that a Senate hearing will jeopardize the rights of the defendants.

SEGMENT 2

ZIEGLER: It seems to me that we should say that if the intent of the Ervin committee is to examine this whole area, not only in 1972 but back to '60, 1964, and 1968, and, as Senator Ervin says, it is not going to be partisan in nature, then, of course, we would be supportive and cooperate.

PRESIDENT NIXON: Is it limited to 1972?

ZIEGLER: Yes.

EHRLICHMAN: The bill of particulars is very specific. It's the presidential election of this last time, and particularly as to the Republicans.

PRESIDENT NIXON: It says that?

EHRLICHMAN: Yes, sir, in the resolution.

HALDEMAN: Does it say Republicans?

EHRLICHMAN: All the way through it. Yeah, there are about ten specifications in that thing. It says Republicans, you bet, and it says the bugging of the Watergate headquarters of the Democratic party.

PRESIDENT NIXON: What about violence at the convention?

EHRLICHMAN: I don't know about the violence, but they had a whole bunch of proposed amendments. Tower was pushing—

PRESIDENT NIXON: All of them failed.

EHRLICHMAN: —to get three and three. And I think they will propose this on the floor—three Republicans, three Democrats.

PRESIDENT NIXON: Why not just say that we—the administration has always indicated willing cooperation with the investigation that is after the facts . . . .

EHRLICHMAN: There's an aspect of this that you may want to allude to, Ron—I don't know. The Watergate defendants are going to claim that Sirica should not sentence them because he exhibited such malice and prejudice. If he does sentence them, they will appeal, even those that pleaded guilty. . . .

PRESIDENT NIXON: Of course, we should have in mind that obviously . . . the scope of the investigation must of course be dependent upon the status of any proceedings that are in the courts and must not under any circumstances be allowed to impede or—well, or interfere with the rights of defendants to get a fair trial and a fair appeal.

EHRLICHMAN: Due regard for the rights of others.

PRESIDENT NIXON: Due regard for the rights of defendants to get a trial.

EHRLICHMAN: Now, that's being advanced to Ervin privately, and I don't know what effect it might have. . . . But what may happen is that one of the defendants will seek an injunction to prevent the hearings from going forward, and then you've got a nice constitutional question of whether a court can enjoin the proceedings of the Congress and it'll get all snarled up. So that's all up ahead somewhere.

PRESIDENT NIXON: With regard to this, the key part is that the administration—I said this long ago—will cooperate with the courts or any investigation of this (unintelligible), but it's one that cannot be partisan and should not be partisan. It must be directed to the activities of both political parties, and it should not be limited to this election. . . .

EHRLICHMAN: In other words, we have never—we've never been opposed to a thorough and fair investigation.

PRESIDENT NIXON: But not limited to this election. It should be the elections of '68 and '64 and '60. Senator Goldwater, you could say, has raised some very serious questions about what happened in 1964 on both sides, and it might be useful if the Senate is really attempting to—I mean, if the Senate committee, of course—I don't want to throw any aspersions to the Senate committee—wants to render a public service it should go back and pick up those charges as well, '64, '60—1960, '64, and '68. . . .

SEGMENT 4

PRESIDENT NIXON: They're going to have Tower and Wilson [?] on the committee on our side.

HALDEMAN: What they were talking about yesterday was Tower and Griffin.

PRESIDENT NIXON: . . . And Griffin has a good image.

HALDEMAN: That's it. He's got a sort of a Mr. Clean type thing. And if it does go on television, he looks like a serious, intense type.

PRESIDENT NIXON: Oh, it'll be on television.

HALDEMAN: . . . [S]ee who they have on the other side [Democratic], but the problem there is that both of them are up for election next time, and they're afraid they won't track.

PRESIDENT NIXON: The problem—that's right. The problem with the—all this is that it is going to be a television story. But, on the other side of the coin, it may—may—wear out the story after a certain length of time.

HALDEMAN: You hear the same old crap over and over, and I just can't imagine that the people really get very interested. . . . Now there's this damn trial judge [Charles Richey] in the civil suit. You know, he's gotten all excited seeing what Judge Sirica did, [and he] has released all the secret depositions. . . .

FEBRUARY 21, 1973: THE PRESIDENT AND HALDEMAN, 12:54–2:13 P.M., OVAL OFFICE

The possibility of Senator Ervin appointing a Republican as majority counsel is momentarily pleasing.

HALDEMAN: Ervin's come up with a slick move on his general—on his Chief Counsel for his committee. He's trying to get [former Republican Senator] Ken Keating, which, weighing the alternatives, may be the best bet for us, because he is—

—the next choice is, oh, Christ, you know his name. I can't remember it—a lawyer [unknown] in New York who solved the problem now, that is a particular type of Republican, ran for governor or something like that years ago.

PRESIDENT NIXON: Oh, yes.

HALDEMAN: Older man.

PRESIDENT NIXON: Older man, yes.

HALDEMAN: And the third one is some Jew. Of course, what he's going for is some prestigious Republican. . . .

FEBRUARY 22, 1973 THE PRESIDENT AND HALDEMAN, 2:35–4:04 P.M., EXECUTIVE OFFICE BUILDING

The President comments about Senator Howard Baker's choice for minority counsel, Fred Thompson.

HALDEMAN: Minority counsel is aware of the way things work in Washington, and we can handle a guy like Sam Dash, majority counsel. Oh, Baker has appointed Fred Thompson, Minority Counsel.

PRESIDENT NIXON: Oh shit, that kid.

HALDEMAN: I guess so.

PRESIDENT NIXON: They are going to lose them all. . . . It's too damn bad the kid (unintelligible).

HALDEMAN: I guess that's the way it is. Is this Fred Thompson the young guy from Tennessee?

PRESIDENT NIXON: Yes.

HALDEMAN: Do you know him?

PRESIDENT NIXON: Yes. He is a young kid.

HALDEMAN: Well, we're stuck with him. Yes.

PRESIDENT NIXON: Yeah, I know.

FEBRUARY 22, 1973: THE PRESIDENT AND BAKER, UNKNOWN TIME AFTER 4:04 P.M., EXECUTIVE OFFICE BUILDING

This is the first meeting between the President and the ranking minority member of the newly formed Senate Select Committee. Baker had let it be known that he worried that his conversations were being bugged. It is unclear whether he knew he was being taped, but the conversation is vague and the recording poor. Nixon labors hard to turn Baker's attention to Democratic campaign practices. Baker vigorously defends his choice of Thompson.

PRESIDENT NIXON: Tell me about your, your hearing, you are going to have a very interesting hearing. All are lawyers, is that right?

BAKER: Nobody knows I'm here except Bill [Timmons] . . . .

PRESIDENT NIXON: . . . I would hope that you would pretty well go in the other thing, there are lots of things out there. . . .

BAKER: The danger of that is that it's a fishing expedition.

PRESIDENT NIXON: Let me say, the Segretti thing, for God's sake, you can find so much stuff on it otherwise. That's all they're interested in. Look at the convicted seven. They have all been convicted. Now, the press is really after a bigger fish. As I say, I have a very sad—I'm not excited about this. . . .

BAKER: I think I have a better chance, I hope, next week—

PRESIDENT NIXON: Who is [Sam] Dash?

BAKER: Dash is the majority's attorney.

PRESIDENT NIXON: . . . Thompson?

BAKER: Yes, Thompson, Fred Thompson, U.S. Attorney from Tennessee.

PRESIDENT NIXON: . . . [I]f Dash gets awfully partisan, our guy could go in there . . . .

BAKER: . . . [H]e's tough. He's six feet five inches, a big mean fella. . .

PRESIDENT NIXON: Smart?

BAKER: Terribly smart.

PRESIDENT NIXON: Good . . . .

PRESIDENT NIXON: . . . I know you'll do a good job. You're exactly right. The main thing is to have no damn cover-up. That's the worst that can happen, more that the substance of this is to prepare. No coverup, but also if it does get rough, then I think you may have to at a certain time turn and get away from this [i.e., Watergate]. You are going to have to get away from this.

BAKER: Right. Right. . . .

MARCH 1, 1973: THE PRESIDENT AND DEAN, 10:36–10:44 A.M., OVAL OFFICE

Dean informs the President that Attorney General Kleindienst is distancing himself from Gray's position of making raw FBI files available to the Senate investigators. Typically, the President responds with familiar anecdotes of the misdeeds of other Administrations, reading his own published account of John F. Kennedy's rough handling of the press.

PRESIDENT NIXON: . . . Did you get Kleindienst?

DEAN: Yes, I have.

PRESIDENT NIXON: Yeah.

DEAN: Because the record is not quite as bad as printed in the paper, for one thing, but he [Kleindienst] has talked to Gray this morning.

PRESIDENT NIXON: Gotten him off of this?

DEAN: Gotten him off of this.

PRESIDENT NIXON: . . . Is that what he was calling me about?

DEAN: I told him—that's right. He wanted to tell you he'd gotten the situation turned around, straightened around. He said he didn't need to talk to you, based on our conversation.

PRESIDENT NIXON: Yeah.

DEAN: He said that Gray, in offering this, had said, one, not that he can turn the files over, but they could come down. But he also did say that this was subject to the approval of the Attorney General. So Kleindienst feels he can wade back in on that, and he told Gray that if it comes up again . . . they'll have to talk to the Attorney General about it, as to what he will or will not make available.

PRESIDENT NIXON: Well, now what are they going to say when [Congresswoman] Bella Abzug [D-NY] asks for the files? How can he?

DEAN: Well, because Kleindienst will say this is not a circumstance or situation. . . .

PRESIDENT NIXON: Kleindienst doesn't realize that. He doesn't realize it's a bad [precedent]. Is Kleindienst—did you tell him what happened in the Hiss case?

DEAN: I did, and I said that I would be sending over that chapter on the Hiss case out of [Nixon's book] *Six Crises.*

PRESIDENT NIXON: Goddamnit, tell him to get the book and read it.

DEAN: Well, I've got it in my office. I can just—

PRESIDENT NIXON: The point is, if you just go there, you could find out. We had no cooperation from the FBI, none. . . .

DEAN: [Presidential aide Clark] Mollenhoff wants to use what you said about executive privilege then.

PRESIDENT NIXON: I didn't attack it then.

DEAN: That's right.

PRESIDENT NIXON: Because it wasn't White House people we were after.

DEAN: I had just recently gotten that excerpt from the record of your speech, and I think we'll be able to very clearly distinguish, particularly if Ziegler gets a question from Mollenhoff, as to what you were talking about then *vis-à-vis* now.

PRESIDENT NIXON: Well, I would say that we ought to say to get cooperation from the FBI and the Justice Department, which we were entitled to.

DEAN: And getting none.

PRESIDENT NIXON: You see, we weren't asking for cooperation from the White House. We were asking cooperation of the Justice Department and the FBI, and they put out an order.

[On the telephone, reading from his book.] Listen to this. And bring me a copy of *Six Crises* right away, please. . . .

"[During the Kennedy Administration], at 3:00 on an April morning, a ringing telephone bell awakened an Associated Press reporter. The man on the other end of the line introduced himself as an agent of the FBI and told the AP man to expect an ugly visit from the FBI. One hour later, FBI agents rang his doorbell.

"Two hours after that, a reporter for the *Wall Street Journal* was routed out of bed by other FBI agents, and at 6:30 a.m. a newsman working for the *Wilmington, Delaware Journal* found FBI men waiting at his office door. The reporters were not involved in any crime. They had merely written that the steel industry was raising prices, and it had become important to President Kennedy to know the source of the story."

DEAN: That's excellent material. That should be out in the domain right now.

PRESIDENT NIXON: Well, Christ, it's an old story.

DEAN: That's right.

PRESIDENT NIXON: The special early morning attentions of the FBI were given as well to the major executives of large steel corporations which had announced price increases. These invasions of privacy were at the order of the President's brother, Robert Kennedy. As Attorney General, he misused his authority. . . .

DEAN: We need somebody. . . .

PRESIDENT NIXON: I don't think we have anybody that smart, frankly . . . . It's like I tried . . . because everybody around here was against or wanted me to soften the stand on amnesty. And I said I'm going to be like Lincoln. I told them, have you ever read [Carl] Sandburg? No, it's too long. I said, Goddamnit, I said, just read one page.

There's one page that Sandburg wrote on Lincoln's position on amnesty . . . . And it was very simply this. He gave amnesty to the South. But when somebody who had gone to Canada was up in front of the White House, and sent a note asking that he be given amnesty, and Lincoln wrote . . . he may return to his country provided he serves in prison for the number of days he was out of the country. That was Lincoln's amnesty. In other words, amnesty for those who fought for the South, either prison sentences or execution for those who deserted or draft-dodged in the north. And that was Abe Lincoln's position. Goddamn people around here won't read anything.

DEAN: Well, the point you made is very good, that we're not scouring—what's really in the public domain right now can put some of these things in perspective, and we should have a team doing that right now. . . . . I've got that over in my office and I'll mark the pages and send them to Kleindienst today.

PRESIDENT NIXON: Go out and bring in to me my speech on the Hiss case. Bring me my speech on the Hiss case that I made in 1951 or '50 in the House of Representatives. Would you do that, please?

DEAN: Yes, sir.

MARCH 1, 1973: THE PRESIDENT AND KLEINDIENST, 10:52–10:56 A.M., WHITE HOUSE TELEPHONE

March begins a crucial two-month period for Nixon. The White House's vulnerabilities are about to be exposed, triggered by L. Patrick Gray's confirmation hearings for the FBI directorship. Attorney General Kleindienst reports on the nomination's progress. Given Gray's yeoman service in trying to suppress the FBI investigation of Watergate, Nixon probably had no choice but to name him. Subsequent revelations in his confirmation hearings provided the Senate Select Committee with further avenues of inquiry into the Administration's cover-up activities. Nixon betrays a certain nostalgia for the days when Presidents controlled—or thought they controlled—the FBI.

KLEINDIENST: I just wanted to give you a very brief report on Pat Gray, the happenings of the first day. I think everything is going fine. Pat might have gone a little bit farther than I would like to have him go with respect to the availability of FBI records to the Senate, you know, to satisfy themselves, but I think we still have control over it with respect to procedures.

PRESIDENT NIXON: Right.

KLEINDIENST: I think his openness and his candor—[Senator] Jim Eastland [D-MS] this morning said that [Senator Sam] Ervin [D-NC] is with him all the way, and I think he is really creating a good environment up there.

PRESIDENT NIXON: Well, the main thing is don't let him get in a position where he feels that he has to—where in order to get confirmed, that he has to go so far with the Senate. One thing—I know, I guess Dean said he discussed it with you and Gray had said he would leave it to the Attorney General, but I should point out if . . . [anybody] has taken the trouble to read what I said about the Hiss case.

KLEINDIENST: I read it.

PRESIDENT NIXON: At the time, that's where I covered it in my speech at Congress, that's where I said it, at the time that we got into the case, Truman issued an order to . . . Tom Clark, the Attorney General, and to Hoover, the FBI, that they were not to cooperate. In the entire course of that investigation, the FBI closed its doors completely. The Justice Department would not cooperate, nobody from the White House would cooperate. But my point is, that was espionage against the United States of America as distinguished between hinkey-dinkey espionage with one party against another. Now, my point is, I think looking back Hoover was right, I mean Truman was right, in the sense that you cannot have a congressional committee that can get at the FBI files, but we have crossed that bridge, and if he goes so far as to say that he will give it to members of Congress, what's he going to say when Bella Abzug says, I want to see the files with regard to the investigation of the riot in Miami, or the Black Panthers? But you see, he must—there must never be—no individual—no individual congressman, no committee, nothing should have rights to FBI files.

KLEINDIENST: He made that clear, that whatever we do in the Watergate case is not to be oppressive, has got to be subject to the approval of the Attorney General and the President, and I think the record is clear enough for us to control it. Incidentally, you ought to go back and read that chapter on the Hiss case again [*laughter*] because what you did, as a result of what Truman did, was just blow them out of the water. . . . [T]heir approach to it was a political approach, and I think we want to avoid that ourselves in this case.

PRESIDENT NIXON: Exactly. Exactly.

KLEINDIENST: That's the very thing we want to avoid.

PRESIDENT NIXON: Oh well, I'm not suggesting that we do what Truman did. Because we crossed that bridge. But I'm simply saying, don't let, don't let Ervin and these boys have a double standard. I'd say all right, now, look here, boys, we are aware of that, do you really realize what we have been up against over the past? Let's remember this administration is being more cooperative than anybody else.

KLEINDIENST: Right. Well—

PRESIDENT NIXON: Well, we wish you well on it. And you are going to, as I have totally said, Dean is the only fellow you should talk to except for me.

KLEINDIENST: Yes, sir.

PRESIDENT NIXON: And I should stay out of the damn thing.

KLEINDIENST: Yes, sir.

PRESIDENT NIXON: But the other point is that I think that you ought to, and then you should talk to Baker and Ervin and be sure that Baker's back, you keep it good and stiff. He's clever, but he has got to remember—that—

KLEINDIENST: He's got to be fucked up a little bit.

PRESIDENT NIXON: He's got to be fucked up because he is so anxious, you know, to get—

KLEINDIENST: They are all thinking about themselves—

PRESIDENT NIXON: Themselves, you know, and being like, looking like great impartial investigators, well, fine, if the other side, is but don't let Howard [Baker] know—

KLEINDIENST: I think in a crunch Howard will do it.

PRESIDENT NIXON: Oh, he wants to be all right. He wants to be all right. He certainly has nothing to gain to go in the other direction. Do you remember [Senator] Ralph Flanders [R-VT]? Those who think that they can go, remember Ralph became a hero in the Washington press corps because he went after Joe McCarthy? Destroyed Ralph. That's what it does. You can't take your own party apart.

KLEINDIENST: I know it.

PRESIDENT NIXON: I don't mean by that that you cover up, but I do mean—to join this, just to pander to these Washington reporters, Dick, and this is the thing you have got to tell Pat Gray, don't do it.

KLEINDIENST: Yes. Yes. I'm meeting with him two or three times today—

PRESIDENT NIXON: Yes. Yes. Well, you understand it—well, that's the main thing.

KLEINDIENST: There might be something specific. As you say.

PRESIDENT NIXON: As you see, Pat doesn't have the sophistication that you have got, just say Pat, don't be drug into this and that.

KLEINDIENST: Right.

PRESIDENT NIXON: I want him to be totally forthright. I want him to be totally forthcoming. He's got to establish the image as a lawman and all the rest, and on the other hand don't go to the point where he wins bravados in the newspapers, in the columns, in the editorials of the eastern press. If you go that far, then you have lost, because they do not want you to do the right thing, they want you to do the wrong thing, okay?

KLEINDIENST: [*Laughter.*] Yes, sir. I won't bother you unless I have to.

PRESIDENT NIXON: No. No. No. Anytime. But let me say, I'm deliberately limiting my communication only with Dean, because you have confidence in him, he never opens his mouth—oh, one other thing that I think Pat, and I'm going to get Ziegler to do it, could play a little bit differently, I don't think he should indicate, of course, the thing that both the *Times* and the *Post* picked up, as you might expect, is that he said he had reluctantly turned the files over to the White House. Well, obviously, Dean, but I have ordered Dean to conduct an investigation. Good God, if he's going to make the files available to Congress, can he do it to the President?

KLEINDIENST: That's the one thing we discussed this morning. I said, for Christ's sake, Pat, the President of the United States, you know, this is his FBI and his department.

PRESIDENT NIXON: My point is that I ordered an investigation, and that's the only one I was getting.

KLEINDIENST: Yes. You ordered that specifically.

PRESIDENT NIXON: Right. Good luck. Good-bye.

KLEINDIENST: Good-bye.

MARCH 2, 1973: THE PRESIDENT AND HALDEMAN, 1:00–1:27 P.M., OVAL OFFICE.

This conversation reveals Nixon's knowledge of the cover-up's details. He and Haldeman discuss Thomas Pappas's role as principal funder of the hush money to the burglars—"this other activity," as the President put it. Pappas, a prominent Nixon fund-raiser, had important ties to the fascist regime of the Greek colonels in

Athens. Without hesitation, Nixon approves Pappas's request that the American Ambassador, who supported the colonels, be retained in his post. But Pappas's most important asset is that, as Haldeman succinctly states, he dealt "in cash." The moment offers an opportunity for lavish praise of their young operations officer, John Dean.

SEGMENT 1

HALDEMAN: The other one Mitchell raised, which I don't believe he did with anybody else, is—I don't know if John Dean's told you or not—one of the major problems on the business John's working on is the question of financial, continuing financial activity in order to keep those people in place. And the way he's working on that is via Mitchell to Tom Pappas.

PRESIDENT NIXON: Yeah.

HALDEMAN: Which is the best source we've got for that kind of a thing. Pappas is extremely anxious that [Ambassador Henry] Tasca stay in Greece. . . . And our plan was, you know, to remove him and put someone else in Greece, but Mitchell says it would be a very useful thing to just not disrupt that.

PRESIDENT NIXON: Good. I understand. No problem. Pappas has raised the money for this other activity or whatever it is. How's he doing?

HALDEMAN: I think it's just—you know, he's (unintelligible) raise money. . . . . [H]e put a thing together over there [Greece] and he just—he sold his company out or something and picked up something else and parlayed that into something, and apparently he's sort of one of the unknown J. Paul Gettys of the world right now.

PRESIDENT NIXON: Great. I'm just delighted.

HALDEMAN: And he's able to deal in cash. . . .

SEGMENT 2

PRESIDENT NIXON: Hell, I'm convinced that Dean is a pretty good gem. I've talked to him two or three times about it.

HALDEMAN: He's a real cool cookie, isn't he?

PRESIDENT NIXON: I don't know about cool, but he's awfully smart. Goddamn, there's no—there's judgment there, you know. He doesn't—he thinks things through and all that. He's not cocky. You see, the trouble with a cocky guy who will come in and have a lot of bravado, you've got a guy who won't check his facts.

HALDEMAN: Dean's just the other way. He does—he hasn't always checked his facts, but he never covers up if he hasn't. He just says he doesn't know. God, he's been through the wringer.

PRESIDENT NIXON: Horrible. . . .

HALDEMAN: The great thing is he's good in dealing with people. He's able to—because all this is a people game, trying to just keep these people on an even keel, not having someone break and go rattling off, and all these Goddamn Watergate seven guys he's had to nursemaid all these months.

[Withdrawn item. Privacy.]

PRESIDENT NIXON: Well, I must say I've been impressed by him. . . . Oh, would you tell Colson, please, that in the future all of his discussions on Watergate, he is to talk to you, Ehrlichman, or Dean.

HALDEMAN: Right.

PRESIDENT NIXON: I think it's very important to get Chuck funneled into the Dean shop, don't you agree? . . . The point is, Chuck will tend otherwise to raise this with other people—what about this, that and the other thing. It's just better, Bob. For example, I'm not talking to anybody but Dean—do you agree?—on this.

HALDEMAN: Yep.

PRESIDENT NIXON: He's a lawyer and all that. . . .

MARCH 3, 1973, THE PRESIDENT AND HALDEMAN, 9:40–10:05 A.M., OVAL OFFICE

By early March, the White House senses that L. Patrick Gray's nomination as FBI director faces growing opposition, and Nixon and Haldeman, who had misgivings about Gray, have little stomach for a prolonged fight.

PRESIDENT NIXON: What's your judgment as to how Gray is handling himself?

HALDEMAN: I don't know. Dean says he's not doing well, that he's letting too much out. Gray—Gray's line is that this is all a tactic, that he's doing it on purpose. For instance, his offer to let them look at the raw files he's doing because he's convinced that Ervin won't allow that to happen and that this is all a clever thing and he turns it all off on Tuesday and Ervin hangs tight and that they've got the votes and that's where they are.

There's two sides to the argument. The Gray side—and it's a question of congressional tactics really—the Gray side is that he's playing sort of a throw it out there and let Ervin snatch it back game that will close the whole thing off on Tuesday and put it to a vote, and that Eastland is sure he's got the votes and will move to vote and it will be on the floor. The . . . concern of that tactic is that [Senator Robert C.] Byrd [D-WV] is taking such a strong anti-Gray position that one has to consider the possibility that Byrd may know he's got the votes and they aren't going to get it out. And Eastland's advice to us on tactics has been almost as wrong as Mitchell's, and Mitchell's has, of course, always been based on Eastland. . . .

Kleindienst, Mitchell and Eastland. The three of them have worked together. The Kleindienst tactics were all based on what Eastland told him was fine. But when it gets to a crunch, Eastland . . . bows to senatorial courtesy and lets the thing go on.

PRESIDENT NIXON: Mm-hmm.

HALDEMAN: And if he does that on Tuesday, Gray's got an awful lot out on the plate that it would be better not to have out on the plate. If, on the other hand, they close it down Tuesday, we're—

PRESIDENT NIXON: You mean on Tuesday they'll have a vote . . . ?

HALDEMAN: Well, they don't have a vote scheduled, but they're going—Gray says that Eastland's plan is to bring it to a vote, because he says Ervin will never let them get into individual senators pursuing the files, which is about all we've got left now. I don't know. I don't think John's [Mitchell] much of an analyst of Hill strategy, and I think those guys over there all tend to worship at Eastland's shrine and Eastland doesn't come through. But Dean has been hitting him hard and Kleindienst has too. Kleindienst disagrees with him [Gray], as I understand it from Dean.

PRESIDENT NIXON: Oh. Kleindienst, what's he think?

HALDEMAN: He doesn't think he should—he thinks he's being too outgoing on this stuff.

PRESIDENT NIXON: Well, he says, for example, . . . a lot of people at the Bureau are disturbed and they're going to get to the bottom of the Watergate thing.

HALDEMAN: Yeah. I understand that.

PRESIDENT NIXON: . . . You know, we might have been better to follow the first hunch and put [D.C. Police Chief] Jerry Wilson in that thing [FBI Director]. . . .

MARCH 6, 1973, THE PRESIDENT AND DEAN, 11:49 A.M.–12:00 P.M., OVAL OFFICE

Dean delivers a progress report on the Gray nomination. Nixon complains that Gray was trying to be "non-political." The President has no desire for such an appointee. Nixon expresses doubts whether Senator Howard Baker will help the Administration in the forthcoming Senate hearings. The two also discuss the question of "privilege" for top White House staff and lawyers.

DEAN: Good morning, Mr. President.

PRESIDENT NIXON: Hi. Say, I wanted to get a brief report on how they're doing over with Gray.

DEAN: Yeah. I don't know what's happened yet this morning. I talked to Pat, oh, maybe four or five times since he was up there last. He said that his policy had been one to cooperate all the way with the committee up to this point. He's turned over for the record everything that was requested, including the things that hit the papers this morning, which I think he should have deferred on. Kleindienst told me that he isn't touching base with him, despite his efforts to get him to touch base, on timing on when he's turned things over. . . .

Today he'll talk about, you know, he's going to infringe upon the rights of individuals. He's going to open sensitive files that have not been sort of groomed for public consumption, if they're going to be put in public form, and they'll harm innocent people, and really close the store down today. That's what he's supposed to do. Now, he was reminded, when—and mentioned it to me. He said, "I know my nomination can be withdrawn."

PRESIDENT NIXON: He did?

DEAN: Gray said to me, when I talked to him on—I guess this was on Friday, he said, John, I appreciate the fact that my nomination can be withdrawn at any point in time, if you all see what I'm doing as improper. . . .

Kleindienst talked to Eastland this morning. I asked him to do that. Eastland says he sees things going well right now, that they have the votes, that [Senators Philip]

Hart [D-MI] and [Birch] Bayh [D-IN] and Kennedy and [John] Tunney [D-CA] have indicated they don't plan to prolong the hearings, particularly until the early hearings are completed, or something like that, on the Watergate, to hold up Gray. Now, Ervin gave an interview this morning with WTOP, the local station out here, saying that he would support the request of Tunney that I appear before they proceed with Gray, and he didn't say he would hang in there all the way. . . . But, of course, the things they're raising about Dean are totally irrelevant to Pat Gray, totally irrelevant. . . .

PRESIDENT NIXON: We're not going to give an inch on that. When are you going to put out the statement?

DEAN: . . . The one thing conspicuously absent from that statement that just occurred to me is we have never treated the subject of former White House staff who have departed who still enjoy the privilege for those times when they were here. I think we ought to—I have a good memorandum from the office of legal counsel on that point, and I think we ought to add possibly one more paragraph to deal with that situation. That takes care of the Chapins, the Colsons, the Strachans. . . .

PRESIDENT NIXON: . . . [Y]ou wonder whether we were right in sending Gray down. What do you think? Were we or not?

DEAN: It gives pause, but I think we're right in the long run, and I think today will be the test, the way he performs up there today, and if that's continued, you know, sort of abandon for everybody else, except for Pat Gray, then I think we really have to reassess.

PRESIDENT NIXON: Well, he's got to determine whether he's going to play [politically?] Godddamn, . . . he's the director of the FBI. There are plenty of men that could direct the FBI if they're going to play it non-politically.

DEAN: That's right.

PRESIDENT NIXON: But Gray has got to—we're not even asking him to be political. We're just asking to give us a fair break.

DEAN: Withhold the store is all we're asking.

PRESIDENT NIXON: He should not be up there and say, well, I've got to be confirmed at the expense of everybody here. Oh, no. That can't be.

DEAN: Well, I, without getting terribly specific, I said, Pat, I said, I've got to be very candid with you. There's a certain degree of disappointment in the way you've performed thus far over here, and I think you can understand why. He said, "John, I know, I know, but let me tell you what the strategy has been all along."

PRESIDENT NIXON: [We have to move forward] now and trying to get [William] Sullivan to scare [Cartha] DeLoach and those other things I spoke to you about?

DEAN: Yes. That's been in the works, as well as the report you asked me for on some of the past activities. I had another long session with Sullivan and . . . I'm going to treat Sullivan at arm's length. I'm not sure about him yet.

PRESIDENT NIXON: Right. Right.

DEAN: And I said want to know everything you know that's been done to that Bureau in the whole time you were there. And he says well, I've got some humdingers, and he gave me a couple more. . . . Lyndon Johnson . . . said, "I want that file changed." And it was just an impossible task for them to try to change it, but yet—

PRESIDENT NIXON: They did.

DEAN: —they did. But he has countless examples of this sort of thing and we'll have those.

PRESIDENT NIXON: I want that report. Well, I guess there's nothing we can do.

DEAN: Well, there is—

PRESIDENT NIXON: . . . [D]o you know whether or not Ervin and Baker have yet talked to Kleindienst?

DEAN: They have not. And I suggested to Kleindienst again—I guess it was yesterday I suggested it—I said, Dick, it seems to me you've got to monitor when it becomes appropriate for you to return the call so the ball is in their court to get the channel open. And he said, John, I will.

PRESIDENT NIXON: Well, the one I'm concerned about is not Ervin. I expect him to be partisan. The one I'm concerned about is Baker.

DEAN: Baker.

PRESIDENT NIXON: Where the hell is he going to be (unintelligible) started shaping up? . . .

DEAN: Well, I think the most important thing for our handling the hearings are, one, any witnesses that go up are well prepared. You know, re-reading your speech on the Hiss case again showed how effective investigators can be if one witness doesn't know what the other witness is saying or there is a dichotomy between witnesses. And that's one thing that can't—you know, whatever they say over there, they've got to hum the same tune, and they're ready to do it. They've done it thus far. Otherwise, they just create problems that are not necessary.

PRESIDENT NIXON: Yeah. Well, you can't do much with Baker. I think with Ervin, . . . they're going to make this big run on executive privilege. The point we have to do is to hammer home the fact that we will furnish information. That is not the issue. The issue is formal appearances before committees, and that we will not give in on.

DEAN: Actually, the forum we're in couldn't be better. The Gray hearings is just an excellent place for particularly myself, the counsel who has sort of a double privilege in a sense, the attorney-client relation always lurks back there, how it would be contrary to the ethics of my—of our profession. . . .

PRESIDENT NIXON: I just wondered—I don't think Gray is smart enough. I'm just not sure. I hope he is.

DEAN: Well, we'll have the test.

PRESIDENT NIXON: He's a decent man, but . . . Did you ever go back and read—I think there's only one copy of it left in the whole Bureau—in the Hiss case . . . we were up against two big men in Chambers and Hiss. The only difference was Chambers was proving Hiss was lying. That's why they killed him. The point is that you couldn't be more right. The witnesses have got to be prepared, because any clever person up there will murder them.

DEAN: Catch them in inconsistencies and then weaken them right away.

PRESIDENT NIXON: And my problem with Baker, I don't think he'll work hard enough to become a good cross-examiner. A good cross-examiner has got to know more about the testimony than his opponent. . . .

MARCH 7, 1973: THE PRESIDENT AND DEAN, 8:53–10:12 A.M., OVAL OFFICE

Nixon is impatient and angry with Gray. He does not want Gray questioned by the Senate Judiciary Committee on his Watergate role, and the President proposes a scheme to Dean to embarrass both Gray and the FBI, and thereby scuttle the Gray nomination.

PRESIDENT NIXON: . . . [L]et's put him [Gray] on the griddle a little bit as to whether he approves or disapproves of certain things. Let me tell you how this is done, the way I would do it.

"Mr. Chairman—I mean Mr. Director—it has been charged that electronic devices were used to—for the purpose of bugging the President—the candidate's plane [in 1968] . . . . I want to ask you. These charges have come to my attention. I want to ask you whether it's true or false." Then say, "Now, Mr. Gray, have you investigated these charges? Do you approve of such things?" Do you get my point?

DEAN: Mm-hmm.

PRESIDENT NIXON: They're [the Senate Judiciary Committee] not up there to conduct an investigation of Gray on Watergate. They're up there to conduct his—to question his competence to be head of the FBI and whether he approves of certain things the FBI has been charged with doing over the years. . . . You have to write the questions out. I'll write them out if you want me do. . . . Keep this fairly simple. . . .

Then take all your [William] Sullivan material. . . . It doesn't make any difference whether it's hearsay or not.

DEAN: That's right.

PRESIDENT NIXON: The game—this game—is not played according to the rules. It's played according to the headlines. . . . Do you understand?

DEAN: Right. . . .

PRESIDENT NIXON: But, you see, what I mean is this. Why don't we now—let's get the stuff out right in this hearing? Now that's a perfectly logical place to do it. In other words, raise questions. . . . . [For example], "in the 1968 campaign, has the FBI, at the request of the White House"—never say who—"at the request of the White House did some electronic surveillance of Vice President Agnew's phone when he was in Phoenix? Is this true or not? . . ."

DEAN: Just the fact that they're making the charge is going to be our headline.

PRESIDENT NIXON: Secondly—that's my point. Then, second, it has also been charged that the White House ordered the electronic surveillance. In other words, I want to put Gray in there. I told him that Hoover had told me, and I'm going to make him lie, because I think Gray's not handling himself well.

DEAN: Mm-hmm.

PRESIDENT NIXON: What he said yesterday with regard to the fact that it was—you know, this jolly well bullshit and all that sort of thing, that it was highly improper for you to be present [during the interrogation of the Watergate burglars]. Well, God-damn it, we're not going to let him get away with that.

DEAN: He even said, went so far as to say yesterday that he had told me he thought so. That is an outright misstatement.

. PRESIDENT NIXON: All right. Well, now we're going to put it to him. He will know he's lying, see, because he knows I told him that Hoover had told me. He knows that he's been told that, because I told Gray specifically. I said I want you to go back and check it. He hasn't done it. Now, you see, what I'm trying to get at here is Gray, and, mind you, it probably is coming to the point that he's either got to—that it's probably not in our interest to let him get in. . . .

DEAN: I know exactly what you're saying, sir.

PRESIDENT NIXON: Or do you disagree?

DEAN: No, sir.

PRESIDENT NIXON: We thought yesterday was the day of truth, and now he turns out worse yesterday than the day before.

DEAN: Well, he did what he said in this regard. He started the argument that he can't turn over any more material, he's harming the rights of individuals, and the like. He did do that. But not with much success, for this reason: Kennedy bore right in on him again on the old stuff. . . .

PRESIDENT NIXON: It's an old story.

DEAN: He's volunteered so much that—

PRESIDENT NIXON: . . . Say, you're going to be the director of the FBI. "Mr. Chairman, I am concerned about the FBI being used by the White House for political purposes not only—I mean through the years. Now I want to know—I mean, Mr. Gray, do you have any knowledge that the White House has been doing it this year. . . . . Is this true or not? Did the FBI do this or not? Do you approve of that? Will you see that that's not done in the future?" And then repeat it, see. Then I would go on, but mainly I'd go into this stuff that is new. Everybody knows about what happened in the Kennedy thing and rooting the reporters out of bed and all that sort of thing. But people do not know some of this other crap, about how Johnson used the FBI. But just go right down the line on some of it—stuff that you think is fairly good. . . . [C]ertainly not the stuff [morals charges] with [Johnson aide] Walter Jenkins, but there's other stuff that's pretty good.

DEAN: Oh, yes. Oh, yes.

PRESIDENT NIXON: . . . And then Gray lies. He lies, and then we will be willing to call and tell him because he lied under oath and then withdraw his name. Do you get my point?

. DEAN: Exactly. . . .

PRESIDENT NIXON: . . . I ordered him when he was in this room. I directed him. I said you are to give a lie detector test to every individual who may have had anything to do with electronic bugging of the President's plane in 1968. No, Goddamn it, he hasn't done that. . . . He didn't do it, did he? Has he used lie detector tests?

DEAN: No, sir.

PRESIDENT NIXON: I told him to get [Cartha] DeLoach in. I ordered him to. Now we're not going to screw around with a thing like this. Hoover would have lie-detected him in one second, you know, if he'd been ordered. What I think is happening here, John, is that Gray—I know the type. He's a nice guy, loyal in his own way. But he's panting after the Goddamn job and is sucking up.

DEAN: As [Presidential aide Tom C.] Korologos says, some of these fellows go up and they get confirmationitis. They change. They're different individuals once they get up there.

PRESIDENT NIXON: All right. It's going to happen now. It's got—do you question these tactics? . . . Do you see what I mean? He's pissed on the White House enough, frankly. . . . . Maybe you don't want to pull in Bobby Kennedy, but, Goddamn it, he's dead. But certainly you could pull in all the Johnson crap. . . . It will worry Gray to death. And then if he does lie, he's to be called, and says, all right. I mean, that was a lie. Under the circumstances, you just have to paddle your own canoe up there.

DEAN: I think the man to do this is probably [Senator] Edward Gurney [R-FL] rather than [Senator Roman] Hruska [R-NB], for this reason.

PRESIDENT NIXON: Because he's so much smarter.

DEAN: He's smarter and Hruska is extremely close to Kleindienst. . . .

PRESIDENT NIXON: Well, does Gurney know you well enough that he won't get up and say it's from the White House? That's what I'm concerned about. I can't—

DEAN: Well, I can have somebody who does know Gurney well enough do it. . . . I'll do it outside.

PRESIDENT NIXON: You can say—somebody on the outside can go and say look, we've got some hot stuff here. It'll help you in your campaign. Use it.

DEAN: I like to believe I've operated around here for about two and a half years now, and no one has ever—I've never surfaced until you decided to surface me. . . .

PRESIDENT NIXON: Hruska's loyal, but a little bit on the pompous side and would be concerned about hurting the FBI. Gurney won't give one Goddamn what happens to the FBI.

DEAN: That's right.

PRESIDENT NIXON: And shouldn't be. But now, on Gray, how about it now? My view is that we should—now, what the hell, where's Kleindienst in all this? What in the name of God is he doing?

DEAN: Kleindienst had been totally unable to program what he calls a bull-headed Irishman [Gray] in this whole thing. We have tried. They had—before the hearings started, they had sit-down sessions to plan this whole strategy. . . . It's beyond Dick's control.

PRESIDENT NIXON: Now listen. I want all communication with Gray cut off. That's the other thing. Give him the cold stuff for a while.

DEAN: All right.

PRESIDENT NIXON: It doesn't do any good to talk to him. . . .

MARCH 7, 1973: THE PRESIDENT AND THOMAS PAPPAS, 10:54–11:01 A.M., OVAL OFFICE

A rare moment: the President personally thanks his good friend Thomas Pappas for helping out "on some of these things that . . . others are involved in"—meaning raising funds for hush money payments. Here Nixon is quite voluble; Pappas, on the other hand, is a man of few words but great deeds in behalf of the President.

PRESIDENT NIXON: Let me say one other thing. I want you to know what I was mentioning last night. I am aware of what you're doing to help out on some of these things that Maury's people and others are involved in. I won't say anything further, but it's very seldom you find a friend like that, believe me.

PAPPAS: Thank you.

PRESIDENT NIXON: Frankly, let me say Maury's clean as he can be.

PAPPAS: I know.

PRESIDENT NIXON: Mitchell is. A few pipsqueaks down the line did some silly things.

PAPPAS: Sure.

PRESIDENT NIXON: But it's down the line. Down the line, they're all guilty. You know that. . . . But nobody in the White House was involved. It's just stupid.

PAPPAS: I spent eight months, did you know that?

PRESIDENT NIXON: Eight months?

PAPPAS: Yes, (unintelligible). Every day at the office I made 12 trips back and forth from the time I started in January.

PRESIDENT NIXON: How did you do it?

PAPPAS: Well, I did it because—well, (unintelligible).

PRESIDENT NIXON: And basically, as you say, we were so shocked—I was so shocked to hear such a stupid thing, mainly because if you're going to bug somebody, for Christ's sake, first, you shouldn't bug them. But, second, if you're going to do it, [why?] the National Committee? They don't know a Goddamn thing.

PAPPAS: That's right.

PRESIDENT NIXON: I thought it was the most [stupid?] thing. But, you know, amateurs. That's what it is. Amateurs. Believe me.

MARCH 11, 1973: THE PRESIDENT AND COLSON, 4:19–4:51 P.M., WHITE HOUSE TELEPHONE

Colson worries that Gray has erred in his offer of raw FBI files to a Senate committee. Colson and Nixon raise issues of executive privilege in order to prevent top aides from testifying before the Senate. They recognize the necessity for sheltering John Dean.

COLSON: But it was a very good trip. As I told Bob, you do get a completely different feeling when you come back and see the jackassery that is engaged in this town. My God almighty. Just lean back, and there is the *Washington Post,* big picture of Kalmbach and Chapin, you know, as if that really had any consequence.

PRESIDENT NIXON: Well, that's all they are interested in. But for awhile—

COLSON: Well, you are killing us on the issues that are important, Mr. President. I'm convinced that you have the country—

PRESIDENT NIXON: Well, we'll get, of course, they are going to have a field day. They are building up this Ervin, like they built up poor old Ralph Flanders. Remember that?

COLSON: Yes, sir.

PRESIDENT NIXON: And they will do the same thing so that he will have his day and they will have two or three months of crap, and that's—we'll survive it, though.

COLSON: Oh, hell yes. I really think whatever damage has been done by that issue has been done. And I think, I really think they can overplay it as a matter of fact. They may just go too far with it.

PRESIDENT NIXON: Well, they are going to push everything from executive privilege, probably. They put it to the contempt line with Dean or something, why, we'll just let it go to the [Supreme] Court. Fight it like hell.

COLSON: Oh sure. I think the Gray thing has a silver lining.

PRESIDENT NIXON: But that Court, if it turns that way, well, I can't believe they would, because they can't—

COLSON: Court wouldn't rule on that, Mr. President.

PRESIDENT NIXON: Well, particularly if there is a double privilege with him. He is both counsel and the other. What the hell, are you going to have him go testify?

COLSON: No. Dean, I think, is unassailable. I think the one that would make a stronger case for them would be Haldeman, Ehrlichman, Chapin, or someone like that.

PRESIDENT NIXON: Perhaps Chapin. The three at top are tougher. But Chapin would be the easiest.

COLSON: Yes. That would be the easiest one to get to.

PRESIDENT NIXON: I'll have to talk to him about it any way. . . .

COLSON: Well, Gray has helped us enormously in that regard. I think, I read in Europe, of course, the dispatches and the wires, and I thought Gray was making a complete ass of himself. I got back, and I still don't think he has handled it very well, but I think there is a great virtue in what's happened with Gray, because what now can be said is look, my God, there is nothing left—we are not hiding behind anything like executive privilege. That's a very important principle for the President to be able to have his own advisors as judges do, as congressmen and senators do, because we have made everything public. We have made volumes of FBI files, an unprecedented. That's never been—

PRESIDENT NIXON: Raw files, incidentally. That's bad, though. As a matter of fact, my God [*laughter*], the American Civil Liberties Union is right for once, the raw file should never be, because that just gossip, hearsay, it's unbelievable. But anyway, it's done now.

COLSON: Well, as I said, I think Gray made a hell of a mistake, in the long term the utility of the FBI has been damaged. . . .

PRESIDENT NIXON: Right.

COLSON: Mr. President, of putting you in a position where we can say now, my God, we did this unprecedented action of making the FBI data available. There just isn't anything else. The only thing else that would be left would be a TV spectacular fishing expedition, political in nature, and that we are not going to permit.

PRESIDENT NIXON: That's right. That's right.

COLSON: I think I can help on the outside. I have talked to Dean about this. . . . Dean has a wealth of research that he has put together. I have told him that I am going to go to work—

PRESIDENT NIXON: You have got to do a lot of this from the outside basically. It shouldn't come from the White House. That's the problem.

COLSON: Well, on this sensitive issue of the Watergate, anything the White House does—

PRESIDENT NIXON: It's dynamite.

COLSON: Is going to be caught.

PRESIDENT NIXON: It's dynamite.

COLSON: I simply have to work as—

PRESIDENT NIXON: Right.

COLSON: Well, I can do both. I can do a little bit on the public side myself.

PRESIDENT NIXON: Sure. No problem on that.

MARCH 14, 1973: THE PRESIDENT AND DEAN, 4:25–4:34 P.M., WHITE HOUSE TELEPHONE

In two short telephone conversations, the President asks Dean to check precedents for Pat Gray's offer to submit raw FBI files to the Senate Judiciary Committee.

PRESIDENT NIXON: Yeah. Yeah. Do you know whether or not there have been any other instances where raw files of the FBI have been turned over to a committee of Congress?

I mean raw files. All right. You call the FBI and tell them I want that in three minutes, they're to have . . . it over here or I'll fire the whole Goddamn Bureau. I mean that. . . .

MARCH 14, 1973: THE PRESIDENT AND DEAN, 4:34–4:36 P.M., WHITE HOUSE TELEPHONE

DEAN: Unless I get a counter-information upon further checking, the answer is no, there have been no formal submissions of FBI material like this ever before. However, there have been informal.

PRESIDENT NIXON: In other words, what they mean is that they have never formally turned over raw files to a committee. Now, informally they have taken the files up and shown them. Jim Eastland, when he, for example, was conducting judge [confirmation] investigations, that, I understand. . . .

What I am getting at is this. I'm going to say that there was always Hoover's practice never to turn over formally to a committee, because he knew this, and he only did it on a basis of total security for the purposes of conducting investigations, and so forth.

DEAN: And there has never been a leak.

PRESIDENT NIXON: And there has never been a leak of those things before.

DEAN: That's right.

PRESIDENT NIXON: And therefore we think that they should be evaluated in terms of that.

DEAN: Mm-hm.

PRESIDENT NIXON: Okay. Well, keep them scared over there.

DEAN: [*Laughter.*] Exactly.

MARCH 14, 1973: THE PRESIDENT AND DEAN, 9:50–10:50 A.M., EXECUTIVE OFFICE BUILDING

In a long rambling conversation with Dean, occasionally joined by Ron Ziegler and Richard Moore, Nixon offered some random thoughts on Watergate and his own role.

PRESIDENT NIXON: Espionage and sabotage. Do you understand? That's the point that I'm making. . . . [E]spionage and sabotage is illegal only if against the government. Hell, you can espionage and sabotage all you want, unless you use illegal means. . . . Can I get away with it?

DEAN: I don't think we'll get away with it forever.

PRESIDENT NIXON: Do you think he knew, Haldeman knew?

DEAN: Yes. . . .

PRESIDENT NIXON: My point is—the main point is that I know that everybody here, and all of Washington, but as far as the country is concerned, they do not want the President spending his time horsing around with all this crap. They want him to be spending his time on something that is a little bit more important . . . .

DEAN: Hopefully there's an assumption that we know all here, the Dean investigation knows everything. We don't. Now we've got some good ideas, but we don't have all the answers.

PRESIDENT NIXON: Suppose you knew all? What the hell does it tell them? I mean, Watergate we know—certainly we must know what happened. We know what happened. We must know that somebody, we were very specific, and I can't—and it had to be at a higher level. We know Goddamn well that Hunt and Liddy. We all know that.

Who, I don't know, and I would prefer not to know, because I don't want to get my friends involved. But I know very well it had to be a higher-up. That's our real problem, and everybody knows it. They wouldn't have done it because Magruder told them to, or Hugh Sloan told them, and we've just got to recognize that. So there is our real problem with Watergate, as I see it, my problem. But I'm taking your word that your investigation showed that no one in the White House knew.

MARCH 16, 1973: THE PRESIDENT AND KISSINGER, 10:18–10:33 A.M., OVAL OFFICE

Conversations between Nixon and Kissinger are mutual support sessions. Kissinger expresses his concerns, but also his ignorance of Watergate affairs; meanwhile, the President, impatiently and defensively, tells Kissinger to "remember the big picture."

KISSINGER: . . . I don't know a damn thing of what really happened in the Watergate thing, but my impression is that—

PRESIDENT NIXON: Well, what happened you know very well, some assholes—

KISSINGER: The stupidity.

PRESIDENT NIXON: As I told you, Mitchell wasn't tending the store and some jackasses did some things and that's all.

KISSINGER: Oh, it's total stupidity. I'm not against—I believe in playing rough. I think it was stupidly done, but that's another matter. What I'm saying is, leaving aside what happened, I think the public respects you for hanging tough. They don't understand all the nuances of all this crap of—

PRESIDENT NIXON: The only problem that we have on that is to appear to cover-up, but I made the point over and over again we will furnish information, but we're not going to have [a spectacle?]. What they want is to have a television show, putting Haldeman up there and bullying him, and they're not going to do that. They're not going to destroy him. They're not going to do it to you. They're not going to do it to any of us. That is what we will not allow. This Congress is not interested in getting the facts. They're interested in embarrassing the Administration, and, Goddamn it, I won't let them do it. . . .

KISSINGER: *Of course.* I remember [Joseph] Califano, who is actually a decent guy. . . . Well, he's a partisan, but he's not like—

PRESIDENT NIXON: Like Clifford.

KISSINGER: Like Clifford. A decent guy, but still very much opposed to you. And I remember [I ran into] Califano in January, and he was practically salivating then at the prospect of what the trial would do to us, because he figured—he said, oh, don't worry. He said, these judges are very much influenced by the newspapers.

PRESIDENT NIXON: Yes.

KISSINGER: In the conduct of their trial. Well, that didn't turn out to be true. Now they have high hopes of the Senate here, probably.

PRESIDENT NIXON: Oh, yes. It's a big deal. It'll be on three months, everybody around here will worry about it. But what we always have to do is to remember the big picture . . . .

MARCH 16, 1973: THE PRESIDENT AND DEAN, 10:34–11:10 A.M., OVAL OFFICE

Nixon continues to rely heavily on John Dean, whose attempts to manage the cover-up are becoming increasingly difficult. Who better for the President to admit to that "the problem is the cover-up" than John Dean? By this time, Dean is seeing the President on a daily basis, offering briefings and information, and sharing frustrations. It is interesting here, in the light of later statements, that Nixon did not want a complete report from Dean, but merely something that could be used for public consumption. But doubts are in Dean's mind, clearly anticipating their famous March 21 meeting: "I should possibly report a little fuller than I really have, so you really can appreciate in full some of the vulnerable points and where they lead to," Dean says. Nixon is unhappy with Senator Baker and "that kid," minority counsel Fred Thompson. The President wants protection on the cover-up issue.

PRESIDENT NIXON: . . . In very general terms, I realize the problems of getting too specific, because then you do open up the possibility of, oh, why didn't you say that, why didn't you say that? But you just put it [a report] in very general terms, you see?

DEAN: Mm-hmm.

PRESIDENT NIXON: I don't know. Do you think that's possible?

DEAN: It's going to be tough, but I think it's a good exercise and a drill that is absolutely essential we do.

PRESIDENT NIXON: Yeah, that's the point. The exercise is important.

DEAN: It sharpens thinking and, as I—

PRESIDENT NIXON: Find out what our vulnerabilities are and where we are and so forth and so on.

DEAN: Right. I would—maybe there will be some time when I should possibly report a little fuller than I really have, so you really can appreciate in full some of the vulnerable points and where they lead to.

PRESIDENT NIXON: That's right.

DEAN: I don't think that should be a written document right now.

PRESIDENT NIXON: Oh, by no means. No. I don't want any damn written document about any of that. . . .

DEAN: . . . I'm going to have Kleindienst pull Baker aside and find out what in the world he's [Baker] talking about when he says on television last night, he says, I was quite surprised when the President said he wasn't going to send anybody up [to testify]. No one knew better than Baker, from his conversation with you.

PRESIDENT NIXON: He lied.

DEAN: Sure. . . .

PRESIDENT NIXON: I told Baker, I said, we would have no—I said I would not allow people to come up in formal hearings. I said we would have written interrogatories. I said we would *discuss* the possibility of having the chairman and ranking member talk, you know. I mean, I went through that.

DEAN: I know you did.

PRESIDENT NIXON: . . . [B]ut I said we would not agree to any appearances before the committee. No. He's trying to be a hero, and, you know, play to the people here. . . . But . . . what in the hell is the matter with Mitchell? I mean, he's supposed to be close to—

DEAN: Close to Baker?

PRESIDENT NIXON: Yeah. I find that somebody's got to get Baker—

DEAN: Pulled around. He's off the reservation, I would say.

PRESIDENT NIXON: I think he must be off the reservation, and I'm kind of surprised that he saw me and then went off. I don't—I want him to know that I won't forget that that conversation ever took place. You remind him about it and so forth. Because I remember it took place, and he knows Goddamn well he lied about it, although he didn't—of course, he didn't say the conversation took place. He recognizes he can't do that. . . .

But I think what it gets down to is what you have here is that Baker and [Senator Lowell] Weicker [D-CT] have predictably—I mean, they read the Washington papers and the rest, run around in the social set, and want to be hotshots. They'll take a potshot even if it is to the embarrassment of the administration. We have that over and over again. It's one of those things. . . .

Baker—I just wonder if he'll survive the election. Baker may not realize it, but by getting on the wrong side of this we will destroy . . . his chances ever to move into a leadership position. We will destroy it. He can't be told that, but—you know what I mean. . . . He's just going overboard and his counsel [Thompson], I noticed, is working hand in glove with [Sam] Dash. Well, Dash is too smart for that kid. . . .

DEAN: . . . [P]eople have not been, for some reason, volunteering to us what has been volunteered to the other side. . . .

PRESIDENT NIXON: . . . I know, for example, that an even friendly paper like the *Detroit News* says that we ought to make some statement. I still think that that is something we ought to consider. I mean, just so we have done it. Do you get my point?

DEAN: Yeah. One point. I have drafted such a document. Back in December I did it.

PRESIDENT NIXON: Right. Do you think it opens up new problems?

DEAN: I think it's something we ought to continually review.

PRESIDENT NIXON: But you see my point. But let me say we've got to forget some of the problems it may raise for other people. But you've got always to think in terms of the presidency and the President should not appear to be hiding and not be forthcoming. Do you know what I mean? . . . The problem is the cover-up, not the facts . . . .

DEAN: What we're doing now, Dick Moore and I were just talking about this this morning, is we're so busy putting out daily fires that we have not really gotten, although we've had some sessions on this, a good master plan to deal with this. And hopefully Dick and I can just get off somewhere—

PRESIDENT NIXON: Get away.

DEAN: —and kick it [a report] around four ways to Sunday.

PRESIDENT NIXON: Why don't you go up to Camp David and do it?

DEAN: Well, that might be a good idea.

PRESIDENT NIXON: You're welcome to go any time.

DEAN: Thank you. And just really kick it around.

PRESIDENT NIXON: Do you need anybody else besides Dick? Would a Mitchell be helpful in that sort of thing?

DEAN: Damn right, he might.

PRESIDENT NIXON: His judgment's pretty good.

DEAN: Yes, it is. . . .

MARCH 16, 1973: THE PRESIDENT AND HALDEMAN, 11:10 A.M.–12:06 P.M., OVAL OFFICE

This pessimistic conversation senses the futility of maintaining the cover-up. Perhaps it is a losing game, Haldeman suggests; "that's sort of my feeling," the President replies. Nixon's frustration is growing as he lashes out bitterly at Baker, Gray,

Mitchell, and Kleindienst. In Segment 2, Nixon realizes that his claim of "executive privilege" is a public relations disaster; the term has connotations that the President is hiding something.

SEGMENT 1

PRESIDENT NIXON: [H]e's [Senator Howard Baker] not handled himself well, and he doesn't realize that he's just going to make himself a hero for a while and he will destroy forever his chances to move up in his party forever. . . . It's just like old Ralph Flanders. He was a hell of a hero in destroying McCarthy. Ralph Flanders, of course, was a old fart at that time. . . . It's funny. It's just the way—Howard Baker has got a character flaw. . . .

HALDEMAN: They think if we just clear it up then everything'll be fine. And they think you're being misguided by your White House staff.

PRESIDENT NIXON: . . . I just told him [John Dean] today, . . . the one thing you have to bear in mind is there's only one thing worse than having any substantive disclosures that have not come out, and that is to have the cover-up exposed. I said you cannot have the President hurt here in a cover-up. I mean, you've got to get—and I said, in any event, you haven't got any choice, the stuff is going to come out anyway. So that's why I feel, as I told him, try to find a way to take the offensive with regard to Watergate, so forth.

HALDEMAN: Well, you know—we've all—I've done it twice with him, and one time we had a lot of time out west when we took two full weeks, and another time a whole day here. . . . But on Watergate . . . if you want it out, the issue is high-level involvement there. It's the question of criminal—. Then you have a problem. And if you start pushing people, you've got people who have got to decide whether they stay with what they've said or change their story, and then we get into a real mess. That's why Dean's put this scheme of containment on the line.

PRESIDENT NIXON: Yeah.

HALDEMAN: I just wonder if it isn't a losing game.

PRESIDENT NIXON: Well, that's sort of my feeling. I mean, it has been for quite a while. . . .

HALDEMAN: It would be a lot better if you get it all out now and get it done than to have them squeeze it out. . . .

PRESIDENT NIXON: My hunch is still right, Gray is a good, straight arrow, wonderful guy, but not very smart. He's not very smart, apparently.

HALDEMAN: [*Laughter.*] He sure hasn't been in this, but he's following a long tradition over there. . . . I don't mean Hoover. I mean Mitchell and Kleindienst.

PRESIDENT NIXON: Yeah. [*Laughter.*]

SEGMENT 2

HALDEMAN: The issue right now, the burning issue . . . is executive privilege and are we going to have Dean go up to the Hill?

PRESIDENT NIXON: . . . The term['s] got everybody—

HALDEMAN: Doesn't work though, you can't—

PRESIDENT NIXON: You can still use the term, the separation of powers, the President's constitutional responsibility . . . .

HALDEMAN: Keep banging on the Constitution, because that's [helpful?].

PRESIDENT NIXON: The constitutional responsibilities. . . . Don't you think so, think that's a much better way.

HALDEMAN: Oh, sure.

PRESIDENT NIXON: I have a constitutional responsibility—the separation of powers.

HALDEMAN: Everyone remembers that. They read about privilege—a bad word.

PRESIDENT NIXON: Very bad word. It means that we've got something they don't have.

HALDEMAN: . . . It's executive right.

PRESIDENT NIXON: Or responsibility.

HALDEMAN: Well, "executive" is a bad word too.

PRESIDENT NIXON: . . . . Separation of powers. It's just hard to explain to somebody that the President has a right to have confidential information imparted to him. Well, then they think, ah, the President knows all about Watergate, but that's confidential. See, . . . that's why that is a privilege. Of course that's not what we're talking about. . . .

HALDEMAN: The point is the presidential assistant has got to have a relationship with the President where, as someone was saying, where the President can haul a guy in, put his feet up on the desk, and tell dirty jokes about congressmen if they want to without figuring that it's going to be put out someday. . . .

MARCH 16, 1973: THE PRESIDENT AND EHRLICHMAN, 3:00–4:47 P.M., EXECUTIVE OFFICE BUILDING

Nixon's problems extend to family matters. His brother and nephew are closely linked to the notorious Robert Vesco, already indicted for various illegal financial schemes. Ehrlichman is in charge of the problem. But Watergate inevitably intrudes. Nixon assures Ehrlichman he was trying "to keep you out of it for other reasons"—probably a reference to Ehrlichman's and Colson's roles with the Plumbers. They discuss their inability to control Senator Howard Baker.

In his memoir, John Ehrlichman acknowledged his daily talks with the President at this time but claimed "he wasn't talking to me about Watergate." But the two regularly review the story, trying to determine what exactly Nixon could reveal. Ehrlichman pushes the President to blame the break-in on John Mitchell. They realize that "Watergate" is far more than the break-in. The President protests he cannot afford a cover-up, yet that and other nefarious activities, such as financing the shadowing of Senator Edward Kennedy, have to be concealed. Ehrlichman concedes that their "extracurricular activities" were not too "savory," but he credits the White House (and himself) for not using the FBI to spy on Kennedy.

EHRLICHMAN: A couple of family problems . . . .

PRESIDENT NIXON: Donny [Nixon, the President's nephew]?

EHRLICHMAN: Don [Nixon] Senior [the President's brother]. . . . But did you know there's been a very vigorous Internal Revenue investigation of the Howard Hughes empire?

PRESIDENT NIXON: Oh, yes.

EHRLICHMAN: Don [Sr.], because of his contacts with [John] Meier back in the old days now comes up as a witness, and the IRS wants to contact him. So they asked me if we had any objection to his being interviewed. I have held off answering until we got . . . in place. . . .

PRESIDENT NIXON: Have we gotten Donny [Jr.] out of the Vesco thing?

EHRLICHMAN: He won't leave. . . . We have no control over Vesco at this point at all.

PRESIDENT NIXON: I see, because we can't—

EHRLICHMAN: Because we indicted him, you know, and he's headed for prosecution. But the kid will not leave. I have talked to him like a Dutch uncle. Eddie [Nixon, the President's brother] has talked to him, and he cannot persuade him that he's hurting himself, you, and everybody else by staying.

PRESIDENT NIXON: What's he do?

EHRLICHMAN: Well, he's a gofer. He just runs errands, that kind of stuff, and they make him feel like a big shot. They let him sit in on meetings and so forth. He says, oh, I'm learning a great deal about business. He says I couldn't get this kind of an education in school.

PRESIDENT NIXON: I thought John . . . .

EHRLICHMAN: Well, we thought we had at one point, and that's probably the last time we talked about it. Ed was going to take him—this was just before the election—Ed was going to take him and go east, travel with Ed, and they were to meet at a certain time and Don didn't show up. And Ed called and he was still down there, and he said, no, I've changed my mind. I'm going to stay here. And I've talked to him twice since.

PRESIDENT NIXON: Well, it's going to come out, so what are you going to do about it . . . ?

EHRLICHMAN: It's a matter of public knowledge. The *Star* has run a story about it, and then it's in the *New Republic* this week, and so on. But they can't let it go. The way the angle of the thing is played is, Vesco has done his best to attach himself to your family by various devices like taking this kid on his payroll and so on and so forth. And nobody has been able to establish him having any wrongdoing. . . .

Vesco . . . was going around hot-shotting, saying that the White House was behind me and so on, and I had to say to that he was to get no special favors or consideration. Just after he got out of jail, he was using Mitchell's name and my name and everybody's name—I've just met him. I don't know him. But his people have been brought into my office. . . . [Murray] Chotiner's been working for him.

PRESIDENT NIXON: What the hell's he doing for him?

EHRLICHMAN: He [Chotiner] comes in. He tried to see me and I wouldn't see him. My assistant [Tod R. Hullin] talked to him, and he had a deal. Vesco would fix us up in South America. He'd act as an operative down there and he'd [do] . . . this and that if we got him off the criminal prosecution. And then there's an element of blackmail, that the worst isn't yet out and that it's going to hurt the Administration if they tell all they know, and this, that, and the other thing.

PRESIDENT NIXON: Like what?

EHRLICHMAN: They really don't specify. For a long time, it was Eddie's involvement, . . . and then there was the $425,000. For a long time, they were—

PRESIDENT NIXON: . . . For Christ's sakes, return the contribution. We shouldn't have taken it. . . .

EHRLICHMAN: Well, Eddie, poor fellow, he was just purely sucked in. . . .

PRESIDENT NIXON: But Murray [Chotiner] disappoints me.

EHRLICHMAN: I know. Yea.

PRESIDENT NIXON: I guess he just can't—

EHRLICHMAN: They offered Colson's firm a 100-grand retainer, at the beginning, and I understand they offered Smathers more than that. . . . And they've got two firms in New York working on this . . . . The SEC told me that it's a very, very tight case. . . . The way this will probably end up, he will go to Costa Rica. . . .

PRESIDENT NIXON: Do you have to run?

EHRLICHMAN: No, no.

PRESIDENT NIXON: Then let me ask you about one other thing.

EHRLICHMAN: Sure.

PRESIDENT NIXON: I've been talking deliberately, trying to keep you and Bob out of this as much as possible of conversations with Dean.

EHRLICHMAN: . . . Well, I've appreciated that.

PRESIDENT NIXON: I've tried to keep you out of it for other reasons [i.e., the Plumbers], and I've—actually, . . . I want to keep him [Colson] out of it because he's involved too.

EHRLICHMAN: Yeah. . . .

PRESIDENT NIXON: Sloan apparently is, apparently pissed off with Magruder.

EHRLICHMAN: Certainly.

PRESIDENT NIXON: Now, the reason he's pissed off at Magruder is he thinks Magruder lied. And Magruder, apparently Magruder, as I piece it together, . . . Magruder was the one that directed Sloan to pay money for certain [persons?].

EHRLICHMAN: I don't know whether that's right or not.

PRESIDENT NIXON: Okay. Now . . . we give him a job in the government. That pisses off Sloan.

EHRLICHMAN: Now there's a jealousy, there's a long-time jealously there.

PRESIDENT NIXON: What jealousy?

EHRLICHMAN: Between Sloan and Magruder.

PRESIDENT NIXON: About what?

EHRLICHMAN: Oh, it goes way back to the time when they were both here. I don't know what the basis of it is. . . .

PRESIDENT NIXON: . . . [A]ccording to my understanding, I understand it, Magruder was quite a talker, has told Dean that Mitchell knew and that Haldeman knew.

EHRLICHMAN: But he doesn't say that when he's talking to Haldeman.

PRESIDENT NIXON: Then what in the hell has he been saying to Dean?

EHRLICHMAN: Jeb is shopping a little different story to two or three people around here. I've never talked to him, but I have the impression that Jeb has said that rather cleverly to Dean, Haldeman's got a problem. And he says to Haldeman, Mitchell's got a problem, or Colson's got a problem. This is what he says to Bob. . . .

PRESIDENT NIXON: Wonderful.

EHRLICHMAN: He's doing it to protect himself. He's looking for backing. . . .

PRESIDENT NIXON: Or do you think that it's more possible that Mitchell was in on it, or possibly that Colson was in on it. I don't think that Haldeman could have been in on it. . . .

EHRLICHMAN: I'll give you my theory of the case. It is that Colson felt the need to know a great deal more about the opposition than he knew. He felt the need to have the ability to know, so his need to have apparatus, and that Colson, either directly to Magruder, which I think is the case, or through Mitchell, did not specify the operation but said I've got to know what's going on, we've got to know what the White House is going on, what the hell are they talking about, who was [Lawrence] O'Brien seeing, so on and so forth. And kept the pressure on. That—Magruder—

PRESIDENT NIXON: But not necessarily doing a bugging.

EHRLICHMAN: No.

PRESIDENT NIXON: I can't imagine Colson doing that.

EHRLICHMAN: No.

PRESIDENT NIXON: That's not Colson's operation.

EHRLICHMAN: That's right.

PRESIDENT NIXON: Colson talks too much, but he is quite discreet in his—that kind of operation. . . .

EHRLICHMAN: Now, Magruder called in Liddy, at least my theory indicates, and he said, Gordon, you've got to get these results for me and get them believable. Liddy said I'll take care of it. Don't worry about a thing. But it's going to cost you.Magruder said how much, and he said 100 grand, or whatever it was. So Magruder called Sloan and said Gordon's going to come down and see you. Give him $100,000. Sloan said, well, what does Mitchell say about that? I can't just lay out that kind of money. Mr. Stans won't let me. So Jeb says I'll have John call you. Jeb called John and said, listen, you've got to call Sloan and clear this—and I'm just making all this up now, but this is the kind of thing I can see him in. He says, John, he's over with Justice. He said, you've got to call Sloan for me and clear the expenditure of $100,000 cash, and Mitchell said well, what's it for. Well, he said Gordon Liddy is going to undertake to get that information that I keep getting badgered about from the White House.

PRESIDENT NIXON: About the Democratic convention.

EHRLICHMAN: Or whatever. And Mitchell says are you sure you can do it? Jeb says, yeah, I think I kind of know how we can do it. I think Liddy can pull it off. And Mitchell said okay, I'll call him. So he calls Sloan and says, go ahead [and give the money]. And it was that kind of an almost casual undertaking. Now we've got a back-room conspiratorial meeting where they said we'll go in the basement and put scotch tape on the locks and all that kind of stuff. And then Liddy, being a kind of a nut, sat down with Hunt and said, okay, how are we going to pull this operation off? And Hunt said, listen I've got five Cubans [who] will come here for that kind of dough and they'll crack the United States Treasury for that. . . .

And that's how she went. Now that's a guess.

PRESIDENT NIXON: We were getting reports—

EHRLICHMAN: But then they were getting reports—Liddy was getting the reports and my hunch is that he was sharing them with Magruder, Colson, and probably Mitchell.

PRESIDENT NIXON: And Strachan. . . .

EHRLICHMAN: But I suspect, without knowing, that Mitchell probably advised himself of the general parameters of the operation through Fred LaRue, who was keeping him—he was sort of Mitchell's eyes and ears. Fred told me about it . . .—he's going to be a witness in this thing, and I suppose Eastland will look after him. . . .

PRESIDENT NIXON: Now, the query I have is . . . even if Mitchell is involved, we can't put it all out, is there something that could be said for at least putting out . . . this is what the facts are as far as we know. . . . Well, Goddamn it, as I've often said, John, first, if the facts are going to come out, let's get them out. I mean let's get them out, because far worse than the facts here is the coverup. Okay, that was my phrase, is the coverup. I don't know.

EHRLICHMAN: Supposing you were to look at it this way, and I've thought a lot about this. Supposing you were to say Mitchell's future, Colson's future, Ehrlichman's future, whoever, is not as important as the integrity of the presidency.

PRESIDENT NIXON: Integrity of the presidency, that's right.

EHRLICHMAN: If you accept the premise, then there is really nothing at all that you can't say.

PRESIDENT NIXON: I believe that.

EHRLICHMAN: And let the chips fall where they may. . . . If you accept the premise that the presidency needs this as an institution, and I have particularly in the last week or ten days more and more come to the feeling that we have more to lose by being cute about this than we have by letting it all hang out in the sense of the presidency. That's who "we" is, the presidency. If you once accept that premise, then I think the way to go is not to try and hold anything back, because there's a very complex set of interrelationships and there isn't any convenient place to draw the line. See, the element we haven't discussed that is a problem here is the money.

PRESIDENT NIXON: Yeah, I know.

EHRLICHMAN: And that's a very complicated fact pattern, which loop reaches out, touches Kalmbach and comes back, while the Segretti loop also reaches out and touches Kalmbach and comes back.

PRESIDENT NIXON: Does it involve Kalmbach in any illegal activity?

EHRLICHMAN: Not that I know of.

PRESIDENT NIXON: Good.

EHRLICHMAN: But he was a fund-raiser, and he raised cash and such. The Segretti thing is troublesome because it gets into Kalmbach's bank accounts, and before there was a campaign committee, as you know, that we operated a lot of money through Herb's bank accounts for all kinds of activities.

PRESIDENT NIXON: Oh, yeah, before we had—in other words, this was money that was—

EHRLICHMAN: Left over from a previous campaign or raised in the meantime, and it was sitting there in boxes of cash and there was a lot of it. And we financed a hell of a lot of stuff of all kinds with that money—polls and investigations and all sorts of stuff. Now, that opens a lot of collateral matters the minute you get into that.

PRESIDENT NIXON: Like what?

EHRLICHMAN: Oh, like the guy [Tony Ulasewicz] we had shadowing Teddy Kennedy for eight or nine months.

PRESIDENT NIXON: Oh, yeah. We don't want to get into that.

EHRLICHMAN: That kind of stuff. . . . Well, it characterizes some of our extracurricular activities as not too savory.

PRESIDENT NIXON: Yeah. And the shadowing of Teddy Kennedy.

EHRLICHMAN: Sure. Now there's only one way to read that. That's—it's to our credit in the sense that we didn't have the FBI do it. But we're not going to get the benefit of the doubt and it's going to make for juicy reading—keep track of a United States Senator in his off hours for nine months. . . .

PRESIDENT NIXON: The Ervin committee presumably goes into that?

EHRLICHMAN: Well, I think you have to assume that they'll go into anything they get a chance to go into. This general counsel of theirs has a statement in the paper today that they intend to follow every lead regardless of where it goes. . . .

So anyway, the hell of it is that even—it comes back to Bob in another way that I've never mentioned to him, but for some time we had [Franz Lane?] on the payroll. . . . He was doing our job on some various task forces in southern California. He was a bagman. He was delivering money. He was in contact with people. He was paying our sleuths . . . .

PRESIDENT NIXON: Well, coming back, though, to the presidency, John, as you know, I remember one other thing, which was Sherman Adams.

EHRLICHMAN: Right. He served him up, didn't he?

PRESIDENT NIXON: In the end. He did a lot that made it pretty easy to do so, but he did it, because Eisenhower, properly so, felt that the presidency had to be protected. And I feel the same way. I mean, I cannot—you cannot . . . figure the President is covering up the Goddamn thing. . . . My view would be that that would be a separate report, what happened and so on, so on, so on, and here is what happened on Watergate. Now, that said, we furnish the statement to the committee. . . . That's one way we could do it. . . .

EHRLICHMAN: Well, it's almost impossible to draw that document—

PRESIDENT NIXON: Dean's working on it.

EHRLICHMAN: —to make it the whole truth, make it consistent with the extensive facts, and have it hold together without going all the way. I mean, you have to incriminate Mitchell to some extent and so on.

PRESIDENT NIXON: Well, . . . he approved it. There's no doubt about that.

EHRLICHMAN: We've been over this a number of times, and every time we've decided no, that we can't do it because there's no way to do an effective job of disclosure and tie up all the loose ends in this thing. . . . It's the nagging loose ends, the little inconsistent fact, the unassailable piece of evidence that wasn't included is always the thing that bites in the end and makes you worry about it.

PRESIDENT NIXON: So you make it more general.

EHRLICHMAN: You have to make it general, and when you make it general, why then it's a cover-up. . . .

PRESIDENT NIXON: I'm thinking basically of the symbolic, (unintelligible) general, (unintelligible) as far as the facts are concerned.

EHRLICHMAN: Could be a letter to you and it could say you asked me, Mr. President, to put in writing a synopsis of the—

PRESIDENT NIXON: A report. . . .

EHRLICHMAN: . . . Maybe what we ought to do is have somebody like Dick Moore sit down and see if he can write a paper on that.

PRESIDENT NIXON: Dean apparently has tried to write it.

EHRLICHMAN: Yeah, but Dean's not as artful as Dick. He's not a writer. Dick could write it from the standpoint of advertising copy. . . .

MARCH 16, 1973: THE PRESIDENT AND COLSON, 7:53–8:12 P.M., WHITE HOUSE TELEPHONE

Nixon confides a great deal in Colson, here using him as a go-between with Senator Baker. Colson is determined to show the President that he is a good soldier, while berating those who fail to defend the President.

PRESIDENT NIXON: . . . Well, you might have a little fun with some of the Senators in a quiet way.

COLSON: I might talk to a few this weekend. I'll also see what Baker is sniffing around on. It may be that he, the message I got from him [said] . . . he would like to talk to me, and he said the real thing he would like to know, he wants to know whether he is going to stick his neck out and get it sawed off.

PRESIDENT NIXON: Well, talk to him. . . .

COLSON: This was a case of step up and become a hero.

PRESIDENT NIXON: We do not want him to get his neck sawed off. He needs to be assured on that. You know, the problem is that many of our guys here are scared to death for fear there is something there that's going to come out that's going to make them look like—

COLSON: Maybe that will stiffen his back. That may be what is concerning him.

PRESIDENT NIXON: Well, also, he has got to know that whatever his views are, he is not going to win if he takes the deal that he is going to participate in an attack on the President.

COLSON: No. And basically, he is not like that. It may be that he is just a little nervous. Maybe I can settle him down, and maybe I'll assure him that no one in the White House knew anything. That's something that may—

PRESIDENT NIXON: That's what he needs to know.

COLSON: I'll take a crack at that and also see if I can line up a few good stalwarts on the hill.

PRESIDENT NIXON: Good. Good luck.

COLSON: Thank you, Mr. President, sir.

MARCH 20, 1973: THE PRESIDENT, DEAN, AND RICHARD MOORE, 1:42–2:31 P.M., OVAL OFFICE

Dean offers an old remedy for dealing with political opposition.

DEAN: It was the parting remark yesterday that gave me thought about the FBI, when you said it's too bad we can't use the FBI. I got to thinking last night, well, we probably can. Why can't we? Isn't there some way to use them?

PRESIDENT NIXON: We've known about this for a long time, but everybody's stayed miles away from it.

DEAN: I mean to have the FBI investigation.

PRESIDENT NIXON: Oh, yes. Of the Congressmen?

DEAN: Yeah.

PRESIDENT NIXON: Christ, and Senators?

DEAN: Yeah.

PRESIDENT NIXON: That's terrific. [*Laughter.*]

MARCH 20, 1973: THE PRESIDENT AND GEORGE H. W. BUSH, 4:09–4:26 P.M., OVAL OFFICE

Republican National Chairman George Bush is not privy to the Administration's cover-up. He believes Watergate is a Washington-New York story, but he adds that in his travels around the country, questions recur about the Administration's claims of executive privilege.

BUSH: We're getting hit a little bit, Mr. President, on Watergate around the country, but we're just saying . . . and I'm just simply saying look we're not going to change the image, and try to get on to the next question. But it's building, and the mail's getting heavier.

PRESIDENT NIXON: What do you think you can do about it? Is there anything more that could be done? Here we sit. We've got hearings coming up. The hearings will make it worse.

BUSH: I got a question when I was speaking to the executives at the Bull Elephants. . . . The guy said to me, well, why doesn't the President—you know, if you're concerned about Watergate, why doesn't the President send Dean? I said, you're confusing two issues. One of them's a great constitutional issue that's going to transcend in importance Watergate. That is the executive privilege, which may be determined by the Supreme Court someday. Don't mix that into an issue that I'll agree with you is a grimy issue. But it's this kind of thing that—the disclosure is what they're calling for.

PRESIDENT NIXON: Why don't you emphasize the point. I'd only say there's no issue of disclosure, not at all. I mean, as the President has said in his press conference, as distinguished from previous administrations, going clear back to Truman, we have cooperated totally with the grand jury. All White House staff and so forth who were asked testified, and gave statements to the FBI and so forth. We've offered total cooperation to the committee. The only question is how we will cooperate. The President has a constitutional responsibility—rather don't use the term executive privilege—a constitutional responsibility to defend the principle of separation of powers. Now that's my job. I have that responsibility.

And they say well, what about [Eisenhower Chief of Staff] Sherman Adams going up? Why did he go up? He was charged with a crime. This is an entirely different matter. Dean is a lawyer, a lawyer who has—nobody's raised any question about Dean being a lawyer. Do you see the point? My point is—my point is, George, that we have cooperated with them, and under the circumstances I would say we are cooperating. We will. There's no question of holding back. It's simply—it's a question, however, of we cannot agree to have members of the White House staff brought before congressional committees and for that precedent to keep repeating. That's really what it gets down to. But point out that we are cooperating. We have offered to. It's up to them. They don't want any cooperation. They aren't interested in getting the facts. They're only interested in [political gains?].

BUSH: . . . But in New York they asked me at a big press conference there, they said something about well, what about Watergate? I said . . . the Watergate issue is mainly one which—where the questions are concentrated here in New York and in Washington. And they go well, what do you mean by that? I said, well, when I go to Kansas City or Cleveland or wherever, they don't ask. They might ask one question at a press conference, and we can sit here for 15 minutes and talk about nothing else. Well, it came out, you know, in the press that I was saying well, it wasn't a national issue or something. So I get letters coming in . . . . And it's the *funniest* damn thing. And you get outside in Kansas, and nobody cares about it.

PRESIDENT NIXON: But if it's anything that's negative to the administration, they are—see, this is basically a much more liberal left-oriented press here than in the rest of the country. The country has its problems, but it's much worse here. . . . I wish there were an answer to Watergate, but I just don't know any. . . . I don't know a damn thing to do. That's the problem. I mean some people say put out some statements. We have—nobody on the White House staff was involved. Nobody believes it.

BUSH: Yeah.

PRESIDENT NIXON: Right. They say let him go up and testify, and they testify and what happens? Then you've broken the executive privilege once and for all, and there's no—you can't run the White House that way. The President can't run his office by having particularly his lawyer go up and testify. In fact, he can't let his lawyer go in any event.

MARCH 20, 1973: THE PRESIDENT AND EHRLICHMAN, 4:26–5:39 P.M., OVAL OFFICE

Nixon broaches the idea of sharing the facts of Watergate with the Republican leaders, but he cannot, of course, tell them about the cover-up and White House "horrors." The President instinctively knows the right thing to do, although he fails to do so. He recognizes that the "money trail" leads straight to the White

House. By now, "Watergate"—the events and the cover-up—are overwhelming the President. Rationalizations strain logic as Ehrlichman describes the spying on Senator Edward Kennedy as "campaign organization." The lengthy conversation again gives the lie to Ehrlichman's later public insistence that he had no knowledge of John Dean's role until mid-April. The President apparently is feeling some stress as pressures mount; clearly, he has a variety of subjects on his mind, including Senator Ervin, executive privilege, and Pat Gray.

PRESIDENT NIXON: Another thing that you've got to think about, I do think you've got to brief our Congress, our leadership, on it. Maybe Dean has to.

EHRLICHMAN: Well, we have to decide what it is first.

PRESIDENT NIXON: Oh, I understand . . . [Y]ou know, it's not really fair to the Gurneys and the leaders on the committee, it's not fair to [Republican congressional leaders Hugh] Scott, [Gerald] Ford, and the rest for them . . . to get caught with their pants down.

EHRLICHMAN: Sure.

PRESIDENT NIXON: Do you agree with that?

EHRLICHMAN: Well, you shouldn't ever tell Scott anything you don't want used against you.

PRESIDENT NIXON: I understand. That is not true—that's true not only with Scott, but all of them. I'm simply saying that—I would do it on a confidential—I would do it on a broad basis. I would hold one of those leadership meetings and say: Now look, you've all been wondering about Watergate and here are the facts, period, and give them the statements. . . .

You can say Haldeman was not, Ehrlichman was not involved. You know what I mean. I'm afraid in the case of Chapin you've got to say what the hell the facts are. And that's what I—Strachan, I would try to ignore that as much as possible. With Colson, you put out what the Goddamn facts are. I don't mean by that that you've got to go into every relationship. For example, I wouldn't go back into the fact of your relationship with Hunt [i.e., the Plumbers] and Colson's relationship with Hunt. That's not relevant to this. That's not relevant to this at all. This involves Watergate and the campaign activities, right? You had nothing to do with Hunt in the campaign or Watergate.

EHRLICHMAN: No.

PRESIDENT NIXON: Colson claims to have had nothing to do with him in Watergate or the campaign. You know what I mean? The only thing I guess that—the only thing there where I guess you do have an anti-side is that tailing of Teddy Kennedy that somebody is going to bring out.

EHRLICHMAN: Well, even there, that would deal with the—that's way, way back. That would deal with the question of money, and you I think do have to have a statement from someone. But I think that statement can come from Stans, and it can deal with these various allegations and charges. . . .

PRESIDENT NIXON: He covers that?

EHRLICHMAN: Yes.

PRESIDENT NIXON: Do you suggest—do you say you used it to spy on Kennedy?

EHRLICHMAN: No, you say Herb Kalmbach had a fund of money which was used for preliminary campaign organization and so on.

PRESIDENT NIXON: Campaign organization.

EHRLICHMAN: That was not accounted for by the committee because it wasn't required to be. It was held in compliance with then-existing law and so on and so forth. . . .

Boy. Oh, Ervin really smacked his colleagues on television last night, called them lazy and egocentric.

PRESIDENT NIXON: Why?

EHRLICHMAN: Oh, [television interviewer Roger] Mudd asked him in a special why the Congress didn't exercise its powers. They were talking about impoundment and spending limits and so on. And he said, " Well," he says, "too many people up here don't want to work an honest day." And he said, "An awful lot of them are very self-centered, very independent, not willing to work as a team." And on and on and on. He really laid it to them. I'd love to get a tape of that and run it every hour on the hour in the Rotunda.

PRESIDENT NIXON: Ervin's seventy-six years old and running for re-election.

EHRLICHMAN: Sure.

PRESIDENT NIXON: That's his true business.

EHRLICHMAN: Mudd [*chuckles*] introduced him and he said, "Now, there's this one character up there in the Senate who's sort of become the central figure in this and he's turned into a media freak. In the last month he's been on the *Today* show twice, on the CBS Morning News, on the CBS Evening News." He gave the whole list of television appearances that he'd made, Meet the Press, you know. And it's true, he's taken every booking that comes his way. . . .

PRESIDENT NIXON: . . . I do feel, though, in some way or other I just have a feeling on Watergate that if there's any way to get out some kind of a statement that will say that I got a statement from somebody. I don't know. . . .

Then why don't we put it out? And that's what I want to do. Basically, that's true. Now the problem I see is that . . . if they put it out, that's a whole lot of the questions. But suppose it does. Let me ask: it's a PR exercise. The whole thing's a PR exercise. So you put that out. There is that thing, that they attack then. Let's go down that. Is that necessarily bad? Isn't it a question—I mean, the point is we can say we were forthcoming. They are never going to let us get off the hook by letting us send up our written interrogatories. . . . I don't know. Is there something wrong with that?

EHRLICHMAN: No, there's nothing wrong with it. The point is that the questions aren't going to go away. There are always going to be questions.

PRESIDENT NIXON: Of course they're not going to go away. I realize that. But at least we will have *some* answers. . . . To me it's a tougher question for me to have to get up and say, what about this? Well, I'm not going to say that we will not furnish this information and we stand on the responsibility to the separation of powers. I'd rather say, "I will furnish a statement; if there are other questions, I will be glad to answer them." You see my point? I just don't know. I don't know about the stonewalling.

Let me put it this way. We've got to look at it in terms of precedents. That's what we've got to look at here. I've got to insist, John, that whatever the facts are, are not hidden. Or do you agree? I don't know. I think I have to do that. Now, I know very well what the problems are here. In some instances people got involved innocently, like Mitchell with his poor stupid wife or some Goddamn thing. That's one thing. . . .

EHRLICHMAN: Yes, and then you've got some defendants in the criminal case.

PRESIDENT NIXON: Well, you've got Hunt.

EHRLICHMAN: Yes.

PRESIDENT NIXON: That's right.

EHRLICHMAN: Who are still erratic.

PRESIDENT NIXON: And you don't know what—also, you don't know how much they know. Do we know? I don't know.

EHRLICHMAN: I don't know how much they know about what went on in 1701 [headquarters for the Committee to Re-Elect the President], for instance, on any angle.

PRESIDENT NIXON: No, that's the point. The point is, to be perfectly frank, I don't give much of a damn what went on in 1701. . . . What I am concerned about, is whether or not Hunt, for example, had something to do with Haldeman or Colson. I just can't believe that—

EHRLICHMAN: I doubt it.

PRESIDENT NIXON: —he did with either.

EHRLICHMAN: I doubt it.

PRESIDENT NIXON: For different reasons. [*Chuckles.*]

EHRLICHMAN: So—

PRESIDENT NIXON: He's (unintelligible).

EHRLICHMAN: Yes. Liddy's apparently all right. This fellow McCord is apparently very erratic, the security man, and he's on appeal, so he's probably all right for the time being. So that's just another loose end. . . .

PRESIDENT NIXON: And you've got of course John Dean. Dean I must say has a horrible job here.

EHRLICHMAN: Yes, he has.

PRESIDENT NIXON: He's gotten all these people together, and I guess it must discourage him to see how hard it is to break through.

EHRLICHMAN: Well, it's that, and it's just the steady dripping on the stomach. Every day he comes back to it and some other dang loose end hits him. So I think the fact that you've been spending some time with him, whether it's been productive for you, has been very good in buttressing him.

PRESIDENT NIXON: He needs it.

EHRLICHMAN: Yes.

PRESIDENT NIXON: He needs it, and also—well, I think you're right, though. I don't believe that—Dean was in, as he said, confidential relationship with everyone he talked to. So he's not telling me everything. He's telling me everything that I need to know. . . .

EHRLICHMAN: . . . . [T]o my way of thinking, we're not any longer in a situation where you can successfully trim your losses, as we have done for a year.

PRESIDENT NIXON: Well, we had to trim them before the election.

EHRLICHMAN: Why, sure, of course.

PRESIDENT NIXON: That was the purpose [of the cover-up]. We knew that.

EHRLICHMAN: Sure.

PRESIDENT NIXON: But afterwards, it seems to me that the quicker, the sooner—

EHRLICHMAN: Well, it's a question of figuring out how to do it without it splashing on you and tying up the corners of it. And I must say, I don't know how to do that at the moment. But I am satisfied that that's a safer direction in the long haul than trying to contrive a defense to the hearing or to counterattack the hearing or somehow or another to hope that the hearings will go lightly, and so on. They won't. . . .

PRESIDENT NIXON: And the media, they have to jump on it, that bunch of vultures. We obviously know that. I'm not complaining about that. It's wrong, but I think it's inevitable they're going to have that kind of a double standard as compared to what they do when you get into Chappaquiddick, or something.

EHRLICHMAN: Yes, and that's the way it's going to be.

PRESIDENT NIXON: Yes. But I don't know how you can just stand there and fight the battle for years this way. But would you go so far as to reverse the situation and have all you fellows go up and testify?

EHRLICHMAN: No—

PRESIDENT NIXON: I guess not.

EHRLICHMAN: —I don't think you can do that. . . .

PRESIDENT NIXON: . . . [Colson] certainly been involved in a lot of things, but he's not probably been involved in this. So why not—I mean, what have we got there? That's the people. Look, who the hell are they after? You know who they're after.

EHRLICHMAN: They're after Bob, me.

PRESIDENT NIXON: Well, not so much you. They don't think you really did—but they're after Bob and they're after Colson and they're after Mitchell. Those are the three.

EHRLICHMAN: They're after anybody that—yeah, that they can tie you to by imputation. . . .

PRESIDENT NIXON: Well, if we need to do any more to buck up Dean, let me know.

EHRLICHMAN: I will. I think he's all right. I think he's okay.

PRESIDENT NIXON: I think he's quite a fellow.

EHRLICHMAN: Yes.

PRESIDENT NIXON: Now let me ask you this. There's only one mistake in judgment, and maybe it wasn't his. Was he the one who felt we ought to push Gray?

EHRLICHMAN: Ought to do what? Push Gray?

PRESIDENT NIXON: Send Gray's name up.

EHRLICHMAN: Yes, yes.

PRESIDENT NIXON: I guess Mitchell influenced him a great deal on that one, Mitchell and Kleindienst.

EHRLICHMAN: Well, Kleindienst doesn't influence Dean.

PRESIDENT NIXON: I think in that connection we have to look at the mistakes, leaving out the judges [nominations of Clement Haynsworth and Harrold Carswell to the Supreme Court]. I think the Kleindienst thing was a mistake and I think Gray was a mistake. Would you agree in that respect—

EHRLICHMAN: I don't know whether the Gray thing was a mistake yet or not. I think it's too early to know.

PRESIDENT NIXON: Oh, you mean that the Gray thing may still prove to be diversionary?

EHRLICHMAN: We may come out all right. This may be drawing off a little of the poison in this deal.

MARCH 21, 1973: THE PRESIDENT, DEAN, AND HALDEMAN, 10:12–11:55 A.M., OVAL OFFICE

This taped conversation profoundly influenced events. John Dean, with his famous "cancer on the presidency" remark, reports to the President on the origins of the Watergate break-in, and the problems of the cover-up. None of this is news or even wrong to Nixon. In a well-known exchange, Dean says that continuing hush money will require a million dollars, Nixon replies they "could get the money... you get a million dollars. And you could get it in cash. I, I know where it could be gotten." This is not a probing or rhetorical comment, as he later claimed; he emphatically means it. He later contended, and Haldeman so testified, that "it's wrong, that's for sure." But that remark was a response to the idea of granting clemency, not to paying money. In the exchange, Nixon is a knowing, informed—not a disinterested, shocked— participant who promptly launches his own "investigation" to find the wrongdoing and the culprits. The conversation ends with Nixon and Haldeman clearly pledging to continue the cover-up. Dean's report to the President is designed to stimulate top-level thinking as to the next White House move. Unbeknownst to Dean, that move developed the new Administration line: on March 21, the President learned of the cover-up, took charge of the investigation, and determined that John Dean had a key role in the planning of the break-in and single-handedly instituted and ran the cover-up on his own writ and authority.

PRESIDENT NIXON: John, sit down, sit down.

DEAN: Good morning.

PRESIDENT NIXON: Well, what is the Dean summary of the day about? . . .

DEAN: Uh, the reason I thought we ought to talk this morning is because in, in, our conversations, uh, uh, I have, I have the impression that you don't know everything I know—

PRESIDENT NIXON: That's right.

DEAN: —and it makes it very difficult for you to make judgments that, uh, that only you can make—

PRESIDENT NIXON: That's right. . . .

DEAN: I think, I think that, uh, there's no doubt about the seriousness of the problem we're, we've got. We have a cancer—within—close to the Presidency, that's growing. It's growing daily. It's compounding, it grows geometrically now, because it compounds itself. Uh, that'll be clear as I explain, you know, some of the details, uh, of why it is, and it basically is because (1) we're being blackmailed; (2) uh, people are going to start perjuring themselves very quickly that have not had to perjure themselves to protect other people and the like. And . . . there is no assurance—

PRESIDENT NIXON: That it won't bust.

DEAN: That, that won't bust. . . . So let me give you the sort of basic facts. . . . First of all, on, on the Watergate: how did it all start, where did it start? It started with an instruction to me from Bob Haldeman to see if we couldn't set up a perfectly legitimate campaign intelligence operation over at the Re-Election Committee.

PRESIDENT NIXON: Hm-hmm.

DEAN: Not being in this business, I turned to somebody who had been in this business, Jack Caulfield, who is, I don't know if you remember Jack or not. He was your original bodyguard before . . . they had . . . protection, an old New York City policeman.

PRESIDENT NIXON: Right. I know, I know him.

DEAN: Uh, Jack had worked for John [Ehrlichman] and then was transferred to my office. I said, "Jack come up with a plan that, you know, is a normal infiltration, I mean, you know, buying information from secretaries and all that sort of thing." He did, he put together a plan. It was kicked around, and, uh, I went to Ehrlichman with it. I went to Mitchell with it, and the consensus was that Caulfield wasn't the man to do this. Uh, in retrospect, that might have been a bad call, cause he is an incredibly cautious person and, and wouldn't have put the situation where it is today.

PRESIDENT NIXON: Yeah.

DEAN: All right, after rejecting that, they said, "We still need something," so I was told to look around for somebody that could go over to 1701 [Pennsylvania Avenue, CREEP headquarters] and do this. That's when I came up with Gordon Liddy, who—they needed a lawyer. Gordon had an intelligence background from his FBI service. I was aware of the fact that he had done some extremely sensitive things for the White House [Plumbers unit] while he'd been at the White House, and he had apparently done them well. Uh, going out into Ellsberg's doctor's office—

PRESIDENT NIXON: Oh, yeah.

DEAN: —and things like this. He'd worked with leaks, . . . so the report that I got from [Egil] Krogh [co-leader of the Plumbers group] was that he was a hell of a good man and, and not only that, a good lawyer, uh, and could set up a proper operation. So we talked to Liddy. Liddy was interested in doing it. [I] took Liddy over to meet Mitchell. Mitchell thought highly of him because, apparently, Mitchell was partially involved in his coming to the White House to work for, for Krogh. Uh, Liddy had been at Treasury before that. Then Liddy was told to put together his plan, you know, how he would run an intelligence operation. And this was after he was hired over there at the, uh, the Committee. Magruder called me in January and said, "I'd like to have you come over and see Liddy's plan."

PRESIDENT NIXON: January of '72?

DEAN: January of '72. Like, "You come over to Mitchell's office and sit in on a meeting where Liddy is going to lay his plan out." I said, "Well, I don't really know as I am the man, but if you want me there I will be happy to." [Clears throat.] So I came over and Liddy laid out a million-dollar plan that was the most incredible thing I have ever laid my eyes on: all in codes, and involved black bag operations, kidnapping, providing prostitutes, uh, to weaken the opposition, bugging, uh, mugging teams. It was just an incredible thing. [Clears throat.]

PRESIDENT NIXON: But uh, . . . that was, that was not, uh, . . discussed. . . .

DEAN: No, not at all. And . . . Mitchell, Mitchell just virtually sat there puffing and laughing. I could tell 'cause after he—after Liddy left the office I said, "That's the most incredible thing I have ever seen." He said, "I agree." And so then he was told to go back to the drawing boards and come up with something realistic. So there was a second meeting. Uh, they asked me to come over to that. I came into the tail end of the meeting. I wasn't there for the first part. I don't know how long the meeting lasted. Uh, at this point, they were discussing again bugging, kidnapping, and the like. And at this point I said, right in front of everybody, very clearly, I said, "These are not the sort of things (1) that are ever to be discussed in the office of the Attorney General of the United States"—where he still was—"and I am personally incensed." I was trying to get Mitchell off the hook. . .

PRESIDENT NIXON: I know.

DEAN: He's a, he's a nice person, doesn't like to say no . . . [to] people he's going to have to work with.

PRESIDENT NIXON: That's right. . . . Who else was present? Besides you—

DEAN: It was Magruder, Magruder. . . Mitchell, Liddy and myself. I came back right after the meeting and told Bob, I said, "Bob, we've got a growing disaster on our hands if they're thinking this way," and I said, "The White House has got to stay out of this and I, frankly, am not going to be involved in it." He said, "I agree John." And, I thought, at that point, the thing was turned off. That's the *last I heard of it,* when I thought it was turned off, because it was an *absurd* proposal.

PRESIDENT NIXON: Yeah.

DEAN: Liddy—I did have dealings with him afterwards. We never talked about it. Now that would be hard to believe for some people, but, uh, we never did. Just the fact of the matter.

PRESIDENT NIXON: Well, you were talking about other things. . . . But you were his advisor, and I, I understand how you could have some, uh, what cam—what are the campaign laws? . . . Haldeman told me you, that you were heading all of that up for us. Go ahead.

DEAN: Now. [*Clears throat.*] So, Liddy went back after that and was over, over at, uh, 1701, the Committee, and I, this is where I come into having put the pieces together after the fact as to what I can put together what happened. Liddy sat over there and tried to come up with another plan, that he could sell. (1) They were talking, saying to him he was asking for too much money, and I don't think they were discounting the illegal points at this, after—you know, Jeb is not a lawyer. He didn't know whether this was the way the game was played or not, and what it was all about. They came up with, apparently, another plan, uh, but they couldn't get it approved by anybody over there. So Liddy and Hunt apparently came to see Chuck Colson, and Chuck Colson picked up the telephone and called Magruder and said, "You all either fish or cut bait. Uh, this is absurd to have these guys over there and not using them, and if you're not going to use them, I may use them." Things of this nature.

PRESIDENT NIXON: When was this?

DEAN: This was apparently in February of '72.

PRESIDENT NIXON: That could be—Colson know what they were talking about?

DEAN: I can only assume, because of his close relationship with—

PRESIDENT NIXON: Hunt.

DEAN: —Hunt, he had a damn good idea of what they were talking about, a damn good idea. He would probably deny it, deny it today and probably get away with denying it. But I, uh, I still—

PRESIDENT NIXON: Unless Hunt—

DEAN: Unless Hunt, uh, blows on him—

PRESIDENT NIXON: But then Hunt isn't enough. It takes two doesn't it?

DEAN: Probably. Probably. But Liddy was there also and if, if Liddy were to blow—

PRESIDENT NIXON: Then you've got a problem . . . .

DEAN: I will go back over that, and tell you where I think the, the soft spots are.

PRESIDENT NIXON: Colson— . . . you think [he] . . . pushed?

DEAN: I think he helped to get the push, get the thing off the dime. Now something else occurred. . . .

PRESIDENT NIXON: Did he [Colson] talk to Haldeman?

DEAN: No, I don't think so. Now, but here's the other the thing where the next thing comes in the chain. I think that Bob was assuming that they had something that was proper over there, some intelligence gathering operation that Liddy was operating. And through Strachan, uh, who was his tickler, uh, he started pushing them—

PRESIDENT NIXON: [Sighs.] Yeah.

DEAN: —to get something, to get some information and they took that as a signal—Magruder took that as a signal—to probably go to Mitchell and say, "They are pushing us like crazy for this from "the White House." And so Mitchell probably puffed on his pipe and said, "Go ahead," and never really re—reflected on what it was all about. So, they had some plan that obviously had, I gather, different targets they were going to go after. They were going to infiltrate, and bug, and do all this sort of thing to a lot of these targets. This is knowledge I have after the fact. [Coughs.] And, apparently, they, uh, they, they had, they had after, they had initially broken in and bugged the Democratic National Committee, they were getting information. The information was coming over here to Strachan. Some of it was given to Haldeman, uh, there is no doubt about it.

PRESIDENT NIXON: Did he know what it was coming from?

DEAN: I don't really know if he would.

PRESIDENT NIXON: Not necessarily. . . . Strachan knew what it was from.

DEAN: Strachan knew what it was from. No doubt about it, and whether Strachan—I have never come to press these people on these points because it . . . hurts them to, to give up that next inch, so I had to piece things together. All right, so Strachan was aware of receiving information, reporting to Bob. At one point Bob even gave instructions to change their capabilities from Muskie to McGovern, and had passed this back through Strachan to Magruder and, and apparently to Liddy. And Liddy was starting to make arrangements to go in and bug the, uh, uh, McGovern operation. They had done prelim—

PRESIDENT NIXON: They had never bugged Muskie, though, did they?

DEAN: No, they hadn't. . . . Now, so the information was coming over here and then, uh, I finally, after the next point in time where I became aware of anything was on June 17th, when I got the word that there had been this break-in at the Democratic National Committee and somebody from . . . our Committee had been caught in the DNC. . . .

PRESIDENT NIXON: You knew what it was.

DEAN: I knew what it was. So I called Liddy, uh, on that Monday morning, and I said, "Gordon," I said, "first, I want to know if anybody in the White House was involved in this." And he said, "No, they weren't." I said, "Well, I want to know how in God's name this happened." And he said, "Well, I was pushed without mercy by Magruder to get in there, get more information, that the information, it was not satisfactory. Magruder said, "The White House is not happy with what we're getting."

PRESIDENT NIXON: The White House? . . . Who do you think was pushing him?

DEAN: Well, I think it was probably Strachan thinking that Bob wanted things, and, because, because I have seen that happen on other occasions where things have been said to be of very prime importance when they really weren't.

PRESIDENT NIXON: Why [unintelligible] I wonder? . . . We'd just finished the Moscow trip. . . . The Democrats had just nominated McG—McGovern. I mean, for Christ's sakes. . . . I don't see why all the pressure would have been around then.

DEAN: I don't know, other than the fact that, uh, they might have been looking for information about—

PRESIDENT NIXON: —the convention. . . .

DEAN: I understand, also, after the fact, that there was a plan to bug Larry O'Brien's suite down in Florida.

PRESIDENT NIXON: Yeah.

DEAN: Uh, so, uh, Liddy told me that, uh, you know, this is what had happened and, and this is why it had happened. . . .

PRESIDENT NIXON: Where did he learn of the plans to bug Larry O'Brien's suite?

DEAN: From Magruder, . . . long after the fact.

PRESIDENT NIXON: Oh, Magruder, he knows?

DEAN: Yeah. Magruder is totally knowledgeable on the whole thing. . . . Mitchell. I don't know how much knowledge he actually had. I know that Magruder has perjured himself in the Grand Jury. I know that Porter has perjured himself, uh, in the Grand Jury.

PRESIDENT NIXON: Porter [unintelligible]?

DEAN: He is one of Magruder's deputies. . . . They said . . . that, uh, Liddy had come over as, as a counsel . . . to do legitimate intelligence. We had no idea what he was doing. . . . He was given an authorization of $250,000 . . . to collect information, because our surrogates were out on the road. . . . [W]e had to have a plan to get information as to what liabilities they were going to be confronted with . . . and Liddy was charged with doing this. We had no knowledge that he was going to bug the DNC.

PRESIDENT NIXON: Well, the point is, that's not true.

DEAN: That's right.

PRESIDENT NIXON: Magruder did know that—

DEAN: Magruder specifically instructed him to go back in the DNC.

PRESIDENT NIXON: He did?

DEAN: Yes.

PRESIDENT NIXON: You know that? Yeah, I see. Okay.

DEAN: Uh, I honestly believe that no one over here knew that. I know, uh, as God is my maker, I had no knowledge that they were going to do this. . . .

PRESIDENT NIXON: Did Bob know? Bob, Bob, now—he wouldn't—

DEAN: Bob—I don't believe specifically knew they were going in there.

PRESIDENT NIXON: I don't think so.

DEAN: I don't think he did. I think he knew there was a capacity to do this but he wouldn't, wasn't giving it specific direction.

PRESIDENT NIXON: Strachan, did he know?

DEAN: I think Strachan did know.

PRESIDENT NIXON: They were going back into the DNC? Hunt never entered the DNC . . . . Why did Petersen play the, play the game so straight with us?

DEAN: Because Petersen is a soldier. He played—He kept me informed. He told me when we had problems, where we had problems and the like. Uh, he believes in, in, in you. Believes in this Administration. This Administration has made him. Uh, I don't think he's done anything improper, but he did make sure the investigation was narrowed down to the very, very . . . . fine . . . criminal things, which was a break for us. There is no doubt about it.

PRESIDENT NIXON: He honestly feels that he did an adequate job? . . .

DEAN: That's right. But see, the thing is, is based on their FBI interviews, there was no reason to follow up. There were no leads there. Colson said, "I have no knowledge of this" to the FBI. Uh, Strachan said, "I have no knowledge of—" you know, they didn't ask Strachan any Watergate questions. . . . Strachan appeared, uh, as a result of some coaching, he could be the dumbest paper pusher in the bowels of the, the White House. . . .

PRESIDENT NIXON: Right.

[Dean then turns to the cover-up.]

DEAN: Uh, Liddy said, said that, you know, if they all got counsel instantly and said that, you know, "Well, we'll ride this thing out." All right, then they started making demands. "We've got to have attorneys' fees. Uh, we don't have any money ourselves, and if—you are asking us to take this through the election." All right, so arrangements were made through Mitchell, uh, initiating it, in discussions that—I was present—that these guys had to be taken care of. Their attorneys' fees had to be done. [Herbert] Kalmbach was brought in. Uh, Kalmbach raised some cash. . . .

PRESIDENT NIXON: They put that under the cover of a Cuban Committee or [unintelligible].

DEAN: Yeah, they, they had a Cuban Committee and they had—some of it was given to Hunt's lawyer, who in turn passed it out. This, you know, when Hunt's wife was flying to Chicago with ten thousand, she was actually, I understand after the fact now, was going to pass that money to, uh, one of the Cubans there.

PRESIDENT NIXON: . . . Well, whether it's maybe too late to do anything about it, but I would certainly keep that [laughs], that cover for whatever it's worth. . . .

DEAN: . . . [T]hat's the most troublesome post-thing, uh, because (1) Bob is involved in that; John is involved in that; I am involved in that; Mitchell is involved in that. And that's an obstruction of justice.

PRESIDENT NIXON: In other words the fact that, uh, that you're, you're, you're taking care of witnesses. . . . How was Bob involved?

DEAN: . . . Bob had $350,00 in a safe over here that was really set aside re polling purposes. Uh, and there was no other source of money, so they came over here and said, "You all have got to give us some money."

PRESIDENT NIXON: Right.

DEAN: I had to go to Bob and say, "Bob, you know . . . they need some money over there." He said, "What for?" And so I had to tell him what it was for 'cause he wasn't about to just send money over there willy-nilly. And, uh, John [Ehrlichman] was involved in those discussions, and we decided, you know, that, you know, that there was no price too high to pay to let this thing blow up in front of the election.

PRESIDENT NIXON: I think you should handle that one pretty fast. . . .

DEAN: But, now, here, here's what's happening right now.

PRESIDENT NIXON: Yeah.

DEAN: What sort of brings matters to the—this is . . . going to be a continual blackmail operation by Hunt and Liddy and the Cubans. No doubt about it. And McCord . . . has asked for nothing. . . . And as you know Colson has talked to, indirectly to Hunt about commutation. [*Clears throat.*] All these things are . . . problems, they are promises, they are commitments. They are the very sort of thing that the Senate is going to be looking most for. I don't think they can find them, frankly.

PRESIDENT NIXON: Pretty hard,

DEAN: Pretty hard. Damn hard. It's all cash. Uh—

PRESIDENT NIXON: Well, I mean, pretty hard as far as the witnesses are concerned.

DEAN: That's right. Now. The blackmail is continuing. . . . Hunt now is demanding another $72,000 for his own personal expenses; $50,000 to pay his attorneys' fees—a hundred and twenty some thousand dollars. Wants it, wanted it by the close of business yesterday. 'Cause he says, "I am going to be sentenced on Friday, and I've got to be able to get my financial affairs in order."

. . . Hunt now has made a direct threat against Ehrlichman, as a result of this. This is his blackmail. He says, "I will bring John Ehrlichman down to his knees and put him in jail. Uh, I have done enough seamy things for he and Krogh [of the Plumbers], uh, that they'll never survive it."

PRESIDENT NIXON: What's that, on Ellsberg?

DEAN: Ellsberg, and apparently some other things. I don't know the full extent of it.

PRESIDENT NIXON: I don't know about anything else.

DEAN: I don't know either, and I [*laughs*] almost hate to learn some of these things. . . . Now, where are the soft points? . . . The Cubans that were used in the Watergate were also the same Cubans that Hunt and Liddy used for this California Ellsberg thing, for the break-in out there.

PRESIDENT NIXON: Yeah. . . . I don't know what the hell we did that for. . . . What in the name of God did that—

DEAN: Mr. President, there have been a couple of things around here that I have gotten wind of. Uh, there was at one time a desire to do a second-story job on the Brookings Institute where they had the Pentagon Papers. Now I flew to California because I was told that John had instructed it and he said, "I really hadn't. It is a misimpression, that for Christ's sake, turn it off." And I did. I came back and turned it off. Because, you know . . . , if the risk is minimal and the. . . and the gain is fantastic, it's something else. But with a low risk and, uh, no gain, . . . it's not worth it.

[Dean then talks about the role of the defendants' lawyers who have been involved, including Henry Rothblatt, F. Lee Bailey, and William Bittman.]

DEAN: . . . [A]ll the principals involved know. Uh, Hunt—some people's wives know.

PRESIDENT NIXON: Sure.

DEAN: Uh, there's no doubt about that. Mrs. Hunt was the savviest woman in the world. She had the whole picture together.

PRESIDENT NIXON: Did she?

DEAN: . . . Apparently, she was the pillar of strength in that family before [her] death. . . .

PRESIDENT NIXON: Great sadness. . . . I said, of course, commutation could be considered on the basis of his wife, and that is the only discussion I ever had in that light.

DEAN: . . . Now, where, where are the soft spots on this? Well, first of all, there's the, there's the problem of the continued blackmail . . . which will not only go on now, it'll go on when these people are in prison, and it will compound the obstruction-of-justice-situation. It'll cost money. It's dangerous. Nobody, nothing—people around here are not pros at this sort of thing. This is the sort of thing Mafia people can do: washing money, getting clean money, and things like that, uh—we're—we just don't know about those things, because we're not used to, you know—we are not criminals. . . .

PRESIDENT NIXON: That's right. . . . How much money do you need?

DEAN: I would say these people are going to cost, uh, a million dollars over the next, uh, two years.

[Pause.]

PRESIDENT NIXON: We could get that. . . . [I]f you need the money, . . . you could get the money. . . . What I mean is, you could, you could get a million dollars. And you could get it in cash. I, I know where it could be gotten.

DEAN: Uh huh.

PRESIDENT NIXON: I mean it's not easy, but it could be done. But, uh, the question is who the hell would handle it? . . .

DEAN: Well, I would think that would be something that Mitchell ought to be charged with. . . . And get some, get some pros to help him.

PRESIDENT NIXON: Let me say, there shouldn't be a lot of people running around getting money. . . .

DEAN: Well, he's got one person doing it who I am not sure is—

PRESIDENT NIXON: Who is that?

DEAN: He's got Fred LaRue, uh, doing it. Now Fred started out going out trying to—

PRESIDENT NIXON: No.

DEAN: —solicit money from all kinds of people. Now, I learned about that, and I said, "My God,"

PRESIDENT NIXON: No.

DEAN: *"It's just awful. Don't do it."*

PRESIDENT NIXON: Yeah.

DEAN: Uh, people are going to ask what the money is for. He's working—he's apparently talked to Tom Pappas.

PRESIDENT NIXON: I know.

DEAN: And Pappas has, uh, agreed to come up with a sizable amount, I gather, from, from Mitchell. . . .

PRESIDENT NIXON: Well, your major, your major guy to keep under control is Hunt. . . . Because he knows—

DEAN: —he knows so much.

PRESIDENT NIXON: . . . [A]bout a lot of other things. . . .

DEAN: All right, now we've got—

PRESIDENT NIXON: —you've got Krogh, and you've got—

DEAN: —now we've got Kalmbach. [Coughs.]

PRESIDENT NIXON: Yeah, that's a tough one. . . .

DEAN: . . . I don't know of anything that Herb has done that is illegal, other than the fact that he doesn't want to blow the whistle on a lot of people, and may find himself in a perjury situation.

PRESIDENT NIXON: Well, if he, uh, he—could because he will be asked about that money?

DEAN: He will. . . .

PRESIDENT NIXON: All right. How do your other vulnerabilities go together?

DEAN: The other vulnerabilities: we've got a, uh, runaway Grand Jury up in the Southern District [New York].

PRESIDENT NIXON: Yeah. I heard.

DEAN: They're after Mitchell and Stans on some sort of bribe or influence peddling—

PRESIDENT NIXON: On [alleged financial swindler Robert] Vesco.

DEAN: —with Vesco.

PRESIDENT NIXON: Yeah.

DEAN: They're also going to try to drag Ehrlichman into that. Apparently, Ehrlichman had some meetings with Vesco, also. [The President's nephew] Don Nixon, Jr., came in to see John a couple of times, uh, about the problem.

PRESIDENT NIXON: Not about the complaint. . . .

DEAN: . . . [I]f this thing ever blows, and we're in a cover-up situation, I think it'd be extremely damaging to you, uh, and, uh, the, uh—

PRESIDENT NIXON: Sure. . . . The whole concept of Administration Justice—

DEAN: . . . [W]hat happens if it starts breaking, and they do find a criminal case against a Haldeman, a Dean, a Mitchell, an Ehrlichman? . . .

PRESIDENT NIXON: Well if it really comes down to that, we cannot, maybe—we'd have to shed it in order to contain it again.

DEAN: [Clears throat.] That's right. . . . Bob and John and John Mitchell and I should sit down and spend a day, or however long, to figure out (1) how this can be carved away from you, so it does not damage you or the Presidency. 'Cause it just can't. . . .

PRESIDENT NIXON: That is true.

DEAN: I know, sir, it is. Well, I can just tell from our conversations that, you know, these are things that you have no knowledge of.

PRESIDENT NIXON: The absurdity of the whole damned thing. . . . Colson et al., and so forth, were doing their best to get information and so forth and so on. But they all knew very well they were supposed to comply with the law. . . . No question. . . . [Y]ou feel that really the man, the trigger man was Colson on this then?

DEAN: Well, no, he was . . . just in the chain. . . . [S]ome people are going to have to go to jail. That's the long and short of it. . . .

PRESIDENT NIXON: You go to jail?

DEAN: That's right.

PRESIDENT NIXON: . . . I can't see how a legal case could be made against you. . . . [W]hat would you go to jail on, what thing?

DEAN: The obstruct—, the obstruction of justice.

PRESIDENT NIXON: The obstruction of justice? . . . I feel, could be cut off at the pass. . . .

Sometimes it's well to give them—

DEAN: [*Sighs.*]

PRESIDENT NIXON: —something, and then they don't want the bigger fish then. . . . I wonder if that [the blackmail] doesn't have to be continued? . . . Let me put it this way: let us suppose that you get, you, you get the million bucks, and you get the proper way to handle it, and you could hold that side. It would seem to me that would be worthwhile. . . .

[The President wants to fight and continue the blackmail to avoid indictments.]

DEAN: Bob and I have talked about just what we're talking about this morning. I told him I thought that you should have the facts, and he agrees. . . .

[Haldeman enters the room.]

PRESIDENT NIXON: I was talking to John about this, uh, this whole situation, and I think we, uh, so that we can get away from the bits and pieces that have broken out. He is right in . . . recommending that, that, uh, that there be a meeting at the very first possible time.

[The President continues the discussion, now including Haldeman, and he looks for ways to maintain the cover-up, including more money payments.]

PRESIDENT NIXON: . . . [Y]our feeling is that we just can't continue to, to pay the blackmail of these guys?

DEAN: I think that's our greatest jeopardy.

PRESIDENT NIXON: Now, let me tell you it's . . . no problem, we could, we could get the money. There is no problem in that. We can't provide the clemency. The money can be provided. Mitchell could provide the way to deliver it. That could be done. See what I mean?

HALDEMAN: But, Mitchell says he can't, doesn't he?

DEAN: . . . A million dollars in cash, or, or the like, has been just a very difficult problem as we've discussed before. Apparently, Mitchell has talked to Pappas, and I called him . . . last night after our discussion and after you'd met with John to see where that was. And I, I said, "Have you talked to, to Pappas?" He was at home, and Martha picked up the phone so it was all in code. "Did you talk to the Greek?" And he said, uh, "Yes, I have." And I said, "Is the Greek bearing gifts?" He said, "Well, I want to call you tomorrow on that."

PRESIDENT NIXON: . . . Now, look [unintelligible] I am, uh, unfamiliar with the money situation. . . .

. . . All right. If you bunker down and fight it, fight it and what happens? Your view is that, that is, is not really a viable option.

DEAN: It's a very—it's a high risk. A very high risk.

PRESIDENT NIXON: A high risk, because your view is that what will happen . . . is that's going to come out. Sombody's—Hunt—something's going to break loose—

DEAN: Something is going to break and—

PRESIDENT NIXON: When it breaks it'll look like the President—

DEAN: —is covering up.

PRESIDENT NIXON: . . . All right. Fine. . . . [L]et me say, I have no doubts about the right plan before the election. And you handled it just right. You contained it. Now after the election we've got to have another plan, because we can't have, for four years, we can't have this thing—you're going to be eaten away. We can't do it. . . . I say the White House can't do it. Right? . . .

HALDEMAN: John's point is exactly right, that the erosion here now is going to you, and that is the thing that we've got to turn off, at whatever the cost and we've got to figure out where to turn it off at the lowest cost we can, but at whatever cost it takes.

DEAN: That's what, that's what we have to do.

PRESIDENT NIXON: . . . [T]he Watergate isn't a major concern. It isn't. But it would, but it will be. It's bound to be.

DEAN: We cannot let you be tarnished by that situation.

PRESIDENT NIXON: . . . I say that the White House can't do it. Right?

HALDEMAN: Yeah.

DEAN: Yes, sir.

MARCH 21, 1973: THE PRESIDENT AND ROSE MARY WOODS, 1:06–1:20 P.M., OVAL OFFICE

Nixon speaks to Rose Mary Woods just after his remarks to John Dean about the easy availability of cash. The tone with Woods is cryptic and dark. While the two know exactly what they are talking about, they are allusive and vague.

PRESIDENT NIXON: Let me ask you something I was checking. We at the present time may have a need for substantial cash for a personal purpose for some things that are outside the political (unintelligible), and so on. Approximately how much do you have at this point in the event (unintelligible)? It would be reimbursed at a later time, but this is something that, I don't know if we wanted it or not, but I got to find out.

WOODS: I know—I deliberately don't remember the thing, but I know I still have that hundred [thousand?], if I'm right. It's not the kind of thing you remember—I'm so worried.

PRESIDENT NIXON: Do you have (unintelligible)?

WOODS: They called earlier and I said it had been used for a special project, so that there'd be no record.

PRESIDENT NIXON: And you have some other as well?

WOODS: Yes. I don't know. I would have to look. I'd have to get in the safe. I don't remember.

PRESIDENT NIXON: But it's a sum you can take. We may have to call on that, and I don't know—. Incidentally, let me ask you, is that in—in what kind of—

WOODS: That's why I've been wanting to (unintelligible) recommend that either you or Pat [Nixon]. I think you gave me about a couple of years, whether to use the thing or not.

PRESIDENT NIXON: Well, I see that that would have to be transferred to something else in order to get it out. Okay. . . . Now, how much (unintelligible), maybe somebody who would know, not here, but we have to use it for certain purposes, and we'll get it.

WOODS: Nobody here knows I have it, because I don't—

PRESIDENT NIXON: Well, I know, and nobody anyplace else knows. Just we have a campaign thing that we're talking about.

MARCH 21, 1973: THE PRESIDENT AND HALDEMAN, 3:05–3:45 P.M., EXECUTIVE OFFICE BUILDING

After the morning meeting with Dean, Nixon and Haldeman review the issues with no recriminations. The recording is poor, but it clearly reveals that Dean's information offered no surprises. The talk is about continued money payments to Hunt and others, and the President—contrary to his later protestations—definitely understands obstruction of justice.

PRESIDENT NIXON: Let me go over a couple of points here that relate to—you're going to meet with whom?

HALDEMAN: Ehrlichman and Dean.

PRESIDENT NIXON: All right. The first consideration, which I guess is what to do about Hunt. I think we've obviously overloaded Dean. Everybody says well, that's Dean's job. Yeah, but now we've really got to step in there. . . .

HALDEMAN: Well, we've been backing him up pretty well. . . . It isn't just Hunt. It's Liddy and that other guy, McCord, and the Cubans. Now [Fred] LaRue has been helping on it, but LaRue . . . will go out and get the money and then LaRue doesn't go out and get the money. He has tried some, but not very much. LaRue is not a very dynamic guy anyway. . . . So Dean finally just goes running pretty much to Mitchell and said I've got to have some money. You guys know I just can't go asking . . . . LaRue has proven Kalmbach can't do it anymore, and shouldn't.

PRESIDENT NIXON: Well, so that's going to impact on Mitchell.

HALDEMAN: Yes.

PRESIDENT NIXON: . . . [P]ut it on the shelf. Dangerous things are going around getting the money. . . .

HALDEMAN: You can't afford to do it. You can't do this, you can't have a fund-raising drive and give everybody certificates and gold pens.

PRESIDENT NIXON: No business [unintelligible] the obstruction of justice.

HALDEMAN: Well, see, I hadn't really thought of that . . . .

PRESIDENT NIXON: I hadn't thought of it either . . . . We are all in it. . . . I think up to this point that we had certain choices, choices before the election, or after . . . . That's gone. Now, the trial in addition to the committee hearing, we have a different situation. And money [unintelligible], possibly through Dean, possibly through [unintelligible]. . . . It's money that's available, it remains in the campaign [funds?], in cash in $100 bills. . . . I can get it. I mean, I can find a way to get it, and I can find a way to get it and give it up, *but* I will not. This cannot be—

HALDEMAN: Consider the cost.

PRESIDENT NIXON: I cannot consider it unless there is an effective change. . . .

HALDEMAN: They've got other ways that they do that.

PRESIDENT NIXON: Like what?

HALDEMAN: Well, apparently that's what Dean was saying; he's learned a lot about this stuff now. He's all ready for next time. They run—as I understand it, the easy way is to pay it to Vegas and run it through the [casinos?] out there and it gets lost pretty easily in there. . . .

Well, Hunt's not the major liability in Watergate, but he's a major liability [elsewhere]. Liddy is the major liability on Watergate, because Liddy is the one that presumably knows where he got his orders.

PRESIDENT NIXON: My concern is the Colson [stuff?].

HALDEMAN: Yeah.

MARCH 22, 1973: THE PRESIDENT AND KLEINDIENST, 2:19–2:26 P.M., WHITE HOUSE TELEPHONE

The Attorney General offers a gloomy progress report on the Gray nomination. Meanwhile, he agrees to "babysit" that "sumbitch," Howard Baker.

PRESIDENT NIXON: Now the point is, on the other hand, Baker wants and does need some, you know, contact, and it seems to me that you're the man. . . .

KLEINDIENST: And I made myself available to him a dozen times.

PRESIDENT NIXON: Really?

KLEINDIENST: Yeah. And, Goddamn him, you know, he's running here and he's running there, and he's just awfully—hard to get his hands on him. But the last time I met was before and then after that conference that I had with him and Ervin, in which I said Howard, I want you to feel free to call me—you know, one problem that he's got in his Goddamn mind, he's afraid to talk to anybody on the telephone. You know, he thinks it's bugged.

PRESIDENT NIXON: Uh-huh.

KLEINDIENST: And I said, Howard, you're not being bugged. [*Laughter.*]

PRESIDENT NIXON: Why of course not.

KLEINDIENST: You know. But that's one of his problems. And then he's also busy, and then he really hasn't focused on this problem. But I think as a result of our last meeting that we really don't have much of a problem. . . .

PRESIDENT NIXON: Let me suggest this. Why don't you get him on the phone and get him down and say, look, you've heard some of this business. He's also lying . . .

that he doesn't have any contact at the White House. And, of course, he didn't want that. That's not his fault—not our fault, I mean. We'd be delighted, except that it would not be the right thing. On the other hand, contact with you is essential so that you can give him a little guidance on various things.

KLEINDIENST: Part of the irritation might be, is that, you know, he gave me a lot of ideas on what he thought you ought to do, and I said, well, the President's already made some decisions.

PRESIDENT NIXON: Yeah, his idea that he wanted everybody to come down in public session.

KLEINDIENST: And I said, Howard, now that the President has already decided that, we've got the fact. Let's you and I figure out a way that we're going to implement it. . . .

PRESIDENT NIXON: . . . We'll keep in touch with you, Dick, basically through Dean, which is the best way, in terms of, you know, what can be worked out with the committee and that sort of thing within our guidelines. But then I think you've really got to be the Baker hand-holder, if you will. It's a hell of a tough job, but if you have to have him move in with you, why do it.

KLEINDIENST: I'll babysit the sumbitch 24 hours a day.

PRESIDENT NIXON: That's right. Get his wife out of the way and keep him in.

KLEINDIENST: Mr. President, let me just talk to you for a second about Pat Gray. . . . Well, the thing is the whole Goddamn thing pretty much hangs on [Senator Charles] Mac Mathias [R-MD]. But Eastland has some questions in his own mind whether if they got him out of that committee—

PRESIDENT NIXON: They could get him on the floor, get him passed, yeah.

KLEINDIENST: —whether or not they could get him passed. . . . You know, Pat wanted to go on the Second Circuit. [Senator] Lowell Weicker [R-CT] wants him to go on it. I asked Jim. I said, well, suppose that we all conclude that we can't get Pat through? Incidentally, I'm not prepared to say that right now. . . .

PRESIDENT NIXON: . . . Then let's leave it this way. You'll handle Baker now, you'll babysit him starting like in about ten minutes?

KLEINDIENST: Just like he's a brother.

PRESIDENT NIXON: All right.

KLEINDIENST: I'll call him when I put the phone down. Thank you, sir.

PRESIDENT NIXON: Okay.

MARCH 27, 1973: THE PRESIDENT AND KISSINGER, 8:54–9:44 A.M., OVAL OFFICE

Judge Sirica imposes severe provisional sentences on the burglars, and he urges them to cooperate to implicate others. Nixon and Kissinger offer a joint chorus of complaint about the lack of respect for civil liberties in the affair and the failure of "civil libertarians"—particularly Kissinger's "Harvard friends," as the President derisively said—to stand up on such issues. Nixon tells Kissinger not to be concerned, but admits the affair "is a worry."

KISSINGER: I don't know a damn thing about the Watergate case and I don't want to know, but where are the civil libertarians? Where are the civil libertarians? Here the judge gives somebody a 55-year sentence in order to make him talk. Where is the protection of the Fifth Amendment?

PRESIDENT NIXON: Where is his—and the poor bastard didn't even have a gun.

KISSINGER: It was a simple case of burglary.

PRESIDENT NIXON: He revoked his bail.

KISSINGER: Two years.

PRESIDENT NIXON: Which didn't work.

KISSINGER: Which didn't work. I mean, a two-year sentence, first offenders, people who would never do it again, so there is no reason. I mean, one knows they're never going to do it again.

PRESIDENT NIXON: Well, the other point is that trying to make them talk, that's unbelievable. But also, for a counsel to a Senate committee to go out and make the charges publicly and then say—well, at any rate, don't you worry about Watergate.

KISSINGER: No, I don't worry about it.

PRESIDENT NIXON: I'm just saying, let me say, it is a worry.

KISSINGER: If you did this to a liberal, if during the McCarthy hearings a liberal had been sentenced to 40 years in prison on a trivial offense in order to make him testify before a committee, you'd have every bloody newspaper—

PRESIDENT NIXON: Let me tell you about the McCarthy hearings. But I'll go back to my famous Hiss case and the rest, which of course your Harvard friends find worrisome. But let me tell you about it. . . . The *New York Times,* the *Washington Post,* all the libs, said the committee—this is no place to investigate these matters. These are serious charges. The place for them to be heard is in the courts. And the only reason I had to go ahead with the Hiss case is that Truman wouldn't bring it to the court. But that's all right. Once he got to the court, I stopped the investigation.

But the point here, these assholes are saying: Oh no, the grand jury isn't enough; the court finding seven people guilty and giving them fifty years isn't enough. It's got to be now try it before a kangaroo court before the Ervin Committee. There's a double standard. The only thing to do is to fight it.

MARCH 27, 1973: THE PRESIDENT AND HALDEMAN, 9:47–10:55 A.M., OVAL OFFICE

Haldeman reports on Hunt's apparent collapse, Magruder's testimony, Dean's involvement, and the idea of appointing a Warren-type commission for Watergate. The President worries about revelations regarding the "Plumbers." Haldeman tells Nixon that Ehrlichman confidently insists there are no problems. This conversation sounds contrived at points, as if the two men want to establish a record. But they intervene with frank admissions, and at times the exchange is surrealistic—as for example, when Haldeman suggests that the whole thing was driven by communists, or when the President suggests putting former Attorney General Ramsey Clark—long an object of Administration criticism and ridicule—on a Warren-type commission.

SEGMENT 1

PRESIDENT NIXON: What's the situation today . . . ?

HALDEMAN: [W]e've had some new developments. It keeps bouncing, but we now have—well, let's see. Briefly, there are three new factors which caused Dean to question—

PRESIDENT NIXON: Whether he could go [testify]?

HALDEMAN: Exactly. And I have not talked with him this morning. I was just on the phone. . . .

Number one, Liddy spent yesterday at the grand jury, took the Fifth Amendment all day. Sirica is going to give him immunity, to de-Fifth him. So you have the question of what Liddy will do without the protection of the Fifth. There's not any great concern on that. They [Dean? Ehrlichman?] think Liddy will still stonewall it and take a contempt if he has to on top of it.

Hunt—Bittman has now informed—I think Dean—that Hunt is ready to fold and is going to pull the plug. Curiously enough, Bittman is now very disturbed about that, because he's the guy that gave Hunt the money. So [*chuckles*] he's now an accessory and [*chuckles*] Hunt's pulling the plug on him. Whether that's—how serious that is remains yet to be evaluated.

The third one is that Magruder has sort of crumbled to the seams as the question—as Dean gets named and the question, the obviousness that Dean's going to be called to the grand jury, and Magruder's at least assumption, if not knowledge, that Dean's testimony will not—

PRESIDENT NIXON: Be helpful.

HALDEMAN: Well, it won't totally jibe with his. Dean won't say anything that will hurt Magruder, except it will be in conflict with some of what Magruder has said.

PRESIDENT NIXON: Yes.

HALDEMAN: Not on the direct point of did Magruder do anything, but on the peripheral points. And that's got Magruder scared to the point where Magruder has apparently told Dean that he's thought this whole thing through and he's now—no, he didn't tell Dean. He called in [Kenneth] Parkinson and [Paul] O'Brien, the two committee lawyers, yesterday, and said: Here's the situation. He has now clarified his memory and figures that he's got to—he's now got to—if they're going to haul everybody up, he's got to clean himself up, too.

PRESIDENT NIXON: Right.

HALDEMAN: And that what really happened on the Watergate was that all this planning was going on and Dean set it up and was involved in it in getting the planning worked out, and they had the plan all set but they were not ready to really start with it, and then Strachan, Gordon Strachan, called him or went through him or something and said: Haldeman has said that you cannot delay getting this operation started any longer, and the President has ordered you to go ahead immediately and you're not to stall any more, you're to get it done.

And that Magruder has chosen to say he believes to be the actual fact now, and he told these two lawyers this. And Dean said: Don't discount Magruder as a witness; he's a hell of a convincing guy, as was evidenced by how he got off on the Sirica trial.

PRESIDENT NIXON: Well, Bob, let's look at the actual facts there. Could that have happened?

HALDEMAN: No.

PRESIDENT NIXON: Ever?

HALDEMAN: I don't believe so.

PRESIDENT NIXON: It couldn't?

HALDEMAN: Not the version about Watergate.

PRESIDENT NIXON: That's what I mean. Could anything have ever happened about, for example, Strachan saying that you said the President? Or even that you told him to do anything on that?

HALDEMAN: See, he can assume when I say something that the President wants it done. But he knows better than that, too. But on this one, the only thing that I had pressured him on this, Strachan undoubtedly did nag him on was getting coverage of the Democratic candidates.

PRESIDENT NIXON: That's right.

HALDEMAN: On their public statements, and that's what he confused. Now, Magruder has asked, asked on Saturday—he met with the lawyers on this yesterday. But on Saturday he asked that Mitchell and I meet with him. He felt it was important that the three of us get together and understand exactly what the problem is that we face. Dean thought then that I should agree to the meeting to keep him on balance, but not rush right into having the meeting. I don't know what he thinks now. Dean gave me this all late last night. . . .

If Magruder went—and he's smart enough to figure this out, in fact. If he went to Sirica now, who believes that he told the truth, and Sirica has said so publicly and privately to Magruder, so Sirica looks a little foolish on it, too. If Magruder goes to Sirica and says, if you'll give me immunity I can nail the big boys—

PRESIDENT NIXON: Right.

HALDEMAN: I think Sirica would give it to him.

PRESIDENT NIXON: Right. The thing that's to me very hard to understand, Bob, is how Magruder would do that to maybe you and the President, because, first, it's hard that he would do that. But the main point is *I can't believe that it's true.*

HALDEMAN: It isn't.

PRESIDENT NIXON: I can't believe that it's true.

HALDEMAN: Dean says it's not.

PRESIDENT NIXON: You know damn well that we—well, the utter shock we had when we heard about the Goddamn thing.

HALDEMAN: Absolutely. And it's understandable that he could now, for his own purposes, confuse things, because he's got what was done mixed with other things, if he actually believes this. Now, he may not actually believe it, either. He maybe just decided—and he may not be intending to do anything on this except fire across our bow.

PRESIDENT NIXON: Blackmail.

HALDEMAN: Well, either blackmail or just, you know, he's sitting out there and he's afraid—

PRESIDENT NIXON: Nobody's covering him.

HALDEMAN: —nobody's paying enough attention to him, and that this will at least get them to look up.

PRESIDENT NIXON: Somebody'd better talk to him. . . .

HALDEMAN: . . . Magruder talked to Dean earlier yesterday before he met with the lawyers, and at that time he was taking a totally different line, which convinces Dean that Magruder is a little psycho or something, I mean, that he's playing a strange game at least, because he said to Dean: "Jeez, John, it's a shame that sonofabitch McCord has hauled you into this, because you and I both know you had absolutely nothing to do with it."

PRESIDENT NIXON: And now Magruder's saying that Dean—

HALDEMAN: To the lawyers, he ties Dean in.

PRESIDENT NIXON: And Strachan.

HALDEMAN: And me.

PRESIDENT NIXON: Strachan, you, and the President.

HALDEMAN: That's right. . . .

PRESIDENT NIXON: Here's where you need the advice of Rogers. How do you appoint the [Warren-type] Commission, who's going to be on it?

HALDEMAN: Well, there are some possibilities there.

PRESIDENT NIXON: Warren?

HALDEMAN: Well, not—he had some ideas. I talked to Ehrlichman about it this morning. He of course went right to that point. And you come up with an interesting thing. You need to get everybody or enough people to agree this is the right thing to do. You can't just have the President go out and say everybody, all the branches of government, are screwed up, so I'm taking it over. It's got to be something that rises even above the presidency in terms of what it is. Well, in the first place, you could put Sam Ervin on it, which would buy off Sam Ervin maybe.

PRESIDENT NIXON: Yes.

HALDEMAN: Maybe you can also put Howard Baker on as the minority member, or maybe you go to an alumnus of the Senate like John Williams [R-DE], who is unassailable. Maybe you have to put Earl Warren on, and then Tom Clark as another Justice. Then you come into the executive branch and take a couple, maybe former attorneys general or something. Of course, Tom Clark is a former attorney general. Maybe put [Eisenhower's Attorney General] Herb Brownell on.

PRESIDENT NIXON: Ramsey Clark, he's a former attorney general. He's getting pretty bad . . . .

HALDEMAN: Well, but you go for that. You set up that thing with maybe a six-man board, two executive branch types, two judicial branch types, and two legislative branch types. And you give them subpoena power, you give them the power to give immunity, and they conduct their hearings, of course, in secret, and you of course waive executive privilege for all people except, of course, the communications with the President, which have to be protected. . . .

Well, this type of a commission is clearly better than the Senate, publicly televised. And they met yesterday and confirmed they would have publicly televised hearings. It's clearly better than that. It's probably better than the grand jury, that's irresponsible people and with leaks through the Justice prosecutors. . . .

PRESIDENT NIXON: Dean's right, you've got to fight the thing. But I don't know how much time we've got to fight it.

HALDEMAN: He doesn't think we have very much. . . . There's a hell of an interest in the communists, the true-believer types, just what I described. They are shaking some of the basic system underpinnings, which is exactly what they'd like to do. . . .

Rogers will argue you also ought to get rid of Kleindienst. . . .

PRESIDENT NIXON: Will he?

HALDEMAN: I think so. He's lobbed that one in a couple of times, what about the problems at Justice. You've got a question of Kleindienst there. Kleindienst ties to Mitchell and so on. So you have that. And then you should be prepared if anybody else is named. . . .

PRESIDENT NIXON: Krogh, because he wouldn't talk. You never know when that may set a guy off, you know what I mean. The guy says: Oh Christ, they're abandoning me.

HALDEMAN: Except Dean talked to him.

PRESIDENT NIXON: Well, right. But then you've got who else?

HALDEMAN: Well, Liddy. You don't know what Liddy—we think he'll hang tight, but you don't know now. Now, Liddy, you see, goes to a lot of other things besides Watergate, too.

PRESIDENT NIXON: Well, what kind of things? [Whispers.]

HALDEMAN: The stuff over here. He was working in the plumbing operation.

PRESIDENT NIXON: That's fine. I'm not going to be a Goddamn bit apologetic about the plumbing operation. Do you think we—well, never mind that.

HALDEMAN: Well, Ehrlichman said he went back through his records on that to see what problems he had, and he doesn't have any. What his records have is a ton of memos from Colson on what we have to do to nail Ellsberg. If Ehrlichman's got the memos, so do other people.

PRESIDENT NIXON: Colson, to nail Ellsberg? How did Colson get into Ellsberg?

HALDEMAN: I don't know.

PRESIDENT NIXON: I didn't even know he was—I thought that was all Ehrlichman's thing. I never talked to Colson about Ellsberg.

HALDEMAN: I think Colson was pushing on it just, you know—

PRESIDENT NIXON: Because it was an issue.

HALDEMAN: Going for the throat, yes. He saw an opportunity. Chuck was in damn near anything where he thought we could make a point. . . .

PRESIDENT NIXON: I'm not going to be one who's going to sit here and second guess. One thing I want to tell you that you've got to watch, too. In fairness to everybody, whether it's Mitchell, Chuck, you, Ehrlichman, Dean, Magruder, the rest, the tendency in a case like this, you know, is for people to say: Well, I didn't, but he did, and so on and so on and so on.

HALDEMAN: Yes.

PRESIDENT NIXON: We all know people did what they felt was right, Bob. That's what I mean. We were trying our best and, frankly, whatever—take Dean. Dean is an absolutely innocent accomplice in the whole thing. Dean, he gave good advice. He said "Don't do it" after it was done. He was just holding the pieces together because he thought that was his job.

HALDEMAN: He could see a higher harm done by it coming apart. . . .

SEGMENT 4

PRESIDENT NIXON: . . . Now, as far as Ehrlichman is concerned, before you go on, he says that, as far as his view, and so forth, of his own, that he's got a lot of memorandums from Colson, but Ehrlichman's not concerned about his own role.

HALDEMAN: He says he did not order it and was not aware of what they were doing until after it was done.

PRESIDENT NIXON: Krogh did know. . . .

HALDEMAN: His thing hangs totally on national security. What he was doing was purely on checking leaks on national security documents. There's no question about that.

PRESIDENT NIXON: . . . But he could just say, I was on national security matters. . . .

MARCH 27, 1973: THE PRESIDENT AND WILLIAM P. ROGERS, 3:27–4:16 P.M., EXECUTIVE OFFICE BUILDING

Secretary of State Rogers and Nixon had a long-standing relationship, going back to Nixon's early days in Congress, and especially during the Eisenhower Adminis- tration. Nixon apparently valued Rogers's advice; nevertheless, he treated him shabbily as Secretary of State, finally forcing his resignation later in 1973. But as Watergate begins to boil over, Nixon has many conversations with Rogers. He is looking for advice, but carefully refrains from confiding everything. Interestingly, the President emphasizes how he never had anything to do with offering clemency. Nixon learns that Rogers is good friends with Judge Sirica, and he urges Rogers to speak to Sirica.

PRESIDENT NIXON: Well, what is your judgment on the subject today?

ROGERS: Well, Mr. President, I think you and I are probably in the same position. Neither of us really know a lot about it.

PRESIDENT NIXON: Well, we know the facts. . . . I think I know who did what and so forth and so on. The problem is how you handle the [situation] and, as you know— let me say I have—you naturally have mixed emotions on the [subject] . . . . We've got several options, none of them good.

ROGERS: None of them any good. Well, I was just talking to Bob [Haldeman] about it. There's a hell of a problem that's inherent, one, for this reason. Everyone that supports you in your immediate family almost was [involved], and prior to that involved getting intelligence from the other side.

PRESIDENT NIXON: That's right.

ROGERS: Now, intelligence is a perfectly proper course to follow, getting intelli- gence on the other side, when it involves listening to speeches, finding out where he's going, what his general attitudes are, what one candidate says about another, all of that. . . .

PRESIDENT NIXON: You try to get advance notice as to what their schedules are so that you won't (unintelligible), try to get what the subjects are. You try to find out from stenographers, newspaper people, everybody.

ROGERS: You try to find out who doesn't like who and all of that sort of thing. Consequently, all your people are involved in that. Somewhere along the line, that got out of hand, and they decided to commit crimes in order to find out what the other side was doing. Now, because of the publicity and interest that's been aroused, if you were involved in intelligence-gathering the implication is that somehow you were involved in Watergate, which is not true. For example, Bob Haldeman obviously was involved in intelligence-gathering. He wanted information, and he wanted information on what candidates were saying. . . .

The second problem is that in an effort to protect you and protect probably unnamed persons, and Bob to protect himself as well, they went, they took some real chances, probably unknowingly, chances which could be construed as obstruction of justice.

PRESIDENT NIXON: That's the problem. That's where their liability comes in, is the obstruction thing. . . .

ROGERS: . . . Now the criminal act itself was minor as hell. I was talking about—

PRESIDENT NIXON: It was an unsuccessful burglary. . . .

ROGERS: Sure. So I mean that part of it isn't too serious. But it's the attempt to cover up later on that can cause trouble. Now you asked me, Mr. President, what to do? One thing I would not do—I'm not sure exactly what I recommend, but I'll recommend something . . . . I don't like the idea of a special panel for a lot of reasons. The principal ones are, first, there's no reason to suspect the court system can't handle it.

PRESIDENT NIXON: Let me say, without going into the special panel, I came down against it—[how are you going to] get good people on it? Second, how are you going to finance it? Third, it's going to take a hell of a hell of a long [time] and the whole thing is just going to hang over. The thing to do is to, if you go that route, . . . is set up a blue-ribbon panel.

ROGERS: That's my second point, though, would be the only time in history this happened this way.

PRESIDENT NIXON: The Warren Commission.

ROGERS: Well, even the Warren Commission wasn't to investigate anybody in the administration.

PRESIDENT NIXON: No, no. That's what I mean, that it was a special panel. You remember we always had the idea of special panels. I think it was even suggested at the time of the 5-percenter thing [during Truman's Administration]. I think it was suggested at the time of the [Sherman] Adams thing, a special panel and so forth. Well, the hell with that. . . .

ROGERS: Too bad [J. Edgar] Hoover isn't alive. . . .

PRESIDENT NIXON: Let me put it this way. Here's what I have in mind. I would like to—I know the grand jury is tough (unintelligible), but, Bill, so [is] a committee of Congress. Goddamn it, you know, a committee of Congress—first of all, a committee of Congress is a double weapon. It destroys a man's character in public, and, second, if a file is turned over, you know, to the Department of Justice for prosecution, they will prosecute the poor guy. . . .

ROGERS: And everybody knows that . . . .

PRESIDENT NIXON: Well, we did it to two people. We did it to Hiss. I did it to Hiss. We did it to the 5-percenters. . . . [I]n the Hiss case, we went forward with the investigation under enormous [pressure?] and editorials in virtually all of the major papers and so forth said the proper place for this to be had was in a court of law, and the reason that we went forward was that the statute of limitations had run. And that's why.

I pointed that out. I said, we can't send this to a court of law because of the statute of limitations. Once they were referred to this committee, then it was up to the Justice Department. See, we nailed Hiss for perjury—that is, at least in our sessions. It was up to the Justice Department to prosecute. The Justice Department would not prosecute, and we continued and that's what broke the Pumpkin Papers, and then they did prosecute. Once they started their prosecution, there was never another hearing in the Hiss case. My point is that the proper place for a hearing, the proper place for a criminal [proceeding] to be heard and so forth is in the judicial system. It's only when the judicial system is not being followed that you can justify a congressional investigation, trying to kick them in the ass . . . .

I think Mitchell authorized it. I don't think he did it perhaps in a very conscious way, but what happened here apparently was that they had this room over there, you know, these people and so forth, and they were supposed to get intelligence, and then they have this wild-eyed scheme involving Liddy. Apparently they discussed such a scheme. It was turned down. And then they discussed it a second time, and Dean was present on both occasions, not [in support]. Dean said this won't go. You just can't go on this course.

Then, at a later time, they went on and went ahead with it anyway, because they said they had to get information and so forth and so on and so on. Now the question is who triggered them to go forward with this cockeyed scheme. My view is that Magruder was the [most] active. . . . Mitchell was all tied up in his Martha problems. So Magruder would probably say that (unintelligible), either that he had pressure from Haldeman, which he will claim, which is not true according to Haldeman. . . . I think it was Mitchell. He's never said. I've never asked him.

ROGERS: That's been my guess. . . .

PRESIDENT NIXON: Why should I ask him? How do I—why should I know? I can't put him in the position of lying to me. He's already lied. . . . You see, Mitchell has said—you see, my only statement on it has been *totally,* I mean totally, honest and candid. I knew nothing about it. I disapproved of it, and no one in the White House was involved, period. I've said that. That is the honest-to-God truth. Now, in terms of what happened afterwards, there is this—there are the questions of did somebody promise them clemency and the rest. *Not me,* not on your damn life. I'd know if the hell I'd promise them clemency.

ROGERS: I would think Colson would probably because Chubby is a very careless man, he has some sort of far-out ideas. . . .

PRESIDENT NIXON: . . . And then, of course, you have the problem of who took care of them financially. On that, it was done right out of various funds that were raised and all this stuff, everybody is aware of that. The way I think they would have to do it, they would have to do it defensively, say that we were trying to help these people because they were entitled to counsel . . . . That's very good. Of course, they say they got it because they were trying to be shut up . . . .

Now I don't believe a [blue-ribbon?] panel would wash at all. I don't believe feeding them up to the committee in executive session washes. That would be just as bad. And I don't believe just holding on and letting it come out drip by drip washes. See, another thing about the Sirica thing [special prosecutor] that appeals to the lawyers is at least it moves [things along]. Because I'm not getting a Goddamn thing done. I've got to get on to other things.

ROGERS: Another thing, Mr. President, on that, people are going to wonder well, why does he do it now. You've got a good reason for doing it now, and that is McCord's statement. . . .

How do you get along with Kleindienst? Would he be all right to do this? . . .

PRESIDENT NIXON: Kleindienst? . . . Kleindienst doesn't know a Goddamn thing about it. . . . Kleindienst is a very good friend of Sirica's, he says, a very good friend of his, so I would think that he could . . . see the judge . . . .

ROGERS: I'm actually one of the closest friends John has, and I know I wouldn't want to do that.

PRESIDENT NIXON: Sirica?

ROGERS: Yeah. I put him [on the bench during the Eisenhower Administration].

PRESIDENT NIXON: Well, he's a good judge, apparently. He's doing what he should, except I think he's gone overboard in a sense, because you don't give a guy 55 years for, you know, for breaking and entering. . . . But, nevertheless, I'm not going to criticize him for being tough. The hell with it. That's the kind of judge we want.

ROGERS: And he's the kind of fellow that the public would respect.

PRESIDENT NIXON: That's right. Well, are you suggesting you could talk to Sirica?

ROGERS: No, I don't think so. I think it's better from Kleindienst. . . . [He could tell Sirica] that if you have any questions about the Department of Justice or U.S. Attorney's office or the prosecutors who have been handling this case, if you feel more comfortable with a special prosecutor to handle it from now on, the President's prepared to work that out to your satisfaction. Or he, Kleindienst, is.

PRESIDENT NIXON: Kleindienst will work with him in getting a special prosecutor that you want.

ROGERS: Right. Three, Kleindienst will work with you to get a special grand jury. If this grand jury is not satisfactory—

PRESIDENT NIXON: You could just say the President has directed that I do everything that is necessary to cooperate with you in getting a special prosecutor, if necessary, getting a special grand jury, if you want, and, finally, getting total cooperation from the White House staff. He wants you to call before a grand jury, a prosecutor, every member of the White House staff who has been named directly or indirectly and question them, because he . . . doesn't want a cloud hanging over the White House. How does that sound?

ROGERS: Good.

MARCH 27, 1973: HALDEMAN AND DEAN, 4:20–4:57 P.M., WHITE HOUSE TELEPHONE

Dean reports to Haldeman that he had become too "hot" to get information from the Justice Department about the grand jury. But he has information on Hunt's testimony. This conversation reflects Haldeman's ongoing need for Dean, his major agent for maintaining the cover-up. Dean has other thoughts: two days later, he decides to hire a criminal lawyer.

DEAN: Well, I'll tell you what I was told after we talked the last time, that it was planned that he [Hunt] was going to give a written statement about some questions they had asked him and take the Fifth on everything else.

HALDEMAN: What is the written statement regarding?

DEAN: Nothing particularly sensitive.

HALDEMAN: And he's taking the Fifth on everything else, huh?

DEAN: Yeah.

HALDEMAN: Okay.

DEAN: Now, it's going to be hard to get a report out of counsel as to what occurred down there until 5:00 or 6:00 or so, because they had a 2:00 meeting in court where counsel were to be present.

HALDEMAN: Oh. So the grand jury didn't meet this afternoon?

DEAN: Yes, they did, but it was after that meeting. All counsel were present in the courtroom and then Hunt was to go before the grand jury after that situation. . . . We have a terrible breakdown in communication with both the committees and now the grand jury. I used to be able to stay plugged in with the grand jury, but I'm too hot to do it now. . . . So I'll call Dick [Kleindienst] right away and see if he's gotten a report.

HALDEMAN: Could [Dean aide Fred] Fielding step in and do that—the point being I'm not sure Dick's fast enough to handle your communications stuff for you.

DEAN: I agree. Let me talk to Fred. Henry [Petersen] too . . . . . Here's the other thing. He probably won't know right now what's happened. They don't report to him hour by hour. He has not injected himself into it, so probably it won't be until later this afternoon we can get a report from him anyway.

HALDEMAN: You don't expect anything anyhow, though.

DEAN: No. . . .

MARCH 27, 1973: THE PRESIDENT AND HALDEMAN, 4:20–5:20 P.M., EXECUTIVE OFFICE BUILDING

The Chief of Staff follows Rogers into the President's EOB, offering his own gloss on Rogers's remarks. The conversation reveals Nixon's interest in details, ranging from the idea of a Warren-type commission, the Vietnam POWs, and lobbying by F. Lee Bailey for a scheme to legalize a client's gold holdings.

HALDEMAN: Dean talked to Mitchell today also, and Mitchell told him he needs to stiffen up. He said you should understand that if you go ahead—if you go up before the grand jury, you've got a problem because you won't be believed, because your story won't jibe with mine, doesn't jibe with mine. And all you're going to do is open up a can of worms. Dean has the distinct feeling that Mitchell was saying to him that Dean should consider adjusting his story so that it fit neatly with Mitchell's. [Mitchell said] just so you understand my position, if I thought I could plead guilty and solve this thing and do it, I would do it, but I cannot go to the grand jury and not tell the truth, because I know how unable I am to lie. He said, if I start doing that, my hands will start trembling and my voice will shake and, he said, I can't get away with it. So he said just so you understand, if I go, I will do the best I can, but I will not change the facts. . . . [He supported the] idea of calling Sirica and lobbying [him] . . . .

PRESIDENT NIXON: Bill [Rogers] is for it, but he says Kleindienst is the one to talk to Sirica rather than me talking to him. . . .

HALDEMAN: Dean is opposed to that because he said lobbing the whole thing at Sirica will scare everybody anyway. That will really scare them, because they will feel they have no chance to prepare, and the judge on his last big case has to make a name. These are my thoughts. He [Dean] thinks the panel idea is much better because they can make a fair assessment of the facts out of the public eye and the court can't.

PRESIDENT NIXON: Rogers is totally against the panel. We'll get no assistance from him . . . .

HALDEMAN: . . . [W]e're obsessed with this thing. . . . In the first place, we've got other stories. All he needs to do is pick up the newspaper. You know what the story is? The last of the prisoners are on their way home. That's the story. If you turn on the television, they'll be interviewing them all over again. They did all night last night again. They keep—they are obsessed . . . and I can't imagine why. It must have occurred to somebody that it's helping us. But they do it anyway, I guess because that's what the people really are interested in [the POWs]. It's a fascinating story. But they get those damn guys on and they're waving their Nixon banners.

PRESIDENT NIXON: They still are?

HALDEMAN: Yes. They sure as hell are. I don't know about this last batch, the ones that are on their way now. . . .

PRESIDENT NIXON: But, you see, Bill's reactions . . . are totally different from Ehrlichman with regard to me stepping out and making a big statement, a presidential statement.

HALDEMAN: . . . What the hell. He's sitting here in Washington, he reads the *Post* and he is sensitive to this crap.

PRESIDENT NIXON: And he talks to these people.

HALDEMAN: If you had a Bill Rogers type out in Chicago and called him in and said, look, what do I do about this, he would think you had lost your senses . . . .

PRESIDENT NIXON: . . . [H]e doesn't want [to see] Sirica, I can see the point of that. The panel thing just doesn't work. . . .

HALDEMAN: . . . [Dean] said there's a new development. F. Lee Bailey called Mitchell today. . . . He represents McCord in the case before Sirica. Fensterwald apparently represents McCord in his dealings with the Hill and then he handles publicity. But Bailey has a thing going. He has a client that has 200,000 tons of gold or something, that he wants to find a way to get legalized, and he keeps talking to Mitchell about that.

PRESIDENT NIXON: That's good. . . .

MARCH 27, 1973: THE PRESIDENT AND HALDEMAN, 6:05–7:10 P.M., EXECUTIVE OFFICE BUILDING

Haldeman reports to Nixon on Colson's negative reactions to a special prosecutor or a Warren-type commission. Haldeman reveals how Colson has labored to appear uninvolved, which evokes a rather sardonic remark from the President regarding "rewriting history." Characteristic finger-pointing goes on here, but the two men talk about their cover-up, although in muttered words and tones. The options are narrowing. Haldeman's concerned, and almost prophetically says: "You fire everybody now, you send them to jail."

HALDEMAN: [Colson said] . . . there is a very clear case for conspiracy to commit perjury, a very clear case for conspiracy to obstruct justice. Both those cases can be made and they can be sustained. As he put it, if a special prosecutor were to go to a Warren Commission, you would ensure indictment and almost probably, almost certainly ensure conviction on those counts for a number of people.

PRESIDENT NIXON: So the Warren Commission's out?

HALDEMAN: He says the problem is, for any practical purposes if you bring in a special prosecutor, even with this grand jury, you can't limit his authority. He basically has—that's how a special prosecutor—

PRESIDENT NIXON: If they call one.

HALDEMAN: . . . The greatest danger we have, Chuck feels, is a runaway grand jury. The best thing we've done up to now was the superb handling of the grand jury that was done the first time. . . . And our objective now totally should be to control the grand jury and to control what happens within the grand jury. And he says the problem on the obstruction thing is that everyone in the White House, maybe not everyone, but a hell of a lot of people are participants in one way or another except himself. He didn't say what he was told to say. . . .

PRESIDENT NIXON: What does he mean, told to say?

HALDEMAN: He claims that he was supposed to get to Hunt and say certain things, and he didn't say them because he didn't need to . . . .

PRESIDENT NIXON: Rewriting history a little better.

HALDEMAN: That's all right. It's good that he takes it that way. Then he says this is why he feels so strongly that the President needs one independent person to advise him who is a good, skilled trial lawyer. He says you've got nobody in here that knows trial law. You have nobody in here who is a criminal lawyer. . . . He said I feel this very strongly, because in the firm I've got some good trial lawyers, and I now see the difference between the way they look at things and the way [others do].

PRESIDENT NIXON: So the President's going to get a trial lawyer. What would that do—so that I know what to say—how to continue to cover up?

HALDEMAN: That's right. And he says, looking at it, the advice I would give, the argument I would make at this point is that the worst thing you can do now is over-react, that if Kleindienst goes to Sirica and says, you know, we're concerned about these charges and all that, it's telegraphing to Sirica proof that the administration is involved in a conspiracy, and Sirica would use the opportunity to go out and blast the Attorney General in the incompetence in the trying of the case and say that he's now coming sucking around trying to put the thing together.

And, worst of all, he would know in his own mind that he had succeeded, and that would give him the confidence to go ahead. He says if you had a criminal lawyer in advising you, a trial lawyer, he would say to you now the main thing is don't give them any unnecessary charges. For God's sake, don't grandstand. Things may get better rather than worse. Sirica is on dangerous ground. He's screwing things up in his coercion of defendants and all that stuff. There's a lot of possibilities here in things he's doing. . . . So I said, well, okay. What you're saying is—

PRESIDENT NIXON: Dig in.

HALDEMAN: There's nothing we can do. He said, well, basically yeah. He said, first of all, get the best criminal lawyer possible, because none of us can render good advice to the President. . . . You can't write this script the way you'd like it. You've got to write it the way it is. And the options you have are for people to go around muttering to themselves the President must be having something to cover up, or to prove that by God he sure as hell did have something to cover up. . . .

PRESIDENT NIXON: So what Colson really sees here—

HALDEMAN: Is to hunker down. He says—

PRESIDENT NIXON: Now you understand it affects him more than anybody else, Bob.

HALDEMAN: He says—what does he say. He argues that it affects Dean most of anybody . . . . Well, Dean has been trying to say that. . . . But he's got immunity, at least until he is fired. He doesn't go to jail and isn't disbarred. And he isn't fired; he resigned. . . . Chuck . . . said Magruder was instructed on what to testify. I said that isn't true.

PRESIDENT NIXON: By Dean?

HALDEMAN: And he said he met with Dean. I said, now, Chuck, you're stating something that is not to your knowledge. He met with Dean, but he met with Dean in order to be questioned in the manner that a grand jury would question him. . . . He asked Dean to throw questions at him so that he would know what kind of thing he was up against.

PRESIDENT NIXON: Right.

HALDEMAN: I said is that a conspiracy to commit perjury, even if Magruder did in fact later commit perjury, or even at the time he was answering Dean's questions commit perjury? He said not if Dean advised him to tell the truth. And I said what if Dean didn't advise him anything? . . . He said okay, I take all that [back], but I will simply say to you there was conspiracy to commit perjury and there was conspiracy to obstruct justice.

PRESIDENT NIXON: The latter one.

HALDEMAN: He says too many people know that those people—that the money was paid to those people. I said all I know is that there were funds raised to try to help them with their lawyers' fees and—

PRESIDENT NIXON: You said that?

HALDEMAN: Yeah.

PRESIDENT NIXON: Yeah.

HALDEMAN: And what's wrong with that? There's nothing that's wrong with that. That is normally done. . . .

PRESIDENT NIXON: Maybe he was—Chuck then must be more—I think he's involved. . . .

HALDEMAN: Absolutely. . . . Chuck says is that you've got to face that the worst— he feels strongly on this—the worst harm to the presidency and to Richard Nixon regarding the Watergate is already done. It's there. There is a cloud. But it's a little black cloud that's there.

PRESIDENT NIXON: That's right.

HALDEMAN: He said, now, if you do any of the things you're talking about, what you most likely will do is seed that (unintelligible) cloud and start a rainstorm that there will be no way to stop it. What I'm saying to you is you've got the cloud; live with it. Just keep it as small a little cloud as you can. . . .

PRESIDENT NIXON: Well, I've said, you know, time and again that so far as the presidency is concerned it isn't the crime, it's the cover-up. . . . That's what Chuck said. . . . Because he thinks the crime will . . . might touch you, it might touch Ehrlichman, correct, and it might touch Dean . . . .

HALDEMAN: Yeah, and then it would go to others.

PRESIDENT NIXON: Strachan?

HALDEMAN: Well, yeah, I guess. . . .

PRESIDENT NIXON: Strachan. Who else? . . . Outside the White House, it would touch Mitchell.

HALDEMAN: And LaRue and Mardian, and Parker—Parkinson and O'Brien. . . . Ehrlichman is in the sense of being involved in the operations [of the Plumbers]. . . .

PRESIDENT NIXON: . . . You say what is worse, the cover-up or the crime. I say cover-up. . . . [W]hen . . . I called up Ehrlichman, he belonged to the let it all hang out school. The argument there is whether you're going to get hung anyway. . . . I think Chuck is right. It's a nasty business and our friends are going to question us about it, and we say look, I'm cooperating . . . . I don't know what the hell you can do but cooperate . . . .

HALDEMAN: But it's a cloud. Sherman Adams was a cloud on Eisenhower.

PRESIDENT NIXON: But he fired him.

HALDEMAN: Okay. But he still was a cloud.

PRESIDENT NIXON: You see, they might say well, why don't you fire everyone? Well, on the basis of what?

HALDEMAN: You fire everybody now, you send them to jail.

PRESIDENT NIXON: Huh?

HALDEMAN: If you fire everybody now, in effect you send them to jail. . . . And that's the danger of throwing any baby to the wolves, is you always just make the wolves more hungry and prove to them that you've got some more babies.

PRESIDENT NIXON: . . . This stuff's all going to be hearsay, Bob. . . .

HALDEMAN: That's right.

PRESIDENT NIXON: [They bring] up with all of the old stuff about the surveillance of Teddy Kennedy. . . .

MARCH 28, 1973: THE PRESIDENT AND HALDEMAN, 8:45–9:00 A.M., EXECUTIVE OFFICE BUILDING

Nixon and Haldeman prepare to meet John Mitchell. The President is anxious for Mitchell to step forward and take the blame for the Watergate break-in. But Nixon, who later lamented that he was not a "good butcher"—William Gladstone's prescription for a great Prime Minister—is reluctant to confront his friend. Haldeman assures Nixon that Watergate still is not "playing" well in the national polls—despite warnings from congressional liaison William Timmons that the situation is growing more dangerous.

HALDEMAN: I didn't know John [Mitchell] was arriving so early.

PRESIDENT NIXON: He's already here?

HALDEMAN: Yeah, he's here. We had told him you wanted to meet with him and asked him to get here as early as he could. . . .

PRESIDENT NIXON: Fine. Well, then, you go ahead. I just wanted you to come (unintelligible) told you, just for—I do not want to be in a position of asking him what happened. . . .

HALDEMAN: I think maybe I will. . . . I think maybe I'll ask him to see if he might get into this whole Magruder thing.

PRESIDENT NIXON: Yeah. Well, you can get to the Magruder thing, but I think what I was going to say to him, we've got to really know what he thinks about this appearance before the grand jury . . . . Also, if we could get into the business with him about what he sees on the Colson business, the business about . . . the two things, obstruction of justice and perjury . . . . I gave a little more thought to that. I think Colson maybe—and (unintelligible)—I think that he is overdoing Dean a bit on that perjury, Goddamn, . . . but I don't think . . . calling Dean and telling him, encouraging Dean on that. I think that's what he's talking about.

HALDEMAN: I think that's it.

PRESIDENT NIXON: On the obstruction of justice.

HALDEMAN: On a solid basis, I think that's right. There is certainly a potential problem in that area, however, in that Magruder's a weak link, and you get to the question of whether Dean would have to admit that he did [suborn perjury from] Magruder. . . . [D]id you see the *Post* story, the Jules Witcover story?

PRESIDENT NIXON: No.

HALDEMAN: On the front page of the *Post,* he surveyed everybody he could find across the country in the way of Republican state chairmen and Senate campaign committee leaders, ticket sellers for the dinners and all that, and all those people say absolutely no problem. Nobody has any interest in Watergate. He talked to the pollsters. Oliver Quayle says nobody gives a damn about the Watergate. Sindlinger says where it used to be during the election only about ten percent was the highest it ever got that said Watergate was a big issue, now it's two or three percent. He said we just can't find anybody who is interested. Look at here's a big story bouncing that we were all absorbed in yesterday, and you look at the networks last night. One network had about 20 seconds.

PRESIDENT NIXON: On Watergate?

HALDEMAN: On Watergate.

PRESIDENT NIXON: Well, that's because there wasn't any news.

HALDEMAN: . . . Every one of them ran six or eight minutes of POWs last night, but the lead story was the POWs were coming home.

PRESIDENT NIXON: I'll be damned.

HALDEMAN: And the *Post* on its editorial page has a thing blasting, a whole column on their media analyst guy, blasting Dash for running around having press conferences and saying apparently the Senate isn't going to be the place where we are finally going to get the truth about Watergate. . . .

PRESIDENT NIXON: My view is what I would like to offer—and I think we've got to have a deal with Ervin to show that we're cooperating. That's what [Senator John] Tower [R-TX] wants, that's what Weicker wants. Why not offer them an informal session. . . at Blair House, the whole committee. They can have and they can take sworn testimony from any member of the staff they want, but it must be on an informal basis. . . .

HALDEMAN: The biggest concern here is we feel strongly that we can make that kind of a deal without a good deal of trouble. And we just don't give that much away.

PRESIDENT NIXON: Who can make a deal? That's the point.

HALDEMAN: Bill [Timmons] thinks he could. He thinks . . . maybe he should do it. . . .

PRESIDENT NIXON: . . . I think we should try to cut a deal with Ervin. I think we—I just have that feeling. Let me put it this way. The rap against the President here basically and the White House staff is that we aren't cooperating. Now that's a bad rap, Bob. It is a bad rap, isn't it?

HALDEMAN: Yes, it is. But it's going to hang on. . . .

PRESIDENT NIXON: . . . Bob, it is true of the staff, but it is true of me in spades. I must not get dug down deep into this sort of thing. Now, one thing that we've got to recognize too, that I think you realize Ehrlichman's good qualities, but I think we have to realize that you've got to be in charge of all this . . . . But in terms of a PR reaction, John Ehrlichman's reactions are not good. . . . We're not looking for something that is sort of a big play in order to settle this thing. That isn't going to settle it. They're going to be crapping on and on for a long time. . . .

HALDEMAN: . . . I talked to Timmons last night on this whole—because he raised the question. He said, "I'm staying out of this and I just want to be sure that's what you want me to do. If you want me to help, I certainly am willing and anxious to help in any way." And he said, "I think we're getting a bad rap up on the Hill, and I didn't realize how intense it is. . . ." He said it appears to them that the only real reason for non-cooperation is to get something covered up. . . .

I was thinking Dean is enough discredited that the Dean report isn't going to mean anything anyway. And I think you cooperating with the people who are looking into it—you've already said you had the Dean report. . . .

PRESIDENT NIXON: Then let's purge that boil now, now that they've stood there, and then we could say either do that or the President is going to take the matter to the courts. Now, which do you want? Do you want this or do you want that? Okay. Good luck.

MARCH 28, 1973: THE PRESIDENT AND HALDEMAN, 12:45–1:45 P.M., EXECUTIVE OFFICE BUILDING

Haldeman expresses weariness over the Watergate affair. Still, he rakes over familiar ground of who did and said what. Similar conversations occur throughout March and April, but their repetition is an indication of the constant concern. The two target Mitchell for primary responsibility for the break-in. Colson continues to fascinate and Haldeman himself is confused as to Colson's role and knowledge. The President does not tip his hand.

HALDEMAN: . . . John [Ehrlichman] talked to Dean on what Jeb [Magruder] had told him. . . . [J]ust trying to lay out what he thinks, what happened here is that the whole intelligence plan was hatched here at the White House by Hunt, Liddy, and Colson. And Colson called Jeb twice to tell him to get going on this thing, and specifically referred to the Larry O'Brien information. Jeb says Hunt and Liddy were in Colson's office and Magruder was in Jeb's office on that phone call . . . . And Liddy told Magruder later that he was in Colson's office when Colson called him. Gordon Strachan probably had a lot of direct dealing with Liddy. . . . He [Magruder] says that there were four people in the White House who had full knowledge of the Watergate operation—Colson, Dick Howard, who worked for Colson, Gordon Strachan, and Haldeman. How does he base that those four people had knowledge? Well, he says Colson, he knows, had knowledge because of the phone call—phone calls. Howard, he knows that knowledge because of conversations he had with him. Gordon Strachan he knows that knowledge because he got copies of what Liddy (unintelligible).

PRESIDENT NIXON: And you?

HALDEMAN: And Haldeman because Gordon Strachan told him that I approved the plan. Now Gordon Strachan says flatly and absolutely that he did not know and that I did not approve the plan. . . .

PRESIDENT NIXON: And you didn't approve the plan.

HALDEMAN: No, sir. I did not.

PRESIDENT NIXON: But I think it's the important thing here that Strachan says it too.

HALDEMAN: . . . Mitchell says also that Magruder told him . . . that Bart Porter talked to Dean about his testimony regarding accounting for the purposes of money, cash, that Porter gave to Liddy, because Porter was the keeper of the revolving cash fund and was instructed to and did give [large?] amounts of cash to Liddy, and he discussed what the purpose of that would be and how it was accounted for and so on with Dean, according to Magruder's testimony. . . .

PRESIDENT NIXON: Oh, but did he [Magruder] actually say that he had said this to Dean? Then that's all public.

HALDEMAN: He worked this out with Dean ahead of time, what he was to say. The problem is Porter perjured himself, and so did Magruder, but what they're both saying is that they worked out their perjury with Dean. Magruder and Porter also talked to Mitchell and to their lawyers about their testimony. This is Mitchell telling me this. . . . He says that Liddy did present—they have a problem on those two meetings in Mitchell's office, because both Mitchell and Magruder have specifically testified that there were no meetings regarding intelligence—

PRESIDENT NIXON: About Watergate.

HALDEMAN: —or proposals. Dean says he has to testify that there were. Therein lies the question. . . . What I said in all this is, this is obviously something that you and John Mitchell have got to talk about. I called John Dean and . . . he said this is something I knew nothing about. . . . The point is, though, after those meetings, Liddy came in with elaborately prepared plans. He, according to Magruder, was told that he would have a million-dollar budget for intelligence operations and to develop plans for how he was going to handle that. And that's what he did. And he came in with big charts that showed what they were going to do and all sorts of stuff.

PRESIDENT NIXON: Who told him he could have a million-dollar budget?

HALDEMAN: That's exactly the point. Who did?

PRESIDENT NIXON: Mitchell?

HALDEMAN: Mitchell says that he did not and that Magruder did not. And they can only assume that Dean told him that, or possibly Colson. Mitchell—I mean Magruder—

PRESIDENT NIXON: Neither of them had any authority.

HALDEMAN: I said how could they. But he said, look, okay, but that's still an interesting question.

PRESIDENT NIXON: Right.

HALDEMAN: Then there's another interesting question, which is apparently Magruder hired Liddy as general counsel for the campaign with no responsibility for intelligence. Liddy is a very peculiar guy and was engaged in very peculiar kinds of things around, which caused Magruder, A, not to like him, B, not to trust him, and, C, to decide to fire him, which he did, in April. . . . Liddy immediately came running over to Gordon Strachan and said Magruder's fired me. You can't do that. It will botch up everything I'm supposed to be doing on the intelligence side, and Strachan told Magruder to rehire Liddy, which he did. . . .

Now, he [Dean] also says that there is a problem that Porter is going to have to testify on when they haul him up to the Senate or somewhere as to what he did with a lot of cash payments that were made. He made a lot of cash payments to Colson, pre-April 7 mostly, and one specific payment of $8,000 to Dick Howard, which Howard has been trying to get him to cover up, and Magruder says he's got to cover it up because it's a very embarrassing situation.

I said, well, what is it? He said he had—Howard had to have $8,000 to buy some books. So what's embarrassing about that? He said well, we can't let it get out. I said why not? He said, he was going around to bookstores all over town buying up a lot of books for some reason.

Well, obviously what that was was Colson trying to hype sales of the [Edith] Efron book [critical of the "liberal-dominated" media] to get it on the bestseller list. So I can't see any problem with that. We can say this was a book that we thought a lot of people ought to have, and we wanted to take some money and get it out for distribution. . . .

They also did—they gave Colson the money . . . to pay for the Kennedy mailing in New Hampshire, which Colson informed him was ordered by the President. And that when Colson told him to make the payment and Jeb said I won't. That's one we shouldn't be involved in. And Colson said this was ordered by the President. He [the President] wants it, Jeb said. . . .

PRESIDENT NIXON: You know, I would be surprised if Colson told we were going to [do that?].

HALDEMAN: Well, I absolutely challenged that. I said that I am certain is not true. Mitchell interjected. I said Colson wouldn't—even if that were the case, Colson wouldn't have said it, and I can't conceive where it would be the case. And if it were not the case, I know Colson didn't do that kind of thing. And Mitchell laughed and he said . . . Colson did nothing but that kind of thing. . . .

But, see, their point is that—and Mitchell feels this strongly—that if they admit to a presentation of intelligence plan, then that admits to prior knowledge of Watergate, even though Mitchell says flatly, and Magruder is kind of shaky on that part, there was no specific mention of bugging Democratic headquarters in that intelligence plan. But there was included in it bugging operations. . . .

PRESIDENT NIXON: So they rejected the plan.

HALDEMAN: One of the things they're worried about is that McCord, who was working on budget stuff, probably made copies of the charts and stuff that Liddy used, and probably worked with him on—because Liddy said I have a million dollars. I've got to work out a budget as to how I can do all this with a million dollars or something. And McCord probably worked with him on that. . . .

Now Jeb intends to stay with his story, which, of course, is what he has to do. . . . Magruder committed perjury. And they've got to explore that. And that hangs on, somehow impeaching Magruder's testimony. I think if we have our people go up with counter testimony, they're going to bring perjury charges for Magruder. . . .

PRESIDENT NIXON: Who can impeach him?

HALDEMAN: Who can impeach him is Colson. . . . I told him I don't think you have any problem with Colson, because Colson's already testified under oath that he didn't know anything about Watergate. So how can he impeach him? . . .

PRESIDENT NIXON: Would you not gather from this that Colson was one of the people involved?

HALDEMAN: Magruder and Mitchell are certainly totally convinced of that. It was obvious that he was involved with some of the activities. Now whether he was directly involved with the Watergate, I still am not convinced that he was. But Mitchell kind of laughed . . . .

MARCH 28, 1973: THE PRESIDENT AND HALDEMAN, 8:50–9:09 P.M., WHITE HOUSE TELEPHONE

Haldeman gives Nixon an update: Hunt has appeared before the grand jury; Baker is unhappy with his White House liaison; Martha Mitchell is causing more problems; Dean recommended that the White House hire a criminal lawyer; he probably will hire one of his own. The two men have little trouble with that prospect. A lawyer, Haldeman suggests, "may show him a way around this, you know, a technicality basis or something like that." Nixon recognizes potential problems with Dean, but he hesitates to undercut him in any way. He's "been a hero," the President noted.

HALDEMAN: . . . [Lawyer and friend of Howard Baker's] George Webster called John Dean and said that Baker's AA, [Hugh] Branson, had asked to see him today.

PRESIDENT NIXON: Why?

HALDEMAN: And he had seen him. And the AA said again that he wants a link to the White House, that Baker is not happy with the Kleindienst contact and wants to be in communication and be helpful. And [George] Webster said it took him about an hour of sort of [talking] around to get this to come out. And Webster—he said, so who should I deal with? And Webster couldn't think of who to tell him, so he said Murray Chotiner.

PRESIDENT NIXON: God! Oh, boy.

HALDEMAN: And he finally called John Dean and told him what he'd done.

PRESIDENT NIXON: Oh, boy!

HALDEMAN: We're now in the position where Webster's—I mean Baker's AA thinks that he supposed to handle his White House dealings with Chotiner.

PRESIDENT NIXON: Never!

HALDEMAN: We've got to get off that track.

PRESIDENT NIXON: Right. . . .

HALDEMAN: Well, that's exactly my point. I said that to Dean, and he said because they don't think Webster's wired in. And I said well, I can assure you Chotiner isn't wired in. . . .

PRESIDENT NIXON: Well, I guess the problem we've got there, Bob, is really with Dean now, isn't it.

HALDEMAN: That's one of them. . . . Did you see what Martha Mitchell did?

PRESIDENT NIXON: No.

HALDEMAN: Because that's what John's problem was.

PRESIDENT NIXON: She call somebody?

HALDEMAN: She called the *New York Times*.

PRESIDENT NIXON: And told them what, that John—

HALDEMAN: Went through a whole thing of they're framing John and I'm not going to let them do it.

PRESIDENT NIXON: Hmmm. That's not bad.

HALDEMAN: Stuff like that, and she says they're not going to pin anything on him.

I won't let them, and I don't give a damn who gets hurt. I can name names. She said they're trying to make a goat of him, a goat.

PRESIDENT NIXON: Who in the world do you think she's talking about?

HALDEMAN: I don't have any idea.

PRESIDENT NIXON: I mean what would you guess?

HALDEMAN: She also said that McCord was bugging their apartment or something.

PRESIDENT NIXON: Her apartment?

HALDEMAN: Mm-hmm, and a few other strange things. I don't know who she would be—

PRESIDENT NIXON: Who the hell she thinks framed him?

HALDEMAN: Maybe Magruder. I don't know whether she—I don't know who Martha liked and didn't like.

PRESIDENT NIXON: Did he say what he was going to do, or just did he say he couldn't do anything about it?

HALDEMAN: Well, he said—I said good grief. I hadn't seen the story. And he said now you know why. You saw the paper so you know why I didn't come by yesterday. And I said no, I didn't see it. And he said, well, [Martha] told me she had called the *Times*. I said good Lord, what did she say, and he said just what you'd expect someone full of whiskey to say. Poor guy.

PRESIDENT NIXON: It's a terrible burden for him.

HALDEMAN: To have that problem on top of everything else.

PRESIDENT NIXON: Terrible burden for John, yeah. Yeah. I don't think she's going to be taken that seriously, frankly. I mean, I think that's the least of our problems, frankly.

HALDEMAN: She, I am sure, has no firsthand knowledge of any—she waltzed into Kalmbach some. She said that they were trying to shut her up or something, and she said don't you think it's curious that it was Kalmbach that took me to the hospital . . . and why hasn't anybody looked into that.

PRESIDENT NIXON: Oh, well. . . . You know, it makes a pretty good case that he has had a difficult wife [*laughter*] and he just didn't remember these things.

HALDEMAN: Yeah.

PRESIDENT NIXON: It doesn't help Magruder any, does it?

HALDEMAN: No.

PRESIDENT NIXON: Hmm. Interesting, interesting. But actually the thing about it, Bob, is that their story is the damn—is the truth. I mean, they didn't approve the damn thing. You know what I mean?

HALDEMAN: That's right.

PRESIDENT NIXON: . . . I think the difficulty in Dean's case is that (unintelligible) he can hire a criminal lawyer and so forth and so on, but where's that going to lead him? I mean, if you look at Dean, why I suppose—

HALDEMAN: Well, he may show him a way around this, you know, that it's a technicality basis or something like that.

PRESIDENT NIXON: I really feel that Dean's—Dean is a damn good thing here. You know what I mean? I think I would stand on that. I mean, I personally would stand back of him on it, that the White House counsel simply can't talk. You know?

HALDEMAN: Well, but he's got to talk on his own charge. I mean, if he's charged directly, unless he takes the Fifth, and then you've got to fire him.

PRESIDENT NIXON: Well, maybe that has to be done. What good would that do? Then the question is about the others.

HALDEMAN: Yeah. And Dean's capable of talking just like Magruder is, if you undercut him very far too.

PRESIDENT NIXON: Oh, Christ, I wouldn't think of undercutting him. Never. He's been a hero, really.

HALDEMAN: Yeah.

PRESIDENT NIXON: Really, he's been a sturdy, like a giant. No, no, no, no, no . . . . I mean, thinking out loud, if he wanted, rather than take the Fifth, say I'm not guilty of anything but I'm not going to get into that because it's such a fuzzy area—you know, lawyer-client and so forth and so on—and I'm just not going to talk about it. . . . Will you keep in touch with him as that situation tomorrow, will you?

HALDEMAN: He's back in town now.

PRESIDENT NIXON: You mean—all right. Be sure he knows we—that he's backed to the hilt, doesn't he?

HALDEMAN: Oh yeah. He's in good shape.

PRESIDENT NIXON: Just thinks this won't work?

HALDEMAN: He just sees what at the moment is a knotty problem that he doesn't see the end . . . .

MARCH 29, 1973: THE PRESIDENT AND HALDEMAN, 12:54–1:34 P.M., EXECUTIVE OFFICE BUILDING

Nixon and Haldeman discuss growing problems with the Senate Select Committee, McCord's sudden importance in implicating Mitchell, Magruder, and Dean, and finally, their concern about Dean's status and their relationship to him. They fluctuate between professions of Dean's loyalty and uncertainty as to what he might do. The President begins his defense of himself in that relationship, denying he ever saw Dean until after the election, ignoring the pivotal September 15, 1972 meeting.

HALDEMAN: McCord's testimony yesterday has all leaked out. All the Republican Senators have refused to tell us what was said there. They say he had a (unintelligible) discussion in secrecy, so they can't tell us anything. . . . Well, even [Howard] Baker was bad. He went up to the press club or something last night, and he . . . confirmed that he [McCord] had named Dean and Magruder.

PRESIDENT NIXON: But they won't talk to us. Well, [let George Webster to] talk to him about it. . . .

HALDEMAN: In the meantime, Baker called the Vice President and obviously this would give some credence to this point that Baker's AA made that he is looking for a way for somebody to . . . get direct communication with the White House, and apparently [through the] Vice President.

PRESIDENT NIXON: Fine.

HALDEMAN: And what he said to the Vice President—the Vice President called me and what he said is that he has a firm conviction—Howard does now—that our stand on executive privilege is very unwise in a public relations sense, that it's hurting us, and that time is of the essence on it, that the President should waive privilege for some people and let them come up. The Vice President said I'm not sure whether I agree with that. I'm passing the message along. . . .

What Baker told him was that the names, the White House names and so forth, were mentioned, as was reported in the paper. In other words, he confirmed it after seeing the newspaper story. And he then said that McCord, however, could only give them as hearsay. He did not have direct knowledge. But he did identify two people from whom he had gotten this information, each of whom did have direct knowledge, and Baker did give the Vice President those names, . . . and he further made it clear that the Senate committee intends to immediately call them in, and that they expect, therefore, to hear direct first-hand testimony that Mitchell and Dean—

PRESIDENT NIXON: If Hunt and Liddy talk.

HALDEMAN: And Magruder, if Hunt and Liddy talk. Hunt and Liddy may not. . . . I then laid out to the Vice President in very brief form our problem, the point that if you waive executive privilege and go up and look what the Senate is doing, and you have the overriding surface problem of, if they get one person up there and they get what they can out of him and chastise him and berate him and all that, and make a show out of it on television, or even if they do it in executive session, they then put it out, obviously, so you have no protection there. . . .

[Baker] says that if the grand jury wants to interview John Dean, and he hopes very much that they will since his name has now been bandied about rather loosely in this thing, that John is very willing and anxious to appear, and the President is, of course, desirous that he appear and waives not only his executive privilege but his lawyer-client privilege, as it pertains to any acts or steps, you know, involvement of Dean himself in anything relating to Watergate.

PRESIDENT NIXON: We have to work out the statement very carefully as to what precisely he does. . . .

HALDEMAN: And then say also that any other members of the White House staff who would presumably come under the posture of executive privilege would also welcome the opportunity, if the grand jury wishes to talk with them. . . .

PRESIDENT NIXON: The way you start this, you might say targets of criminal conduct. . . .

HALDEMAN: . . . Weicker's having a press conference at 2:30 today, which had the Vice President also worried that Weicker's going to blast the committee's leaks . . . .

We found out inadvertently that an individual for the last some weeks every day at noon drops off a brown envelope at a newsstand, at the Senate newsstand, stops by the newsstand at 12:30 every day and leaves a brown envelope, which every day between 3:30 and 4:00 is picked up by another individual and taken away. And that's been going on for some weeks. And the individual who drops the envelope is an employee of the Judiciary Committee, Senate Judiciary Committee, a staff member. They don't know who the person is who picks it up.

PRESIDENT NIXON: Probably press.

HALDEMAN: But inadvertently, presumably, a girl who works in the newsstand yesterday—I think it was yesterday—opened the envelope thinking it was something else, and it contained Watergate materials. She sealed it back up. She realized it wasn't for her. She thought it was her envelope or something, she says. So she got to put it back, and a man came and picked it up at 3:30. [An] observation crew is watching the drop and the pickup today and will put a tail on the pickup, the Secret Service is doing it. . . .

One wouldn't think that would have anything to do with Watergate, except this girl says that the materials were about the Watergate. . . .

PRESIDENT NIXON: . . . Dean can't avoid this grand jury.

HALDEMAN: He feels that he can't—cannot.

PRESIDENT NIXON: Cannot.

HALDEMAN: Well, we're back to that hangup, and it's a super hangup, and it's gotten worse now because Liddy—I mean, what's his name—McCord has testified that there was a meeting that Dean says there was. He said who was there and he said when it was, and he said there was charts presented by Liddy and all that. Now that's again hearsay, except in this case McCord may have or has seen the charts, and they have called McCord back for next Wednesday and told him to bring evidence, and one of the Senators afterwards told a reporter to check what McCord's going to bring back. That's your story. . . .

PRESIDENT NIXON: Dean's problem—Dean's problem, Mitchell in effect is asking Dean to commit perjury. Is that what he's saying? . . . . Dean's recollection was that it [plans for a Watergate break-in] was brought up and they had a million dollar [budget] and Mitchell just laughed and thought it was turned off.

HALDEMAN: But it wasn't.

PRESIDENT NIXON: They would not finance it. . . .

HALDEMAN: Well, that's one—but then there's the question of the second meeting. Then there's the question of the second meeting. . . .

PRESIDENT NIXON: Well, so they don't remember the second meeting. You said yes, there was a second meeting. Dean was there. Dean came in at the tail end of the meeting. What happened there was no go-ahead—

HALDEMAN: —was the revised presentation of a revised plan, which Dean also says he rejected, Mitchell agreed.

PRESIDENT NIXON: Dean was not making the decisions about it?

HALDEMAN: Dean ties me into this too. No, he wasn't making the decisions, but he was sitting in [the] same [room and said] . . . you should not be talking about this with the Attorney General, and this is ridiculous. And then Dean says—and I'm sure it's probably true—that he came by my office when he came back, and he said they had a presentation of an intelligence plan that was just out of the question and I told them so, and it's been turned off and I think we should stay out of any further discussion. They obviously are, you know, on the wrong track. . . .

PRESIDENT NIXON: And you should testify to that. . . .

HALDEMAN: I had knowledge that, of course, that there was a general effort to put together some intelligence-gathering.

PRESIDENT NIXON: But then they would say, "Well, now, Mr. Haldeman, did you know that there was some bugging involved?"

HALDEMAN: No, absolutely not.

PRESIDENT NIXON: Dean did not mention that. . . .

HALDEMAN: . . . Dean cited to me some of the examples of the far-out things, but I don't remember them and I don't recall that he did. He may have. If he did, it didn't make any impression. I wasn't concerned with it because Dean said it was a far-out consideration and dropped. . . .

PRESIDENT NIXON: I never saw Dean, I know that. I never saw Dean or Magruder until after the Goddamned election. . . .

HALDEMAN: I think we've got to offer Dean up to the grand jury. They're going to get him anyway, and we've got this problem regardless. I don't know how we deal with that problem, and maybe our offering him accelerates this problem, because if that's all it does, he's got to go. . . .

PRESIDENT NIXON: Mitchell says he has to.

HALDEMAN: Nobody argues the question of whether Dean is going to have to go to the grand jury. If Dean is named, which we now have—well, we don't know for sure, but we sure as hell for every practical purpose know that he is—

PRESIDENT NIXON: Well, we could say that he waives executive privilege with regard to any matter involving any personal charges against him about the Watergate. . . .

HALDEMAN: . . . I've got a thing here, George Bush just called. It must be from the President at the President's earliest possible convenience. This is the most urgent request he has ever made of the President. This [request] is an outgrowth of discussions he's had with Gerry Ford and Bryce Harlow. We'd like to have at least Ford and possibly Harlow attend the meeting. He doesn't necessarily have solutions but feels that this political advice and any the others would like to give is of the utmost urgency. . . .

PRESIDENT NIXON: Can you handle this for me?

HALDEMAN: Sure. But that's the point. It's our people that are, you know—

PRESIDENT NIXON: Yeah. . . . I've got to leave tomorrow, but would it be useful for me to sit down and talk to George Bush about this?

HALDEMAN: Well, it would be useful to you, and I don't know why it would be useful to George. I think maybe I can talk to him.

PRESIDENT NIXON: Well, you could see whether—Ehrlichman should get him and Ford. May I say there at least you can get that much of the congressional thing and get them in and say this is the situation. . . .

HALDEMAN: It's just hurting you too much now, or it's coming close to hurting you, it's getting to the point where it's going to hurt you. . . . And that obviously you're protecting somebody. Now that's what you are doing, and the question is who. And I'm not sure we satisfy the vultures when you're the first piece of meat and you say nobody in the White House was involved. So let's call that, so everybody in the White House is cleared. In the course, let's say we all go to the Senate and get cleared there. Then they say okay, then where did it go. . . .

PRESIDENT NIXON: Call him [Bush] back immediately and tell him I'm keenly aware of this and I'm working on the problem. . . .

MARCH 29, 1973: EHRLICHMAN AND SENATOR HOWARD BAKER, 3:30–4:05 P.M., WHITE HOUSE TELEPHONE

Baker complains to Ehrlichman that no one is in charge. The President and his top aides, of course, are well aware of what has happened, and they cannot afford to tell Baker.

EHRLICHMAN: . . . I have had vibrations that you were concerned that you didn't have anybody that you could, you know, talk to down here, and if that's so and you wish to, I'm available to you.

BAKER: No, that's not quite right. The vibration I got, whenever it was emanating, was that I—to be frank, John, and I'm not being critical—I was afraid that nobody's really in charge. I kept getting information and feedback from three or four different sources, and it suddenly dawned on me no one person's calling these shots.

EHRLICHMAN: I get you. [*Laughter.*]

BAKER: That's what concerned me.

EHRLICHMAN: Well, you will probably continue to get that sense of it because there are a great many people who are sort of first-party-concerned around.

BAKER: But somebody, John, really somebody needs to be in a position to have the broad overview of every piece of this puzzle.

EHRLICHMAN: Well, apparently, as of this afternoon I'm the fall guy.

BAKER: I'm delighted.

EHRLICHMAN: [*Laughter.*] And so I don't know what's gone before, but the President said that he listened to the Vice President loud and clear and he called me in and said I'd like you to get into this, and so that's the reason for this telephone call. . . .

MARCH 29, 1973: EHRLICHMAN AND DEAN, 5:35–6:24 P.M., WHITE HOUSE TELEPHONE

This is a telephone conversation that interrupts the next one. The two men are knowing conspirators. Ehrlichman is aware of Dean's knowledge of the 1972 meetings in Mitchell's offices, in which Magruder and Liddy discussed the Gemstone plans, which included the Watergate break-in. Ehrlichman understands the consequences for the White House. He and Dean agree that the only solution, now as much as ever, is for John Mitchell to step forward and assume full responsibility and hope that will be the end of the story.

DEAN: . . . What I wanted to bring you up to date on, first of all, how would you handle the question, if called, were you aware, either before or after the fact, of meetings in the Attorney General's office?

EHRLICHMAN: Well, you'd have to answer that flat-out, I would think.

DEAN: I mean, how would you answer it?

EHRLICHMAN: You mean on the basis of hearsay?

DEAN: Yeah.

EHRLICHMAN: Oh, I'd have to say I was aware that there had been some. I had been told of one.

DEAN: Okay. Bob's in the same situation, right?

EHRLICHMAN: Yeah. You told me about one.

DEAN: These arguments that I should, you know, that I'm getting a lot of pressure to go down and do them, and I'm not capable of doing. And I'm assembling an argument as to why it's infeasible to even consider it [a grand jury appearance].

EHRLICHMAN: Oh, well, I would never suggest to you that if you went you would do anything but say what's true.

DEAN: I understand. I understand. But you understand the consequences of that.

EHRLICHMAN: Well, that was what I was trying to explore with you on the phone earlier.

DEAN: Well, I was talking to [CREEP lawyer Paul] O'Brien about it a little bit further.

EHRLICHMAN: Mm-hmm.

DEAN: And what it'll do is open a open war pissing match between Magruder, Mitchell, and Dean and the White House. The ultimate solution to this thing is—to deal with the problems from post as well as anything pre-—is something that John Mitchell's unwilling to face. He has this lingering hope that he can pull this out.

EHRLICHMAN: Mm-hmm.

DEAN: It's occurred to me—I don't know . Has the President ever talked this over with John?

EHRLICHMAN: Not that I know of.

DEAN: Well, it's a thought. I've mentioned this to Bob too, that that might be the ultimate solution.

EHRLICHMAN: Well, my thought here is this, that, regardless of what, you know, Mitchell's frame of mind is, that sooner or later you're going to be subpoenaed to that grand jury, and maybe you don't agree with that.

DEAN: Well, that's what O'Brien is saying, that maybe it won't happen. He's following pretty closely the tidbits that are coming out in the press on McCord. McCord apparently, and upon close reading, has said that he understood Liddy was going to a meeting in Mitchell's office. He didn't actually say that he was at a meeting. Maybe this is reading too much into a press report. We haven't seen any transcripts or anything of that nature.

EHRLICHMAN: Mm-hmm.

DEAN: The next thing I wanted to know, were you aware of Weicker's press conference?

EHRLICHMAN: No.

DEAN: Jeez. He was supposed to go out and criticize the press for the leaks. To the contrary, he went out and praised them for the beautiful, diligent job they're doing on this whole thing, and the fact of the matter was that the man that ultimately was responsible for this is sitting in the White House today.

EHRLICHMAN: My word, meaning whom?

DEAN: I don't know.

EHRLICHMAN: They didn't ask him?

DEAN: He wouldn't reveal names, but he's done this independent investigation. It's kind of a McCarthy-type style. . . .

EHRLICHMAN: Hum. Well, I think really the basic question here is one of prophecy, as to whether or not you're going to be called or not. If you are, then obviously the best position to be in is that you volunteered. If you aren't, then O'Brien's—

DEAN: If you volunteer, it's sort of like you—well, I can appreciate the fact you want to go down and cleanse your name, sort of willing to do that at any time. But, however, the grand jury has charged me with nothing right now.

EHRLICHMAN: I understand.

DEAN: Denied everything.

EHRLICHMAN: See, the angle would be one can't expect probity, fairness, and guarantees of rights before a committee of the Senate that does the kind of things this committee's done in the last couple of days. My safe refuge is at the grand jury.

DEAN: Well, but I really wonder if now is the time to volunteer that.

EHRLICHMAN: Well, of course that's the question. That's the basic question. And I gather you and O'Brien feel that it is not.

DEAN: I think we ought to wait and see how—there's always the chance I won't be called. . . .

MARCH 29, 1973: THE PRESIDENT AND EHRLICHMAN, 5:35–6:24 P.M., EXECUTIVE OFFICE BUILDING

The President and his aides often spoke in coded language. Nixon cryptically refers to that "other activity," namely the work of the Plumbers, and already he is versed in the familiar "national security" defense of his actions. The "national security" imperative here, of course, involved a break-in of Daniel Ellsberg's psychiatrist's office. Public knowledge of the Plumbers still was a month away.

The President fights hard to prevent Dean from testifying to the grand jury. Nixon and Ehrlichman sense the danger posed by Pat Gray. Gray fights mightily for his confirmation, telling Ehrlichman that he can be invaluable for providing protection for the Administration.

SEGMENT 1

PRESIDENT NIXON: . . . I've never asked Mitchell about Watergate, never asked him whether he was involved. I don't want him to tell me, frankly, a lie. . . . Finally they said he signed off on it, whatever that meant. . . . I would venture to say that Mitchell was never aware, never gave a specifically approved plan. That's what I would think. My view is that what happened is that he just didn't have a tight control on the shop. Magruder busted it up. Do you agree?

EHRLICHMAN: I assume so. I don't know that, but I assume so. The thing here, it seems to me, is—

PRESIDENT NIXON: But Haldeman, I know him. Colson, I believed him. And you I know. And, as far as the other activity, you know . . . .

EHRLICHMAN: We could defend that as national security.

PRESIDENT NIXON: This is national security, you bet we have. We've got all sorts of activities because we've been trying to run this town by avoiding the Jews in the government, because there were very serious questions.

EHRLICHMAN: We had leaks . . .

PRESIDENT NIXON: Because there were leaks in the government itself.

EHRLICHMAN: I went the other day through some of those files, and that was at a time when we had a fellow named William Sullivan on the one side, and Hoover and somebody else on the other.

PRESIDENT NIXON: I remember. We couldn't get it done then. Hoover didn't want to go for the Ellsberg case, didn't want to face the [situation?] Remember that?

EHRLICHMAN: That's true.

PRESIDENT NIXON: For review, so we had to get it out.

EHRLICHMAN: We finally crammed it down his throat.

PRESIDENT NIXON: I know.

EHRLICHMAN: That's right.

PRESIDENT NIXON: So the investigation had to be undertaken for the national security of this country. . . .

SEGMENT 2

EHRLICHMAN: . . . I have been asked the applicability of executive privilege in the case of a White House staff member, past or present, charged with wrongdoing.

PRESIDENT NIXON: Charged with wrongdoing. Right. Charged—rather than wrongdoing—with illegal activities. I like that word. Wrongdoing is [un?]ethical. Illegal activities aren't legal, if you know what I mean.

EHRLICHMAN: Charged with illegal activities. I want to make a brief statement on that subject.

PRESIDENT NIXON: Yeah, that's right. We have already put a statement—our previous statement referred to executive privilege as it related to the Congress, right?

EHRLICHMAN: Right.

PRESIDENT NIXON: . . . Here it has been our policy in this investigation to date, and it will continue to be our policy, that any present or former members of the White House staff—the White House staff; don't say the President's—will cooperate fully with the grand jury. And that there will be no executive privilege with regard to—no executive privilege with regard to, ah, questions relating to any illegal conduct upon the part—charges of illegal conduct upon the part of former or present White House staff members. Are we giving away any ground there that we don't have to give away?

EHRLICHMAN: It would be argued that we are in effect inviting grand jury attention to the Colson-Dean charges. . . .

PRESIDENT NIXON: All right, fine. Now let's see what our option is. Our option is to wait until you try to work a deal out with Ervin. . . .

EHRLICHMAN: . . . [C]an I change the subject just a minute? This bears on this. And then we can come back to it. I just had Pat Gray over because, as your suggestion, we went through your scenario with Timmons about the possibility of [his not being confirmed]. Timmons tells me that Eastland tells him on the QT that he probably can't get Gray confirmed in the committee as matters now stand. Gray, on the other hand, is still battling. He's just provided Eastland with a whole lot of documentation about their rigorous investigation of the Watergate. . . . And Eastland told him that he could get him out of the committee and tabled, and that he would be tabled until after the completion of the Ervin Select Committee investigation. This is very attractive to Gray.

PRESIDENT NIXON: He wants to stay on?

EHRLICHMAN: He wants to stay on then.

PRESIDENT NIXON: Oh, shit.

EHRLICHMAN: Now, he's [insistent?] about this. He says I think the President's got to consider who he wants to have holding the levers of power at the FBI during the Ervin Select Committee hearings, and he says he's certainly better off with a friend like me than he is with some stranger coming in there and trying to get control of things. Now, that all translates to me into if I leave there and somebody gets into that attic, they're going to find stuff that they wouldn't find if I stay there. Now, I said, then, to Pat, look—and Bill went through the options, four options—table and kill, table him, pass, or defeat. And I said I think the President's got to have a crack at this, don't you, Pat? He said absolutely. He certainly does, and I hope he [does?] soon and let me know what his decision is.

He's still battling. He's still contriving. He's got guys working on his confirmation and so on and so forth. Bill Timmons tells me that Gurney is moving away from Gray. They could get him back. . . . There are two or three others that they could get. They could get McClellan and Eastland, and that might be enough to pull it off. But Bill says frankly the way to do this, if the President decides that Gray ought to be tubed, is just to relax. And Eastland is being pressed by Byrd to bring it on in the committee in a week or so. If he does and we don't go to extraordinary lengths, why he's dead. . . .

PRESIDENT NIXON: Hopefully.

EHRLICHMAN: And, you know, that we'd not hear anything from him. But God only knows what's squirreled away over there. I want to talk to Dean and see what his reading on that is, because I just don't have any idea. I can't believe that Gray's suppressed anything. . . .

MARCH 30, 1973: THE PRESIDENT AND HALDEMAN, 1:43–2:53 P.M., OVAL OFFICE

Senator Lowell Weicker [R-CT] made it clear that Nixon could not count on unquestioning loyalty from the Republican members of the Senate Select Committee. Nixon and Haldeman believe that Weicker has made use of personal campaign contributions, and the two discuss how to exploit the item. Heightened suspicions are rampant within the White House. Nixon and Haldeman discuss the maneuvers and finger-pointing of others—Mitchell, Dean, Magruder, Ehrlichman—while at the same time they defend their own interests.

SEGMENT 1

PRESIDENT NIXON: I want you to get the [goods?] on [Senator Lowell] Weicker. I think we've got to play a tough damn hard game on him. And he is not a strong man.

I want to know who the—if the man that delivered—the bagman was gone out of the campaign, find out who delivered the money. . . .

HALDEMAN: The bagman's [Jack Gleason?] in town.

PRESIDENT NIXON: Can he be asked?

HALDEMAN: Hell, yes. I just don't want to ask him. I'm getting him asked.

PRESIDENT NIXON: You are getting him asked. I want you to be sure to do that, now.

HALDEMAN: Yes, sir, I am.

PRESIDENT NIXON: Who did he deliver the money to? Have they done the checking on his financial statements and everything?

HALDEMAN: As best we can, yeah.

PRESIDENT NIXON: Is his income tax being checked yet, or have we got our man [new IRS head, Donald Alexander] in yet?

HALDEMAN: We nominated him, but he isn't confirmed. He isn't there.

PRESIDENT NIXON: Well, you know damn well he [Weicker] didn't report this income, so we'll just say that.

HALDEMAN: Oh, he'll get around that. He'll just say it was a campaign contribution.

PRESIDENT NIXON: Oh, I know. I know. But if he didn't report it as a campaign contribution he's broken the law. See my point? . . .

SEGMENT 2

HALDEMAN: It's funny. Boy, the raw human stuff keeps—as you grind people against the wall, it starts coming out. Mitchell—that's why I was not so sure you ought to have Ehrlichman in with Dean. I don't know whether this is true, but Mitchell says that Dean doesn't trust Ehrlichman, he thinks Ehrlichman is maneuvering to—

PRESIDENT NIXON: Sink him?

HALDEMAN: —sink Dean. Now, Dean thinks that Mitchell and Magruder are maneuvering to sink him. That's what he tells me.

PRESIDENT NIXON: I don't think Ehrlichman is maneuvering to sink anybody.

HALDEMAN: No, I think Ehrlichman will maneuver to keep himself clear.

PRESIDENT NIXON: You're damn right he will, and everybody does.

HALDEMAN: And he should.

PRESIDENT NIXON: Everybody—

HALDEMAN: As long as he doesn't pull anyone else in, and I don't think he will. And I don't think John [Ehrlichman] has—

PRESIDENT NIXON: John wouldn't do it at the expense of somebody else.

HALDEMAN: No, sir. . . .

APRIL 9, 1973: THE PRESIDENT AND HALDEMAN, 9:47–11:49 A.M., OVAL OFFICE

The two men acknowledge the taping system, and are confident that it will not reveal anything detrimental to them. This may be the origins of Haldeman's notion that the tapes could be exculpatory and helpful to the President—a partial explanation for Nixon's later refusal to destroy them. The times are growing more tense,

and the President's logic is strained and his thoughts sometimes are incoherent, or at least unconnected. Nixon rambles over the familiar ground of Watergate, but John Dean slowly emerges throughout the month as their primary culprit.

SEGMENT 4

PRESIDENT NIXON: . . . [F]rankly, I don't want to have in the record [that is, the tapes] discussions we've had in this room on Watergate. You know, we've discussed a lot of that stuff.

HALDEMAN: That's right.

SEGMENT 5

PRESIDENT NIXON: . . . [W]e ought to (unintelligible), prove we never discussed anything from—

HALDEMAN: Oh, yeah, you can prove, but who are you going to prove it to? For any practical purpose, what are you going to do?

PRESIDENT NIXON: That's right. When you think of all the discussions there have been in this room, that Goddamn thing never came up.

HALDEMAN: They could also argue that . . . well, we discussed that in the Lincoln Sitting Room or somewhere in the Executive Office Building, where you didn't have it [i.e, the taping system].

PRESIDENT NIXON: I really dreamed, as I told you, [Democratic Senate Leader Mike] Mansfield heard about it, and I said, you know, it's terrible what you've done to Haldeman here. I said, you know, I know he was with me, and I said, he was with me in Florida when we read about this thing. And I said, Mike, . . . we thought the Goddamn thing was a joke. People wearing gloves and everything, and that's the honest to God truth, and I said *what in the hell* is this. . . . I don't know whether Ehrlichman called and said no, it isn't a joke. [*Chuckles.*] You remember?

HALDEMAN: Yeah.

PRESIDENT NIXON: Ziegler went out and called it a third-rate burglary.

HALDEMAN: A third-rate burglary.

PRESIDENT NIXON: Right, so he must have thought it was a joke.

HALDEMAN: Right.

PRESIDENT NIXON: . . . John Dean's concern, as I understand it, really is what he did afterwards, all his activities in which he did basically coach the witnesses (unintelligible). Well, he did help get some money.

HALDEMAN: His concern is his potential technical violation in the money.

PRESIDENT NIXON: Money going to them? . . . Mitchell ought to step up to that and say he did it.

HALDEMAN: And that it was for legal fees and family support for men who were going to jail and having to hire lawyers.

PRESIDENT NIXON: Not for the purposes of getting them not to talk. Hell, Christ, they all pled guilty. That has to be.

HALDEMAN: But John [Dean] also feels that they have no interest in going after that.

PRESIDENT NIXON: The grand jury?

HALDEMAN: Mm-hmm.

PRESIDENT NIXON: But not Ervin.

HALDEMAN: No, and that's obviously now McCord's purpose [in his letter to Judge Sirica on March 26]. That's the disservice of the McCord stuff, whether it's hearsay or not, is that . . . he lobs all these possibilities out and then it gives them a basis for going in to explore. They can say, well, we have to run this out now. It is only hearsay, but we have to confirm it's not true. . . .

PRESIDENT NIXON: Well, what really is involved here? My guess, Bob, is that Dean—there isn't any way he could probably avoid pulling the plug on Magruder, unless Magruder, according to John, under some statute if he were to go before the grand jury and said I refreshed my recollection and I was wrong. That would avoid criminal liability for perjury. . . .

HALDEMAN: Dean's point, and John [Ehrlichman] I think basically agrees, is that they're not really interested in perjury anyway.

PRESIDENT NIXON: They just want to prove—

HALDEMAN: They want to settle a case. They're not out to try and hang people for technical stuff.

PRESIDENT NIXON: I think that could be right. In other words, the U.S. Attorney wants to prove that they went after the case and found who did it. For them, Magruder would be high enough.

HALDEMAN: Probably, although the editorial drumbeat now is building to say that throwing Dean and Magruder to the wolves is not—

PRESIDENT NIXON: Satisfactory, yeah.

HALDEMAN: I think they're starting to see that that's a possibility.

PRESIDENT NIXON: My God, you mean they seem to know that Dean and Magruder are going to be thrown to the wolves, is that the point?

HALDEMAN: . . . They probably think—they anticipate that's one possible out. I think what they're doing here is starting a water fight. They're taking—they sit down and say now what might they do, and then let's shoot that down. And then they say now, what else might be, and we'll shoot that down. Because that's sort of what they've done. They've . . . tried to hang it directly on individuals, and then they moved to say well, he wasn't directly involved, but he knew about it. . . .

They use the hearsay thing to get a guy in, and then they back off of the hearsay thing and then try to tie him up some other way. They've done it with Magruder. They've done it with Dean, done it with Mitchell, done it with me. They haven't done it with Colson, which is really kind of interesting. That's another reason that he [Colson] was so damn stupid to do the lie detector thing. As of now, he's—unless it's an obsession to get back in the headlines—he's been out of the thing, which is a pretty nice place to be.

PRESIDENT NIXON: Yet earlier he was in the White House. Why do you think they haven't done it?

HALDEMAN: I don't know. I can't understand why they dropped him.

PRESIDENT NIXON: Because there's more ties to him than anybody else in this whole thing. He's the guy that's closest to Hunt and Liddy, for that matter.

HALDEMAN: Not really to Liddy.

PRESIDENT NIXON: Is that right?

HALDEMAN: Well, that's what he says. I don't have any reason to believe otherwise. Nobody was close to Liddy. One thing Dean points out that I hadn't known is that Liddy hates Magruder with an abiding passion.

PRESIDENT NIXON: Why?

HALDEMAN: They didn't get along.

PRESIDENT NIXON: That's right.

HALDEMAN: Magruder fired him. And Magruder is just a different type of guy than Liddy is. . . . And he and Liddy just didn't—and Liddy's view is that Magruder was lashing him all the time to do more, get more stuff, do more stuff and all that, and that's what led to Liddy making mistakes. Liddy never intended to use McCord or any personnel from the committee in what he was doing, apparently, but he was under—and he intended to use more skillful operators, and he had to go—he wasn't given enough money and all that, so he went with less skillful. Well, Hunt was pretty skillful, I think, or he was supposed be. . . . That's one of Liddy's lines, apparently, that he told Dean right at the very beginning, was that he had been lashed so hard to do stuff that he had done it too fast.

PRESIDENT NIXON: Dean didn't talk to Liddy, then, did he?

HALDEMAN: Once, right after the Watergate.

PRESIDENT NIXON: Oh, he did? Who did Liddy tell him at that time was responsible? Did Liddy tell him? He didn't mention any higher-ups except Magruder? He mentioned Magruder. He didn't mention Mitchell?

HALDEMAN: I think that's right.

PRESIDENT NIXON: And he didn't mention the White House, did he?

HALDEMAN: No. No. Dean asked him directly. The first question or—you know—what happened is Liddy—I don't know. Dean can tell you the story. It's—

PRESIDENT NIXON: I don't want him to tell me anything.

HALDEMAN: It's a clear, specific story. Liddy called him or he called Liddy right after—I mean in the next couple of days after the Watergate, and said I've got to talk to you or something. And Liddy came over here and Dean said let's go for a walk. And they went for a walk down 17th Street, and he said all of a sudden that—that Liddy was trying to untangle it, and he says all of a sudden it just kind of went good, and his story was that he had been under this enormous pressure to produce information, and that he had bungled . . . . He'd used inept people, he hadn't been given enough money to do the job right, and the thing had screwed up and he went into this whole business of, you know, the bug wasn't working right on the phone and they had to go back in and fix it and all this stuff.

And Dean immediately said is anybody in the White House involved in this, and Liddy said no, no one. And Dean then said—no, then he didn't ask, but Liddy said that it was Magruder that had been lashing him to do this. I don't think—I think Dean purposely didn't ask him if Mitchell was involved. . . .

PRESIDENT NIXON: Right.

HALDEMAN: I don't think Liddy specifically said he was. The thing is that he—

PRESIDENT NIXON: Magruder's story would then be that he was lashed by the White House, if he wants to say that. I don't know what good that does him.

HALDEMAN: And that would build the Weicker theory, that, okay, Haldeman didn't do it, didn't even know about it. That's built in the *Washington Post* story yesterday. That's—the [Robert U.] Woodward piece this time too, that maybe Haldeman didn't know about it, but Haldeman was—had a bunch of these eager guys around who were busting their ass to try to please the higher-ups, and were engaging in activities that followed the theory where it was understood that the higher-ups would never know the means by which this information was gained, but we win favor with them by providing them with the information.

PRESIDENT NIXON: That's a pretty reasonable theory, in a way.

HALDEMAN: Well, that's—I also argue that's a theory that we can live with, if we can get it moved down to the right level. . . . This whole thing—see, if you have doubts in your own mind, I wonder in my own mind whether maybe I did know something about the Watergate thing. I have no conscious knowledge of it, but the whole Dean thing convinces me I did, because the only thing I could have known is through Dean.

PRESIDENT NIXON: That's right.

HALDEMAN: And I'm convinced Dean didn't know and his reactions to this other thing is such that—

PRESIDENT NIXON: What's that? His reaction to?

HALDEMAN: His reaction to Liddy's telling him about it.

PRESIDENT NIXON: Well, the only thing that either of us was trying to reconstruct was, you know, the only discussions that we ever had in here was when you would come in and say don't ask about how we're getting this or something or other, and I thought, my God, maybe it was something. . . .

HALDEMAN: I don't by any means think they've given up on me. . . . The *New York Times* has a big editorial saying this terrible thing that they did to me and all that, but then it goes on to say that, although the committee—the point that they have no evidence now (unintelligible), that in no way clears Haldeman. . . .

PRESIDENT NIXON: In other words, you're guilty until proven innocent.

HALDEMAN: No. It's that I'm innocent until proven guilty, and I haven't been proven guilty, but they don't rule out the possibility that I still may be. . . .

PRESIDENT NIXON: I don't see how Mitchell can stand there and—what's he going to do, Bob, about it?

HALDEMAN: See, Mitchell's got a worse problem than I do on that, when they get him up there and they say, Mr. Mitchell, you were chairman of this thing. You were running the campaign. Is it conceivable that a quarter of a million dollars of the money for which you were responsible could have been allocated to this without your knowledge? He's got a tougher time than I do. I can say absolutely, I had no control or knowledge of allocation of money and had nothing to do with it.

PRESIDENT NIXON: That's right. . . .

HALDEMAN: I wasn't on the budget committee. . . . No, sir, I was not. But that's—the question is who was. The answer is Magruder was. The question is who did Magruder report to, and the answer is he reported to John Mitchell.

PRESIDENT NIXON: That's right.

HALDEMAN: And he did. And every bit of evidence that—as Dean was saying, almost the only contact he had with Magruder, which certainly was true of me, during that whole period was when Jeb would call asking how to handle some problem with Mitchell. In other words, he was calling to ask for guidance on how to deal with John on getting something worked out. But John has said—and I've checked this and he has—he has said under oath again that until he moved over to run the campaign he had nothing to do with the management of the campaign. That is just absolutely, totally, 100 percent untrue. Well, you know that's untrue, because you talked with him about it. He came in here from time to time, not very often. . . .

PRESIDENT NIXON: Well, in my view, despite the howls and the screams and the editors and all the rest, it's going to come down to the fact, it would seem, Dean will testify. His testimony will put Magruder in a hell of a spot. Magruder then will have to choose. I don't think they will grant him immunity. John Ehrlichman doesn't think he will (unintelligible). If they don't, he'll have to go to trial, he goes to trial.

HALDEMAN: If he goes to trial, you have the real danger of Liddy being a witness against him. Liddy will, but he won't—he says he won't—

PRESIDENT NIXON: Be a witness?

HALDEMAN: Yeah. Liddy has—see, from what Dean tells us, Liddy has told the entire story to the prosecutors.

PRESIDENT NIXON: . . . Ehrlichman doesn't quite believe that, but that's—

HALDEMAN: Well—

PRESIDENT NIXON: But Dean thinks—that's what Dean thinks.

HALDEMAN: Dean believes it, and Ehrlichman has no more reason not to believe it than Dean has to believe it.

PRESIDENT NIXON: I agree. I agree. . . .

SEGMENT 6

PRESIDENT NIXON: So John Dean really thinks it's going to come out and it's going to reach Mitchell, does he?

HALDEMAN: He thinks it's possible at the moment. . . . He shares my view that they don't really want to make a case against Mitchell. That's why I think a Mitchell statement might be the way out for the Justice Department too. If Mitchell would say well, I didn't know about it, but it was done under my thing and that's a terrible thing to have had happen, I'm sorry about it. . . .

PRESIDENT NIXON: And Mitchell (unintelligible) at the same time absolve the White House.

HALDEMAN: Mitchell says I did authorize the money, and I did authorize an intelligence operation, but I sure as hell didn't authorize bugging the Democratic National Committee. I'm not that stupid, let alone dishonorable.

PRESIDENT NIXON: In fact, I explicitly did not authorize it.

HALDEMAN: I rejected it. There was some discussion of this kind of activity—not the Watergate bugging but of the idea of doing this kind of surveillance and so forth—which I rejected as not being feasible at the meeting that John Dean and Jeb Magruder attended, so both John Dean and Jeb Magruder know I rejected that, that idea, which is true. Now, how they could possibly have gotten so confused as to decide to do it anyway is beyond me. It indicates, at the worst, some evidence of not the best management on my part, and I must confess to that. As the guy responsible, I have to say—

PRESIDENT NIXON: He's got to say that. How can he do anything else? Is he just going out there with a great stone face and say I knew nothing about it?

HALDEMAN: Well, legally that is probably the best—

PRESIDENT NIXON: Legally, but also—

HALDEMAN: John's problem is less legal than it is otherwise.

PRESIDENT NIXON: Yeah. He maybe doesn't—he's out of government now, so he doesn't much give a damn in a way. . . . I think that may be his attitude here, of what the hell, boys will be boys.

HALDEMAN: Maybe he's convinced that they can't make the case on him and so that's it.

PRESIDENT NIXON: Right.

HALDEMAN: They've either got to convict him or they don't convict him. . . .

PRESIDENT NIXON: . . . Now the only guy that's playing (unintelligible) the alone game is now Colson. Isn't he?

HALDEMAN: Mmmm.

PRESIDENT NIXON: God, that must burn Mitchell's ass.

HALDEMAN: Yes, I'm sure it did. It did mine. . . .

APRIL 9, 1973: THE PRESIDENT AND HALDEMAN, 2:05–3:00 P.M., EXECUTIVE OFFICE BUILDING

This is a fragment from a poor recording in the Executive Office Building, discussing the taping system, in the light of—as Haldeman said—the President's "new position."

HALDEMAN: The way I've heard is that I forget is that they have, you know, the Secret Service locator signal, when they first put it in the office here, and that also activates this thing. So that it only works in this office when you're in it, or if another office when you're in. . . . From now on it will only be when you turn it on. The other thing that they have on there which was—which we instructed, by the way, is your telephone here and in your oval office. And I think in your new position—

PRESIDENT NIXON: Can we (unintelligible) those?

HALDEMAN: The same thing. This is the same thing. You can take those off if you want . . . . I remember now, this is something a conversation, because there's some conversation (unintelligible) talking about the (unintelligible) Camp David. There's nothing like that. (unintelligible). They will monitor—there's no way that they can. There's nobody there. This is all done automatically. . . .

PRESIDENT NIXON: . . . I think in the future that I want to have a thing that would record my telephone conversation—

HALDEMAN: Taken off your phone?

PRESIDENT NIXON: (unintelligible) let's mark it and (unintelligible) the tape, and all the rest have been destroyed.

HALDEMAN: Oh, on the phone tape? In other words, record them all and then destroy them periodically, right?

PRESIDENT NIXON: Right, right, because let's say this tape I'd like to have recorded, I think that would be worthwhile, that's my intention to do (unintelligible) but—

HALDEMAN: I don't think—see, you can put that thing on the phone anywhere, and there's no problem. If you set up your other thing at Camp David, let the military know you have it, as well as the Secret Service. . . . You can't see it, it's just a little wire that goes on there.

PRESIDENT NIXON: It goes on there then I just put that on?

HALDEMAN: You put the telephone however way you want to record it and it records and you turn it off.

PRESIDENT NIXON: Oh, it does?

HALDEMAN: You haven't turned it off. . . .

APRIL 9, 1973: THE PRESIDENT AND EHRLICHMAN, 7:55–8:07 P.M., WHITE HOUSE TELEPHONE

Ehrlichman negotiates with Senators Ervin and Baker over guidelines and topics for the upcoming Senate investigation. Ehrlichman describes that meeting, confident that the White House can control events.

EHRLICHMAN: . . . We went an hour and a quarter, very cordial, very friendly. Ervin's attitude was very, very good.

PRESIDENT NIXON: When are you going to meet again?

EHRLICHMAN: We're going to meet again Wednesday. He's agreed that any announcement that comes out of this meeting you may make, or somebody may make in your behalf. He will say nothing to the press. . . . I was afraid that he would try and steal the ball. But he's in a very good frame of mind. We spent most of our time talking about John Dean.

PRESIDENT NIXON: I figured that, yeah.

EHRLICHMAN: And the way we resolved it is that [Leonard] Garment and committee counsel are to get together tomorrow and try and work out a system by which Dean's information can be taken without violating executive privilege.

PRESIDENT NIXON: So he wouldn't have to appear up there.

EHRLICHMAN: Well, they're not saying that, and I'm not saying that he will, and we're at sort of a Mexican standoff. So the idea was that the staff would explore various devices like interrogatories and things of that kind, and see if they could come to any sort of an understanding with Garment. I'm sure they can't. But it was a way of keeping the issue alive until we get together again on Wednesday.

PRESIDENT NIXON: Right.

EHRLICHMAN: Ervin kept saying he doesn't want a confrontation. He said that there are some very serious charges against Dean which would involve him, because I said, you know, the basis on which we want to proceed here is that anybody that has a serious charge leveled against him will appear. He said, well, that includes John Dean. And I said well, I don't understand that to be the case. So then he unloaded on me a little bit on Dean.

PRESIDENT NIXON: Mm-hmm.

EHRLICHMAN: And they have a witness who alleges that Dean tried to recruit him for political espionage. They have another witness who claims that Dean showed FBI reports to Segretti.

PRESIDENT NIXON: That's not true.

EHRLICHMAN: But, you see, these are the kinds of things that—

PRESIDENT NIXON: Right. We know that isn't true. John Dean told me it wasn't true.

EHRLICHMAN: Well, I suspect that it's hearsay twice removed. . . .

PRESIDENT NIXON: What about the other things? How'd you leave that? . . .

EHRLICHMAN: Oh, yes, scope [of the hearings] was no problem. He agreed with that out of hand. And we'll try and devise some language, which I'm going to write out, that—

PRESIDENT NIXON: The scope is Watergate and what else?

EHRLICHMAN: And political espionage and political financing.

PRESIDENT NIXON: Financing? . . . Are they going to go into the Democratic stuff on that?

EHRLICHMAN: Yes. Yes, they are.

PRESIDENT NIXON: Did you tell him—you told him that they've had some cash funds too, haven't they?

EHRLICHMAN: And then Baker hung back afterward and said that the more of that kind of stuff that we could get for him, the better. And he particularly—apparently you told him about bugging the airplane, and he really wants to hold that out till the very last and then drop that on them right at the end.

PRESIDENT NIXON: Yeah, well, of course, we can only make that as an allegation, you know. Everybody's going to deny it.

EHRLICHMAN: We'll have to work on that one, see if we can't develop some evidence of some kind.

PRESIDENT NIXON: [William] Sullivan [from the FBI] backed off of that to an extent. They all back off. . . .

EHRLICHMAN: . . . Baker was a lot of help—in fact, Baker was of enormous help all through this thing today. . . . The rules of evidence—we're going to try and draft some exclusionary rules of evidence that will keep hearsay out and will keep out the thing that Bob was concerned about, about conduit people testifying to things that were told to them. They are not only agreeable but enthusiastic about having [Leonard] Garment in attendance . . . And television, interestingly enough, is discretionary. If a witness objects, then it will be in the discretion of the committee, but it is conceivable that any given witness could ask that the lights be turned off. . . .

PRESIDENT NIXON: Did Baker help you any on [Dean]?

EHRLICHMAN: No, Baker did not help me. He feels Dean should come. And so he and Ervin ganged up on me on that one. But I hung very tough. I said that I didn't think there was going to be any motion on that, that it was not a question of suppressing any substantial information that related to Dean's own conduct, that written interrogatories or affidavits or things of that kind, and then I got them into specific examples.

I said, now I know you're hung up, Senator, on this business of Dean sitting in with witnesses when they're interviewed by the FBI. We'll give you the dates, the places, and the names of the witnesses on a piece of paper so you'll know exactly who those were. But I said surely you don't want Dean to come up there just to badger him about that. What you want to elicit is the time and place and who was present. We'll give you all that. No problem. . . .

PRESIDENT NIXON: [E]very one of those [witnesses] is a Goddamn headline that smears somebody and you can't catch up with it. . . .

EHRLICHMAN: And then Ervin gave me a very pious, long assurance that he wanted to protect everybody and he was going to try and be a fair judge and without fear or favor and all this business, you know. . . . I think he's got a very exalted sense of himself, that he's the fairest guy that ever came down the pike.

PRESIDENT NIXON: This may help us a bit.

EHRLICHMAN: I think it may, and I think Baker has the kind of relationship with him that will tend to keep him honest. . . . And when I brought up the business about the Democrats, why Ervin chimed right in and said just because I'm a Democrat, I'm not going to keep that out. We gotta let all this come out. He says, I'm very concerned about my own reputation, and the reputation of this Select Committee. It's my committee. And he said we're not going to favor one side over the other here.

PRESIDENT NIXON: Mm-hmm. On the Democrats, the point we've got to do is to— what Baker's got to realize is that he's got to ride hard on this disruption, and that is the sabotage [of Nixon's campaign].

EHRLICHMAN: Well, I stayed behind with Baker for about ten minutes, and we talked about that.

PRESIDENT NIXON: Does he realize that's a Goddamn good thing to hit?

EHRLICHMAN: Oh, absolutely, and he wants some help in developing where the financial support for some of these disrupters came from and so on. And so we'll have to turn some people loose to try and track that down.

PRESIDENT NIXON: Yeah.

EHRLICHMAN: I said, well, you can subpoena [McGovern campaign contributor] Henry Kimelman and some of these McGovern people.

PRESIDENT NIXON: That's right.

EHRLICHMAN: He said don't worry. He says, I've thought of that. He apparently is very—he's got a big old Tennessee boy as the minority counsel [Fred Thompson] who's made friends with Ervin. . . .

PRESIDENT NIXON: Ervin will take him in like Flynn. . . . The more I think about this, I've got to stay one step removed from the Goddamned thing. . . .

EHRLICHMAN: Baker also said that he felt that it would be possible to insulate you from any contact with this as long as neither Bob nor I were involved. And I said, well, there's no question about that, Howard. I can assure you for my part that neither Bob nor I were involved, and I think you'll see when this is all done that there will be no question about that. Well, he said, if that's the case, then, he said, I think the President's going to come out of this looking very good.

PRESIDENT NIXON: What the hell is the matter with that asshole [Senator Charles] Percy [R-IL], (unintelligible) reach out this morning or yesterday and say that if Haldeman in any way was involved—what the hell is that? I mean, that's like saying if a fellow is guilty, then he should be hung. What the Christ is that?

EHRLICHMAN: Well, Percy is doing everything he can to move away from you. He's getting as far away from the administration as he can get and still be a Republican.

PRESIDENT NIXON: He realizes that that's his track to the nomination.

EHRLICHMAN: Sure. Sure, that we've never going to help him.

PRESIDENT NIXON: So what do we do, then, with him? Are there a few things that you can do?

EHRLICHMAN: Well, there will be opportunities, I'm sure. . . .

PRESIDENT NIXON: In Illinois—now, look, in Illinois you've got—basically you've got Percy, you've got [Senator Adlai] Stevenson [D], and you've got a Democratic governor. Now, for Christ's sakes, I'd just cut the shit out of Illinois. . . .

APRIL 10, 1973: THE PRESIDENT AND EHRLICHMAN, 12:48–2:00 P.M., OVAL OFFICE

Nixon reviews the story with Ehrlichman, as he did with Haldeman. He feigns ignorance of events and explains away criminal conduct with disclaimers such as "It's all right" and "It can be justified." He is exasperated with Mitchell's stonewalling, what Ehrlichman—Mitchell's antagonist—calls "pulling the covers over his head." The two discuss providing information to Senator Baker. The President worries anew about Howard Hunt's possible exposure of an "earlier venture"—meaning, of course, the Plumbers and their illegal operations.

SEGMENT 2

EHRLICHMAN: Well, I think the less personal participation you have in this right at this juncture—the better.

PRESIDENT NIXON: I better not talk to Dean. It is not necessary. Dean knows that I care about him.

EHRLICHMAN: Well—and we're—we're in touch with him. He's not abandoned by any means. . . .

PRESIDENT NIXON: He's going to say what, that he and Mitchell worked together?

EHRLICHMAN: He's going to say that he and Mitchell worked it out, that's about right. Yep.

PRESIDENT NIXON: This money was contributed by whom?

EHRLICHMAN: Well, I'm not going to answer that. I have an idea. I think some of the [Herbert] Kalmbach's contributors came through with most of it. I suspect that, what's his name, [Fred] LaRue, either put up some of it or got somebody to put up some of it.

PRESIDENT NIXON: What would Dean answer?

EHRLICHMAN: He probably said he doesn't know. And I don't think he does. . . . Well, Mitchell knows. He may not know where Kalmbach got his.

PRESIDENT NIXON: This was money in other words that was raised?

EHRLICHMAN: They went around to contributors after the elections in effect.

PRESIDENT NIXON: This is money then that was not reported as a contribution to the campaign? Well—

EHRLICHMAN: As far as I know. . . .

PRESIDENT NIXON: I'd like to have him—I'd like to have that run by him to see what he says, how he—how he gets himself into that position, did he ask or, you know, what the hell, does he have a right under—I mean as a member of the White

House staff—he had a right to help him [Mitchell], a perfectly legitimate thing. Well, I can see through Mitchell on a thing like this with—Mitchell (unintelligible) of course we weren't trying to shut them out. These people were people that had been employed by the committee, and they engaged in illegal activities. We felt they were entitled to assistance until they had a trial, which took a long time to get to trial, and that was all, gentlemen. That's what he has to say.

EHRLICHMAN: Yeah.

PRESIDENT NIXON: Hush-up money—didn't seem to work, did it?

EHRLICHMAN: Well, more than that. These defendants had a right to be quiet. It wasn't as if they weren't exercising a right. He can weave that in there.

PRESIDENT NIXON: Well, it's quite true. The defendants didn't have to talk. I mean we didn't—(unintelligible) they were—was anybody asking them to talk at this point? . . . .

EHRLICHMAN: . . . And instead of working on all those people to get them lined up, as Magruder is trying to do with his people, Mitchell is sitting up in New York and pulling the covers over his head. . . . I just don't see how he can pull it off. There's just way too many loose ends. . . .

PRESIDENT NIXON: I can't believe Mitchell can be so blind to this Goddamn thing.

EHRLICHMAN: Well, he's—I'm sure he's not blind in functional sense, he's blind in the emotional sense. You know, he's turned this off, I suspect, or else he's decided it's his best posture to just stonewall all of us. . . .

Baker swears by this minority counsel of his. This fellow Thompson and—

PRESIDENT NIXON: Says he's tough—

EHRLICHMAN: Says he's good and tough, a lot of experience and so forth. One thing I asked Len [Garment] to do is size the guy up, when he talks to him . . . .

PRESIDENT NIXON: . . . I guess, John, we just got—got—everybody just got through this thing—the real key thing to this thing now is Mitchell. Mitchell has got to decide, because he—I don't think he's going to get all these guys to stand up there and lie, that's what it gets down to.

EHRLICHMAN: To possibly pull it off. . . .

PRESIDENT NIXON: . . . The one really that's going to pull the plug on Colson is Hunt. . . . I don't think he'd [Hunt] pull the plug on his earlier ventures for us, do you?

EHRLICHMAN: He would have done it by now if he was going to do it. . . .

PRESIDENT NIXON: That's right. So, . . . what is Hunt going to do? What does he say with his so-called February ultimatum? Well, we'll cross that bridge when we come to it. . . .

APRIL 11, 1973: THE PRESIDENT AND BILLY GRAHAM, 10:00–10:08 A.M., WHITE HOUSE TELEPHONE

The President reassures an old friend. A year later, after the first release of tapes, Graham complained that "situational ethics" had infected the highest levels of government, and reflected that perhaps he had been "used" by Nixon.

GRAHAM: And I know dear old Sam Ervin. He's been a neighbor of mine all his life, and, of course, this is his great moment of glory.

PRESIDENT NIXON: Sure. Well, we'll let him have it.

GRAHAM: [*Laughter.*]

PRESIDENT NIXON: He'll dig away, and he'll make a lot of headlines and he'll irritate a lot, but those things also pass. The main things about those, of course, as you know, the campaign people—I can assure you nobody in the White House is in, but campaign people, they sometimes do silly things.

APRIL 12, 1973: THE PRESIDENT AND EHRLICHMAN, 2:30–3:45 P.M., EXECUTIVE OFFICE BUILDING

Dean now is a serious problem, yet Nixon is loath to dismiss him, hoping to keep his loyalty and silence. The President and Ehrlichman agree they need Leonard Garment as Counsel, knowing he is well-liked and has no Watergate involvement. Nixon and Ehrlichman rehearse a scenario that will have Dean accept a leave of absence. Ehrlichman directly criticizes Haldeman, saying that he must fight the accusations against him and protect the presidency, and also take a leave. Ehrlichman believes that he is free from any Watergate liability, but of course he has knowledge of the Plumbers, hush money, and other misdeeds. At first, Nixon rejects the idea of dismissing Haldeman, but Nixon slowly becomes enamored of the idea as essential to ending the affair. "We've got to think the unthinkable sometimes," he says.

SEGMENT 2

EHRLICHMAN: . . . We have Chappie Rose [Nixon's former law partner] coming down to sit with Len Garment on senatorial hearings. . . . I felt strongly from the beginning that we had to have somebody there. I just think this guy Ervin is such a shark—

PRESIDENT NIXON: And a total partisan.

EHRLICHMAN: Absolutely.

PRESIDENT NIXON: I never believe this crap that [Senator] Baker utters . . . He is a difficult, mean southern politician, and I've known about him.

EHRLICHMAN: No question.

PRESIDENT NIXON: Partisan, vicious, and clever. . . . Very clever. . . .

EHRLICHMAN: He's nicing Baker. He's nicing the committee staff, and he's getting along with the boys he has to get along with. . . . But he's nobody's dummy. He went through that draft of mine last night in about 15 minutes, and he picked out most of the clues just the first time through. . . .

PRESIDENT NIXON: Coming back to the . . . Dean thing . . . . Do we call Dean in and tell him this?

EHRLICHMAN: What do we do? . . . Basically he should take a leave. . . . [T]hat's a probable suggestion.

PRESIDENT NIXON: I think as a matter of fact, while it is of a half-way nature, it's the only decent thing to do, and also it seems to me it's decent to gain something out of it, at least some indication we're trying to find somebody else . . . . It's an opportunity to get somebody else working on the problem.

EHRLICHMAN: I wouldn't burden anybody else. [Fred] Fielding [Dean's assistant] can go ahead and run that as acting counsel. . . .

PRESIDENT NIXON: I was thinking of putting somebody in his place, [not involved in] Watergate.

EHRLICHMAN: Well, I would put Len [Garment] there.

PRESIDENT NIXON: . . . Except he was Mitchell's law buddy, I suppose.

EHRLICHMAN: He was in your law firm and he's been here. He has credibility.

PRESIDENT NIXON: He has high credibility. He really does.

EHRLICHMAN: He made a very strong impression apparently on the committee staff and they reported to Ervin and Baker who congratulated me yesterday on Garment's selection.

PRESIDENT NIXON: Dean would say on the basis of what? That he needs the time . . . . [*Anticipating Dean's comment*] "I cannot at this time since I have . . . become a subject of the investigation myself. . . . I do not believe that I—I am not the one who can carry on an investigation for you, Mr. President—for the President on this matter. And I, therefore, believe that I should take a leave of absence until [I am] . . . absolved of any charges which are—in my view—are wrong (unintelligible) against me. I ask that you give me a leave of absence with pay." . . .

EHRLICHMAN: I think it's better, it shows some confidence in him to say leave with pay.

PRESIDENT NIXON: Yeah. Then, you see, when they do hit him, he resigns. If they hit him , and he's involved, I think, as Magruder charges, under the circumstances I submit my resignation. Or we get him off of it right now and get somebody else who's conducting this—who has high credibility. Now, I think that step should be taken like very soon. . . .

EHRLICHMAN: Let me kick this around before we get together here.

PRESIDENT NIXON: . . . All right. So much for that. Let's come back now to the Haldeman business . . . .

EHRLICHMAN: You did ask me to put the worst face on it. The worst face, of course, would be (unintelligible) little pieces making up a big picture. No one of these is big. Every one of them can be explained, but you've got Haldeman connected to Segretti, Haldeman connected to the bugging through the intelligence reports coming to him.

PRESIDENT NIXON: And through Dean asking him about support for the defendants, which is a *small thing.*

EHRLICHMAN: See, everything is cumulative. . . . You have—I suspect this. I don't know this. I suspect if you really ride him hard, an interrogator could break Dean down to say that during a period of four meetings, during which the intelligence operation was planned, he was possibly reporting to Haldeman. And the reason that I think you can do that is you could lay a circumstantial web compelling the answer "yes" to the Haldeman questions. He was not the conceiver at the White House. He wasn't the one who was making the demands. . . .

He says that during that period of time, he did not know anything about that planning operation. All he was interested in was the results, and the only results he was really interested in was the verbatim of what the candidates were saying against each other in the primaries.

PRESIDENT NIXON: Which, of course, Christ, it's so Goddamn obvious it should have been done by somebody else. Nevertheless, well that's perfectly alright.

EHRLICHMAN: Well, he says, I didn't know anything about this Liddy—Liddy, schmiddy. I didn't know who Liddy was during that period of time. . . . I didn't know these fellows were talking to Mitchell about—

PRESIDENT NIXON: You asked him the specific question whether Dean, in cross-examination was asked, did he ever report to Haldeman that he discussed the security operation and turned it down?

EHRLICHMAN: Haldeman says no. . . . On the other hand, when I broached this with you is I think I can make Dean say yes on cross-examination. It appears so illogical that he—that he wasn't. We'd make it appear that he, Dean was running the campaign. . . .

PRESIDENT NIXON: Dean actually could answer it another way. He could say, look, I was the counsel. I was sitting in on it in that fashion. . . . I did not discuss it with Haldeman because—because it was turned off, I didn't report it.

EHRLICHMAN: The way you get at that then: "Well, Mr. Dean, you're responsible for keeping the President out of legal trouble, aren't you?" "Yes, sir." "You sat in a meeting where a man named Liddy proposed a million dollars' worth of kidnapping and wiretapping and assassination and on and on and on and on, and you didn't jump in a taxicab and rush back to the White House and burst in on Bob Haldeman and say, you know what those crazy guys on the committee are doing?"

PRESIDENT NIXON: [Anticipating Dean.] "No, I didn't because I thought it was so ridiculous. The Attorney General said, absolutely not. We have all sorts of crazy schemes that I don't raise."

EHRLICHMAN: "No, I understand. I understand that. And when was the next time you saw Mr. Haldeman immediately after that?"

PRESIDENT NIXON: "Well, I probably saw him the next day."

EHRLICHMAN: "What did you say to him?"

PRESIDENT NIXON: "Well, I can't recall."

EHRLICHMAN: "Well, Mr. Dean, didn't you rush up and grab Mr. Haldeman by the elbow and say, Bob, I was in the craziest meeting yesterday you ever saw? Do you know what they have over there? They've got a crazy man who wants to kidnap people and plant bugs—"

PRESIDENT NIXON: Quite unlikely, actually. Bob maybe told the truth . . . . [Bob] works like I do. You don't bring up things unless they're matters to act on. We don't come in and gas around about stuff. . . . Let's come off Haldeman. Come off those things. You say that's the worst case. What's the best case?

EHRLICHMAN: Well, the best case is we'd anticipate each one of these mosaics—each one of these tiles in the big picture that they're going to try and paint and shoot them down. That's the only way I know how to do it. Plus one other thing, and that's the thing that the movie star does when he's got a paternity suit going. He goes out and he gives a million dollars to some charity, and he hires a PR man and programs, and all that kind of stuff, and you put a good face on it to try and combat the bad face, which is the big picture. . . .

It seems to me we ought to try and get the [*Chicago*] *Trib* and anybody else that'll run a story about the real Bob Haldeman and the kids, and the bright side and the happy side, you know, the good. And not for the nation. That's a Washington story; it's preconditioning of this committee. We ought to be sure the committee sees it. We have to work that dimension.

PRESIDENT NIXON: Haldeman has to give some interviews.

EHRLICHMAN: Sure he does. And he's got to also, I think—and I think this is entirely proper. He ought to make calls on this committee. I don't know what the niceties of that are. . . . And as a matter of fact, if I were him I'd go call on Weicker, too. . . .

PRESIDENT NIXON: Now, you understand here. That is the strategy, of going all-out.

EHRLICHMAN: That's correct. The way I see it—and it's very hard for me to be objective about this, terribly hard. But he's your Siamese twin, and to sever the alter ego is—can be a very difficult operation.

PRESIDENT NIXON: So was [Sherman] Adams.

EHRLICHMAN: Yes.

PRESIDENT NIXON: Even more so. . . . Adams was Haldeman and you. . . . And a little bit of Henry [Kissinger].

EHRLICHMAN: Oh, hell. I could spin out of here tomorrow and it wouldn't touch you 10 percent what it would if Bob were involved.

PRESIDENT NIXON: Or what Adams did to Eisenhower.

EHRLICHMAN: That's right. . . . We're very close to this thing and we're in the heart of the storm right now and it's very furious. But in the eight-year context, my hunch is that this is going to hurt you less than the Adams thing hurt Eisenhower.

PRESIDENT NIXON: Because his came right at the end. . . .

EHRLICHMAN: You will have all kinds of masterpieces that will come after this.

PRESIDENT NIXON: Let me . . . just ask the question . . . Why shouldn't Haldeman ask to leave? . . . You see, we've got another problem here. . . . Haldeman's ability to be effective with people is seriously [weakened] at the moment.

EHRLICHMAN: Yes. . . .

PRESIDENT NIXON: He cannot fight his own battle as well as he ought to fight it if he's here. You know what I mean. If he's here, Bob carries a huge load. In other words, the strategy would be, the strategy would be this kind of strategy. It would be . . . along this line: Haldeman and Dean would say: "By God, we're tired of this sonofabitch and we're going to go out." Haldeman then would go out and he might sue, among other things.

EHRLICHMAN: Yeah.

PRESIDENT NIXON: And bring a lawsuit. You know, he'd go down and say, I'm going to sue you people . . . . If he says I want to do it, I want to ask for a leave, he says that I've been smeared and so forth, I am innocent, and it's not fair for me to be the target of the poison and so forth, and I will return, Mr. President, only when this committee—not when this committee—only when these charges are proved false.

EHRLICHMAN: Yeah, yeah. The other thing it does, it puts you in a position to signal vindication, which is—

PRESIDENT NIXON: Or in a position, if the worst comes to worst, simply to say: Bob, you just quietly go.

EHRLICHMAN: . . . Well, it's got a lot to be said for it.

PRESIDENT NIXON: I think, let me say this. We've got to realize, John, that, much as they're after Mitchell and so forth, they're after Haldeman more because they know it gets to me.

EHRLICHMAN: Sure. . . .

PRESIDENT NIXON: Also, he's at the White House, and so forth. You see, it puts Haldeman on the offensive. He says, my God, I'm not going to take this, I'm going to get out here and I'm going to fight. . . . They want to fight, I want to fight. . . .

He takes the time then to see the press, he takes the time to do all these things. . . . That's the tragedy of the moment. Just at a time when we got Bob—we got him on a schedule and we got him out of all the East Wing crap, you know, and we got him out of the line of fire there, and we've got him so that he can concentrate basically on the big plays, the things that I say he ought to do, now we've got this thing. But let's face it. The amount of time that he's having to spend on this at the present time is tearing him up, and it will tear me up. There's your problem, John. We've got to think the unthinkable sometimes.

EHRLICHMAN: Yeah, yeah. Well, I don't find that unthinkable. I see a lot of advantages to it. . . . That's a pretty big medicine. But as I say, I certainly don't reject it out of hand.

PRESIDENT NIXON: . . . Here's the thing I dread. I dread it coming up on Bob as it did on Adams. I know what that did to Eisenhower. And Adams, Eisenhower stood by him and stood by him and stood by him. Eventually, the Republicans en masse, led by Styles Bridges, forced, forced him. Now, Goddamn it, this is nothing compared to that. There's nothing personal against Haldeman.

EHRLICHMAN: That's right. . . .

PRESIDENT NIXON: If you wait four months, John, then, by golly, wait four months and you'll fight the Haldeman fight for four months, then have to have him go, that would be—in other words, there's the line: Battle, fighting, and so forth and so on; or Haldeman fights on the outside. . . . You talk of the fact that the effectiveness of the presidency and all that sort of thing. You've got to realize we've got to live this year, too. We've got a few things coming up with the economy and the summit with the Russians, and there are some pretty Goddamn big plays at the present time. It also— it also tends to get the Watergate purity thing lowered in decibels—a hell of a lot lower decibels. I'd like to screw that committee. . . . Just trying to think it through. I don't know of anything that we could do that would be more disappointing to Ervin than to have Haldeman take a leave.

EHRLICHMAN: Yeah.

PRESIDENT NIXON: You know, Ervin would like to bring the President to his knees and have him forced to fire him as a result—[*mimicking Senator Ervin's drawl*] "as a result of mah committee's investigation, it is clear that Mr. Haldeman has to go." Look what it does to Weicker.

EHRLICHMAN: [*Also mimicking Senator Ervin*] "I don't want to inflict any hardship on the President."

PRESIDENT NIXON: [*Continuing*] "I know he's got a hard job, and so forth." I think we've got to think about this. . . .

APRIL 13, 1973: THE PRESIDENT, HALDEMAN, AND EHRLICHMAN, 2:50–4:20 P.M., EXECUTIVE OFFICE BUILDING

The three men drearily review various principals and deeds. The one bright spot is when Ehrlichman assures the others that the U.S. Attorney's office would make every effort not to involve the "presidency." But by this time the prosecutors had interviewed Dean and Magruder as "cooperative" witnesses.

EHRLICHMAN: They [the U. S. Attorney's office] advised my counsel that I am not a target. And he said you have to rely on something in this life, and he said that's pretty good, stable, reliable practice. So he says: I feel as comfortable as one in my position can feel under the circumstances. He [Ehrlichman's lawyer] said, "More than that, they have said informally that nobody in the White House is a target."

PRESIDENT NIXON: Why then would they ignore the fact that LaRue got money from the White House?

EHRLICHMAN: They aren't ignoring it. They aren't ignoring it. They're going to indict him for it. Well, they don't care if—it wasn't money from the White House. It was their own money being returned.

PRESIDENT NIXON: I know, but you know what I mean. I'm just trying to—I don't see why they don't bring the White House in. I'm trying to pick Dean's—

EHRLICHMAN: All right. He [Dean] says this. He says, "You have to understand these two guys, [Assistant U.S. Attorneys Earl] Silbert and [Seymour] Glanzer." He says, "Believe it or not, they really care about the presidency and about the institution. He's known them for a long time, and he said they're a couple of professionals who are working along. They realize that they've got a terribly dangerous mine in their hands and they have to carry it carefully." And he says, "I am morally convinced . . . that these guys are going to do everything they can to indict the guilty parties without having it splash on the President. . . ."

HALDEMAN: Everything they have done from the day they started on this case corroborates that. . . .

APRIL 13, 1973: THE PRESIDENT AND HALDEMAN, 5:48–5:58 P.M., WHITE HOUSE TELEPHONE

In this fast-paced conversation, the striking thing is that at this late date, the two men sound as if they are in a state of denial. But they know one important reality: Dean is talking to prosecutors and revealing everything. Howard Hunt also has decided to give information to the grand jury. A subsequent conversation follows with Ehrlichman as part of this moment, one in which the President and his top aides desperately seek a strategy to cope with the rapid collapse of the cover-up.

PRESIDENT NIXON: Colson's in with Ehrlichman, apparently. He said he had something urgent to talk about.

HALDEMAN: Yes.

PRESIDENT NIXON: I don't know what the hell it's about.

HALDEMAN: I don't know. He came over with his—

PRESIDENT NIXON: Attorney.

HALDEMAN: —Jewish friend [David Shapiro].

PRESIDENT NIXON: That's one thing I'm a little disturbed about.

HALDEMAN: Yes.

PRESIDENT NIXON: Aren't you?

HALDEMAN: I am.

PRESIDENT NIXON: I just don't know what the hell they're up to half the time. Colson thinks he—he is smart, but, you know, sometimes you just—Colson talks pretty freely and you never know.

HALDEMAN: Yes.

PRESIDENT NIXON: Whatever it is. What do you—analyzing this Dean thing and so forth, it's your view that Dean probably didn't know at the time after the election what the crew of three [?] was, is that right?

HALDEMAN: I don't think he knew for sure.

PRESIDENT NIXON: That's what he guessed it might be?

HALDEMAN: I think so. Well, we all guessed.

PRESIDENT NIXON: Didn't think he had any choice. Well, we didn't really, did we? We thought it was some screwballs. I mean, that was—in fact, if I thought about it at all—and I'm afraid I didn't think enough about it—but remember, I saw that: Oh, this is just nuts, you know. Of course, I didn't dream that Mitchell knew anything about it.

HALDEMAN: No, I'm talking about after the election. Back at the beginning, I think that's right. But as—

PRESIDENT NIXON: No, no, no. I mean when we first heard about it.

HALDEMAN: Oh, yeah, that's right.

PRESIDENT NIXON: When Dean had his conversation. Oh, after the election we all knew, yeah. I mean, we all had a pretty good idea. But I mean right after, in June for example, when we first heard about it and Dean had his meeting, I don't think any of us really thought that Mitchell could possibly be involved, did we?

HALDEMAN: I think that's right.

PRESIDENT NIXON: Or Magruder, for that matter.

HALDEMAN: That's right.

PRESIDENT NIXON: We thought that these guys just went off on a caper.

HALDEMAN: Yes.

PRESIDENT NIXON: Well—

HALDEMAN: I'll tell you, though. I've just listened to this Magruder tape, the stuff—

PRESIDENT NIXON: Tell me what you think of it.

HALDEMAN: There's nothing—it's all there. It's an extremely valuable thing to have, because he flatly says that he did it and that he—he says he's got 100 years' worth, 100 to 125 years' worth of jail sentence ahead of him on perjury alone, and he says, "When I talk I'm going to tell the truth."

PRESIDENT NIXON: So he's going to get off the perjury?

HALDEMAN: Yes.

PRESIDENT NIXON: That's what Ehrlichman told me, that he was going to talk. So that's that.

HALDEMAN: No, he said he hasn't decided yet whether he's going to talk or say nothing. He might go the Fifth, I suppose, and say nothing.

PRESIDENT NIXON: Yeah.

HALDEMAN: But it would appear that he's thought through and prepared for and his lawyers are advising him to talk. And he says, "When I talk, it won't in any way implicate Haldeman and absolutely in no way implicate the President, and there was no involvement and no knowledge of either," and so forth.

PRESIDENT NIXON: Well, in this respect, Bob, he is telling the truth.

HALDEMAN: But he says it will hang Mitchell. . . .

PRESIDENT NIXON: Boy, you know, the real problem is John [Mitchell]. Goddamn, I feel for him.

HALDEMAN: Yes.

PRESIDENT NIXON: And jeez, if I were advising him I'd advise him to come forward and say, "Gee, I've told the truth all along, but I take the responsibility for this thing," you know.

HALDEMAN: That's his way out.

PRESIDENT NIXON: He really ought to do that, rather than go and hard-line this damn thing. He says: I didn't know about it, I didn't approve it, but I take the responsibility for it, right?

HALDEMAN: Yes. Then they'd let him off. They'd say: Well, you know, this great man was—

PRESIDENT NIXON: That's right.

HALDEMAN: —screwed up and ill served by his people, and that's too bad.

PRESIDENT NIXON: That's right.

HALDEMAN: Obviously he had other pressures on him and, you know, one of those things. . . .

PRESIDENT NIXON: . . . I really ought to stay away from it, you know, because basically it isn't just the consumption of time and the rest, but I really don't know what the hell did happen, you know.

HALDEMAN: Yes.

PRESIDENT NIXON: I don't really know, you know. And I feel for all these people. I'd like to do something to save them all, but there isn't a Goddamn thing you can do, is there? Do you think of anything?

HALDEMAN: No, I don't. . . .

PRESIDENT NIXON: Let me tell you, yes, that's tough. Any tougher than [Sherman] Adams? No. My God, Adams was Eisenhower's alter ego. He was with him at the heart attack. He was President actually.

HALDEMAN: That's right.

PRESIDENT NIXON: You know, let's face it. And it was personal venality and not just a caper. This is just a caper, you know, like your poll showed.

HALDEMAN: Yes.

APRIL 13, 1973: THE PRESIDENT AND EHRLICHMAN, 6:16–6:31 P.M., WHITE HOUSE TELEPHONE

Ehrlichman tells how Hunt will testify to the grand jury. Again, Ehrlichman maneuvers to have Mitchell take the blame for the break-in. Obviously, the White House still hopes to contain a cover-up, a prospect dimming considering Dean's activity, a situation that the President still hopes to reverse.

EHRLICHMAN: . . . Well, I have quite a tale of horrors to tell. The bit of information that they had was that Hunt has decided to tell all to the grand jury Monday at 2:00, that he, the way they put it—and it's not conclusive, but my suspicion is that [William] Bittman, his lawyer, made a deal with the government so that Bittman does not get caught in this obstruction of justice business. But he will—

PRESIDENT NIXON: Bittman, Hunt's lawyer?

EHRLICHMAN: Right. He will implicate the [Re-Election] committee lawyers, [Kenneth] Parkinson and [Paul] O'Brien, as the bagmen and the transmitters of money through Hunt to the Cubans and to Hunt for Mrs. Hunt for other people, and so on and so forth.

PRESIDENT NIXON: Why will Hunt do this, do they say?

EHRLICHMAN: They think simply because he has no incentive to stand mute now. He sees the whole thing going up in smoke and he just doesn't want to be the only guy holding the bag. . . . Now, all of this, this whole hour I just spent with these fellows [Colson and David Shapiro], was a "sink Mitchell" operation.

PRESIDENT NIXON: Well, I hope you laid into them a little, John.

EHRLICHMAN: I did, and I have, for what it's worth, I have Colson's commitment that he will do nothing, say nothing, make no move, without prior approval at this point. . . . Now, Liddy and Hunt had a conversation, according to Hunt. This fellow Shapiro has interviewed Hunt and Hunt told him this. Liddy and Hunt. Hunt says, "This is a screwball operation, this Watergate thing; I don't think I want to go forward with it." Liddy says, "Well, Howard, we have to; we can't call it off now. Mr. Mitchell has specifically instructed that we do and we must go ahead. . . . Also, Hunt tells Shapiro the reason Liddy is sitting there without saying anything is he has a blood oath from Mitchell that he's going to get a presidential pardon.

PRESIDENT NIXON: Shit. Isn't that something. . . . Mitchell you think—you know, he might have done it, though.

EHRLICHMAN: Well, I don't know. But in any event, that's what Hunt will say Liddy told him, you see. That's the problem. Another thing Hunt will presumably testify is that he was advised to leave the country by John Dean right after this.

PRESIDENT NIXON: Was he?

EHRLICHMAN: I think he was. Well, I don't know whether John advised him. I think somebody must have, because he went to ground and he was missing for a long time. Now, they have several—they have several suggestions. They say, first of all, what's going to happen is that by Wednesday of next week, if Hunt goes in like this, this is sure to leak and there'll be a big front-page story about some of these allegations.

PRESIDENT NIXON: Right.

EHRLICHMAN: Lots of congressional excitement, lots of thrashing around among Republicans.

PRESIDENT NIXON: Right.

EHRLICHMAN: Next, they say the only thing you can do is beat this thing to the punch, and they have several suggestions.

PRESIDENT NIXON: Fire Dean.

EHRLICHMAN: Well, no. . . . The first thing Shapiro says is to restate very clearly that criminal conduct is not embraced within executive privilege, it never was intended to cover it.

PRESIDENT NIXON: Well, that isn't for me, but that's for somebody else to do that.

EHRLICHMAN: Yes, but he means from here.

PRESIDENT NIXON: In the White House, right.

EHRLICHMAN: And the Justice Department. . . . . Secondly, someone—Colson says me; Shapiro says Fred Fielding or somebody—but somebody comes in to you and lays out the damaging evidence. The U.S. Attorney is given the damaging evidence by somebody in the President's behalf. Next, the President's man goes to see Gordon Liddy and says, "Gordon, I don't know what you may have been promised, but obviously no one had authority to promise you a pardon. The only way you could be entitled to any consideration in a case of this kind would be by coming clean, by telling the truth, and the President very much wants you to tell the truth, always has wanted you to tell the truth, regardless of—"

PRESIDENT NIXON: Maybe we'd have you or—

EHRLICHMAN: Yes.

PRESIDENT NIXON: I see.

EHRLICHMAN: Then you have stolen a march on Hunt, you have broken the case by persuading Liddy to come clean. He is the key to the Watergate thing. The focus is all on Watergate with Liddy. And you have demonstrated your desire that all come out.

PRESIDENT NIXON: That's their plan. Well, how's this all affect Colson?

EHRLICHMAN: [*Laughter.*] Well, I don't know how it all affects Colson. Hunt has got to talk a lot about Colson, I would guess.

PRESIDENT NIXON: That's the other point. He wants to keep Hunt solid.

EHRLICHMAN: One marginal piece of news that they brought in that has Colson a little shook is that McCord has told the U.S. Attorney that he participated in an operation with Hunt to go out to Las Vegas, leave their airplane with the engines going standing by, go into town, bust [Las Vegas reporter] Hank Greenspun's safe—

PRESIDENT NIXON: Jesus Christ!

EHRLICHMAN: Yes—steal some stuff from it, jump back in the airplane, and come on back; and that Colson masterminded it.

PRESIDENT NIXON: What in the name of God would that be?

EHRLICHMAN: I can't imagine. But Colson stoutly and devoutly maintains that he never heard a thing about it, never heard of it before, never heard of Hank Greenspun before, and so forth.

PRESIDENT NIXON: Yeah, yeah, yeah. You see, you've got to analyze all of this, John, as you of course know, in terms of what Colson and Shapiro are thinking. . . .

EHRLICHMAN: As I say, it's another Mitchell tubing. Their whole point is that some time between now and 2:00 o'clock Monday afternoon you have to sink Mitchell, and that every minute counts.

PRESIDENT NIXON: I have to sink Mitchell? How do I do it?

EHRLICHMAN: In order to detach yourself from it, because otherwise Hunt will have conclusively sunk him and nothing you could do thereafter could get out ahead of it. . . .

PRESIDENT NIXON: How do we handle that, the presidential pardon thing? We just deny it?

EHRLICHMAN: Flat-out deny it, vigorously, strongly.

PRESIDENT NIXON: But frankly, frankly, it's not only a flat-out denial, it's totally true. Mitchell has never discussed the Goddamn case with me. . . .

EHRLICHMAN: I think I had better let Dean know this, in case he doesn't know it. . . . Because this will change some of this aftermath business, I think, because Hunt is an actor in that aftermath business.

PRESIDENT NIXON: You mean that Dean then would say that he participated in the aftermath?

EHRLICHMAN: Well, I don't know if it would change his testimony any. But he certainly ought to be aware that it's happening.

PRESIDENT NIXON: You've got to figure, what will—put yourself in Magruder's and Mitchell's place. What are they going to do? Now, are they going to—is Mitchell going to sit here with Martha and the rest?

EHRLICHMAN: I don't think so.

PRESIDENT NIXON: What do you think he's going to do?

EHRLICHMAN: I think he'll come in.

PRESIDENT NIXON: Huh?

EHRLICHMAN: I think he'll come in to the U.S. Attorney. I think Magruder's ready now.

PRESIDENT NIXON: Come in and confess?

EHRLICHMAN: Sure.

PRESIDENT NIXON: Yes, but what are they going to do? If they're going to piss on the White House, that's what I'm worried about.

EHRLICHMAN: Oh, I see, I see. . . .

PRESIDENT NIXON: All right, fine. What does Mitchell say? What the hell does he do? He doesn't want to hurt the President, that's for damn sure. This is a decent man.

EHRLICHMAN: Well, if I were Mitchell I'd get on a plane and I'd come down here and ask to see you, and I'd come in and say, "Well, I put this meeting off as long as I can, and now you've got to know what happened."

PRESIDENT NIXON: Right, right.

EHRLICHMAN: "And it's up to you as to what I do from here."

PRESIDENT NIXON: You see, you can be very considerate about a former Attorney General, you know.

EHRLICHMAN: Sure.

PRESIDENT NIXON: That's the point that he's got to realize. But Goddamn, he may just decide to stonewall it and fight it through. He'll never win on that, will he?

EHRLICHMAN: Well, I can't see that he would. . . .

PRESIDENT NIXON: I really think Colson is deeply concerned about Hunt, don't you?

EHRLICHMAN: Yes, I'm sure he is.

PRESIDENT NIXON: Or did you sense that from your meeting?

EHRLICHMAN: He had Hunt talk to Shapiro a long time in the day. . . .

PRESIDENT NIXON: Well, what the hell. He [Hunt] probably figures he isn't going to get a presidential pardon. . . . You know Goddamn well I can't give him a pardon. . . . They're looking right—and Colson's sort of made all these protestations perhaps to him, and he knows damn well we can't come through on them, because Colson has no commitment. . . . So Hunt then will pull the plug. Isn't that really Colson's concern, that Hunt will pull the plug on him?

EHRLICHMAN: He didn't say so, but I'm sure it is. I'm sure it is. And he's probably doing everything he can to get a line around Hunt at this point.

PRESIDENT NIXON: But at the present time, for God's sakes, keep him from talking. You know what I mean. . . .

EHRLICHMAN: Yes.

APRIL 14, 1973: THE PRESIDENT AND KISSINGER, 12:02–12:30 P.M., EXECUTIVE OFFICE BUILDING

Kissinger defends Haldeman, his frequent ally in the personal and bureaucratic turf wars with Secretary of State Rogers.

KISSINGER: . . . My view is that Haldeman should under no—my view is that he should be held onto if it's humanly possible. If he cannot be held onto, then he should resign ahead of the group. . . .

PRESIDENT NIXON: I wasn't clear. I wouldn't say that. What I meant is that that would be a rough intention. But he's entitled to a chance. . . . He's had two rough days, but he'll survive them. . . . The point is it's going to come out if we cooperate or not.

KISSINGER: No, no, I'm not talking about cooperating. I was—

PRESIDENT NIXON: No, no, no, no. What I meant is, appearances before the Congress or not, it's going to come out. That's what I'm talking about.

KISSINGER: But if it's going to come out, then the question is whether once and for all to take some brutal measures.

PRESIDENT NIXON: There's no more brutal measures, I'm afraid, than [sacrificing] John Mitchell and Jeb Magruder. It's likely to work this way in two weeks. . . .

KISSINGER: . . . This thing can be contained.

PRESIDENT NIXON: You think it can be?

KISSINGER: That's right. . . . I grant you that the people who did the bugging are bad guys. That's why they need protection.

PRESIDENT NIXON: Sure, that's why you protect communists.

KISSINGER: I said that's what the constitutional protections are there for.

PRESIDENT NIXON: That's what McCarthyism was about. . . . I have to worry about it because it gets to me personally. I mean, it hits me personally. I'm not referring to polls. I don't give a shit about that. I'm not referring to attacks in the press. Of course, I am concerned about the human factors. Good God, Mitchell's a decent man. Magruder's a decent man. All these Goddamn people who were doing this were, they were misguided, they were wrong. They were doing it for what? You get my point? . . .

APRIL 15, 1973: HENRY PETERSEN AND EARL SILBERT, 4:00–5:15 P.M., WHITE HOUSE TELEPHONE

Assistant U.S. Attorney Earl Silbert was the lead prosecutor in the Watergate investigation, and Henry Petersen, Assistant Attorney General for the Department of Justice Criminal Division, was his superior. The recording probably was made during one of Petersen's frequent visits to the President at this time. While we do not know whether Nixon was present during the conversation, the recording certainly was available to him and Haldeman. Petersen was reporting regularly to Nixon on the progress of the investigation, apparently oblivious for quite some time as to the President's own involvement.

PETERSEN: . . . How are you coming?

SILBERT: Well, [Charles] Shaffer [Dean's lawyer] was in the middle of summarizing his position. [*Laughter.*] . . . And his positioning is hardening a little, in the sense that if John [Dean] is believable, we have an obstruction case against Haldeman and Ehrlichman, in the sense that they knew everything that was going on.

PETERSEN: If—if John Dean is believable, you have an obstruction case against Haldeman and Ehrlichman?

SILBERT: Well, let me say this to you. They knew everything that was going on. That is, all the plans, like the Magruder plans and, you know, they were—like Ehrlichman was present—again, going through the same stories about the (unintelligible), get rid of—Hunt get out of town. He and Haldeman are in on the money. I mean, Ehrlichman and Haldeman are in on the money, clearly. I mean, the $350,000 comes from Haldeman, and he's putting it in that Haldeman told him to get it back over there and that they knew that the money was coming—I mean, the demands were being made and finally they had to give this money up.

It was Haldeman's decision to send it all back to the committee, and he told John [Dean] to do it, and that's when John called Strachan. Strachan, you know—Strachan's testimony so far is inconsistent with that. He says it was his own idea, Haldeman hardly even knew the money was there, and he just decided to bring it back, and he just called up—I mean, his story is basically not too believable, that is Strachan's.

But John's is much more credible because he says, "Yeah, I gave it to LaRue because LaRue was giving all the money, and that's why the money went to Larue." Whereas Strachan can say, well, I knew—he doesn't even return it to the Finance Committee, which is normally where it would go back. He returns it to LaRue. And why does he return it to LaRue? Because LaRue is—I mean, Strachan's explanation is, well, he was a senior campaign official. But in any sense, money ought to go back to a person in the Finance Committee.

PETERSEN: Does he say Haldeman said to?

SILBERT: To give it to LaRue?

PETERSEN: Yes.

SILBERT: No, not that. He says give it back, send it back to the committee and get a receipt. That's what Haldeman said. But there is a, uh, there's been a face on the money. Dean . . . had advised Haldeman at the first two meetings that took place in the Attorney General's office, you know, it's just intolerable. And he says, well, he says, Haldeman agreed and we should have nothing to do with it.

PETERSEN: But nobody stopped it.

SILBERT: Huh?

PETERSEN: But nobody stopped it.

SILBERT: Nobody stopped it. . . .

APRIL 15, 1973: THE PRESIDENT AND HENRY PETERSEN, 8:14–8:18 P.M., WHITE HOUSE TELEPHONE

Petersen provides more information on Dean's cooperation with the prosecutors. Here Nixon learns that Dean intends to pull Haldeman and Ehrlichman down with him. Nixon suggests that he meet with Dean; "I want to be sure you understand that you know we're going to get to the bottom of this thing," he says. Petersen agrees, but also thinks the President should tell Liddy's lawyer to have his client cooperate. Liddy, however, remains determined to carve out a reputation as the only accused Watergate figure who would not do so.

PRESIDENT NIXON: . . . Anything further you want to report tonight before our meeting tomorrow at 12:30?

PETERSEN: Not anything especially that I didn't give you today.

PRESIDENT NIXON: Nothing to add to what we had earlier?

PETERSEN: That's right. They concluded the meeting with Dean.

PRESIDENT NIXON: Right.

PETERSEN: His counsel says he will not permit him to plead.

PRESIDENT NIXON: Permit him to plead, what do you mean by that?

PETERSEN: To plead guilty. In other words, he'll go to trial.

PRESIDENT NIXON: He's going to plead not guilty, huh?

PETERSEN: That's right, unless we come to some agreement with him.

PRESIDENT NIXON: I see.

PETERSEN: His counsel's position is that it would be a travesty to try Dean and not try Ehrlichman and Haldeman. But the basic information . . . is not much more than I gave you.

PRESIDENT NIXON: Well, let me ask you this. Based on this, though, you mean that inhibits you from using the information, then? Or do you use it, or how do you do it? You use it for leads, but you can't use it unless he pleads, right?

PETERSEN: We cannot use it for any purpose unless he pleads. . . . [T]hat's incorrect. Unless we strike some agreement with him. He had a call from Ehrlichman. Ehrlichman wanted to meet with him tonight—

PRESIDENT NIXON: I see.

PETERSEN: —at about 8:00 o'clock. We advised him he would have to make his own determination, but suggested he not.

PRESIDENT NIXON: I see.

PETERSEN: He then through his counsel informed us that he was writing a note to you in which he would say, one, that what he was doing was in your best interests and that that would all become apparent as this situation unfolded. . . .

PRESIDENT NIXON: Let me ask you this. Why don't I get him in now, if I can find him, and have a talk with him?

PETERSEN: I wouldn't see any objection to that, Mr. President.

PRESIDENT NIXON: Is that all right with you?

PETERSEN: Yes, sir.

PRESIDENT NIXON: All right. I'm going to get him over, because I am not going to screw around with this thing, as I told you. . . . But I want to be sure you understand that you know we're going to get to the bottom of this thing.

PETERSEN: I think that the thing that—

PRESIDENT NIXON: What do you want me to say to him? Ask him to tell me the whole truth? . . .

PETERSEN: Yes, sir. And there's one other thing. That is that a signal from you might bring out the truth from Liddy. . . .

PRESIDENT NIXON: A signal from me? What do I do?

PETERSEN: He went to John Mitchell and indicated, I am told, that he would do whatever he was told to do.

PRESIDENT NIXON: I've never met the man. I don't know what I can do with him. How do I give him a signal?

PETERSEN: Well, I can do it for you. . . . [W]e'd just go and say that we've discussed the situation with the President of the United States and he said it was vitally important that you tell us everything you know.

PRESIDENT NIXON: I get it. Okay. . . .

APRIL 15, 1973: HALDEMAN AND LAWRENCE M. HIGBY, 8:18–8:25 P.M., WHITE HOUSE TELEPHONE

Higby, Haldeman's principal aide—"Haldeman's Haldeman," as he was known— conveys a message from Dean to the President, urging him to cooperate with Henry Petersen.

HIGBY: Hello, Bob.

HALDEMAN: Yeah.

HIGBY: John Dean just called me. He had a message he wanted to relay to the President through you. He would not speak directly to you.

HALDEMAN: All right.

HIGBY: He said: Point one: "I hope you understand that my actions are motivated totally out of loyalty to you and the President."

HALDEMAN: "You."

HIGBY: "You." "And if not"—

HALDEMAN: Wait a minute, wait a minute. "Totally out of loyalty"—

HIGBY: —"to you and the President."

HALDEMAN: Yes.

HIGBY: —"and, if not clear now, it will become clear."
"Two"—

HALDEMAN: Wait a minute.

HIGBY: "Ehrlichman requested to meet tonight, but I feel it's inappropriate at this time."

HALDEMAN: Okay.

HIGBY: "I am ready and willing to meet with you,"—meaning the President—"at any time to discuss these matters." . . . "You"—meaning the President—"should take your counsel from Henry Petersen, who I assure you does not want the presidency hurt." That's the end of his message. He was calling me from his home, the operator said. . . .

HALDEMAN: How long ago was this? Just now?

HIGBY:: Yes, sir.

April 15, 1973: Ehrlichman and L. Patrick Gray, 10:16–11:15 p.m., White House Telephone

Ehrlichman informs Gray that Dean has told the prosecutors that Gray may have destroyed evidence Dean had given him. Gray contends that Dean had told him the envelope contained only "political" materials, and that he had not seen them. Ehrlichman is anxious to separate himself from this episode, for he had told John Dean to "deep-six" the envelope.

EHRLICHMAN: . . . Pat, this is John Ehrlichman.

GRAY: Yes, John. Good evening.

EHRLICHMAN: Did I find you at home?

GRAY: Yes, I'm at home.

EHRLICHMAN: I wanted to tell you that John Dean has apparently decided to make a clean breast of things with the U.S. Attorney. One of the questions that apparently they've been asking him is about the envelope that he turned over to you.

GRAY: Yeah, well, he better deny that.

EHRLICHMAN: Well, he's apparently pretty much on the record on that. I thought I'd better alert you to it.

GRAY: What the hell am I going to do about that?

EHRLICHMAN: I don't know. Is it still in being?

GRAY: No.

EHRLICHMAN: I see. I don't know.

GRAY: I was told that that was purely political and I destroyed it.

EHRLICHMAN: I see, okay. Well, it probably was.

GRAY: Is there any way you can turn him off? . . .

ERHLICHMAN: No. He's out of any orbit that we [*laughter*] [re]cognize around here. So I just wanted to alert you to it.

GRAY: What other things do you think he's going to talk about?

EHRLICHMAN: Well, he's putting the best face on his relations with Petersen that he can, because Petersen has sort of moved in on the prosecution.

GRAY: Was he doing things with Petersen, too?

EHRLICHMAN: Yes.

GRAY: I see.

EHRLICHMAN: You might want to take a look at your hole card where he's concerned, because I don't know all the ins and outs of your relationship or, you know—

GRAY: The only thing I can do with this is deny it.

EHRLICHMAN: Okay.

GRAY: You're not going to back him up, are you?

EHRLICHMAN: I can just say I don't know anything about it except what he told me. But he has spent all day today with the U.S. Attorney. So that's about all I have to tell you for the moment. I'll keep you posted if I can. . . .

APRIL 15, 1973: EHRLICHMAN AND GRAY, 10:16–11:15 P.M., WHITE HOUSE TELEPHONE

Ehrlichman has further advice for Gray.

EHRLICHMAN: . . . Pat, John Ehrlichman again. Listen, I've been giving some thought to our conversation. I just don't think that there's any way to do anything but level on this if you're asked. There are just too many collateral facts. If it's the fact that that was just full of stuff irrelevant to any business of the Bureau, why, you know, that's reason enough.

GRAY: Well, that's what I was told. But I didn't look at it.

EHRLICHMAN: Right. I just don't see how you could get yourself crossways in the testimony in this thing, for fear you'll get caught up in it. So I just encourage you to just state the facts.

GRAY: I'd state it a different way, that at no time did he [Dean] indicate that this was from Hunt's material.

EHRLICHMAN: Yeah. So you didn't know where it came from?

GRAY: No.

EHRLICHMAN: I see. Just that it was papers that he wanted to turn over to you?

GRAY: Yes. . . . That it was purely political things and had no bearing on the subject of Watergate.

EHRLICHMAN: Uh-hmm, uh-hmm. I think if I were you I'd stick to that. I obviously can't tell you what to do, but I was a little troubled by our conversation and I didn't pick it up fast enough when you said that. So I just thought I better call you back.

GRAY: Yeah. I don't know all the other collaterals there are that are involved in this.

EHRLICHMAN: Well, the thing is moving so fast, I'm frank to confess I don't, either. But I just hesitate to get crosswise on something of that kind. I'll talk to you later. . . .

APRIL 17, 1973: THE PRESIDENT AND DEAN, 9:19–9:25 A.M., WHITE HOUSE TELEPHONE

The President believes that Dean still is useful to him. Apparently, he thinks he can charm Dean and command his loyalty.

SEGMENT 2

PRESIDENT NIXON: . . . [Magruder will] be their first star witness. You know, their procedure there apparently is to have him go out and make a statement in open court, confess in open court and make a statement, apparently. I didn't know they could do that with a guilty plea.

DEAN: That's because Sirica's insisting on it. . . .

PRESIDENT NIXON: That's what they said. Sirica was asking—Sirica would ask him the questions anyway, so they said, we'll just make him make a statement. I wonder about that procedure. It's a little tough, isn't it? It's very risky as far as jeopardizing— I mean, I would think that Mitchell et al. would have a pretty tough constitutional— I mean, have a good constitutional question there, wouldn't they?

DEAN: I think they would indeed, if they're named in open court like that.

PRESIDENT NIXON: Give me a little feeling on that. Don't let them know I'm checking on that.

DEAN: I understand.

PRESIDENT NIXON: But give me your—do a little run-down.

DEAN: I'm digging on that for you.

PRESIDENT NIXON: I'll call you about 2:30 or 3:00.

DEAN: All right, sir.

PRESIDENT NIXON: Okay.

DEAN: Thank you.

PRESIDENT NIXON: I hope you got a good night's sleep, as well as you can these days. But let me say, like I told the other boys: I said, God, you know, it's tough for everybody, John. All of you are good friends and, I said, you have fought the good fight, and you'll live to fight another one. That's the important thing.

DEAN: Indeed.

PRESIDENT NIXON: Right?

DEAN: No problem there. . . .

APRIL 17–18, 1973: THE PRESIDENT AND KISSINGER, 11:45 P.M.–12:04 A.M., WHITE HOUSE TELEPHONE

The President has been to a late-night dinner affair. Returning to the White House, he makes several calls, seeking out aides to offer him comfort. Kissinger proves particularly accommodating, telling Nixon that history would remember him for more than Watergate. Kissinger's tone is mournful, while the President seems particularly sad, perhaps on the verge of tears. He knows, for example, that Haldeman must go. He begins his denial of knowing anything until Dean informed him of

events on March 21. Change is very much in the air. On April 17, Press Secretary Ron Ziegler decisively transformed the story when he said his previous Watergate remarks were "inoperative."

SEGMENT 1

PRESIDENT NIXON: . . . Goddamn, I think of these good men.

KISSINGER: That's right, who wanted to do the right thing.

PRESIDENT NIXON: Well, it's going to splash on a lot of them. Anyway—

KISSINGER: Well, I think the way you have positioned it now is the right way to do it.

PRESIDENT NIXON: Of course, Garment, as you know, was having the idea that I should get up and announce that I'd fired Haldeman, Ehrlichman, and Dean, without waiting until they get up the main—the real culprit is Mitchell, of course. He's in charge of the whole Goddamn thing, and John Mitchell should step up like a man and say, "Look, I was in charge; I take the responsibility," period.

KISSINGER: Exactly. All the more so, as doing the opposite won't help him any.

PRESIDENT NIXON: No. They're going to get him.

KISSINGER: No, I think to fire Haldeman would make him the villain.

PRESIDENT NIXON: Well, in the end he probably will have to go, Henry. They're going to rip him up good.

KISSINGER: Well, if that's the case then he should get out before.

PRESIDENT NIXON: Well, but not until I have absolute evidence. I'm not going to fire a guy on the basis of a charge made by Dean, who basically is trying to save his ass and get immunity, you see. That's why I had that phrase in there [in a White House statement] that no immunity should be granted to a top person. . . . He has no right to do that.

KISSINGER: That's absolutely—I mean, I think that is outrageous. No, I just have no way—I have no good feel for where—I think you would not have improved the situation if you had suddenly, without any preparation, turned on all your associates.

PRESIDENT NIXON: Well, we have two or three hard months ahead. It's going to be real rough.

KISSINGER: Well, the major thing now, Mr. President, if I may say so, is to protect the presidency and your authority.

PRESIDENT NIXON: That will be hard.

KISSINGER: That is absolutely essential.

PRESIDENT NIXON: Some of these people will even piss on the President if they think it will help them. It's pretty hard. I'm the only one, frankly, of the whole bunch who really didn't know a Goddamn thing about it until March, when finally Dean came in and said, well, here's where it is, which he should have done months ago.

KISSINGER: Well, they were in over their heads and they tried to, instead of stepping back and assessing where they were, got in deeper and deeper.

PRESIDENT NIXON: That's right.

KISSINGER: But I think the absolute—I mean, to protect [the presidency].

PRESIDENT NIXON: Well, if we can. If we can we will, and if we don't, what the hell.

KISSINGER: We can, Mr. President.

PRESIDENT NIXON: Maybe we'll even consider the possibility of, frankly, just throwing myself on the sword—

KISSINGER: No—

PRESIDENT NIXON: —and letting Agnew take it. What the hell.

KISSINGER: That is out of the question, with all due respect, Mr. President. That cannot be considered. The personality, what it would do to the presidency, and the historical injustice of it. Why should you do it, and what good would it do? Whom would it help? It wouldn't help the country. It wouldn't help any individual involved. With all respect, I don't think the President has the right to sacrifice himself for an individual. And it would of course be personally unjust.

PRESIDENT NIXON: Well, maybe. . . .

KISSINGER: It's impermissible to touch the President. That cannot be permitted, at whatever price. I'm sure that even Bob [Haldeman], that Bob wouldn't want that.

PRESIDENT NIXON: Oh, no, Bob is willing to—Bob and John both are willing to throw themselves on the sword over there. When they do, they're going to fight like hell.

KISSINGER: But one of them ought to stay.

PRESIDENT NIXON: I would hope so, but I'm afraid it can't be Haldeman. I'm afraid the only one that possibly could be saved would be Ehrlichman, and that's tough, too.

KISSINGER: But I think you've positioned it correctly, that as evidence comes out. For you to fire them all now would look like panic.

PRESIDENT NIXON: Well, that's the [Leonard] Garment line [to dismiss all the top aides]. What do you think of his line?

KISSINGER: Well, Garment wants you to fire Haldeman, Dean.

PRESIDENT NIXON: And Ehrlichman.

KISSINGER: I don't know whether he wants you to fire Ehrlichman, too.

PRESIDENT NIXON: Yes. . . .

KISSINGER: Well, if there's a good chance that they'll have to go as a result of what happened, then I don't think you should fire them; they ought to resign on the grounds that their usefulness is impaired, that they have to be above, like Caesar's wife. . . . But I think it does you credit to have stood as you have. And in any event, today you were right to go no further.

SEGMENT 2

PRESIDENT NIXON: Well, don't you get discouraged.

KISSINGER: Mr. President, I'm not discouraged.

PRESIDENT NIXON: You do your job. Two or three of us have got to stick around, try to hold the Goddamn fort.

KISSINGER: You have saved this country, Mr. President. The history books will show that, when no one will know what Watergate means.

PRESIDENT NIXON: Maybe, although our enemies say, well, this proves that we obstructed justice. Oh, well.

KISSINGER: Oh, and in six months no one will know it any more. It's a human tragedy for Haldeman and Dean and a few of those fellows. Haldeman is a big man, Mr. President.

PRESIDENT NIXON: Dean is the real, the fellow that's really going to be the loose cannon, because he's trying to save his ass, trying to get immunity. That's why I had in that little phrase that no immunity should be granted to any top person. . . . And that's going to burn his ass, because then he'll thrash out about everything you can imagine. . . . Although Ziegler made an interesting point. He [Dean] has Goddamn little credibility. After all, he was making the report.

KISSINGER: That's right.

PRESIDENT NIXON: He was the one that said there was no involvement, and that's what we relied on. . . .

KISSINGER: I'd just fire him as soon as it comes out, and let him scream from the outside.

PRESIDENT NIXON: I guess so, we will, when the time comes. Well, you know, nobody really will know what they put a President through on a thing like this.

KISSINGER: Well, it's inhuman, Mr. President. These bastards know damn well that you couldn't have known about it, if one considers all the things you had to go through. You couldn't be a police judge, too. You're running the government, you're doing all the negotiating, you're carrying a bigger load than any president has. On top of it, they want you to—

PRESIDENT NIXON: Good God, we were going to Russia and China and ending the war and negotiating. I wasn't even thinking about the Goddamn campaign, you know. I had nothing to do with the damn campaign, as you know. . . . That's the tragedy. I wish to Christ maybe that I had, but if I'd been spending time in the campaign maybe we wouldn't have pulled off Vietnam.

KISSINGER: If you can't rely on your own people to tell you the facts, then it's rather difficult. Exactly, if you had done that we might still be in the war.

SEGMENT 3

PRESIDENT NIXON: And in the meantime, put your arm around Haldeman and Ehrlichman.

KISSINGER: You can count on it, Mr. President. I've been standing by Haldeman. I didn't know Ehrlichman was in trouble, too. . . . No, you can count on the fact that I'll stand by them. But the major person to stand by now is you.

PRESIDENT NIXON: We shall see. But at least old [Frank] Sinatra gave them a lift, and I thought the dinner was rather nice.

KISSINGER: Oh, the whole evening was beautiful. . . .

PRESIDENT NIXON: Well, sleep on it. I'll try to get some ideas. I don't think Garment's judgment is very good, you know what I mean. He panics so easily. You know, he panicked on Cambodia and everything else earlier.

KISSINGER: That's right, that would be my opinion. . . .

PRESIDENT NIXON: Unh-uh.

KISSINGER: If you get some evidence that makes it look that these fellows can't be helped—

PRESIDENT NIXON: If it's hard evidence, though. Goddamn it, I'm not going to—

KISSINGER: If you've got hard evidence.

PRESIDENT NIXON: It's got to be corroborated. I ain't going to let them do it on a basis of—

KISSINGER: Then you ought to fire the people against whom you have evidence and the others ought to consider resigning.

PRESIDENT NIXON: Yup. Well, it'll be a great day on the other side for all of our enemies, won't it? The *Times,* the *Post,* the rest—shit.

KISSINGER: That's right, Mr. President. You have to gather the wagons and pull it through, as you've done so often.

PRESIDENT NIXON: Well, what's really disturbing is comparing this Goddamn thing with Teapot Dome, for Christ's sake, which was thievery on a massive basis. That isn't what this is all about.

KISSINGER: That's right, Mr. President, and in a year that will be clear.

PRESIDENT NIXON: It'll take that long, I'm afraid.

KISSINGER: It might be less. I think the major thing now is to get the pus out of the system. You cannot let it be squeezed out a little at a time. . . . Once you have all the facts, I think you should consider then at least cleaning at least that part of the house that must be cleaned.

PRESIDENT NIXON: Right.

KISSINGER: However painful.

PRESIDENT NIXON: Right, right. Okay, Henry.

April 18, 1973: The President and Haldeman, 12:05–12:20 a.m., White House Telephone

The President quickly follows with a call to his Chief of Staff. The tone is much the same, but they raise familiar matters of substance. Here, of course, there is no talk of Haldeman's resigning.

PRESIDENT NIXON: Hello.

HALDEMAN: Yes, sir.

PRESIDENT NIXON: I just wanted to say, keep the faith. . . .

HALDEMAN: Well, I think we've reviewed what the worst is and what's in between and all, and I think we can deal with whatever it is, and the thing now is to just play it as it lies day by day and see where we come out. . . .

PRESIDENT NIXON: . . . [T]omorrow afternoon we ought to meet again and really look hard at what's coming and look at the names and so forth, you know, and just be prepared for it. I think, too, that you've got to consider the Dean thing and what it lands—I don't know whether somebody really oughtn't to talk to him. I don't know whether I should, but he must think about that as to whether it's worth doing or not, because he's obviously on the kick of saving himself. And the U.S. Attorney is going to have a tough problem. I think the U.S. Attorney will, my guess is, will give him the immunity.

HALDEMAN: You think he will?

PRESIDENT NIXON: Well, I would think so, Bob. And then of course, if the U.S. Attorney is giving him immunity so that he can tell the truth, that doesn't bother me. But if he gives him the immunity in terms that it's an incentive for him to lie, that's the thing.

But they'll of course have their other witnesses and so forth to try to corroborate it. I do hope—one thing, the other thing we've got to do, Bob, is to get some kind of a line with regard to this whole business of helping the defendants. I just feel some way that ought to be able to be done, you know what I mean? I don't know whether there is any way, though; is there?

HALDEMAN: Well, I don't see anything other than the basic point that, you know, as it's been discussed all along, that it was the fees and the support and that's it. . . .

PRESIDENT NIXON: . . . You remember when he [Dean] came in and had this information about [William] Bittman. You were there, but they would say, well, right at that moment the President should have probably turned that over to the U.S. Attorney, you see?

HALDEMAN: No.

PRESIDENT NIXON: Why not?

HALDEMAN: Because you didn't know what you had and you weren't in any position to turn it over to him.

PRESIDENT NIXON: Well, on the ground when he said, "Look, they want money for their fees," and so forth and so on. And he said, well—and I suppose we did. In fairness, we were saying, well, what can be done, you know. And the way Dean might put that is that, well—you've got to figure that maybe he could say, well, he was in the President's office and told the President that. That of course he shouldn't be able to do. . . .

But then he'll of course report that he reported it to Ehrlichman, Ehrlichman said he couldn't do anything, and that it was discussed with Mitchell, right? Was he present in the room at that time, you know, when Mitchell said, well, it's taken care of?

HALDEMAN: Yes. It was John [Ehrlichman] that he talked to.

PRESIDENT NIXON: You were present—Ehrlichman present?

HALDEMAN: Uh-hmm.

PRESIDENT NIXON: Well, it shows, I suppose, knowledge. Why didn't you go tell the President, then?

HALDEMAN: Well, there again, you can argue because there was—it was a separated amount specifically for fees and for a family problem he had.

PRESIDENT NIXON: Right. Well, give that one some hard thought, because I suppose Dean will lob that one in pretty soon.

HALDEMAN: Yes. That's almost beyond belief.

PRESIDENT NIXON: If he has immunity he'll do it. If he doesn't, he may not want to. But the way he's operating, it's very interesting. Of course, the problem is that he talked to me and that day I talked Goddamn freely with him. I said, "Well, what the hell; where are you going to get it, you know?" And he said, "We don't have the money." "How much is it?" "That'll be a million dollars." And I said, "good God," I said. And then we went into the blackmail thing. He said this is blackmail, and I said we can't be blackmailed, or somebody said that or he did, you've got to say, to his credit, didn't he?

HALDEMAN: I'm not sure he did. I'm not sure he said we couldn't be.

PRESIDENT NIXON: Couldn't be blackmailed?

HALDEMAN: It's just a question of whether you go down that route. . . .

PRESIDENT NIXON: But let's sit down and just put on a piece of paper what the vulnerabilities are, how many people. As I see it, at the present time they've got clear cases in terms of prior knowledge of LaRue, Mitchell, Mardian, Magruder, possibly the lawyers. What do you think? [Paul] O'Brien?

HALDEMAN: I guess so. I guess they must. . . .

APRIL 20, 1973: THE PRESIDENT AND HENRY PETERSEN, 11:32–11:40 A.M., WHITE HOUSE TELEPHONE

This conversation is representative of Nixon's attempts to manipulate and exploit Assistant Attorney General Petersen. Petersen, a career official, is in awe of the President. He occasionally reminds Nixon that he remembers the President's disclaimers about trying to cull out secret grand jury testimony, Nevertheless, Petersen continues to provide useful information for Nixon and his aides.

PETERSEN: . . . Mr. President, how are you?

PRESIDENT NIXON: Hi. I wanted you to know that I have directed Ziegler, because of these damn grand jury leaks, that in any talks I had with you that I specifically do not want to know what in substance was said.

PETERSEN: I understand.

PRESIDENT NIXON: So I want you to bear that in mind, because I don't want to be in a position where I might inform somebody else, you see?

PETERSEN: Mr. President, to refresh your recollection, you told me that very early in our early meetings, and I've abided by it.

PRESIDENT NIXON: But I want you to be sure that you remember that and we said it. The second point is, what I would like to know is, you have Mitchell today?

PETERSEN: Yes, sir. He's in the grand jury now.

PRESIDENT NIXON: How long will that be, do you think? Will he be there several days or one day?

PETERSEN: Will he be there several days? No, he will not be there several days. I don't know. We may have to recall him.

PRESIDENT NIXON: I see.

PETERSEN: My guess is he'll be out of there today.

PRESIDENT NIXON: Right. The other thing that occurred to me, just as a matter of strategy, which you might impress upon, it seems, the prosecutors. It seems to me, Henry, the dragging of this thing out is going to make your problem increasingly difficult, with the leaks and the statements that Magruder and Dean are making publicly, and all that sort of thing. I know, obviously, you're trying to get the corroboration and that sort of thing and get down the four corners and nail it all down. But I am inclined to think—I don't know what your views are, and I'd be glad to know them. But if I were sitting in that spot, your spot, I would try to accelerate the thing if you know pretty well what's going to happen. Or do you agree with that? I don't know.

PETERSEN: Well, I agree with it, but I don't agree with it that it's practical. . . . We don't have control of the situation, that's our problem. . . . Every individual involved in this has a lawyer. Every one of them has to be scheduled. . . . Every one of them is reluctant. Every one of them has to be recalled. The grand jury transcript has to be reviewed each day in the light of what's gone before.

PRESIDENT NIXON: I get it. . . . The other thing is that the calling of Mitchell early I think was a good idea, don't you think, just to get it done with?

PETERSEN: Well, I think so.

PRESIDENT NIXON: Now wait a minute. you haven't heard Magruder yet, have you?

PETERSEN: Well, we've got his statement *in extenso*.

PRESIDENT NIXON: No, no, but I mean you haven't had him before the grand jury. . . .

PETERSEN: We haven't decided on that yet, because Dean is still in arm's length negotiation.

PRESIDENT NIXON: Oh, is that right?

PETERSEN: He hasn't really decided to be a witness yet.

PRESIDENT NIXON: And that brings you back to that critical problem, doesn't it?

PETERSEN: Yes, sir.

PRESIDENT NIXON: It occurs to me that one other thing you've got in Dean as we want to be fair to individuals in all this case is that I suppose that—it would seem to me that you could distinguish that whatever he did as basically work product, you know, and so forth and so on as counsel is one thing. What he did as an activist is something else again. I suppose that distinction is something you're bearing in mind, that he's bearing in mind. In other words, if Dean's conducting an investigation, I'm just trying to figure. I'm figuring now, I'm just trying to think about his own vulnerability. Dean conducts an investigation, that's one thing. When he's involved as an activist say in the cover-up process, that's something else again. But is there any distinction there that can be made? I haven't talked to Dean, so I'm just asking you.

PETERSEN: It may be that—certainly to the extent that he's involved as an activist, but—

PRESIDENT NIXON: If he has information, he has to give it.

PETERSEN: That's the point. Well, you know, if it's information with respect to a violation of the law.

PRESIDENT NIXON: Right. . . . I'm not talking about his testimony. I'm talking about his own legal liability, and there his liability runs only to his activism, unless he was suppressing a violation of the law. Then he's guilty of that, too, suppressing information on the violation of the law.

PETERSEN: That's true, but that becomes a very refined doctrine, Mr. President.

PRESIDENT NIXON: Right, right.

PETERSEN: If you know a fact which fact is the ultimate object of a conspiracy—

PRESIDENT NIXON: I get it.

PETERSEN: —and you perform an act which may be in a sense neutral in other circumstances, but can be construed as aiding and furthering it—

PRESIDENT NIXON: Right, right. Well, as I told you, as far as Dean is concerned—and this is true of any of these—there is absolutely no—there's no—with Magruder because I didn't see him at all. But as far as any others, Haldeman, Ehrlichman, and so forth, . . . there is no privilege whatever except for conversations with the President. . . . And anything national security. But that's the only thing. But otherwise, you just go right to the heart of this damn thing. . . .

APRIL 25, 1973: THE PRESIDENT AND HENRY PETERSEN, 8:56–9:01 A.M., WHITE HOUSE TELEPHONE

Nixon regularly complains to Petersen about leaks from the U.S. Attorney's office. Typically, he demands lie-detector tests, but Petersen manages to stave off the President's demands.

PRESIDENT NIXON: Another thing I wanted to ask you, just for my own guidance. I noticed something in the paper this morning about these continuing leaks, you know, which I know must distress you—

PETERSEN: Yes, sir.

PRESIDENT NIXON: —(unintelligible) that made your story. And it occurred to me that the least you should do to make the record—you know, it's very easy to change the court reporters. But the least you should do is to take the three members of the prosecuting team and put them to a lie-detector test. Now, I do that with members of my staff and I'm therefore directing you do that to them. All right?

PETERSEN: Mr. President, I'd like to talk to you more about that this evening.

PRESIDENT NIXON: Do you think you know who did it?

PETERSEN: No, sir. But I'd like to talk to you more about that this evening, before we get into that.

PRESIDENT NIXON: Well, the only problem that I'm concerned about here is that, the way the leaks are coming out, I mean, it gives the impression that we really aren't getting at it. You see what I mean? I just want you to be—

PETERSEN: I understand, but I think we ought to discuss that more.

PRESIDENT NIXON: All right.

PETERSEN: I think there's terrible significance to that.

PRESIDENT NIXON: Yeah. You're afraid to do that, then, huh?

PETERSEN: I'm reluctant. I think we ought to talk about it more.

PRESIDENT NIXON: Well, the only thing is, I remember, you know, our mutual friend Edgar [Hoover] used to put his people to one. . . .

You know, I don't ask you what goes on, but I can read it in Jack Anderson's column.

PETERSEN: Well, that's right, and that's terrible. . . .

APRIL 25, 1973: HALDEMAN AND STEPHEN B. BULL, 11:06 A.M.–1:51 P.M., WHITE HOUSE TELEPHONE

Haldeman is auditing tapes of past conversations, and he orders Appointments Aide Stephen Bull, who has full knowledge of the system, to prepare some tapes for his listening.

HALDEMAN: . . . You get ahold of the guy you talked to on that stuff and pull out of the file, have him deliver to you the material [tapes] for the period from March 10th to March 23rd. You know what I'm talking about?

BULL: Yes, sir. Telephone?

HALDEMAN: The whole shot. Have them put it in a suitcase or something. I don't know what form it's in. But put it in some kind of bag so it isn't obvious, and have them bring it to you. And also, get a machine that is technically capable of listening to it. . . . The smallest and most simple such machine.

BULL: All right, fine.

HALDEMAN: We don't need stereo and living color.

BULL: I'll tell you when I have it, then.

HALDEMAN: All right, and do it as quickly as possible.

BULL: I'll do it right now.

HALDEMAN: Thank you.

APRIL 25, 1973: THE PRESIDENT AND KLEINDIENST, 3:14–3:16 P.M., WHITE HOUSE TELEPHONE

The Attorney General tells the President that the judge in the Daniel Ellsberg trial must be informed of the Plumbers' break-in of Ellsberg's psychiatrist's office. Nixon asks to see Kleindienst alone.

KLEINDIENST: . . . I've got to see you right away.

PRESIDENT NIXON: Why?

KLEINDIENST: It came to my attention this morning the implications of Dean's statement to [Earl] Silbert with respect to the Ellsberg case. I think just as a matter of law we've got to do something—

PRESIDENT NIXON: Right, fine.

KLEINDIENST: —and I've got to talk to you about it.

PRESIDENT NIXON: Fine. All right. Come right over.

KLEINDIENST: Can I come over now?

PRESIDENT NIXON: Fine.

KLEINDIENST: Do you want me to bring Peterson, or shall I come by myself?

PRESIDENT NIXON: By yourself. . . .

APRIL 25, 1973: THE PRESIDENT AND KLEINDIENST, 3:35–4:10 P.M., EXECUTIVE OFFICE BUILDING

Kleindienst reports that the Department of Justice must notify the judge in the Ellsberg case about the Plumbers' activities. "We can't have another cover-up, Mr. President," the Attorney General reports. While Nixon realizes the futility of maintaining that cover-up, he nevertheless rationalizes the break-in of Ellsberg's psychiatrist's office just as he had Watergate: it was stupid and nothing was gained, he insisted. Furthermore, he asserts that the purpose of the break-in remains a "national security" matter. The burglars, of course, were looking for derogatory material on Ellsberg. John Dean, however, is paramount in the President's mind, so much so that he tells Kleindienst that Dean had ordered the break-in of

Dr. Fielding's office. The two conclude by discussing Dean's immunity. Two more conversations follow on the telephone. The beleaguered President facetiously suggests turning his office over to Spiro Agnew.

KLEINDIENST: [Henry] Petersen came in this morning and gave me a memorandum from [Earl] Silbert to him dated April 16 . . . .

PRESIDENT NIXON: With regard to the—my directions with regard to not having national security stuff come out?

KLEINDIENST: No, no, no. That's the problem. "This is to inform you that on Sunday, April 15, 1973"—this is Silbert writing to Petersen—"I received information that on a date unspecified Gordon Liddy and Howard Hunt burglarized the offices of a psychiatrist—"

PRESIDENT NIXON: That's correct.

KLEINDIENST: "—of Daniel Ellsberg to obtain the psychiatrist's files on Ellsberg. The source of the information did not know whether the file had any material information or whether any of the information or even the fact of the burglary had been communicated to anyone associated with the prosecution."

PRESIDENT NIXON: I want to tell you, nothing was [communicated]. Go on.

KLEINDIENST: The problem we see in that, Petersen then has a notation here that he advised [Kevin T.] Maroney—Maroney is in the internal security division—and requested information as to whether or not any such information like this was in the possession of the government and used in the Ellsberg prosecution. On April 18, John L. Martin, who is in the internal security division—I guess at Maroney's request—on the subject of *U.S. v. Ellsberg,* writes Maroney: . . .

"Today I was informed by you that an allegation has been made that the office of Daniel Ellsberg's psychiatrist had been burglarized by certain defendants convicted in the Watergate case. I am familiar with all the reports, memoranda and other investigational materials in the case of U.S. versus Ellsberg, and based on my familiarity with these materials I am able to state without equivocation that I am completely unaware of any information developed in this case could have possibly emanated from such a source. Furthermore, today you and I called James Wagner, who supervises the FBI investigation in the case, and he informed us that he had absolutely no knowledge of any alleged burglary or any information which could possibly have come from such a source. I also checked with Dave Nissen"—he's the prosecutor in California—"and he advised that no information has come to his attention during the course of this case which could have emanated from such a source."

Two problems. One is a legal problem which is clearly established by court decisions. And one is a factual problem.

PRESIDENT NIXON: Yeah.

KLEINDIENST: The legal problem, under the (unintelligible) case, that if the prosecution comes into possession of information during the prosecution of a matter—

PRESIDENT NIXON: That was falsely obtained—

KLEINDIENST: Or any—

PRESIDENT NIXON: Illegally obtained.

KLEINDIENST: Illegally obtained that could in any way affect the rights of a defendant, the prosecution has to tell the judge about it, let him have an *in camera* hearing to determine whether it was (unintelligible) such information and advise the defendant and his attorneys. . . .

PRESIDENT NIXON: Let me tell you the problem with the Ellsberg case. Petersen may have told you, and I wanted to see you alone because I had—you trust Petersen and I think I do, but I'm not sure. Do you?

KLEINDIENST: Yeah, I trust him.

PRESIDENT NIXON: Fine.

KLEINDIENST: Within the limit of his—

PRESIDENT NIXON: Yeah. I told Petersen at the time that . . . you can go into anything. I don't care who the hell it hurts—Haldeman, Ehrlichman, Nixon, Kleindienst, Mitchell. . . . But you cannot go into confidential (unintelligible), and national security matters, if they are determined to be that. Right? National security matters. . . .

Now, under the circumstances, with all the leaks and everything else that is developing, the initiative was undertaken at the White House, under the proper direction, to see what the hell, whether Ellsberg is lying, leaking, or what the hell he's doing. That's what you call, or what we call, the plumber operation. Without any knowledge of anybody, these crazy fools went out and they went into the psychiatrist. They got nothing. It was a dry hole. Now, what happened there is, however, that Dean was aware of that, because Dean was the one that implemented the whole thing. When I say implemented, he carried it out.

Petersen asked me, and I told him about this, that I am not holding—Dick, you know, I'm not going to be obstructing justice here, believe me, ever. And I said that's the fact. I said—he said, [did you] do anything to communicate to the prosecution? I said absolutely nothing, from my information, because they got nothing. But, I said, the fact is there was a burglarization of the psychiatrist's office which produced, apparently, nothing that was relevant to the case. Now that was the fact without question.

KLEINDIENST: . . . If we tell them, this is going to be out in the street tomorrow or two days from now, a week, and the law clearly dictates that we have to do—it could be another Goddamn cover-up, you know.

PRESIDENT NIXON: Right.

KLEINDIENST: We can't have another cover-up, Mr. President.

PRESIDENT NIXON: I don't want any cover-ups of anything. You know that.

KLEINDIENST: Now we have two alternatives, I think—

PRESIDENT NIXON: Right.

KLEINDIENST: —both of which would be the same. Number one is that we inform just the prosecutor. And, incidentally, at this point Silbert would have to take the position that he cannot reveal the source of his information. As a result of this deal with Dean, he can't. The judge I think could tell Silbert you can do it; at the outset I think that we would have to communicate to the judge that from a source that we cannot reveal it is come to the attention of the government that the office of the psychiatrist of Ellsberg was burglarized.

PRESIDENT NIXON: Right.

KLEINDIENST: We do not have any information from it. We got none, but we do not have definitive factual information on that, that he could have an *in camera* hearing to determine, you know, the facts as to whether there was any taint in Ellsberg's trial.

PRESIDENT NIXON: Exactly.

KLEINDIENST: And let Ellsberg and his attorneys be advised of this. That's alternative number one, and the one I recommend. Alternative number two would be to instruct Nissen to dismiss the Ellsberg case. You cannot dismiss cases any more just because you want to. The judge could ask for a reason for it, at which point Nissen would then say the reason. That, to me, is an undesirable alterative, because I think a hearing on this would demonstrate, based upon everybody in the Department of Justice, that we have no such information. . . . The judge could also issue an order against the Ellsberg attorneys to make no reference publicly to such an *in camera* procedure. . . . It seems to me, Mr. President, we've got to do this this afternoon. We've got to do this before we run the risk of this getting out in the streets. . . .

PRESIDENT NIXON: What is Dean—what's he doing, pointing a gun basically at Ehrlichman?

KLEINDIENST: I don't know, sir. Since that Sunday, (unintelligible). The only reason why Petersen brought this to my attention is I'm the Attorney General in the Ellsberg case. He is the Watergate case; I am the Ellsberg case.

PRESIDENT NIXON: Let me say I want no coverup. Good God Almighty, as far as I'm concerned, we had no—we had no alternative, but to conduct the investigation, conduct our own. . . . The fact that these people, who were designated to do it, burglarized the office of a psychiatrist. Shit, it's the dumbest Goddamn thing I ever heard of. . . .

KLEINDIENST: Well, I also like to check my judgment . . . . I don't have very many friends in this town or in the world, but . . . [U.S. Circuit Court Judge Roger Robb is] my friend and counselor . . . .

PRESIDENT NIXON: Excellent man.

KLEINDIENST: He did it not as a judge. He did it as a personal friend of mine. I could not give him all the details or facts, but I gave him the substance of it, and he said there's only one course that can be pursued, and that's the one that I had arrived at independently. . . .

PRESIDENT NIXON: Liddy and Hunt have done so much, though, that I guess this is just one more thing. . . .

KLEINDIENST: It used to be under the law if the Department of Justice went into court and filed an affidavit that we have now information that could possibly be tainted, you know, the act was done but we got nothing out of it, that's the end of it. . . . .

PRESIDENT NIXON: It's gonna kill the case.

KLEINDIENST: Oh, no, I don't think so. I don't think so. . . .

PRESIDENT NIXON: The other point is that Liddy and Hunt, of course, or Dean could say he was ordered to by Ehrlichman.

KLEINDIENST: Sure. *He could say he was to by you.*

PRESIDENT NIXON: No, he won't do that, you can't (unintelligible), because I didn't tell him . . . .

KLEINDIENST: I'm not saying he could do it truthfully, Mr President . . . . Do you think he would not try to implicate you?

PRESIDENT NIXON: I think he would implicate anybody.

KLEINDIENST: You think that he would try to implicate you?

PRESIDENT NIXON: But I don't—well, let me put it this way. Dean has enough trouble. I didn't know about it. He never discussed it. I hadn't seen Dean until February. I never had a conversation.

KLEINDIENST: But the fact of the matter is you think that this young man, that's threatened to do that, would say it nonetheless?

PRESIDENT NIXON: I think any individual would do anything to save [himself]. . . .

KLEINDIENST: I've got to do this, Mr. President. . . .

PRESIDENT NIXON: I know, I know. But at the present time the problem involved is the presidency, and we all know that, Dick, decent men like yourself and Ehrlichman and Haldeman, and I thought Dean. . . . But the main thing is, Goddamnit, I was just talking to Henry [Kissinger] about SALT. Shit, we've got big things going on, and I cannot allow this office to. . . .

Dean runs in there, let's see what his motive is for telling Silbert this.

KLEINDIENST: His motive is to create an environment whereby he will get immunity.

PRESIDENT NIXON: Can it be given?

KLEINDIENST: Sure, we can give him immunity. . . . Petersen has asked me the same question, and he even comes up to the point where a trump card of Dean would be that I'm going to implicate the President, and I told Henry at that point you have to tell Dean to go fuck himself. You're not going to blackmail the government of the United States and implicate the President in the Ellsberg matter.

PRESIDENT NIXON: Christ [*laughter*], *I haven't the slightest idea about the Goddamn thing.*

KLEINDIENST: I'd say that you can't tell a dumb little kid like this . . . .

PRESIDENT NIXON: He's [Dean] not that dumb. He's clever as shit, but—

KLEINDIENST: Well, he's clever, but he's not smart.

PRESIDENT NIXON: He's not smart, you say?

KLEINDIENST: Apparently he's clever, but he's not real smart.

PRESIDENT NIXON: [*Pause.*] Dick, the only one in our shop, believe me, the only one that knows anything about this is Ehrlichman. . . . [W]hat the Christ would you learn from his [Ellsberg's] Goddamn psychiatrist? How would that affect his guilt?

KLEINDIENST: Well, he could confess to a psychiatrist. . . .

PRESIDENT NIXON: Coming back to Dean, you know, you know him better than I do, Dick. (Unintelligible), but you've always trusted him, haven't you?

KLEINDIENST: I trusted him. . . . Up until two weeks ago, I thought that he was one of the most able, fine, decent, honest, sensible young kids.

PRESIDENT NIXON: I know. All of our people around here did. They said—you know, they set Dean in charge of this *whole Goddamn thing.* Dean was in charge. I must say, in fairness to him, though, Dick, he thought he was doing what was right during the summer, because basically he was trying to protect our mutual friend, John Mitchell. You and I have got to be quite honest with each other. Dean had to know. I think Dean knows a hell of a lot more. I think Dean was involved himself. . . .

KLEINDIENST: He would have gotten himself out of it. He would have taken himself away from a position that has confidentiality with you. . . . But then, having made that mistake, Mr. President, the one thing I cannot forgive him for, no matter what the state of his conscience is, that he gets over there and talks to the U.S. Attorney in a way that impinges upon or takes advantage of his confidential relationship with you. . . .

PRESIDENT NIXON: Well, basically, as you say, I am not going to be concerned about anything I talked to him about. I think, quite frankly, that Jesus Christ, all I did was say John, write a report, get me the deal. He's never been able to do it, and I think the reason is he was involved in the subornation of perjury with Magruder. Second, he was involved in the payoffs, and he may have in the first instance thought that they were humanitarian. . . .

KLEINDIENST: And I think all of them must have felt the judgment, after those arrests, that a complete disclosure at that time would have affected the outcome of the election. . . .

PRESIDENT NIXON: . . . You know, he's [Dean] still trying to make a deal . . . . I will not be in a position of having the President of the United States blackmailed by anybody. I've been trying to get to the bottom of this thing, believe me, and I think it hurts me the most—first and foremost, I know that it's going to do John Mitchell in, and you know it too.

KLEINDIENST: Sure. He could go to jail.

PRESIDENT NIXON: Huh?

KLEINDIENST: He could go to jail.

PRESIDENT NIXON: Could he really?

KLEINDIENST: I think so. . . .

PRESIDENT NIXON: But I didn't try to protect him. I tried my best. You know, I urged Dean. I said, even in July, I said, for Christ's sakes, I said, let's get a report on it. . . . Dean assured Ziegler that the White House is not involved. But I think I see how Dean assured Ziegler of that. He was involved. He was involved, right? And then he got others involved. And what would you do with Dean at the present time? Immunity?

KLEINDIENST: No. . . . Nobody else implicates the President of the United States except John Dean, and John Dean turns out to be the very, very weak, selfish, self-directed, you know, the link in the whole operation. . . . [T]he reason why you would immunize John Dean is to get his testimony, and unless he's going to come forward to testify with respect to other people's conduct, there's no reason to immunize him. See, so you don't really gain anything. . . . Now he, according to Henry, has said if he can't work this out that he wants to talk to Henry Petersen and play his final trump card. . . . But I told [Henry]—[pause]—that at that point if it's you [the President], just tell the son of a bitch to get his fucking ass out.

PRESIDENT NIXON: Well, it's his word against the President of the United States.

KLEINDIENST: And I said the same thing about me. I said, if he says a Goddamn word about me, just tell him to get his ass out. And I said you do the same thing about yourself. You can't let a little guy like this for his very intense, deep, selfish motives—you know, blackmail, you know, people who are innocent of this Goddamn thing. He just can't do it. . . .

APRIL 25, 1973: THE PRESIDENT AND KLEINDIENST, 7:22–7:25 P.M., WHITE HOUSE TELEPHONE

PRESIDENT NIXON: . . . Well, I do think it's important to let the prosecutor know, as it's passed on that this was a national security investigation of very great sensitivity. I just—I think it's important that that be known, you know what I mean, so that he could use some restraint in terms of like trying to get—get in the sources and all that sort of thing. Understand, I'm not trying—

KLEINDIENST: I think that's a good suggestion, and I didn't really make a point of it. . . .

PRESIDENT NIXON: The point being that, look, this is a national security investigation. It involves great sensitivity, and to have it—we're just giving it for information. None of this was ever presented to the prosecution. You can give absolute assurances on that. And under the circumstances—

KLEINDIENST: I get the point.

PRESIDENT NIXON: And I think the judge should know that too. Do you get the point?

KLEINDIENST: Yes, sir.

PRESIDENT NIXON: It's very important. . . .

APRIL 25, 1973: THE PRESIDENT AND KLEINDIENST, 8:20–8:23 P.M., WHITE HOUSE TELEPHONE

PRESIDENT NIXON: Did you get your call through to [Ellsberg case prosecutor David R.] Nissen?

KLEINDIENST: Yes, I did.

PRESIDENT NIXON: Fine. What did you point out to him?

KLEINDIENST: Well, I pointed out to them, you know, the essential nature of it. What their strategy is right now is to first try to persuade the judge [Matthew Byrne] that we ought to have this as a post-trial hearing—you know, wait until the case is over, the verdict's in, and have a hearing on this. . . . .

PRESIDENT NIXON: That's good. Let me say one other thing. I don't know how you can get this to the judge, but I think it's very important for him to know that this is a national security investigation of the highest importance. It really is, you see.

KLEINDIENST: Right.

PRESIDENT NIXON: You know that and I know it.

KLEINDIENST: And that's what we would intend to do. But our primary objective, you know, is to downplay it, get the trial over, have a post-trial hearing.

PRESIDENT NIXON: Post-trial for the purpose of what?

KLEINDIENST: Well, determining whether there was any tainted evidence. . . . What we want to do is to say, Judge, here it is. No information came to the Department. Under the law, we can't make that determination. We would—we bring this to your attention. We would like the trial to go ahead and continue. If there's a verdict of acquittal, that ends it. If there's a verdict of guilty, then we'll have a post-trial hearing to determine whether there was any tainted evidence.

PRESIDENT NIXON: Now, on that point, though, the acquittal, and the rest doesn't make a hell of a lot of difference, but the main point, Dick, is I just want Nissen to know that this is a very important national security investigation, which it was. . . . Okay. Well, sleep well, boy. . . .

KLEINDIENST: Hang in there, Mr. President.

PRESIDENT NIXON: Good luck. What the hell, you know. People say impeach the President. Well, then they get Agnew. What the hell? [*Laughter.*] Is that all right?

KLEINDIENST: There's not going to be anything like that.

PRESIDENT NIXON: All right, boy. Fine. . . .

APRIL 25, 1973: THE PRESIDENT AND HENRY PETERSEN, 5:37–6:45 P.M., EXECUTIVE OFFICE BUILDING

Despite the President's hectic conversations with Kleindienst about the Ellsberg case, Dean is Nixon's primary concern, as reflected in a lengthy conversation with Petersen sandwiched between the visit and calls with the Attorney General. Nixon labors to persuade Petersen he is a disinterested party, while pumping him for information. He boldly asks Petersen for a summary statement of the case against Haldeman. Nixon realizes that he must confront the probability of removing his top aides.

PETERSEN: Now, there have been some negotiations by Dash, Sam Dash, with Dean's lawyers. And Dean's lawyers have asked Dash this question. If we decide to cooperate with you, how soon can you assemble the committee? And Dash has given them assurance that if he gets that agreement, that he could convene the committee on 14 hours' notice. . . .

PRESIDENT NIXON: The committee is trying to get Dean. . . .

PETERSEN: Dean's lawyers are trying to play the committee against us and *vice versa*. . . . Did I tell you about the documents that Gray destroyed?

PRESIDENT NIXON: Oh, yes.

PETERSEN: And I told you what those documents purport to be?

PRESIDENT NIXON: What do they purport to be?

PETERSEN: They purport to be—

PRESIDENT NIXON: About Watergate?

PETERSEN: For the fraudulent—fraudulent cables from the State Department which reflect that John Kennedy, when—when he was President—was actively involved in the murder of President—

PRESIDENT NIXON: Diem?

PETERSEN: And they're concocted out of whole cloth. Now, that comes from Dean. Gray says he never read them. He got back to his office and tore them up and put them in the waste basket.

PRESIDENT NIXON: Why does Gray—why did Gray do that? Just because—

PETERSEN: Gray said that it was just a question of trust in Ehrlichman and Haldeman and—and Dean—excuse me. . . . He came over to the office and they said these are some documents. . . . . They're politically sensitive and they ought to be destroyed here. . . . But we discussed this once before, and you indicated, God, I hope we don't have to bring that out. I share that, but Dean is using them and Dean's lawyers are using it. And I wrote to Pat Gray and I told him that he's probably going to have to deal with it before the grand jury on this issue. . . . Mr. President, the other thing—

PRESIDENT NIXON: Have you met McCord?

PETERSEN: No, sir. I haven't met any of them personally.

PRESIDENT NIXON: Hunt? Do you know him? . . . Liddy?

PETERSEN: Oh, yes.

PRESIDENT NIXON: You met him? What's he like?

PETERSEN: Well, Liddy is a very bright man, Mr. President.

PRESIDENT NIXON: Bright and crazy.

PETERSEN: He's the type of fellow if you give him a specific legal job, he comes out marvelously precise, well-written and brilliantly thought-out . . . . You give him a general problem, he comes out with all the wrong answers. . . .

PRESIDENT NIXON: . . . [I]f there was one person that had really no knowledge whatsoever about Watergate, it was I.

PETERSEN: Mr. President, I believe that. . . .

PRESIDENT NIXON: I don't think that anybody is suggesting that I had knowledge of Watergate, not even Dean. That I had knowledge of it. . . . People forget that is the time that I was—the election was the least of my concerns. My major concern was getting the war in Vietnam over. We were negotiating like a son of a bitch. They were keeping it from me, and I'm glad they did, as a matter of fact. . . .

PETERSEN: . . . We made a mistake early in this investigation—Kleindienst and I—in not coming to you directly in person. . . .

PRESIDENT NIXON: Well, in June or July I told Ehrlichman and Dean—and Dean—I said, get this damned story out. I said . . . let it out. I says, I don't know what the hell it is, but get it out. . . . But Dean I suppose at that point was probably primarily concerned about Mitchell—primarily. Maybe he was concerned somewhat about himself. I don't know. Maybe about himself. I just don't know what your judgment is. But anyway, he carried himself. He is the man that had the responsibility.

But on the other hand—on the other hand—he didn't tell me. Frankly, I didn't ask him, and he—but I had told him I didn't know who (unintelligible). It was not basically—well, I got on the case myself. And it was March 21st when I had this conversation with Dean, and to his credit because I asked him. I asked him. I said, John—I even asked him. I said, John, write a report on this thing, take it to the Cabinet, take it to the congressional leaders as to what the hell this is all about. I said, let it hang out, whatever it is. So, he came and it was that time that he made what he calls "cancer at the heart of the presidency." . . . Then he went into . . . about Kalmbach operating and items of money. . . . I didn't know who the hell was doing it. . . .

But on March the first—I mean March the 21st, that was the date that I started my personal investigation. . . . And then I went into a long conversation with Dean on it. And I was frankly (unintelligible) what in the hell this was about. Who was going to get it and so forth, the upshot of which I said, well, you can't go down that road. . . . I said, that's blackmail. I said, why does—why do you have to be concerned about Hunt? Is it because of Hunt's . . . knowledge of the Ellsberg and other matters (unintelligible) all national security because I have told you I can assure you that Hunt to my knowledge and to Dean's knowledge was engaged only in national security activity while he was at the White House. That is what we call a leak operation which he apparently was involved in and on that case, the Ellsberg thing. . . .

Well, I want you to know about that conversation because I want you to know how to deal with Dean. . . . I got this problem. I've raised the problem with you very candidly about the question of immunity. That's your decision. But, Henry, he can't make the immunity thing on the basis of blackmailing the President.

PETERSEN: I agree, Mr. President.

PRESIDENT NIXON: The President. Now, if he's blackmailing—if your purpose is to get—to get the dope on Haldeman and Ehrlichman, you get it. You understand?

PETERSEN: Yes.

PRESIDENT NIXON: But he says, look, I won't say that I talked to the President about the question of whether or not we could get this money and the President said, well, we can get the money, et cetera, et cetera. I want you to know that he was told that this is a road you can't go down, and if you don't believe me on this—understand I don't ask you to believe me any more than anybody else. I don't lie to people.

PETERSEN: Neither do I, Mr. President. You may throw me out of here sometimes for what I say, but I'll never lie, Mr. President. . . .

PRESIDENT NIXON: I just wanted you to know that because if anything comes up, if he starts anything about the fact that there's any other discussion with the President—with the President—with regard to paying off Hunt and so forth . . . . Because basically—basically you'd be frankly letting him blackmail the President and we'd be living with that the rest of our lives. I'll be damned. I'm not going to do that because I—believe me—I am not going to—I would never approve the payoff of Hunt after the fact.

PETERSEN: I'm going to have my office wired.

PRESIDENT NIXON: Huh?

PETERSEN: I'm going to have my office wired unless they absolutely refuse to come there. Then I will record conversations with them. . . . Very vital conversations. That's the only thing I can think of, and if that kind of attempt is made, then we'll have a recorded record. . . .

PRESIDENT NIXON: . . . Well, you get it done. I want you to know that we're going to get this out because the presidency has got to go ahead here, and I've got enormous problems. . . . I've got to meet with the Russians in June and [West German Chancellor Willy] Brandt next Tuesday, [French President Georges] Pompidou on May the 31st, and deal with the economy and the rest. We cannot let this stinking damned thing kill the presidency. . . .

The second thing. Can you for these eyes only give me your evaluation—your case against Haldeman? . . . [G]ive me a little sheet of paper. Would you do that for me?

PETERSEN: It's still—it's still being completed, but I can give you what we have to date, yes, sir.

PRESIDENT NIXON: I'd like you to give me your evaluation of—I understand—I'm talking about the legal evaluation. All other judgments are beyond that.

PETERSEN: I understand. . . .

PRESIDENT NIXON: I want to know what your case is. I haven't asked for that much . . . . When could you have that for me by? Today? Tomorrow? Today is Wednesday. . . .

PETERSEN: By Friday evening.

PRESIDENT NIXON: Friday evening? I don't want to rush you. . . . Do your best to give me an evaluation because I want to think about it and study about it and make the right decision at the right time. . . . Now, in the meantime, I have got the problem of Dean, Haldeman, and Ehrlichman which I think we're going to have to separate it. The way Dean has gone now—you got to separate him from the Haldeman and Ehrlichman thing . . . . My point is—well, let me put it this way. . . . Resignation, leave of absence, and so forth, all of which I can consider (unintelligible). Do you want to do that? Because I can assure you—Goddamn—if they are—if they're in this thing, they're either indicted or named as non-indictable co-conspirators, *that's it.*

PETERSEN: I understand that . . . .

PRESIDENT NIXON: As far as Haldeman and Ehrlichman are concerned, I'm not protecting them, but the process must run. . . . Now, the problem on Dean is a different problem. Here you and I are sitting on information. There is no question about Dean's guilt, is there? Is there any question on that?

PETERSEN: No (unintelligible).

PRESIDENT NIXON: In other words, he's indictable as of today. The only question is whether or not you immunize him.

PETERSEN: Well, he's indictable based on what he's told you. He's not indictable on the basis of what he's told us. . . .

APRIL 26, 1973: THE PRESIDENT AND KLEINDIENST, 12:16–12:21 P.M., WHITE HOUSE TELEPHONE

The President talks about the Plumbers and Ellsberg, complaining, as always, that J. Edgar Hoover had let him down in this case. But he fears John Dean's knowledge of the group, despite Kleindienst's insistence that Dean had no credibility. Here Nixon begins to worry about Dean's "trump card," later variously known as his "black box" or "lock box." This subject recurs throughout conversations during the next two months and, in part, explains Nixon's obsession about maintaining control over documents.

PRESIDENT NIXON: . . . I forgot to tell you, please give me a call on any development on that California thing.

KLEINDIENST: Yes, sir, I will.

PRESIDENT NIXON: On the decision, so that we'll know how to react here.

KLEINDIENST: I'll keep you posted. . . .

PRESIDENT NIXON: We've done the right thing, and these clowns get out and do such stupid Goddamn things as that, we've got to take the blame for it. You know.

KLEINDIENST: Yes. Well, I think we can obviate a lot of that in this situation, though.

PRESIDENT NIXON: How?

KLEINDIENST: Well, I think the fact that, you know, when it came to our attention—i.e., yours, mine—you know, we made an immediate disclosure.

PRESIDENT NIXON: Oh, yeah, that, of the event. But I mean the fact that it was done, you know.

KLEINDIENST: Oh.

PRESIDENT NIXON: The fact that it was done. As you know, it was not authorized. This is a case where these guys had the responsibility when they were at the White House to conduct an investigation of the Ellsberg thing due to the fact that Hoover would not. And so they go out [*chuckles*] and do this sort of thing.

KLEINDIENST: Right. Well, we've just got to live with that.

PRESIDENT NIXON: Yeah. Just say this was totally unauthorized.

KLEINDIENST: Right. . . .

PRESIDENT NIXON: Dean is basically what the problem is . . . . I mean, here's a desperate man who has misled and so forth and so on, and there's an old story: you don't strike a king unless you kill him. . . .

KLEINDIENST: I'm not worried about it, Mr. President. The only thing I don't want us to do is to encourage him in believing that he feels that we're worried.

PRESIDENT NIXON: Yes.

KLEINDIENST: Because then he could do—

PRESIDENT NIXON: Well, he says he's got his—what does he call it, a big bomb?

KLEINDIENST: Trump card.

PRESIDENT NIXON: His trump card. Well, his trump card could be anything.

KLEINDIENST: That's right.

PRESIDENT NIXON: Petersen says maybe it's him, maybe it's the Attorney General. I don't think so. I think what his trump card is, he's got all this information on Ehrlichman and maybe that the President has denied immunity to him in order to protect Ehrlichman and Haldeman. That could be a trump card.

KLEINDIENST: I don't even want to speculate about it.

PRESIDENT NIXON: Or he could say that—I suppose another thing, that, well, he informed the President on March 21st, which that's what of course triggered my whole reaction, that he informed on the fact that Hunt's people were requiring money, which was my first knowledge of it, believe me, of the whole thing. But of course, that's not going to be a damn good trump card, because that's the day I took over the investigation myself.

KLEINDIENST: That's right.

PRESIDENT NIXON: And frankly, just for your information, I relieved him of it.

KLEINDIENST: That's why we think all he has is just a blatant desperate attempt at blackmail, and he is at that point—if we deny him that, then he's going to crumble his own little house, Mr. President. . . .

PRESIDENT NIXON: He either crumbles it or he then flails out in the wildest possible way. . . .

KLEINDIENST: And it might ultimately come out to the benefit of everybody.

PRESIDENT NIXON: Why would you think that? Because—

KLEINDIENST: Well, just in terms of credibility and the whole—

PRESIDENT NIXON: Because basically he is not going to be believed, in my opinion. Or do you think he will? Can he establish believability now, after—

KLEINDIENST: No, sir. I've just tried too many lawsuits and seen too much human behavior to be worried about him.

PRESIDENT NIXON: Okay, boy. . . .

APRIL 26, 1973: THE PRESIDENT AND KLEINDIENST, 4:50–4:51 P.M., WHITE HOUSE TELEPHONE

Despite Nixon's oft-repeated contempt for Attorney General Kleindienst, the President nevertheless exploits him for information until the very end. In three phone conversations on April 26, the President discusses Dean's attempts to obtain immunity, the dealings with Ellsberg trial judge Byrne, and the need for an immediate resignation of Pat Gray. In the last conversation of the evening, Kleindienst tells Nixon that Gray has destroyed evidence. While Gray's name had been withdrawn for nomination to head the FBI, he continues to serve as Acting Director. The President urges Kleindienst to force Gray's immediate withdrawal, which comes the next day. The last part of Nixon's talk with Kleindienst includes his distortions about his relationship to John Dean.

PRESIDENT NIXON: . . . I wondered if you had anything further on the coast matter?

KLEINDIENST: I haven't received a report back.

PRESIDENT NIXON: Okay, boy.

KLEINDIENST: It's still, it's only—well, it's now 2:00 o'clock there. Would you want me to call you later on this evening?

PRESIDENT NIXON: Yes, probably. . . . All I want to know is procedure, you know. Let me say, six of one, half a dozen of the other, Dick, as far as I'm concerned. Let's get the Goddamn thing hung out there.

KLEINDIENST: Sure, and I think the thing is pretty much up to the judge anyway. . . . As soon as I get word on it, I'll call you, Mr. President. . . .

PRESIDENT NIXON: Fine. As far as you're concerned, there's two possibilities, as you have indicated, going one way or the other. I think I understand it. And I don't know the law, but you know it and I've got to depend on you for the law, boy. . . .

APRIL 26, 1973: THE PRESIDENT AND KLEINDIENST, 5:53–5:55 P.M., WHITE HOUSE TELEPHONE

PRESIDENT NIXON: . . . The other thing, Dick, I was going to call you about is, you know the situation, which I think I should talk to you about because it involves Pat Gray, involving his being given the contents of some of the contents of Hunt's safe.

KLEINDIENST: I just learned of that for the first time. . . .

PRESIDENT NIXON: That's in the *New York Times* and so forth. And Gray just destroyed it, you know. . . . Don't you feel that under the circumstances, that Gray—I mean, I don't think I'm overreacting, but—under these circumstances would really have to resign? What do you think, or how do you handle this one? You want to think about it, talk to Henry Petersen, call me back?

KLEINDIENST: I'd like to think about it overnight.

PRESIDENT NIXON: Well, the point is—well, we're not going to have him do it tonight, I guess you're right. . . . And we'll—let me say, though, that I know this is one of those things, but believe me, I want the whole damn thing out. Don't you? Tough as it is.

KLEINDIENST: It's going to come out anyway, whether we want it or not.

PRESIDENT NIXON: Well, sure, sure, it's going to come out. But Dick—

KLEINDIENST: It's a fact of life right now.

PRESIDENT NIXON: Dick, for crying out loud, Goddamn it, if these damn things happened I as President have got to get them out, you know. . . . That's my responsibility.

APRIL 26, 1973: THE PRESIDENT AND KLEINDIENST, 7:44–8:02 P.M., WHITE HOUSE TELEPHONE

KLEINDIENST: . . . Henry and I are down here at my office with Pat Gray. . . . Let me give you his version of it before we discuss the ramifications of it and I describe his attitude. Several days after the apprehension of the Watergate burglars, he was asked to come over and met in John Ehrlichman's office with him, and there was Dean. Part of the conversation was with John Dean, Ehrlichman saying nothing.

John Dean says, "Pat, here are some highly sensitive and very secret files that were in the possession of Howard Hunt that had nothing to do with the Watergate case. They are of a very, very secret, sensitive nature." He did not describe their contents. "They should not be put in the FBI files and they should never see the light of day. Here, you take them." That's the substance of it. Pat took the documents from John Dean. Then he stayed there with John Ehrlichman. Ehrlichman said nothing about the documents, and they were talking about the apprehension and concern that you had about leaks from the FBI.

Pat then left that office, went home, had a few trips to make, left them at home. When he came back on a Sunday night—I think this occurred on a Thursday or a Friday. When he came back on a Sunday night, he then took the documents down to his office without looking at them, tore them into bits, put them in his burn basket, and they were destroyed. That's Pat's story. . . .

PRESIDENT NIXON: He will not say that he was ordered to destroy them?

KLEINDIENST: No. Pressed upon cross-examination as a result of what Dean said, he said that, "I had to gather from Dean as being, you know, a representative of the President of the United States, that I had to just infer from his remarks that, since they were never to see the light of day, they were of such a highly sensitive nature, and could not be put in the FBI files," he just concluded himself he ought to destroy them. Now, that's quite a bit different, you know, than getting a specific direction.

PRESIDENT NIXON: Yes.

KLEINDIENST: I think if you know Pat as I do, you press him to the wall and Pat would say that the only fair inference that I could gain from my conversation with John Dean with Ehrlichman present was that they had to be destroyed. He would not say—

PRESIDENT NIXON: It was Dean that told him this?

KLEINDIENST: Yes, yes. But he would not say that he was specifically ordered to destroy them. . . . So now we are talking in this vein: Pat, if you testify before a grand jury, we all have to assume that that's going to go out and hit the streets. . . . So suppose that this very statement that you gave us, that you made public tomorrow. You just got the press in and said, this is what happened. What would that do with respect to your ability to look after, manage, the Federal Bureau of Investigation? He said it would be a disaster. So I said, "Pat, that's where we are logically. If it should come out—and indeed it is because of all the leaks that we have—isn't that where we are?" He feels that for him to resign is an admission of guilt of some kind.

PRESIDENT NIXON: Right.

KLEINDIENST: And I said, "Pat, as far as I can see you haven't done anything criminally wrong. But in light of all the facts and circumstances of the Watergate case—"

PRESIDENT NIXON: His ability to conduct the office.

KLEINDIENST: "It creates just an impossible situation for you to manage that Bureau." And that is where we wound up before I called you, because I told him—

PRESIDENT NIXON: Right, I understand, I understand.

KLEINDIENST: —that I wanted to—he's in the other room with Henry—to report to you what he said and the context of it. Pat Gray, as you know, is a soldier and he's going to do any Goddamn thing [you ask of him].

PRESIDENT NIXON: I know, I know.

KLEINDIENST: Henry and I . . . feel and we're trying to get across to Pat without just denuding him is he's got to resign. How do you want us to proceed tonight?

PRESIDENT NIXON: But how would we do it? He should say nothing tonight.

KLEINDIENST: Oh, I'm not talking about tonight. I'm trying to make a decision tonight.

PRESIDENT NIXON: Yeah. But in terms of the resignation—and I know Henry's always raising a problem of what about Ehrlichman in this case and I raised the problem with Dean, what about Dean? And he says—Petersen is going to—they're going to have to get Dean. You know what I mean. Dean's lawyers are still saying they're going to want immunity and all that sort of thing. . . . Can you give him immunity, Dean?

KLEINDIENST: Hell, yes. . . . But you won't, will you?

PRESIDENT NIXON: I don't want to give him immunity. . . . I never saw him [Dean] personally till—never saw him about this, and then it was about—because of the Gray confirmation thing—until February 22.

KLEINDIENST: Is that right?

PRESIDENT NIXON: Never.

KLEINDIENST: You never discussed this matter with him at all—

PRESIDENT NIXON: Never.

KLEINDIENST: —until February 22?

PRESIDENT NIXON: That's right.

KLEINDIENST: That is a very—

PRESIDENT NIXON: Or February—wait a minute. Let me just check my book here. 27th—27th.

KLEINDIENST: Of February?

PRESIDENT NIXON: 27th of February. That's right.

KLEINDIENST: You mean he was not in your office?

PRESIDENT NIXON: Never, except one time, to sign my wills.

KLEINDIENST: Is that right?

PRESIDENT NIXON: That's right. Look, that's the way we work here. You know, I mean, I put a man in charge, and that's—

KLEINDIENST: You know, to listen to this little bastard he's in there talking to you four times a day.

PRESIDENT NIXON: Oh, he has been since then. He was—

KLEINDIENST: But even last summer, you know.

PRESIDENT NIXON: Last summer, I never—well, let's get one thing straight. [*Spoken with emphasis, pausing between words*] I, the President, never saw John Dean once except for the signing of the wills. . . . And that was on August 14. August 14 I signed my wills. That's the only time I ever saw him. . . .

APRIL 26, 1973: THE PRESIDENT AND HENRY PETERSEN, 5:56–6:17 P.M., WHITE HOUSE TELEPHONE

Between calls with Kleindienst, the President speaks to Petersen, asking his opinion on dismissing Gray. The two discuss Dean again. Neither wants him to have immunity for quite different reasons: Petersen believes he must plead guilty to prove his credibility, while the President is fearful of what Dean will say if he is immunized.

PETERSEN: . . . Dean tells me, and he told me this well before, Ehrlichman had told him to destroy these documents.

PRESIDENT NIXON: Dean says that Ehrlichman told Dean to destroy them?

PETERSEN: That's right. And Dean said, "You know, Goddamn it, I wasn't going to do it."

PRESIDENT NIXON: That's the so-called "deep six" thing?

PETERSEN: That's right. And that he Dean wasn't going to do it, so they both in effect gave it to Gray.

PRESIDENT NIXON: Well, I don't know. I'm not going to try to tell anybody to change his story and so forth. That is, understand, we want the truth. But I just can't believe, I just can't believe that anybody—I can't really believe that anybody's going to believe that the Director of the FBI was handed some documents and told to destroy them. You know what I mean?

PETERSEN: Well, he's going to come out looking awfully stupid, to say the least.

PRESIDENT NIXON: My God, yes. And that he did it.

PETERSEN: That's right.

PRESIDENT NIXON: I mean, destroy them. I mean, I bet you Edgar Hoover's got every doodle that anybody ever had around . . . somewhere in his file. . . .

[Pat Gray] said he refreshed his recollection and said, yes, I did get the documents and I was told to destroy them? That's what Pat Gray now says, is that correct?

PETERSEN: Yes, sir.

PRESIDENT NIXON: Well, I don't believe that. I don't know whether—see, the point is when you say that Dean and the deep-six thing and so forth, you haven't said Ehrlichman. I mean, you haven't had that corroborated yet, because basically Ehrlichman was in the room when this happened, and Ehrlichman of course knows. I'm going to have to talk to him about this and ask him. The point, the point that I make is this. Whether or not—does Dean corroborate Gray's story? That's one thing I'd like to know. Does Dean say that in the presence of Ehrlichman that he or Ehrlichman or both told Gray, these are politically sensitive, unrelated to Watergate, and they should be destroyed? Does Dean say that? That's the whole point, you see.

PETERSEN: Generally, but I can't say . . . .

PRESIDENT NIXON: Because, hell, Dean isn't going to—well, let me put it this way—assuming he had, why the hell is he going to implicate himself in such a thing as that? He can let Gray take the rap.

PETERSEN: Of course, his story to me at the very early time before this was even a celebrated cause was that Ehrlichman told me to destroy them.

PRESIDENT NIXON: And that he didn't.

PETERSEN: But he didn't do it.

PRESIDENT NIXON: Right, right.

PETERSEN: That's when he told me, "Goddamn it, I wouldn't lie for Ehrlichman, whatever I might do for the President."

PRESIDENT NIXON: That's right, right. Right, right, right, right, right.

PETERSEN: So there is some corroboration of the destruction aspect.

PRESIDENT NIXON: I see, I see, but that was not done.

PETERSEN: That's right. At least Dean didn't do it, that's right. . . .

PRESIDENT NIXON: All right. On the Gray thing, it seems to me that Gray, that you should have your meeting with Gray immediately, the three of you. Don't have him make a statement, however, until—I don't know if he should even make one tonight. You know what I mean.

PETERSEN: Yes.

PRESIDENT NIXON: I'm not sure I would react that soon. I don't know, but at least that was Dick's feeling, that maybe we shouldn't act tonight. But under the circumstances with the destruction of the documents story, even though it was done with no venal intent, this is stupidity of an unbelievable degree.

PETERSEN: I agree.

PRESIDENT NIXON: And he'll have to resign. And who would be the best—who is the second man over there?

PETERSEN: Mark Felt's the second man at the Bureau. Let me say one thing, Mr. President. You know, I don't give a damn whether I get that job or not.

PRESIDENT NIXON: I understand.

PETERSEN: You know, I think, next to the presidency of the United States, it may be the toughest job in America. . . . I don't want to see anybody from the inside take that job. . . .

PRESIDENT NIXON: It's got to be cleaned out. But my point is, my point is, this is not the time, this is not the time. I'm not ready to name Gray's successor. I'm still searching, you know.

PETERSEN: I agree. . . .

PRESIDENT NIXON: . . . Well, finally, one thing else. What about your meeting with

Dean? Isn't it about time to get that done with and get this thing rolling? How does that stand? When are you going to meet with him? . . . I mean, you've got to decide the Dean thing. And let me just say one thing on that. The decision is yours if he comes to you, but don't be concerned about what he calls any—what do you call it— trump card or blank check and so forth. There's not going to be any blackmail here.

PETERSEN: Okay.

PRESIDENT NIXON: Don't you agree?

PETERSEN: My problem is wholly one of proof, Mr. President.

PRESIDENT NIXON: What's that?

PETERSEN: My problem is wholly one of proof. I've got Magruder, he's an affected man, he's ready to plead.

PRESIDENT NIXON: Right.

PETERSEN: That means I've got Magruder head to head against Dean.

PRESIDENT NIXON: Right.

PETERSEN: You know, until I can get—

PRESIDENT NIXON: Magruder's and Dean's stories vary, do they?

PETERSEN: No. But if I have to use Magruder against Dean, that's basically all I have, if Dean insists on going to trial. So I mean, we're trying to bring Dean around to the point where he'll plead [guilty].

PRESIDENT NIXON: You want Dean to plead.

PETERSEN: Then when I've got the two of them pleading, then—

PRESIDENT NIXON: Then you've got a case.

PETERSEN: Then I've got the case against the other principals.

PRESIDENT NIXON: That's right.

PETERSEN: Never mind Ehrlichman and Haldeman. We're still short on them.

PRESIDENT NIXON: I know you are, you're still short on both of them.

PETERSEN: That's right.

PRESIDENT NIXON: But you've got to get—but the point—I understand and I'm not trying to tell you how to run the case. The only thing I'm trying to see is how I can still sit here with—I mean, I'm wrestling with the Ehrlichman and Haldeman problem naturally, as you suggest. But I also have to wrestle with the Dean problem, because I'm aware of information, as you are, of these, I agree, arm's length conversations. . . . [L]et me put out that Dean now has about as much, I'm afraid, in view of what has happened here, he has got about as much credibility as Magruder, that much. . . .

PETERSEN: That's one of the reasons we'd like him to plead.

PRESIDENT NIXON: That's right. You'd like him to plead, okay. . . .

APRIL 27, 1973: THE PRESIDENT AND KLEINDIENST, 4:14–4:16 P.M., WHITE HOUSE TELEPHONE

Gray resigns from the FBI on April 27 following the disclosures of his destruction of documents. Kleindienst proposes that Mark Felt take over as Acting Director of the FBI, but Nixon overrules him, distrusting Felt and insisting that he has the power to appoint an FBI Director personally loyal to himself.

KLEINDIENST: . . . In view of Pat's resignation, Mr. President, it would be my recommendation that I just administratively permit Mark Felt, who—

PRESIDENT NIXON: No, I tell you. I don't want him. I can't have him. I just talked to Bill Ruckelshaus and Bill is a Mr. Clean and I want a fellow in there that is not part of the old guard and that is not part of that infighting in there.

KLEINDIENST: Will Ruckelshaus do it?

PRESIDENT NIXON: He'll do it as acting director until we get a full director. See, I'm making a search, as you know, and he says he'll take it for that long. Don't you think that's a good thing?

KLEINDIENST: Ideal.

PRESIDENT NIXON: Now, his only problem is, he says what the hell am I going to say? He says, I knew Mitchell. But, I says, hell, everybody knows Mitchell. I mean, he hasn't worked there since 1970. . . . And he was there never during the campaign. But don't you think Bill would be a good one?

KLEINDIENST: Ideal.

PRESIDENT NIXON: Ideal. And I'm going to name him Acting Director of the Bureau, and I'm going to have it announced from over here. Is that all right?

KLEINDIENST: Sure. But, Mr. President—

PRESIDENT NIXON: Yeah.

KLEINDIENST: Under the rules and regulations and the law, it's an appointment that I administratively have to make.

PRESIDENT NIXON: Oh.

KLEINDIENST: So I think your announcement should be that you have directed me to designate him.

PRESIDENT NIXON: So under the rules and regulations of the law, it's an appointment that the Attorney General has to make. Is that right? . . . I make the announcement that I have directed the Attorney General to make him the Acting Director until a successor [is named].

APRIL 27, 1973: THE PRESIDENT AND HENRY PETERSEN, 4:31–4:35 P.M., WHITE HOUSE TELEPHONE

Petersen warns the President that Judge Matthew Byrne, presiding over the Ellsberg trial, will expose the role of the Plumbers. Petersen tells Nixon that "everybody should go"—meaning Haldeman and Ehrlichman, as well as Dean. While Nixon recognized before that his closest aides would have to leave, Petersen's words precipitated prompt action.

PETERSEN: . . . I just wanted to call you and give you a report on that—on the Ellsberg case.

PRESIDENT NIXON: Yes.

PETERSEN: Judge Byrne had opened it up last night and was inclined to the view that disclosure to him was sufficient.

PRESIDENT NIXON: Yeah.

PETERSEN: And then apparently overnight he changed his opinion.

PRESIDENT NIXON: Right.

PETERSEN: And read the memorandum from Silbert to me in open court, indicated that the defendants were entitled to a hearing on it, requested disclosure of the source, which I've authorized, and asked for all the information the government has. We don't have anything.

PRESIDENT NIXON: No. I mean, there was no material, was there?

PETERSEN: Well, that's right.

PRESIDENT NIXON: As far as we know. . . .

PETERSEN: [W]e're going to have the Bureau interview Dean. . . . And Ehrlichman to see if they know anything about it. . . . And in fact we just gave the—see if we can locate the psychiatrist, Ellsberg's psychiatrist, to see whether or not there was a report of a burglary and what have you.

PRESIDENT NIXON: Yeah, right, right, right.

PETERSEN: And do the best we can.

PRESIDENT NIXON: Right, right. Thank God you didn't get anything—you never knew of anything he ever got. . . .

PETERSEN: Mr. President, you asked me for something.

PRESIDENT NIXON: Yeah, a piece of paper, if I could get it.

PETERSEN: I don't think I can produce. I'll tell you why. Most of the information— almost everything they have—

PRESIDENT NIXON: Is not corroborated. Yeah.

PETERSEN: Except that which I've already given you in writing. . . . It's all grand jury.

PRESIDENT NIXON: I see. I get it. I get it. Well, I can't have it, then. That's right. That's right. Well, under the circumstances, then, we'll just have to leave me in a spot where I've just got to, you know, look at matters. You see, the problem I have, I'm trying to get my own investigation, and yet I don't want the grand jury stuff. That's for darn sure.

PETERSEN: That's right. And that's what—you know, it's a direct conflict. . . .

PRESIDENT NIXON: Yeah. Now, where does the Dean thing stand? . . .

PETERSEN: Our negotiations with him are, you know, just no place. We're not getting any further. I have to say at this point, Mr. President, that you cannot jeopardize our position with Dean by anything you might do now.

PRESIDENT NIXON: Mm-hmm.

PETERSEN: There's no basis for me to ask you to withhold any longer so far as he's concerned.

PRESIDENT NIXON: Mm-hmm. I see. Well, I just don't know what to do on that one, do we?

PETERSEN: No, sir.

PRESIDENT NIXON: Because he's in effect saying that he goes provided the other guys go and so forth. And that isn't the proper way to do—I mean, nobody can tell me that. You know what I mean? I can—the others can say well, they'll go if he goes. [*Laughter.*] . . .

PETERSEN: . . . You know, I think the longer you wait, the worse it gets.

PRESIDENT NIXON: Right, right. All right. . . .

APRIL 27, 1973, THE PRESIDENT AND ZIEGLER, 8:22–9:24 P.M., EXECUTIVE OFFICE BUILDING

Press Secretary Ziegler assumes greater importance as a confidant now that his mentor, Haldeman, is on the way out. The President speaks of the "presidency" as if it were separate from his own doings; at the same time, of course, he blurs any distinction between the abstraction of the institution and his own interests. The two men consider the unthinkable—impeachment; and they also talk about Haldeman and Ehrlichman's resistance to resigning. Ziegler and Nixon rehearse lines from the President's forthcoming speech.

SEGMENT 1

PRESIDENT NIXON: . . . I can't have a new attorney general right in the middle of this Goddamn thing. We—you see then that I—then that gives me the time to appoint a new Attorney General. I don't think I'll have a chief of staff. I may just decide to do it myself. . . .

I can do quite a job of that Goddamn press, I hate to do it, but I will. I have to. But tell me this, in spite of all their vindictiveness and so forth, they—the press still wants the President to come out all right? I mean—I mean my—except for [television commentator Martin] Agronsky and a few others, they don't call for impeachment so far. I heard on the Agronsky show they had—

ZIEGLER: They didn't call for impeachment. They referred to it, you know, the wording.

PRESIDENT NIXON: Christ, impeach the President on John Dean—John Dean's word. [*Pause.*] I wonder what documentary stuff Dean's talking about. He claims he's got some documentary stuff. You know, it must be some Goddamn memos from that fucking Colson. What do you think? . . .

ZIEGLER: *John Dean against the presidency of the United States,* the President's counsel has lied to him? The President counsel misled him? The President's counsel distorted something, is willing to make a charge against the President of the United States and sticks it to him?

PRESIDENT NIXON: Who didn't tell him tell until March 21st.

ZIEGLER: That's right.

PRESIDENT NIXON: You were all going to write a Dean report. And he doesn't start—(unintelligible) and before March 21st, and then to his credit. He came in, there, there's a cancer in the heart of the White House, on the heart of the presidency. [Dog barks] King! He says—I give him credit. But he was really, then after that is when he went to Camp David and decided he better save his own ass.

ZIEGLER: I understand that too.

PRESIDENT NIXON: But he did say that. . . . Goddamn, get off of me! [*To the dog.*] . . .

SEGMENT 2

PRESIDENT NIXON: . . . But they can't want frankly to see Agnew be President.

ZIEGLER: That's right.

PRESIDENT NIXON: No, really. You know—well, I don't think of impeachment, good God Almighty, the point is they've got to want this country to succeed. The whole hopes of the whole Goddamn world of peace, Ron, you know, where they rest, they rest right here in this damn chair. . . . Dean was magic. You've got to give him credit. We all said he did a helluva good job, right? Didn't we?

ZIEGLER: Yes.

PRESIDENT NIXON: But I guess his job—what happened there? He went—you can't blame him. I mean the payments to the defendants. The rest, I guess he thought that was his job, too. Then he really got involved with Mitchell, wasn't that it?

ZIEGLER: Yes, sir.

PRESIDENT NIXON: Mitchell was the guy they were protecting, not the White House.

ZIEGLER: That's right. . . .

PRESIDENT NIXON: . . . [T]he press has got to realize that. . . whatever they think of me, they've got to realize I'm the only one at the present time in this whole wide blinking world that can do a Goddamn thing, you know. Keep it [the world] from blowing up. . . .

ZIEGLER: Yes, sir. . . .

PRESIDENT NIXON: [*The President complains that Haldeman and Ehrlichman are reluctant to leave.*] . . . I tried to be subtle, and I tried to be kind and I tried it other ways. I think John [Ehrlichman] tottled him off on some of those lines. What the Christ happened here? Bob usually has such good judgment. What the hell happened? . . .

ZIEGLER: Well, [he] lost perspective of the presidency, not because he was thinking too much of himself.

PRESIDENT NIXON: But Ehrlichman said this is going to hurt you if I get out, and I gave him the arguments of, look, you fellows can't do your job. And Bob made the point to me today, he said look, half of me is worth one of anybody else, and he is exactly right.

ZIEGLER: But that isn't the point.

PRESIDENT NIXON: Half of him is damaged goods. That's what he doesn't realize, you see, he's damaged goods. Right?

ZIEGLER: That's right.

PRESIDENT NIXON: You can't have damaged goods in the White House. You can't have them in the White House.

ZIEGLER: That's right.

PRESIDENT NIXON: No way, that's what neither of us realized. He's a bright individual, but the presidency is the only way to go, I agree on that. . . .

SEGMENT 5

PRESIDENT NIXON: In other words, we're trying to contain the Goddamn thing, because we've got to remember this is a continuing battle. Look, if we went in sackcloth and ashes and fired the whole White House staff, [Speechwriter Raymond] Price must realize that isn't going to satisfy these Goddamn cannibals. They'd still be after us. Who are they after? Hell, they're not after Haldeman or Ehrlichman or Dean;

they're after me, the President. They hate my guts. That's what they're after. You don't agree? . . . .

My point is, though, Ron, that at this point, just moving all-out at an earlier date would not have solved the problem. Now at this point you've got to move on it on stages. We've done one stage, and now we hit this stage. And now we have the opportunity now to get a chance to talk with a few people and be able to move on it—plus an Attorney General, new FBI Director. . . . You can tell [Pat] Buchanan and you can tell Ray [Price] that the President's already—give him my [speech] outline. . . . And you can tell them I want it ready by—what time did I say— seven o'clock?

ZIEGLER: Seven o'clock. He'll come up [to Camp David] tomorrow night, then. I'll come up with him, if you like.

PRESIDENT NIXON: You come up too. . . . Tell him make it *strong,* not cross, not apologetic. Just say this is the fact. I assume the responsibility. Be a president and not a peon. You tell him that. Goddamnit, Price does not usually understand this. He nor- mally—you know, sometime he doesn't, but he thinks that you've got to be in sack- cloth and ashes.

ZIEGLER: I told him that, there has to be a very firm tone about that. . . .

PRESIDENT NIXON: Well, Goddamn, Price is . . . is totally wrong. You can't do that. The President can't come before the country and say, look, I made a horrible mistake and please forgive me, my friends. . . . You realize that if the President comes in and apologizes, and I'm very sorry—Kennedy didn't do that in the Bay of Pigs. He says I take responsibility, da, da, da, and I ask for your support. . . .

There'll be more tomorrow, Sunday stories. . . . We aren't going to take this crap. I mean it. They're not going to attack the President. They can attack the President's men, but they must not attack the President. . . . [*New York Times* writer Seymour] Hersh, you can't talk to him?

ZIEGLER: Well, no. The people to hit on is Clifton Daniel, Scotty [James] Reston. I mean, he'll cry, but if you go to Scotty Reston, [and tell him he] can't run a story like this in the *New York Times* . . . on . . . speculation about the President of the United States. You have an obligation as a major newspaper to journalism and so forth. . . .

PRESIDENT NIXON: . . . Let's build up the speech. I'll have a hell of an audience for that speech. . . .

ZIEGLER: Yes, sir. People trust the President, they respect the President. The pres- idency at this moment is not involved. . . . The presidency's not involved in politics now. The presidency's not involved in a battle to prove whether or not they were right or wrong in doing this or that. The presidency right now is involved in the ending of an era of the greatest achievement in a generation, the achievement of peace.

PRESIDENT NIXON: I know.

ZIEGLER: And of concluding in the next few years in a spark of statesmanship and accomplishment, what you've already done the last few—

PRESIDENT NIXON: That's a line, incidentally, that I think would be a great conclu- sion, if he says I have often thought of the legacy I would like to leave. . . . The great- est [legacy] is peace, and I will work for that until my dying day. Another is, you know, justice . . . . But also, above everything else is integrity. You must believe in the President. You must not lose confidence in the White House. There must be no white-washing going on.

That's what I have in my head, that that's the reason I have taken personal responsibility for this investigation and personal responsibility for everything that has happened. And we will do everything necessary to investigate this and to restore, you know, respect and so forth and so on.

ZIEGLER: Respect for the presidency.

PRESIDENT NIXON: Yeah. Okay, good.

APRIL 28, 1973: THE PRESIDENT AND ZIEGLER, 8:21–8:41 A.M., CAMP DAVID TELEPHONE

The President prepares to cut loose Haldeman and Ehrlichman, but the moment is excruciatingly painful. He is reluctant to face the two men. Press Secretary Ronald Ziegler effortlessly moves into the growing vacuum. He had been Haldeman's protégé, but he instinctively offers complete loyalty to the President. For his part, Nixon kindly bolsters Ziegler's spirits. But Ziegler is not privy to Nixon's shadow world as Haldeman and Ehrlichman had been. Now, with more revelations, and the White House appearing increasingly vulnerable, Nixon believes that without the cover-up things would have been worse. He knew that, as he put it: "there's a helluva lot of other crap going to hit."

SEGMENT 1

PRESIDENT NIXON: That's quite a collection of headlines this morning, isn't it? . . . The Gray, the Gray headline. And then of course the Ellsberg thing broke. And then, God, they got poor Ehrlichman on that Vesco thing. He's got a hell of a good defense, but they don't play the defense much, do they? . . .

ZIEGLER: The Ruckelshaus appointment seems to be received well.

PRESIDENT NIXON: I hope your morale isn't down, Ron.

ZIEGLER: No, sir, mine's not.

PRESIDENT NIXON: Huh?

ZIEGLER: I don't mean to sound that way, I hope.

PRESIDENT NIXON: Right. No, no, no. I didn't mean you did, but I just want you to know. What the hell, we've just begun to fight, haven't we? . . . The way I feel now is that it's almost as well. You know, it's a funny thing about timing, funny thing about timing. You know, if we had had this move earlier and all this shit had broken it would have been awful bad. . . . You get my point? . . . You've got to let the other side play their hand a little bit and then crack, you know what I mean. I mean, you can't—it's a mix, because it appears that maybe the President knew and didn't do something or they waited. But on the other hand, we might have made a sort of a bland statement when, after all, there's a helluva lot of other crap going to hit, you know.

ZIEGLER: That's right.

PRESIDENT NIXON: And that's that. But anyway, that's that. But you know, this is the time for strong men, Ron. . . . Don't you get panicky, you know, and so forth. And our day is going to come. . . . Because we're going to clean a lot of things up. I notice an interesting comment by Liddy, I mean Hunt, in this paper this morning, to the effect that he will not, unless he is given immunity, won't testify. What's that line, to show that maybe we're covering up if we don't give him immunity. Well, that's not my decision. That's the decision of the U.S. Attorney, and I've told him he can do it—I mean, the Deputy Attorney General. I've told him he can do what he Goddamn pleases.

ZIEGLER: That's right. The way you've looked at this thing, Mr. President, this thing we discussed, is all of these guys now who are trying to throw these threats out, the presidency of the United States doesn't have to put up with that.

PRESIDENT NIXON: We're not going to. . . . If the immunity thing comes up, you say: The President has stated a view. He has expressly told Mr. Petersen that the decision, however, is one that must be made by the chief Justice Department official, and he can make any decision that will get to the bottom. That's all I want. The President wants to get to the bottom of this. I'd keep hammering the fact that I am determined that the chips fall where they may, that I am going to root this out, root it out root and branch, or whatever it is.

ZIEGLER: Right.

PRESIDENT NIXON: I was rather sorry to see Billy Graham join in the chorus of saying do something, you know. I was really surprised to see him say that.

ZIEGLER: Without their calling, I was too.

PRESIDENT NIXON: Because he had indicated to the contrary. Not that he wasn't concerned, but to the contrary about his views about it. But I suppose that's just a straw in the wind. He's probably jumping ship, don't you think?

ZIEGLER: Oh, I don't know that he's jumping ship. It's hard to see what context he put it in. I'm sure he's still very much there.

PRESIDENT NIXON: Yeah, but he just feels that this is the only thing to do. Right now, though, when you talk about a special team to prosecute and so forth, God, it's too late. The grand jury's too far along the line and they're going to indict. And when they indict, that's going to answer an awful lot of questions. My view is that people are going to be really surprised to see a former Attorney General, among others, get the axe. What do you think?

ZIEGLER: Well, the scope of it, sure. . . .

PRESIDENT NIXON: They get Magruder and LaRue. Now, the point is if they don't indict Haldeman and Ehrlichman, I suppose they'll say, well, they're covering them up. We'll see, we'll see, we'll see. . . .

SEGMENT 2

ZIEGLER: Are Bob and John coming up today?

PRESIDENT NIXON: That's what they tell me. That's what they tell me. You know, I don't know, I don't know. As you know, this is going to be a painful session. God, I don't—do you see—Jesus. Do you see anything, now that they, with all of this, that they really should hang on? What's your feeling on that?

ZIEGLER: My feeling is the same, Mr. President.

PRESIDENT NIXON: That they better move now or the time will be gone?

ZIEGLER: Yes, sir.

PRESIDENT NIXON: Move on the high ground? Hmm?

ZIEGLER: Yes, sir, I think so absolutely. It seems it must be done. The alternative, of course, would be to—

PRESIDENT NIXON: Say we'll wait until the grand jury.

ZIEGLER: We'll wait for the grand jury, and then hang and stand and battle it out on that basis. But that is—

PRESIDENT NIXON: That's right.

ZIEGLER: —that's a battle you enter into knowing you're going to lose. It's a battle—

PRESIDENT NIXON: A battle you're going to lose because it's a question of the President getting at least one head ahead of the power curve.

ZIEGLER: That's right.

PRESIDENT NIXON: One step ahead of the power curve. . . .

ZIEGLER: And the battle, as I was saying, that can be won is the battle from the standpoint of moving ahead with the major weapon, doing the job of government, the job of the administration.

PRESIDENT NIXON: Yes.

ZIEGLER: That can be won.

PRESIDENT NIXON: That'll be after, after. That's true. We've got a lot of big things left to be done. Truman didn't. But the point is that can only be done after we do the cleaning up on this Goddamn thing. We can't start that really, Ron, until after the grand jury indicts. Don't you agree?

ZIEGLER: Well, that's true, right, which is fairly close.

PRESIDENT NIXON: Yes, two or three weeks away, I guess, three weeks perhaps, depending upon Dean. Dean is the key to the whole thing, and [Paul] O'Brien to a certain extent, because he can talk about the payoff business. Ron, let me ask you a question. I'm trying to think of what the hell this fellow Dean talks about that he's got, does he say "documentary"? Or no. What was the kind of proof he's supposed to have?

ZIEGLER: Substantiating.

PRESIDENT NIXON: Written evidence, yeah, yeah, yeah, yeah. . . . The main thing, let me say, all the crew, you know, they're all sort of worried and everything.

ZIEGLER: Right. . . .

PRESIDENT NIXON: . . . Quite remarkable, you know, even in a place like Meridian [Mississippi], that we'd get quite a reception like this, with all the shit that's breaking. How do you figure that out?

ZIEGLER: Well, I don't think—

PRESIDENT NIXON: I don't know what the hell it is. Well, of course, Meridian is out of the way and they're all more interested in POWs and love of country and all the rest, and they don't—they think that this is political shit.

ZIEGLER: I think the story on Meridian, I think that the significance of Meridian, is the fact that the American people, as reflected in Meridian yesterday, had respect for the presidency, they want to see the presidency succeed, and they have respect for a firm, strong presidency. I mean, that's what they had to—

PRESIDENT NIXON: But that's why this [forthcoming] speech is very important. . . .

ZIEGLER: And that's what we're fighting against here. We're not trying to—well, let me put it this way. It has not permeated the country yet, but it will.

PRESIDENT NIXON: Yes, yes. Well, some, but it's going to permeate it more, Ron. Sure, sure, sure. It did with Truman, it will with us. But the point is, everything it permeates, these days even more than in those days—I mean, yesterday's story is very old news because television, television. . . . Well, looking back to Truman, they lost confidence in him totally toward the end, you know, the old man, although he was able to name Stevenson [for the 1952 presidential nomination] even then. . . .

ZIEGLER: What was Truman doing? Nothing.

PRESIDENT NIXON: That's right, that's right. That's right, he had already finished the Marshall Plan and the Greek-Turkish loan, and he was in the Korean War. . . . So he was in a hell of a spot. We've got economic problems, but those problems are at their worst now and will probably get better, despite the stock market and everything.

Well, old boy just wanted to cheer you up a little.

ZIEGLER: Well, thank you, Mr. President.

APRIL 28, 1973, THE PRESIDENT AND HALDEMAN, 8:43–9:01 A.M., CAMP DAVID TELEPHONE

Haldeman and Ehrlichman's downfall proceeds with astonishing speed; nevertheless, their dismissal is difficult for Nixon for it provides an impression of wrongdoing as close to the President as possible. The President is determined that his aides come to Camp David to submit their resignations, but Haldeman manages to defer the visit one more day. He assures Nixon that other aides have no copies of the President's personal memos to Haldeman. The President considers William Rogers for Attorney General, but is hesitant to ask him until he is certain that Haldeman and Ehrlichman will resign.

SEGMENT 1

PRESIDENT NIXON: . . . I was wondering what time you and John could be up here?

HALDEMAN: Well, I haven't talked with John yet this morning. We're both trying to finish up our—

PRESIDENT NIXON: Statements.

HALDEMAN: —written things. Then we've got our lawyers are standing by to go over the stuff with us, and then we can get up as soon as we do that. Let me raise the point of today versus tomorrow again. You feel strongly that today is better?

PRESIDENT NIXON: Yes. I do for a reason. Bob, the most important thing that I have got to do is to make that speech, and I've got to get this—well, no. I guess if we make the decision today that doesn't make a helluva lot of difference. I've got to work on it and write it.

HALDEMAN: Well, I assume that decision's made.

PRESIDENT NIXON: (unintelligible) get it made, all right.

HALDEMAN: The question—and we got into this in some discussion last night—

was that the concern of writing—it again gets to this Dean question, which really does bother—

PRESIDENT NIXON: Yeah, I know.

HALDEMAN: —the legal guys.

PRESIDENT NIXON: I know.

HALDEMAN: That if we go today and ride through the 48-hour period—

PRESIDENT NIXON: Yes, it looks like—

HALDEMAN: —with Dean sitting here and us out—

PRESIDENT NIXON: Yes, that's problem.

HALDEMAN: —we've got a problem. But if we go tomorrow—

PRESIDENT NIXON: Then we just move on him right away.

HALDEMAN: —and then move on Monday with Dean, it looks like a logical sequence and it moves right into your speech on Monday night.

PRESIDENT NIXON: Right. Tomorrow's fine, John—Bob. Tomorrow's fine. . . . I'm not going to damn anybody. You know what I mean? I'm not going to mention or fail to damn, because if I mention I've got to then get into other things. No, the talk's going to be more—I've done a lot of thinking about it.

HALDEMAN: It's got to be broader than just specifics.

PRESIDENT NIXON: That's right, that's right. It's going to be a pretty good talk, Bob. . . . And the other thing, you know. We knew it was there, but we didn't know that it was going to come out. And it's best to hit after they have blown a lot of their wad, you know what I mean.

HALDEMAN: Sure.

PRESIDENT NIXON: And then crack it. See my point?

HALDEMAN: Yes.

PRESIDENT NIXON: The timing situation. That's what we did with the fund [from 1952, that is, the "Checkers" speech], you know. I kept waiting and waiting and then finally hit. So I want you to know that I feel that our timing is probably about right, about right.

HALDEMAN: I think so, too. . . .

SEGMENT 2

PRESIDENT NIXON: . . . On Dean, I've been doing some thinking about it. I'll tell you what it is. I've got a very tough plan for him. I mean, it will be handled properly, you know what I mean. I'm not going to—the way we've thought it through, it's going to be very peremptory. . . . I'm not going to see him. I'm not going to have—he can't come dicker with me. I've got it all worked out in my mind, the fact that when I have Garment see him I'll say the U.S. Attorney has said that I should not talk to anybody who is—I mean, I should not talk to him because he's discussing, he's negotiating with them and that he, the U.S. Attorney—I mean, the Assistant Attorney General, is the only one who can make any decision, and I've told him the decision is his and that he is to make his own mind up based on getting at the truth. I'm just leaving it right there with him. And they're not about to give him immunity. It's interesting, there was a story in the paper this morning indicating if he didn't get immunity he wasn't going to talk. You know, that's sort of a two-way sword.

HALDEMAN: Yes.

PRESIDENT NIXON: I suppose he's [Hunt] trying to say, well, if he doesn't get immunity we're covering him up—covering up for others, right?

HALDEMAN: Could be. . . .

PRESIDENT NIXON: That's all right. I don't think the public—but the public doesn't give a shit about that. . . .

Here I think maybe you're going Monday—I mean Sunday, Sunday.

HALDEMAN: Uh-hmm.

PRESIDENT NIXON: And I'll just have—

HALDEMAN: It looks like it sets the events in motion.

PRESIDENT NIXON: Yeah, it sets them in motion. And I'm going to have Garment go in and tell Garment he's going to get a lot of threats and he's to say: Fine, that's all right, John [Dean]; go out and do what you want. Here it is. The President is—

HALDEMAN: I'm not so sure he will get all the threats on this one.

PRESIDENT NIXON: What's that?

HALDEMAN: I think if John and I are on leave that Dean isn't going to resist it.

PRESIDENT NIXON: Really?

HALDEMAN: I don't think so. I don't think—I think he'll hope that he doesn't—you know—

PRESIDENT NIXON: Your move's going to surprise the hell out of him.

HALDEMAN: It'll surprise him, and then you've got a question of which way he'll go. He might be smart enough to move to request a leave himself.

PRESIDENT NIXON: Well, he doesn't have much time.

HALDEMAN: That's right.

PRESIDENT NIXON: You'll have Sunday night, and then there's that. But he may request a meeting with me and I'll say nope. Garment can go in and deliver the notes. I'll just have the note prepared.

HALDEMAN: Yeah.

PRESIDENT NIXON: And that's a brilliant idea. I'm going to do him [Dean] in a way that's at arm's length, arm's length—no more talks.

HALDEMAN: You need that for your own record.

PRESIDENT NIXON: I sure do.

HALDEMAN: Depending on how things bounce. But you need to do it, and it seems to me this comes pretty close in a way that doesn't antagonize him any more than you have to. And you've laid a groundwork by our going.

PRESIDENT NIXON: A small thing, but it's interesting that neither the *Post* nor the *Times* ran that story that they were bouncing around there. They said that Dean's—that they learned from the U.S. Attorney that Dean's lawyer or Dean had implicated the President or something like that. They didn't run it. I wonder why?

HALDEMAN: I don't know. I wonder if they really have it or if that's something they're just lobbing out. I still have the feeling they're throwing a lot of stuff around now to see how it bounces. . . .

PRESIDENT NIXON: . . . I wanted to ask you a question. You know, I mark things in news summaries now and then, you know, to do this, Good God, check on this, what the hell's this guy doing, and so forth and so on.

HALDEMAN: Yeah.

PRESIDENT NIXON: It was not your practice to just make multiliths of those and send them to fellows like Dean and so forth? They don't have the verbatims of that stuff, do they?

HALDEMAN: No. They have—what they have is a memo from the staff secretary saying it's been requested that you check such and such.

PRESIDENT NIXON: Does it indicate the President has requested?

HALDEMAN: No.

PRESIDENT NIXON: Good. That's fine.

HALDEMAN: And it doesn't ask for a report back to the President. It says: Please report back to the staff secretary on your actions, or something, by April 15th.

PRESIDENT NIXON: Good, good. Well, that's perfectly all right.

HALDEMAN: And then the originals of those go into your file. . . . That was standard procedure.

PRESIDENT NIXON: Could I suggest, then—could I suggest, then, that you—first, as far as the decision, can I just, just in terms of my writing, which is terribly important—I've just got to go forward. Can I assume that the decision is made?

HALDEMAN: Yes.

PRESIDENT NIXON: I mean, you and John have made the decision, right?

HALDEMAN: Yes.

PRESIDENT NIXON: Second, can I—you would not want to come up until tomorrow, then?

HALDEMAN: Yeah.

PRESIDENT NIXON: You would come up tomorrow, is that right?

HALDEMAN: At least that was the strong feeling last night.

PRESIDENT NIXON: Right, right.

HALDEMAN: And I think that—

PRESIDENT NIXON: Now, if there's any reversal on the decision I need to know.

HALDEMAN: Right.

PRESIDENT NIXON: Well, no. I'll tell you what. I was talking to [William] Rogers today, that's the point. But I don't want to talk to him unless—you know, and then have any reversal or anything of that on this decision.

HALDEMAN: Yeah.

PRESIDENT NIXON: Well, let me put it this way. Let's just say it's made. Shall we do that?

HALDEMAN: Yes.

PRESIDENT NIXON: Fine, on this basis. And can we have that understanding now?

HALDEMAN: Yes, sir.

PRESIDENT NIXON: Fine. So I could talk to Rogers [about becoming Attorney General or maybe Chief of Staff], fine, see what he had in mind, what he wants to do. What I had in mind, frankly, with him—I don't know. I have the feeling that if we could get him to move, Goddamn, that would have a damn good effect, wouldn't it?

HALDEMAN: I think so.

PRESIDENT NIXON: Yeah.

HALDEMAN: I think it really would. I think you can really mountaintop him on it and he'll buy it: You know, there is a crisis here of enormous proportions and this is the way for him to finish his service to the Nation now, is by moving in and cleaning this up; and he's the one man of impeccable authority in whom you have total confidence.

PRESIDENT NIXON: That's right.

HALDEMAN: That can do it.

PRESIDENT NIXON: And he has a free hand.

HALDEMAN: In all the world.

PRESIDENT NIXON: A free hand in doing the FBI, following up on—if he needs a special prosecutor, he gets him.

HALDEMAN: That's right. . . . I think it would just be a master stroke, enormously good around the country. . . .

PRESIDENT NIXON: Remember, the decision is made and I'm going to write on that assumption.

HALDEMAN: Okay.

APRIL 28, 1973: THE PRESIDENT AND WILLIAM ROGERS, 9:02–9:07 A.M., CAMP DAVID TELEPHONE

Nixon and Secretary of State William Rogers had been close allies in the Eisenhower years, when Rogers served in a variety of posts, including Attorney General. While Nixon relies mostly on Kissinger for foreign policy matters, Rogers remains an important confidant. Nixon values his advice.

SEGMENT 1

PRESIDENT NIXON: Well, I don't want you to get all ready to throw in the sponge because of the gaggle of headlines this morning. These are inevitable things, you know, that were going to happen.

ROGERS: Yeah.

PRESIDENT NIXON: That Gray thing, you remember I told you about that.

ROGERS: Yeah.

PRESIDENT NIXON: It's one of those things. But I wanted you to—I was wondering if—if you might have time to drop up and we could have a little talk.

ROGERS: Sure, I can do it. . . .

PRESIDENT NIXON: I wanted to tell you, so that you can have this thought in mind: John and Bob now are going to make their move. I worked it out with them finally, and they're going to make it—they're going to come up and see me Sunday with their letters. They're going to—it's going to be a leave of absence. They realize that it's going to be more than that, but, you know, they feel that it's the only right thing to do.

ROGERS: Yes.

PRESIDENT NIXON: I mean, the arguments we made, that they've got to get through the grand jury and then they're going to say, well, in view of this, it's too much time, and so on and so on. So they're going to do that Sunday and it'll come out Sunday night for Monday papers. Then I'm going to move on Dean. I'm just going to move on him in a peremptory way, but the same way. Then I am planning, for your information, I am going to do a broadcast Monday night, which I am now working on, which I think is the time to do it because I—not for the purpose of saying everything that happened, but because I just—I just want the country to know that I'm in charge, that this is—we're getting to the bottom of it, you know, and all that sort of thing, and that anybody—I'm going to call on anybody that knows anything about it to come on it.

It'll be a pretty good speech, actually, a pretty good speech. But it will be Monday night. . . .

APRIL 28, 1973: THE PRESIDENT AND HENRY PETERSEN, 9:13–9:25 A.M., CAMP DAVID TELEPHONE

Nixon also talks to Henry Petersen during this flurry of telephone calls from Camp David. Their relationship has many dimensions, and here Petersen gives Nixon some legal education on use immunity. Nixon repeatedly tells Petersen that the decision to immunize Dean is Petersen's alone, although the President does not hesitate to make his views known. The Justice Department and the prosecutors, like Nixon, oppose immunity, but they fear that Dean would lose his credibility as a witness. Interestingly, Nixon does not hint that Kleindienst, Petersen's superior and friend, will be dismissed.

PRESIDENT NIXON: I'm at Camp David. I'm working and I'm not going to tell you what, but, as you know, I don't come here to look at the Easter lilies. But things are going to work out. . . . I don't want any stories indicating that I'm here and that people are coming to see me, which they will be.

PETERSEN: Sure.

PRESIDENT NIXON: The second point related to that, I am not going to see Dean. I am not going to see him, because, in my view, I cannot be—I remember that conversation that we had that I cannot be in a position where he will want to come in and try to talk to me about how he's going to plead.

PETERSEN: I subscribe to that. . . .

PRESIDENT NIXON: That doesn't put any burden on you that you don't want now. I don't want to pass the buck.

PETERSEN: That doesn't put any burden on me that I don't have by law.

PRESIDENT NIXON: It's the truth. My third point on that, I noted his rather interesting story to the effect that if he didn't get immunity he wasn't going to talk. I wonder if that's a gun at our head in terms of thinking, well, if he doesn't get immunity, we're covering up.

PETERSEN: Yes, sir, I heard that story.

PRESIDENT NIXON: Yeah. How do you analyze it?

PETERSEN: Well—

PRESIDENT NIXON: In a way, though, you know, he doesn't have to get immunity in order to talk, does he?

PETERSEN: Oh, no, but he also has Fifth Amendment rights.

PRESIDENT NIXON: Right, right.

PETERSEN: That's the only way we can take those rights away from him, is immunity.

PRESIDENT NIXON: Oh, I see. I see. That's right. That's right. And your immunity can be limited or total or half?

PETERSEN: No. It applies to everything he says.

PRESIDENT NIXON: Like use immunity, you mean?

PETERSEN: Yes, sir.

PRESIDENT NIXON: Well, that isn't going to help him a helluva lot, Henry. I mean, that isn't going to help him a helluva lot, for example on the—you know, the subornation issue. That's the one that I think he's got—I mean from my limited knowledge of the law, that's a tough one, isn't it?

PETERSEN: Well, it would cover—it would cover anything that he disclosed to us and, as a practical matter, we, as the sovereign extending the immunity, would be almost in an impossible situation to prosecute him, even if we came in with evidence from an independent source. . . .

PRESIDENT NIXON: In other words, if you give him even use immunity, he gets it?

PETERSEN: That's right. Yes, sir.

PRESIDENT NIXON: I see. I see. Well, all right. The decision is yours, just remembering also that your obligation is to not see that he gets an incentive to get after innocent people.

PETERSEN: I understand. . . .

PRESIDENT NIXON: That's right. The situation on the other thing that I think remains about as it is, the judge apparently is going forward with the Ellsberg thing, is he, with the trial, despite the—this thing. I mean, the FBI is talking to the individuals, and then the judge will—is that the way that's normally done? I want to be sure there's nothing abnormal about that. . . .

PETERSEN: [A]ssuming we can get the inquiry done in time, we'll have to make that available to the judge, and then he'll either do one of two things, depending on the quality of the information. He'll either order an evidentiary hearing or dismiss the case outright if it's blatant. Assuming it's not blatant, then he's going to give the defense an opportunity to—

PRESIDENT NIXON: To argue on that point?

PETERSEN: Well, to conduct an evidentiary hearing. . . .

PRESIDENT NIXON: Would that be in open court?

PETERSEN: Yes, sir, but that would also mean that Liddy and Hunt would probably be subpoenaed and they might very well take the Fifth Amendment. The judge might order us to immunize them. They could then still refuse to talk and be held in contempt. . . .

PRESIDENT NIXON: Possibly Ehrlichman? Ehrlichman possibly, you say?

PETERSEN: Ehrlichman possibly, yes.

PRESIDENT NIXON: Yeah. If Dean says he did it under his direction or whatever the hell it is, right.

PETERSEN: I have only an oral report, but I understand Ehrlichman told the Bureau that he heard of this incident but had no independent knowledge of it.

PRESIDENT NIXON: That's right. That's what he—well, for whatever it's worth, I asked him, as you can imagine, immediately, and I said what the hell was this thing? He said he heard of it, he had no independent knowledge of it, and once he found it out, he said for Christ sakes knock this crap off. But nevertheless [*chuckles*], that's irrelevant.

PETERSEN: Yes.

PRESIDENT NIXON: Well, it's relevant. It's relevant. Let him go out and talk. Okay. That one will move, then, and we'll go forward with the trial and we'll get it. I hope you will help my—our old friend Mr. Clean in the FBI.

PETERSEN: Bill Ruckelshaus?

PRESIDENT NIXON: Yeah.

PETERSEN: We're good friends, Mr. President.

PRESIDENT NIXON: Yeah. And just tell—now with Bill, as you know, I gave him *carte blanche*. Of course, I said don't start a new investigation, but I said for Christ sakes, I want you to really do anything. I mean, don't leave a Goddamn stone uncovered. And that's for you too. You understand that.

PETERSEN: Well, I don't think—I think he respects me, and I respect him.

PRESIDENT NIXON: I think the rest of the country respects him too.

PETERSEN: And we like each other on top of it. I don't think there's going to be any difficulty there at all. . . .

PRESIDENT NIXON: . . . One final thing to get your thoughts on. You know there's sort of an increasing sort of clamor developing—I don't know how much it is—with regard to a special prosecutor and so forth. I don't know. My view is still negative, negative because I think that you—I mean you and the prosecuting team are going balls-out, hell-bent for election to get the facts, and that once you—once the grand jury quits and you indict that that's going to be pretty clear. . . . Give me your honest view about this thing. Should I consider it?

PETERSEN: Well, I still have the very difficult practical problem that even if you put one in, there's going to be an awful lot of time lost. . . . The credibility issue is becoming much more severe, much more severe. . . . Both within and without government. One of the things that I've been discussing with Kleindienst and frankly I told [U. S. Attorney Harold H.] Titus that we'll set up a decisional-making organization, a panel of three, composed of me, Titus, and someone at my rank in the Justice Department to pass on these critical decisions. . . .

PRESIDENT NIXON: Could you put—could you pull perhaps maybe one from outside, maybe a judge?

PETERSEN: Well, that's the other possibility, is to bring somebody from outside. I don't think we can do it with a judge. I think that flies in the face of separation of powers doctrine, even with a retired judge that still has the authority to sit judicially. . . .

PRESIDENT NIXON: How about bringing in [prominent "establishment" figure] John McCloy?

PETERSEN: That'd be fine. . . .

PRESIDENT NIXON: If you want, have Kleindienst give him a call and tell him that the President wants him to do it, if that's what you want to do. . . . Let me just say one other thing. You know, that story that was floating out last night, let me say, boy, don't let anything like that—I mean, it might come out, but don't you let it without letting me know. I'm not going to have anybody [John Dean], I mean, threatening the President. . . .

PETERSEN: All right. Have a good day, Mr. President.

PRESIDENT NIXON: Thank you. You bet. And you too.

APRIL 28, 1973: THE PRESIDENT AND ZIEGLER, 11:10–11:21 A.M., CAMP DAVID TELEPHONE

With the approaching dismissals, Nixon is stressed and weary. He hopes to persuade William Rogers to take over as Attorney General. Yet he wavers on the question of resignation or leaves of absence for his top aides, as well as what he will do with Dean. Despite protestations that Dean cannot intimidate him, Nixon fears Dean's potential for damage. Ziegler again demonstrates a new confidence in dealing with the President.

PRESIDENT NIXON: . . . I'm going to see Bill Rogers right now.

ZIEGLER: Yes, sir. I wanted to—I had a nice long talk with Bob [Haldeman], and I wanted to pass this on to you, if I may, before you give your talk.

PRESIDENT NIXON: Yeah.

ZIEGLER: I think he indicated to you that both John and Bob are very comfortable now about the decision.

PRESIDENT NIXON: Of a leave of absence.

ZIEGLER: Yes, sir.

PRESIDENT NIXON: But not resigning.

ZIEGLER: Right, a leave of absence. So that is past. In other words, there's no further problem with that. In thinking of the timing and discussing this in very frank terms with Bob, something he mentioned sparks me in a way that it is something that I know you are considering, but I would like to say from an overall standpoint seems to be the master stroke in all of this.

PRESIDENT NIXON: What's that?

ZIEGLER: That is, if action is taken which is action typical of President Nixon before the speech, which is dramatic in itself—

PRESIDENT NIXON: I should announce it, you mean?

ZIEGLER: No, sir. Can make the speech the final breaking point, breaking off point for the President. What I have in mind simply is this. If, for example, over the weekend Rogers is named as the Attorney General—

PRESIDENT NIXON: Yeah.

ZIEGLER: If over the weekend Rogers is in a position where he takes charge of the prosecution. And if Rogers is then in the position to name a special prosecutor, that action in itself will then allow the presidency to totally remove itself from this whole process. And the reason I wanted to make this point is, one of the—it's something you should be aware of. One of the things that [Robert U.] Woodward [a *Washington Post* reporter] said the other day and one of the things that I think we can anticipate coming, is a run at Petersen and a run at the investigation.

PRESIDENT NIXON: Yeah.

ZIEGLER: Woodward made the point that they have some information on Petersen, not in relation to this but in relation to action he took in a previous case, a fairly recent case, where he can come under some criticism.

PRESIDENT NIXON: Yeah.

ZIEGLER: And that in itself could perhaps, you know, tend to not, you know, carry things through in a positive way, but—

PRESIDENT NIXON: The difficulty with a special prosecutor, it'll be months before they could ever learn the case.

ZIEGLER: But the thing of it is, it's not starting a new investigation—

PRESIDENT NIXON: Yeah.

ZIEGLER: But it would be picking up from where it stands now.

PRESIDENT NIXON: Mm-hmm. Mm-hmm. Yeah. And then you mean not have them resign? . . . Their leaves have got to go forward now. . . .

ZIEGLER: That's correct. And then, on Monday or after this is announced, Sunday afternoon or whenever, move vigorously on Dean.

PRESIDENT NIXON: Well, on Dean, my thought was, on moving vigorously on Dean was to simply have, rather than the firing—just to have Garment coldly go in and say the President is accepting your resignation—not resignation. You are placed on leave of absence and I'm taking over your duties, John, until this thing is cleared up.

ZIEGLER: Well, one thing I think in the scenario I'm just mentioning, particularly on the Dean thing, based on the information you have in terms of Dean would be to have Garment go in and say, because of the moves we're taking, we're accepting your resignation, you see.

PRESIDENT NIXON: Well, I think he should be treated the same as the others. I don't know. But basically, let's face it. They've got this problem. Dean—Dean—well, maybe you're not as worried about that. Dean knows a helluva lot about Rogers—I mean, about Haldeman and Ehrlichman, I mean, most of which I think he can—they can handle. He also has one gun pointed at the President, in the fact that conversation I told you in which he did discuss the possibility of—told me about that damned thing, his conversation about well, Hunt needs money, and that was on the 21st of March.

ZIEGLER: I'm not worried about that at all.

PRESIDENT NIXON: He started our investigation so he could say well, the President had—knew all that information and sat on it and didn't do anything.

ZIEGLER: But you did.

PRESIDENT NIXON: No, I know I did. I conducted—but why didn't I turn that over immediately to the Attorney General?

ZIEGLER: Because you were determining what—

PRESIDENT NIXON: What the facts were. . . .

ZIEGLER: Now you're turning it over to a man [Rogers] who is highly respected and it would be a master stroke, I think.

PRESIDENT NIXON: Yeah. Well, I don't know whether Rogers would ever do it.

ZIEGLER: Well, in terms of Secretary Rogers doing it, I think—

PRESIDENT NIXON: If he won't do it, maybe I may get Richardson to do it.

ZIEGLER: Well, the main thing on Rogers I think is this gives him an opportunity, and I think Rogers would want this, to—he's had an opportunity to serve as Secretary of State through a very key period—

PRESIDENT NIXON: And he used to be Attorney General.

ZIEGLER: Well, but this gives him an opportunity in terms of serving the President to give you a chance as President to move on with your work and for him to step in and play a very key role in bringing things back into order.

PRESIDENT NIXON: Well, let me talk to him to see whether there's any possibility of it, Ron, and I'll call you back on it.

ZIEGLER: In other words, he has an opportunity to help the President in pulling this thing together.

PRESIDENT NIXON: Right. Right. Okay. . . . I just talked to my daughter Tricia, who came up to tell me—you know, she's a sweet child—and told me the family and Pat that they felt strongly that Haldeman and Ehrlichman should resign.

ZIEGLER: Yes.

PRESIDENT NIXON: Of course, the feeling they should resign is very strong, as you know. But, Ron, don't you think the leave of absence is almost going to in the public mind be the equivalent to resignation, or not?

ZIEGLER: Yes, sir.

PRESIDENT NIXON: Or not?

ZIEGLER: Well, it won't be quite there, but you've thought this through so much, Mr. President. It is your wisdom.

PRESIDENT NIXON: Well, frankly it isn't my wisdom. It's the fact we've got two guys that say we may be sending them to jail.

ZIEGLER: That's right.

PRESIDENT NIXON: And I've got to think of that.

ZIEGLER: Yes, you do.

PRESIDENT NIXON: I think they are innocent.

ZIEGLER: Yes, sir.

PRESIDENT NIXON: And I'm just not going to do that. . . .

APRIL 28, 1973: THE PRESIDENT AND ZIEGLER, 5:35–5:45 P.M., CAMP DAVID TELEPHONE

The President reports that Rogers will not be Attorney General. Whether he declined, or Nixon withheld a formal offer, is not entirely clear. Yet Nixon is gleeful that he has an "equally good" idea for a candidate. Rogers had recommended that Haldeman and Ehrlichman's usefulness was over, and they must resign, and not be offered leaves of absence. Nixon passes this on to Ziegler, expecting him to convey the news to Haldeman. In any event, Nixon is determined to force the "resignations."

PRESIDENT NIXON: I want to talk to you in confidence. The Bill [Rogers] thing will not work out. There are reasons that I don't need to go into, but it won't. But I am working on another thing that is equally good. I won't tell you what it is.

ZIEGLER: All right. Okay.

PRESIDENT NIXON: But it's awfully good.

ZIEGLER: Okay. . . .

PRESIDENT NIXON: In the case—and it does involve a replacement of the Attorney General—in the event that it does work, I'm just thinking about the fact that it might better, rather than to—I guess I've got to put Kleindienst on the rope on that, too—better to have the Haldeman-Ehrlichman thing than the Dean thing, and my announcement on Monday, and then hit that on Wednesday—in other words, to just keep the ball rolling to show that I'm acting. Because, you see, it takes quite a bit of moving around to get Kleindienst out and somebody else in right away. But I just want you to know that that's one possibility. The other possibility, if we can get it ready, would be that I would announce it in my Monday night talk. . . . How are they coming on their speech thing and so forth?

ZIEGLER: Well, he [Raymond Price?] is moving along, I think, and is going to have it ready by 7.

PRESIDENT NIXON: Fine. Any other developments I should know about?

ZIEGLER: No, nothing of major importance in the scope of all of this. The direction of the story seemed to be going to the plumbers operation.

PRESIDENT NIXON: Yeah.

ZIEGLER: Specifically the Pentagon Papers break-in, but also the cable [forged by Howard Hunt] regarding the death of or the overthrow of Diem.

PRESIDENT NIXON: Yeah, which was some sort of a fake, wasn't it?

ZIEGLER: Yes. . . .

PRESIDENT NIXON: Yeah, yeah. Let me tell you one interesting observation that Rogers had with regard to Dean which I think is interesting. . . . He said he remembered in the Eisenhower Administration they had a rule to the effect that if any individual was charged that he would be required to go and testify freely. If he claimed, however, or asked amnesty or, you know, so forth, that he would have to resign. . . . And he suggested that the way that we ought to handle that is to have Garment go to Dean after this thing has happened and say, all right, Haldeman and Ehrlichman have agreed to go and testify without any, you know—testify freely. . . . And if you, John, want to go testify to the grand jury, fine. If you, however, want to go and ask for amnesty then, of course, we'll have to have your resignation, because a request for amnesty, which of course is crystal clear, is really a request—is an admission of guilt.

ZIEGLER: Sure.

PRESIDENT NIXON: Now I say well, that makes Dean more of a loose cannon, and he says we all have to realize that. But, he says, you know, his old point. It's going to come anyway. And I think it gets back to your point. So he is a loose cannon. I just can't believe that Dean at this point is going to have—he's going to raise hell, but I don't think he's going to have that much credibility. I don't know. What do you think?

ZIEGLER: No, not on the move you are contemplating here.

PRESIDENT NIXON: Yeah. But doesn't that make sense to you as a way to handle it? You cannot possibly give Dean a leave of absence and let him say, all right, go get amnesty.

ZIEGLER: Right. . . . The Secretary felt that the overall resignation was the best way to go?

PRESIDENT NIXON: Yes. . . . And this is what they are prepared to do now, as I understand. You got that impression from talking to them today? . . . They're not backing off of that, are they?

ZIEGLER: No, no.

PRESIDENT NIXON: Yeah, because that's what we're going to have to do. Do you have any idea when they're going to be up here?

ZIEGLER: I guess tomorrow afternoon.

PRESIDENT NIXON: Mm-hmm. Mm-hmm. Good. The Secretary [Rogers] thought, incidentally, that it should be, should be brief, brief, and you have to indicate the new direction. You know, he is strong on that idea, the very same thing you said, a new direction, he said, not only in dealing with the press but with the Congress and the Cabinet and so forth. . . . But I think he's right, which gets back to my point that I think really as far as Chief of Staff I've got to be the Chief of Staff.

ZIEGLER: Mm-hmm.

PRESIDENT NIXON: How does that sound to you?

ZIEGLER: Well, I think in the new way of operation, fine, but as President you've always been, you know, been the Chief. I think in terms of—

PRESIDENT NIXON: Yeah. Then you have various people that do various things. But my point is not have one guy that appears to be the block. . . . That is the problem with Haldeman.

ZIEGLER: —because it would be so difficult to find another man like that. In other words, they don't duplicate Bob Haldemans.

PRESIDENT NIXON: And they don't duplicate John Ehrlichman.

ZIEGLER: That's right. That's correct.

PRESIDENT NIXON: Bill thought, incidentally, that the Ehrlichman thing was enormously complicated by the Hunt thing, by the point. He said, look—the thing we talked on the phone. He said, if they did this and if Ehrlichman knew they did it, and then they weren't fired, and went on over to the committee, this is going to be very, very tough, not in a legal way, for Ehrlichman but in terms of coming back. . . .

We don't know when the son of a bitch [Hunt] left after he did this, do we, how soon it was or how long he stayed on?

ZIEGLER: No, I really don't have those dates. John would have that, I suppose.

PRESIDENT NIXON: That's something we have to have in mind. Fine. Well, anyway, you keep the faith.

ZIEGLER: Yes, sir.

PRESIDENT NIXON: The world will still go round. We've got to make it go, Ron.

ZIEGLER: Absolutely.

PRESIDENT NIXON: You're not losing confidence, are you?

ZIEGLER: Absolutely not.

APRIL 28, 1973: THE PRESIDENT AND EHRLICHMAN, 6:33–6:54 P.M., CAMP DAVID TELEPHONE

Haldeman prepares to go quietly; Ehrlichman, however, balks. Here he pleads for separate consideration and time alone with the President. Their conversation is

strained and tense. Haldeman has informed Ehrlichman that they are not being given leaves of absence. Nixon raises the question of Howard Hunt's fake cables regarding Presidents Kennedy and Diem, insisting he knew nothing about this, and places the blame on Colson. Ehrlichman responds testily, telling the President he did know, and that he clearly is uninterested in the problems of others.

SEGMENT 1

PRESIDENT NIXON: . . . I had a long talk with Bill Rogers today and he made a suggestion that I think puts the Dean thing in a context that will maybe appeal to you. . . . [H]e thought that the way to present it to Dean was to say, Mr. Ehrlichman and Mr. Haldeman are going to take leave and testify freely about this matter. You can do likewise if you want to testify freely. If you want to take immunity, why, we want your resignation. In other words, so it's really going to be a resignation, because he isn't going to go in and testify freely.

EHRLICHMAN: Well, he's all over the papers today saying that he is.

PRESIDENT NIXON: That he's going to testify freely?

EHRLICHMAN: Yes, sir.

PRESIDENT NIXON: Without immunity?

EHRLICHMAN: Yeah. That's what he's saying.

PRESIDENT NIXON: Well, I know—I wonder. All right. That's going to be a different game then. But we shall have to see. . . .

EHRLICHMAN: Right. He's got a lot of problems and I don't know how you reconcile it, but I think you have to anticipate that he would stare Garment down on that one.

PRESIDENT NIXON: Start a what?

EHRLICHMAN: I say if Garment were sent to tell him that, or whoever it was, why he would stare them down. . . .

PRESIDENT NIXON: Yeah. Yeah, well, let me just say then I'll have to think of something else then. All right, pal. I'll think of something by that time. What time will you and Bob be up here, do you think?

EHRLICHMAN: At your convenience. We just arbitrarily picked 11:00, if that's a good time for you. . . . I know that we're sort of coupled like Siamese twins in this, Bob and I, but I do have a couple of things I would like to—

PRESIDENT NIXON: I understand, John. Fine. Of course you can have some moments alone. Now let me ask one thing. Ron said that the interest today is sort of—is moving toward the California Plumbers operation. Is that right?

EHRLICHMAN: Well, I don't know. I haven't been following it.

PRESIDENT NIXON: Yeah. On that one, I mean—well, we can talk about it tomorrow. Do you have any thoughts about it at the moment?

EHRLICHMAN: No, I really don't. I assume that that could run quite far.

PRESIDENT NIXON: Yeah. It's a question of—basically I suppose the question is who was in charge. Was Dean in charge?

EHRLICHMAN: No, I was.

PRESIDENT NIXON: Yeah.

EHRLICHMAN: And Krogh and Young, of course, ran the operation.

PRESIDENT NIXON: And the purpose was to look out for leaks.

EHRLICHMAN: Sure.

PRESIDENT NIXON: But from what I understood from what we have heard to date as far as so-called electronic surveillance is concerned none of that—maybe it was contemplated, but none was tried, as far as we know, from the White House. It was from the FBI. Is that approximately correct?

EHRLICHMAN: That is correct.

PRESIDENT NIXON: That is correct.

EHRLICHMAN: As far as I know, that's right.

PRESIDENT NIXON: Mm-hmm. As far as this operation in California, do you know when he [Hunt] left?

EHRLICHMAN: No, I don't.

PRESIDENT NIXON: In other words, after he—after it happened and you learned about it, did you have Liddy and him in and talk to them about it?

EHRLICHMAN: No, no. No indeed.

PRESIDENT NIXON: How then did—

EHRLICHMAN: I never saw them again.

PRESIDENT NIXON: How then did it get turned off in effect?

EHRLICHMAN: I talked to either Krogh or Young.

PRESIDENT NIXON: Yes. And did they inform you of the fact that they had done it?

EHRLICHMAN: Yes.

PRESIDENT NIXON: What—in a word, what happened? They had done it? They had acquired nothing or they had?

EHRLICHMAN: Right, got nothing. . . .

PRESIDENT NIXON: And they wanted to go back again.

EHRLICHMAN: Right.

PRESIDENT NIXON: And you negatived.

EHRLICHMAN: Right.

PRESIDENT NIXON: Right. Well, that's a solid position, I think, isn't it?

EHRLICHMAN: Well, it's what actually happened.

PRESIDENT NIXON: No. What I meant is—no, I know it's what happened. But what I meant is, I'm just . . . saying that as far as your part of it was concerned that you—that this was something you never authorized.

EHRLICHMAN: That's right.

PRESIDENT NIXON: You learned that they tried something like this. You said that is absolutely out and you're not to do it.

EHRLICHMAN: Right.

PRESIDENT NIXON: That's right. That's right. Well, let me say, in terms of—I realize the cases are different and we should talk about it.

SEGMENT 2

PRESIDENT NIXON: I had a good talk with Rogers, and he feels strongly that Kleindienst must go soon.

EHRLICHMAN: Will he step in there?

PRESIDENT NIXON: No, but I have another thought that is quite intriguing. I'll tell you about it if it works out. I'll know within a couple hours. I mean, it's one I think you'll like, if it works. [Rogers] won't for reasons that I think are good, I mean mainly the fact that he's so Goddamn close to me you know what I mean—in terms of in a sense, he is in a public sense, you know, and all that, despite all that. But nevertheless, whatever the reason is, he isn't going to do it. But I have another name, John, that has not occurred to any of you. It occurred to me late last night, and I just busted in on him today and we've been calling the Chief Justice and a few others today on it. It may be something that'll work. I'll know within a couple hours. As a matter of fact, if I get an affirmative on it, I'll call you back and let you know.

EHRLICHMAN: That's great. Thank you. I think that's very healthy, to make that change.

PRESIDENT NIXON: Now, on that, let me ask you this in terms of my talk. It was not my thought to mention you or Bob in the talk.

EHRLICHMAN: I would agree with that.

PRESIDENT NIXON: I don't want to talk anything about that. It was not my thought—however, on the AG [Attorney General] thing, I'd have to—it was my thought probably to do that Wednesday or, of course, if I could get Kleindienst lined up and so forth, I could bust that in the talk. . . . Just for purposes of my thinking, which would you think would be better?

EHRLICHMAN: I'd put it in the talk. The more motion you can show in the talk, the better. . . .

PRESIDENT NIXON: Well, just pray that Rogers has success in the telephone call he's going to make in about a half hour. . . . Did you have a good talk with your lawyers this morning?

EHRLICHMAN: Yes. We've drawn two letters, one each, which we think are—

PRESIDENT NIXON: And yours are different now, I guess.

EHRLICHMAN: Oh, yes, indeed. . . . We've been at work all day on it, but they are pretty well honed. I think you will find they are all right.

PRESIDENT NIXON: You see, your case is totally differentiated in a very important way. You had nothing to do with the campaign.

EHRLICHMAN: That's it.

PRESIDENT NIXON: That's the point that I meant. You had nothing to do at all with this whole damn period before June 19. You had nothing to do with the—well, except for the call to Kalmbach, you had nothing to do with the—

EHRLICHMAN: And that was after, you see.

PRESIDENT NIXON: No, no, no. But I mean you had nothing to do with the so-called cover-ups.

EHRLICHMAN: No. That's it.

PRESIDENT NIXON: But at that point you don't—you—certainly nobody would have considered that a cover-up. Right?

EHRLICHMAN: Right.

PRESIDENT NIXON: Isn't that the position?

EHRLICHMAN: That's it exactly.

PRESIDENT NIXON: Yeah. With regard to the papers, I'm just looking at yours in terms of your lawyer and so forth, what you did turn it over to is your statement with regard to Gray. You had no reason to think that the stupid bastard was going to burn the stuff.

EHRLICHMAN: None whatever. . . .

PRESIDENT NIXON: . . . [In] the plumbers operation, the papers said it was something regarding some letter that Hunt prepared from, allegedly a fake letter from Kennedy on the Diem thing or something.

EHRLICHMAN: Yeah.

PRESIDENT NIXON: But that, of course, is totally, totally out of our ken. Have you ever heard of such a Goddamn—

EHRLICHMAN: Yes, sir. [*Sarcastically.*] That leads directly to your friend Colson. . . .

PRESIDENT NIXON: Goddamn it, I never heard of it, John. What, that a fake letter was—

EHRLICHMAN: No. It's a cable.

PRESIDENT NIXON: But a fake one?

EHRLICHMAN: Yeah.

PRESIDENT NIXON: From John F. Kennedy?

EHRLICHMAN: Well, that is what it is alleged to be.

PRESIDENT NIXON: Oh, my God. I just can't believe that. I just can't believe that. The whole—you remember, you were conducting for me—you and Young were conducting a study of the whole Diem thing and the Bay of Pigs thing.

EHRLICHMAN: That's right. That's correct.

PRESIDENT NIXON: But, John, you will—if my recollection is correct, I just said get the facts.

EHRLICHMAN: Well, I don't know where Colson got this inspiration, but he was very busy at it.

PRESIDENT NIXON: And he had told you that there was a fake letter or a fake cable?

EHRLICHMAN: Yes. . . .

PRESIDENT NIXON: I should have been told about that, shouldn't I?

EHRLICHMAN: Well, I'm not so sure but what you weren't.

PRESIDENT NIXON: By whom?

EHRLICHMAN: I don't know. I don't know.

PRESIDENT NIXON: No. I wasn't told about anything, a mistake. I mean, the only thing I was ever told about it, you remember I said the thing that you did for *Life* magazine? . . . That's the only thing I ever heard about the Diem thing.

EHRLICHMAN: Well, that's a part of that transaction.

PRESIDENT NIXON: But was the fake thing in that?

EHRLICHMAN: Right. That's what I believe. I could be wrong on this.

PRESIDENT NIXON: You didn't know there was anything fake in that, though, did you? You didn't tell me anything about that, John.

EHRLICHMAN: Well, I'd have to go back and check my notes. But my recollection is that this was discussed with you.

PRESIDENT NIXON: Well, I'd be amazed at that. I mean, I must say that I knew that a lot was done. I mean, I knew that we were making a study, but I didn't know that we were putting together something that was totally fake to send to *Life* magazine or something like that on Kennedy and Diem.

EHRLICHMAN: Well, I could be wrong on this. I'll try and get the time to check my notes tomorrow before I come up.

PRESIDENT NIXON: Yeah, yeah. Well, I've got to know about that. If I'm in—I mean, if I'm in that kind of a position, I'm in a position I just didn't know about, believe me. I have—throughout this thing, I must say, I have not known (unintelligible)—I didn't know about the Watergate and I didn't know about the other thing. But I knew that we were checking all this. But my God, I didn't know they were faking stuff involving that on Kennedy.

EHRLICHMAN: Well, as I say, I got this second-hand.

PRESIDENT NIXON: From Young or Krogh?

EHRLICHMAN: No, no, no. I think Chuck told me one time.

PRESIDENT NIXON: Well, he sure didn't tell me. You didn't tell me, did you?

EHRLICHMAN: I don't know whether I did or not. As I say, I'd have to go back and check. . . .

PRESIDENT NIXON: Another one of those things. Well, thank God. Thank God it wasn't used. . . .

EHRLICHMAN: Yeah, that whole thing, that Hunt—and it was mostly a Hunt-Colson thing—ran off in a lot of strange directions that I really don't have a lot of information on.

PRESIDENT NIXON: You know, the thing about that is that Colson never told me about Hunt, that he knew Hunt, until after the Watergate thing.

EHRLICHMAN: Is that right?

PRESIDENT NIXON: I never heard of E. Howard Hunt, no, sir, no. No, sir. . . . I had understood he said he doesn't know Hunt well, or something like that. I think that's apparently been his line. . . . But afterwards he said he was an intimate friend.

EHRLICHMAN: Yes, yes. Well, we'll—I can get back into that or not, depending on what you'd like.

PRESIDENT NIXON: You are now, just so that I can get my own thoughts, you feel that I should go—the time should be Monday for the broadcast, right?

EHRLICHMAN: I think the sooner the better. . . . I gather from Bob that this leave business is a closed subject as far as you're concerned?

PRESIDENT NIXON: Yes, it has to be. I can't see any way to handle it otherwise. I think it's separable up to a point, but whatever the subject, whatever the problem is on this thing about the file thing with the Gray thing is, I mean, even though I know what the facts are and I know your story is right, I think it's something that we've just got to get cleared up. And I just don't think—I had a long talk with Rogers on that. Now, he's been an advocate of separability and he was, really—he has been—you know, I mean he was open to it. But we went into it and, John, I just feel that that's what we have to do.

EHRLICHMAN: Do you have anything from Petersen at all that we don't know about?

PRESIDENT NIXON: Nothing, nothing. And he will not tell me. You see, I closed my own door there, damn it, by saying I didn't want to know what was in the grand jury. . . .

This is the way I feel I have to move, John. I guess one of the prerogatives of the President is to make mistakes, you know, and sometimes you have to make some. I've made my share, but on this one I just feel it's the right thing to do, that the leave thing is the right thing at this point, if it's properly worded.

EHRLICHMAN: Well, you take a look at what we have. . . .

APRIL 29, 1973: THE PRESIDENT AND KISSINGER, 10:19–10:25 A.M., CAMP DAVID TELEPHONE

Kissinger calls the President, insisting their achievements will far outstrip Watergate in historical importance. But Nixon prefers to discuss substantive matters rather than future historiography. He reveals his choice of Harvard man Elliot Richardson as Attorney General, and then not so subtly reminds Kissinger of the telephone taps on aides and reporters that Kissinger had earlier requested. The President lets Kissinger know that he, too, is involved in the Administration's now-questionable tactics.

KISSINGER: Hello, Mr. President.

PRESIDENT NIXON: Hi, Henry. How are you?

KISSINGER: Okay. I didn't have, really have anything. I just wanted to call you to tell you I was thinking of—

PRESIDENT NIXON: Oh, sure. Well, that's fine, Henry. Now you get on with your business, and I'll work. Don't you worry.

KISSINGER: I have no question about it.

PRESIDENT NIXON: Yeah, yeah, yeah. Got some awfully tough calls to make, but I'll make them. . . .

KISSINGER: Well, Mr. President, no one can undo the achievements, none of these packs of jackals.

PRESIDENT NIXON: Well, look, and in the end—

KISSINGER: It is the achievements—

PRESIDENT NIXON: —and in the end—let's not. In the end, remember, within a year people are not going to be thinking of this. They're going to be thinking of what we've been doing, Henry. So don't you worry about that.

KISSINGER: In three months, Mr. President, no one will be able to—

PRESIDENT NIXON: Frankly, people are getting Goddamn sick of it now, you know.

KISSINGER: I think in fact—

PRESIDENT NIXON: I've noted people—I just have a feeling that even now, you know, you pick up a paper and it's Watergate, Watergate, Dean charges this, somebody charges that, who broke into the psychiatrist's office. Wasn't that the silliest Goddamn thing?

KISSINGER: Well, I think it's the *Post* and the commentators are keeping it going. . . .

PRESIDENT NIXON: I've got something to tell you in the greatest of confidence, I've decided on and I'm going to have to work it out today. I've got to get a new Attorney General, of course.

KISSINGER: Right.

PRESIDENT NIXON: And actually, not because Kleindienst is involved, but because Mitchell is and he's so close to him and he also is close to other things. And the man who is totally qualified and is impeccably, would be trusted by the so-called damned establishment is Elliot Richardson. I've got to move him out of Defense, and I'm trying to get Dave Packard to come back as Secretary of Defense. Now, that's just for your information.

KISSINGER: Right.

PRESIDENT NIXON: But I'm working on it. That's my decision. That's what I'm going to do. . . . First in his [Richardson] class at Harvard Law, attorney general, lieutenant governor, one of the most—and I'm going to give him a free hand. I'm going to tell him to clean every son of a bitch—see, I'm going to clean—and I'm going to put in a new FBI director, too, you know. I've got Ruck[elshaus] over there for a while, . . . but that's only temporary. . . . I'm going to get the most mean sonofabitch I can find and put them in the FBI and then let all hell break loose. Now, there's one area, of course, where you and I have to be concerned about it and where we've got to stand firm as hell. As you know, Henry, we did do—we did do some surveillance with the FBI on these leaks, you remember?

KISSINGER: Oh, yes.

PRESIDENT NIXON: And they were approved, approved by the Attorney General and so forth. When they come out, we've just got to say. Of course, you remember the whole business. People have forgotten.

KISSINGER: That was in '69.

PRESIDENT NIXON: Well, it was whenever the damned Ellsberg case was.

KISSINGER: Right.

PRESIDENT NIXON: When Ellsberg came, remember?

KISSINGER: Right.

PRESIDENT NIXON: And then right after that, why, God, the place was leaking like a sieve. So we did checking and so forth and so on, and so on and so on and so on. '69 and early '70, I think. I don't know whether it was in '70 or not. When was Ellsberg, '69?

KISSINGER: No, Ellsberg was '71. I don't remember any FBI work on the Ellsberg case.

PRESIDENT NIXON: Well, in any event, '69 and '71, too, then. Maybe we can get it—well—

KISSINGER: The '69 ones I knew about. . . .

PRESIDENT NIXON: But they were done, and I've got to defend those as national security leaks and we've got to do it in the future, you know. By golly, when we've got leaks I'm going to order bugging. Don't you agree?

KISSINGER: Well, if it's a question of national security, approved by the Attorney General, I don't see what anyone can say about it.

PRESIDENT NIXON: That's correct, correct. The problem we've got with some of this in the Ellsberg stuff, you see, Edgar Hoover wouldn't do the job because [Patricia] Marx, his closest friend's daughter, was married to Ellsberg and wouldn't do it, and that's why some of that crap was done in the White House. But that's too bad. That's just one of those things. I just want you to know. When that comes out, don't back off. You know what I mean. Anything that's national security we're going to fight like hell for.

KISSINGER: Right, absolutely. No, I will certainly not back off.

PRESIDENT NIXON: Yeah, we don't have to. Okay, Henry. Thanks for your call.

KISSINGER: Right, Mr. President.

APRIL 29, 1973: THE PRESIDENT AND WILLIAM ROGERS, 10:26–10:36 A.M., CAMP DAVID TELEPHONE

Nixon once admitted that he was not a "good butcher," given his reluctance to confront people directly and act decisively against them. Nowhere is this more apparent than when he has to dismiss Haldeman and Ehrlichman. Friendship certainly dictated a lot of this behavior, but the President must have feared the consequences of abandoning the two. In several calls that morning, Rogers insists that Nixon demand resignations. Haldeman and Ehrlichman, he claimed, had been a problem for the Administration for some time; indeed, Rogers personally had suffered from Haldeman's brusque manner. In the first conversation, Nixon persuades Rogers to help him through the confrontation with the aides by joining the meeting, but an hour later, Rogers calls to beg off. Throughout both conversations, Rogers struggles to strengthen Nixon's resolve. Finally, in a third call, Nixon asks Rogers to review his speech, as he had numerous times for the President.

PRESIDENT NIXON: Now, let me ask you. I think that, the more I think about it, that what I ought to do is to announce Elliot in the little talk.

ROGERS: Yeah, I do, too. . . .

PRESIDENT NIXON: And I thought that in announcing him, too, that I have among his duties I'm going to, you know, to oversee this entire investigation of this and all other activities, et cetera; and second, to assist me in a nationwide search for the best possible man as a permanent Director of the FBI. . . . I already have a man in mind, as you know, if he survives Ellsberg. . . . [Federal Judge Matthew] Byrne. . . .

ROGERS: [Richardson] is a man you have confidence in, the public has confidence in, he has a reputation, attorney general of his State, United States Attorney.

PRESIDENT NIXON: . . . Well, with Elliot, would you say that I should bring him up here? . . . [S]hall we leave [David] Packard, not mention the Packard thing [as Secretary of Defense] at this point?

ROGERS: I'd ask Elliot what he thought about him. . . .

PRESIDENT NIXON: Ehrlichman is hanging terribly tough, and I want to just get your judgment on this question again as to—you have no—you believe that they both must, at the very least, take a leave of absence?

ROGERS: Yes, I do. As a matter of fact, my own preference is for resignations. . . . I just think . . . that they've got to go, and the sooner the better, I think.

PRESIDENT NIXON: And Ehrlichman, too?

ROGERS: Yes.

PRESIDENT NIXON: Can't really separate it?

ROGERS: No.

PRESIDENT NIXON: Could—let me ask you. I'm seeing them at 2:00 today, and I'm going to talk to Ron. Would it be asking too much, if I really need some backing, for you to come up and help me talk to them about this thing a little?

ROGERS: I'll be glad to do it. I had planned to come up and get there around 1:00 or something like that.

PRESIDENT NIXON: . . . If you're here at 1:00, that'll really help a lot. How would you—how would you just go about talking to them? I mean, I'll talk to them, but what will you say? Just lay it—you see, the point is that—

ROGERS: Well, I didn't realize that they were—I thought the thing was all agreed to.

PRESIDENT NIXON: Well, Haldeman yes, but Ehrlichman, I talked to him last night on the phone and he said he wanted to raise the question with me again, you know what I mean. He feels that not only his case is separate, but I think he probably wants to give the President hell for not getting at this himself earlier, and this and that. You know how it is. He's not behaving well, frankly, not behaving well, to my surprise, to my surprise.

But my point is that—my point is he must not think of this in terms of—you know, for example, I had asked Petersen to give me a further sheet of paper. I said: "Now, what the hell is this you've got here?" And Petersen came in Friday and he says: "I can't because it involves, that would involve disclosing from the grand jury." Well, their attorney, according to Ehrlichman, says that Petersen's horsing me, he can give me that. The problem is Petersen maybe can't, due to the fact that he knows damn well I'll give it to Ehrlichman and Haldeman.

ROGERS: That's right. No, I don't think you should be put in that position. . . .

PRESIDENT NIXON: I mean, isn't the reason for resigning—tell me—tell me in a word what you think it is, what they've got to be told, will you? And then let me—what would you say to them? Would you just brainstorm it just for a minute with me? What the hell should they be told?

What would you tell Ehrlichman, even though he says, "Well, look, on Gray I didn't do anything; on making the call to Kalmbach, I was only doing—you know, I wasn't covering up anything; and that's all I had to do with it. And as far as the Plumbers operation was concerned, the purpose of that, I didn't approve anything illegal; I was simply doing what was necessary in order to protect the national security, and that was my duty," buh-buh-buh. All right. What do you—how do you answer him?

ROGERS: Well, I thought that the rationale—I didn't realize that they were being reluctant. They can't perform their duties now, for Christ's sakes. The whole government is at a standstill because these guys are reluctant.

PRESIDENT NIXON: Yeah. No, but they say that half of them is worth two of anybody else, that nobody else can do it.

ROGERS: Nuts.

PRESIDENT NIXON: And they think they're sort of indispensable and so forth, you know. That's the line.

ROGERS: Well, that's the trouble. That's what's been the trouble all along. . . .

PRESIDENT NIXON: They say the reason they can't perform their duties is that I left it uncertain. Of course, I haven't; they've left it uncertain.

ROGERS: You know, when we first talked they said they'd do whatever you wanted. . . . They'd do it for the good of the government. . . . And you've hung in there with them too much too long. They should have done this two weeks ago. Now, now you've decided and you've taken a course that I think serves everyone's interest. And they ought to abide by their decision. They said they'd do whatever you agreed on. . . . Well, what they are now saying is they'll do anything you want them to do as long as you agree with what they want done, which is nothing. Well, I can't—

PRESIDENT NIXON: Well, it's because—it's the lawyer's influence. The lawyer is telling them over and over that if they resign it's going to really prejudice their case, and so forth and so on. . . .

ROGERS: Well, I'm amazed [at their attitude], I really am. . . . [I]f they're going to do it this way, make it difficult for you, then I think you ought to just ask for their resignations, and say so. I didn't realize. I thought the whole thing had been agreed on. I'm really surprised.

PRESIDENT NIXON: Well, it had, but Ehrlichman's coming apart. . . .

APRIL 29, 1973: THE PRESIDENT AND ROGERS, 11:46–11:52 A.M., CAMP DAVID TELEPHONE

ROGERS: Hello, Mr. President.

PRESIDENT NIXON: Hi, Bill.

ROGERS: I just wanted to—I'm thinking over what we talked about. I think you ought to give a little thought to whether you should have somebody else, anybody else, there [for the forthcoming meeting with Haldeman and Ehrlichman], for the following reasons. Not that I'm ducking the responsibility.

PRESIDENT NIXON: Yeah.

ROGERS: But I think that if the going gets tough I can be a lot more helpful to you if I'm not in the discussion. For example, when I had the other discussions with these two fellows they both told me that you didn't know anything about this and you were not involved. So if they should turn on you, I'd be in a position—now, I don't want to hear anything else. I have no idea what they'll say if they get desperate.

Secondly, I don't really want them—I know there have been some leaks to the effect that I advised this and that. I haven't told a soul, so it must be coming from somewhere else. I don't want them to feel that—

PRESIDENT NIXON: You gave them the axe.

ROGERS: —that this was my decision. . . . And it seems to me that you shouldn't have to convince them. . . .

PRESIDENT NIXON: Yeah. Let me say this. All right, let me ask you this. Ron and I just talked a little about this. He's just come down awful hard on the resignation side now. He just says that the leave is going to just attract more flies and so forth and so on. I ask you again, is the leave an option or should I just say, fellows, you've just got to go? . . .

ROGERS: That would be, that's my recommendation. It's tough for me because you're so close to it and so close to these men and so forth. But my own judgment is that they should resign now. I don't think there's a possibility—I don't think it'll hurt them any with the grand jury. I think if they do it, I don't think—I think they'll be able to say, you know, I wanted to be sure that the President wasn't hurt, I wanted to be sure the government wasn't hurt, therefore I voluntarily resigned.

PRESIDENT NIXON: Yeah.

ROGERS: But I won't be too upset if it's a leave of absence. I think it's a lot—it's a lot more effective and a lot more convincing if all of them resign, the three of them. . . . Well, I'll be up and we can talk about it. But I wanted you to think about it.

PRESIDENT NIXON: Are you coming up?

ROGERS: Yes, yes.

PRESIDENT NIXON: You'll come up, but you—well, the point is, let me ask you this. If you would come up, and then if we get into a donnybrook then could I ask you to come over and help? Would you mind doing that?

ROGERS: Well, I don't really think it should be a donnybrook.

PRESIDENT NIXON: No.

ROGERS: This is one of those situations where you've given a hell of a lot of thought to it. It seems to me you should just say, "I've thought it over, I know how tough it is, and you told me that you'd do whatever I decided on, and this is what I decided on and this is my judgment," period.

PRESIDENT NIXON: Right. . . . Would you mind if Ron just talked to you a bit about the thing?

ROGERS: No.

PRESIDENT NIXON: And see. I'm not trying to—

ROGERS: Another thing, Mr. President, I think I can be helpful in helping reconstitute things is—

PRESIDENT NIXON: That's right.

ROGERS: —as long as I'm not—as I don't get in a pissing match with them.

PRESIDENT NIXON: That's right, unless—you don't get in it with them. I understand, okay. . . .

APRIL 29, 1973: THE PRESIDENT AND ROGERS, 12:28–12:30 P.M., CAMP DAVID TELEPHONE

PRESIDENT NIXON: Bill, suppose—one thing that could be helpful, if you wouldn't mind, if you could maybe come up around 4:00 o'clock, and I'd like to—[Raymond] Price is working on the draft.

ROGERS: Yes.

PRESIDENT NIXON: He's spent some time, of course, and I just went over the first, not the second. But as you can imagine, I'm having a hell of a time trying to get it done. I made up all the first outline a couple days ago and he's coming along and he's got a pretty good draft. But I remember how helpful you were at the time of the fund in the 1952 campaign [that resulted in the "Checkers" speech]. Would you mind coming up ? . . . And frankly, I might not even see you, but—

ROGERS: That's all right.

PRESIDENT NIXON: But if you could look over Price's draft and make suggestions—

ROGERS: Okay. . . .

APRIL 29, 1973: THE PRESIDENT AND ZIEGLER, 12:49–12:52 P.M., CAMP DAVID TELEPHONE

Ziegler has spoken to Haldeman and conveyed the decision that the aides had to resign. Haldeman offered to explain the decision to Ehrlichman. The President

worries about Ehrlichman's finances, and later offers them jobs with his yet-to-be-created foundation.

ZIEGLER: Yes, sir. I talked to Bob. . . . And told him that your decision was to ask for the resignation, and you had talked to Rogers and thought this through for now three weeks, you feel that a leave of absence would be detrimental to them and to the presidency, and that you intended to ask them for their resignations. And he said—I told him that you recognize that their lawyers don't agree with this approach and that they don't agree with this approach, but the President feels clear in his mind now that this must be done and that's what he wants. And Bob said fine, he understands, he feels it's the wrong decision, but he will abide by it. And in terms of John, he said, "I think John is going to be more difficult in accepting this." And I said, "I believe the President recognizes that, but is prepared to stand by his decision." And Bob said, "I'll do what I can with John."

PRESIDENT NIXON: Good. A big man.

ZIEGLER: He sure is.

PRESIDENT NIXON: Big man. You think, in other words, he's going to go talk to John, I presume?

ZIEGLER: He's going to talk to him on the helicopter. But the point is I told him that was your decision and Bob said: I understand the decision. . . .

PRESIDENT NIXON: . . . I don't know what the hell you do about—you know, one problem, it's a real one for John particularly, is I don't know what the hell we do for money for them in this period. Ron, what the hell do you do about that?

ZIEGLER: I don't know.

PRESIDENT NIXON: They haven't got any money. They may have—I mean, that's why the leave appealed to John particularly. Well, it didn't—nothing appealed, but—

ZIEGLER: Well, I think that in terms of money I'm sure that there's a way to—

PRESIDENT NIXON: Friends?

ZIEGLER: —friends to advance them money.

PRESIDENT NIXON: Okay, thank you. . . .

APRIL 30, 1973: THE PRESIDENT AND RAYMOND K. PRICE, 10:42–10:52 A.M., CAMP DAVID TELEPHONE

Nixon and speechwriter Ray Price discuss a draft of the President's upcoming talk to the nation that evening. The President has high hopes for Elliot Richardson, and he discusses his willingness to assume responsibility for the unfolding events.

PRESIDENT NIXON: Oh, yes, yes, it's better for me not to announce Richardson, that's right, that's right. Put them all on the same day, that's the way it is. Don't you think Richardson's a good choice?

PRICE: I think he's splendid, I think it's a first-rate move.

PRESIDENT NIXON: Yeah. It's better than [William] Rogers; I thought of him too. But even though it isn't true, everybody would think he's sort of a Nixon crony, and he would do what I said, which he would never do. But Richardson nobody figures he's a friend—well, what I mean is a personal friend. And he's sort of Mr. Integrity, Mr. Clean. He's a little tortuous at it. He's a hell of a fellow.

PRICE: Yeah, they're smart guys.

PRESIDENT NIXON: Oh, God, smart as hell. When I say tortuous, you know, he takes a long time to say something [laughter], because he's thinking so carefully.

PRICE: Um-hum.

PRESIDENT NIXON: But he'll do one hell of a job.

PRICE: Um-hum. I think that's a very good move.

PRESIDENT NIXON: He will be infinitely trusted. . . . So . . . the work you've done is so important. Was Rogers helpful?

PRICE: Yes, he was. Yes, he was. And he also said he thought that everyone—the general tone was . . . just about the right amount of sackcloth and not so much and so forth.

PRESIDENT NIXON: Oh, hell, as far as sackcloth, I would be willing to go a lot further. But, you know, I mean, I really—I have—I always had this weak[ness], I'm one of the few men in Washington that never blames the secretary when the poor damned secretary misspelled a word. I mean sometime the boss is always to blame, so the boss did it, hell, I appointed Mitchell and I appointed Haldeman. I appointed Ehrlichman. I appointed Dean. Christ, these are all my people. Colson. If they did things, they did them because they thought—they thought that's what we wanted. And so I'm responsible.

You know, but the boss can never pass it on. The President—the only problem is that if you get sackclothed too much then, you know, you no longer can be President. That's what—where Rogers I think was. He didn't want—or am I right, isn't that what his concern was, that if you go too far in terms of saying, well, I take all the blame, and I don't blame these poor fellows and all that, then you think well, Christ, this poor damn, dumb President why didn't he resign? Which might not be a bad idea, the only—

PRICE: [*Laughter.*]

PRESIDENT NIXON: —is—the only problem is, I mean you get Agnew. You want Agnew?

PRICE: No, I think—I think we'll be going around on this.

PRESIDENT NIXON: I doubt it. But any way, whether we do or not, we're doing the right thing, the right thing. God damn, we're going to get this sonofabitch routed out one way or the another. Okay. Good enough. . . .

PRICE: I really sympathized with you this weekend.

PRESIDENT NIXON: Huh?

PRICE: I said I really sympathized this weekend when I know it's been an awful tough set of decisions.

PRESIDENT NIXON: The decisions it was yesterday having to talk to Bob and John. But they're great men, fine men trying to do what was right. Okay. Ray, thanks. . . .

APRIL 30, 1973: THE PRESIDENT AND HALDEMAN, 10:16–10:20 P.M., WHITE HOUSE TELEPHONE

In a tense, highly emotional speech on April 30, 1973, President Nixon announced the "resignations" of Haldeman and Ehrlichman, "two of the finest public servants it has been my privilege to know." He allowed Kleindienst to resign, and he dismissed John Dean, who was talking to prosecutors about "Mr. P[resident]." After the speech, Nixon fields a number of telephone calls from Haldeman, Rogers, Richardson, Billy Graham, Colson, and *Reader's Digest* editor-in-chief Hobart D. Lewis. The hour is late, Nixon is distraught, and his conversations are taut and often poignant. His slurring of words only accentuates the powerful emotion of the moments. "I love you," he tells Haldeman. Yet to others, he complains that Haldeman and Ehrlichman would not voluntarily resign. "Get some sleep," Rogers tells the President. Kissinger applauds the speech, but in his memoir he was closer to the truth when he wrote "no one could avoid the impression that he was no longer in control of events." A few days earlier Nixon told Ziegler, "It's all over, do you know that?" Nixon later wrote that "from that day on the presidency lost all joy for me." Nevertheless, in the following days, Nixon resumes his defiant fight for his presidency.

PRESIDENT NIXON: Hello?

HALDEMAN: Hi.

PRESIDENT NIXON: I hope I didn't let you down.

HALDEMAN: No, sir. You got your points over, and now you've got it set right and move on. You're right where you ought to be.

PRESIDENT NIXON: Well, it's a tough thing, Bob, for you and for John and the rest, but, Goddamn it, I'm never going to discuss the son-of-a-bitching Watergate thing again—*never, never, never, never.* Don't you agree?

HALDEMAN: Yes, sir. You've done it now, and you've laid out your position. You've laid out—you've taken your steps. . . .

PRESIDENT NIXON: An interesting thing. You know, we haven't heard a—the only Cabinet officer that has called—and this is fifty minutes after the thing is over—is Cap [Caspar W.] Weinberger, bless his soul.

HALDEMAN: Hmm.

PRESIDENT NIXON: All the rest, you know, are waiting to see what the polls show. Goddamn strong cabinet, isn't it?

HALDEMAN: Oh, you better check and be sure, because they may—you know, we've had a—

PRESIDENT NIXON: No, no, no. They know. They know. They know who to call, you know. They know they can get through. But, in any event, I just wanted you to know that Cap called and he was all the way.

HALDEMAN: Good.

PRESIDENT NIXON: But let me say you're a strong man, Goddamnit, and I love you.

HALDEMAN: Well—

PRESIDENT NIXON: And, you know, I love John and all the rest, and, by God, keep the faith. Keep the faith. You're going to win this son of a bitch.

HALDEMAN: Absolutely. . . .

PRESIDENT NIXON: God bless America. I mean, I'm sure it must have driven you up the wall. It didn't drive me up the wall, but I felt that way.

HALDEMAN: No, sir, not at all. No. I'm all for that, completely agree.

PRESIDENT NIXON: I don't know whether you can call and get any reactions and call me back—like the old style. Would you mind?

HALDEMAN: I don't think I can. I don't—

PRESIDENT NIXON: No, I agree.

HALDEMAN: I'm in kind of an odd spot to try and do that.

PRESIDENT NIXON: Don't call a goddamn soul. The hell with it. Let me just say, getting this call from you—when I haven't heard from any Cabinet officer except Weinberger, now or afterwards, and thank God—and no staff member.

HALDEMAN: Well, now when I called, the board said they were instructed not to put any calls through. So—

PRESIDENT NIXON: The hell with that. I told them to put all the calls through.

HALDEMAN: Well, that may be why you haven't gotten them, though, because that's what she told me.

PRESIDENT NIXON: All right. I'll change it. I'll change it.

HALDEMAN: All right.

PRESIDENT NIXON: Fine. But God bless you, boy. God bless you.

HALDEMAN: Okay.

PRESIDENT NIXON: I love you, as you know.

HALDEMAN: Okay.

PRESIDENT NIXON: Like my brother.

HALDEMAN: Well, we'll go on and up from here.

PRESIDENT NIXON: All right, boy. Keep the faith.

HALDEMAN: Right.

APRIL 30, 1973: THE PRESIDENT AND WILLIAM ROGERS, 10:20–10:32 P.M., WHITE HOUSE TELEPHONE

PRESIDENT NIXON: Hi, Bill.

ROGERS: Gee, that was terrific, really superb.

PRESIDENT NIXON: Don't give me that shit, you know.

ROGERS: No, I really mean it.

PRESIDENT NIXON: You and I have been through—it's kind of rough. You know, afterwards I shouldn't have done it, but, you know, I thanked, you know, the operators and the rest.

ROGERS: Yeah, I know.

PRESIDENT NIXON: And all of a sudden, I sort of, sort of broke down a bit. I don't do that. You know, I'm not that kind of a man.

ROGERS: Oh, hell. I tried to get you right away, but your damn system there, it's tough to get through. . . .

PRESIDENT NIXON: We've been trying to get through to you all day. I mean, I told

Rose, Goddamnit, any Cabinet officer is to get through from the minute after this speech, and the only one I've heard from is Weinberger. So I wonder what the hell's happened to everybody else.

ROGERS: I don't know what the Goddamn system is. . . . Anyway, I thought it was superb. I don't know how you—I don't see how you could have done it any better. I think it's the best delivery I've ever seen you give. I thought the delivery—

PRESIDENT NIXON: What parts of it did you like, Bill?

ROGERS: Oh, I liked all of it. I just thought it was great.

PRESIDENT NIXON: You didn't mind the God bless America? That was my intuition at the last. I just sort of felt that way.

ROGERS: No. I thought it was—I thought it was great. I suppose some of the, you know, Christ, the editorial writers may not like it, but the public is going to love it. That's what counts. And I thought the whole tone couldn't have been better. I didn't think it was—I didn't think it had any rough spots in it. I didn't think that you had any sackcloth and ashes or anything of that kind. No, I thought it was superb. I couldn't improve on it. I just thought it was great. Adele [Rogers] was watching.

PRESIDENT NIXON: What did Adele think?

ROGERS: She thought the same thing. She thought it was critical.

PRESIDENT NIXON: She's a smart woman. You married a smarter wife than you are, you know, like I did.

ROGERS: That's right. [*Laughter.*] How'd you think it went?

PRESIDENT NIXON: I don't know anything about it, you know. I've got—you know, I've been through a hell of an experience. You know, I was just reading [Sherman] Adams's memoirs.

ROGERS: Yeah.

PRESIDENT NIXON: And Adams, you know, to his credit, did come in and say, look, I'll resign.

ROGERS: Yeah.

PRESIDENT NIXON: But Haldeman and Ehrlichman didn't, and I had to tell them they had to resign. And that was a Goddamn tough son of a bitch. . . .

Incidentally, the Cabinet thing, they were putting out Thursday, but I told Steve [Bull] to move it to Wednesday. I think we ought to get it over quickly.

ROGERS: I think it's probably better.

PRESIDENT NIXON: Is that all right with you?

ROGERS: Right, right.

PRESIDENT NIXON: Because you're the cabinet now, boy. [*Laughter.*] No, no bull-shit. You know that.

ROGERS: Incidentally, I think things look pretty good for [David M.] Packard [as Secretary of Defense], if you still want him. I think you ought to give him a call. . . . I talked to [Senator John] Stennis [D-MS]. I talked to [Senator Mike] Mansfield [D-MT]. I talked to [Representative] George Mahon [D-TX].

PRESIDENT NIXON: What'd they say?

ROGERS: Oh, they thought he'd be great. They thought he'd be great. . . .

PRESIDENT NIXON: Good of you to call, Bill. You've been a—

ROGERS: Well, Mr. President, that was a great speech. Get some sleep now.

PRESIDENT NIXON: Great.

APRIL 30, 1973: THE PRESIDENT AND BILLY GRAHAM, 10:20–10:32 P.M., WHITE HOUSE TELEPHONE

PRESIDENT NIXON: I had to tell Haldeman and Ehrlichman to resign, which they wouldn't do voluntarily, and that was tough.

GRAHAM: Well, your sincerity, your humility, your asking for prayer, all of that had a tremendous impact.

PRESIDENT NIXON: Do you really think so, Billy?

GRAHAM: I really—I'm telling you the truth, and I'm not trying to just encourage you. I know you get all that. But I really mean it.

PRESIDENT NIXON: Well, that's good of you, Billy. You have been a friend—

APRIL 30, 1973: THE PRESIDENT AND ELLIOT RICHARDSON, 10:34–10:36 P.M., WHITE HOUSE TELEPHONE

RICHARDSON: . . . Well, I was very—I thought that was really great.

PRESIDENT NIXON: Well, you're very kind to say that.

RICHARDSON: In a real sense your finest hour.

PRESIDENT NIXON: I tried to call you, actually—I mean, you know, I just—just learned, you know, about this, because, you know, the lines have been jammed, and I just learned about five minutes ago from Steve Bull that you had called. And I said, for Christ sakes, why don't you put it through? Then he said, well, we had other calls on, you know, and I was on the phone. Good God, my God, Billy Graham and eighteen other people, but I just wanted you to know I hadn't cut you off because of that.

RICHARDSON: Well—

PRESIDENT NIXON: Because you can always get through. I want you to know, you can always get through, believe me.

RICHARDSON: Well, I thank you, Mr. President. And I was very moved and touched by what you said about me—

PRESIDENT NIXON: Oh, well.

RICHARDSON: And I can assure you that—well, you know what I mean.

PRESIDENT NIXON: I know.

RICHARDSON: I won't let you down.

PRESIDENT NIXON: Do your job, boy, and it may take you all the way.

RICHARDSON: You know, it so happened that I was having a party here tonight for the military assistants who have been with [Deputy Defense Secretary] Bill Clements and me and who were just leaving for new jobs. And so all the [Joint] Chiefs were here.

PRESIDENT NIXON: Right.

RICHARDSON: And we all watched and listened to you together.

PRESIDENT NIXON: What did they think?

RICHARDSON: I've never—I don't think I've never ever been with a group of people who were more moved by an occasion like this.

PRESIDENT NIXON: Really? Really? . . .

RICHARDSON: And I won't let you down, Mr. President.

PRESIDENT NIXON: Oh, I know that. I know that. That's why I named you. [*Laughter.*] . . . .

RICHARDSON: I have the feeling that I think I can do it right. I really do.

PRESIDENT NIXON: Of course you can. Of course you can. Elliot, the one thing they're going to be hitting you on is about the special prosecutor.

RICHARDSON: Yeah.

PRESIDENT NIXON: The point is, *I'm not sure you should have one.* I'm not sure but what you should say you assume the responsibility for the prosecution and maybe bring that nice fellow [first name unknown] Hastings or whatever his name is, say he's—but whatever you want. Good God, if you want, you know, to exhume [one Chief Justice] Charles Evans Hughes, you know, do it. I don't mind. [*Laughter.*]

RICHARDSON: Okay. Well, I'm thinking about it, and I met with Henry Petersen this afternoon.

PRESIDENT NIXON: Right.

RICHARDSON: And I talked with him about it, and I'll think about it some more.

PRESIDENT NIXON: Do what you want, and I'll back you to the hilt. I don't give a damn what you do, I am for you. Do you understand? Get to the bottom of this son-ofabitch.

RICHARDSON: I do. . . .

PRESIDENT NIXON: Thank you for calling and give my best to your lovely wife.

RICHARDSON: I will. Thanks.

APRIL 30, 1973: THE PRESIDENT AND HOBART D. LEWIS, 11:04–11:06 P.M., WHITE HOUSE TELEPHONE

LEWIS: I just wanted to tell you that was a tremendous job.

PRESIDENT NIXON: You always say that.

LEWIS: No, I don't. I certainly don't. In any case, I think this was the best of all, and the toughest. Just—

PRESIDENT NIXON: You know, having to tell two men who didn't—who refused to resign, to tell them they had to was the toughest thing tomorrow—yesterday.

LEWIS: Of course.

PRESIDENT NIXON: And they are great men.

LEWIS: Of course they are.

PRESIDENT NIXON: But I had to do it.

LEWIS: Well, you're going to miss them.

PRESIDENT NIXON: Oh, well, the hell with missing them. You can fill any position, Hobe.

LEWIS: Sure. Nevertheless, it was the only thing to do, just the only thing to do.

PRESIDENT NIXON: You didn't think the speech was too emotional, huh?

LEWIS: No, it wasn't. It had to be emotional. I thought it was exactly right, the right tone of voice, and you've got everybody pulling for you, because you cleared the air on the whole thing. Without any question, it was the best job you've ever done.

PRESIDENT NIXON: I hope you liked God bless America at the end.

LEWIS: Well, of course.

PRESIDENT NIXON: I believe that, you know, very deeply.

LEWIS: I know. Well, it was very clear that your feeling about the whole thing was so sound and so sincere, so honest. You just absolutely put the cold light of day on the facts.

PRESIDENT NIXON: Right. Isn't it a shame it's all about a crappy little thing that didn't work?

LEWIS: No, of course.

PRESIDENT NIXON: Didn't work. Nobody ever got a Goddamn thing out of this damn bugging.

LEWIS: No Goddamn thing, of course—just a bunch of schoolboys.

PRESIDENT NIXON: Assholes. . . .

APRIL 30, 1973: THE PRESIDENT AND COLSON, 11:24–11:28 P.M., WHITE HOUSE TELEPHONE

PRESIDENT NIXON: Incidentally, on this—you know, all this business about, you know, the Plumbers operation, good God, that's totally justified, isn't it?

COLSON: Yes, sir.

PRESIDENT NIXON: Or is it?

COLSON: Well, I don't think there's any doubt about it. I don't intend to talk about it. They—I don't think they can make me, because that's, at least what I know about it, it's a national security operation, and Ehrlichman talked to me about that some time ago, and that was something that I wouldn't discuss. I wouldn't have any reason to discuss it.

PRESIDENT NIXON: Right. You just say—but you say look, we were protecting the security of this country.

COLSON: That's right. . . .

PRESIDENT NIXON: Well, God bless you and keep your faith, boy.

COLSON: Mine's with you, sir.

PRESIDENT NIXON: Fine.

COLSON: And the country's is, Mr. President.

PART FOUR

WATERGATE: THE PRESIDENT UNDER SIEGE

MAY 1973 – JULY 1973

The day after the resignations of Haldeman and Ehrlichman, the President was re-energized, determined to fight to preserve his presidency. In calls to a variety of aides, he cheered them on, making clear his own resolve. He vowed to conduct his own "investigation," to find out what really happened—as if the March 21 conversation was all news to him. Until the collapse of his presidency, Nixon steadfastly maintained that he had become the principal investigator, uncovering the trail of wrongdoing by disloyal and incompetent aides. John Dean's destiny was to be the President's scapegoat. Throughout the remainder of these tapes, Dean became Nixon's favorite demon, and the President constantly complained that Dean had told him nothing prior to March 21, and that he knew nothing about a cover-up.

Nixon nevertheless managed to defend the cover-up, insisting that it was "perfectly *proper* to give money for the defense of people. It is not *proper* to give it to shut up." He insisted that Dean "never told us" that was the purpose of the hush money. Now, Nixon had no hesitation to assign others their share of the blame. "We've had some bad advice," he told Haig. But a lot of the Dean problem, he argued, was because "Haldeman and Ehrlichman were relying on him" too excessively.

Besides the Dean material, the most striking thing in this period was the introduction of General Alexander Haig as Nixon's Chief of Staff, replacing H. R. Haldeman. Press Secretary Ronald Ziegler also assumed a more substantive role. The President was very much at ease with his young aide, although he never really confided his own criminal culpability to Ziegler. On occasion, Ziegler tried to offer words of moderation to quell Nixon's anger. But Haig was the dominant force in this period. Unlike Ziegler, he was expert at fueling and manipulating the President's hostilities. Nixon and Haig never frankly discussed the President's liabilities and vulnerabilities, but as the weeks wore on, it is apparent that Haig knew exactly what they were.

Haig insured his preeminent place by taking command of the President's legal defense, using his old West Point friend, J. Fred Buzhardt. Buzhardt was a veteran Capitol Hill staffer and he had served as Counsel to the Secretary of Defense. Without doubt, he had absolute loyalty to Nixon, but he worked with the President through Haig. Other lawyers, such as Nixon's old friend Leonard Garment, constitutional law expert Charles Alan Wright, and later, James St. Clair, who handled the President's impeachment defense, had no access to Nixon except through Haig. The President early on sensed that he was outgunned in legal resources by his adversaries. "We don't have a good, sound mature lawyer around," he told Haig early in May.

During this period, the President saw Haldeman, but Haig maintained a wary eye on their meetings. Haldeman already had listened to tapes of the President's conversations. Although Haldeman had joined in the famous March 21 meeting with Dean only in the last few minutes, he had a clear fix on what had transpired. Now, the two men developed their own interpretation of the conversation and Dean's motivation. Haldeman persuaded Nixon that the tape could exonerate him— used selectively, of course, and at the President's will and discretion.

The Senate hearings began on May 17. Nixon pretended to be disinterested, but he received regular briefings on the proceedings from Haig and Buzhardt. He was angered from the outset by what he perceived as a lack of loyalty from Senator Howard Baker, and the incompetence of the minority legal staff, headed by Baker's protégé, Fred Thompson. From the outset, the prospect of Dean testifying weighed heavily on his mind. Later in June, the President relished the preparation of a White House assault on Dean's integrity and ethical shortcomings. But he rarely underestimated Dean, realizing what a dangerous and formidable witness he could be.

There was occasional talk of resignation. At times, Nixon sounded like Uriah Heep, a man put upon, and unappreciated by an ungrateful nation. Let Agnew have the presidency, he said, undoubtedly with tongue in cheek. But the ploy invoked prompt objections from his aides. Kissinger told him that he could not resign, not over this "chicken shit stuff." When he said to Haig that maybe it would be better if he were to just "check out," Haig promptly responded that "it would be the greatest shock this country ever had." At times, there is a facetious, teasing quality to Nixon's talk; yet it is difficult to avoid the realization that Nixon fully comprehended the reality of such a possibility—some fifteen months before it happened. Whatever defenses were devised for him, Nixon always sensed their futility and his endangered, exposed position. For example, when Buzhardt promoted the idea of a "national security" blanket defense to exonerate the President's actions, Nixon remarked: "I be-

lieve somehow I have to avoid having the President approve the break-in of a psychiatrist's office." Such explanations clashed sharply with Nixon's treasured self-image
as a man of "law and order."

Although Nixon remained in office for a little more than a year after these tapes
concluded, we see by July 1973 that the President was a lonely, isolated man. Rose
Mary Woods, his longtime secretary, and Charles "Bebe" Rebozo, a trusted friend,
seem to offer him the rare uncomplicated, absolute loyalty and friendship he so desperately needed. And try as he might to get on with the business of the presidency, it
was Nixon himself who "wallowed" in Watergate.

May 1, 1973: The President and Alexander M. Haig, 5:43–5:44 P.M., White House Telephone

The day after dismissing his aides, Nixon holds brief conversations with such old friends as Herbert Klein, Robert Finch, and William Rogers, and with new advisors such as General Alexander Haig, that reflect his varying moods. He is profoundly upset when he learns that FBI agents had sealed Haldeman and Ehrlichman's offices to prevent any removal of papers. The new White House counsel, Leonard Garment, orders this action, but Nixon angrily rescinds it. Unlike the dispirited, distraught conversations of the previous days, here Nixon is re-energized, eager to do battle again.

PRESIDENT NIXON: Hello. Is the Pentagon still surviving today? Right, right. How's the reaction to the thing last night? All right, stay calm. Good. You think it was the right thing to do, huh? Remember we talked last night, but you still feel better today? But, your morale is good, huh, Al? O.K., well, let's get on with the business, boy. Everybody, chin's up. Right. I'll try, boy. Thank you.

May 1, 1973: The President and Stephen Bull, 5:53–5:54, White House Telephone

PRESIDENT NIXON: Yeah. Give Bob Haldeman a call and tell him I'll meet with him about those FBI guys—you know, being outside the door. . . . Second, that I want him, and he can relay it to John, he and John and the family (unintelligible) are invited to use Camp David for the weekend if they want. . . .

May 1, 1973: The President and Herbert G. Klein, 5:55–6:24 P.M., Executive Office Building

SEGMENT 1

PRESIDENT NIXON: Herb, come in.

KLEIN: Yes, sir.

PRESIDENT NIXON: . . . Let me bring you my concerns. I want them to get you on and get you up to the Watergate proceedings. And, I'm afraid that's all they'll talk about.

KLEIN: That's exactly what they will say.

PRESIDENT NIXON: And, there isn't a Goddamned thing you can say, but here's the line: . . . I want you, totally, just to say that all you're interested in is [my] being in charge of the investigation. . . . You didn't know a Goddamned thing about it, any more than I did, unfortunately. And, so why the hell should you get involved? You know what I mean?

KLEIN: I appreciate that very much. . . .

PRESIDENT NIXON: Well, what do you think? I think right now, I'd let them all jackal around. But, you carry the big burden, you've done it brilliantly, well and articulately—everybody knows you're an honest man, before too long, maybe very privately, you can say such things—you know what I mean, I wouldn't mind that, but I'd do it privately in a background way. But there's one thing that really disturbs me is when somebody leaks out the fact that those FBI guys are standing in front of Ehrlichman and Haldeman's offices—that is a bad thing—that is just reflected on those men. I was so pissed off. . . . I walked in and the guy blocked my way (unintelligible) and I said what the hell are you doing here? . . . Nobody is going to steal anything around here. They're my papers—not Bob's. *They're mine.*

SEGMENT 5

KLEIN: [Senator] Jim Buckley's [R-NY] raised a couple of questions.

PRESIDENT NIXON: What questions did Buckley raise?

KLEIN: Well, Buckley raised a question about making sure that what Ehrlichman had done was above all an examination (unintelligible).

PRESIDENT NIXON: For Christ sake, Christ, you fire the top two guys (unintelligible) and say, here it is—here's my new prosecutor, here's the new FBI guy. Good God, you can't do anything else here. What else do they want us to do? Fire the whole staff? Not going to do it. And, this is not the biggest story I've heard. There are other stories. . . . [B]y God, the President—the hardest thing in the world is for an administration to investigate itself and by God, we're doing this thing on chicken shit over nothing. But, we're doing it. . . .

SEGMENT 9

PRESIDENT NIXON: . . . I told Steve [Bull] that you might also call Bob.

KLEIN: I sure will.

PRESIDENT NIXON: Tell him how I raised hell about those Goddamned FBI men.

KLEIN: Yes, I will.

PRESIDENT NIXON: I prefer (unintelligible) that I read the cabinet out. I said, by gosh, next time, but for the grace of God, go any of you. And, that's true.

KLEIN: Couldn't be more definite.

PRESIDENT NIXON: Well, it's true. I mean—[OMB Director Roy] Ash—I defended Ash, I've defended many people, [Secretary of Agriculture Earl] Butz . . . . Rough talk, but they sort of get the feeling that well—you know a lot of those faces didn't like Bob because he was the boss. And, they didn't like Ehrlichman because he had to overrule them. But, damnit Herb, that's the wrong attitude. They're members of the *damn team.* . . . I don't let people piss on my people. I won't let them piss on anybody.

MAY 1, 1973: THE PRESIDENT AND ROBERT H. FINCH, 6:45–6:47 P.M., WHITE HOUSE TELEPHONE

Only Nixon's voice is heard on this tape.

PRESIDENT NIXON: I hope your morale is all right. OK. Take two men [Haldeman and Ehrlichman] that are so selfless and so dedicated, you know that I'd have to say all right, fellows, you know they're innocent—you have to leave, but we had to do it, Bob. That was a hard Sunday, and I'm going to have to get up for a speech. Did it come over all right on television? Were you out there? What kind of effect did it have? What have you found today? Have you talked to other people? You'd say it was positive then? He and the special prosecutor. And, that [Senator Charles] Percy [R-IL], he cooked his goose with me when he came out and said, "well, we've got to have [a Special Prosecutor to work with] Elliot [Richardson]." Well, my God. That son-of-a-bitch. I think you're going to find the morale among your people—I always just say, we just have confidence in the integrity of the presidency. One of those rare presidents who has the guts to conduct an investigation of his own people. Yeah. It's true. Then they're going to realize that this whole Watergate thing was about a crappy little thing—that everybody shouldn't have gotten that excited about. It will pass, it will pass. . . .

MAY 1, 1973: THE PRESIDENT AND ROGERS, 7:19–7:22 P.M., WHITE HOUSE TELEPHONE

Only Nixon's voice is heard on this tape.

PRESIDENT NIXON: Yeah. Oh, Bill, just [to] get your judgment before I give Elliot a call. You know, with regard to this sort of sense of the Senate resolution about a Special Prosecutor. I think Elliot should stay one jump ahead of that. I told him he could do what he wanted but I told him that he's a prosecutor himself. But, do you think he should simply say that he plans to once the grand jury finishes—what's your advice on that? . . . He shouldn't rush into that because, basically, we know the problems of the Special Prosecutor—it isn't a question of trying to get justice done—but it's a question of delaying it. Good. [Unintelligible] It attacks the new Attorney General—that's why the hell we appointed him, Bill. All right, well, we're not worried about it—just one round in the battle. Right?

MAY 1, 1973: THE PRESIDENT AND RICHARDSON, 7:24–7:32 P.M., WHITE HOUSE TELEPHONE

Only Nixon's voice is heard on this tape.

PRESIDENT NIXON: What I was going to say is that on this sense of the Senate thing [calling for a Special Prosecutor], it seems to me—and I've been thinking about it myself is basically, appointing you, of course, can name an individual . . . in this area, with the authority to do what you want, of course, but what you might do is indicate your desire to discuss the matter with congressional leaders or to name the head of criminal division [Henry Petersen]. What's your thought about it? That's right. You can do—what I mean is . . . you want to name somebody, that's your prerogative. . . . You are basically a man who is responsible. You are the Attorney General. I do think that the selection of Petersen would make sense. You know what I mean? But, uh, the point is one way you might finesse it would be to find your man there and say [you have] the responsibility, but [a Special Prosecutor] reporting directly to you—something like that. And, incidentally, it's still good in terms of the Senate. . . . I'm not trying to tell you how to do it, but let me say that you had absolute authority to do that. . . . Well, anyway, I just wanted you to know that I thought about it, and that I didn't have any good answer but it's part of the battle. You might give Bill Rogers a call and talk to him and getting his views on it. . . . You'll work on that tomorrow, will you? Good deal, good deal.

May 3, 1973: The President and Kleindienst, 8:51–9:09 a.m., Oval Office

The President confers with his now-dismissed Attorney General and instructs him in what Richardson should know about the Plumbers and the President's knowledge. Curiously, Kleindienst tells Nixon that Dean had mentioned that he never saw the President between the break-in in June 1972 and February 27, 1973.

KLEINDIENST: We have two memoranda [regarding the Ellsberg trial] chasing around my department for, by this time, ten days, unbeknownst to me.

PRESIDENT NIXON: Yeah.

KLEINDIENST: One, Silbert to Petersen disclosing what his unnamed source, *i.e.*, Dean, said. And another one from a guy named [John L.] Martin to [Kevin T.] Maroney, the deputy assistant attorney general, saying that we looked through our files and we got nothing on him. And so they've actually gone through our files. Now if they made a complete check to see if there was any evidence given to the Department of Justice and . . . there was none. . . .

PRESIDENT NIXON: We did exactly the right thing.

KLEINDIENST: My dear friend—

PRESIDENT NIXON: I want you to, I want you to, I want you to make it clear that— if you would, if you would just be sure to tell Elliot [Richardson]—that Dean had been saying a lot of things about this and you were checking them out. And that's what happened. For nine days, you were checking them out. . . .

KLEINDIENST: Incidentally, I've had two press interviews since the Department put this thing out and I said I came and told you and without any hesitation you said, "Give it to them." I also said that the reason I took nine days was we wanted to make a thorough check . . . whether we had any such information. . . . That's what Petersen brought to my attention

PRESIDENT NIXON: All right, you covered it. I just want Elliot to know that I didn't have any information, you understand?

KLEINDIENST: Oh—

PRESIDENT NIXON: Because Dean, Dean has the impression, got the impression or is under the impression that Dean had told me in March. I don't know when the hell Dean—Dean—Dean mentioned so many Goddamned things when he's around here on the Ellsberg and the rest, I don't know. . . .

When I had talked to [Henry] Petersen, and I had several talks with him in this period, I said, "I think you should know," I said, "I want you to know" when he got ready to question Hunt, I said Hunt was working on some national security items—I didn't know what national security items; he was in elite operations. I said, "In your questioning of him in the, in your questioning of him in the grand jury, you can go into anything you want, but you must not go into national security, which of course is my responsibility." He said, "I understand, I understand." . . .

But they, that Hunt did work on the Ellsberg case, that was one of the main things they were working on, you know, through our dear friend John Mitchell. But anyway, he [Petersen] said "Do you have any evidence that they ever got, ever go to the prosecution? Did they ever get any evidence?" And I said, "It is my information that they never got anything."

KLEINDIENST: That's right.

PRESIDENT NIXON: And nothing went to the prosecution. And that's what I want you to tell Elliot.

KLEINDIENST: I shall.

PRESIDENT NIXON: Tell him that, as far as the President is concerned, that he was, that the Justice Department was fully informed of everything he knew. And this was what Dean had told me. See, Dean—I didn't see Dean until the 21st of March. That's when Dean came in and began to tell me some of the things that he hadn't told me before. Sonofabitch. And now he's making up things. He's making up things all over the place.

KLEINDIENST: He told me you hadn't seen him from June 17th until sometime in March, except to sign a codicil of your will, I was astounded. And—

PRESIDENT NIXON: [*Raising his voice*] I saw him once—the sonofabitch—

KLEINDIENST: Sonofabitch.

PRESIDENT NIXON: —I saw him once for five minutes, not because of the will itself, which was not written by him as it was written by my attorney—

KLEINDIENST: He was there to execute the will.

PRESIDENT NIXON: He was there as a witness. . . . But my point is, I didn't see him until the 27th of February, 27th of February. But the other point is, I want Elliot to have the absolute assurance that, as far as the President is concerned, he [Nixon] had *no* information whatever about this thing, and as soon heard about the information, he talked to Petersen. . . .

I think the only chinks in the armor there is that, that I may have told, or somebody, or Dean may have told somebody that he informed me earlier of the fact that Hunt and Liddy worked on the Ellsberg case. Now, if that comes up, it comes up. But I told Petersen immediately, you know, I told Petersen. Petersen was aware of it. And, uh—

KLEINDIENST: No problem with that.

PRESIDENT NIXON: Well, but I want you to know, though, because I told Petersen and Petersen was aware of it, and his question was, was anything obtained in terms of the prosecution and I said, nothing, and I remember this talk was at Camp David. I remember Petersen's sigh of relief and he says, "Oh, thank God." . . .

But be sure you tell Elliot, tell him that you've never seen anybody cooperate with anybody more than I have and I've leveled with him all the way along. *And I have!* I haven't got anything to cover up. I (unintelligible)—this Goddamned thing. God-damned firing people's ass outta here right and left.

Another one I'd like for you to, uh, what you've gotta keep under control here is, you've gotta tie in with Leonard Garment, who I've got working on this, because Dean, you know, is yakking around him. And you could say, look, the President's only, the President's only knowledge of this thing, the only knowledge—believe me, I never even knew about the Ellsberg, this crazy thing that happened at the psychiatrist's. . . . Ehrlichman knew about it but didn't tell me, thank God. I'm glad he didn't; I don't want to know about such things. Neither do you.

KLEINDIENST: No. . . . I thought, the way you were looking at me, that you thought I was the one that sent those fucking FBI agents to be stationed in front of Haldeman's and Ehrlichman's office.

PRESIDENT NIXON: I know you didn't.

KLEINDIENST: I had nothing to do with that, Mr. President!

PRESIDENT NIXON: I know you didn't. . . . Nobody's interested in any files, you know. They're my files; *they belong to me.*

KLEINDIENST: Jesus Christ, if they were gonna take them, they'd have done it the day before! It's so ridiculous!

PRESIDENT NIXON: Forget Garment. You just be sure that Elliot's aware of that shit. . . .

MAY 3, 1973: THE PRESIDENT AND ZIEGLER, MAY 3, 1973, 10:30–11:01 A.M., OVAL OFFICE

Nixon tells his Press Secretary that he was unaware of the Plumbers' break-in of Dr. Fielding's office, although Ehrlichman knew. Nixon is furious that his new counsel, Leonard Garment, ordered FBI agents to seal off Haldeman's and Ehrlichman's offices. Ziegler pleads with the President to see Garment for a few minutes about an important legal matter. He also reports that Haldeman is reconciled to accepting his dismissal; Nixon, however, adds that Ehrlichman is proving more difficult. Ziegler focuses on the matter at hand: distancing the President from his discredited advisors.

SEGMENT 2

PRESIDENT NIXON: Ehrlichman said [Plumbers co-leader David] Young was on his [Kissinger's] staff. Well, that's true, Young was on the NSC staff. So, he [Kissinger] says, how (unintelligible) do I get into this? I said, "Tell the truth," I said, "Tell the truth that Young was on your staff originally." And that, however, he was needed on the domestic council and so he was transferred to Mr. Ehrlichman; however, under the system they didn't have any budget for it there, so he remained temporary on the payroll. Nothing wrong with that.

ZIEGLER: No.

PRESIDENT NIXON: You can handle that.

ZIEGLER: Oh, sure.

PRESIDENT NIXON: And Young ended up—I want you to take a very strong position on these national security things up there, right? Listen, I don't know what, I don't think that they, Hunt and Liddy, did anybody. I think that story is phony; that's one Dean probably just guessed up. . . . Ehrlichman doesn't know anything about it . . . . I don't think Krogh does. But the point of the matter is, the fact of the matter is, that if they did, it was because the Attorney General was running down these Goddamned leaks on national security and we're gonna continue to. If I see a story, if we leak, for example, our SALT position paper to [the *Washington Post*'s] Chalmers Roberts, he [Kissinger? Another leaker?] probably is gonna be gone. Goddamnit, we're gonna find out how it got outta here! You understand?

ZIEGLER: Sure, sure.

PRESIDENT NIXON: And don't be apologetic!

ZIEGLER: No, I'm not, I'm not.

PRESIDENT NIXON: I know you've always said, . . . that we don't bug, haven't bugged the newsmen since you've been in here. That's not true.

ZIEGLER: That's what I believe.

PRESIDENT NIXON: Not true. The FBI has. You said that, "to my knowledge,"that's what you probably said. . . . We probably bugged editors, if we could we could get them, but that's the way it is, but—on this, I would simply say I had no information on that—. . . .

ZIEGLER: *We did.*

PRESIDENT NIXON: But we also had to use our White House capabilities. We used every capability in the country to find out. That's always been done that way, you know. The White House—we investigated every department and every department was ordered to carry out its own investigation. That's true. Defense was ordered to carry out an investigation; State was ordered to carry out an investigation. Everybody carried out an investigation—did you know that?

ZIEGLER: No, I— . . . I think everyone understands that and has a—

PRESIDENT NIXON: I think people appreciate it too, but I'm sorry about Krogh. I told Ehrlichman yesterday that I thought he shouldn't resign because of it—

ZIEGLER: Krogh? . . . He took a leave, I think. . . .

PRESIDENT NIXON: Well, all right, fine. Tell him that that's what I think and be very positive, and say everything he did was in the national security area. You see, here's the only problem, is that there was this silly Goddamned burglary and the question was, whether or not from a legal standpoint, he should have immediately reported the burglary. . . . Well, he didn't, because, in national security investigations, they burglarize *all the time.* . . .

Well, they go in, they, they do everything because it's in the national security interest. But he [Krogh] should take—he should *not* resign—I don't want him to resign, actually, he should just take a leave until this matter's cleared up. And do it very quietly. Young is no longer in government, so we have no problem.

ZIEGLER: Okay. I have one other point I raise with you, not as an advocate but just— . . . Rogers and Len and Richardson met yesterday. First of all, I'd like to say in terms of Len, he knows you're upset by the FBI thing, without question.

PRESIDENT NIXON: Well, I'm just upset about the symbolism.

ZIEGLER: The symbolism, he understands that. . . . Well, let me make a point on Len first. Len is, I'm convinced, not leaking—

[Withdrawn item. Privacy.]

ZIEGLER: Len's not after Bob and John either. Len is moving in, I think, a very responsible way, so—

PRESIDENT NIXON: All right.

ZIEGLER: —that's of course for you to judge, but Rogers—Len, after talking to Rogers, they went over how to handle the executive-privilege matter, which you have just raised here. There's a question about this—

PRESIDENT NIXON: I signed a (unintelligible) piece of paper there.

ZIEGLER: You did? Well, Len's point is, after discussion with Rogers last night and also after meeting with John Wilson [lawyer for Haldeman and Ehrlichman], I think, that Wilson needs guidance from Len, is what Len points out to me. . . . And after discussion with Rogers on this, and Richardson. As to how he could proceed and how they should proceed on the whole executive-privilege matter. . . . Rogers supports this. . . .

PRESIDENT NIXON: Do I have to call Wilson?

ZIEGLER: No, no, no. What Len says is that he feels that he needs about five minutes with you, just to go over three questions, in terms of what he does as White House counsel. He makes the point, "Look, Ron, I'm the White House Counsel, I don't want to bother the President, . . . but for *his* protection, for the President's personal protection, I do have to at least spend a moment—"

PRESIDENT NIXON: Well, of course he should.

ZIEGLER: —"with him to—"

PRESIDENT NIXON: He knows he can come to me.

ZIEGLER: And then I called Rogers and I said, "Now, is this necessary?" And Secretary Rogers said, "Ron, I think it is, just so that Len, in his representation of the White House and the President on the whole area of executive privilege and on down the line, that he has the straight, you know, straight direction." So I bring that to you as a passage of information. I think it would be good for you to see—

PRESIDENT NIXON: Isn't he down there with them today with the U.S. attorneys?

ZIEGLER: No, he's not. But see, this is, it's this area that Wilson needs guidance apparently and Len needs guidance—Len's been meeting with John Wilson to try and work this out.

PRESIDENT NIXON: What I wrote out was a little memoranda to Len today to say I want everybody to cooperate and I want Len's cooperation. I said that executive privilege was waived with the exceptional cases of communications between the president or the president and national security.

ZIEGLER: I can't judge what that means, because I just am not confident in that area of executive privilege or the legality. But Len and the Secretary had, apparently, a long talk about this whole area last night, fully recognized the national security, you know, matter, and how it should be handled and the fact that it should be handled. But I think it would be worthwhile for you just to spend five minutes with Len—

PRESIDENT NIXON: Mm-hmm.

ZIEGLER: —for him to go, you know, over this. So that he is proceeding, uh, in accordance with your direction. I think it would be good to at least hear his point of view too on this, in terms of how to handle the executive privilege thing.

PRESIDENT NIXON: Does he want to throw everything out?

ZIEGLER: No! Absolutely not.

PRESIDENT NIXON: If he wants to do that—*these are my papers!*

ZIEGLER: No sir, Mr. President, there is no stronger, there is no stronger advocate on protecting the presidential papers than Len Garment, believe me.

PRESIDENT NIXON: Let me say, there is, I mean, the executive privilege is all national security matters.

ZIEGLER: He insists on that, Len insists on that. . . . Len insists on two things: he insists on executive privilege, . . . and above all, he insists on *absolute, total protection* of the presidential files.

PRESIDENT NIXON: That's right.

ZIEGLER: And uh, he also uses another word, he says not only "protection" of the presidential files, but no potential poaching in the presidential files [*a nervous laugh*].

PRESIDENT NIXON: I'm gonna keep them myself; they're *my* files. They don't belong to Haldeman and Ehrlichman. Or Dean. . . . Bob and John—pray for them; they're good men, though, they're honest men.

ZIEGLER: Yes, they are. . . . Bob told me, you know, that he agreed with the decision after it was made. Did he tell you that?

PRESIDENT NIXON: You told me. . . . See these are very moral men. . . . They don't drink, they don't smoke, they don't screw around, they love their families, they're very, you know, Christian Science–type of people. And damnit, it just burned their tails to get involved in all this. . . .

ZIEGLER: Well, you see, it's easy for people on this staff to sit over there and said they would've resigned; it's easy for me to sit here and say I would've resigned, when you're not confronted with it, based upon the set of circumstances that they are— there's no question in my mind that it was the right thing to do. . . . I know Bob and John are very moral men and I owe a great deal to both of them. Bob, in terms of talking to me, said "we made the right move, Ron," he said. . . .

Mr. President, I think—without dwelling on this any longer—I do think, I do think that, in this—let me just say, I trust Bob, er, Bob Haldeman and John Ehrlichman. Of course I trust them; I've trusted them for four-and-a-half to five years. From your standpoint, your personal interest, though, you, I believe, bogged down and burdened with this Watergate thing, but I do know that—

PRESIDENT NIXON: The stories are going to continue. . . . Dean'll come out again and thrash again and say that "I told the President" and Bittman, Hunt's lawyer, and I'll just say that he told the President that, er, Hunt's lawyer wanted $120,000.

ZIEGLER: We've talked about that; that is not a problem.

PRESIDENT NIXON: Why? They're not gonna believe him?

ZIEGLER: They're not gonna believe him. . . . [I]n this process is this very delicate point we're involved in right now. This is Rogers's argument and Garment's argument and Richardson's argument. This period we're going through right now is so crucial from the standpoint of protecting you, so that it does not appear that there, at this time, you are taking steps to associate yourselves, as much as you love them and respect them, associate yourselves—yourself, sir—with two of the men who are—of course, in our minds, innocent—but through a combination of circumstances and the convergence of events, it could appear—

PRESIDENT NIXON: Yeah, but that doesn't go so far, when you say "go so far" as to have FBI agents running around the White House. . . .

ZIEGLER: It was a mistake. Len [Garment] knows it was a mistake; he overreacted. It was a process he was trying to put into place. He blew it. And he knows it. He knows your feeling about it, and he absolutely, you know—he knows it. . . .

PRESIDENT NIXON: —have them sitting in the hall.

ZIEGLER: But, but, but we didn't have them sitting in the hall. I mean, there were other ways to do that. It happened that it leaked out this way and it didn't work out well. Uh, I'm convinced it didn't leak from Len.

PRESIDENT NIXON: Oh, well, I'm not gonna blame anybody. . . .

MAY 3, 1973: THE PRESIDENT AND BARRY M. GOLDWATER, 11:19–11:24 A.M., OVAL OFFICE

Senator Barry Goldwater had a great deal of stature and influence. Here he commiserates with the President about unfair media coverage. Goldwater is a bit wary during this brief conversation, perhaps because of his son's links to John Dean. In time, Goldwater will abandon Nixon altogether.

PRESIDENT NIXON: Well, you know, Barry, that you've been such a staunch soldier in this whole thing, and these, you know, jackass things happen and God, what they did to you in '64 was nothing compared to what I've been doing here.

GOLDWATER: I was lucky. . . .

PRESIDENT NIXON: . . . It's hard to call on my two trusted aides and say "Boys, you've gotta leave," but I did it. You think it was right?

GOLDWATER: Much as we didn't like to see it, I think you can take pride in these. We did the right thing. . . . I had breakfast with about 40 newsmen this morning and of course that's all they could talk about. Why weren't you guys this enthusiastic when you were doing it to me? Where were you when Bobby Baker was around? Uh, where were you when Johnson was becoming an overnight millionaire? He says, only Republicans you can get nasty with. So I said, "Maybe they won't do it to you"—

PRESIDENT NIXON: I know, I appreciate it.

GOLDWATER: Personally, I doubt they'll do anything for you. . . .

MAY 3, 1973: THE PRESIDENT AND LEONARD GARMENT, 11:30–11:59 A.M., OVAL OFFICE

Garment apologizes for bringing in the FBI to seal off Haldeman's and Ehrlichman's offices. As the President's counsel, he urges the President to use executive privilege as a "scalpel" rather than a "blunt instrument." But Nixon is uninterested in such fine distinctions and focuses instead on his adamant position that all White

House papers belong to him. Once again, Nixon bluntly lies about his relationship to Dean—and to his new lawyer.

GARMENT: First, I want to, uh, apologize for the way I handled that FBI thing. But I—I—I really didn't think of it—

PRESIDENT NIXON: I thought it was Ruckelshaus—

GARMENT: No, it wasn't that. It was me.

PRESIDENT NIXON: The only thing that I was concerned about was that, in the halls—

GARMENT: They shouldn't have been in the halls, but I didn't know—

PRESIDENT NIXON: I talked to Ehrlichman and I talked to Bob, and—

GARMENT: No, no, it was my fault. . . .

PRESIDENT NIXON: Yeah, you were right to do it, you were right to do it.

GARMENT: . . . [I]f I knew what I know now, I'd have gone at it differently. I over-reacted, sorry, I understand your feelings about it. Haldeman was just strong as steel the next day when I saw him, admirable reaction to the whole thing, so don't be worried about this guy. He said "don't be worried about this, you did the right thing to protect the president and be professional about it." So I'm sorry.

PRESIDENT NIXON: Forget it. Don't even mention it. Harm's done.

GARMENT: The harm's probably done. . . .

PRESIDENT NIXON: The most important thing is this, if I may say so, that we've got to recognize on those papers and so forth, that they do not belong to Haldeman or Ehrlichman or Dean—they belong to me. And I am not going to allow anybody, and that includes Elliot Richardson or you or anybody ever to look at those papers.

GARMENT: Got it.

PRESIDENT NIXON: You understand? *They're mine.* They're under lock and key, and incidentally, that also covers Henry's. All those national security papers, I am not going to frankly allow them to be put out there. My papers—

GARMENT: They're your papers.

PRESIDENT NIXON: You understand the point. . . . Okay, that's all I wanted. That's why the FBI thing worried me a little because I thought, well, they're gonna have the FBI clawing through my papers?

GARMENT: If you ever believe anything I've ever said to you, in all of the years we've known each other, believe me on that. I give you my solemn word. I'll try to be solemn. The problem is, now, Mr. President, the same one here, about how to protect the privilege and how to protect you and how to deal with the privilege. It is a scalpel, rather than a blunt instrument, to the extent that when it's used in a blunt way, it will lose its effectiveness, because then it creates impressions of power. So knowing that we have a whole parade of scenes going at this point: the grand jury, the FBI inter-rogators, and Matt Byrne, proceedings in the Senate, those fellas were rushing with all kind of people.

PRESIDENT NIXON: Right.

GARMENT: And with the privilege problem, they—from time to time—and not knowing what one of these damn fools are going to say and you know, before they crank their camera. I took counsel, basically, with Bill Rogers because he is, he's a for-mer Attorney General, he's very practical, he understands what the problems are. And his very strong feeling was to figure out what the priorities are: gotta protect the President, gotta protect the conversations between the President and his staff, . . . and then beyond the core of concerns is the avoidance of any appearance of trying to—

PRESIDENT NIXON: cover-up.

GARMENT: —cover-up. . . .

PRESIDENT NIXON: What do you suggest as a procedure?

GARMENT: What Rogers has suggested and [what] I think is essentially this: basi-cally, I'll summarize what it is and we can go through it, that the witnesses before the Ervin Committee, informal discussions that are going on now with the committee, the staff investigator, and before the grand jury and in the FBI interrogations, deter-mine privilege in the first instance, knowing . . . that they can't reveal conversations with you, and knowing that they can't turn over any presidential papers, that they don't have them and they can't turn them over, and that the area in which you'll be able to raise privilege would be essentially national security concerns. . . . I think they would be consulting their own lawyer about—they understand the general ground rules here. If they have any real questions, then I think—

PRESIDENT NIXON: The problem is, . . . as I understand it, the President, it's the President's privilege and not theirs—is that right?

GARMENT: Well, that's—

PRESIDENT NIXON: Not true?

GARMENT: It, in a sense, that's correct. . . .

PRESIDENT NIXON: . . . [I]n the time of the Pentagon Papers, we had a broad-based, what we called a "leak operation". We ran practically—most of it through the Bureau. These two clowns [Hunt and Liddy] were used also. However, I—let me say—I don't, I can't tell you what I think they did. I asked Ehrlichman specifically, I said "John, did these guys do any *bugging?*"

GARMENT: Unbelievable.

PRESIDENT NIXON: He said, "no." I see the paper this morning that apparently Dean, (unintelligible), says they did bug. But he's saying that basically on hearsay. . . . I have to say, if they did, the most important thing is that the whole Hunt and Liddy thing never produced a Goddamned thing.

GARMENT: Right.

PRESIDENT NIXON: *Nothing!*

GARMENT: Nothing.

PRESIDENT NIXON: Now, take this Water—take this psychiatrist thing. The reason it came—if you talk to John [Ehrlichman] or read his FBI interview—the reason it came to John, he tells me, is that what happened—[*laughter*] these clowns apparently wanted to go to the psychiatrist and then they didn't get what they wanted. And then asked to go back in.

GARMENT: To go back in? [*Laughter.*]

PRESIDENT NIXON: And he, and then John said, "No, knock it off!" That's what John Ehrlichman told me. . . . Now, when did I learn—when did I—the first I ever heard about the Goddamned thing—I mean about the whole Watergate. The first time—now let's get another thing very clear about this so that you'll know where we stand on Dean. . . . Dick, Dick Kleindienst would say, uh, you know, "How often did you see Dean, you know, the summer and so forth? I said, "Once." I said, and it's true, from January the first, 1972, until February the 27th [1973], . . . I saw him for five minutes when I signed my will. Five minutes. But Kleindienst said, "well, Dean gives the impression that he's sitting in there on your lap every day!" . . .

But he didn't! . . . All that I know is that, in the period—in the March 21 period, you know—Dean came in and . . . that's when he told me about Hunt and all that crap, you know, and raising funds for them, and that's when I started my own investigation. Uh, the fact he says, you know, Hunt and Liddy were involved, in some of the leak operations—I knew they'd been on the White House staff—and they said some of that stuff is involved, may be involved, in the Ellsberg case. That's all—just like that.

Later, later, when Hunt was called before the grand jury, I talked—this was in April—I talked to Petersen at Camp David. I said, "I just want to say one thing." I said, "You can question me with the grand jury about anything that has to do with Watergate," but I said, "but national security matters are not the province of this grand jury." He says, "I totally agree. We're staying out of national security matters." Not knowing then what the hell it was. Then Kleindienst came in finally on Sunday, as he said he has reported it to you. And said, "Look, we now apparently, based apparently on what Dean or I or somebody had told him, had conducted an investigation for ten days, had found that there had been this break-in." And the way they found it is a curious thing, from what I now—from what I hear—apparently there was a picture taken—did you hear about that?

GARMENT: In front of the office.

PRESIDENT NIXON: Did you hear about that?

GARMENT: I heard generally that they came out [of Dr. Fielding's office] with a picture [of the ransacked office].

PRESIDENT NIXON: The CIA—the CIA—his camera, you see, but crazy Hunt borrowed a camera from the CIA when he was working there. He returned it to the CIA. There was a roll of film in it. The roll of film had a picture of these two clowns standing in front of the psychiatrist's office. . . . But, but let me just say this—you've got to, you've got to have confidence in me—

GARMENT: I have.

PRESIDENT NIXON: I know you do.

GARMENT: Absolutely.

MAY 8, 1973: THE PRESIDENT AND ZIEGLER, 8:21–9:23 A.M., OVAL OFFICE

The President prepares Ziegler for a news briefing. He claims that his memory is "unclear" on the origins of the Ellsberg break-in, but is confident, or maybe just hopeful, that Ehrlichman will not involve him. Nixon and Ziegler discuss John Dean and the March 21 meeting. Following form, Nixon maintains that Dean had brought him "news," and he promptly launched his own investigation. Dean had

leaked information about the crucial September 15, 1972 meeting, but Nixon again denies that they had met before February 1973. "Why didn't he tell me before?" Nixon complains.

SEGMENT 3

PRESIDENT NIXON: . . . [W]e had leaks, for example, on—(unintelligible), we have national security, and the President's—the President gives instructions to everybody. He says, I received instructions. Everybody was to—to take all possible steps to (unintelligible). I ordered—directed the Cabinet to do so. I directed the Security Counsel to do so. I told everybody in the Administration as a first priority to avoid the release of national security matters. . . .

One other point I'd like to raise if I could. It's very important. They're [the media] going to ask when I had knowledge of the fact that there was a burglary. You know, not burglary, but you know, out there. And, as I told you, my recollection is unclear. I just don't remember when I heard. . . . You see, John Ehrlichman, I think really in a way, it was to cover his own (unintelligible) to a certain extent, is—and I told him, I said, John, I do not recall damn things as well as you do, but I think he's talking about two different things. I was aware that Krogh was conducting an operation. I had no awareness whatever of going out to Los Angeles or whatever to look in the Goddamned office of a—

ZIEGLER: psychiatrist's office. . . .

PRESIDENT NIXON: Is it—don't you think we had better check with Ehrlichman to say, to say that our position here is that I did not learn of this—I mean, I did not learn of the burglary—you know what I mean—until I began my own investigation? . . . Yeah, that he informed me of the burglary.

ZIEGLER: Well, I'm sure he didn't. . . .

PRESIDENT NIXON: . . . [J]ust like I am talking to you at this moment, I trusted him . . . I talked to Dean this way. The only thing that I have concern about that he could raise hell about is the crazy damned business that (unintelligible).

ZIEGLER: Well, I know, but nothing happened, and the investigation resulted—of course, the other thing you have to keep in mind—

PRESIDENT NIXON: . . . I said you can't give this guy clemency (unintelligible) that's out of the question. . . . Let us say that if I told you [Dean] to go get that [a million dollars], and where you get it and so forth and, of course, nothing like that was discussed. But if so, we would have to deny it anyway.

ZIEGLER: True.

PRESIDENT NIXON: . . . [I]n talking to Bob, . . . I might say I had no knowledge of the break-in, I had no—

ZIEGLER: The Ellsberg?

PRESIDENT NIXON: Exactly, the break-in, until my own investigation in March. And that is the [truth?]. I didn't know—I didn't know the White House people had broken into the Goddamned psychiatrist's office. John and Ehrlichman didn't come in and tell me. Believe me. Nobody told me. Did you know about this?

ZIEGLER: No, sir.

PRESIDENT NIXON: Are you sure?

ZIEGLER: I'm absolutely sure. . . . And I was stunned when I heard that Hunt and Liddy had done that, and I was absolutely totally stunned, and I told Ehrlichman, and I said—this is during the period when we were beginning to make the decision—you were—they had to leave. I said—John, *you cannot stay and survive around here if you had awareness of a break-in,* as insignificant as it was, and it was related to national security, because of the environment. Remember those discussions we were talking about? . . .

PRESIDENT NIXON: I—I—I could—I could defend a bugging—

ZIEGLER: Sure.

PRESIDENT NIXON: —but not a—not a burglary. Well, for national—

ZIEGLER: You could even defend a burglary for national security. . . . But it happened to be conducted by Hunt and Liddy. . . . Who became later involved in the Watergate, who also were involved in a whole—an awful lot of other stuff allegedly, like the Cuban—I mean the—

PRESIDENT NIXON: The problem we've got, I must tell you this, Ehrlichman has an—has given—has (unintelligible) the national security files, as I've told you. I don't know how much of that is Hunt and Liddy stuff.

ZIEGLER: I don't think it matters.

PRESIDENT NIXON: I'm never going to give it out. They'll ask for it. National security—I'm going to stand like a rock. . . .

ZIEGLER: Mr. President, this is where you really need—and Al and I were talking about this. This is where you need—Al's not a lawyer, I'm not a lawyer. Len Garment is okay, but—

PRESIDENT NIXON: too emotional. . . .

SEGMENT 4

ZIEGLER: . . . Now, these—Len tells me that Fred Thompson, the minority counsel—

PRESIDENT NIXON: Yeah.

ZIEGLER: —wanted to meet with me privately to find out what I told—what Dean told me, and I've got him nailed on that.

PRESIDENT NIXON: What did Dean tell you? . . .

ZIEGLER: They simply are interested in finding out how I got my guidance from the brief. Well, [Gerald] Warren and I are going to sit down with him for about forty-five minutes and just document how we got the guidance. And there's absolutely no question we went through the files over and over and over again, and Dean refers to the President's statement in San Clemente, referred to the Dean report. . . .

Len said that they went out of their way three times in the conversation, we want to talk to Ron privately, totally privately, and Jerry, for the sole purpose of determining what Dean said in terms of guidance. Strictly limited to that. That there's no other reason, and he said they went on and on and on and out of their way to state that. So I think we should do it.

PRESIDENT NIXON: We should be very forthcoming. Well, there comes the charge. Okay. Assuming that that's the charge that's made, assuming he has a document he has written at Camp David, forty-three pages in length, in which he recounts the conversations we've had, that we went over (unintelligible) executive privilege, there's no question that that was blackmail. Well, . . . you've got to really smash it once and for all. He may mention that [Thomas] Pappas was in the office the week before. You know how to handle that. . . .

ZIEGLER: Figure it's the worst. Let him say, I walked into the President's office and said to the President, Mr. President, you are totally aware, aren't you, sir, about the money, we've been paying to the defendants. We need more money. If not, they're going to blow. And he did this in January or February?

PRESIDENT NIXON: Never did.

ZIEGLER: You said figure the worst. Did it in March, did it some other time or during the course for the period that he was working on this at some point, he said something to you that in the context of today could mean something. The best way to deal with John Dean—

PRESIDENT NIXON: Why didn't he say it before?

ZIEGLER: Excuse me?

PRESIDENT NIXON: Ask, why didn't he tell me before.

ZIEGLER: The best way to deal with Dean, is some day—you don't rush right out and deal with Dean. In the—whenever it is, two months from now, whenever this develops, the President of the United States, to look directly into the camera, or wherever, in a press conference or out here in the press room and say, ladies and gentlemen, . . . I had a man on my staff who was my counsel and who was a trusted aide, and in the course of that, I talked freely with him, not about illegality, not about wrongdoing. That man has taken much of what I said in the sanctity and the privileged sanctity of the Oval Office and attempted to use that for his own self-service—serving means in order to discredit the Presidency of the United States. That will not be done. That cannot be done. I reject everything which he states took place. . . .

In the *Newsweek* article, for example, Dean says he was not aware of the—of the—he was not asked to conduct an investigation. On two occasions Gerry [Warren] said Dean was lying, I mean, because he said on two occasions he said that John Ehrlichman told him that the President wanted to get—to look into this immediately, on occasion after occasion.

PRESIDENT NIXON: *Oh Christ, we all assumed he was conducting an investigation.* And thanked him for carrying such a big load, or whatever it was. Oh, no. He—I think Dean is going to overstep, he's going to lie too much here. Even the little thing that Jack Anderson pointed out that he was he in the office on September 15. Hell, no, he wasn't in the office on the September 15. Haldeman wasn't even in the office. . . .

You know, the interesting thing was a lot of the time—we started meeting the 27th of February, and we were talking about executive privilege, and we were talking also about Dean's fight with Pat Gray, you know, that—actually trying to defend him—and I was pointing out to him, I said, if you were conducting an investigation for the White House, you would have had to have these things.

ZIEGLER: Yeah, the FBI files.

PRESIDENT NIXON: That's what I said. . . . [S]o what the hell—if he wasn't conducting an investigation, why did he get the FBI files? Why did he sit in on the conversations of the White House staff?

ZIEGLER: Sure.

PRESIDENT NIXON: That was the purpose of it. He's had conversations and got the FBI files. Well, get ready when he cracks. I don't know why he flipped up the *Newsweek* crap to begin with. . . .

MAY 8, 1973: THE PRESIDENT AND HAIG, 9:23–10:16 A.M., OVAL OFFICE

On May 4, the President announced that General Alexander Haig would assume Haldeman's tasks on an "interim" basis. A week after the dismissal of his chief aides, Nixon has easily transferred his confidence to Haig. The President congratulates himself on his April 30 actions; clearly, he is prepared to have Haldeman and Ehrlichman stand trial. Haig provides Nixon with the supportive talk that the President needs. He assures the President that the polls show that people do not want the presidency destroyed; there is, Haig said, a bipartisan consensus on this matter.

PRESIDENT NIXON: Basically, you know, the more you think about it, Al, it's the right thing.

HAIG: I think it is.

PRESIDENT NIXON: Goddamn it, it's just more of the same. It's just crap. You know what I mean? Don't you agree?

HAIG: I agree. I think it's just crap. It's going to ultimately resolve itself to discrediting that son of a bitch [Dean], and I think the weight of the Presidency and the—

PRESIDENT NIXON: Did you see the Harris poll, by any chance?

HAIG: No, I didn't see it.

PRESIDENT NIXON: Ron . . . said that by a vote of 59 to 31, they thought the President should be given the benefit of the doubt on this matter and should be allowed to finish his term. You know, the next three and a half years. But the other interesting thing is by a vote of 77 to 13 they opposed suggestions that the President resign.

HAIG: *Of course. My God.* . . . It's unthinkable. It's unthinkable. . . .

PRESIDENT NIXON: Oh, they may, but, you see, only one person there trying to do that. You realize that. That's Dean. And Goddamn him, we got to figure out the very worst he's going to say and be prepared to hit it at a proper time, but no sooner and let the son of a bitch go. They're not going to give him immunity. . . . If he doesn't get immunity, he's got to be worried about his own skin, how much he wants to admit.

HAIG: That's right. That's exactly right.

PRESIDENT NIXON: But you know, the other thing is if one—one disloyal President's counsel, a lawyer, of all people, not just a—a Henry Kissinger walking out, you know, as a disgruntled person, people will understand it. But the President's lawyer? Jesus Christ. I mean, this is a—

HAIG: Well, he's a sniveling coward.

PRESIDENT NIXON: I think we can destroy him—we must destroy him.

HAIG: Have to.

PRESIDENT NIXON: We never can allow this to happen—even if I was guilty as all hell, but I'm not (unintelligible). I was dragged into this, sonofabitch, because of stupid people. Well-intentioned stupid people.

HAIG: That's something entirely different. Here, we've got a vicious little coward who's trying to protect his ass at any cost.

PRESIDENT NIXON: And therefore he's got to be destroyed.

HAIG: And he's emerging as that type of character.

PRESIDENT NIXON: You really think so?

HAIG: Yeah. . . .

PRESIDENT NIXON: . . . I'd rather have a lawyer advising me and advising Ziegler what to say and let Ziegler handle it right here.

HAIG: I think so. There's no way of breaking it out without—

PRESIDENT NIXON: We might break it out, but let's—I thought that over, and don't you agree, let's just decide that we not try to do that. However, let us ask [H. Chapman "Chappie"] Rose [Nixon's former law partner] on a temporary basis just to come in as a special assistant to the President. . . . Would you call him and counsel him and just meet him here, and he'll be the guy to just handle all these matters.

HAIG: And, what's, Garment can work for him, and Garment is very—gets along very well with him. In fact, Garment leans on him. So I think it's an excellent solution short-term. . . .

PRESIDENT NIXON: Has Richardson gotten any word of special counsel yet?

HAIG: No, he has not, but he—that was well done yesterday. He handled that well. I could check that this morning and see—

PRESIDENT NIXON: The thing you should do with him, so that I don't want him to be out of touch with me.

HAIG: No. I'll call him.

PRESIDENT NIXON: I don't want him to feel that—that—just say, the President thought you handled the announcement just right. That he deliberately wants to keep this at arm's length at this point. That—you know what I mean? If he had any—wants anything, he can run names by or thoughts—

HAIG: Well, he knows quietly that he's to appoint no one without checking.

PRESIDENT NIXON: Well, I'd just like to know something about it. The other thing is tell him I know that the question of the immunity for Dean has raised, he's to know that the prosecutors and I had told Petersen after I made my statement . . . that that's a decision they must make, and it depends on their judgment as to how they investigate the truth. But immunity must not be used as an incentive to lie. You know what I mean? . . . I want him to know that's the decision of the prosecutors. I want them to know that the President—that I said that consistently, as of the [April] 16th, on the 16th, I said it's your decision, whatever you can do to get to the bottom of this thing. I want them to know that, Al. As far as I'm concerned, it's six of one and a half dozen of another on immunity too. I think in one way, you can say you can give him immunity, it isn't going to be as rough. On the other hand to give this fellow immunity from prosecution, I'm inclined to think he could even be right. What do you think?

HAIG: I think that's it totally. That's the way he's trying to play it. That's why— that's the incentive for—

PRESIDENT NIXON: Leaks, attacks on the President?

HAIG: It's bad. It's the worst thing we could do, and I hope they don't do it. . . .

PRESIDENT NIXON: But, Al, there's something to be said, you know. I didn't have to see a Harris poll to realize it, I mean, apart from anything else. The country doesn't want the Presidency to be destroyed.

HAIG: No.

PRESIDENT NIXON: I mean, the country rallies around the President. They rallied around Kennedy at the time of the Bay of Pigs, that horrible disaster. You know what I mean? That doesn't mean they like presidents when they have terrible problems, but on the other hand, they realize we've done some quite considerable things for this country, you see. . . . And they know we've got some other great things to do too.

HAIG: It hasn't been very long since November where they registered how they felt.

PRESIDENT NIXON: Well, it also hasn't been very long since—let's face it, since the end of January when we had the peace announcement. It hasn't been very long since the 28th of March when all the prisoners came home. . . .

[Haig then raised the problem of White House and Cabinet morale since November when Haldeman, in Nixon's name, demanded Cabinet and staff resignations.]

PRESIDENT NIXON: You mean [the] transition since November?

HAIG: Yes. That's where the problem started, really.

PRESIDENT NIXON: Basically what happened, I must take some of the blame there. Haldeman and Ehrlichman were a little too rough [*chuckles*].

HAIG: They were rough, very rough. . . .

PRESIDENT NIXON: We thought—we thought that was the right thing to do then. I was part of the decision.

HAIG: It would have been, had we hadn't had this other problem [Watergate] on top of it. . . . The two together was too much.

PRESIDENT NIXON: That's right. If we hadn't had this other problem, it would have been like we planned. After all, you won the election; everybody should have shaped up.

HAIG: We would have had a—we would have had great discipline, we would have had a tightly knit team. . . . But this other thing was too much for the traffic to bear.

PRESIDENT NIXON: Well, this other thing sort of came on top of them, and everybody thought, well, now's a chance to get these sons of bitches.

HAIG: That's right.

PRESIDENT NIXON: And everybody hates the White House staff, now.

HAIG: Oh.

PRESIDENT NIXON: You know, the Cab-—when I say hates them, the Cabinet usually, the Congress is always saying—they always—they don't like to blame the President, but they like to blame his staff for every damned silly thing that happens. I'll tell you, . . . what the hell, a bigger move could I have had than to have had the Attorney General resign, and Haldeman and Ehrlichman resign?

HAIG: Couldn't have been any more.

PRESIDENT NIXON: And I did it, right? . . . You still think it was the right thing to do?

HAIG: Yeah. You had to. You couldn't—you couldn't have operated, I don't think, with both of those men being named. . . .

PRESIDENT NIXON: That doesn't mean that every time anybody comes under attack, he goes. In other words, we've got to defend our people when they come under attack. On the other hand, the White House staff has got to be like Caesar's wife.

HAIG: Exactly. Has to be.

PRESIDENT NIXON: That was the sad thing about Bob and John, because they're both wonderful men, and they are guiltless. . . . I think . . . they had just built up too much—they had no friends, let's face it.

HAIG: They had no friends. . . . They were waiting. They were waiting to pounce. You had no way of holding those men, and you can see it in the editorials and everything else, that this animosity was building against both of them. It was building even without this. . . .

PRESIDENT NIXON: And yet, despite—I raised the question rhetorically, was it the right thing to do? I think we gained quite a bit out of, one, the action where I finally did have to lower the boom on two of my most trusted associates, [two] when I took the resignation of the Attorney General and appointed Elliot Richardson and when I made that speech to the country and said I take responsibility. I think that had to help us out.

HAIG: It did help us. It turned off what would have been a very bad stampede. That stopped. The stampede has stopped. . . . They will whack away, and they'll continue, but it's not the same kind of thing. Your responsible people want this thing stopped. . . . You got a bi-partisan census.

PRESIDENT NIXON: Well, you take care of that.

HAIG: Good.

MAY 8, 1973: THE PRESIDENT AND DONALD M. KENDALL, 12:43–12:56 P.M., OVAL OFFICE

Kendall, CEO of Pepsico, was an old friend of Nixon's, a former client, who had been Chairman of Businessmen for Nixon. Here he offers some advice to his friend, from the perspective of an outsider.

KENDALL: . . . . [T]here's still a lot of people who question your involvement. . . . The only thing now that people believe is not what you put out in the press, it's what somebody picks up on a leak. I mean that's the only thing they believe, so what I think you ought to do is that you want to write a memorandum to Haig. Tell Haig all the anguish, the personal problems you had going through this period, and what has happened, and the reason your position of this is that you don't want this same type of thing to ever happen again in your administration, or anything that comes up that is going to affect the integrity of this office—

PRESIDENT NIXON: I got it.

KENDALL: You want to know about it—that you don't want him to make that type of mistake. . . . And you want to blister Haldeman and Ehrlichman and this, I know, is a tough thing for you to do. But, what you have publicly defended—Haldeman and Ehrlichman, which people admire . . . . Well, you have no choice because you've got to think about the office. I mean, this is not—

PRESIDENT NIXON: They both are going to be found not guilty. . . .

KENDALL: Well, it's a horrible thing. I mean these two guys' lives are—

PRESIDENT NIXON: Hurt, not ruined.

KENDALL: They're not ruined, but uh—

PRESIDENT NIXON: That's right. I think that's a good idea. I get exactly what you mean. . . .

KENDALL: What you do is you get the thing—you get the memo out. You give me the memorandum. I will guarantee that Jack Anderson will print it. . . . What you do is you go through the personal agony that you have in the past. You review that for him which is not the thing to do and telling Haig that you don't want this to happen again—in other words you go through all the problems that you've had the last few months and what it meant to you to do it with Haldeman and Ehrlichman and then you have to blister them and say that they let you down by not keeping you informed and that you don't want something like this happen without being informed of all the details because this attacks the integrity of the office . . . .

PRESIDENT NIXON: I think it's a very good idea. I'll write something—

KENDALL: And, then he does a complete story about it [and] Anderson comes out with it. . . .

MAY 8, 1973: THE PRESIDENT AND HAIG, 12:59–1:47 P.M., OVAL OFFICE

For the first time, Nixon gives Haig a lengthy report on the fateful March 21 meeting with Dean. Nixon may have heard the tape, or Haldeman, who did hear it, may have briefed him. The President's account had some important omissions and some important lies. "The purpose of the conversation was to get at what he had been up to," Nixon tells Haig. The President characterized Dean as a man with something to hide; he "[left] out that he was involved," Nixon insists. But, in fact, Dean had initiated that meeting, and made his own culpability in the cover-up quite clear. Now six weeks later, the President furiously turns on his former counsel. Curiously, Haig secures an admission of the September 15, 1972, meeting with Dean—one that had made "no earthly impression" on Nixon. The new Chief of Staff consolidates his power at the outset, undermining other White House aides.

PRESIDENT NIXON: . . . I do not remember ever seeing Dean. Bob Haldeman told me that I only saw him on the one occasion when I signed my will. . . . The worst thing, far worse than . . . involved in this even obstruction of justice, is perjury. . . . Well, I'm glad you told me. . . . [Haldeman] should have told me more about this thing as it turned out. But, boy, don't ever keep anything from me I need to know. Don't bring me crap that I don't need to know. You know what I mean. . . . I know what the hell this stuff is. I am confident I've told you everything that I know about my—my own conversations with Dean for whatever it's worth. . . . March 21st was the critical day. He came into the office and on that day did reveal a hell of a lot of things except leaving out that he was involved. Like he didn't go into the fact that he had fixed this. I told you the testimony for Magruder. Now that later comes up, that he did coach Magruder, which he was not supposed to have done. He did, however, say that that's when he—he said this is a terrible cancer on the presidency. Dean says the way this thing is growing, we've got to do something about it. . . .

And he also told about the—the fact that the defendants had—and that money had been raised for the defendants. . . . . That was late or early summer. And then both Ehrlichman and Haldeman had approved the transfer of $350,000 back to the committee, which is when he presumed—he assumes. He doesn't know . . . . And—and this is the critical point—that this fellow Bittman, Hunt's lawyer, was now demanding more money for his attorney's fees.

It was then that I got into a discussion which I deliberately led him on, about I said, well, suppose you could get it. How much—how much you going to need? You're going to have to do it for four years, aren't you? So, that would cost a million dollars. So, you could get a million dollars, but how are you going to get it delivered to him? And how—you can't provide—you can't produce—clemency. . . . [F]ortunately, Bob does recount—remembers the conversation better than I—but what I'm getting at, the purpose of the conversation was to get at what the hell he had been up to. And I said, well, there's nothing we can do about it. . . .

What I did do—what I did do, I said, now, John, we've got to—I've got to have a full written report on this case. That's when I sent him—then the following day I sent him up to Camp David, and I said, take your time. Write a report so that we can—tell the truth about it. I said, "I want the *whole* truth. I want the Segretti thing out. Let's get that story out. Let's get out the story about whether the—to the extent that the White House is not involved"—because he was still contending on the 21st that despite these things, that first, there was no White House involvement—either Haldeman or he—in the planning of the Watergate, and second, that from a legal standpoint, there was no White House involvement by Haldeman or Ehrlichman themselves in obstructing, you know, through collecting money for the defense because they were doing it presumably for attorney's fees.

But then the question arises as to whether it would now become obstruction, and the point was, the Bittman part. . . . Bittman had gone to apparently the attorney for the committee [Paul O'Brien or Kenneth Parkinson?] and had asked—and told him that he had to have the money, and that came into Dean. Dean (unintelligible) reported to me as a matter of fact. . . .

It was his job to tell me what the hell was up. And it was when—it was actually then in my own mind, as I reflect back, that triggered my own investigation of this Goddamn case is because, as I told you then, the word—the only word you could (unintelligible) basically is blackmail. You can't blackmail—and frankly it just wouldn't work. I said, let's suppose you could get it. I said we could get the money. I said, but how—how would it work? A million dollars paid to a jackass that's in jail to keep you from talking?

Well, this was the purpose of this. I'm talking about Watergate (unintelligible) Hunt saying he talked about other things that he was engaged in. In other words, if there's such (unintelligible), he's blackmailing Ehrlichman. I said, but Jesus Christ, for a man to go out and put that up, which he will do, which we must assume he may do, is of course, a terrible thing to do. . . .

Now, how would you answer anything like that? I don't know. I don't know. I can't do it. I can't get up and say, look, I'm not a crook, something like that. . . . Here's the guy who for nine months we were counting upon, who was supposed to be making the reports. Here's the guy, and so forth and so on. And then he comes in for the first time nine months later reports this sort of thing—

HAIG: . . . An investigation was launched and the man was told to write up a complete report. That was the kind of activity that he had been involved in, and that's it. It's got to be.

PRESIDENT NIXON: You know, the problem that he has with this—of course, the minute he gets immunity, he won't have that problem. The problem he has with this whole thing, this involves him in the whole, you know, criminal—I mean, not really. He's reporting to me what somebody else is doing, but you see, the problem it presents to us basically is the charge that the President was aware of or gave approval of a coverup. You got the point? Or of obstruction of justice. There's the charge that you could expect from . . . Dean, but I think we can manage it. . . .

HAIG: I think that's (unintelligible), and we have two guys down [Haldeman and Ehrlichman]. . . . You see, they know the realities. In some instances, it is troublesome for them, but [you must] anticipate they know the institution has got to be protected and that you have to be protected. . . .

PRESIDENT NIXON: Well, the main thing you have to know, as I said before, is you've got to know, first, leaving out the morality, I would never be so stupid to say, look, let's go out and raise $120,000 for the purpose, after Hunt had already been convicted and keeping it quiet for four years because that would simply be a bottomless pit, also particularly since there was even talk of clemency hanging around, which I knew we couldn't fulfill. That was also in the conversation, as I told you.

So, in other words, in the conversation [we discussed] blackmail. There can be—the clemency thing won't hang up, and second, how the hell—how the hell do you do the money? In other words, basically it was my way of getting the Goddamn facts out. That's what I'm really trying to say. . . . I think at that point I only just thought it was a hopeless mess. Dean had reached that same conclusion then on March 21st. When he went to Camp David, I think he was trying to think how the hell can we write it in a way (unintelligible) report which does absolve the White House. . . .

I think what happened is that he realized, as he started to write his report, there was no way he could write the Goddamn thing that didn't incriminate himself. That's what happened. So, then he told his lawyers and decided to tell all, but he should have told us.

HAIG: That's right.

PRESIDENT NIXON: That's the point.

HAIG: That's right. He was scrambling for cover, and I think that's pretty (unintelligible).

PRESIDENT NIXON: Well, he—basically he's trying to save his own skin.

HAIG: Wherever—wherever we wind up, wherever we can through innuendo and what have you, is manage it. That's the basic judgment here. There's enough Goddamn at stake in terms of the country and the interest of the country. . . .

PRESIDENT NIXON: It has to be managed. That's the whole point. There's a question of whether it's manageable. . . . The hopes and dreams of a hell of a lot people in this country and the world are going right down the tube, and we're not going to let that happen now, not with this kind of a son-of-a-bitch. That's really what's involved here.

HAIG: Precisely what's involved. . . . I have a feeling that it's going to—it's going to be—and if he does his best, it's going to surface in a confused and contradictory way. At his best, assuming the worst case where that son-of-a-bitch is just trying to (unintelligible), I still think it's going to be a very confused. . . .

PRESIDENT NIXON: You know, I can't for the life of me remember that damn conversation of the [September] 15th. I can't remember. Thank God you told me. . . . Dean will have undoubtedly a memcom on that. . . . They'll be pretty rough. How do you answer those?

HAIG: Well, it will be as credible as he is. Anything that he writes himself as interpreted by him I think is very vulnerable. . . . Because of (unintelligible) his motives. . . .

PRESIDENT NIXON: His motivation to me is to save his ass. Some people are going to wonder what the hell is his doing. Also, it might be the President's counsel who had to resign and the President's people are not going to be on the side of the Goddamn counsel. He'll try to say, well, I had to do this because the President is trying to defend Haldeman and Ehrlichman, which is true. I mean, I was defending Haldeman and Ehrlichman. I was defending men I believed to be innocent.

HAIG: Well, you couldn't do less and no one would expected you to do less.

PRESIDENT NIXON: That's right. . . . Well, would they say, Al, that we were trying to cover up some presidential papers? But, no, they can't. We can't—we can't let them get in the White House files. No way.

HAIG: No way. . . . It just can't be and it won't be.

PRESIDENT NIXON: What if, for example, Hunt goes and testifies he has documents that he made or investigations he made, they are in the White House files?

HAIG: . . . It wouldn't hurt us. . . .

PRESIDENT NIXON: Well, we could say that except for the national security stuff. . . . I think we've got to hold firm. . . . Don't you agree, or do you?

HAIG: Well, I think we have to look at each—each case.

PRESIDENT NIXON: That's right. . . . [A]ny—any conversations—any conversations that will be—that relate to this problem are not privileged.

HAIG: That involve criminality—

PRESIDENT NIXON: Involve illegal activities. Involve illegal activities are not privileged. Involve charges of illegal activities. I would say that any conversations that involve charges of illegal activities are not privileged. That's the way I think it ought to be. How do you keep the national security out of that, though? . . . You see there basically, even if it's illegal, we want to keep them out. . . .

HAIG: We've got to refine this down very carefully, and that's the issue we have right now. What do we give in guidelines in return for snuffing out the Senate thing and keeping it strictly in the grand jury?

PRESIDENT NIXON: It's gotta be kept in the grand jury . . . . [Y]ou could declare war on Cambodia or Thailand or Mexico, but it's not going to divert attention from this son-of-a-bitch. You know that, Al. . . .

HAIG: He's [Dean] smart. He doesn't move till he knows where he's going. . . .

PRESIDENT NIXON: Well, I suppose the papers, if they involve meetings, memoranda on Watergate, we should oppose the matter, but we wouldn't allow Haldeman's memorandums on Watergate to go down there would we?

HAIG: No.

PRESIDENT NIXON: We have to stand firm on presidential papers, say, Kennedy's memoranda for example, and things of that sort. Good God, don't we?

HAIG: Yes, sir, we do. And we have to stand firm because *the Goddamn presidency* can't run in the future with this kind of challenge (unintelligible). . . .

PRESIDENT NIXON: I suppose they'll then say they're incriminating documents.

HAIG: Well, they could take a look at it case by case, and if it's—there was such a thing. But we'll be in the dark . . .

PRESIDENT NIXON: Well, boy, it's a hard day.

HAIG: Yes, sir.

PRESIDENT NIXON: And there will be others, but we'll fight the good fight.

HAIG: Yes, sir.

MAY 8, 1973: THE PRESIDENT AND ZIEGLER, 5:16–5:42 P.M., OVAL OFFICE

Nixon is more at ease with Ron Ziegler, certainly, compared to the more stilted conversations with Haig. Here, the two men discuss the "snake," John Dean, and Nixon's plans to "destroy" him. Again, Nixon is determined to prevent access to presidential papers, but he wavers some on his earlier insistence on an absolute privilege for executive conversations.

PRESIDENT NIXON: I think somebody has got to take him [Dean] on, somebody—the damned Senators. All right? . . . See, that's our problem. . . . I think he is showing a little frayed at the edges, but I don't know. But I don't see [why] people are really playing him up as a great hero. . . . Shit. What the hell. I thought we were getting everything out. . . . My position, Ron, as you know, has been that all along. I mean, I haven't tried to contain anything. I said, that's—you got to let it hang out. . . . I was the one who was insisting on a Goddamn Segretti report [and on] the Watergate. I said, get it out, get it out. What did Haldeman say? Excuse me.

ZIEGLER: Well, but too at that time, what you were talking about getting out was certainly not the scope of things that people are talking about now. You weren't aware of it.

PRESIDENT NIXON: I wasn't aware of the Goddamn—of the Goddamn money business. Unfortunately, though, I'm afraid Bob and John's lawyer on the money. I don't think they intended it, you understand. . . . I don't think that Bob when he turned over the 350 [$350,000] intended it to be hush money. [He thought] it's for the committee. You know, they need it for [polls] and so forth and so on, and I don't think that Ehrlichman, when he approved the calls from Kalmbach, intended that it be hush money.

ZIEGLER: I'm sure of that.

PRESIDENT NIXON: The purpose was to allow Kalmbach to raise money for this. When I saw Tom Pappas here in March, I said, thanks for his help, you know, the help he was giving John Mitchell. I just thought he was helping John Mitchell, you know, with his funds, you know. . . .

ZIEGLER: At the time that you made the comment in your press conference, Mr. President, that—about the Kennedy complicity with the overthrow and murder of Diem—

PRESIDENT NIXON: Yeah.

ZIEGLER: —you did not base that on that cable. You based that on the information that you had been aware of. . . . But I'm just thinking—did Colson or someone—

PRESIDENT NIXON: Never. Never, never, never, never, never, never. No. No, I was basing that—do you want the real truth? I was basing it on the book [*Our Vietnam Nightmare*] that I had read by the [*New York*] *Herald Tribune* reporter that died, Marguerite Higgins. If they want to read the book, that's what it is. Marguerite Higgins and others published—that were written at the time. Oh, and the other one is Kennedy's—and another book, that [first name unknown] Smith book, *Kennedy's Twelve Great Mistakes,* you know that one? . . .

Did I use the term "the Kennedy complicity"?

ZIEGLER: Kennedy complicity in the overthrow and murder.

PRESIDENT NIXON: That's right, yeah.

ZIEGLER: But the murder was a result of the overthrow.

PRESIDENT NIXON: That's right. That's right. Well, nobody questions it.

ZIEGLER: No, of course, not.

[Withdrawn item. National security.]

PRESIDENT NIXON: Goddamn. That Colson thing. Colson is—he said he just told him to improve the wires, or something. *Oh Christ, he's looking like a Goddamn fool.* . . . What can he say? He'll make quite a witness, won't he? He says if Hunt misinterpreted—maybe. I think Hunt probably did—did whatever out of loyalty, but Colson may have said make it clear or—what do you think, probably did happen? What's your guess? You think that Colson told him to take over?

ZIEGLER: Yes. I do. . . .

PRESIDENT NIXON: Please God, make sure you get across to the *New York Times* I had no Goddamn knowledge whatever . . . .

ZIEGLER: But they understand that.

PRESIDENT NIXON: . . . Just say that's all my own study of the situation. That isn't the first time I said that. I said that—I said that during—in 1960—before the 1968 campaign I made that charge. I said that.

ZIEGLER: Right.

PRESIDENT NIXON: That the greatest mistake—there was a speech that I made in 1967—'66 and '67. I made speeches in '66 and '67.

ZIEGLER: Where you referred to the murder? . . .

PRESIDENT NIXON: I said that—that was not new. It was not new. I referred to that based on you can say the books by Marguerite Higgins. If you want to read it, it's one of the classics. . . . You see, the point was—it's the complicity of the overthrow, you see, and then the murdered followed.

ZIEGLER: Sure. . . .

PRESIDENT NIXON: . . . Ron, Al is greatly concerned about our . . . you know, executive privilege and the whole thing. He went too far in that statement and in the light of Dean's conference [with the prosecutors] over the weekend, . . . we're going to have to give some on that. But I don't know. Is that—because it might be if he says that he thinks we are committed and now it looks as if we consider conversations with the President with regard to illegal activities are privileged. And I don't—do you sense that as much as he does?

ZIEGLER: Well, that—that seems to be a bone of contention to him, and the press is writing on—

PRESIDENT NIXON: Yeah. Well, we can give some on that, you know. But we cannot commit the presidential papers.

ZIEGLER: Never.

PRESIDENT NIXON: Never. You understand that?

ZIEGLER: Never, never, never. . . . You'd have anarchy if they got into presidential papers. . . . They can't get in the presidential papers. Never. You'd have the end of constitutional government. . . . *Never.*

PRESIDENT NIXON: But conversations with the President.

ZIEGLER: Even conversations with the President—how can you conduct business? You didn't feel that, for example, me as a staff [member], I could come in here and talk to you in the sanctity of the Oval Office and you could explain or discuss—

PRESIDENT NIXON: I think what we could do is to loosen it up in terms of—

ZIEGLER: The Watergate.

PRESIDENT NIXON: You mean, conversations with the President on Watergate? Loosen that up? Or you could say conversations that our staff—

ZIEGLER: Criminal activity—

PRESIDENT NIXON: Yeah. It sort of makes you wonder about—you've got to keep control of anything that has to do with the executive—I mean, the national security (unintelligible) even when it's criminal.

ZIEGLER: Well, there's only one criminal thing involved there.

PRESIDENT NIXON: I think. [*Chuckles.*] You know. I never know. Suppose if there's something else (unintelligible), we'll pick it out and give it to them, but nothing else. I'm not going to give them [phone] taps of what [J. Edgar] Hoover did. . . .

ZIEGLER: [W]e're moving into a point—I'd say we'll be there maybe in about four or five days—where he'll show his hand far enough where we can give some very real consideration to some very constructive leaking of our own positions.

PRESIDENT NIXON: You mean—like leaking what?

ZIEGLER: Well, just how it happened, what, you know, his position was inside of the White House.

PRESIDENT NIXON: Destroy him, you mean.

ZIEGLER: Begin to do—

PRESIDENT NIXON: His destruction is going to be, you know, you got to say he did—got the problem of whether or not he suborned perjury, for example, with Magruder. Magruder has already probably testified to that. . . . I think he was up to his ass in this whole thing himself and probably didn't tell Haldeman everything. He says they knew every inch of the way.

ZIEGLER: I'm—the more and more that I think of this, think about it—and I'll have to say that my view has wavered here a little bit—I've questioned, as much as I like Bob and John, some of their judgments in this thing.

PRESIDENT NIXON: Sure.

ZIEGLER: And—but I've got a feeling here that the real snake in the wood is old Johnny Dean. And if you look back over his record—and I suppose if you look at it as an individual now, knowing about all of this, the fact that he didn't flag the President—or how many times have you said something and you say [that you have] to be flagged on it or you say—you say it to a staff man who has any guts about him at all—and I've heard you say this over and over—to say—say, fine, Mr. President, I'll do that. But if this happens, this will take place. Over and over again.

PRESIDENT NIXON: Yeah.

ZIEGLER: *He didn't do that.* . . . until March 21st. . . .

MAY 8, 1973: THE PRESIDENT AND HAIG, 6:30–7:37 P.M., OVAL OFFICE

Nixon and Haig agree that Buzhardt will handle the Watergate legal defense. Despite vast resources at his command, the President complains about the inadequacy of his legal team. Nixon was feeling outgunned, for good reason. Department of Justice lawyers confronted him; and now the formidable legal staff of the Senate Select Committee had broadened the inquiry against him. A month later, the newly formed Special Prosecutor's office added another fifty-plus lawyers.

PRESIDENT NIXON: We—we know it's going to be bad. . . . [F]rom what he's already said, the crap he put out in *Newsweek.* Well, you know he's going to take everything in the meeting he had with me and twist it and turn it. Right?

HAIG: And that's fine and we'll take it on. We're going to beat the son of a bitch.

PRESIDENT NIXON: We have to do it. I just—I don't know. I just don't want me to have to do it. I think that the idea of—like I told Ron a few minutes ago, I hope people aren't going to suggest that by tomorrow or the next day I go on national television and answer John Dean.

HAIG: Absolutely not.

PRESIDENT NIXON: I can't do that. . . . I think if you want to really destroy this office, have me out there fighting John Dean. Somebody else has got to fight him.

HAIG: That's right. That's exactly right, and it's not your task to do that. In fact, it's ludicrous. . . . We'll work out the way. That's why we'll get this thing through, get a, beef-up our capability with a real tough guy who operates and works—

PRESIDENT NIXON: I think Buzhardt would be good. Get him over into it right away. I agree, and get [Nixon's former law partner, H. Chapman] Rose for every—every hour we can get him. . . . Well, I wish I knew of another name. Isn't it something here that—to be President of the United States and Goddamn White House under assault and not have a name. . . . Now, with Buzhardt, you've got a guy that you know that is loyal and everything. I'd rather take a loyal guy and put him to work on this.

HAIG: And a smart guy.

PRESIDENT NIXON: And a smart guy and a loyal guy and somebody that is not from the outside that we could really have the inside. I think that's [the] best thing to do, Al. . . . See, if we had Bob—John Ehrlichman here—now, Ehrlichman's mind is very good. He'd have a strategy to work with them. We don't have—we don't have a good sound, mature lawyer around right now on the staff. . . . Now, on this executive privilege thing too, we've got to write it certainly in a way before the grand jury so they don't get into presidential papers. That is the problem. . . . What did Chappie [Rose] say about that?

HAIG: He said, that's right. He said, but remember, as long as you control it, you can decide what to give them. And if you decide—

PRESIDENT NIXON: Yeah.

HAIG: —that it's to your advantage to give them something, fine. If it isn't, you just don't give it. So, he said, you shouldn't just make a straight prohibition. . . .

MAY 8, 1973: THE PRESIDENT AND HAIG, 6:59–7:37 P.M., EXECUTIVE OFFICE BUILDING

The President launches a vicious tirade against John Dean, a tirade that masks his fear that Dean has "a Goddamn safe full of documents." In later conversations, this notion appears as Dean's "trump card," his "black box," or his "lock-box." Typically, such conversations are sparked by the presence of another person, one who would fuel Nixon's anger. Alexander Haig is the perfect foil.

SEGMENT 1

PRESIDENT NIXON: I think Dean's out to kill us. . . . He's got a lot of cards. He's got a Goddamn safe full of documents.

HAIG: That would be very dangerous.

PRESIDENT NIXON: Don't be surprised about his documents, because this man's a consummate liar, I can tell you, lying about so many things. He's likely to say things about Haldeman and Ehrlichman that just aren't true, let alone me. . . . Now, the other man that we might get into this is [John] Connally. I didn't mention it to him, but, you know, we just have to say, "John, we have a problem we want your advice on." Connally is a mean, tough, son of a bitch. He's got tremendous judgment and all the rest. . . . There's nothing more important to this country that he could do than this, mash this son of a bitch Dean.

HAIG: The most important job we have.

PRESIDENT NIXON: God, why would (unintelligible) be concerned about, Al, about a man who *worked for us,* for Christ's sakes? It isn't like a little Goddamn yeoman [Charles Radford] that did that horrible thing to Henry [who spied on Kissinger for the Joint Chiefs of Staff in 1971]. *This son of a bitch was counsel.* This is like [Kissinger aide Helmut] Sonnenfeldt, right, or you?

HAIG: (Unintelligible)

PRESIDENT NIXON: Right. God Almighty. I think that has got to have some effect on the country. I don't know. Or I guess, is the country all crazy? Is it all crazy?

SEGMENT 2

PRESIDENT NIXON: Goddamn it, if we've got the record, Al, we must always be sure our guys have got it. Haldeman must never lie, never. Ehrlichman must never lie. Nobody must lie. *Goddamn it, this Goddamn thing has got to be brought out* [*pounding table*]. The President is not in it, was never in it. I've been trying to keep this sonofabitch—well, it's unbelievable. We've had some bad advice. I must say that a hell of a lot of the problem with Dean and so on, good God, basically, Haldeman and Ehrlichman were relying on him. You understand?

HAIG: That's the counsel, that's what he's here for.

PRESIDENT NIXON: They relied on him. He should have told us, said, "Look, Christ, there's a hell of a lot of problems about these guys wanting money for their defense and all the rest." He didn't put it that way. I mean, it's perfectly *proper* to give money for defense of people. It is not *proper* to give it to shut up. [*Shouting.*] He should have told us. That's the whole point. He never told us.

HAIG: That's the problem. That'll show, though. I mean, how could it be otherwise but that the inadequate son of a bitch was at the switch. . . .

PRESIDENT NIXON: For nine months. But let me say, don't assault him too soon. Let him get on a little further. But then his legs have got to be cut off on national television like nobody's business, but not by me. I cannot take on the little asshole. Agnew? Connally? Connally won't? I don't know. I don't know. Agnew may.

HAIG: I think Agnew would want to and he'll do it. I think Connally will do it if it's necessary. . . .

PRESIDENT NIXON: What we might do is really get Connally into this thing. I think maybe when he comes in you ought to brief him on the whole Goddamn thing. You know, it isn't all that complicated. I explained a little of it to him. But say, for Christ's sakes, here it is, this Goddamn Dean out here attacking the presidency, and we can't allow it. The President, he should have known, but he was very busy with other things.

SEGMENT 4

PRESIDENT NIXON: What the hell's Agnew doing? He's never spoken up once on this Goddamn thing. Connally's got to speak up. That's the thing to do. Even those *assholes* in the Senate. Good God, I've got to stay out of this, Al. I mean, the thing— as you know, we've got to make some grave, very grave decisions, and I must not be, and you either, consumed by this sonovabitch Goddamn thing. Let's get the facts on those damn papers and get them as fast as we can. If the Goddamn judge doesn't give them to us, fine. Assume the worst. Assume they're everything. And then destroy this man, and I mean destroy him. . . . Dean is a bad fellow. Ehrlichman [*sic:* Haldeman] made a very bad call putting him in the Goddamn job.

MAY 9, 1973: THE PRESIDENT AND HAIG, 9:40–10:02 A.M., OVAL OFFICE

The President continues his attack on Dean, but more important is his struggle to control his papers, which includes those of his key aides as well. The conversation

includes the range of topics nagging at Nixon: Dean's "black box," his legal defense; questions of immunity, executive privilege, and control of documents; the media; LBJ's bugging; and the forthcoming Senate hearings. Nixon's anger and rage are at a peak.

SEGMENT 1

HAIG: Now, what we've got going now is a very comprehensive game plan on taking this thing on. We've got to start now building a backdrop, but not to shoot our big guns yet on Dean. . . . I think [John] Connally would be a great guy if he can go out and just put in the context of drawing on the [Senator William] Proxmire [D-WI, who had been critical of the attacks on the President] thing, draw back and, by God, we're in the process of inhibiting justice and truth and are involved in an orgy of very irresponsible press activity. And that kind of a thing we can hint and do can be picked would be very helpful.

[Withdrawn item. Privacy.]

PRESIDENT NIXON: We may not be able to get Connally to take that on, but you can talk to him frankly that he must make up his mind.

HAIG: That's right. . . .

PRESIDENT NIXON: . . . Oh, a couple of points I wanted to make. One thing that's very important in terms of working on this executive privilege thing—is there anything—any time we can get ready to meet today to determine what we do with regard to the person? Has Dean made a deal with the Senate yet or not?

HAIG: No, he has not.

PRESIDENT NIXON: He has not. He's still waiting.

HAIG: And as I understand it, they have not even delivered the notice to the Attorney General, which they have to do. . . . Now, what I have here is—Buzhardt is on his way over right now.

PRESIDENT NIXON: Right, right.

HAIG: And he'll meet with Chappie [Rose] and—

PRESIDENT NIXON: Good.

HAIG: I'm trying to move on this Italian fellow.

PRESIDENT NIXON: [Justice Department lawyer Donald E.] Santarelli?

HAIG: He's had quite a relationship with Dean but I think he turned on him very violently some months ago.

PRESIDENT NIXON: Find out. If that's the case, we may have something that's very good there. . . . Santarelli is supposed to be a brilliant, mean, rough son of a bitch—

HAIG: Everybody agrees that he's first class. He's a poor administrator but he's a great mind and a great fighter, a good legal head. So, that will give us a first class team.

PRESIDENT NIXON: Yeah, yeah. I just mention to you this. I just caught Bob [Haldeman] this morning, wished him well, poor guy. But he mentioned one thing on executive privilege, and I want to be sure you understood. He said that—I said, Bob, be sure—as you know, we're going to have to lighten that up some that—you can't just say conversations with the President where illegal actions are discussed or privileged and so forth. He said, yeah, I can, but he says, one thing I must not—we must not give on and that is my notes. . . .

And I just want to be sure that you, Bob, and everybody in this whole staff understands, that no note is made but any—even in that meeting in there, it belongs to those people. It belongs to the President. You know that. Now, that was [Lyndon] Johnson's rule. It's my rule too. I mean, their notes—those are not notes—Bob Haldeman's notes prepared for the President, you know what I mean? And his notes of his meetings with the President are not—cannot be subject to being—

HAIG: They are all in our files and in our vault, and they—and I told this to Len. I said, we are not turning over any notes, any documents, any presidential or Haldeman—

PRESIDENT NIXON: Ehrlichman. . . .

HAIG: You know, in a public sentence, we don't want to say that. We just aren't going—when the issue comes up specifically and they ask for this or that, that's executive privilege. . . .

PRESIDENT NIXON: We don't want to make a public statement. . . . Goddamn it. Some—executive privilege is going to be—I think that someone—let me put it this way. There's no way you can get off the whole privilege hook if you turned over the whole White House. . . . Now, let's face it because every time they said, well, wouldn't you do this, wouldn't you appear the Ervin Committee and that will solve it. I mean, nothing has solved it. In my view stand for some of the privilege then, God-damn it. Let them scream about it. I don't think that's—provided your position—our position is reasonable.

HAIG: That's right. All we want to do is take a—take a reasonable position, but a responsible—

PRESIDENT NIXON: Yeah. We're giving—we're giving them the men. We're letting them question all the White House aides. We are freely—we're letting them testify freely, and you know, and without any privilege on matters affecting this matter. And we are going to expand that to include on any matters—any discussions the President's involved—you know what I mean—involved with illegal activities because there we've got—there's an advantage for us to say and they will say they were not. Do you get my point?

HAIG: Absolutely. Now, that's—that's what they're going to start on, first order of business, how to handle the congressional—or the Senate immunity issue.

PRESIDENT NIXON: Yes, the Senate immunity issue and the Senate hearings, to get the Senate hearings—not only the immunity issue now, Al, they've got to get the issue. But then they've got to get the lawyers for Bob and or Mitchell—sorry, particularly Bob's lawyer and so forth. Somebody's lawyers have got to get those Senate hearings delayed on the basis of this. . . . The best way in my opinion is for the defendants, Bob, et al, for them to take the lead and say, look, our rights will be jeopardized if these hearings go forward. Now, that's the best way. That's what ought to happen, rather than the White House putting its shield up around them. . . .

HAIG: Right.

PRESIDENT NIXON: . . . [T]he prosecutor—the prosecutor should join in. . . as a separate thing, as a prosecutor [saying] hearings might jeopardize the rights of those people as well as the chances to convict the guilty. . . . Now, and incidentally then only as a last resort, should executive privilege be used as the device. See, that third thing is if the prosecution, the prosecution won't do it. If Haldeman's and Mitchell's lawyers will not do it, see, then the White House simply moves and drops the blanket of executive privilege on saying we will not allow anything. We will cooperate with the committee on all matters that it has jurisdiction over except the matter currently being considered in the—in the criminal justice departments and that we—that we have been advised that—we have been advised that this might jeopardize the rights of some people, et cetera. And, therefore, until those matters—those proceedings are completed, executive privilege is asserted.

HAIG: That's generally the way we outlined it yesterday.

PRESIDENT NIXON: Yeah. Now, that means executive privilege with regard to appearances of all White House people. That still doesn't stop Mitchell. That's all right. That would stop Dean. Executive privilege is asserted.

HAIG: No. That doesn't stop Dean. We've got—we just got—

PRESIDENT NIXON: What I meant, that would stop him from testifying. . . . That's the last resort. Now, the best way, of course, is for the Attorney General, as soon as he is confirmed, to negotiate with this—with the Ervin Committee. That's what Petersen was talking about earlier, he should negotiate with the Ervin committee.

HAIG: That's right. . . . That's what I think. I, uh, that's one of the mistakes we made last week. . . .

PRESIDENT NIXON: . . . [Y]ou and I both know that the main thing we've got to do is keep our iron hand on the presidential papers for any other reason. National security, national security.

HAIG: That's essential.

PRESIDENT NIXON: National security—that's what the *Times* and others are nibbling about Ellsberg—Goddamned people stole those Pentagon papers, and now they want to get out there and the whole Goddamned files and we're not going to allow—we were trying to stop them. We're not going to allow that. You know that—that's, that's too hot. That's too hot, Al. . . . It would really destroy (unintelligible) government, wouldn't it? I mean Goddamn it, we've got leaks all the time. What the hell do we do, for example, we—

[Withdrawn item. National security.]

HAIG: We know that (unintelligible).

PRESIDENT NIXON: Huh?

HAIG: It just would be inconceivable that ever got out and its always been true. You know this isn't any different than with any other presidency or any other—you just do not do it. You can't.

PRESIDENT NIXON: . . . One point Mitchell made was not too [smart?] was when he said he did not approve of a separate White House investigation on the Pentagon Papers deal. Now Mitchell was totally aware of it, and I can tell you because—that I told you that bizarre story that Edgar Hoover refused to investigate because [Louis] Marx, Marx's daughter was married to that son-of-a-bitch Ellsberg. He refused and Mitchell said, well you'd better get it done and out of the way, so that's why we conducted the investigation over here. It was as simple as that. But—

HAIG: Yet the frustration we had at that time, in the White House, after months of the most serious leaks—*nobody* could have sat here and not moved to stop it.

PRESIDENT NIXON: We had to do something. We had to do something in order to stop it. We had to get the types of people that did it, it was a tough deal, but you had to do it. My God, it was awful. Well I guess that Dan Ellsberg. Well, I guess . . . [they] will build a monument to him [Ellsberg] on Harvard Square. . . . Finally, come back always to the fundamental plan, Al, that whatever the son of a bitch Dean throws, we got to defend this office and this presidency and let's go forward and do whatever we were elected to do.

HAIG: No question.

PRESIDENT NIXON: We weren't elected to fart around on this thing. We weren't elected to be obsessive and wallowing in it, and so forth, right?

HAIG: Exactly right, and that's what we're going to do, and we're going to have about another two weeks of hell, and . . . then I think it's going to turn.

PRESIDENT NIXON: No, you think it might turn in two weeks? I doubt it. I don't mean I doubt it—I meant—these things are going on for months now. You know, they're going to have hearings up there and they start going on for months. . . .

HAIG: You know, . . . it can't, it can't go on.

PRESIDENT NIXON: You know, when you really come down to it—as I noted when I read some of the incoming letters and wires, the media has been highly irresponsible in the way that it has played this up as being the biggest Goddamned crisis in (unintelligible). Well now, it is a big crisis, after all the Attorney General and the Director of the F.B.I., and two top White House aides—those are important as fish go—that's a big deal. . . .

SEGMENT 2

PRESIDENT NIXON: . . . If I thought the whole government is coming apart, I would resign. They're going to have to drag me out of here, you know that.

HAIG: But it isn't anything like that. That's what my major concern is. I think a lot of people think that this thing is worse than it is, and it's just sheer nonsense and it's even permeated some of our staff and some of the cabinet. Yesterday we started knocking this out. Yes, sir, I think your speech last night was confident, Goddamn it, and that's the way we ought to be. You know, this is just insanity and these cabinet guys have got to understand this Goddamned thing.

PRESIDENT NIXON: . . . Remember your friend, [William] Sullivan?

HAIG: Yes, sir.

PRESIDENT NIXON: But, Sullivan is supposed to be prepared for Dean—some of the dirty tricks of [Lyndon] Johnson and so forth, in the FBI. . . . You get Sullivan in and say, now look here, we're getting it bad down here. We want to know everything you got on what Johnson and Bobby Kennedy did. It's worth trying, isn't it? . . . I was thinking of this—something to counterattack. . . .

HAIG: I wouldn't talk to Sullivan directly about it, but I can get it.

PRESIDENT NIXON: You could? . . .

Hoover would not even look into the Ellsberg. He did not want to prosecute him. Anyway, just wanted to tell you, though—let's really be the hardliner now. The more I think about it, . . . what the hell's Dean got in the black—well, I'm sorry, I don't care what the hell he's got in the black box. . . . [W]e've got a hell of a lot of good witnesses up there—that are going to say that Dean's a liar. And, he has been lying, too.

HAIG: That's right—lying through his teeth. He's got one conflict after the other in his testimony. . . .

MAY 9, 1973: THE PRESIDENT AND ZIEGLER, 12:31–12:34 P.M., WHITE HOUSE TELEPHONE

The following is a typical discussion between the President and his Press Secretary regarding Ziegler's press briefings. The status of presidential aides' papers remains in contention. They also discuss the interpretation of popularity polls.

PRESIDENT NIXON: Hello.

ZIEGLER: Yes, sir.

PRESIDENT NIXON: Survive your briefing?

ZIEGLER: Oh, yes, I did. . . . You know, we went around on the Dean thing, and I said we want our papers back. That's basically the line [*laughter*] I said—not because of the content but because they belong to the White House.

PRESIDENT NIXON: Yeah.

ZIEGLER: And they said do we know that Haldeman and Ehrlichman don't have papers? I said we have no reason to believe that they do.

PRESIDENT NIXON: That's right.

ZIEGLER: Then we went along the line of—

PRESIDENT NIXON: Of course, the Haldeman and Ehrlichman papers, whatever they are—well, their own papers are available, actually, to—well, their own, if they don't have to do with me, they can do what they Goddamn please with them. But basically anybody in the White House who produces papers for the President, they belong to the President. . . . The only problem we've got with Dean's papers, Ron, is that if this is a self-serving document he's put out, he's going to get it out anyway.

ZIEGLER: That's right, sure.

PRESIDENT NIXON: So therefore we would treat that differently. But we must never give an inch on Haldeman and Ehrlichman's papers. Don't you agree?

ZIEGLER: . . . The fact of the matter is, the Haldeman and Ehrlichman papers are all under supervision at their request, so there can be no question of their personal papers and also the presidential papers. . . . Then, on the court thing in California [the Ellsberg case], I simply made the very direct stern statement that the fact of the matter is that the material was provided to the court at the direction of the President. . . . And then I said in terms of phone calls, the many phone calls that we receive in my office as a part of, you know, taking some of the calls, the vast majority of them on the subject are supportive of the President—what he has done in the last four years, what they want him to continue to do. So I think that line, you know, get the support—

PRESIDENT NIXON: Did the Harris poll get any play, the one you mentioned?

ZIEGLER: Yes, it did. Oh, yes, sir. It got play on TV last night, got good play.

PRESIDENT NIXON: Of course they had some negatives, but did they get across that point that they didn't want the President to resign?

ZIEGLER: Yes, sir. Absolutely, yes, sir.

PRESIDENT NIXON: And that 59 to 31 thought that he ought to continue the work?

ZIEGLER: Right.

PRESIDENT NIXON: Okay.

ZIEGLER: We survived, and we're going to continue to.

PRESIDENT NIXON: Damn right. Okay.

MAY 9, 1973: THE PRESIDENT AND ZIEGLER, 6:03–6:08 P.M., WHITE HOUSE TELEPHONE

Nixon and Ziegler comment on what they saw as a rare cooperative moment from the media. The White House had launched a counterattack, defending the Plumbers and other deeds as necessary to cope with national security perils.

PRESIDENT NIXON: . . . You think then you can't really start discrediting this fellow [Dean]. . . .

ZIEGLER: I talked to some members of the press corps this afternoon, and I don't think we're going to have to do too—I think our major risk—and I may be wrong on this—but our major risk is moving too abruptly to discredit him. I think he's doing it himself. Hank Truitt from *Newsweek* was just in here, and he said, you know, there's no question about the fact that this guy's moving in a totally self-serving way and is tending to discredit himself. That's moving without our initiative.

PRESIDENT NIXON: I see. . . .

ZIEGLER: And Truitt was really in there. He said, Ron, you know, he said I think something people are overlooking here is the national security aspects from a positive standpoint. I said, "you're Goddamn right, Henry. You think back to the period in '71 and so forth, when documents were being stolen from the government. There was massive leaks prior to a summit and so forth. Of course there was concern about it." He said, yeah. He said people are tending to forget that. So that's the line.

PRESIDENT NIXON: Sure.

ZIEGLER: People are beginning to move. He said he thinks that things have met a—reached a plateau on this.

PRESIDENT NIXON: Yeah.

ZIEGLER: And that people are starting to get into perhaps a better perspective and thinking about other things.

PRESIDENT NIXON: Sure. Well, what the hell.

MAY 9, 1973: THE PRESIDENT AND HAIG, 6:35–8:26 P.M., EXECUTIVE OFFICE BUILDING

On May 4, the President announced that General Alexander M. Haig, Jr. would be "interim" Chief of Staff, a position that he had largely assumed almost immediately

after Haldeman's dismissal. Haig was an experienced turf fighter and a master of intrigue. He had been Kissinger's deputy, and had given Kissinger ample cause to wonder about his loyalties. In this lengthy conversation, Haig is at his ingratiating best. He establishes distance between the President and Haldeman. He skillfully convinces Nixon to name J. Fred Buzhardt as the primary White House lawyer for Watergate matters, effectively squeezing out Leonard Garment, the newly named White House Counsel. Buzhardt and Haig had attended West Point together; moreover, Buzhardt was an experienced Senate staffer (with Strom Thurmond and the Armed Services Committee) and had served as counsel to defense secretaries Laird and Richardson. Haig and Nixon agreed that Buzhardt would be the primary lawyer. Buzhardt joins the meeting and Nixon lays his charm on him, and appears to confide in him—all designed to secure his loyalty. Nixon offers his standard defense of himself, insisting that he was not involved in Watergate. His lack of candor is puzzling, for Buzhardt would eventually hear the tapes and know exactly the President's liability. Nixon offers his version of the March 21 meeting with Dean, emphasizing that it was Dean who said that "we" could get the money, when, of course, it was Nixon who did so. Nixon understands that at this time it is his word against Dean's. The President begins to distance himself from Ehrlichman. The conversation ends on an eerie note. Nixon and Buzhardt recognize the possibility of impeachment, but see it as a perverse opportunity to win a vote of confidence. Altogether, it was an auspicious beginning for Haig and Buzhardt.

SEGMENT 1

PRESIDENT NIXON: Boy, I'm sorry you had such a long day.

HAIG: Well—

PRESIDENT NIXON: How'd you do?

HAIG: This was a three-way circus of necessity with [Fred] Buzhardt, who's, incidentally, just great.

PRESIDENT NIXON: Aren't you really glad you got him?

HAIG: Yes, for more reasons than I can say. . . . Now, this is tough medicine. Bob has taken out with him all his notes and burned them, burned copies of them.

PRESIDENT NIXON: What do you mean, taken them out of the office?

HAIG: Yes, and his lawyers have them. And the concern that Buzhardt has is . . . that means we've lost the executive privilege on documents, because what they can do is just hold him in contempt, throw him in jail, put out a search warrant, or in any other physical way insist on the documentation. While we held the documents, they were all here, in a technical sense we could prevail with executive privilege. But we cannot now.

PRESIDENT NIXON: Have they asked him for the documents?

HAIG: They have not yet.

PRESIDENT NIXON: Well, he better get them back here.

HAIG: Yes. Well, I think I better go on with the whole thing, because that's just one side of it. The next thing is that they're in a terrible dilemma because there's nobody that can defend you in the sense of defending the President, because they don't know how serious it is. I told them that it isn't, it isn't serious. . . . Their great fear every time as we go down the road, A, is the documents will be compromised. They're concerned about that very easily. . . . The second thing is that John [Ehrlichman], we found out today, turned over to the grand jury his investigation.

PRESIDENT NIXON: John.

HAIG: And that's very incriminating stuff for the people down. It's marginal in the case of John, but very bad for Colson all the way down. . . .

PRESIDENT NIXON: For himself? . . . I'm not concerned about this. This one does not bother me.

HAIG: And I'm not either.

PRESIDENT NIXON: But that was inevitable, that he was going to take it to court and he's turned it over.

HAIG: But you see, they're document-conscious. . . . And their view is that this afternoon Bob's going to—they're going to ask Bob for these documents. And they said if he takes the position that, no, they can't have them, they'll say: Well, have you got them? Then he'll have to answer yes. And then they can put out—then they'll put him in jail or hold him in contempt. Now, his lawyer will get him out of jail, of course. But we're in a tough position. . . .

PRESIDENT NIXON: Why in the name of God did Bob take them [documents]?

HAIG: Well, of course, I'm sure he's studying before he testifies to be sure it's right.

PRESIDENT NIXON: And he's still safe. I think he's got a (unintelligible). We can claim privilege on those documents. I don't know; maybe.

HAIG: They said that if you had physical—

PRESIDENT NIXON: [Lyndon] Johnson used to insist, Al, that every note made be picked up after a meeting and it belonged to him, the notes made by the staff belonged to the President. And that's the whole idea. You've really got to have the paper. . . . Al, listen. Let me tell you something. . . . The one conversation that Dean has, the only one, was the one on March 21st that I told you about. And that conversation, if you saw it in cold print and heard it by Dean, it would look very incriminating. But by Bob Haldeman, it's going to be exactly the opposite, because what happened is he [Dean] came in and . . . he proceeded to go down the line. And that's when he got in for the first time—he didn't get into his own incrimination as I told you about, his suborning of perjury and all that, but he got into this business of the use, the raising of funds for the defendants.

And I . . . said, "Look, that's not legal, is it?," I asked him. And he said, "Well, if . . . the purpose is to shut them up." And then he raised the one point, the one point of a *current* thing. He said, for example—and I repeat it to you now so that you'll know it just as a cold-hearted fact, no more. He said, "Bittman, the attorney for Hunt, is open to a bribe." Hunt—Hunt needed attorney's fees, attorney's fees and other money. . . . And he said, . . . "Bittman says to [Paul] O'Brien that if he doesn't get it that Hunt will then begin to talk about some of [the actions] of the administration, other than Watergate." I said, "Well, what do you mean by those things?" And he starts going into that, a little of that crap, you know, and so forth.

And I said, "Well, suppose you get the $120,000; how's this going to work out?" I said, "That takes care of them now; what happens for the next four years?" And—I'm repeating this so that you'll know exactly what my recollection is—and Bob's is the same. And he said, " Well, it'll take, a million, probably a million dollars, and we could probably get that." I said, "Well, how would you get it to him? Give it to a Cuban committee or something?" "No, we're not very good at that sort of thing. You know, we've got to take the money to Vegas and wash it, send it around," and all that kind of crap—which again indicated that he knew what the hell was going on. . . . I finally said, I, thank God, had in the conversation Bob Ehrlichman [*sic*: Haldeman]. He says, "well, first, it won't work; second, it's wrong." And then I also had in there, I said, "Clemency," I said, for example, "Hunt wants clemency." I said, I couldn't even think of clemency until after 1974, I couldn't even think it, I said, even consider it. I said, therefore—so this whole thing of, this won't work. . . .

I worry about it because I know how Dean might try to interpret it. Dean was not—Dean, on the other hand—you see, Al, that was the first time, after nine months of investigation, that Dean came to me and said money was being raised for the purpose of getting people to hush up. I never knew about Bob's transfer of 350,000. He never told me about that. I never knew about the fact of the so-called the launching of, getting Kalmbach to raise funds. I'm sure that doesn't show up. . . .

SEGMENT 2

PRESIDENT NIXON: Well, now, in other words, what we could do here is that, even [with] Bob's documents, we could say at this point—we could exert executive privilege even though he's got it, or we can't?

HAIG: He [J. Fred Buzhardt] says we can't sustain it because executive privilege is no more than your power. Existing power is what really executive privilege is, that you've got more troops and (unintelligible). In this instance, the documents are out of the White House. They're not under presidential control. The originals are, copies are not. And if they say Bob, do you have your notes, and he says yes, . . . they'll say we're going to subpoena those. We must have them. And if he won't give it, then they can hold him in contempt and throw him in jail unless [he complies]. But they have the legal authority then to break executive privilege.

PRESIDENT NIXON: Well, we seem every day to come to a harder place, don't we?

HAIG: Well, no. I think we're getting very close to the point where we've got a strategy. . . . Absolutely. I don't think so for a minute. But . . . if you're getting your counsel from people (unintelligible).

PRESIDENT NIXON: Bob or John you're talking about?

HAIG: That's right. And Dean. . . . Counsel [Buzhardt] will support you. He's totally dedicated to only your interest, and I have great respect for Bob, but I can't expect him or his lawyer to be objective here, despite their loyalties. . . .

PRESIDENT NIXON: . . . [I must be] my own man.

HAIG: Your own man. . . . [B]ut what can happen is the wrong piece of paper [Haldeman's notes], interpreted in that forum, could be very damaging. On the other hand, that same piece of paper, under our control. . . . I wouldn't give total trust to this man [Leonard Garment], . . . not because I wouldn't trust him but because I don't trust his judgment.

PRESIDENT NIXON: . . . No, no. He'd be all excited. . . .

HAIG: . . . [I]f Bob's papers are either obtained by the court or at some point they are compromised.

PRESIDENT NIXON: . . . Let me say this, Al. I am not concerned myself about anything incriminating in anything that I've done. I mean, I know what I've done. I mean, I've told you everything I did. You know what I mean. I frankly—I was not informed, and I don't blame people for not informing me. They just [thought I] was too busy with other things. And that's the reason—and probably if I had been informed, I must say maybe I wouldn't have done anything anyway. Let's face it. You know how busy we were in September and October and November, Jesus Christ, December and January. I didn't worry about this Goddamn Watergate.

HAIG: That's right.

PRESIDENT NIXON: I wouldn't let people talk to me about it. . . .

HAIG: There's not that much material [Haldeman's notes], I am sure. But if he [Buzhardt] could screen it and make—

PRESIDENT NIXON: Screen Bob's notes for just on the Watergate, you mean?

HAIG: Yes. Well, they'd be together. They'd have different things. He could take all the other worldwide things out, and I'm sure that's where more trouble would be than in the Watergate, in many instances. But I have confidence in this Buzhardt. . . . I said why can't I do it. I said why don't I just take them and screen the stuff out. And he said no, you can't do that because you're not legal counsel . . . and we'd have another litigation problem in court. . . .

PRESIDENT NIXON: . . . I would never have Len go through any of these documents. . . .

[Phone rings. Haldeman and Haig speak.]

HAIG: Bob, have you got copies of your notes out of the building here?

HALDEMAN: Nope.

HAIG: Do your lawyers have them? . . .

HALDEMAN: They don't have copies of my notes. And I don't think they told your people they did.

HAIG: Well, my people—well, you know when I say that, my people, Buzhardt says that your lawyer said that he had copies, that the originals were in the vault, and that he had copies of them, and, if the President agreed, he'd show them to you—to Buzhardt. Now, what they were worried about—

HALDEMAN: He has some stuff of John's.

HAIG: Well, he gave him copies of John's investigating.

HALDEMAN: That's all he has. . . . He has some notes from John on, you know—

HAIG: Well, they have to be back. . . . See, you understand you were asked if you had any notes, you couldn't take executive privilege on them, if they subpoena them from you, because they're outside of White House custody.

HALDEMAN: Well, in the first place, that's wrong. You know, you'd better get a better lawyer than you've got [Garment]. There are two different things. One is the question of whether I have custody, and the other is the question of whether they're covered by privilege. And the fact of the matter is that, A, I do not have custody. I do not have the notes. I did—have not made copies of them, and I have no copies outside and the lawyers have no copies.

HAIG: Well, okay. That's good. You know, they came in with an entirely different story.

HALDEMAN: I don't believe that. . . . I believe that your lawyers did, because I believe that Len Garment's capable of anything. But I don't believe my lawyers told Len Garment that, or Fred Buzhardt.

HAIG: Well, Chappie, Buzhardt, and Len were all in the session and came out— and came over sort of concerned about it.

HALDEMAN: Well, I think they're confused rather than concerned. . . .

HAIG: Okay. This fellow Buzhardt is very good. You know, I really feel a lot better.

HALDEMAN: Well—

HAIG: He's oriented totally on the problem here.

HALDEMAN: Yeah. What I think you ought to do is, we ought to get Garment and that idiot ass kisser [Douglas M. Parker] of his out of the way and let our guys meet with Buzhardt at some point. . . . There were no copies made of any of my notes, except one or two xeroxes that I made in Room 522 [of the Executive Office Building] the other day, and I left them there.

HAIG: Mm-hmm. Okay. . . .

HALDEMAN: . . . [W]hat I do have is some extracts from those notes, and just don't tell anybody I have those. I'm going back to 522 tomorrow and I'll put them back in. . . . But they're still privileged, and you can hang awful tight on that privilege. Look, you're kidding yourself if you argue on the custody question only. You've got to argue both. Each of them holds. . . .

HAIG: Yeah. That's helpful. I've got a better feel now.

HALDEMAN: So don't worry about any copies of notes. I have none.

HAIG: Good. Okay.

[End of conversation.]

HAIG: I'm sure he's telling the truth. He said he doesn't have anything. He said he may have some extracts from his notes and . . . . He said his lawyers have not seen them. . . .

PRESIDENT NIXON: Would you be sure to let Buzhardt know right away?

HAIG: I'm going to ask Buzhardt. . . .

PRESIDENT NIXON: I would like you to get Buzhardt on the phone right now and tell him that there is no problem. . . .

HAIG: Fred? Fred Buzhardt, please. He's in Len Garment's office.

PRESIDENT NIXON: I just want you to be sure. We've got to start using one man here, and you've got me thinking Buzhardt. Now, the second thing is, I still think Buzhardt can go through them. . . . .

[Phone rings.]

HAIG: Hello? Fred? Say, Fred, a few people got the wrong reading, apparently, on these documents. I ought to talk to you as soon as I leave the President's office, but Bob doesn't have them. He does not and has never had, other than about three pages of extracts of notes he made on his notes. . . . Now, Goddamn, we've got to be careful as hell. I gather his lawyer told you this. . . . All right. Bye.

[End of phone conversation.]

HAIG: . . . I have a feeling that Bob's lawyer doesn't explain himself very well.

PRESIDENT NIXON: He's an old man. . . . Well, what did Bob think, that Garment had done him in? What did he say?

HAIG: He said that ass-kissing sonofabitch. Every time he talks to my lawyer there's some problem. I don't trust him.

PRESIDENT NIXON: I'm awful glad you came over here, Al, tonight. It's good for us to get this—you should always bring these things right to me, because—and I don't want you, and you must never have any doubt about my being afraid of anything here now. You know what I mean? I'm not afraid of anything—Bob's notes. I'm really not. Except for the fact that we had a hell of a lot of free discussion about this thing. You know what I mean? Not on paying anybody off (unintelligible). But, I mean, good God almighty, we can't have his notes of his conversations with me, any more than this conversation. You don't want that in a courtroom. . . . Bob's lawyer doesn't like Len. . . . Bob's lawyer is basically, is anti-Semitic. That's part of the problem.

HAIG: Well, sometimes Bob is too.

PRESIDENT NIXON: Yeah. Buzhardt, incidentally, should get with Bob's lawyer and win his confidence. I really think maybe I ought to get Bob over here. He's not going to the grand jury until Monday. . . . You say that Bob's lawyer felt that something, whatever documents Bob showed him was very incriminating to Bob? . . .

[Phone rings. Haldeman to Haig.]

HAIG: Another problem here: allegedly your guy told Garment and Chappie and Buzhardt that there was a four-pager. . . . A four-page extract or document that he had seen, that had it come out that he would have been very upset and it would have been extremely damaging.

HALDEMAN: I don't know what that would be.

HAIG: Me neither.

HALDEMAN: Did he say it was something of mine or something of John's?

HAIG: No, something of yours, something of yours that you had either given to them or shown them.

HALDEMAN: Okay. I know what it is.

HAIG: You know what it is? . . .

HALDEMAN: . . . [I]t's not the 21st; it's a phone call from Dean and it's—what it is is Dean's—it's a phone call Dean makes to me where he outlines his theory of the case, and it's on about the 26th, I think.

HAIG: I see.

HALDEMAN: When he's up at Camp David.

HAIG: Right.

HALDEMAN: And we're down at Key Biscayne. . . .

[Pause. Haig confers with the President.]

HAIG: On the 21st thing, the President wanted you to tell me how you viewed that exchange. . . .

HALDEMAN: Oh, I think it's difficult to explain. He knows that. . . . Yeah. I think it can be done. If it comes out, we'll just have to deal with it, but there's no reason for it to come out.

HAIG: Right, right. Okay.

HALDEMAN: I think that the lawyers don't even know about. . . . No. The 21st thing they don't. . . . What they have is the thing on the 26th, which was a conversation I had with Dean.

HAIG: Okay. . . .

HALDEMAN: Our lawyers were trying to shake up your lawyers.

HAIG: I got you. I got you.

HALDEMAN: Because our lawyers were very distressed with the idiocy of the approach that your lawyers had come up with [on executive privilege] . . . . And in order to convince these clowns (unintelligible) trouble, they lobbed a few bombs across their bow.

HAIG: Bob, we better put Buzhardt in touch with your guy and get Garment out of this thing.

HALDEMAN: I couldn't agree with you more.

HAIG: And have them sit down and talk.

HALDEMAN: That's the solution, and I think you ought to put Buzhardt in touch with me too. . . .

[End of phone conversation.]

HAIG: . . . Bob's lawyer was just trying to get Buzhardt and Garment frightened, because Garment said we think we ought to lift the executive privilege. So they said if you knew—they were telling them fairy tales. Bob said that his lawyer doesn't know about the discussion on the 21st. His lawyer doesn't know. And the document his lawyer was referring to that was very damaging was a summary of a telephone conversation from Dean at Camp David to Bob in Key Biscayne on the 26th. That was it. . . . [T]hey were exaggerating in order to keep Lenny Garment from lifting executive privilege. . . . Bob said that what was involved was his lawyer attempting to scare— and the document he's referring to was not the 21st but the 26th. He says it's a total breakdown of any confidence in Garment, and that's dangerous, to have him feeling this way.

PRESIDENT NIXON: Bob said he had a total breakdown?

HAIG: He said his lawyers did. They just don't trust him. And that's bad.

PRESIDENT NIXON: We can put Garment on some other things, let him work on the public relations aspect. Do you know what I mean? Buzhardt had better be mine. Well, Garment [will] understand that we need one man. . . .

HAIG: He understands. I think there's enough work there that you're going to need Garment to do some [things], but Buzhardt ought to be the man that holds the information and makes the basic [decisions], which we're going to have to make a few of, and certainly have to decide on what to do about the Senate next Thursday. We've got to get that action blocked or postponed. And we're going to have to get some work done on the Hill. I'd like to tell Buzhardt to go up and have this discussion with [Senator John] Stennis [D-MS].

PRESIDENT NIXON: All right. . . . You mean Stennis would talk to Ervin? Is that what you mean?

HAIG: I think so. I'll have to get his strategy in detail. . . . But he [Buzhardt] generally knows what he's talking about on the Hill . . . He's dedicated to you, Stennis is. . . .

PRESIDENT NIXON: Well, let's put Buzhardt and put [aide Tom C.] Korologos and everybody concerned that these hearings have to be—what argument does he think about postponing it—because it's going to interfere in the processes of judges?

HAIG: The Goddamn committee first insisted that we appoint a special prosecutor. We sit down and appoint a special prosecutor, are in the process of doing it. No sooner do we start that then they usurp the whole Goddamn thing and make [it] his [Richardson's] task, before he even takes it on, an impossible one by conducting a television circus, at the risk of the witnesses, the facts.

PRESIDENT NIXON: That's right. We've got to fight the hearings. And if we don't— if we don't—we'll fight it. By fighting it, even if we lose, we will help discredit.

HAIG: That's right. It will all come out just that way. But I think we can—I think we can stop it. . . . What I had hoped to do was have Bob talk to this guy Buzhardt, and Bob's lawyer talk to him, and let them build some confidence in [Buzhardt and see that he] is not a self-serving politician. You see, that's Bob's concern. . . .

PRESIDENT NIXON: Well, Bob knows. Bob's totally loyal. . . . And I just thank my lucky stars, just thank God that Bob was in the room when I talked to Dean. . . . He wasn't the whole time. But, you see, I called him in when Dean—see, Dean started to come in and tell me the story. . . . I think Bob and I can sit down and try to reconstruct the damn thing the way it really was.

HAIG: That may be the best thing. It would be well if I could bring Buzhardt in at some point to talk [to Bob]. . . . [*Raises the Ellsberg case issues.*]

PRESIDENT NIXON: Oh, the burglary thing.

HAIG: The plumbering.

PRESIDENT NIXON: The plumbering thing is basically something that they're not going to have—this grand jury's not going to indict anybody on that. No. It's just embarrassing to him. What is embarrassing to him in this case—he has two vulnerabilities. . . . One is that he was present at the time that the documents were handed over to Gray from Hunt's safe. . . . The other thing is that Ehrlichman and Haldeman as well, at the request of John Mitchell, which was relayed through Dean, right after the burglars got in, called Kalmbach in California, who did special fundraising, and authorized him to raise some money for the attorneys' fees. Now that also, in my opinion, is manageable, at that stage. Now that was very early, you understand. . . . That is Ehrlichman's total involvement in Watergate, in my opinion, as far as I can see.

HAIG: That's right. That's about all. . . .

PRESIDENT NIXON: Don't you think it would be well if perhaps I had a little talk with Bob alone first? . . . And then I'll get you in, because Bob—he deserves that. Do you know what I mean? I don't want to talk to John, John Ehrlichman, because John's on his own now pretty much. He's got to play the battle out. See, Bob took the resignation thing, for your information, Al, he took it hard, but he took it well. John was very difficult.

HAIG: Well, they are both fine men.

PRESIDENT NIXON: They are splendid men, but John just felt he wasn't, frankly—

you know, he just felt, Goddamn it, I'm not guilty of anything. . . . But they would have killed him. . . .

HAIG: It's just like Elliot Richardson. If he loses this battle to become Attorney General, he can't be Secretary of Defense. He would have been voted no-confidence. Now that's not going to happen. . . John's name got dragged into that thing and it was innuendo. He had some involvement. . . .

PRESIDENT NIXON: Do you want to bring him [[J. Fred Buzhardt] over now? . . . But let me say that I do not believe, on reflection, that I should have him, even him, paw through Bob's notes. I'm not even sure I'd want you to, Al.

HAIG: I don't want to. . . .

PRESIDENT NIXON: I would just as soon that—understand, this is not any sense of guilt or anything of that sort, but there is always the chance of misinterpretation when you're not there and hear the inflections or what has gone before or what the hell— the nuts. Do you know what I mean? I can assure you that you've got to have confidence in your clients, but I just want you to know that I just don't think it's a good idea.

HAIG: It's not, no. That is a judgment that you make, sir. I would never want to do it, under any circumstances.

PRESIDENT NIXON: But think I will have Buzhardt talk to Haldeman. I think that's good. Talk to Bob. That's good enough. That's good enough, because he won't get any surprises out of Bob's testimony. . . .

[Buzhardt enters room.]

PRESIDENT NIXON: Let me say that I am really delighted that you could come over and try to work on this very complicated case. It's complicated, but the main thing you have to do is to have, as I told Al, you've got to have confidence in your client. I just want you to know I didn't know anything about the Goddamn Watergate, as far as the so-called—the whole business of payments and all that crap is concerned. It was in March when I finally got a whiff of it, on March 21, and started my own investigation. That's it.

So on the other hand, as I said in my radio talk or television talk the other day, I take responsibility for it, because anybody—after all, I hired John Mitchell and Haldeman and Ehrlichman, who I don't think are guilty. . . . But I think they may have been caught in it by—in a tangential way, which may get them in this very mushy area of conspiracy to obstruct justice, which, as you know, is very broad and hard to prove. It's hard to prove, I understand. . . .

BUZHARDT: (unintelligible) John Ehrlichman—

PRESIDENT NIXON: The report that he made?

BUZHARDT: Yeah. And the notes of his . . . investigation.

PRESIDENT NIXON: I understand he gave that to the jury.

BUZHARDT: To the grand jury and to the Senate committee.

PRESIDENT NIXON: He gave it to the Senate committee? . . . That's all right.

BUZHARDT: But that will be a very damning document. . . .

PRESIDENT NIXON: For whom?

BUZHARDT: For both . . . Ehrlichman and Haldeman, for Dean, Mitchell, Magruder, and some of the others. . . .

PRESIDENT NIXON: Well, the question there—let me ask you this from a legal standpoint. If the funds are raised for the purpose that they were at a very early point—this is like what Haldeman and Ehrlichman told—approved Kalmbach raising money—something which they didn't tell me, incidentally—I would have approved it, had they asked, but they didn't. I had a rule that nobody ever discusses money during my campaign, and that's a damn good thing at this point, isn't it? But, anyway, that kind of activity is not in itself a crime, is it?

BUZHARDT: No crime. But you get to the point that you—

PRESIDENT NIXON: Are trying to get—

BUZHARDT: —are trying to suborn perjury or hush—or try to keep them from talking. That's what the obstruction is. You have to prove the obstruction, and that will be very difficult to prove [from] Haldeman and Ehrlichman. . . . It is going to be difficult to prove for the simple reason . . . most of the evidence is hearsay, somebody down the line.

PRESIDENT NIXON: That's right. . . . [W]hat I need is one man to basically [advise] the President on this. . . . And I would like for you, in that connection, to sometime, maybe tomorrow or the next day, to have a good talk with Bob Haldeman. . . . I will ask him to talk very frankly with you. Now I want to talk a bit about the paper situation. . . . Haldeman does not have his papers out. What he did have was an extract, apparently, of some [conversation]. He must have written a summary of—he may have written something out.

HAIG: It was a telephone conversation he had with Dean at Camp David.

PRESIDENT NIXON: On March 26.

HAIG: He had that. But his lawyers, his lawyers were so outraged at the proposal. . . .

PRESIDENT NIXON: . . . [John] Wilson probably is a great old guy and a very good lawyer. Wilson does not trust Len [Garment]. A part of the reason for that is that—maybe I'm Jewish so I don't know if he can trust me or not [laughter], but he's violently anti-Semitic. So when you get with the proposition of distrust, it's unbelievable. We've had this throughout now. . . .

Ziegler has often said that Wilson's misleading us. . . . For that reason, I think it's very important to have Len in the General Counsel role. You know, leave him right where he is, doing the various things he does. He can work the Ervin Committee and all that sort of thing. But I . . . want you [Buzhardt] to basically be the personal and confidential role that we have to have, not on papers. I have a very strong feeling about that, not because I am concerned about—I mean, everybody sees it in its entirety—but the problem is, because if you start adding through the notes that Haldeman made or that even Haig has made, let alone Henry Kissinger when I've talked to him, it will be an *unbelievable mess.* I don't care how carefully they are gone through. Now Haldeman, as I understand it, Al, is going to have everything back in the White House, correct?

HAIG: Yes, sir. He said the one little four-page summary that he has he's going to get back. . . .

BUZHARDT: I think it would be better if he got that back. I thought he had the summary for the purpose of preparing his testimony. They didn't get to him in the grand jury today. . . . They had John all afternoon. He thinks he's through, but he wasn't sure. But certainly [the notes should be] back in here where it's in your custody. So he has the problem of access, if the question arises and it's here. Then your executive privilege means something because it's in your possession.

PRESIDENT NIXON: That's right. Well, let me say this. If it's here, Bob has a perfect right to come here any time. After all, he can come in and look at his papers. Do you understand that?

BUZHARDT: Right.

PRESIDENT NIXON: And so does John.

HAIG: He's been doing it.

PRESIDENT NIXON: And Dean has not [chuckles]. Dean has taken most of his out, apparently, whatever he made up. But that's what we'll do then. Bob understood that, that he was to get his summary back here too?

HAIG: Oh, yeah.

PRESIDENT NIXON: And he'll do that first thing. . . . You see, that's the good thing about having Fred working here right now. But what I want to do, Fred, is to have executive privilege. I don't mind giving up conversations with the President if anything involving illegal activity is involved. Do you know what I mean? You can't—we're not going to hide a damn thing. But I don't want anything too damn formal. The main thing is here in terms of papers I think we simply have to say that presidential papers—and those are privileged. I mean, they are. They are not Haldeman's papers. They're mine. There's another reason for that too.

[Withdrawn item. National security.]

PRESIDENT NIXON: . . . I think your [Buzhardt's] idea of talking to Stennis appeals to me very much. But what the hell good will that do? Stennis is not on the committee.

BUZHARDT: I talked to Senator Stennis last Thursday morning for two and a half hours. He wanted to talk to me then—let me be very frank—about whether [Stennis] would be willing to come help you. You don't have a more dedicated supporter.

PRESIDENT NIXON: There is no more dedicated Stennis man than Nixon.

BUZHARDT: . . . But he is prepared, I am quite sure, to go to great lengths for any thought that could [help] you. He would not like to go back on a small issue. He would not like to go back on a budgetary problem or something of that type, but on a major policy issue he will become very active, even at this stage. Now Senator Stennis's history has been in the Senate. It depends on which way you look at it. They call him the conscience of the Senate; others call him the undertaker, depending on which way you look at it. But he has handled almost all of their major problems in the Senate. He's the one voice for their own protection. They've never been in a position to question him when it came to what was the right thing to do for the Senate.

Now, he himself has been a party to questions of executive privilege more than anybody else . . . . He's a former judge and if there's one man that rivals Senator Ervin or outdoes him, certainly in respect to his colleagues, from a judicial point of view, it's Stennis. If Senator Stennis organizes the people in a positive way, to tell Senator Ervin there are some very valid arguments for withholding these hearings, that's why he would be your best bet to pull it off. I would certainly seek his advice.

PRESIDENT NIXON: Well, let's try. I'd try as quickly as you can. Now, the point about it is this. The arguments for this are, frankly, this whole judicial process, we are going forward with an investigation. But, God, they're going to indict a former Attorney General of the United States, and I have chopped off the heads of my two top advisors. What the hell more do they want? You know what they want. They want blood. Stennis doesn't want that. The point is, the point is that I was an investigator at one time, and I remember in the Hiss case we continued to investigate until the grand jury indicated, until the grand jury got into it. Then we quit. Do you understand?

BUZHARDT: Yes.

PRESIDENT NIXON: Because we wouldn't have *thought of gaining more. You can't do that.* We couldn't continue to have witnesses before a committee at a time they were appearing before a grand jury. And that's what's involved here. . . .

But at this time they've got to act in the interest of the Senate itself, let alone the country. But they're going to—let me put it this way. We have to make a run at this, even if they—because if it fails, the committee goes ahead, then we've got to attack the committee. Do you understand?

BUZHARDT: We'll have to.

PRESIDENT NIXON: We'll have to, because the committee will have a Goddamn show up there at a time that Mitchell, Haldeman, Ehrlichman, their damn lives are at stake before a grand jury. That's just wrong, isn't it? . . .

BUZHARDT: It's badly wrong, and they shouldn't do it. I anticipate that some of the Republicans on the committee will be as big a problem as the Democrats, except Senator Ervin, who has gone a bit senile, quite frankly.

PRESIDENT NIXON: Ervin's going senile? . . . Well, the difficulty with some of the Republicans is I don't know what we could do with them, but, God, maybe something ought to be done. They're—Baker ought to be responsible on this, but the trouble we have there is he is a publicity (unintelligible).

BUZHARDT: Put the bit in his teeth and he sees the publicity. He sees the publicity. . . .

PRESIDENT NIXON: Well, let's start with Stennis. I would think in this instance Goldwater would be worth trying. Goldwater would be very helpful.

BUZHARDT: Goldwater would be very helpful.

PRESIDENT NIXON: . . . [W]e better just start with Stennis first. Now, how do we do this? This is going to be that basically it's going to prejudice the rights of all these people.

BUZHARDT: I think we can get help from a lot of folks, many of them Democrats.

PRESIDENT NIXON: Well, they're essential.

BUZHARDT: I mean even from outside. Larry O'Brien.

PRESIDENT NIXON: Right. . . .

BUZHARDT: Mr. President, you should know I think Elliot [Richardson] has some problem with my going on this job. . . . I talked to him briefly. He had some problem. He has to stay at arm's length from the White House, which is the main thing in his position.

PRESIDENT NIXON: I see. . . . Oh, we can find somebody else to do the work. . . . And we're taking a lot of heat and we're going to take a lot more. But the main thing you've got to realize is that . . . I made Haldeman and Ehrlichman resign because people said they couldn't do their job effectively any more. . . . I said maybe I should resign too. He [John B. Connally] said no, you don't have that luxury, and I guess that's the problem. The President has got to stick in there. Al was saying a moment ago maybe they'll try to impeach you. I don't know for what, trying to obstruct justice, I guess.

BUZHARDT: It's conceivable. . . .

PRESIDENT NIXON: Right. . . . Well, they tried to impeach me before, you know. . . . That's right. What does it take for impeachment?

BUZHARDT: It takes a majority vote of the House.

PRESIDENT NIXON: That's what I mean. I think I could win it in the House.

BUZHARDT: We can win it in the House. . . . You know, the day may come. If they raise too much ruckus, and (unintelligible) really put it down, then you can get a vote of confidence. It's a hard way to get a vote of confidence, but that may come some time.

PRESIDENT NIXON: It may. But let me say that that would have, in my opinion, quite a traumatic, (unintelligible) traumatic effect on the country. . . .

BUZHARDT: It would.

PRESIDENT NIXON: And a tragic effect, you know what I mean, to try to impeach the President of the United States for—for why? . . . Thank you for your help. See you later, Al.

MAY 9, 1973: THE PRESIDENT AND HAIG, 11:07–11:09 P.M., WHITE HOUSE TELEPHONE

Haig knew his man: the President does not want any compromise on the executive privilege issue. Nixon has a light-hearted warning for Haig regarding the new lawyer, Buzhardt: "And if he turns out to be a John Dean, we'll fry your ass too."

PRESIDENT NIXON: I want you to know that I've told Bob that the only man now that will deal with him is Buzhardt.

HAIG: This is what we had to do.

PRESIDENT NIXON: We had to do it. We're going to get Garment the hell out of this thing now. I mean, you know, leave him in a lot of other—you know what I mean.

HAIG: We'll just keep him out of it.

PRESIDENT NIXON: But he's just too jittery. . . . But let me say that on the executive privilege thing, though, I just talked to Bob and, Al, we can't give an inch on written documents, not an inch. So I don't want Buzhardt or Garment or anybody else to come in to me and say look, public opinion will be hurt, think we've covering up. All right. We'll cover up till hell freezes over.

HAIG: We can do it. We can do it. . . . I think he [Fred Buzhardt] understands this now. I had a talk with him after we—

PRESIDENT NIXON: Did he get the point?

HAIG: Yeah. He had been greased over [by Garment]. It was just bad even getting him broken in about it. . . .

PRESIDENT NIXON: Well, I want to set up a meeting with him, although we shouldn't do it tomorrow, with him and Bob at a place where they can meet conveniently. . . . And maybe on Saturday. How would that be?

HAIG: I think that's fine, and he should talk to Bob before he talks to any of Bob's lawyers.

PRESIDENT NIXON: Oh, yes. He should talk to Bob before he talks to any lawyers. Oh, no, no, no, no, no. This fellow is our friend, and he's my friend and totally trustworthy. And if he turns out to be a John Dean, we'll fry your ass too.

HAIG: Well, that's fine. [*Laughter.*] I deserve it.

PRESIDENT NIXON: Okay.

HAIG: All right, sir.

MAY 10, 1973: THE PRESIDENT AND HALDEMAN, 11:21 A.M.–12:05 P.M., WHITE HOUSE TELEPHONE

The President and Haldeman remain in close communication. Here, Nixon tries to find a way to support Haldeman and Ehrlichman through the still-unformed Nixon Foundation. The conversation is extraordinary, as the two men contrive their own understanding and meaning of John Dean's March 21 meeting with Nixon. The tension and strain of these days are enormous, given the staff turnover, the growing crescendo of accusations leaked from Dean's meetings with prosecutors, further revelations about the Plumbers, and the concern over incriminating documents that might be in White House papers. Yet, this meeting has a calm, almost rehearsed air about it. Nixon and Haldeman offer ready explanations for the Dean meeting, and they delude themselves in fascinating ways. Haldeman, for example, insists that there was no September 15, 1972, meeting with Dean, noting that the White House Telephone log is missing for that day, and accuses Dean of having stolen it.

SEGMENT 1

PRESIDENT NIXON: Hi, Bob. How are you?

HALDEMAN: Good. I'm sorry. I wanted to tell you . . . one is you had raised the point of the Foundation and, you know, the situation on that. The ideal situation for John and me, if it can be worked out, which it can be as far as the Foundation is concerned, but I don't want them to do it unless—without your knowledge and it may at some point require your indication of concurrence—is if they—if the Foundation would retain me as a special consultant for something and John as a special counsel for something, a one-year retainer that would just be from the time we leave here until a year from that time, it will cover an awful lot of things, including maintaining our security clearance, access to files, accessibility to you or whatever you want, but with total separation.

PRESIDENT NIXON: When would you do this? Start when?

HALDEMAN: Start as soon as we leave here, which is next week I guess. Or we could leave a hiatus. Start July 1 or something, if we wanted to. . . .

PRESIDENT NIXON: I wouldn't want to have it done and then have a big flap over— I don't know. . . .

HALDEMAN: We have both an income problem and an access problem. . . . [T]he Foundation has an overriding interest in having an accurate—

PRESIDENT NIXON: That's right.

HALDEMAN: —thing on the Watergate matter, which is going to be a major factor in the history of it.

PRESIDENT NIXON: Good.

HALDEMAN: Now, that can be done without any announcement I believe and it probably should be.

PRESIDENT NIXON: Who could do it?

HALDEMAN: [Leonard] Firestone.

PRESIDENT NIXON: Just tell him I want it done.

HALDEMAN: Firestone will take care of it, and they want to do it. There are Firestone and [Taft] Schreiber [prominent Nixon supporters] are very interested.

PRESIDENT NIXON: Do it today—immediately.

HALDEMAN: If there's any money—Roy Ash [former Director of the OMB] is anxious to take care of the money.

PRESIDENT NIXON: Don't announce it. Do it. . . .

HALDEMAN: And the other thing is I don't know that you ought to get into this but you ought to be aware of it. . . . But Stans's position—and we'll take care of it externally—this has nothing to do with me. It has to do with the other little people in this. Stans's position is that the committee—and they gave a budget—committee that's deciding this, out of that $4 million and a half, of whatever it is they have—is taking care of the legal fees of committee staff people who are having to have counsel.

As of now, they have decided tentatively that they will not take care of the legal fees of other than committee people who are brought in, such as White House staff people or other agency people. They're willing to reconsider this and I think they're going to. In my view they should—

PRESIDENT NIXON: Absolutely.

HALDEMAN: —because you can't take a guy like Gordon Strachan . . . or any of these other people that they have to get lawyers and ask them to pay their own legal fees. . . .

PRESIDENT NIXON: No. I want the whole damn Watergate thing handled by that way. . . . Let me say that I think—I think that the Finance Committee [of CREEP] should take care of all legal fees, Good God.

HALDEMAN: I won't raise any of this kind of crap with you again. . . .

PRESIDENT NIXON: . . . We wanted to . . . think of what we could do about stopping those committee hearings. I think that we can. What I mean is I think that Ervin has got his bit in his teeth. Let me just say this. [*Exhales loudly.*] If the committee does go forward with those Goddamn hearings, then your lawyers, Goddamnit, I hope, put the Watergate thing together and *raise holy hell, mistrial, Jesus Christ.* Do you understand, Bob? . . .

HALDEMAN: . . . But the thing there is I'm not at all sure that the hearings are that bad anyway. Sure, they're going to have to cover all the facts of the Watergate blunder, but [everyone] knows all that anyway. That's not going to be very interesting. Then when some of us get on, I think we can be very effective.

PRESIDENT NIXON: Very effective. That's right. In fact, you may be better [in the committee than] in the courtroom.

HALDEMAN: Oh, I don't think there's any question because you have much more freedom than the courtroom where you've got to stick to just the evidence where here you have to stick—you can get much more self-serving. . . .

PRESIDENT NIXON: . . . Let me ask—say one other thing. On that September 15th conversation that we had in here, it occurred to me you must have made notes on it.

HALDEMAN: I'll have to go over it. That's one of the things I'm in here for. I don't recall any. See, I've checked—see, when I went through my file—and there's something strange about this because I went through the file. I went through your—you know, I have a copy of . . . the schedule log. And in that I just went through it and I didn't see that, but there were several weeks missing from that log. And I asked them to put those back in, and they're now back in and Dean is on there. But I don't know that that's the week that was missing, but I don't know that it wasn't. And I didn't— I looked damn carefully. I went through it three times looking for all the Dean meetings.

Now, another factor. On—when this was blowing up in the mid-April period when you had John Dean over at the office and then when you had Dean in for—you know, to maybe resign and that sort of stuff, during that period, Dean asked the staff secretaries office for a log of the times he met with the President, the dates that he met with President. And under their practice, an individual is entitled to that information. A senior staff member if he asks the file—for a record of his meetings with the President, he can get them. He can't get anybody else's. He asked for that and he got a memo from this guy [David] Hoopes who handles that record that lists his meetings with the President, and it shows the August 14th [signing of the President's will] meeting and then it doesn't show another meeting until February of '73.

And I find that very curious. In other words, Hoopes or the archivist's in search of it did not find any on September 15. Why? I don't know why but there's something funny there.

PRESIDENT NIXON: Is it possible that he saw you and not me?

HALDEMAN: Possible, but it doesn't show up in my log either. I've got to check other logs over there, but I went through my log too. Now, I don't keep a log myself, but my secretary kept a record of who went in and out of my office.

PRESIDENT NIXON: The thing is that I don't recall the Goddamn conversation—

HALDEMAN: I don't either. . . . Dean has no evidence—from both the Senate and the investigators—that Dean has no evidence that ties the President into either the Watergate or the coverup. . . .

They also have a thing from them saying that there's—that Dean's safe deposit— they know what's in Dean's safe deposit box, that is, some national security documents. They know what they are and they're not—prosecutors—someone in the prosecutor's office. [*New York Times* reporter] Seymour Hersh—he's got a pretty good line into there. He's been accurate on everything he's printed. . . . I think what they are is something related to the Hunt business or something that was a bombshell at one point, but that bomb has gone off now.

PRESIDENT NIXON: Well, you know, the more I reflected on our conversation last night on the whole damn March 21st meeting, Bob, if Dean. . . .

HALDEMAN: We can do that now. . . . I came in the middle of the discussion that you had—had—and I knew you were doing this—had scheduled the day before, this meeting with Dean with the understanding that he is to give you a full account of everything related to Watergate because it was becoming clear that McCord stuff and all that Dean had more information than you had been given, and Dean indicated that to you also apparently in these earlier meetings you had been having with him with Moore as you were trying to look into how we could get this cleared up and a public statement made on it.

So, you said, look, I want the whole facts. So, he came in and gave you the whole facts and he went through a recitation of how he instructed the things that have taken place apparently and as to what he thought the jeopardies were of the various people involved, including people in the White House. And then he indicated he thought there were some jeopardies, potential jeopardies, and circumstantial linkage in terms of the 350 [thousand dollars] that I was—had dealt with.

PRESIDENT NIXON: Was that mentioned in the conversation?

HALDEMAN: I think so, yeah. And then he indicated to you that there had been some blackmail incidents, what he regarded as blackmail incidents involving this, but one of those was—was—as an example, this thing of Hunt's where he had made this direct threat against Ehrlichman, that he was going to reveal what he had done for Ehrlichman if he wasn't given a payment.

PRESIDENT NIXON: $21,000. . . .

HALDEMAN: I'm not going to say that it was discussed with you because I don't discuss those discussions with you, but that you then were very much—this was a totally new area to you and were very surprised about this and very much interested in the—

PRESIDENT NIXON: That's where we could say the President came out of his chair.

HALDEMAN: . . . This was [the time] that you probed deeply into in trying to draw out of him—and he was reluctant to put it out. You weren't getting a full thing right at the outset from him. You kept saying, but what do you do? How do you—you know, raising money is no problem. . . . You were asking a lot of leading questions designed to draw Dean out because it was apparent that Dean was sort of treading a thin line in how he was talking with you in that meeting. You had told him to give you all the facts. He was not giving you all the facts. He was giving you a selected few of the facts and you were pushing to get more information. And you asked about how they did these, what they did, who?

Then you were trying to find out who else was involved, and he volunteered at some point that you were probing in this that he had been in communication with Mitchell about it—

PRESIDENT NIXON: That's right.

HALDEMAN: —which you also found very interesting. You wanted to see what—what was involved there. And there was some discussion of his conversation with Mitchell.

PRESIDENT NIXON: I wouldn't mention [Thomas] Pappas.

HALDEMAN: I won't in regard to all this. And that as you go into this, it becomes very clear and that as you look at subsequent days, he confirms that that the President was realizing here that there was a problem within the White House where he had been assured up to that point that there wasn't. . . . [Y]ou were probing Dean *hard* to find out what was happening. And the upshot of that was you said to Dean—and that's why I think you called me into the meeting. You said to Dean, I want you to have a meeting with Mitchell and Ehrlichman and Haldeman. See, at this point you didn't know what Mitchell's involvement was in this. . . . And neither did Dean I don't think.

PRESIDENT NIXON: Is that what I said?

HALDEMAN: You said, I want the four of you to meet and I want Dean to give Mitchell and Ehrlichman and Haldeman the same total facts that he's given me.

PRESIDENT NIXON: Well, did I say that?

HALDEMAN: Yeah, and you were still suspicious I think of what we were getting. I think you wanted to smoke out where Dean fit and where everybody else fit as a result of that. So, you had us meet with [him]—the next day. . . . He didn't go into as much detail with us as he had with you, though. And then we got to how little we knew about this and how do we get this out? . . . And at that point it was left that it would take him a couple days to write up a full report.

PRESIDENT NIXON: After you and Mitchell met, that's right. But on the 21st, the key thing is we did not tell Dean, look, go have a meeting tomorrow and raise the money for Bittman.

HALDEMAN: Oh, no. . . . [M]oney in this meeting came up a couple times in the meeting, but it was not the subject of the meeting. It was an example.

PRESIDENT NIXON: Except I did go into it about the million dollars. I said that, well, we could get it to—how you going to get it to them. I remember that. . . .

HALDEMAN: Sure.

PRESIDENT NIXON: What about clemency? I said, you can't give clemency before, I said, before the election actually, before '74, you know, or something like that. I mean, the point is that—

HALDEMAN: You were poking on what Dean had in mind. You didn't understand what he was talking about and neither did I.

PRESIDENT NIXON: I remember saying, first, it's wrong. Second, it won't work. That's right. I mean, this sort of a thing. Then I said, I want you to sit down and tell me everything and then let's get something here to get this—

HALDEMAN: Get this out because we can't get into—if there's blackmail going on, that's not something we can tolerate.

PRESIDENT NIXON: Because, incidentally, Dean was very hard on that. Remember, he said that is blackmail.

HALDEMAN: Yeah.

PRESIDENT NIXON: So, that could be our defense. . . .

HALDEMAN: Well, Dean had several idiotic schemes in the process of this. . . .

PRESIDENT NIXON: Let me say I'd be very interested in seeing if you're running, to run over and take a look at your September 15th [log?]. There's something phony about it. . . .

HALDEMAN: Haig went through the log and it wasn't in a thing. He went through another one and it was. I'll tell you what I think is possible is that—that it wasn't there and that somehow Dean figured out how to get it written into the log. In other words, he got the sheet from them and found out there wasn't a meeting, decided this was a useful thing to use, and got it written back in.

PRESIDENT NIXON: My God. My God.

HALDEMAN: And this thing is so weird that I don't discount any possibility.

PRESIDENT NIXON: Well, let me say this. First, check your own files. You made notes of every meeting, Bob. You always did at a meeting sitting in here with Dean to make notes.

HALDEMAN: I went through that stuff.

PRESIDENT NIXON: And you already checked that? . . . Son of a bitch. . . . He's lying. . . .

HALDEMAN: . . . [D]id you watch the Senate hearings on television? First of all, I think most people won't watch. Well, they'll watch some of it on the news.

PRESIDENT NIXON: Oh, shit, yes.

SEGMENT 2

PRESIDENT NIXON: Well, let me say this. I was going to say to you that without being sentimental, I miss you and John both around here because you're both strong men. And it's—but it was good to talk with you. . . .

SEGMENT 3

PRESIDENT NIXON: If John Dean goes on the stand and says the President knew all about this whole thing from the beginning, which I didn't, or if he says on September the 15th (unintelligible), on that day I told him that we're paying off the Cubans, or some Goddamn thing, we've got to fight the son of a bitch to the death. You understand?

HALDEMAN: Yeah.

PRESIDENT NIXON: Because I don't remember the conversation. You don't remember the conversation.

HALDEMAN: No, sir, I sure don't.

PRESIDENT NIXON: I don't remember the fact of the meeting. Now, I did remember the 21st meeting. . . . The only faulty memory I had on that was I was absolutely convinced it was in the late part of the day, but it wasn't. It was in the morning. . . .

HALDEMAN: Poor Ehrlichman. Jesus, he's got all these Goddamn—you know, one thing after another. At least mine stays on the same track.

PRESIDENT NIXON: Yeah.

HALDEMAN: His keep squirting out from under him.

PRESIDENT NIXON: Like he's got now with Krogh.

HALDEMAN: Krogh and the Pentagon and the CIA now saying that he authorized giving the stuff to Hunt which I think he has a letter from [CIA Deputy Director General Robert] Cushman saying that he didn't because Cushman, you know, first recalled that Ehrlichman called. When Ehrlichman called him back and said, you know, when did I call you? Cushman, well, I don't know that it was you. Someone called me.

PRESIDENT NIXON: Who do you think, Krogh?

HALDEMAN: Probably Krogh. . . . I think he has or that Hunt called himself. Hunt made—see, that's what they say, is Hunt called and then represented that he was working on Ehrlichman's authority. Now, that I'm sure is correct.

PRESIDENT NIXON: Yeah.

HALDEMAN: Yeah, that other stuff. You know, he [Hunt] got disguises and all that stuff.

PRESIDENT NIXON: Ehrlichman didn't call the CIA.

HALDEMAN: Ehrlichman's story, as I understand it, was that [Robert] Cushman called him after this had been going on and said, "we've got all this going on. We can't keep on doing this," and John said you're absolutely right. We shouldn't be. Cushman then said, "well you authorized it." And John said, "I don't believe I did, Bob." And Cushman said, "well, you called me." John said, "no, I don't think so." Cushman said, "well, somebody called. Maybe it wasn't you." And then John said, "well, I wish you'd clear that up." And Cushman later . . . wrote John a memo saying just to clear up any misunderstanding, I do not—. . . .

PRESIDENT NIXON: Bob, I don't think people give a shit about the CIA thing. I don't really think they care. I don't think they care about bugging Ellsberg—I mean, about running into the psychiatrist. I really think they [don't] give a shit. I know that they care much about bugging the Goddamn Pentagon—I mean, the—

HALDEMAN: Watergate.

PRESIDENT NIXON: Watergate. I think the cover-up deal was a problem and the obstruction of justice was a problem in the sense that it looks like we're tried to—what I mean—we were not carrying out *the law,* so-called.

HALDEMAN: Yeah.

PRESIDENT NIXON: That is a problem.

HALDEMAN: That's because of—you can contest it I think or I can certainly. You shouldn't at all, but I can contest that a certain degree of naivete and ignorance in it in that I didn't—I didn't vigorously pursue it, but I wasn't hired here as a vigorous pursuer of law and order. I had to keep the Goddamn joint running.

PRESIDENT NIXON: As a matter of fact—as a matter of fact, too, as a lawyer, the idea of obstruction of justice had never occurred to me when I heard about payments for these defendants.

HALDEMAN: And to me either. . . . What that proves to me is, as a layman who is an administrative officer here in the White House, is that this man was the counsel to the President. This man was our legal man. . . . [W]hen a lawyer comes and tells me this is what should be done now and he's the man in charge of the case, then for Christ's sake, I do it. How the hell do I know?

PRESIDENT NIXON: That's right. That's right. . . . You weren't having any other lawyers. This was your counsel. . . . And your damn counsel was misleading you.

HALDEMAN: That's right.

PRESIDENT NIXON: John Dean said to turn over the 350 [thousand dollars] didn't he?

HALDEMAN: Well, I said that—that I wanted the 350 turned over to the committee, and John Dean worked out the ways and means of doing it. I told my man to work with John Dean—

PRESIDENT NIXON: And John Dean decided that the 350 was needed for the defendants.

HALDEMAN: That's right, which was fine with me.

PRESIDENT NIXON: That's right. You had no objection.

HALDEMAN: And at no time did he say there was any illegalities of what I was going to say. He is a lawyer. . . . He instructed Strachan where to take the money and how much to deliver at what time. . . . I didn't know until after the fact it was—was delivered and didn't care. All I wanted was the money back, and I was turning to the lawyer to work out the legal means of getting the money turned over to the committee. And that's how he said to do it, so that's how it was done. And at no time in that process did that lawyer ever say to me there is some question about the legality of this, but we'll do it anyway, or this is illegal, but I'll work it out, or anything. . . .

PRESIDENT NIXON: You might let me say why this is so important to you. It's terribly important in terms of your intentions. . . . Basically your intentions—you can't be accused of illegal intent if you didn't know something was illegal. . . . Unless they say your intent was—well, to shut them up, but he didn't say that's what they wanted it for.

HALDEMAN: No, sir, and it was not my intent. I thought they were going to talk, and I didn't care if they talked. . . . And I had no motive to shut them up. I knew nothing about the Watergate. You knew nothing about the Watergate, and I was told by Dean, on whom I was relying, that nobody else in the White House knew anything about the Watergate. I knew that somebody in the committee did because obviously someone had to do it. I didn't know how high up it went. I had some ideas, but I wasn't privileged to discuss those ideas with somebody because I might have been wrong, and I still think I probably am wrong. I still don't think I know what really did happen there totally. I don't know what Dean's involvement was now, the more I see of this. Alright.

In all of that, what do I do? I turn to the lawyer and say what is the proper thing to do. How can we get this out? My interest is the political interest, the public relations interest, the point that this is a political problem in terms of news stories that are spec stories that are coming out that are harmful. How do we deal with these? I asked the lawyer.

Ziegler does the same thing. Ziegler goes out there day after day and says nobody in the White House was involved. Every time he did that, before he went out, he said to John Dean, am I correct today in saying nobody in the White House was involved? Yes, Ron, go on out and say it. That's what—that's the fact. . . .

PRESIDENT NIXON: It's got to be worked out, just knock his [Dean's] Goddamn brains out.

HALDEMAN: We're holding that as a possibility. We think we may decide to go on television yet and do a thing or something like that, too.

PRESIDENT NIXON: Really? . . . A guy that could help is [John] Connally. I got him as a special adviser, and I knew that he's trustworthy. . . . I think he's trustworthy, but I think also his judgment is pretty good, [although he] tends to be explosive.

HALDEMAN: Yeah, but that's not all bad either. But, look, I think you should be, though, moving with complete confidence in this. I know that's hard to do because of all this shit that hits every day, but I just start out—before I pick up the paper in the morning, I say to myself—I don't even look—I don't listen to the radio because it just—you get all jangled up by all these little things. But I read the papers thoroughly and before I start in the morning, I just say to myself, there's going to be another pile of shit in here and don't get excited about it. Read through it and then coolly and coldly dissect it. And I do. I underline and I go back and work back on the facts on it each day, and I satisfy myself that it's a bunch of shit, which it is, every day. . . . If you'd look at it that way, instead of doing it the way Garment is of, you know, Jesus, what will we do now—

PRESIDENT NIXON: Did you see what the *New York Times* said today? You see their editorial today. You see their editorial? Screw it. . . . [NBC's John] Chancellor is lying, of course, that this is so much bigger than Teapot Dome. Sonofabitch. You think of Teapot Dome and the hundreds of millions were stolen and all that sort of thing. . . .

HALDEMAN: That's the way he makes it bigger. He runs through this litany of all the people who have had to resign as a result of this. . . .

PRESIDENT NIXON: That's right. The media has forced them out.

HALDEMAN: And we I think have got to admit it. We've got to say the media had a monumental victory, temporary, on this and they did. One of things they wanted me to do and they succeeded, they got some of us out that could have been helpful to you.

PRESIDENT NIXON: Well, they also wanted to destroy the [presidency]. But the main thing is that all this crap about the President should resign. . . .

HALDEMAN: Don't even listen.

PRESIDENT NIXON: Nobody should even ever raise such things. . . . I can't do it. Let me put it this way, I don't care what comes out, I don't care what kind of charges are made, all that sort of thing, Bob, you were elected and have a job to do, and frankly, many of them are begging me to do it—you can't do what I—what I can do right now. You just can't do it.

HALDEMAN: There's no question.

PRESIDENT NIXON: And also if I walk out of this office, you know, on this chicken-shit stuff, why it would leave a mark on the American political system. It's unbelievable. . . . But the other thing is—the other thing, if they ever want to get up to the impeachment thing, fine, fine. . . . My point is if they get to that, the President of the United States, my view is then *fight like hell*.

HALDEMAN: You're damn right, and win it.

PRESIDENT NIXON: Fight it. And we must remember that impeachment is not new for me. . . .

MAY, 10, 1973: THE PRESIDENT AND HAIG, 12:31–12:45 P.M., OVAL OFFICE

Reality escapes the President and his advisors. First, Buzhardt suggests that Nixon name Senator Sam Ervin as Special Prosecutor to coopt the Senate investigation. They also consider a longtime Nixon foe, former California governor Pat Brown, for the position. Then Nixon and Haig settle on former Missouri governor Warren Hearns. Nothing, of course, comes of these ideas, but Nixon and Haig believe they can impose their choice on Elliot Richardson. Finally, the two men close with colorful blasts at the bureaucracy and the President's various enemies, all of whom, they believe, are determined to destroy him.

SEGMENT 1

HAIG: . . . Now, [Fred] Buzhardt came up with an ingenious thing that's worth thinking about. He said, the guy—the name number one as a prosecutor should be Ervin himself. He said, he's a jurist. He's impeccable. He can't do any more damage there, and the son-of-a-bitch would be hard-pressed to turn it down. I told him this yesterday afternoon. I said, Goddamn, that looks a little contrived. And he thought about it all night and he came back and he said no. He said, the more I think about it, the better—

PRESIDENT NIXON: He's got the staff. He's got everything. He's got the work already. He doesn't have to start all over again.

HAIG: It would just totally frustrate this thing.

PRESIDENT NIXON: That's right. Did you pass that on?

HAIG: I haven't. I wanted to ask you first.

PRESIDENT NIXON: Oh Christ, let's try it.

HAIG: I've got [former Missouri Governor Warren] Hearns and [former California Governor Edmund G. "Pat"] Brown (unintelligible).

PRESIDENT NIXON: Yeah. Hearns would be better than Brown.

HAIG: Hearns is better. . . .

PRESIDENT NIXON: He's a tough, fine, fine prosecutor. I mean, Hearns I think is the best one I've suggested.

HAIG: And he and Buzhardt happen to be very close friends. . . .

SEGMENT 3

PRESIDENT NIXON: . . . I think we're now beginning to see where we come out. I mean, let's just face it. Sure, we're going to have a rough time here. It always bores me a little to have people say the obvious, that things are going to be sort of rough, you know, and I guess they have to say that, like these congressmen and so forth. But, Al, . . . it isn't the Goddamn Watergate that bugs these people. They said if you just make a statement, they will cooperate with Ervin. So I did, and it satisfied them for 24 hours. Now, they say if you'll just make a statement about Haldeman and Ehrlichman. That will satisfy everybody. I did. That satisfied them for 24 hours. And now what do they want? They just want more. What they want is our head.

HAIG: That has been the battle all along.

PRESIDENT NIXON: That's what this is about, and that's why we've got to keep our perspective and not panic. And by God, I just may hold the line on executive privilege until hell freezes over. . . .

SEGMENT 4

PRESIDENT NIXON: I hope Richardson can see the point of who's going to be in charge.

HAIG: He got the message today, flexibility. . . .

PRESIDENT NIXON: Just say that this [Hearns] is a name that has been checked out down here, tell him that he should know that Buzhardt—throw Buzhardt's name in there. I said, he's a partisan Democrat who supported McGovern, and I think that will be for that reason—and a very fine lawyer, probably the most respected by the Democratic Governors. That's Hearns. Hearns is the best man for this job.

HAIG: I agree we ought to put him one and then the other guy [Brown] two, if you fail on him.

PRESIDENT NIXON: That's right.

MAY 10, 1973: THE PRESIDENT AND HALDEMAN, 3:24–3:26 P.M., WHITE HOUSE TELEPHONE

Haldeman complains directly to Nixon about Garment's role.

PRESIDENT NIXON: . . . How'd you get along with your lawyers? Okay? . . . They don't mind Buzhardt, do they?

HALDEMAN: They're—well, it depends. I've got to talk to them and find out. If he reported the meeting to Haig as it was reported, then they do, because the report you got on that meeting was highly erroneous. . . .

PRESIDENT NIXON: The point was—no, no, no, you can't blame Buzhardt for that. He was only in it for the last 15 minutes.

HALDEMAN: No. He was in it for the entire meeting, and Chappie Rose wasn't in it at all. And I was told Chappie Rose sat in the meeting. So we're getting some bull-shit from somebody, and this is what pisses me off with the chickenheads over there.

PRESIDENT NIXON: You mean that basically—you say Chappie was not in the meeting.

HALDEMAN: [*Raises his voice.*] Chappie Rose was not in the meeting at all, unless he was under the rug.

PRESIDENT NIXON: Yeah.

HALDEMAN: And Buzhardt was in the entire meeting.

PRESIDENT NIXON: And so was—

HALDEMAN: And so was Garment and so was that little shit that follows Garment around kissing his ass.

PRESIDENT NIXON: [Douglas M.] Parker, yeah. Okay, I'll get that to Haig.

HALDEMAN: [*Abruptly.*] Okay.

PRESIDENT NIXON: Okay.

MAY 10, 1973: THE PRESIDENT AND WILLIAM ROGERS, 5:01–5:04 P.M., WHITE HOUSE TELEPHONE

Nixon comments on the indictments of Mitchell, Stans, and Robert Vesco. Mitchell and Stans were charged with three counts of conspiring to obstruct justice and six counts of perjury regarding a secret $200,000 contribution by Vesco to CREEP in March 1972.

PRESIDENT NIXON: Good God, when they today indict that poor damn Maury Stans and John Mitchell for the most utter stupidity and insanity in that Vesco case.

You know, when I stop to think what in the world is the matter with those guys, Bill, why in the name of God, Vesco is a cheap kike, it's awful.

ROGERS: Yeah, but why in the hell didn't they—had they ever read about the Sherman Adams case. Sherman Adams got kicked out for just making one phone call.

PRESIDENT NIXON: One phone call. But these guys, you know, they took contributions and screwed around and so forth, and, Goddamn it, well, in this case they should have told me at least.

ROGERS: I know it.

PRESIDENT NIXON: Told me. But they didn't.

MAY 11, 1973: THE PRESIDENT AND ZIEGLER, 8:27–9:16 A.M., OVAL OFFICE

Throughout this month, the President spends time explaining his actions to his new confidants. Before May, his conversations with Press Secretary Ron Ziegler rehearsed daily press briefings. But in the new situation, Nixon seems to be more at ease with Ziegler than with Haig. Meanwhile, Ziegler's confidence in speaking to, and even correcting, the President grows steadily. Here, he questions the President's usual condemnations of the media, pointing out that some were friends, and that others could be used. Nixon, who fancied himself a master of understanding the media, listened to Ziegler's assessment that the press "orgy" will pass. Ziegler emphasizes the differences between Watergate and past presidential problems. This is a frank, candid conversation, largely devoid of Nixon's proclamations of self-pity.

SEGMENT 2

ZIEGLER: . . . [G]ood play, and the radio this morning was very good and the news reports are starting—just as we expected, they're starting to come around. The President is making moves that will bring them—you know, starting to bring the thing into, you know, control and moving out of this. And that's the sense—

PRESIDENT NIXON: Well, the press has been hysterical.

ZIEGLER: Orgy.

PRESIDENT NIXON: Orgy. It's almost unbelievable. It's an emotional trauma beyond belief—15—10 to 15 minutes every night.

ZIEGLER: Well, it's just like—

PRESIDENT NIXON: I was talking to [Charles "Bebe"] Rebozo last night. He told me—he said—he said, believe it or not, he had—now, of course, this doesn't mean anything. He said he had three friends out to dinner who were Democrats. They were switching to Republicans because they were so sick of the media that they couldn't stand listening. . . .

ZIEGLER: [Conservative columnist Nicholas] Thimmisch said it's all about Nixon. . . . He told me a story that I had never heard before. . . . He said, well, you know—he said, I used to work at *Time* magazine. He said, Hugh Sidey used to do the files and he used to, you know, cover the 1960 campaign. And he said, one time Jack Kennedy walked down the aisle of the airplane and said—[Press Secretary Pierre]

Salinger had gone out. They said they weren't going to campaign anymore—it was the summer—because it was too hot. And then Kennedy walked out a little later. And the press said, why aren't you going to campaign anymore this weekend. Kennedy said, well, he said, I guess we better go to the beach. He said, all the niggers have gone to the beach. And, you know—

PRESIDENT NIXON: So, they killed the story.

ZIEGLER: Repeated it in a memorandum. . . . So the point he's making is that although, you know, the news media as a whole—it's not anti-Nixon.

PRESIDENT NIXON: Really?

ZIEGLER: Yes, sir. . . . He said, in 1972 the President had 85 percent support of the news media. And he said that—he said that the news media also, you know, can be tapped, can be played—this is what we're talking about—can be used. . . . Well, he just senses that they have had their orgy, and he feels that it's passed. . . .

PRESIDENT NIXON: I would think some of the newsmen like Thimmisch, our friends, would realize that—that I've got to go through a hell of a thing and have—not show flappability, you know. You know what I mean? I really haven't. I haven't given them a Goddamn inch.

ZIEGLER: He knows that. . . .

PRESIDENT NIXON: . . . Well, getting back to this point, Ron, let's be quite candid [about] the media or the left. It isn't really Haldeman and Ehrlichman and Mitchell, Stans and our campaign they're after. Don't you really think that what they're trying to do is to destroy not so much the [Administration?] but what I stand for. They realize—you know, we beat them so much on their gravy issues. . . . Do you think—do you think they support what I stand for—the media? . . .

ZIEGLER: First of all, you have to divide it down, at least in my mind. First of all, there's the liberal set, which have been decimated, the Katharine Grahams and the [columnist Thomas] Bradens—

PRESIDENT NIXON: Yeah, that's right. . . .

ZIEGLER: They would be—from their standpoint, their motive—

PRESIDENT NIXON: Is destruction.

ZIEGLER: —is destruction. However, the news media as a whole cannot be lumped into that.

PRESIDENT NIXON: Including TV?

ZIEGLER: Well, some TV cannot be lumped into that group.

PRESIDENT NIXON: Maybe Chancellor.

ZIEGLER: John Chancellor—

PRESIDENT NIXON: He goes back and forth too.

ZIEGLER: John Chancellor is a guy who is a personality who likes achieving it to the top.

PRESIDENT NIXON: . . . I don't feel—have any feeling against them, you know. If I were Katharine Graham, I'd hate Nixon too. . . . You realize the Times has always been on the other side of the issue—

ZIEGLER: Sure.

PRESIDENT NIXON: —of everything that I've ever stood for? Every campaign they've opposed. Well, in any event, if that is the case, isn't that what the larger battle is about? The larger battle is really we're just trying to kill the President. [Loud ex-

hale.] *That's very, very tough.* That's what we must not let them do. . . . But I kept getting at the fact that the attack is on the presidency—on the President and what he stands for, what he stands for. Ron, you realize what we stand for is a hard line foreign policy, a hard line policy of law and order. . . .

SEGMENT 3

ZIEGLER: . . . What you stand for is something that the American people supported by the largest mandate in history. . . .

PRESIDENT NIXON: Well, another thing—another thing—what I stand for is in the best interest of the those press guys in the foreign policy field. Let's forget the domestic stuff. I know you can argue about whether or not you should have a legal services center. That's a legitimate thing, or an OEO thing, or whether or not you should have busing. We can all disagree on that, Ron. We can all disagree as to whether you set wage and price controls. But who the hell can argue about that? The fact that at this present time in world history, the United States has the opportunity, either if you win or lose, the greatest chance that history has ever had to build a structure of peace in the world. . . . *Only us.* And I'm the only man that can do it. There isn't anybody coming along the pike. Can you imagine Teddy Kennedy making the kind of decisions that I have to make? John Connally, yes, if we get him nurtured up to that.

[Withdrawn item. Privacy.]

PRESIDENT NIXON: Well, what I'm saying is this. Goddamn it, whatever our weaknesses are, I know this foreign policy field. . . .

ZIEGLER: But now the national news media has been—this is true of—of the press, free press. They get caught up in the emotion of it all, and that's true. I'd say three of these pricks in the briefing room had done one ounce of investigative reporting or primary reporting on the whole Watergate matter, but they [are] caught up in it. For what? That's the orgy I'm talking about. It's not the motive to get the President. It's not the motive to destroy the President or what he stands for.

PRESIDENT NIXON: It's the Watergate story.

ZIEGLER: It's the Watergate. And this is what I think we—we—we have to deal with because in the next three and a half years, if we understand this phenomenon of the press—and it's true. Look at Congress too—we can use them. . . . My view is that will not achieve the thing if we move into a harsh offensive against them. Now, that doesn't mean—

PRESIDENT NIXON: I agree with you.

ZIEGLER: I'm not talking about being in a position of weakness. I'm not talking about misunderstanding. And you've sewn this up absolutely in the Cabinet. Dealing with the press, dealing with the Congress does not mean that you're ever going to get them to be your friends, but use them. It's just like how boring it is and anything that is done oftentimes, just sit down and have a cocktail with some guy you don't like but you need something he's got. . . .

PRESIDENT NIXON: . . . [B]ut in terms of what they [Haldeman, Ehrlichman et al.] did, it's chicken shit. I mean, it's nothing. It is about—you know, it's what Bobby Kennedy did to me in '60 and '62, what Johnson did to Goldwater. Buzhardt would say, Christ, it was unbelievable what they did to him in '64. We know that's the case. That sort of crap.

ZIEGLER: I agree that

PRESIDENT NIXON: But, on the other hand, the question is all that happening, you can't help but run off and say, well, the President must be a crooked son-of-a-bitch too. Do you think we can avoid that in the end? . . . Some of it rubs. Some of it doesn't. You know what I mean. It doesn't all rub. I mean, the fact we're investigating it, we're going on. People don't want to believe that about the President. That's why audiences react as they did the other night. Shit, they don't want to believe that.

ZIEGLER: . . . I think whoever is telling you—I'd just as soon talk frankly to you. Whoever suggests to you that—that this is—first of all, obviously in terms of scandal, in terms of someone receiving money and so forth, it's minuscule, but it's also, Mr. President, broader than the wiretapping activities of the previous administration.

PRESIDENT NIXON: Well, it's broader. No, no, not that more was done, but a hell of a lot more have been exposed.

ZIEGLER: That's true.

PRESIDENT NIXON: Well, listen—listen. My God, the Kennedys and Johnson used the FBI, Hoover told me, in a shameful way. We didn't do that.

ZIEGLER: No, but—

PRESIDENT NIXON: for political purposes.

ZIEGLER: They probably did more in terms of wiretapping and that type of activity than we did. It wasn't exposed, but this case goes beyond that.

PRESIDENT NIXON: That's right.

ZIEGLER: This goes to the activities. It's not focused on wiretapping really. It's— that's where the play is now, but it goes to the activities of—

PRESIDENT NIXON: Colson.

ZIEGLER: —of the Colson-type thing. And it goes to the activities of the Hunt and Liddy type, which is beyond the wiretapping.

PRESIDENT NIXON: That's right. . . . I'm quite aware of this. I know it isn't just wiretapping.

ZIEGLER: The—we used wiretapping in a *very legitimate way.* The Kennedys and Johnson, as I understand it, used it more indiscriminately. However, you then move to the other aspects of this case, which is what we're dealing with here.

PRESIDENT NIXON: Chicken shit. That's right. I mean, the Canuck letter [false accusations against Senator Muskie] and the [Henry] Jackson [concerning homosexuality] letter. Right? That kind of crap.

ZIEGLER: That kind of stuff. Then you add the cover-up.

PRESIDENT NIXON: Oh, the coverup. Oh, God, of course. That's the worst, my understanding. But I—I lump that in the wiretapping.

ZIEGLER: That's right.

PRESIDENT NIXON: It's all a part of the same deal. So, but how does it sort out?

ZIEGLER: It sorts out just where we are now. It sorts out that the matter is being investigated. It's being dealt with. You've addressed it. You are moving on in terms of your activities, and that is the way we're going to win. The only way we're going to win this is we—we're starting upward. The only way we're going to win is to—to keep the—as you say, keep this matter in perspective, but recognize it fully as to what it was and how it happened and why it happened.

PRESIDENT NIXON: That's right. . . . And also, we've got to get some attention on the fact that we—the other side were not virgins. . . . But I would be absolutely firm, Ron, on the fact, yes, there was wiretapping for the purpose of getting at national— highly classified national security documents that would jeopardize the ending of— our interests to end the war and that sort of thing. . . .

ZIEGLER: SALT.

PRESIDENT NIXON: That's right. And wiretapping [of journalists and NSC staff] was used.

ZIEGLER: [During the] India–Pakistan [conflict].

PRESIDENT NIXON: Yeah, is used and used properly. Now, the tricky area is whether or not it can be used legally by—outside of the FBI. . . . When the FBI uses it, they don't have to have a court order for this purpose, the national security, for certain parts. The Attorney General can approve it. Mitchell has put us on a bit of a spot there by saying he never approved any from the White House. That's not true.

But I would just say—I just wouldn't get into that. I would say I'm not going to get into that, but we were—we were making every possible effort to get these leaks, you know. And I would go on the offensive on that very, very strongly on this. I'm not going to go into it. I have no information about it and so forth because we're never going to put that out. . . . I think they're in the vault along with the India-Pakistan story. That's in the vault. I'll never put it out. I consider that in the national security and it's going to lay buried as a helluva lot of other things. . . .

MAY 11, 1973: THE PRESIDENT AND HAIG, 9:19–10:10 A.M., OVAL OFFICE

Nixon and Haig discuss the Administration's history of wiretapping of National Security Council and media people. William Sullivan, formerly the Number Three man in the FBI hierarchy, provided information for Haig. For Haig, the stakes are simple and old-fashioned: "good, strong Americanism versus left-wing sabotage." Nixon apparently understood. The two are concerned that Elliot Richardson is getting "goosey." Finally, they consider some possible nominees for the FBI directorship in a rather desultory manner.

SEGMENT 1

HAIG: . . . Well, we'll have to see how the hearing goes today—[William] Sullivan is over there. He's just going to say this is a result of J. Edgar Hoover's deception to the President and national security leaks and if this is the kind of thing that, uh, had always been done—traditionally.

PRESIDENT NIXON: . . . Sullivan told you that's what he was going to say? Mitchell discussed it too?

HAIG: The Attorney General approved every single tap that was going on. . . . I'm not at all worried. Goddamn it, and we may ultimately have to counterattack with some of that stuff. Put it out—what we were doing. But, you see, when the time is up, people start to get filled, then we've got to take the counter-offensive, because, Goddamn it, what's at stake here is good, strong Americanism versus left-wing—

PRESIDENT NIXON: Left-wing—

HAIG: Creeps—sabotage. Hell, we were sabotaged this stuff (unintelligible) talk— that was treason. . . .

PRESIDENT NIXON: I didn't tell Hoover to tap this, tap that or—

HAIG: He did. He developed lies. When one guy's name would surface, and it was suspicious, that put a tap on him. . . .

PRESIDENT NIXON: . . . [Y]ou think Sullivan will be a good witness?

HAIG: Yes, I do. . . . Oh, I think he'll say that J. Edgar Hoover, uh, there were leaks—looked like they were coming out of the White House staff or someplace in the government, and that J. Edgar Hoover authorized these taps. Uh, that the reports of them as they always have been provided to the White House—came over memos from J. Edgar Hoover to the President which were delivered initially to, uh, Kissinger. . . . [W]ell, initially he saw them all.

PRESIDENT NIXON: But, hell, he [Kissinger] was reading everything.

HAIG: Right. Then, it was changed after about four months and we got only what's involved NSC people.

PRESIDENT NIXON: Right.

HAIG: And, they started going directly to John.

PRESIDENT NIXON: Ehrlichman, right.

HAIG: Then, they were terminated when it became—the Supreme Court ruling— made tapping a questionable activity. We terminated it, as I understand it. We were—

PRESIDENT NIXON: Yeah, terminated, then the Hunt thing [plumbers] started after that.

HAIG: Well, that's the trouble. So, it's not too good to draw on the purity of this thing.

PRESIDENT NIXON: Yeah. The Hunt thing is tough . . . . I don't know, Ehrlichman says they did not tape, but I don't know. . . .

HAIG: I would suspect he didn't.

PRESIDENT NIXON: So, I think we're making him look better—maybe (unintelligible) he was going to do a second story job, so-called at the Brookings Institute, which he didn't do and he was going to try to do something in Georgetown, which he did not do. . . . We have nothing on Hunt on taps. . . . And, don't you believe [Mark] Felt leaked this to the *Times?*

HAIG: That's the report Elliot had and Sullivan told me that that's what's going on.

PRESIDENT NIXON: Well, [Felt] used the leak to *Time* magazine. He's a bad guy, you see.

HAIG: Very bad. He's got to go.

PRESIDENT NIXON: He's got to go. . . . You still don't have anybody worth a damn at the FBI. . . .

HAIG: Got to get an outsider and we ought to get the dean of the law school [name unknown] . . . cause he'd be holier than Caesar's wife and uh—

PRESIDENT NIXON: Well, let's get the dean of the law school . . . . Sullivan could help a lot . . . . I think he knows about the Johnson tappings in 1968. . . .

HAIG: He knows everything. . . . And he is 100 percent behind you. . . . He's a patriot, that's why.

PRESIDENT NIXON: What's he think of Felt? What's he think he's up to?

HAIG: Thinks he's trying to—

PRESIDENT NIXON: Be head of the Bureau. . . .

HAIG: I don't know whether to believe these guys—except I have great confidence in Sullivan. For years, he's been really the best man in the Bureau.

PRESIDENT NIXON: But, Hoover didn't like him—Hoover fired him.

HAIG: Because he kept pressing Hoover to do the things that had to be done in the reforms. . . .

PRESIDENT NIXON: So, Sullivan is going to say that Hoover talked to the President? Actually, what happened is that Mitchell ordered it, you see. I, he—Hoover talked to me about it and I said get the dope, you know. Do the best you can. . . .

HAIG: Sullivan's perspective of this is what he's got inside the department where he was and Hoover called him in and said we're going to do this. . . . He's an honest, straight, patriotic guy, and this happens to be totally on the straight patriotic action, and it's going to be portrayed that way. That's good. It's the lack of knowledge on this thing that—

PRESIDENT NIXON: . . . Well, it's tough. We don't know whether you can take the line. Just don't put it out. Elliot, uh, you can't have Elliot get goosey and decide he doesn't want to be Attorney General. That would be a terrible blow. . . .

HAIG: Bring [former CIA Director] John McCone in or somebody like that.

PRESIDENT NIXON: Oh. Another lawyer. Is Elliot that goosey?

HAIG: No, I don't think so. I think he's confident. I think he's—but, he gets—he just had—well, they keep in touch with him everyday so he doesn't get to thinking things are going on that aren't going on. . . .

SEGMENT 2

HAIG: And, that's the way this thing has to be presented—my God, this has been done by Kennedy, Johnson—

PRESIDENT NIXON: And, we did less of it. . . .

HAIG: It would be an absolute travesty and tragedy, and I—that's what I told Elliot—Goddamn it, I happen to know he had started bleating to me about the situation. I said, "Elliot, I happen to know about these taps." I said, "Goddamn it, Henry was serviced with them. They involved our people. We fired two people on the head of them—you know, we got rid of them and we had other grounds too" . . . . [T]hat's straight prudent—protection of the national interests, and it was totally above board. The Attorney General approved every one.

PRESIDENT NIXON: Right. . . .

MAY 11, 1973: THE PRESIDENT AND KISSINGER, 10:15 A.M.–12:03 P.M., OVAL OFFICE

Nixon and Kissinger often talked about the various aspects of "Watergate." On this occasion, the President not so subtly reminds Kissinger of his own part in wiretapping.

SEGMENT 1

PRESIDENT NIXON: We'll survive it, Henry, you know that.

KISSINGER: I know it and as soon as we can get people focusing in on government we're going to—

PRESIDENT NIXON: Which is hard. We will, but you have to keep your confidence up. . . . The people that really watch are going to watch you and they're going to watch me, of course, and they'll watch Haldeman, Ehrlichman, and they'll watch Haig, and that's about it.

KISSINGER: You don't have anything to worry about with us, Mr. President. . . .

PRESIDENT NIXON: But, we've been through hell before, and this is worse hell. Goddamn, Mitchell, Stans indicted, for Christ sakes. For a cheap little crap on a (unintelligible). And Vesco didn't get anything. [*Shouting.*] *They didn't get anything. We indicted them.* . . .

SEGMENT 2

PRESIDENT NIXON: Don't let anyone get you down, Henry, or all you're going to hear is Watergate, Watergate. You know it just breaks out all over the place and God, they throw Maury Stans and John Mitchell are indicted. . . . As I've said to you, didn't get anything, didn't get any money, Vesco got indicted too. *Shit!* It's stupidity, insanity.

SEGMENT 3

KISSINGER: You see this—as soon as the public feels we're governing, then all of this will look like a bunch of dogs snapping at the heels.

PRESIDENT NIXON: Yeah. The difficulty with all this is not the novelty, not its depth, but its width.

KISSINGER: Yes.

PRESIDENT NIXON: The fact that, basically, you take Haldeman and Ehrlichman—as you know, there's no two more loyal, able guys in this place. Christ, they've never done dishonest things in their whole Goddamned life. They're tangled in it because they were here. And, frankly, uh, it's true of others. It's a very sad thing and I feel very badly about it. But, I still think I had to do what I did. I had to sink them.

KISSINGER: It'd be impossible if you hadn't.

PRESIDENT NIXON: . . . I don't mean to be Polyannish, but there's a curious American reaction to it, . . . particularly [for] a president and it always is sympathetic. Kennedy got the massive reaction to the Bay of Pigs. I was so surprised, you know, I thought he'd go down and get the shit kicked out of him. I don't mean the same thing, but not only in our telegrams, in our mail. . . . It's the most emotional, strong public support. They want the President to win, they don't buy the President to do this Goddamned crap. I'm not in it, Henry, you know that.

KISSINGER: I know.

PRESIDENT NIXON: Now, there's one place I have to, and you're in it too, as you know. . . . That is in the national security area, but it is time to accept it and so forth and so on. And, basically, we've got all that stuff here. . . .

KISSINGER: It was read to Haldeman and he showed me copies of it. . . . He showed me copies . . . .

PRESIDENT NIXON: I know why he said it—you read parts of it. I wouldn't ever spend my money on such stuff. But, Ehrlichman . . . was the one who actually did it, but my point is it was done.

KISSINGER: Right.

PRESIDENT NIXON: And it's done. It will have to continue to be done.

KISSINGER: Oh, you had never—

PRESIDENT NIXON: There were massive leaks. . . . Nobody was tapping Ellsberg. . . . They were tapping [National Security aide Morton] Halperin, whom you had discharged, basically—oh, you let him resign, and they got it and that was before Ellsberg's Pentagon Papers thing blew, and they found Ellsberg and Halperin were buddies.

KISSINGER: Well, for your information, I knew about the FBI tap. . . . I knew nothing about the operation that Ehrlichman was conducting with Young [Plumbers]. . . . But the FBI taps, I'm going to take the position that those—there was no reason to suppose those weren't legal taps.

PRESIDENT NIXON: Oh, they were. . . .

SEGMENT 4

KISSINGER: But I think it's against our interests now to get the National Security Council apparatus tied into Watergate.

PRESIDENT NIXON: Oh, we won't, but the point is—the point is it has been tied in as a result of this—this story to the effect that there was a—that there was a tap on Halperin. You see?

KISSINGER: That still makes it an FBI–Justice Department thing.

PRESIDENT NIXON: What's that?

KISSINGER: That still makes it an FBI–Justice—

PRESIDENT NIXON: I know, but the point is why?

KISSINGER: To prevent leaks.

PRESIDENT NIXON: Right, and leaks from where?

KISSINGER: Well, from here and elsewhere.

PRESIDENT NIXON: That's the point. That's—when I say the National Security Council, that's why—you won't have to get into it, but I just want you to know that that's what we anticipate. But don't be offensive about it. You're Goddamn right this was done. We had to do it. We have to prevent leaks. I mean, how can we conduct a foreign policy in regard to China, in regard to Russia? Suppose some of the stuff leaked out on China? Suppose this conversation we had right here leaks in some way? Suppose some of the things I said to you about China and read to you and you read to me about China and Russia—suppose that got out? . . .

KISSINGER: Oh, no question—

PRESIDENT NIXON: . . . We didn't have the Congress with us. We didn't have the press with us. We didn't have the bureaucracy with us. We did it alone, Henry.

KISSINGER: That's right.

PRESIDENT NIXON: Now, Goddamn, what I mean is—what I meant is that you have to have security and you've got to have confidence in your men.

KISSINGER: Of course, the accumulation of stupidities is so great. This NSC—this FBI [?] tactic didn't have to come out at all if Judge Byrne hadn't got started on it. . . . I think you just have to endure it now.

PRESIDENT NIXON: We'll endure. . . . I could survive personally. . . . [T]he reasons we got the biggest majority in history, the people were still for those reasons. They're still for those policies. We have an obligation to carry those out to ourselves and for the free world. If we don't deliver, the chances for peace and freedom to survive in this world for the next thirty or three hundred years may be seriously jeopardized.

Now, Henry, with that—those stakes on—we cannot allow the crappy business about Watergate and campaign crap—we cannot allow that to destroy the presidency of the United States. Sure, I could walk out of here tomorrow and people say, resign, resign. That's an easy thing to do, isn't it? So, I would resign. So, what do you have there? Agnew. Right? [*Laughs.*]

KISSINGER: You can't do that. . . . You can't resign.

PRESIDENT NIXON: I wouldn't think of it. I wouldn't think of it anyway from a personal standpoint. Hell, I'll stay here till the last Gallup polls. . . . Goddamn it. We're here to do a job and we're doing the right thing. You know it and I know it.

KISSINGER: Mr. President, this thing has got to be over sometime in the next month at least; no more new revelations can come out. . . .

MAY 11, 1973: THE PRESIDENT AND HAIG, 12:07–12:43 P.M., OVAL OFFICE

The White House receives startling news on May 11. CIA Deputy Director Vernon Walters, a longtime Nixon friend, had prepared a series of "memcoms" (memorandum communications) in July 1972, detailing the White House's attempts to have the CIA thwart the FBI investigation of the Watergate burglary. Immediately, the Administration seeks to impose a national security blanket over Walters' memos. Lengthy conversations follow to consider damage control. "This was a Dean plot," the President insisted. The *New York Times* published the material the next month, and while they anticipate the August 1974 revelations of the "smoking gun" tape of June 23, 1972, the documents had little impact at the time. Haig uses the situation to enhance his command and to further segregate the President from his former aides. The President, for his part, is anxious to draw apart from Ehrlichman, who was deeply involved with the Plumbers.

SEGMENT 1

HAIG: We have—have some very fast actions here this morning.

PRESIDENT NIXON: Yeah.

HAIG: Walters was called back by [outgoing CIA Director James] Schlesinger from his trip to the Far East about CIA involvement with the White House, primarily through Dean. Walters came in to me and gave me eight memcoms of the meeting here with Haldeman and Ehrlichman in July of last year, and a series of subsequent meetings with Gray and Dean. I—when I read them, I thought they were quite damaging to us. I said, what are you doing with these and where are they? He said that Schlesinger had ordered him to take them over and deliver a copy to me and a copy to the Attorney General. So, I immediately called Buzhardt in and we both read it. And we said, these papers can't go anywhere. We sent him back to the agency, told him not to take any telephone calls, return here immediately with every copy. And these are vital national security matters and cannot go anywhere.

PRESIDENT NIXON: What did these deal with, Al?

HAIG: They deal with Dean's efforts to—to get a CIA cover for the Watergate defendants.

PRESIDENT NIXON: But were Haldeman and Ehrlichman trying to do it too?

HAIG: Haldeman and Ehrlichman's discussion was in the direction of having Walters go directly to the Attorney—or to the Director of the FBI—

PRESIDENT NIXON: Yeah.

HAIG: —and tell him that this involved national security matters and that he should quiet down about the investigation.

PRESIDENT NIXON: Right. . . .

HAIG: And that it had gone far enough and it was getting wider. It was beginning to get into CIA business, Mexican money. . . . Walters refused and he kept saying—

PRESIDENT NIXON: Thank God.

HAIG: That's right. He kept saying, you're going drag the President into this this way. You are—

PRESIDENT NIXON: That's right.

HAIG: And I will not be a part of this.

PRESIDENT NIXON: That's right.

HAIG: So, then he went to Gray. They told him to go to Gray. He did and he had just arrived over at the Agency. Because they told him that it was involving CIA and he hadn't had a chance to check and he did exactly what he was told. He went to Gray, and Gray said, no, I don't know of any CIA involvement. You better check that. But he also quoted a discussion he had with you in the memcom, which isn't helpful for our purposes.

PRESIDENT NIXON: Who? Walters?

HAIG: No, no, no. Gray did. He said, I called the President and told him this case was bad. It involved people high up in the White House and he should clean house. This is July.

PRESIDENT NIXON: John Ehrlichman, yeah.

HAIG: Well, he didn't mention any names. . . . Then there were subsequent, numerous contacts by Dean going in there—

PRESIDENT NIXON: What did he say I said?

HAIG: That you didn't say anything. . . . There's nothing—no incriminating statements from you of any kind. . . .

SEGMENT 2

HAIG: The—then the subsequent memcoms are approach after approach by Dean in July and August, trying to get the CIA to put these defendants under CIA mantle, including the—

PRESIDENT NIXON: This is Dean?

HAIG: Yes, this is Dean. Including telling the—

PRESIDENT NIXON: This guy did some business for himself.

HAIG: Oh, unbelievable, unbelievable.

PRESIDENT NIXON: There is more and more of this stuff that doesn't sound like Ehrlichman and the rest. Let me tell you my conversation. I remember my conversation with Gray to this day. He called me. No. I called him, as I told you, about the other thing. He said, there's some stuff in the White House—there are people in the White House you ought to—he didn't say clean house. But what he said is that there are some people in the White House, he said, that aren't you giving you all the facts here. And I said, well, Pat, you have got to go out and get the facts. I didn't tell him—

HAIG: Well, we had that, you see, and Gray confirms that, and press ahead.

PRESIDENT NIXON: What's that?

HAIG: Press ahead with the investigation is what you told him. . . .

PRESIDENT NIXON: I told him that he was to press ahead with the investigation.

HAIG: So, but in any event, it's very—these things are very damaging to Dean.

PRESIDENT NIXON: Yeah.

HAIG: Now, Walters is very clean. He flat refused each time and he—

PRESIDENT NIXON: But the point is, are they damaging to Haldeman and Ehrlichman?

HAIG: A little bit, a little bit, yes, apparently by innuendo, yeah, quite—

PRESIDENT NIXON: I mean, do they mention the President?

HAIG: No, except for the way Walters transcribed what Gray said to him. . . . He's got it in a memcom. Now, I've got all the memcoms and he's on his way back and he's going to give them to Buzhardt. These memcoms cannot get out under any circumstances.

PRESIDENT NIXON: Yeah, right.

HAIG: Now, I've called Schlesinger and I've told him that Buzhardt would be in touch with him but that we are reviewing these memcoms for—for executive privilege due to the whole broad character of it. He said, I understand completely. And I said—now, the next thing Buzhardt said we have to immediately get in touch with Bob's lawyer and John's lawyer—

PRESIDENT NIXON: Yeah.

HAIG: —and tell him about this and be sure they know what we're doing.

PRESIDENT NIXON: That's right.

HAIG: Then after we make the assessment of the discussion with Bob and John, we are going to tell Walters to go over to [Henry] Petersen and say, the Agency has been under attack here. I've been called back and I am prepared to testify. . . . And Walters is very good. . . . Everything he says is going to help you.

PRESIDENT NIXON: Huh?

HAIG: Everything he says is going to help the President.

PRESIDENT NIXON: Yes.

HAIG: That I'm sure.

PRESIDENT NIXON: I know. As I told you, I was a babe in the woods when they told me about this thing. I frankly thought it was a CIA thing. . . .

HAIG: Now, the FBI has gotten to a point with the trial [Ellsberg] in California. Of course, it's going to be a mistrial, and we want it to and the quicker the better. . . .

PRESIDENT NIXON: That's right. Get it over with and forget it.

HAIG: That's right. So, we have the option now to burn his [Judge Matthew Byrne] ass for the reports on the wiretap on Ellsberg.

PRESIDENT NIXON: Don't give them. . . .

HAIG: . . . [Acting FBI Director] Ruckelshaus is trying to get to me. I don't want to talk to him until we've got a strategy lined up.

PRESIDENT NIXON: Right.

HAIG: His guy, the same fellow I talked about last night, spilling his guts all over the west coast, the newspapers—

PRESIDENT NIXON: [Mark] Felt.

HAIG: Including the names of the newspaper people Joseph Kraft and Henry Brandon, and all those people. And Ruckelshaus feels that we've got to make some kind of a statement on this that's got to be associated with Watergate and it's going to be interpreted. . . .

PRESIDENT NIXON: Right, and what did he say?

HAIG: He would say that, yes, J. Edgar Hoover, the Attorney General the reason for taps, one led to another. . . .

PRESIDENT NIXON: Yes, and they were—the taps were because of leaks of national security documents—national security documents. The newsmen were tapped only for the purpose of determining who was leaking to them. . . . Their names came up, that there—that no implication whatever should be attached to any of the newsmen because basically the purpose of it was the purpose of the leaks that occurred.

HAIG: I think we have to do this and we should let Ruckelshaus do it.

PRESIDENT NIXON: Right. He should put it out (unintelligible).

HAIG: Well, it probably ought to be done tomorrow and concurrently with that, you know, during this investigation even when it might be known. There have been leaks of this information before the investigation was completed and among those was this man who's being discharged.

PRESIDENT NIXON: Felt.

HAIG: Fire his ass. . . .

PRESIDENT NIXON: Blame it on Felt. . . .

HAIG: Sir, he's going to do it whether we fire him or we keep him, and if we fire him and discredit him, everything he says from thereon is going to be—

PRESIDENT NIXON: [Does Ruckelshaus] want him fired?

HAIG: Yes. Now, I haven't talked to him, but I got that indirectly.

PRESIDENT NIXON: Yeah. We have to play the game. Look, now we're clean on this thing.

HAIG: I know it.

PRESIDENT NIXON: I'm clean on this thing. I didn't do anything about this CIA thing. This was a Dean plot, period.

HAIG: Oh, yeah.

PRESIDENT NIXON: He cooked the thing up and apparently talked to Haldeman and Ehrlichman about it, and I'll bet you that they didn't approve the Goddamn thing.

HAIG: But you see, Walters's testimony is going to help. He's going to say constant pressure from Dean. "I [Walters] kept saying you are going to drag the President into this kind of thing. You must get me a written instruction." He never got it, which *ipso facto* proves that Dean was operating on his own.

PRESIDENT NIXON: He's never had anything from me in writing.

HAIG: Never had—never had anything that he could say the President wants this. The President is behind it. He doesn't even drag in, according to Walters, Bob or John. Now, John is a little—he's in more trouble on this than Bob is. Bob—

PRESIDENT NIXON: How is John in more trouble—

HAIG: Well, because he apparently was the man that was talking about the trial, getting in—getting the investigation snuffed out in the meeting that Bob and John had, you know, that the thing is getting too wide. Well, we have to leave it up to Walters and that is a problem.

PRESIDENT NIXON: But Walters's memcoms should not get out. Don't you agree? . . . He will testify and what will he say, though, about his memcoms? . . .

HAIG: He's going to say, oh, yes, I made notes, if they ask him.

PRESIDENT NIXON: Of course, he's got a photographic memory. He said I made—I made notes there.

HAIG: "I [Walters] made notes but I turned them over because they involved a lot of discussion of covert techniques and things of the national security"—and we'll just take executive privilege on it. Now, Buzhardt says he doesn't think they'll ask because Walters is so good and so quick and he'll have his calendar. . . .

PRESIDENT NIXON: And also he recalls everything. Walters says I recall everything and he says I can't—my notes, whatever notes, involves—I made some notes which are secure. They do involve, however, covert—other covert activities and so forth . . .

Second point. Regarding the other thing, Walters is going to testify.

HAIG: Schlesinger . . . instructed him to turn his memcoms in. It's known over in the CIA that he [Dean] was the guy who called over there. . . .

PRESIDENT NIXON: He [Walters] did lay it on Dean?

HAIG: That's right. That's right. And he's a—is very helpful to the President. . . . Our problem is to be sure and have Bob and John describe the purpose of the meeting in July.

PRESIDENT NIXON: With Dean.

HAIG: With Walters. See, they called Walters over, Bob and John together. . . .

PRESIDENT NIXON: . . . Do his [Walters's] memcoms indicate that Bob and John cooked up the scheme and told Dean to carry it out? Was that the deal?

HAIG: Yes. If you read these papers, you would get that impression because of the way the sequence—the timing. The first big meeting was—the first time Walters was exposed was to sit in front of John and Bob.

PRESIDENT NIXON: Yes.

HAIG: And he was told to go over and get Gray to tone down the investigation.

PRESIDENT NIXON: Because of the CIA.

HAIG: Yes.

PRESIDENT NIXON: Well, John's [Ehrlichman] reaction to that could be very well that he was concerned about Hunt and the things that he had been investigating. Now, that's perfectly proper, you know what I mean, to tone it down in terms of those—of that.

HAIG: That's right, and Hunt in the meantime has been running around over at the CIA and Walters cut him off because he was asking for things that were not right. . . .

PRESIDENT NIXON: . . . I'm trying to think of what Dean is going to say. Do you think that Dean has got these memcoms?

HAIG: Nobody has. No one has. . . .

PRESIDENT NIXON: I see. I see. Well, the point is, who the hell do you think was the culprit? Do you think maybe Bob and John? Well—

HAIG: No, I don't think so at all.

PRESIDENT NIXON: He [Dean] could have been trying to cook the Goddamn thing up with Walters.

HAIG: I don't know about John [Ehrlichman], but Bob I'm sure, absolutely not. There's no way. Okay. There's another thing that we have to be very careful on and we have to know where John stands. That's why I don't want to move on any of this.

PRESIDENT NIXON: Yeah.

HAIG: He's generally a little—it indicates he may have been in on the strategy for the (unintelligible).

PRESIDENT NIXON: John?

HAIG: John. And again, it's just innuendo, but that's why we have to—

PRESIDENT NIXON: Well, look, don't have Buzhardt talk to him. . . .

HAIG: Buzhardt has told me, for God's sake, don't talk to him.

PRESIDENT NIXON: For you not to?

HAIG: Yeah. He said, "don't or you're going to end up as a key witness discredited very quickly." . . . You know, I'm willing to do that and that's a risk, though.

PRESIDENT NIXON: Well, maybe I better talk to Bob. That's possible. Not to John. I don't want to talk to John but I could talk to Bob. . . .

HAIG: Well, to get a feel for how they're going to play that. That meeting—that's a very crucial thing. . . . The FBI is going to see Bob and John—Bob at 5:00 tonight.

PRESIDENT NIXON: About this thing?

HAIG: No, not about this, but about those [NSC] taps, and we've got to know how to play that one too.

PRESIDENT NIXON: Yes.

HAIG: So, we've got to coordinate all. They're all linked together.

PRESIDENT NIXON: On the taps, get Buzhardt to play those as solely national security. . . .

HAIG: See, I talk to Larry [Higby] and I keep Larry cut in and he goes to Bob right away.

PRESIDENT NIXON: Yeah, I know. I know. Why don't I just—I just think I better get Bob and have a frank talk with him. I know that that could be off the record.

HAIG: What we think, you know, is that John [Ehrlichman] is not trying to—it's inconceivable that he would but—

PRESIDENT NIXON: Trying to say that I ordered this [CIA cover-up]?

HAIG: Yeah, that he wouldn't try to protect himself.

PRESIDENT NIXON: Oh, my God. Well, that's unbelievable. . . . I didn't do it.

HAIG: No, of course not. But I say we just have to—and what he says, how he describes that meeting it's important that we know.

PRESIDENT NIXON: . . . [L]et's suppose I called him [Haldeman] in and said, look, concoct a story to the CIA and get Walters off of this thing, so forth and so on. God-damn it. He can't say that. . . . It's totally privileged to begin with.

HAIG: It's totally privileged.

PRESIDENT NIXON: But beyond that, it is not true. Second, it's privileged, totally privileged. It's terribly detrimental. . . . All right. What—get—for my own guidance, what do you want me to tell Bob . . . ? First, do you want me to tell him to see Buzhardt?

HAIG: Yes.

PRESIDENT NIXON: This afternoon?

HAIG: Yes. It's important. . . .

PRESIDENT NIXON: Let me ask you to see if—see if we can have Bob over so that I can see him by one o'clock. Have him slip into the Executive Office Building office. . . .

HAIG: You don't want people to see him talking to you. I really don't think you should. . . . I just don't think it's a good idea to have too much evident contact. He could come in here and get in easier. I think he could get in here [Oval Office] easier. . . .

PRESIDENT NIXON: Well, one crisis every hour, but you're all right, aren't you? Well, I still think we're on the way up.

HAIG: I think we've got a bridge now to get people concerned about the truth . . . . We were going to ask Bob whether or not it's all right for us to get these [NSC] taps and these reports of these sixteen taps, you know, the earlier one. . . .

PRESIDENT NIXON: Let me put it this way, Al. You look at them. I'd rather have you rather than Buzhardt. And then give them to him.

HAIG: See, there's nothing in them.

PRESIDENT NIXON: Huh?

HAIG: There's nothing in them. . . .

PRESIDENT NIXON: Well, do you know?

HAIG: I know every tape [from his days as Kissinger's deputy].

PRESIDENT NIXON: All right, fine. Give them to Buzhardt then. It's done. . . .

MAY 11, 1973: THE PRESIDENT, HALDEMAN, AND HAIG, 12:53–2:02 P.M., OVAL OFFICE

In the just-concluded conversation, Haig warned the President that it was inadvisable for him to see Haldeman. But Haig lacked the power to prevent it and Haldeman arrives to see Nixon. The conversation appears to reinforce Haig's command. Nixon and Haldeman review their "story." Nixon covers himself regarding the plumbers. The two maintain they did not concoct the fake CIA cover story; they do acknowledge their intent to limit the Watergate investigation for fear it might unveil other White House activities. Nixon insists that Buzhardt understand "that the purpose of that talk had nothing to do with not pursuing the Watergate burglary. It had to do with not getting into the national security aspects." Passionately, Nixon adds: "I want him to believe." Nixon continues to worry about Ehrlichman's loyalty. Haldeman says he did not know Dean dealt with Walters. In effect, Haig now has full knowledge of the cover-up and is part of the new one to conceal the old.

PRESIDENT NIXON: Robert, how are you, boy? I'm glad to see you. . . . Uh, I wondered if you've got this fill in on this latest flap, uh—

HALDEMAN: Yeah.

PRESIDENT NIXON: Just, just talked to Buzhardt. . . . We want to keep Al a little bit away from it. . . . On—on the situation, let me say first that it was a Buzhardt thing—trust him completely. He's alright for now. He's on our side here in on this. . . . [James] Schlesinger has called [General Vernon] Walters back from a trip so that he would be available to discuss this matter [the CIA's role in Watergate] with [Henry] Petersen, you know. . . . In fact, there was a discussion between Walters and [Acting FBI Director L. Patrick] Gray about possible CIA cover and/or involvement in this matter. . . . Apparently, Walters had several memcoms that he has made. Fortunately, he's a loyal fellow and brought them back; they're in the White House at the present time, including the memcom of the meeting when Helms . . . —Helms, you, Ehrlichman, Dean—at which point that the, uh, discussion was there were—where some of the discussion was the effect that Walters ought to do what he could to—that, that—this Watergate-is-getting-out-of-hand thing. . . . [T]he main thing I wanted to tell you, I want to talk to you about is this so . . . when you and John will be asked about it, . . . you will be on track in terms of what the story really is. The story is that they—that Hunt had been with the CIA—our story is that he had done some national security work—

HALDEMAN: Right.

PRESIDENT NIXON: The story is that you didn't know what the situation is and that's why you asked this guy here, but you at no time ever suggested to Walters that Walters should, uh—and basically—put out a cover story that it was the CIA business. And set Gray to go along with those lines. . . . Now, Walters is like a rock. . . .

[Withdrawn item. National Security.]

Walters is going to say that what happened was that he met here and that he was asked to talk to Gray and he did talk to Gray about this matter, but determined there was no CIA involvement. . . . [T]hese memcoms are mostly Dean hammering him over and over and over again—Goddamnit, you've got to do something about getting (unintelligible) CIA cover-up of this thing. Now, as I told Al—I'll say this again—points up the Dean thing. But, the point that I make, . . . I'll sit on them [the memcoms] till hell freezes over. . . . [T]he point is—

HALDEMAN: What do we do about Helms?

PRESIDENT NIXON: . . . What was the conversation with Helms about?

HALDEMAN: It was about the problem of these people being former CIA people. The question of whether there was any CIA involvement—we didn't know.

PRESIDENT NIXON: If you were asking that question, you were raising problems.

HALDEMAN: We raised our questions. We were raising the concern—I forget why, but Bay of Pigs came into this. It was a concern making the point to Helms— if this— if these people are drawn out. See we had a concern at that time with Helms, Hunt, and Liddy, . . . and the Cubans.

PRESIDENT NIXON: Yeah, well, John—Bob—just be sure that you and John [Ehrlichman] talk exactly that way. . . .

HALDEMAN: Yeah. The thing I wonder is that if we ought to look at—one of us ought to look at Walters's memcom, because it would be accurate.

PRESIDENT NIXON: It would be accurate—(unintelligible) some of it, he says, well, I, Al, has looked at it. Al believes that some of it would be damaging. . . . Walters said he always asked, well, does the President approve, wants you to do any of this, and he couldn't get anything in writing from Dean on that. Thank God, thank God that everybody—

HALDEMAN: I don't care about the Walters stuff with Dean, I don't know what Dean's up to. . . . There was concern about Bay of Pigs coming out—you told us, you know, get in Helms on this promptly because Helms—I think you had some knowledge that I didn't know about—that Helms was concerned about some Bay of Pigs stuff at that point in time because Helms blocked at that meeting, and said, well OK, I'm not concerned about the Bay of Pigs because no matter what comes out or something. That's the part I remember clearly is Bay of Pigs stuff.

PRESIDENT NIXON: Well, I remember you saying that because CIA people were in this, to get them in. . . . Now, that doesn't bother me—it would only would bother me if . . . Walters were told to go over to Gray and say, look cool your investigation. In fact, here's the problem, and then Congress will understand. . . . The problem with the memcom does not involve you, but it does potentially involve John [Ehrlichman], according to Al. . . . [I]t could . . . appear that John was trying to get Walters to talk to Gray to basically make it appear more like that there's more of a national, of a CIA and other kind of a thing. . . . I hope you talk to John. . . .

John should say his only concern was the whole CIA involvement and so forth and wanted to be sure that the—this investigation of Watergate didn't get out, as he put it, didn't get out of hand. John used that term, apparently, in the conversation. . . .

HALDEMAN: Getting out of hand had nothing to do with apprehending the Watergate criminals and trying them. Getting out of hand had to do with exactly what's found out—

PRESIDENT NIXON: Yeah.

HALDEMAN: —which is we believe all this Pentagon Papers—

PRESIDENT NIXON: That's right.

HALDEMAN: —investigation-type set-up, leave the Plumbers operation-type stuff.

[Haig enters.]

PRESIDENT NIXON: . . . I just want to be sure that John [Ehrlichman] doesn't communicate that the President directed him to get Walters to get Gray to turn this off. . . .

HALDEMAN: John would never indicate that.

PRESIDENT NIXON: First, it wasn't true.

HALDEMAN: . . . What the President tells us to do is not—not public—for public consumption.

PRESIDENT NIXON: Except that I always preface that by saying . . . that the President had nothing to do with it. You know what I mean? I can say that I don't have the slightest involvement. But, basically, Bob, I think . . . we've found the thing you talked to me about the other night, or yesterday. It seems to me that more and more that Dean proves to be the guy, frankly, that's connecting the whole Goddamned story and it's astonishing. . . .

HALDEMAN: Hell, he knew what he doing (unintelligible.)

PRESIDENT NIXON: I suggested getting in Walters and Helms. . . . I don't know why I suggested it. You think it is the Bay of Pigs?

HALDEMAN: And, that's the only thing I remember really about it was the concern about the Bay of Pigs stuff and Helms—

PRESIDENT NIXON: And Helms said he wasn't concerned. . . . [T]here's no problem in this. No, I think we did it just straight arrow on this sort of thing. He assured me there was no problem on the thing.

HALDEMAN: In that meeting, that we had with Helms present and Walters, Ehrlichman did do all the talking so that whatever Walters says would have in the memcom would basically been Ehrlichman. I don't think I said much.

PRESIDENT NIXON: That's right. There's nothing to this but—let me say there's nothing on you in it.

HALDEMAN: Well, I'm not—that's not my concern. My concern is how to deal with the implications of each of these. See, I don't worry about—I've got the facts in this. I worry about the implications in each one, cause that's what they like. They don't pay any attention to those facts, you know. The implication of there even being such a meeting poses the problem obviously. But, it's perfectly rationalized, what the hell? It looked like—and the FBI—we were told—I was told by Dean, uh, and I think it was in the papers that the FBI was convinced, for months, that this was a CIA operation. . . . Or, if there were CIA embellishments to it, which was another possibility. . . . That's why I would sure like to look at that memcom, if I can. I would like to see what he implies. . . .

PRESIDENT NIXON: . . . But, let me tell you, Bob, as I told you yesterday, and I want you to know how much that meeting meant to me in the Lincoln Room last night. I, I've kind of reached a—where you kind of reach low spots sometimes in life. . . . It just was good to talk to you and to know that we had no choice. I don't mind the choice. That is to fight like hell. Finally, we're right, and we're not going to allow this stuff.

HALDEMAN: We can't—we can't. We just can't let those—all this breastfeeding—this isn't the worst scandal in history—

PRESIDENT NIXON: You're right.

HALDEMAN: —and all this kind of crap. It isn't the worst scandal—it isn't really a scandal.

PRESIDENT NIXON: It's broader, but no deeper.

HALDEMAN: It's broader because—because it's unraveling. These are unrelated things, really. Like Krogh's [Plumbers] operation, they tied that into Watergate. Doesn't have a fucking thing to do with Watergate.

PRESIDENT NIXON: But neither did Vesco. . . . And here was poor Mitchell and Stans, isn't that a crime? . . .

HALDEMAN: The Grand Jury is terrible. . . . [I]t's a terrible thing to think that you're in a big, dark room with these—these hostile people here and these merciless prosecutors and they tear you up and you—you have no lawyer there. You're all alone and feel like the bull in a bull fight, . . . there's nobody there that's on your side and you're accused of something. You don't know what you're being accused of.

PRESIDENT NIXON: . . . It could be terribly, terribly jeopardizing whatever's in this memcom, indicating that we were—the memcom's not going to get out, I can assure you. It'll be burned first but, uh—

HALDEMAN: Don't worry.

PRESIDENT NIXON: . . . But John must not indicate that the President said set up cover with the CIA. Bob, we never talked about a fake cover with the CIA. We never told Pat Gray this or that. We, frankly, did not know. You know that.

HALDEMAN: Well—that's right. I think that John raised the question of whether there was a CIA involvement—whether this running, unravelling—this did pose a problem for the CIA. . . . Incidentally, you've got a strange thing there with [former CIA Deputy Director] Bob Cushman too. . . . Cushman today is filing a sworn affidavit that says that Ehrlichman called him on July 7th [1971] and told him to provide the CIA support for Hunt and Liddy. . . . Ehrlichman says he did not make that call. And, when Cushman first recalled that Ehrlichman did or even talked to him and said Bob, I didn't make that call. And, Bob [Cushman] said well somebody from the White House did. I thought it was you—that it was you or Dean or somebody who called me, and that was the way that was left. . . .

PRESIDENT NIXON: Yeah.

HALDEMAN: And, so Cushman wrote him about it, as I understand it from John. This says I did not—I do not recall that it was you who called me. I know that there was a phone call. Now, at least today, but had sworn an affidavit saying Ehrlichman was involved, I think. I don't know.

PRESIDENT NIXON: But, uh, has John sworn to the contrary?

HALDEMAN: Probably. . . .

PRESIDENT NIXON: . . . When I heard, uh—when I was informed of this thing afterwards, the CIA was in the thing. I told, uh, Bob [Haldeman] to meet with Helms and Walters to find out—is that true?

HALDEMAN: Yes, sir.

HAIG: And, that's exactly the way it should be. . . .

PRESIDENT NIXON: And, I remember, I said, yep, find out what the hell the score is. And we didn't know, we didn't know. I thought maybe, Christ, that we were getting a bad rap cause these Cubans and so forth, we didn't know. Believe me, that's how unknowledgeable I am. I don't think you knew.

HALDEMAN: And, as I said, there was something—

PRESIDENT NIXON: All Helms said—Helms, Helms said, that's how it is. This is the meeting when you didn't even mention Helms when you were in before, so I was trying to think I thought you said—there was a meeting in which Walters, Dean, Ehrlichman, Haldeman—

HALDEMAN: No, no, no. Dean was not there.

PRESIDENT NIXON: That's curious because that looks like I ordered Walters, my old friend, over to do some cops and robbers. Do you think I would call Helms into something that I wanted to screw up?

HAIG: Never. . . .

PRESIDENT NIXON: And I said—I said to them, my God what the hell, is the situation here? I said if it leads, and I said, because the CIA gets involved or CIA people are involved—we don't want the CIA to be pulled into this *Watergate bugging*. Now, that basically is where—is that approximately what your recollection is of what I said—or is, Bob?

HALDEMAN: And, there was—as I mentioned there's a—in the back of my mind, there is a Bay of Pigs connection in this. . . .

PRESIDENT NIXON: Al, . . . Walters and Helms were called for the purpose of seeing that the investigation, ah, delved into Watergate but did not get into the covert operations of the CIA. Other covert operations—I didn't—none of us knew what in the hell they were. Is that basically what the thing is?

HALDEMAN: Yeah, plus we didn't know—I didn't know any specifics but I knew there had been this project with Hunt working on the leak business. The plumbers operation. We didn't want to get into that.

PRESIDENT NIXON: That's right.

HALDEMAN: We didn't want to pursue Hunt and Liddy. . . . They have arrested them. They had them there. They had them on the thing. Well, maybe they hadn't yet.

HAIG: You see Walters in his discussions with Gray—uh, keeps hitting upon the fact that some middle/lower White House guy—he's referring not by name to Dean—he's constantly trying to involve the White House in things that will involve the President. And the efforts from that and all that Walters would testify to, would be that Dean was there. . . .

HALDEMAN: I don't believe I had any knowledge from Dean that he was dealing with Walters at all. . . .

PRESIDENT NIXON: . . . I just wonder if there are copies [of Walters's memcoms] bouncing around some place.

HAIG: He said, "no," that these are his personal memcoms. Now [Defense Secretary James R.] Schlesinger has seen them and [incoming CIA Director William] Colby has seen them. Schlesinger ordered him this morning to deliver them to Elliot Richardson and to me—copies to each. Thank God, he stopped here first.

PRESIDENT NIXON: Yeah.

HALDEMAN: So, they didn't go to Elliot?

HAIG: No, and I called Schlesinger and said (a) they shouldn't because Elliot is not the Attorney General [not yet confirmed].

PRESIDENT NIXON: That's right.

HAIG: And (b) we are assessing these for national security and what we should do later today—and you finish your coordination with Buzhardt so he's comfortable. . . .

PRESIDENT NIXON: Well, hell, we got to keep Colby—if Colby's seen the damn things, he's got to get lined up on this too. How do we do that? . . . Is Elliot going to want to see the memcom . . . ? Is Elliot going to insist on seeing them?

HAIG: He can't see them because we've got them and they are under executive privilege and they'll stay that way. That's the only thing we can do. . . . It would be damaging now because of the sequence of time. First, you have a big, high-level meeting with Helms and Walters. And, then suddenly these contacts start with Dean who is really a bad guy.

PRESIDENT NIXON: And then Dean would say he was ordered to. . . .

HALDEMAN: The other point the lawyers make, which you just should keep in mind, our lawyers made, and they've been studying—and your guys I'm sure will and come up with the same thing—is the executive privilege is an objective and selective judgment on the part of the President.

HAIG: Right.

HALDEMAN: And it can be made case by case, totally selectively. It can be made paper-by-paper. Obviously, you weaken your case every time you let the bar down at all. You make it harder to keep it up for the next one. . . .

PRESIDENT NIXON: . . . I don't want Buzhardt to have any implication from just reading that Goddamn paper that what this is basically a cover-up on the part of—that first paragraph, where it says the President told Haldeman to get the CIA—what did it say to do?

HALDEMAN: Talk to the FBI about not pursuing this further or something to that effect.

PRESIDENT NIXON: But Buzhardt understands that the purpose of that talk had nothing to do with not pursuing the Watergate burglary. It had to do with not getting into the national security aspects. . . .

HALDEMAN: That's it, and that's our biggest problem in this case. Every time, on every event it's been the Goddamn implications. And you never get a chance to give the facts. . . . And then they live on the implications. . . .

PRESIDENT NIXON: I suppose our loose cannon out there now is Gray. . . .

HAIG: Gray. Gray is a cannon. He's the guy I'm worried about.

HALDEMAN: He's trying to clean himself up.

PRESIDENT NIXON: . . . [W]ell, it doesn't make any difference. We've done everything we could to save him and so forth. . . . Gray apparently, we think, has testified to the effect that he was ordered by the CIA—what is it, Al, that Gray is—what do you hear that he is supposed to have said? . . .

HAIG: I thought he said that you had discussed this with him and you told him to go on with the investigation. . . .

PRESIDENT NIXON: What does it say there about Gray?

HAIG: This is very good. This says. . . . [reading from Walters's memcom]: "Any attempt to involve the FBI or CIA in this could only prove the more [enduring?] wound and would achieve nothing. The President then said I should get rid of whoever is involved, no matter how high. Gray replied that that was his recommendation. The President then asked what I thought, and Gray said that my views were the same as his. The President took it well and thanked Gray. . . ."

PRESIDENT NIXON: Can we get Walters to say that? . . . That's damn good stuff because, frankly, it'll leak out. . . .

HAIG: He's going to be superb.

HALDEMAN: Because Walters is so positive. His recollections are so sharp and so—

HAIG: He's so bright. . . .

PRESIDENT NIXON: Well, now, doesn't that hearten you a little about my role, Al? . . . Would you please mark that for Buzhardt so that he sees that point that I told Gray? Or has he seen it? Or do you think Buzhardt needs to see such things?

HAIG: I am not worried about Buzhardt.

PRESIDENT NIXON: Well, I don't care if you're worried. I want him to believe.

HAIG: He believes.

PRESIDENT NIXON: Well, be sure to mark that.

HALDEMAN: I think the President means really believe, not just believe him because he wants to.

PRESIDENT NIXON: No. Goddamnit, I'm not covering anything up. I want Buzhardt, by God, to read that point. Now that's something that hasn't been written lately. That's something that was written at the time. That's what Pat Gray said and what I said in the conversation with Gray. Now, Goddamnit, that's my role, and that's what I told everybody in this whole Goddamn shop. You know what I mean? I said oh, sure, don't get people involved if they're not involved. . . . Believe me, Al, that shows you how naive we were about it at the time. We actually thought the CIA was in the Goddamn thing. I must have thought so.

HALDEMAN: Well, the FBI thought so for months.

HAIG: I thought so. . . .

[Haig leaves.]

PRESIDENT NIXON: . . . We didn't order a cover-up by the CIA [*chuckles*], and you know that.

HALDEMAN: Right.

PRESIDENT NIXON: The more I think of it, I think what happened is that Dean in some way got into this thing and then he started to operate and go into business *on his own*.

HALDEMAN: Yeah.

PRESIDENT NIXON: Or do you agree?

HALDEMAN: I think that must be it, because I don't see what else it could be at this point. That's what all the trails lead to now. And, if that's the case, they'll find that out. . . .

PRESIDENT NIXON: . . . I don't give a damn what happens here, but fight this through to the finish. I mean, they are not after the shit that's out there. They're not after you, they're not after . . . John Mitchell, they're not after even John Dean or, needless to say, Ehrlichman. What they're after is, they're not after me as a person, but they're after what I have stood for and do stand for. That's what they're after. And they're trying to destroy—

HALDEMAN: And that we have to fight.

PRESIDENT NIXON: For example, on this national security thing, we have the rocky situation where the sonofabitching thief [Ellsberg] is made a national hero and is going to get off on a mistrial. And the *New York Times* gets a Pulitzer prize for stealing documents. . . . They're trying to get at us with thieves. *What in the name of God have we come to?* . . .

HALDEMAN: Three different things they are after me on.

PRESIDENT NIXON: What are they, do you know?

HALDEMAN: One's on this. Oh, one's on the Goddamn [James] Hoffa thing. They want to talk to me about Hoffa.

PRESIDENT NIXON: What in the name of Christ are they on the Hoffa thing about?

HALDEMAN: I don't know. I don't know what I did on Hoffa.

PRESIDENT NIXON: Well, I gave him the clemency. But that was the recommendation of the Department of Justice. . . . There was no Goddamn question on that. Do you think Dean has said something on that, do you think?

HALDEMAN: Could be.

PRESIDENT NIXON: Good. I'm glad they're getting into that [laughs].

HALDEMAN: Then I've got a subpoena to appear in the Federal court in Illinois.

PRESIDENT NIXON: What's that about?

HALDEMAN: In the matter of the murder—of the plan to murder several dozen people.

PRESIDENT NIXON: On what grounds are they getting you there?

HALDEMAN: The airline crash where Mrs. Hunt died. They apparently have me as a factor in crashing the airplane or something. [Exhales.] . . . .

PRESIDENT NIXON: Keep the faith.

HALDEMAN: Yes, sir. . . .

PRESIDENT NIXON: God.

HALDEMAN: Never worry.

MAY 11, 1973: THE PRESIDENT AND HAIG, 2:26–2:47 P.M., EXECUTIVE OFFICE BUILDING

The President and Haig have a tense discussion about the use of the CIA for the cover-up in June 1972. Lurking in the background is Nixon's knowledge of what came to be known as the "smoking gun" conversation. Buzhardt apparently has convinced Haig that Haldeman and Ehrlichman have serious problems. Now, the President wants General Vernon Walters to contain the damage, not only to protect Haldeman and Ehrlichman, as he says here, but himself as well. Again, he lies about the events in June 1972 with the CIA and Pat Gray, but Haig, impassive and silent, may sense the truth. One week after firing his top aides, Nixon appears to be "back," ferociously fighting to defend his position. "[I am] the one person that's totally blameless in this," he says.

PRESIDENT NIXON: Let me tell you why I wanted to see him [General Vernon Walters]. I would just as well not to, but you can get across to him I have no concern about the facts, but I want Walters particularly to reassure [the CIA's William] Colby and [James] Schlesinger, because I don't want them to have any idea. You see, Al, you can't have your top people, they can read a memcom like that and read all the most sinister implications, and even with regard to the President. Now if you read them all—you've read them all—there aren't any implications with regard to the President, particularly with regard to the [L. Patrick] Gray [matter].

HAIG: Yeah, Mr. President, it is very damaging to Bob and John. . . .

PRESIDENT NIXON: Because of what? They were trying to cover up it and put it on the CIA?

HAIG: Well, that's his [Buzhardt's] judgment. He's read them [Walters's memcoms] very carefully. . . .

PRESIDENT NIXON: Buzhardt must not feel that, by golly, it's not damaging to the

President that Bob and John as my agents did something that I wanted them to do. Because, Goddamnit, I didn't want them to do anything like this. I'm not trying to blame them, but, for example, if Walters—Walters has got to be sure that on these memcoms, first Elliot Richardson will sure as hell ask—will sure as hell ask for them, won't he?

HAIG: No, not necessarily.

PRESIDENT NIXON: Now, what I think that Walters should do is to make up a sanitized version, saying, with all the national security stuff out, here is the recollection. Goddamnit, give it to Elliot Richardson at a later time, not now. Not now. When he asks.

HAIG: . . . I don't trust Walters to do that.

PRESIDENT NIXON: You don't?

HAIG: These memcoms are so detailed, so precise, you know. . . .

PRESIDENT NIXON: Right. Oh, no, no, no. I don't mean that he gives anything to the Senate—I mean to the committee. Goddamnit, Al, I don't want my staff, I don't want Elliot, I don't want Colby, and I don't want Schlesinger to have any doubts about the President, Goddamnit. . . . I'm not in this *Goddamn thing*. That's what burns me up.

HAIG: There's no way they would have.

PRESIDENT NIXON: Jesus Christ. Well, they could have. I mean, the first paragraph of that bothered me, because, look, Bob and John were saying, well look, the President wants you to contain this sonofabitch. *Sure,* I may have wanted them to contain it, because I had heard the CIA was involved. That's why I had Helms—Helms here. But the point is be sure you tell Walters that he must lean very, very hard with Elliot, with Colby, with Schlesinger, and with Petersen on my conversation with Gray.

HAIG: That's right.

PRESIDENT NIXON: Where I told Gray to get off his Goddamn ass and take it as high as was necessary. Now Walters has a photographic memory.

HAIG: He has?

PRESIDENT NIXON: Yeah. . . . [D]on't you agree that was a pretty strong statement, wasn't it?

HAIG: Very strong.

PRESIDENT NIXON: Where I said, "however high it goes." . . . Now does Buzhardt realize this? . . . Goddamnit, that's what I told Dean—I mean Gray, right on the phone. I was in this office at the time, and he called, and I called him. And I told him. I said, "take it as high as necessary." Al, that's the way I deal. You know that. . . . And I do my best to try to get to the facts. . . . And, incidentally, I don't think Bob and John are guilty on this. . . . I think what happened is that they were trying to sort of limit the damage, and they were—

HAIG: Buzhardt—

PRESIDENT NIXON: Why? Does he think they're guilty?

HAIG: He thinks that they are guilty and they don't think they are. . . .

PRESIDENT NIXON: . . . Screw it. He's [Haldeman] a decent man, Al. . . . Jesus Christ, I could have sunk Henry out a hundred times for the screwy things he's done, but I would never do it. . . . [Y]ou know that. [Joint Chief of Staff Chairman]

Admiral [Thomas] Moorer [who had spied on Nixon and Kissinger in 1971], I could have screwed him on that and been a big hero, you know. I could have screwed the whole Pentagon about that damn thing, and you know it. Why didn't I do it? Because I thought more of the Services. You know that. By golly, that's the way I deal. I want you to know that. There ain't going to be any of that. But Buzhardt is not thinking in those terms.

HAIG: No, he is not thinking in those terms. . . . He senses that Bob is strong and John is not. . . .

PRESIDENT NIXON: But with regard to Walters, and Walters—I think Walters should be reassured, Colby should be assured, Schlesinger. Or do you think they need reassurance? Would they—but, God, if they do, I'm not going to appoint [Colby as CIA Director, Schlesinger as Secretary of Defense, both of whom were nominated the next month]. Believe me, I'll withdraw it in the morning. . . . But they knew this before. Now Richardson is a horse of another color. How about having this fellow Walters go down and talk to him? Walters is a big weapon. Walters is very convincing. Walters is a total loyalist. He is a total believer in the President. Don't you agree?

HAIG: There's no question about that, none whatsoever.

PRESIDENT NIXON: Well, then, Goddamnit, use him. You don't agree?

HAIG: Bob and John—

PRESIDENT NIXON: —will be involved.

HAIG: [They must] pay the price here.

PRESIDENT NIXON: All right. They're going to pay a price. I understand. How will they pay a price? . . . I am sure John Ehrlichman never approved any of those Goddamn meetings. I am sure that he would have told me if he had.

HAIG: But I'm also sure that—

PRESIDENT NIXON: Dean did it.

HAIG: That Dean did it. . . .

PRESIDENT NIXON: All right. John and Bob both say it [sending Walters to Gray] involved national security and so forth. I'll bet they win on that issue. . . . They may be indicted, but they'll never lose the case.

HAIG: No.

PRESIDENT NIXON: I don't want to get in it with Buzhardt for reasons which you understand. I trust him and all the rest, but, Goddamnit, after the Dean episode I don't trust anybody. Do you understand? . . .

All right, Al. That's the way it's going to be. . . . Jesus Christ, I can't trust Garment, Buzhardt, Price, anybody. Jesus Christ, I don't know who the hell we're talking to any more. But if there's one person that is totally blameless in this, I thought Watergate was the stupidest goddamn thing I ever heard of. I heard of this crazy Cuban thing. I thought it was true. I really did. I really thought it was probably a CIA, because I couldn't think we could have done something that stupid. All this payoff crap. I thought, well, they're taking care of their fees and all this. Believe me, I knew nothing about it, no Goddamn thing. And I was busy with other things. But the point that I'm making is this. I'm not going to blame other people for my bad judgment in picking them.

[Withdrawn item. Privacy.]

PRESIDENT NIXON: . . . It bothered the hell out of Henry. I hope State was bugging him too. And he ought to figure that he was bugging State. Don't you agree? . . . But how do you think we handle this? I want Walters particularly to hit the point that the President was totally in favor of an all-out investigation, particularly with Gray. . . .

HAIG: Yeah.

PRESIDENT NIXON: I told Gray to get off his Goddamn ass, and I said, Pat—because he said I think you're being misled by some of your top people. I said Pat, go after them. I don't care who they are, as high as you want. Now, Goddamnit, for a President to say that when some of his friends could be involved has never been heard of before.

HAIG: That's right. That's right. . . .

PRESIDENT NIXON: . . . You're right that I shouldn't see Walters, . . . but get his ass down there. Believe me, I want you personally, or somebody, to call Petersen, he's to see Walters this afternoon. . . . Now, Walters has got to be sure Helms knows. Helms's ass is out here. His whole career is out here, and Helms knows that Walters's conversation is correct and, second, that Helms told me later the CIA was not involved. I mean, in a very brief meeting in the Oval Office, after the meeting he said I just want you to know the CIA's not involved. I said thank God. That's what I said. That's all there was to it. But he's got to be damned—Helms would never agree that to falsify cops and robbers things. He's never going to say that he participated in a cover-up. . . .

Now, who is going to have Colby in this . . . . Goddamn him. I don't want him screwing around in this thing. He's either going to stand up or he's not going to be nominated. And I have very little other power, but, Goddamnit, I can nominate people. . . . If they have any doubts about the President, let me tell you, I'll withdraw their Goddamn nominations in the next five minutes, believe me. I'm not going to have any screwing around (unintelligible). Elliot Richardson, they say, is very goosey. *If he's goosey, screw him. Out, out, out.*

HAIG: Who said he was goosey? . . .

PRESIDENT NIXON: But he's got to be all the way with the President. No question. This is a time for strong men. . . . Is Colby strong?

HAIG: Colby is a strong defender.

PRESIDENT NIXON: Good. He's just got to know that—and I want Walters to go over and talk to him, because Walters is very persuasive, and say, for Christ's sakes, the President is trying to do his best to get to the bottom of this Goddamned thing. . . .

MAY 12, 1973: THE PRESIDENT AND HAIG, 12:37–12:54 P.M., WHITE HOUSE TELEPHONE

The President, still alarmed, fears a public revelation of General Vernon Walters's memcoms. To Haig, Nixon reiterates his theme: "can we survive it?"

HAIG: . . . Now, I've been over these memcoms again very carefully, and I've asked Buzhardt to do it again himself. He's coming over here shortly. My judgment is that there is absolutely no way that we can permit these to leave the building under any circumstances. . . .

PRESIDENT NIXON: Well, I suppose our problem is whether somebody else has got them.

HAIG: Yeah. Well, what happened—and this influences that judgment also—is that when Cushman went up to Armed Services, [Defense Secretary James R.] Schlesinger sent his memcoms to the committee. That's on another subject, of course. But they're going to hit Schlesinger—or hit Walters—tomorrow and ask for his memcoms. . . . So we're going to just have to take the heat, Mr. President. . . . And it's going to be—

PRESIDENT NIXON: —be hot.

HAIG: —some criticism.

PRESIDENT NIXON: That's nothing. We can take it.

HAIG: Listen. Compared to what would happen with these papers, it's essential.

PRESIDENT NIXON: I understand. Well, we just—the only thing I was—Walters is confident in the fact that he didn't give a copy of these damn things to Helms.

HAIG: Yes, he is. He's confident. Now, he said they were locked in his safe while he was abroad and, unless there was some real hanky-panky, he's confident. . . .

PRESIDENT NIXON: What is the difficulty in it in terms of the President in the damn thing?

HAIG: Well, it's just that first paragraph of the thing, which—Haldeman says the bugging affair—

PRESIDENT NIXON: Yeah.

HAIG: *(Unintelligible)* making noise, and we're maximizing it, and it's leading to a lot of important people.

PRESIDENT NIXON: He said it would lead to a lot of—go ahead.

HAIG: Right. And then Helms said there was no CIA connection. He contradicted it right off the bat, you see.

PRESIDENT NIXON: Yes.

HAIG: And Haldeman said that the whole affair was getting embarrassing and that the President wished—it was the President's wish that Walters call on Acting FBI Director Gray and suggest to him that, since the five suspects had been arrested, that this should be sufficient, that it was not advantageous to have the inquiry pushed, especially in Mexico.

PRESIDENT NIXON: Yeah, that's bad.

HAIG: Just cannot have that.

PRESIDENT NIXON: Well, it may get out, if it gets out, and let's be ready for it when it does.

HAIG: Well, you see, I don't think it will. And it's all going to revolve on Bob and John in the context that we discussed it earlier. So that's where this thing is. It's coming up again. But we knew that and we've known it from the beginning.

PRESIDENT NIXON: Yes. Well, the idea that Haldeman—of course, in a sense he was sort of using the President's name—

HAIG: That's right.

PRESIDENT NIXON: —which everybody does.

HAIG: Now, you see, this is hearsay. . . . And this wouldn't come out in the courtroom under direct testimony. But if you have a piece of paper, . . . you've given hearsay evidence firm credibility. That's why we have to stick to the way we're going. Now, it won't evolve that way if it ends up on direct testimony. Walters will build a wall and, to the degree that that kind of innuendo has been struck from this, then it makes it easier for Bob and John in that context, and hopefully we're going to manage it so that the thing is put in its proper context.

PRESIDENT NIXON: Well, I always figure, as we must, it seems like everything gets out. I don't know. But I think that Walters, who I think we've got a good man, and Helms, Jesus, he's just got to stand firm on this.

HAIG: I think in large measure, especially for this first session, he can—everything he has is hearsay, so it's not worth a damn in this.

PRESIDENT NIXON: No, but Helms in terms of having the memcom and himself so—

HAIG: Well, that's all right, too, because it's hearsay.

PRESIDENT NIXON: No, I know, but—

HAIG: If he had a copy it would be bad. . . .

PRESIDENT NIXON: Yes. So when does he get back [from Iran] and you can get him basically under control, get the Goddamn copy and keep it here?

HAIG: Well, Buzhardt's going to contact him as soon as he's in. I think he's coming in tonight. . . . I asked Walters if there were any other copies anywhere, and he said no, and no one has held them physically but him.

PRESIDENT NIXON: Of course, there's the possibility, as I also said, Al, that Helms made a copy. But you thought that he may not have made a memcom himself.

HAIG: Oh, he may have made a memcom of that session, yes, he may have. And that's important. That's why Buzhardt's going to contact him.

PRESIDENT NIXON: And say that that should be—

HAIG: Should be put in the same category.

PRESIDENT NIXON: The same category. Because basically the Haldeman thing, the Haldeman thing says it may lead to Mexico and so forth and so on. But you can point out that we were not trying to—we were concerned, despite what Helms says, we were concerned about the fact that a whole gaggle of CIA people were in this thing. . . .

HAIG: That's right. It is obviously the context in which it was put in or he wouldn't have taken the position he took. The difficulty is he denied it, you see.

PRESIDENT NIXON: The difficulty is he denied it there.

HAIG: Yes, and alleged to have denied it the day before with Gray. . . .

PRESIDENT NIXON: And then they [Haldeman and Ehrlichman] said that Walters should go—even in spite of that, they said Walters should talk to Gray?

HAIG: Yes. It's very bad the way it's on that—

PRESIDENT NIXON: Very bad.

HAIG: —piece of paper.

PRESIDENT NIXON: Well, if that gets out it's going to be pretty rough. But we could survive it, can we?

HAIG: I'm sure.

PRESIDENT NIXON: Even survive that, huh?

HAIG: Yes. . . .

PRESIDENT NIXON: Incidentally, Buzhardt should, in addition to Haldeman and Ehrlichman, and this isn't a top priority because he could do it tomorrow even, he should have a talk with Colson, you know.

HAIG: Yes.

PRESIDENT NIXON: To see what the hell Colson sees coming down the pike here. . . . And particularly with regard to Colson and Hunt. See what I mean?

HAIG: Exactly. I agree with that. I've told him that already.

PRESIDENT NIXON: That's right. And be sure that Colson knows that he's on our side. Colson knows he's on our side, he knows Buzhardt is. . . . All right, boy. Well, keep your old chin up. . . . And as I tell you, if the Goddamn thing gets out it's just going to get out, Al.

HAIG: That's all right.

PRESIDENT NIXON: It isn't all right. But we can survive it.

HAIG: We can survive it in very good shape.

PRESIDENT NIXON: We can survive it. It will be very embarrassing because it'll indicate that we tried to cover up with the CIA.

HAIG: That's all right. . . .

MAY 12, 1973: THE PRESIDENT AND HAIG, 12:59–1:03 P.M., WHITE HOUSE TELEPHONE

Now that Buzhardt and Haig are convinced of Haldeman's and Ehrlichman's criminal involvement, Nixon looks to link Dean and make him the primary culprit in the cover-up.

PRESIDENT NIXON: Oh, Al. One other thing. Refresh my memory: Dean was not present at that meeting now, was he?

HAIG: No, no, he was not.

PRESIDENT NIXON: That was good. And he has no memcom? I mean, he has none—he doesn't have—

HAIG: He was not there. . . . But what he would have would be contacts with John [Ehrlichman] subsequent to it. . . . And there is reference to it in his contact with Walters. He said "in conjunction with your meeting yesterday, I've got to talk to you, and you can call John Ehrlichman if you want to check on that"—which Walters did, and John said go ahead and see him. . . .

PRESIDENT NIXON: . . . But on the other hand, that would have again been—I'm just trying to put our face on it. The normal procedure, Dean was in charge of the Goddamn investigation for us.

HAIG: Exactly right.

PRESIDENT NIXON: And so he said, talk to Walters about the thing.

HAIG: Exactly. And that's why—

PRESIDENT NIXON: Dean of course, he may go out and say, Ehrlichman told him to keep this thing under the hat and all that sort of thing, right?

HAIG: That's right, that's right.

PRESIDENT NIXON: He's not going to be believed. I mean, . . . that would be Dean versus Ehrlichman. . . . And Walters's conversations with Dean you say are, his memcoms on that are—well, which is important, not on these memcoms because that's all Dean could know—are clean.

HAIG: Very helpful and very clean.

PRESIDENT NIXON: Why are they helpful? You mean—

HAIG: Helpful in the context that here was the real bad guy that was putting the wrong kind of twist into it, and the fact that he couldn't ever—you see, if he had had presidential authority—

PRESIDENT NIXON: Yeah.

HAIG: —when he got continually stymied, God, he would have used it ten times over.

PRESIDENT NIXON: And Walters kept saying, I would have to have presidential authority.

HAIG: Well, he kept saying: Look, you're trying to drag the presidency into a matter to resolve staff incompetence, and you can't do this. . . .

MAY 12, 1973: THE PRESIDENT, HAIG, AND ZIEGLER, 5:15–5:47 P.M., CAMP DAVID TELEPHONE

Nixon and Haig review Elliot Richardson's list of prospects for Special Prosecutor. Cynicism is rampant. Haig suggests Arthur Goldberg, a man of impeccable liberal credentials, but, Haig noted, someone who is "obnoxious and doesn't wear well with the people, which would be good for our point of view." The two men continue to rake over the Walters memcoms. The President finds the topic difficult. For his part, Haig seems knowledgeable about the CIA incident, but here he brushes it off.

HAIG: . . . And of course then we've got to get the damned prosecutor named, uh, the quicker the better.

PRESIDENT NIXON: Uh, Elliot has no, uh, further suggestions on that, I suppose. . . . Well, 'cause see, he's not supposed to give them to us anyway.

HAIG: No, he's not, but I know, I know how he feels about [Missouri governor Warren] Hearns. I got that through the back door.

PRESIDENT NIXON: He doesn't like that, huh.

HAIG: No, unfortunately, Hearns has never had any, any courtroom experience at all.

PRESIDENT NIXON: Ah, okay, good. Out. . . .

HAIG: I'm thinking Arthur Goldberg would, might, needn't be so bad, believe it or not.

PRESIDENT NIXON: I think he'd be fine. . . .

HAIG: He's got a great view of the presidency; he's a little bit obnoxious and doesn't wear well with the people, which would be good for our point of view.

PRESIDENT NIXON: Yeah, God, I hadn't even thought of him, I think he'd be excellent. . . .

HAIG: Yeah.

PRESIDENT NIXON: Excellent.

HAIG: And I think he's on that list that he had.

PRESIDENT NIXON: Right, good, good.

HAIG: But I'm gonna find out the list; I just want to ask him directly, but I'm getting it, I'm getting it.

PRESIDENT NIXON: You had any further thoughts on uh, uh, the uh, uh, the Walters thing, uh, anything further on that?

HAIG: Except, no, but except that we've reviewed it entirely and there's absolutely no question about keeping these things where they are. . . .

PRESIDENT NIXON: But the key point, the ultimate weapon, though, in this one, Al, is the last word of that thing. Read that to me again, where it said uh, where it said "whoever, however high it goes," remember I said, uh,—

HAIG: Yes, the President then said [to Pat Gray], "Then I should get rid of whoever's involved, no matter how high."

PRESIDENT NIXON: And that was his recommendation.

HAIG: Gray replied that was his recommendation. The President then asked what Walters thought and Gray said that Walters's views were the same as his. The President took it well and thanked Gray.

PRESIDENT NIXON: Well, that's not bad, is it?

HAIG: No, not bad.

PRESIDENT NIXON: You know, when you—the uh, obviously—you know, I mean, I'm not trying to gloss over something that's tough, that's bad, but you see what I mean, it's—good God, what else would I say?

HAIG: That's right.

PRESIDENT NIXON: I mean, it's a tough thing I said I didn't know who the hell was involved. . . . Yeah, but the difficulty was that there was a preceding meeting in which Walters going over to see Gray could be read as being—

HAIG: Innuendo, right.

PRESIDENT NIXON: —the innuendo that he was going there for the purpose of covering up. Right?

HAIG: That's exactly right.

PRESIDENT NIXON: Right. On the other hand, Walters, Walters says he did not go there for that purpose, right?

HAIG: That's right. . . .

PRESIDENT NIXON: And actually, and I remember clearly my talk with Gray where Gray said, . . . "Some of your people," he thinks "are disserving you" or something like that.

HAIG: That's right and it is in there.

PRESIDENT NIXON: Is that right? . . . And I said, uh, you know, take it as high as— and then I asked him if he'd talked to Walters, uh, uh, because basi— I'm trying to find what the hell the facts were. And then he said, and then go as high as you, whoever it hurts, hurts.

HAIG: No, see, Wallace doesn't have that here, but we're—uh, it was, it was stated, I believe, by Gray. . . .

PRESIDENT NIXON: . . . [W]hen [Gray] warned me that people were disserving me, none of that, none of the news stories picked up the fact that I thanked him or any-thing of that sort? Or, they just left it that he had warned me and that was all, huh?

HAIG: No, no, no, not at all. When you weaved in the stories, each one with a little different twist, you told them to go on with the investigation. . . .

PRESIDENT NIXON: Yeah, it does. It does show that I did do it.

HAIG: Yes, sir, yes, sir.

PRESIDENT NIXON: Because you see, I know, I know Gray so well and I know what I told him.

HAIG: That's right.

PRESIDENT NIXON: And I—I didn't uh, I told him throughout, I said, Pat, you've gotta do your job, you know. . . . I know that Gray wouldn't have deliberately done anything that, you know, to hurt, because he knows better—first, he's, first, he's loyal to the President, but beyond that, he knows the truth. . . . My point is, too, that we, we're gonna win it because basically, take this whole comedy on this Goddamned Gray/Walters/CIA thing. Al, you were there at the time, for Christ sakes, I thought the Goddamned CIA was in it.

HAIG: That's right.

PRESIDENT NIXON: You know. I, I didn't know, I didn't know.

HAIG: The papers were full of it. . . .

PRESIDENT NIXON: They were all full of it, so I said Walters ran it, right, as far as I was concerned, and of course, I would've been delighted if they were *(laughs),* you know, rather than having a political thing. But—

HAIG: Right.

PRESIDENT NIXON: —and I said, "Let's find out." But the purpose was not to say "Go over and concoct," you see, the other way you could put it is that we were trying to concoct a story that the CIA was involved when actually they were not. Well, for Christ sakes, I wasn't trying to do that, Al. You see what I mean?

HAIG: Well, your perspective and interest, you see, would be entirely from, there-fore from Dean.

PRESIDENT NIXON: That's right.

HAIG: Dean, who had been up to his ears in monkey business—

PRESIDENT NIXON: Yeah.

HAIG: —and had one perspective.

PRESIDENT NIXON: That's right, that I was trying to find out whether the CIA was in it. And the only way to do that was to get him and Gray together and find out.

HAIG: Exactly.

PRESIDENT NIXON: Oh, well, let me talk to Ron. . . .

[Ziegler enters.]

PRESIDENT NIXON: Oh, hi, Ron, how'd your, you were able to sort of hit the Gray thing a little today, or?

ZIEGLER: Yes, we worked on that all day. . . .

PRESIDENT NIXON: . . . I'm trying to find out from the CIA what the Christ they're doing and what the FBI is doing, you know, and so forth, but Dean's motive was ap-parently entirely different. He must've been trying to figure, well, how do you get the CIA and, you know, involved here and there.

ZIEGLER: He's the bad apple. . . .

PRESIDENT NIXON: Okay, boy.

MAY 12, 1973: THE PRESIDENT AND HAIG, 6:48–6:56 P.M., CAMP DAVID TELEPHONE

Haig is convinced that the White House can keep Walters in line and defuse the impact of his memcoms. Nixon is nervous about how they will be received.

PRESIDENT NIXON: . . . Bob and John, if they were gonna, if for example, their purpose was to get the CIA to fake a story that the last person they would've had in that office had been Helms.

HAIG: I *couldn't* agree more.

PRESIDENT NIXON: See, that's my point.

HAIG: You have to know the realities of the thing.

PRESIDENT NIXON: Yeah, you see, my point is, you and I, all of us knew that we thought, we considered Helms to be basically a, well, let's face it, an establishmentarian.

HAIG: No question.

PRESIDENT NIXON: And so they, you mean, the idea that Bob and John would call in Helms and say, "Look, we, the President wants you to fix this thing, sir." Understand—I think it's very likely that Bob could've said—I'm sure that, I'm sure that Richard— uh—that the fellow is, his memory is fantastic, and he could say, "Look, this thing is getting out of hand and five people in and let's don't get the CIA dragged into the Goddamned thing and"—

HAIG: Right.

PRESIDENT NIXON: "— and Walters oughtta talk to, with uh, the fellow over at FBI and get the damn thing uh—uh—see what's going on." Uh, I mean, I mean, I just, I just don't, I just don't want you to, or Buzhardt, particularly to . . . lose faith in the two guys. You see what I mean?

HAIG: Good God, that's the last thing in the world.

PRESIDENT NIXON: Yeah.

HAIG: Uh—

PRESIDENT NIXON: Because you see, my point was that, they got, the I agree with you. If you read the cold print, it looks terrible. But when you know the realities, see—like even my comment with regard to, "Well, have you talked to Walters?" Hell, I had known that they had seen Helms and so-and-so. And they prob—what I mean is, obviously, they would've told me.

HAIG: Sure.

PRESIDENT NIXON: Somebody would've told me, "Look, we've talked to them about the CIA on this, uh, on, and that Walters is gonna talk to uh to that." So, in other words, it's a pure aside, is, you see what I'm getting at? And yet—

HAIG: And that's why—

PRESIDENT NIXON: —and yet you read it in the context of the thing and it looks terrible. . . .

HAIG: I don't think so. He's got, see, really, he's [Walters] been very good. I'll tell you, he's, we've had a couple of knotty ones that we never brought to your attention—

PRESIDENT NIXON: Is that right?

HAIG: —they were just pretty Goddamned touchy and uh—

PRESIDENT NIXON: Good.

HAIG: —he handled them very well.

PRESIDENT NIXON: . . . . [T]he point is, you just gotta know, I'm not asking for to say anything is untrue but I just, I just don't want, I don't want him [Walters] to go in and say, "Look, they called us in and tried to ask to fix the case and I, we wouldn't do it." . . . Yeah, and also, we have to realize that what happened is that then Dean, probably on his own, uh, I don't, I mean I don't blame you too much, he thought, he probably thought he could probably be a smartass, uh, he started to think, well, maybe we can put this whole damn thing over in the CIA.

HAIG: That's right, but he had got (unintelligible) all the way up to his neck and he said a lot of things.

PRESIDENT NIXON: But the point is too that, having done that, see, going to say that—but then Walters, in his later things, turned him off. Isn't that really what happened?

HAIG: Yes, absolutely.

PRESIDENT NIXON: And Walters points that out flatly in his things.

HAIG: Very clearly, and—

PRESIDENT NIXON: —and I want to be sure that Schlesinger and Colby don't get the idea that Haldeman and Ehrlichman are just a—you know, part of a Goddamn, I mean, conspiracy here. Because they really aren't.

HAIG: No, I don't believe that they—

PRESIDENT NIXON: You know, that, basically, let me tell you, they didn't know about it, as you know, and I know they wouldn't have uh—neither man would've, you know, engaged in such a damn thing. You understand what I'm—I'm not just being loyal to good people but I do know this is the truth. . . .

MAY 13, 1973: THE PRESIDENT AND HAIG, 10:48–11:10 A.M., CAMP DAVID TELEPHONE

The White House starts a dangerous precedent: General Robert Cushman's memcoms involving CIA help to Howard Hunt in his dealings with Dita Beard, the ITT lobbyist, will be surrendered, while Walters's memcoms won't be. Nixon discusses "Mexican" money, but earlier conversations indicate his knowledge that Dwayne Andreas was the source of the money.

PRESIDENT NIXON: Yeah. Incidentally, on the other subject that I was talking about. I feel so very strongly about that, you know, Walters and his so-called memcoms over it that I just want to be very sure that you and Buzhardt and so forth and Schlesinger and Colby do not misunderstand that thing from anybody's standpoint, not mine, not Haldeman's, not Ehrlichman's because, Goddamnit, we were trying to find out, and there was a helluva lot of talk to the effect that the CIA was in the sonofabitch.

HAIG: You're precisely right.

PRESIDENT NIXON: Al, you remember, I mean, we were told the White House—we know the White House wasn't in it. We were told by Mitchell that they weren't in it. And we thought, well, what in the name of Christ was it. And then we heard about Mexican money or something like that. And I said, well, get Walters the hell over. But as I said, if they were going to do anything, concoct some crazy scheme with Dean and—so he can work on—do you think for Christ sakes they would have had Dick Helms in the office, as I told you. It's all ridiculous. Now you put it together, Goddamnit, it looks as if, well, the President called them in and said now let's see if we can get some scheme whereby we can pin this whole damn thing on the CIA. . . . And, Goddamnit, and I hope that Buzhardt didn't feel that way.

HAIG: Buzhardt hasn't been questioned at all about it, and you have to keep in mind, sir, when a guy sits down at a meeting that may have had some dangers in it for him, he's going to slant his memcom in the most self-serving way he can.

PRESIDENT NIXON: Sure.

HAIG: But if, you know, when you get into what I call testimony, the man can't—even for his own good—can't slant anything that way. . . .

PRESIDENT NIXON: He can't and he won't because he knows damn well what happened and he knows that I never gave Walters any orders ever to do anything, you know, about a damn, I mean, on this thing. And I never gave [Pat] Gray any except to, you know, to go out and go to the top. . . .

. . . [T]he memcom, as you well know, is something that is written at the time when self-serving things and anybody that writes a diary out always writes the diary, you know, to suit himself.

HAIG: Exactly right. And that's, you know, that's what we—

PRESIDENT NIXON: A diary is no evidence. Huh?

HAIG: It's no evidence and neither is a memcom in a real sense.

PRESIDENT NIXON: No. But outside the government, memcoms, if they made—you say that they can get a hold of. Well—or can they?

HAIG: I know that you're—

PRESIDENT NIXON: Maybe they ought to stand firm on those. I mean, even—you understand. We've got these here. So we've got possession. But—

HAIG: You mean, as a general rule?

PRESIDENT NIXON: That's right.

HAIG: . . . [Y]ou did furnish Cushman's memcoms to both the committee and the grand jury. Now they weren't expected to do any harm at all.

PRESIDENT NIXON: Yeah. But why did he [Cushman] do that?

HAIG: Well, I don't know. Now he's on notice now and he's not going to pull anything like that again.

PRESIDENT NIXON: In other words, Cushman had what? A memcom—

HAIG: —of his earlier discussions here with whoever it was that asked for certain equipment, you know, or—

PRESIDENT NIXON: Oh, this was on the Hunt thing. . . . You know, you really wonder, though, how you can justify giving them Cushman's and not giving them Walters. How do you do that, Al? What's Buzhardt say?

HAIG: Because what Walters discussed was not just a little bit of equipment for somebody but national security matters.

PRESIDENT NIXON: Discussed national security matters. Yeah. As for discussing national security matters, now I will discuss other matters but not those.

HAIG: You see, I asked Buzhardt could we peel off certain ones and just give them those. He said no. We just can't do that because—and then we can hold the others. He says you're better off in a broad statement that they contain national security.

PRESIDENT NIXON: . . . Remember, last week you were disturbed about the fact that maybe we'd gone too far and on our rules of engagement. I'm not so sure. I'm not so sure about our—but we're going to get heat. Even if we spilled all of our guts out, you know, I mean, testicle by testicle, we'd still get heat for cover-up. . . .

HAIG: Goddamnit, we'll just hold firm.

PRESIDENT NIXON: That's right. That's right.

HAIG: And, as a matter of fact, I think you can see in today's Sunday paper there's sort of a slacking off of the whole thing.

PRESIDENT NIXON: Al, that'll be true until we get another story. That's good though. That's good. And slacking even for one day gives us a respite, doesn't it, Al?

HAIG: It does. It does.

PRESIDENT NIXON: Gives the country a respite from it. It shows that the country is still going forward.

HAIG: Oh, God. The country is just—

PRESIDENT NIXON: And it is.

HAIG: —fed up with all this. It just wants to get on with the thing. . . .

MAY 13, 1973: THE PRESIDENT AND JOE D. WAGGONER, JR., 4:21–4:30 P.M., CAMP DAVID TELEPHONE

The President talks to a steadfast supporter, Democratic Congressman Joe D. Waggoner, Jr., from Louisiana.

PRESIDENT NIXON: You know, it comes to the point where you just, you know, I haven't said too much because I always believe in waiting and striking at the right time. I did that one TV last week, but—I just hated to do it but I had to let Haldeman and Ehrlichman go and I hope they're vindicated and I think they will be. But nevertheless, you can't have anybody that they're—any charge, you know, around them.

WAGGONER: No, sir. You had no other choice, Mr. President, under the circumstances.

PRESIDENT NIXON: But there, I'll tell you, we're—when I start to fight, these boys will know they're in a fight, let me tell you.

WAGGONER: That's the way I like to hear you talk [laughs].

PRESIDENT NIXON: Now, I'm on television in every other way there is. . . .

WAGGONER: I don't understand why these people who are convening these grand juries, these judges, who charge these grand juries, I don't understand how they'll just continually let these people keep talking.

PRESIDENT NIXON: Well, let them leak.

WAGGONER: That's right.

PRESIDENT NIXON: And, also, I don't understand, Joe, how the Senate in good conscience, can possibly let a hearing go forward and bring before the committee people that are going to condemn Mitchell and, you know, and others. Why, hell, if Mitchell doesn't get a mistrial, I'll almost bet on it right now, you know.

WAGGONER: Yes, sir.

PRESIDENT NIXON: The same with Haldeman and Ehrlichman. How could you as a lawyer get a fair trial for a man if the damn thing has been all blurted out on television and all week long, you know, and hearsay?

WAGGONER: Well, of course, they'll turn Ellsberg loose for this sort of thing, but they won't turn one of ours loose. . . .

MAY 14, 1973: THE PRESIDENT AND ROSE MARY WOODS, 11:10–11:25 P.M., OVAL OFFICE

A touching conversation with the President's ever-loyal secretary.

PRESIDENT NIXON: Hi, Rose.

WOODS: Hi.

PRESIDENT NIXON: Let me ask you to do something, Rose. Do you—have I, and anything that I heard of, and I'm referring only since the 27th of February—have I ever written any memorandum to Dean? Do you recall anything ever being written?

WOODS: I don't think I ever remember you writing Dean. I don't think you ever have.

PRESIDENT NIXON: I don't he ever did. Has nothing been charged and that sort of thing. I just want to be sure that we know that all of our files do show this. Would you go check that for me?

WOODS: Sure. . . . I was going to tell you one thing. I won't put it in a memo. Dr. Hutschnecker [Nixon's psychiatrist in New York] called me and just said that he's thinking of you all the time and if there is anything on God's earth that he can do. We've had so many calls, you know.

PRESIDENT NIXON: They may kill me in the press, but they will never kill me in mind. I'm going to fight these bastards to the end.

WOODS: Oh, yeah. And as I told you yesterday—

PRESIDENT NIXON: We're going to beat them.

WOODS: Jeane Dixon [a self-styled "seer" or prophet] tells us that May and June are going to be pretty bad. June may be worse than May. But everything will turn out fine and to be of stout heart and all that.

PRESIDENT NIXON: Of course, it's going to be hard, Rose. But—

WOODS: It's going to be very hard.

PRESIDENT NIXON: That's why we have been brought into this world.

WOODS: Well, you particularly, and you'd be surprised how many people say, you know, God does bring the hardest problems to the strongest men.

PRESIDENT NIXON: That's right.

WOODS: I think all, particularly everybody who's really into it, I'm just praying that God has given you enough strength to take this.

PRESIDENT NIXON: I've got the strength.

WOODS: And all I get to help you with is have it with your thoughts.

PRESIDENT NIXON: Well, you know, really it's too bad this all happened. We can all have hard feelings about John and Bob. . . . Dean always impressed me. . . . He was nice to people on the staff and so forth and so on.

WOODS: (Unintelligible) too many.

PRESIDENT NIXON: But for him to rat like this, you know, and try to say there was no Dean report. Christ, he told Ziegler fifty times before a briefing no one in the White House was involved. . . . *Who the hell were we relying on, Rose? Who were we relying on?*

WOODS: Your friends. You have to rely on.

PRESIDENT NIXON: That's right. . . .

MAY 14, 1973: THE PRESIDENT AND ZIEGLER, 1:25–2:05 P.M., EXECUTIVE OFFICE BUILDING

Most of Nixon and Ziegler's conversations before early May involved preparations for media briefings. But after Haldeman's departure, Nixon also discusses substantive issues with Ziegler and, surprisingly, Ziegler challenges the President on occasion, particularly to moderate his growing anger. Here, Nixon rages at familiar issues—the press, the FBI, the wiretaps of the Kennedy and Johnson administrations, and Henry Kissinger. At the end, Ziegler warns the President of his own caveat: the Administration will destroy itself if it is consumed by Watergate events. Ziegler is anxious to protect Nixon—particularly from his own anger—unlike Haig, who fuels the President's rage. Nixon seems to like Ziegler; certainly, Ziegler moves into Haldeman's place as Nixon's most trusted sounding-board.

PRESIDENT NIXON: What else? Did they get after anything that was interesting that involves the national interest? Did they care about Henry's trip [to Hanoi] or Le Duc Tho or not? Unbelievable.

ZIEGLER: They're obsessed. . . .

PRESIDENT NIXON: Screw them, screw them. It'll be our day.

ZIEGLER: Sure.

PRESIDENT NIXON: And we're going to treat them with the contempt they deserve. Believe me, you understand. Ron, have no illusions. These assholes are out to destroy us aren't they?

ZIEGLER: I have no illusions.

PRESIDENT NIXON: No, no.

ZIEGLER: I have no illusions about their obsession. I have no illusions about how they stand. . . . No question about the fact that there was a great deal of concern back in '69 and '70 and '71 about leaks of national security data.

PRESIDENT NIXON: That's right. . . . Absolutely, *of course there was that.* Understand, I don't remember assigning it to [Egil] Krogh, or anybody else. I assigned it to somebody. I said: You ought to ask by number of targets. He said, that may include— Ron come on, don't be defensive about it.

ZIEGLER: I was not at all defensive. . . .

PRESIDENT NIXON: . . . Listen. I've been after this Goddamn staff for a long time. I'm going to ask you to do something. Haldeman never did it, Ehrlichman never did it, nobody else, because this Goddamn Kissinger is always stopping them. Now, look. I want the Diem and the Bay of Pigs [documents] totally declassified and I want it done in 48 hours. Now, you tell, you tell Haig that, and it'll drive him up the wall, too. But I want it done. Do you understand? This is ten years old. Declassify it. We've got a couple of assholes working on this thing. You see any reason why it shouldn't be declassified, Ron? Huh?

ZIEGLER: No, I see no reason it shouldn't be declassified.

PRESIDENT NIXON: I want them to start getting off their ass to start declassifying things, and about next week we'll say, anything that's ten years or more old, we're just going to get out. But now you follow up on that. Will you do that?

[Withdrawn item. National security.]

PRESIDENT NIXON: Did you ever read that little book? Read Henry Fairlie's book if you want to know, or read the book about the 13 Kennedy mistakes, if you want to know. But the second point: Now, I have just ordered Haig to tell that son of a gun (unintelligible) Ruckelshaus before he gets through the rest of the day that, by God, for the FBI to put out the story on us and to say they can't find the records on Kennedy and Johnson—now, I want you to leak a story this afternoon, and I want you to take this down, leak a story this afternoon that the records of massive bugging of newsmen by Kennedy and Johnson have been destroyed or cannot be found. Now, that's true, Ron.

[Withdrawn item. Privacy.]

PRESIDENT NIXON: Ron, they did *five times* as much. You know that. Kennedy bugged them in the Goddamn business of the steel thing [U. S. Steel's 1962 price raises], you remember? Can you get that out to anybody?

ZIEGLER: I think so.

PRESIDENT NIXON: . . . We've got to get the idea out, Ron, that there's a search on for the records of massive bugging of newsmen during the Kennedy–Johnson period, and we find that the records are missing. Now, Goddamn it, Ron, you've got somebody. Give it to [Kenneth] Clawson. . . . You know, as I read my news conference statement, in fact, there's been 102 national security taps in the Kennedy administration, 88 in Johnson, and 75 in ours, which is what they gave me to say. Goddamn it, it's true. Now Ruckelshaus went back to the FBI records and they can't find the records there. You see what I mean? Now, you know they're lying to protect their ass, aren't they?

ZIEGLER: Probably so.

PRESIDENT NIXON: Now, with regard to this whole business about Ruckelshaus, does the President know these records were here? And the answer is no, I didn't know the fucking records were here, no. Nobody'd ever told me a Goddamn thing about the records. You understand that? And I didn't know. . . . The second point, did Hoover threaten the President and so forth? That's sheer—you know, that's hogwash. He never did. I don't think this was solved. The solution was with lower people in the FBI. I'd just say it looks to me like lower echelon FBI politics. That's what I would say.

Did the White House—did the White House—I've already told you that Haig put it in that the White House totally cooperated with this investigation to find where these Goddamn files were, once they started it. You know, but Ehrlichman was *gone,* shit. I mean, we could have had them in two minutes if he had told us. No chance. . . .

ZIEGLER: I think that's about all. They're going to focus in on Henry.

PRESIDENT NIXON: Good. Well, Henry's strong. Let me tell you quite—Henry ordered the whole Goddamn thing [wiretapping]. He ordered it all, believe you me. He was the one who was in my office jumping up and down about "This and this got out," and buh, buh, buh got out. I didn't give a shit about the (unintelligible), but he did. I said, all right, investigate the sons of bitches. And he read every one of those taps until the very last one, every one. I never saw a one, never. I never wanted to see them, you know what I mean? Never. They didn't bring those things to my attention. . . .

. . . Well, he [Kissinger] read this damn stuff. [Shouting] *He reveled in it, he groveled in it, he wallowed in it.* If he quits, starts playing games, we're going to let him have the hook, too. No, no, no, no. . . . Well, I want the story to lead this afternoon that there are hundreds of FBI taps in the Johnson and Kennedy administration that are missing. And that'll force that fucking Ruckelshaus to get in and find them. You see what I mean?

ZIEGLER: Right.

PRESIDENT NIXON: And then you tell a newsman to get in and ask Ruckelshaus: Now, give us the record of the number of taps that were done in this period; where are they, who has possession of them? Do you understand, Ron?

ZIEGLER: Yes, I do.

PRESIDENT NIXON: Goddamn, you *got to fight.*

ZIEGLER: Right.

PRESIDENT NIXON: That's the trouble with our people. They don't know how to fight. You see, with your idea in the new year of getting along with the press, which I approve of, don't believe that you don't have to fight with a thing like this.

ZIEGLER: Oh, I understand that. I understand that. The new era of getting along with the press was totally to our self-interest. . . . Let me just say this, Mr. President. Let me follow up on that. The new era of getting along with the press, of cultivating the press on what we think, makes it a lot easier to do this kind of thing.

PRESIDENT NIXON: Yes, I know, because then you've got somebody to listen to you. But remember, now. Just say hundreds of—just say scores of files are missing in the FBI, that investigation. Now, get that story out, in the Johnson and Kennedy administrations. Just say—use the term: Over one hundred files are missing. Let them fucking play a little with that a little bit. Let's get a little attention on the fact that this business about us was just not Hoover. Shit, Hoover was playing with Johnson and Kennedy, as he did with every previous president, except probably Eisenhower. You see my point? . . . Ron, the best defense is a hell of an offense. For God's sakes, can't you get out this afternoon on a crash basis the fact that the whole FBI is looking now for the missing Kennedy–Johnson taps?

ZIEGLER: You've got it.

PRESIDENT NIXON: Look, I've asked you to do many things. You can do the rest. Most of them, you tried. . . . On this one, this is—believe me, I've never had anything that's of the highest priority.

ZIEGLER: I understand, I understand.

PRESIDENT NIXON: It's important. Don't you agree?

ZIEGLER: It is. . . .

[Telephone call from Haig.]

PRESIDENT NIXON: . . . Tomorrow's story indicates that I was in charge of even the Ellsberg thing, is that right? . . . [*To Ziegler.*] He [Haig] said that the letter to Hoover [from the White House] said: "Help Krogh, help the plumbers." Dumb shit. How do you handle that? It's the [*Washington*] *Star.* Did you see the *Star* story? . . .

ZIEGLER: It hit on this, how Krogh—the thrust of the story was a letter to Hoover simply saying that Krogh was the guy in charge of this bit of investigation. And then it goes on to say that this indicates that the President had a personal interest and concern about getting an investigation and about leaked papers. . . . The story refers to the fact that we wrote to Hoover in '71 and said Krogh is the guy who's in charge of this. . . .

But then the story goes on—does not go on to say that you were aware of all the Plumber activity or the Ellsberg break-in at all. It simply says that, as a result of activities conducted by what became known as the Plumbers, you know, the Ellsberg burglary took place. It does not suggest awareness on your part or involvement in that. It simply suggests—

PRESIDENT NIXON: Well, I guess it's part of the problem. They said, did the President know? Of course not. The President knows a hell of a lot of things, but does he know what the Christ some dumb assholes are going to do? . . . What the Christ. Krogh's an honorable man. How did you handle it today? . . .

ZIEGLER: I said, Krogh's already pointed out that he was involved in it. . . .

PRESIDENT NIXON: . . . Haldeman was great that way. You know, he went through so much, but he never bothered—but I should be bothered with what's necessary. Christ, what can I do about a story that says "help Krogh"? Goddamn to hell, I didn't tell them to go fuck up the Goddamn Ellsberg place. . . .

ZIEGLER: Bringing it all in to you. We've got to knock that off. The other thing is that all this talk about strategies and so forth—we'll put that together and at the right time, when we've got a file, then we bring it to you and discuss it with you. . . .

PRESIDENT NIXON: There are missing files over there.

ZIEGLER: Yes, sir. That's right. But as you said in Florida and as you said at Camp David, if we allow ourselves to be consumed by this—

PRESIDENT NIXON: We'll destroy ourselves.

ZIEGLER: We'll destroy ourselves.

PRESIDENT NIXON: I think we'd better get off of it. . . .

MAY 14, 1973: THE PRESIDENT AND HAIG, 3:10–3:51 P.M., EXECUTIVE OFFICE BUILDING

General Haig relays information that Lyndon Johnson reportedly used the Secret Service to tap phones. Nixon finds this intriguing.

HAIG: I talked to [William] Sullivan. . . . He said you ought to know that the people around Ruckelshaus are all Hoover men. . . . I asked him about previous taps. I said, are they over there, Bill? He said yes. The file of taps should be there—they were there when I left—that ran from Roosevelt right on through. He said the heaviest tapping period was in the '40s.

PRESIDENT NIXON: The '40s? Well, it would be, yes, the war.

HAIG: But he said it was a pretty healthy slug, including the Truman Administration, and—

PRESIDENT NIXON: Eisenhower.

HAIG: And Eisenhower did it.

PRESIDENT NIXON: Kennedy did it.

HAIG: Kennedy did probably more than Eisenhower.

PRESIDENT NIXON: Yeah. We didn't—I don't think Ike did too much. . . . .

HAIG: The trouble with Johnson is that . . . he knew he was vulnerable, so he used the Secret Service.

PRESIDENT NIXON: He used the Secret Service for tapping? I'll be Goddamned. . . .

MAY 14, 1973: THE PRESIDENT AND LAWRENCE M. HIGBY, 5:20–5:43 P.M., EXECUTIVE OFFICE BUILDING

"Watergate" was never about personal financial gain, as Nixon repeatedly said. But Watergate's generic quality expands with revelations about the President's income-tax liability resulting from backdating the gift of his vice presidential papers, and governmental expenditures of more than a million dollars for house and ground improvements at the President's Pacific estate, San Clemente. In a conversation with Larry Higby, Nixon reacts passionately to media leaks of his financial irregularities from the Ervin Committee, persuaded that his enemies will pursue him on any number of issues.

PRESIDENT NIXON: Hi, Larry. Yeah. Did you hear about that—

HIGBY: Mr. President—just incredible . . . .

PRESIDENT NIXON: Well, you know, you think that a committee though—for God's sake, this is the President of the United States—says that the President used a million dollars of unrecorded funds to buy his property. It's just a *total Goddamn lie.* A total lie. . . . . I don't have a damn thing. This is why I don't own anything, I don't own stocks or bonds. All my money's in real estate, you know what I mean, not—this is just unbelievable that that would come out of the Senate Committee and Ervin himself wouldn't slap it down.

MAY 14, 1973: THE PRESIDENT, HAIG, AND ZIEGLER, 6:28–7:27 P.M., OVAL OFFICE

More concern with Richardson, Walters, and the charges of unwarranted use of government funds to improve the President's properties. This prompts a discussion between Nixon and Ziegler about dealing with the media. Finally, Ziegler offers a spirited defense of Leonard Garment, the President's counsel, the object of intra–White House intrigues, most notably by Haldeman and Haig.

PRESIDENT NIXON: . . . The only thing I can guess, Ron, that it could be is there might be some of Hunt's crap in there, although I don't know. . . .

ZIEGLER: I don't know that we should even be concerned about Hunt's crap.

PRESIDENT NIXON: Well, I know. Suppose there is? Goddamnit we order a security thing and Hunt did things he did, but believe me. He didn't do any breaking into somebody's psychiatrist's office as far as we know.

HAIG: We don't have a problem with [Elliot] Richardson.

PRESIDENT NIXON: Is that right? Does he want to resign?

HAIG: No. He made public in the hearing . . . the names of four people [as Special Prosecutor]. We don't have any others. But he, also, says that White House aides called him. Just a couple of other [names] and then he turned [them down].

PRESIDENT NIXON: Well, for Christ sakes. He didn't need to do that. . . .

HAIG: Well, Len [Garment] called him on one and he got somebody else.

PRESIDENT NIXON: Yes.

HAIG: And when I called him I said this would be a good man. . . .

PRESIDENT NIXON: Let's forget it. Let's forget it. That's just a small thing. Let him believe that there's a hog on ice. I don't like him pissing on the White House. That's all. But everybody else is doing it at the moment. All right. Fine. Let's get him confirmed, if we can. . . .

All right. What else do you got?

HAIG: Well, we got a problem with the testimony that Walters gave.

PRESIDENT NIXON: How come?

HAIG: Well, what he did apparently was—

PRESIDENT NIXON: Where? Today?

HAIG: Yes. He twisted it in a way that was bad for Bob and John.

PRESIDENT NIXON: Is it bad for the President, too?

HAIG: No, no. . . .

PRESIDENT NIXON: I think that Walters has misconstrued it.

HAIG: Well, this is what the problem is. Every sonofabitch is a self-server. His memcom was clearly—

PRESIDENT NIXON: It said what? (Unintelligible)

HAIG: Oh, yeah. Len [Garment] says he's a—I pulled Len off the phone. He's talking to Fred Thompson. I said you're not—

PRESIDENT NIXON: Oh shit, he's dumb as hell. Fred Thompson. Who is he? He won't say anything. . . . I'm surprised that Garment can't get—he's talking to Thompson now?

HAIG: That's right and Dash.

PRESIDENT NIXON: Trying to get them to get a statement out. So, what do you think Walters did? Walters deliberately put Haldeman's and Ehrlichman's tit in the ringer on this. That makes me sick. . . .

ZIEGLER: . . . I think we've got to keep our eye on the main ball and that is that a lot of these little men, not referring to Haldeman and Ehrlichman, but the McCords and the others, are putting—creating an environment and an atmosphere that allowed for this story on the [San Clemente] house to run, you know.

PRESIDENT NIXON: You're saying that . . . in other words, you can charge the President with anything.

ZIEGLER: That's right. No. We cannot—as I mentioned to you earlier and Al and I have talked about this—we can't lose sight of the major goal here and that is protection and the preservation of the presidency. And that's going to rest to a great extent on public opinion; right?

PRESIDENT NIXON: Yes.

ZIEGLER: And we're going to have to stop . . . getting ourselves, to the degree we can, bogged down in this day-to-day bouillabaisse and keep our eye on the broader picture. But the problem is in all of this, Mr. President, is that we're consuming our day and, I think, Al would agree with this because we don't have—we are operating totally absolutely in the blind. We don't know what our target is. We don't know what our enemy is. . . .

PRESIDENT NIXON: . . . I'm very realistic about this and you've got to be realistic, too. We're just going to take a hell of a battering. This is difficult shit. And so what— and we're going to take a lot of attrition in this period. But they will not shred us. . . . Because we will come back. You want to remember, presidents before have taken care of batterers and they come back and that's about where we are at the present time. The only reason we won't come back, however, is . . . they happen to be right. In other words, if I had a billion dollars of stolen money in that house or I had put campaign money in that house or if I'd, you know, faked the CIA thing or I'd, you know, tried to get the defendants paid off; then that would be a different matter. But I haven't, you see. That's the whole point.

ZIEGLER: That's right. And there's got to be a—there has to be a formula here which we haven't come upon yet because we have to be in the convergence of these events plus the political aspects of all of this. *There's got to be a way to deal with it.* I don't know the answer to that yet. . . .

PRESIDENT NIXON: But I can't go at it every day. You see, if I do it every week, as people have said—I said, look, I'm doing nothing [but] Watergate. Look, I did it two weeks ago on television. I did it last week. . . . Now, what the hell do they want this week? . . . I think that every time I do that, that raises more doubts. Haldeman and Ehrlichman, I had to do. Do you think we were right to go in that fire or would it have been better to do that in the middle of day?

ZIEGLER: No. I think that one—that had to go that way. . . .

PRESIDENT NIXON: But, you know, when you really come down to it, . . . [all] they've got is brother Dean. You know that.

ZIEGLER: What they've got is Dean?

PRESIDENT NIXON: Yeah. That's all. What the hell else do you think they have?

ZIEGLER: Nothing. . . . I'll tell you this. There's one guy—I sound like I'm uptight about it. But one guy who's a fella who's really standing up to this thing, and I know as well has been poisoned to some degree and I think—

PRESIDENT NIXON: Who? [Leonard] Garment?

ZIEGLER: Well, it's Garment. Garment in his own way—

PRESIDENT NIXON: Well, he's a loyal [lawyer?]

ZIEGLER: He's a lawyer—loyal.

PRESIDENT NIXON: Loyal.

ZIEGLER: A loyal fella.

MAY 14, 1973: THE PRESIDENT, HAIG, AND ZIEGLER, 8:20–9:15 P.M., EXECUTIVE OFFICE BUILDING

As the Senate hearings are to begin, the President is angry about the growing talk of Dean's allegations and also the charges that he had used public monies for his personal improvements of his properties. "Don't react in a jumpy, panicky way every time something comes up," he tells Haig. And then he proceeds to rage about the "libel of unbelievable pretension" against himself.

PRESIDENT NIXON: . . . But now you and I've got to get on with the business of this Goddamned country. We can't be obsessed with it. Today we had to be. Tomorrow I want . . . a list of what Dean's documents are. But, beyond that, nothing else. Do you understand? Screw it all. I don't care what Walters says, and I don't care what Helms says. And I don't care what other people say. And you mustn't care. You and I have got to get on with the business of this damn country.

HAIG: That's right. . . .

PRESIDENT NIXON: That's right. Buzhardt's in charge, and at the end of the day he can tell you well, we had this and this pack of shit today and this pack of shit tomorrow.

HAIG: That's the best way.

PRESIDENT NIXON: Otherwise, we're going to be in the middle, Al, of every stinking little thing. And we can't do this. We've got to run the country. . . . We're going to take attrition. Look, I was talking to Ron before you came in, and I said now, Ron, he's worried about the fact that we're taking some attrition in the press and the polls. Screw it. We're going to take it for another two months, and then we'll come back. Don't worry about it. Don't react to the Goddamn attrition. Al, we just do the job. Don't you agree?

HAIG: I'm convinced that's the best solution to this problem.

PRESIDENT NIXON: Don't react in a jumpy, panicky way every time something comes up.

HAIG: The more we react, the more these bastards will (unintelligible).

PRESIDENT NIXON: Except on one thing. On this million dollar thing, we've got to attack them, assault them, and destroy them. Don't you agree? . . . Because that is a libel of unbelievable pretension. . . .

HAIG: There'll just have to be a major blast. We can't do it any other way, but nothing defensive.

PRESIDENT NIXON: Oh, defensive? Good God. They've libeled the President of the United States that he stole a million dollars. *Shit. It's totally untrue.* [Shouting] Now this is one where we've got to get the committee by the balls, and they just must retract it. They've allowed that kind of a libel to lay twenty-four hours here without retracting it. Do you see my point, Al?

HAIG: We put them on notice. . . .

MAY 14, 1973: THE PRESIDENT, ZIEGLER, HAIG, AND HIGBY, 8:56–10:50 A.M., OVAL OFFICE

The President is concerned about John Dean's files. He wonders whether he might have written to Dean to protect Haldeman and Ehrlichman and ensure that Hunt did not speak. Nixon and Ziegler discuss the current banter about Dean's alleged fears of going to jail.

PRESIDENT NIXON: . . . But you see, Ron, I must say that—and don't worry too much about it. . . . I mean, certainly we have to take the beating and let them beat you down. But the main thing is we've got to save this office and do our job and over a period of time people will, though, perhaps be more concerned about how we do the job on the big things than they are how we handle this chicken shit thing.

ZIEGLER: No. I agree. I agree.

PRESIDENT NIXON: So you see, I just don't know if you could—I don't know that you can ever clear the other thing up, like, no Dean report, oh shit, the resignation. Did the President know? Did he know what? About the cover up, you mean? The CIA thing? Even that will be knocked out. The cover up? That's a tough one because, basically, the President's own attorney helped to raise the money for it. Tom Pappas helped us all to raise the money for it as it turns out, particularly in March. Was it—do you know what I mean? It's just one of those things. . . . There's no way you're going to ever get across to the true meaning. The country on the other hand may eventually have more confidence in the President despite what he does. I think that's about where it stands. . . .

ZIEGLER: But you see, this is my point here. Throughout all of this, Mr. President, I think perhaps we have—and I made this point to you before. I think through March and into April we have allowed, perhaps, this matter to become more complex than what it really is. In seeking the solution, I think people were saying that we should be concerned about whether or not did they find, you know, this FBI thing or the Ellsberg burglary and so forth. Hell, it's all out and it is an insignificant thing. Do you see what I mean? I think that's the point I'm making. Now I am totally convinced, also, that the move for Bob and John to resign—

PRESIDENT NIXON: —was still right?

ZIEGLER: You're absolutely right. Where would we be today?

PRESIDENT NIXON: I don't know. Not many, but some say, well, look, you had a buffer at least—

ZIEGLER: —a buffer for what? . . .

PRESIDENT NIXON: . . . What did he [John Dean] tell you that he thinks he's got in his lock box? . . .

ZIEGLER: Well, he wrote up something in Camp David [about?] the campaign. . . . I know the word gets moved around on the Hill about the guy. . . . Well, just that this guy is a little flipped out. You know, they talked about his cheating in college. A lot of people—the press is going after that type of thing. How he conducted himself in college, not only scholastically but morally.

PRESIDENT NIXON: The way he fell out of his law firm? . . .

ZIEGLER: I defended him based on my conversation with him, but also people look at it as very strange. If the press guys look at it as very strange for a guy to be concerned about going to prison because of his—

PRESIDENT NIXON: —because of sex.

ZIEGLER: Yeah. Because of the sex thing. It's not very virile for someone to be thinking in those terms.

PRESIDENT NIXON: Let me just ask you to do something. [Pauses] The files that I have, my personal files, I've kept in several places, I think. And I wrote—let me put it this way. They don't have to look at any name for the—I guess it doesn't make any difference. What difference does it make? I'm going to say this to you, if I ever wrote—anything I've ever wrote to Dean regarding this, it wouldn't have been anything that I can't defend in the proper context. But is it worth really looking for? . . . Maybe I wrote a memorandum to him saying, look, do everything possible to be sure that John and Bob don't get involved, or everything possible to see that Hunt doesn't talk. Do you know what I mean? You get to the point where you just sort of wonder what you might have—you know, dealing with a rat like this. . . .

MAY 14, 1973: THE PRESIDENT AND LAWRENCE M. HIGBY, 9:47–9:53, P.M., WHITE HOUSE TELEPHONE

The President's darkest secret is in jeopardy: CIA Deputy Director Vernon Walters's June 1972 memoranda are about to be made public. In a conversation with former Haldeman aide Larry Higby, Nixon worries about the "implication" that the White House tried to have a CIA cover for the Watergate break-in. The President is apprehensive and tentative throughout the conversation.

PRESIDENT NIXON: I got your report and the thing I think that I particularly think you should get ahold, get uh, get Bob and John alerted to is that they must not allow, on the basis of the fact that it was national security, this implication to be out that they, you know, were trying to have a CIA cover-up for this Goddamned thing, you know what I mean?

HIGBY: Mm-hmm.

PRESIDENT NIXON: And so I think on that, they just, should just hit it hard publicly, say this is, you know, you understand what I mean? . . .

HIGBY: Yeah, I—the only thing is, I think Bob's position has been all the way through on this thing and has held him in good stead so far, that the truth's gonna come out and what I, what he says publicly, really isn't gonna make that much difference. They hit him on it, from what he told me, today in the latter part of the [McClellan Sub-Committee on CIA Oversight?] hearing, and he very precisely said that he only had one meeting and explained as much as he could without getting into national security what it was about. Uh—

PRESIDENT NIXON: Did he?

HIGBY: —stressing that he had to draw the line on a good portion of it because it was, because it was national security.

PRESIDENT NIXON: But you see, he must not leave the implication, Larry, neither he nor John, that they, on the basis of national security, are, are uh, you know, uh, have participated in any effort to have the CIA cover up this Goddamned thing, which they weren't trying to do.

HIGBY: Right. In other words, what you're suggesting is a blanket, sort of a statement that just flatly puts it down.

PRESIDENT NIXON: Well, they gotta consider that because I don't want them to take a look at the news in the morning and so forth and I don't want them to do anything that'll jeopardize their legal thing, but I—

HIGBY: Right.

PRESIDENT NIXON: —think that, on the other hand, they must, must not have, hanging out there, any implication that they, uh participated in or ordered or encouraged a, uh you know, a CIA uh, uh cover-up for this Goddamned thing. *Which is what they didn't do!*

HIGBY: Right.

PRESIDENT NIXON: They were simply trying to get the Goddamned facts.

HIGBY: Right.

PRESIDENT NIXON: Right?

HIGBY: Right. Precisely. And also, as I understand it, prevent, prevent uh some, from what could've been some subsequent national security problems had the thing continued down the line, which was, which was the point I think Bob was trying to make. That eventually you're going to cross over the area of you're no longer in Watergate, you're in a national-security area and I think he was trying to make that point to Walters also.

PRESIDENT NIXON: Yes, I know, right. Well, you know, what I mean, is that all this is in the public area as well as the private area and so forth, and I'd tell them don't do anything to hurt their case but uh, have in mind the fact that they must not let, that must not leave hanging out there any implication that they—Haldeman or Ehrlichman —either one, were involved in trying to use the CIA as a cover-up for this thing. They were not, they were trying to get the Goddamned facts. . . .

HIGBY: I understand, understand precisely what you're saying. . . .

PRESIDENT NIXON: Yeah, you know, and basically, uh, Bob and John, uh, they don't attack Walters, but they just simply say, "Look, he may have misunderstood. We had no intention to do anything, Goddamned thing here." . . . Dean, on the other hand, did follow up in a way that was totally, you know, he tried—you know, what he tried to do, he tried to—

HIGBY: Hell, yes.

PRESIDENT NIXON: He went over and tried to get Walters to agree to put these people on their payroll, to pay their legal expenses, and all that. But Goddamnit, Bob and John never acc—, suggested such a Goddamn thing. . . .

MAY 15, 1973: THE PRESIDENT AND HAIG, 12:24–1:00 P.M., OVAL OFFICE

Nixon and Haig maneuver to have a hand in the nomination of a Special Prosecutor.

SEGMENT 1

PRESIDENT NIXON: Hi, Al. Well, what's new today?

HAIG: We've had a little activity. . . . We've looked very hard at Elliot's situation and it may be another week or ten days.

PRESIDENT NIXON: All right.

HAIG: He's probably going to get through. But he—it's a possibility he wouldn't.

PRESIDENT NIXON: He not being confirmed?

HAIG: Well, it's a possibility.

PRESIDENT NIXON: On what ground? I named [supported the idea of] the Special Prosecutor.

HAIG: Well, I think we ought to think very hard on an independent prosecutor. It might be a good—

PRESIDENT NIXON: Just have Elliot back off of it.

HAIG: That's right. And have you do it. . . . I was so Goddamn discouraged about the way he did that thing yesterday morning. . . . He went out of his way.

PRESIDENT NIXON: To kick the White House.

HAIG: To kick the White House. . . .

PRESIDENT NIXON: Why don't we do this? Why don't we get Elliot—let Elliot give us a recommendation of a name. In other words, just change the—and then direct it to the Department of Justice who will cooperate. . . .

HAIG: That would unplug his appointment as Attorney General very quickly. I'm just not sure that we haven't got ourselves a problem here. He wants to come out of this as Mr. Clean. In other words, clean up the thing instead of you. You've got to demand, that is, taking the action. You know, this is sensitive, touchy stuff. But I don't trust the sonofabitch. . . .

PRESIDENT NIXON: Well, how could we—why don't we find a tactic to get an independent prosecutor or a special prosecutor named here? . . . And name [Judge Harold R.] Tyler. I mean, if he's a good man, name him. I don't care who the Christ does that. I really don't. . . .

SEGMENT 2

PRESIDENT NIXON: Have you given any more thought to this independent prosecutor thing?

HAIG: Yes, I have. And I'm—Elliot is not available. He's on the Hill, but Buzhardt says it's perfectly legal. We could do it. You know, I think it's got some good, good pizzazz to it. You've got to be in charge.

PRESIDENT NIXON: That's right.

HAIG: The next thing you'll know we'll be boxed there with a guy who's playing his own game.

PRESIDENT NIXON: He won't be telling us anything.

HAIG: Right. Well, he's at the point now any time you talk to him you know you're talking for the broadcast no matter what you say to them. . . .

PRESIDENT NIXON: We thought we were being very strong when we made the speech two weeks ago and I appointed Elliot Richardson and accepted the resignation of Kleindienst so that Richardson was named as special prosecutor. But it wasn't strong enough, was it? It didn't turn out that way. I mean, it didn't give them just enough *blood* that they wanted more.

HAIG: It's usually the way those things go. . . .

PRESIDENT NIXON: Yeah. It's a terrible damn thing to appoint an independent prosecutor to prosecute members of your own administration. . . .

MAY 15, 1973: THE PRESIDENT AND HAIG, 2:10–2:15 P.M., WHITE HOUSE TELEPHONE

The President's former aides escalate their finger-pointing at one another. John Ehrlichman insists on his innocence and is particularly eager to blame others. His target now is Charles Colson, as well as John Dean.

HAIG: . . . [W]e have a little problem with John [Ehrlichman]. Uh, John called me uh, and he's been going over his notes. And I think our best bet is to have Buzhardt get with Colson fast. . . .

PRESIDENT NIXON: Oh, what are, what's John's—

HAIG: Well, . . . there's some reason to expect that Dean is gonna lead to Colson and not to Bob and John.

PRESIDENT NIXON: Oh, uh, who thinks that, John?

HAIG: Uh, he's not sure, he's not sure. . . . But it's just something we have to be prepared for if it does. . . . And I told him not to talk to me about it on the phone—. . . I didn't want the details, but uh, I think he's having a feeling of being probably hard-pressed by, by Walters's testimony. Quite frankly, he is.

PRESIDENT NIXON: Sure he is.

HAIG: He's been very badly damaged.

PRESIDENT NIXON: Yeah. Well, what does he feel we should do?

HAIG: Well, I think what he's thinking in his own mind is that, uh, what's the source of the CIA involvement, and uh, and what was done—you see, it looks, what it looks like is that he triggered Dean to do specifically what was mentioned in general in the meeting.

PRESIDENT NIXON: Yeah.

HAIG: And I think he feels in his own mind, probably—he hasn't, he didn't say that, but I think there's probably a feeling in his mind that Colson may have been the one that triggered Dean.

PRESIDENT NIXON: Well, the main thing is he certainly, he knows that, he's not suggesting that I did it, for Christ's sake?

HAIG: Oh, God no, no, no, no—

PRESIDENT NIXON: Jeez, I didn't know anything about it. [*Laughs.*]

HAIG: No, no, no, no.

PRESIDENT NIXON: [*Laughs.*] I mean, that's just the stupidest Goddamn thing. Oh, he thinks Colson may have triggered Dean. . . . [H]e would never have triggered Dean to do this, never.

HAIG: No.

PRESIDENT NIXON: Never. . . .

MAY 15, 1973: THE PRESIDENT AND HAIG, 3:44–3:51 P.M., WHITE HOUSE TELEPHONE

Nixon and Haig are unhappy with Elliot Richardson. The Attorney General–designate has asserted an independent role for himself in naming the Special Prosecutor he had promised the Senate, and the two men in the White House sense the danger to their authority.

PRESIDENT NIXON: . . . Have you been able to get any more thought to the idea of the independent prosecutor? You've got so many other things up in the air, you haven't had time to work on it.

HAIG: Yeah, well I have, I've had another talk with Buzhardt on it and uh, it's a mixed bag. We have to be very careful because of, uh uh, Elliot.

PRESIDENT NIXON: Yeah.

HAIG: We don't want any disaffections here.

PRESIDENT NIXON: No, no, no, no—we don't want Elliot quitting.

HAIG: No, no that's right. . . . Apparently three of the four on his list have already turned it down.

PRESIDENT NIXON: Is that right?

HAIG: Yes, so we may, that's another problem we have to be sure we have a viable man. And the uh—

PRESIDENT NIXON: Boy oh boy. . . .

MAY 16, 1973: THE PRESIDENT AND KISSINGER, 9:07–9:25 A.M., OVAL OFFICE

The President and Kissinger commiserate again about leaks and the National Security Council wiretaps. Kissinger dutifully recoils at the prospect of Nixon's resignation.

PRESIDENT NIXON: Let me say this. What I want you to know. You've got to go away with great confidence, Henry, and assurance always and you know we've got a helluva battle over here because of these things. But these things run a course and this will run its course.

KISSINGER: I'm beginning to think the public must be getting sick and tired of it.

PRESIDENT NIXON: Yeah. Christ, there's something new every day, you know. Now it's the CIA wanting to do this shit.

KISSINGER: And then they—Haig and I went on the offensive yesterday on these—

PRESIDENT NIXON: Which you should.

KISSINGER: —National Security wiretaps.

PRESIDENT NIXON: Those are totally legal.

KISSINGER: We said they were legal. We had the duty to do it. What is wrong with the National Security—

PRESIDENT NIXON: Well, the point is—I think—the next thing you can say had we had—I mean, the leaks the least as it was, seriously impaired some of our negotiations and that they be allowed to continue, the great initiatives might not have come up.

KISSINGER: That's what I am saying.

[Withdrawn item. National security.]

PRESIDENT NIXON: Let's not worry about it. We didn't—the idea that it was ever used. Some jackass Senator said that perhaps—what he was saying is that it was used politically.

KISSINGER: Never.

PRESIDENT NIXON: Those taps never saw the light of—I never saw them, you know. I didn't even know what the Christ was in those damn things. The only one I ever saw was the first one on [journalist Henry] Brandon and it was certainly much of *nothing*. Do you know what I mean? Hell, they didn't have anything on Brandon.

KISSINGER: They have none. But Brandon wasn't ours anyway. It was J. Edgar Hoover's.

PRESIDENT NIXON: I know. Well, nevertheless, he did a lot of taps.

[Withdrawn item. National security.]

PRESIDENT NIXON: They were legal, but Henry, it's a rough time, I know. A rough time for all of us around here. . . .

KISSINGER: Your presidency will be remembered for its great achievements.

PRESIDENT NIXON: And that was in Herb Klein—he's over at the *Times*. The editors, they say that they all asked him whether or not the President should resign, you know. . . . I wouldn't give a damn if they proved red-handed that I was there in the Watergate, you know, and wearing a red beard, collecting the evidence. Hell, I wouldn't even consider—the President of the United States isn't going to resign—

KISSINGER: Cannot resign.

PRESIDENT NIXON: —not over this chicken shit stuff.

KISSINGER: You cannot resign.

PRESIDENT NIXON: That's ridiculous.

KISSINGER: The horror of this thing . . . . The disparity between the minor league crap that these guys did and the consequences, the amateur and the stupidity, I mean, nothing they could ever done. That's the worse of it.

PRESIDENT NIXON: They never accomplished anything. . . .

KISSINGER: It was a little trick and treat.

PRESIDENT NIXON: Break in, but then they went into the Democratic Committee. What happened? They didn't get any big time information, no big breaks, nothing. That was a total failure. In other words, they're compounding their failures and then, of course, attempting to cover up failures. . . . They're giving John and Bob a bad rap on Walters's testimony. As a matter of fact, it was Dean that went over and tried to push all that crap. . . .

KISSINGER: Bob and John are fine men. . . . The stupidity, Mr. President, is the worse of it.

MAY 16, 1973: THE PRESIDENT, HAIG, AND BUZHARDT, 9:54–10:23 A.M., OVAL OFFICE

Nixon receives an update on Richardson's search for the Special Prosecutor. Again, he expresses concern about the Walters memcoms.

SEGMENT 3

PRESIDENT NIXON: Let me ask you on Richardson. . . .

HAIG: I had a long talk with him last night.

PRESIDENT NIXON: If there's anything he wants, we'll do. So you think he wants to talk, too?

HAIG: Yes. He wants to talk. He thinks he's fairly close now. He read to me his charter for the special investigator.

PRESIDENT NIXON: Right.

HAIG: It's very autonomous. At this point there's only three guys left now.

[Withdrawn item. Privacy.]

PRESIDENT NIXON: That's bad news.

HAIG: And I just don't know. I'm afraid to tell him that he [unknown] is bad news. . . .

PRESIDENT NIXON: Our candidate, he's a—

HAIG: Well, we've got to get someone who's outside and that is not traceable here.

[Withdrawn item. Privacy.]

HAIG: I don't want to say what we'll do if we've got—if you've got yourself a bad apple here.

PRESIDENT NIXON: Ask [Robert] Finch if he knows of a liberal.

[Withdrawn item. Privacy.]

PRESIDENT NIXON: Who is not particularly for Nixon. Somebody that could call Richardson—

[Withdrawn item. Privacy.]

PRESIDENT NIXON: . . . Now this damn thing is a chicken shit thing the more you put it in perspective. Take the Walters thing. So they tried to get the CIA to cover it up. So what's wrong with that? *It was wrong. It was stupid. And it wasn't done.*

HAIG: And it was not done. It was not done. . . .

PRESIDENT NIXON: All right. All right. Now these—we're going to sit on that Walters memoranda until hell freezes over. . . .

MAY 16, 1973: THE PRESIDENT AND JOHN B. CONNALLY, 10:31–11:35 A.M., OVAL OFFICE

Nixon likes John Connally, and the Texan is a rare visitor whose advice Nixon genuinely seems to respect. Connally skillfully points out the political weakness of Nixon's top aides, believing this is the source of the problem. Connally strikes the right chord for Nixon as he emphasizes that Watergate essentially is a PR problem.

CONNALLY: Let me, for your deliberations and your own private thoughts, let me try to characterize where you are in a little different term.

PRESIDENT NIXON: Sure.

CONNALLY: Watergate is a generic term now. . . . It encompasses a lot of things and I don't say this maliciously at all. You see individuals. What you have here—if it hadn't been a Watergate project, it would have been something else because it was almost a rebellion in the town among the press, the Congress and finally the bureaucracy against—

PRESIDENT NIXON: The White House. Yeah.

CONNALLY: —the autocracy of your staff. . . .

PRESIDENT NIXON: I know. I agree with you totally.

CONNALLY: And this is the whole thing that's happening in the country right today, in the press here. This is all part of this. It's more than just Watergate. Hell, it'll just determine then—of course, they have to let loose now. The truth of the matter is that the press is going to destroy themselves if they keep on because they're going to overplay this thing. But I—but you got some more damn rough days to come.

PRESIDENT NIXON: Sure. Pretty bad in the indictments.

CONNALLY: Sure.

PRESIDENT NIXON: And they'll indict Mitchell. They'll indict Magruder, possibly Haldeman, possibly Ehrlichman. . . . They will not make cases against Haldeman and Ehrlichman. They can't, in my opinion. They will in Mitchell. . . . But we're not going to give them another Goddamn thing. What I mean, we're not giving them is any presidential papers. They can't have—there wasn't much in the files there. Do you know what I mean? . . . But we're cooperating every way you can imagine, John, every way we can—

CONNALLY: I think the hearings will be a blessing in disguise. You should go on and let them—let them do it.

PRESIDENT NIXON: They're stars of tomorrow. . . .

CONNALLY: What I'm saying—that's all. It's—all I'm saying is that it's more than Watergate.

PRESIDENT NIXON: Right. So you must correct it by doing more than answering Watergate. . . .

CONNALLY: That's all I'm saying. And this means that you have to restructure your staff to present a new persona.

PRESIDENT NIXON: Also, it has to mean that I have to get out and say some things. I can't do it now. . . . I am stuck for two weeks until that damn grand jury indicts.

CONNALLY: I think that's right.

PRESIDENT NIXON: And then when they've indicted, then I am perfectly free to say, gentleman. I'm not going to say anything. . . . Period. And I never want to speak on the issue.

May 16, 1973: The President and Haig, 12:34–1:25 P.M., Oval Office

Richard Nixon often manages to lapse simultaneously into expressions of self-pity and a militant rhetoric toward his enemies. Unlike Ziegler, Alexander Haig provides a perfect foil for those moods.

SEGMENT 7

PRESIDENT NIXON: . . . Little sonofabitch [John Dean] is in everything. . . . I think he is deeper in a lot of this stuff.

HAIG: Well, he's the linchpin . . . and that's why he's so desperate. That's why you could demolish him. The job is done.

PRESIDENT NIXON: . . . Just think what would have happened if the whole thing had come out and blown up in our faces without having done anything. Do you know what I mean? About my conducting an investigation. I must say the moves haven't helped us much. Oh, yes, they have. Yes, they have. When you come right down to it, my announcing on April 17th that I was going to do—that I had conducted my own investigation and we were going to cooperate with the committee. Then my announcement on—then making the television speech on Haldeman and Ehrlichman. . . . It doesn't satisfy your enemies. . . .

HAIG: Those bastards are—they have just beaten us so badly, brutalized over four years of being wrong.

PRESIDENT NIXON: Yeah. They've lost.

HAIG: . . . [T]hey lost the people. The whole country turned around . . . during this four years.

PRESIDENT NIXON: That's it.

HAIG: It returned to sanity.

PRESIDENT NIXON: The country—we turned away from the Great Society. It turns away from an obsession about the blacks. And it's starting to turn away from the crime and drug syndrome, the dirty movies, et cetera. It turned away from, you know, the whole (unintelligible) peace thing. I mean, it turned a little character.

HAIG: That's right.

PRESIDENT NIXON: That's what really kills these people. There's been a very fundamental change. . . .

MAY 16, 1973: THE PRESIDENT, HAIG, AND BUZHARDT, 3:02–4:08 P.M., OVAL OFFICE

On the eve of the Senate Select Committee hearings, Fred Buzhardt informs the President of another looming bombshell, apparently one of John Dean's "trump cards." Longtime Nixon aide Tom Charles Huston had formulated a plan in 1970 for inter-agency coordination of domestic intelligence, with the policy being centrally directed by the White House. Huston, a deeply committed right-wing ideologue, signed his memos, "Cato the Younger," and Nixon characterized his work as "inflammatory." Openly contemptuous of the existing bureaucracies in various agencies, including the FBI and the CIA, Huston said that they "must be treated as the enemy," but realized that such men as J. Edgar Hoover had to be courted and treated gently. The plan involved surveillance and actions against domestic organizations, including wiretapping and surreptitious break-ins. Hoover recognized a bureaucratic turf war, since he regarded domestic investigations and counter-intelligence operations as FBI territory. He objected to signing on, unless Nixon provided a personal endorsement, and when the President balked the plan died. CIA Director Richard Helms considered the plan "basically Richard Nixon's doing, and he called it the Huston Plan." Buzhardt sees the impending revelation as opportunity. The President can remind the country of the perilous times, and he can then justify the Plumbers and even Watergate as necessary to combat domestic subversion. The discussion is long and convoluted; eventually, however, Nixon realizes the futility of such arguments.

PRESIDENT NIXON: Come in, Fred. Don't it seem like we always have problems? So let's see what this one is.

BUZHARDT: It has nothing to do with Watergate. Let's start with that. Nothing to do with Watergate unless somebody draws an inference of connection. What it is basically, Mr. President, is your inter-agency intelligence group plan—

PRESIDENT NIXON: Right.

BUZHARDT: —for supplementing domestic intelligence—

PRESIDENT NIXON: Right.

BUZHARDT: —plus the documents about the—which include a summary, a memorandum on the recommendation, the memorandum back when Bob stating the method of approval and implementation. One memorandum analyzing Mr. Hoover's objections, methods, approach. Some of the language appears quite inflammatory particularly one of [presidential aide Tom Charles] Huston's memorandums.

PRESIDENT NIXON: Everything he wrote was inflammatory.

BUZHARDT: So, it's very unfortunate. I think it presents a serious problem.

PRESIDENT NIXON: All right.

BUZHARDT: As you know, I guess—well, by far the most serious thing is the approval of the surreptitious entry which is described in Huston's words. It's nothing short of perjury and illegal if the document exists. And objects on that ground but saying clearly the advantages outweigh the risk. Hoover should be overruled. It's in language that will be quite inflammatory. . . .

PRESIDENT NIXON: This is Huston's language, not mine?

BUZHARDT: This is Huston's language but Haldeman going back and saying your recommendations are approved by the President on all counts. There was only one recommendation that was disapproved and that was the use of military undercover agents. That was turned down. Now, I think, frankly, that this will be used by the [Senate] committee really to supersede the whole Watergate thing.

PRESIDENT NIXON: Yeah.

BUZHARDT: It puts a new light, I think, on the fight.

PRESIDENT NIXON: Yeah.

BUZHARDT: I would suggest it be handled in a much different fashion. I think you can't let this dribble out.

PRESIDENT NIXON: No.

BUZHARDT: It's my own belief that you have to make your case for doing it. Think of the environment that it was done in. You have to lay it on the record and there are a number of ways you could do it with something approaching a state paper, perhaps with a summary by you, say that with the leadership or otherwise. I think you should be accompanied at this point by a relaxation to the maximum extent of executive privilege because you can't have the plan and then have anything that appears to cover up. I think we should work up into the maximum extent possible, the best darn approach.

PRESIDENT NIXON: Yes, sir. I hear you.

BUZHARDT: On across the board or in some way we define it's not related to this or the Watergate affair.

PRESIDENT NIXON: Yeah. Except . . . we can't relax with regards to Walters' memorandum, can we?

BUZHARDT: We're going to have to, Mr. President. . . . I just talked to them [White House lawyers] this morning. The court is not going to permit it. The only way you'll hold it is by having it in your possession. And to defy a court order at this point—

PRESIDENT NIXON: I get it.

BUZHARDT: —would be—

PRESIDENT NIXON: Well, problems and problems, aren't they.

BUZHARDT: I really think that the only choice is to really go out to get this thing and get on. It may precipitate action by the House [for impeachment]. If so, you should make your case in the strongest possible terms. Give everybody all the ammunition you can to help you, and then let's go fight it. Just take them on and fight this thing head-on. Actually, it gives us a better case because the issue can now turn on the threat to national security during this period. The document is a good one. It lays out the threat very well. . . .

The purpose of this document was to give you a study showing you what the threat was, what the present capabilities intelligence were, what the shortfalls were, to review all limitations existing then on the intelligence community and to give you the pros and cons of changing those limitations. . . . Then the implementation went forward with all the recommendations on its expanded electronic surveillance—

[Withdrawn item. National security.]

BUZHARDT: —increased use of agents for penetration by the Bureau—

PRESIDENT NIXON: All right.

BUZHARDT: —surreptitious entry—

[Withdrawn item. National security.]

BUZHARDT: —selected internal security targets here in the country.

PRESIDENT NIXON: Was that all approved?

BUZHARDT: Yes, sir.

PRESIDENT NIXON: By what? By Haldeman?

BUZHARDT: That was all approved. He said the President has approved the recommendations. The recommendation was for you to sign off on each one of Haldeman's memos as you prepare and implementing. A document saying the President has approved them and let's handle them like this. It's up to the present time. You did not sign the option plans

PRESIDENT NIXON: I did not sign the option plan?

BUZHARDT: No, sir.

PRESIDENT NIXON: What did I sign?

BUZHARDT: You signed nothing in this package. Haldeman wrote the memo to Huston.

PRESIDENT NIXON: Well, I can't get involved in the middle of a thing. . . .

BUZHARDT: . . . [W]e've got to anticipate the battle. Load up and go for it.

PRESIDENT NIXON: I agree.

BUZHARDT: . . . But at least we've got a case to make now and it will overshadow Watergate.

PRESIDENT NIXON: [*Laughter.*] . . . Well, as a matter of fact, . . . I don't ever remember anything about surreptitious entry of selected targets here and there. I mean, that sounds like gobbledygook-gook from bureaucracy or something like that. But I'm sure it was there. You know how this could have happened, though?

HAIG: Oh, God. Very easy. . . .

PRESIDENT NIXON: Yeah.

BUZHARDT: [Senator Ervin's] a civil liberties man.

PRESIDENT NIXON: Yeah.

BUZHARDT: We'll hear police state, Nazism, everything come out of this fella. So we—

PRESIDENT NIXON: We need to think Dean's told them what was in the documents?

BUZHARDT: Yes. . . .

HAIG: Now, the issue here is that—there are two things that have to be ironed out. One is that, Goddamnit, make a pretty good case that we had flabby, ineffective internal security at the time and there was riots in the streets—

PRESIDENT NIXON: It was right after Cambodia—

BUZHARDT: It was just after Cambodia and we just got to Kent State.

HAIG: That's right. The second thing, you know, we've got to tie into the—Fred, you can't go with this until you can get the lines carefully traced the best way you can on the Watergate situation. Something we can see [connecting] the break-in at the psychiatrist's office after this. . . .

PRESIDENT NIXON: Hell, I don't know whether we can avoid it. I don't see—I believe somehow I have to avoid having the President approve the break-in of a psychiatrist's office. I guess there's—

HAIG: Well, you didn't approve it.

BUZHARDT: You didn't approve that specific one.

PRESIDENT NIXON: Yeah. But I approved a policy.

BUZHARDT: But, you know, the policy is you. . . .

PRESIDENT NIXON: When did this—how long did this go on?

BUZHARDT: Mr. President, the unit—at least the intelligence unit still exists. Henry Petersen mentioned it to me this morning. He didn't get into specifics. He said the damn operation they had over in internal security is still there and I don't think it's any damn business of ours. I don't know what to do with it. It's surprising to me. At the time I hadn't read the documents. So I didn't really know what he was talking about. [Former Assistant General Robert] Mardian can tell us the most about it, I suspect. . . .

PRESIDENT NIXON: If you can get Huston, I think Huston—and just going to have to level with you as to what was done. That's my view but recollection was damn little was done. Haldeman ought to be able to help right you on that. Let the papers— damn, what the hell. Well, we never have any little problems around here, do we?

BUZHARDT: No, sir. All big ones.

PRESIDENT NIXON: Well, that's all right. I'd rather have this than have a part—be part of Watergate. . . .

BUZHARDT: . . . [Y]ou're going to pick up a lot of support on this. They're going to have to rally to your support. This document has got Helms' signature on it, Hoover's signature on it, . . . [and other intelligence leaders'] signature on it.

HAIG: Yeah. And we're responsible, ladies and gentlemen.

PRESIDENT NIXON: Yeah. And approving all this stuff.

BUZHARDT: No, sir. But they recommended the rules.

PRESIDENT NIXON: Including the break-ins?

BUZHARDT: Yes, sir. Everybody except Hoover. He demurred on that. But the rest of them were right there and as they say it was urgent and they state their own ties, the bureaucracies, and that part of it has got to support you. . . .

PRESIDENT NIXON: So Dean pictures that's his trump card [the Huston Plan memoranda]?

BUZHARDT: Yes, sir. That's his trump card.

PRESIDENT NIXON: Well, we thought he had one.

BUZHARDT: Yes, sir.

PRESIDENT NIXON: The rat. . . . What the hell does he think he's going to do with it? . . . Destroy the President?

HAIG: That's the reasoning.

BUZHARDT: That's what he thinks.

HAIG: Right-wing conspiracy.

BUZHARDT: That's what he thinks.

PRESIDENT NIXON: Huh?

HAIG: Right-wing conspiracy.

BUZHARDT: Raise the right-wing conspiracy and destroy the President. . . . The district attorney has them and Ervin has them. We'll never get them out of Sam's pocket. I already know. I've got the call coming in. I haven't talked—but I know Ervin is going to refuse to let them go. . . .

PRESIDENT NIXON: Get Huston in and say, now, what the hell happened under this damn thing. . . . Believe me, if nothing did happen, it's too Goddamn bad. They should have done something. Do you know what I mean?

BUZHARDT: Right.

PRESIDENT NIXON: We have a helluva problem.

BUZHARDT: That's right.

PRESIDENT NIXON: I knew this was going on. Didn't you, Al?

HAIG: No, I didn't, sir. I knew that there was—

PRESIDENT NIXON: A plan? I see.

HAIG: I knew there was an inter-agency group. . . .

PRESIDENT NIXON: [W]ell, actually I knew it was going on. . . .

BUZHARDT: I think we ought to think, give some thought to wrapping the psychiatrist's office into this [Huston Plan] and justify it. . . . We've got a major leak there, we got a threat to the national security. It's either wrap it in there, Mr. President, and hang it on this hat and the whole case than to have to defend it separately. I think we may want to think about whether we just put this one under the umbrella.

HAIG: We're going to have to take a look at that. . . .

PRESIDENT NIXON: Well, then to admit [*sighs*] that we approved . . . illegal activities. That's the problem. . . .

BUZHARDT: We want to be prepared and we want to keep our eyes and ears opened to see if we can't get some feel for how the thing is being played.

PRESIDENT NIXON: And how they're going to play it.

BUZHARDT: And how they're going to play it. I think we need to get the feel for that. . . .

PRESIDENT NIXON: [K]eep me posted. . . . I guess what we have to do is to just say yes.

HAIG: I don't know.

PRESIDENT NIXON: Let me tell you some things that are—I don't like furthering that sort of crap inherently. . . . If they want to make an issue—if Ervin and the Committee want to make an issue out of a plan we have to avoid domestic insurrection, I don't know.

HAIG: Mr. President—

PRESIDENT NIXON: I think if we just—we just fight about it.

HAIG: —we'll just have to fight it. Let me say, you know, I've been through all this with Senator Ervin on this precise point. . . . And this was the '68 riots. . . . And my job was to try to get him to understand the environment that existed when Washington was being burned down, the use of military people for intelligence collection at that point.

PRESIDENT NIXON: That's right.

HAIG: He and his entire committee were totally insensitive. . . . [T]hey played the civil liberties [line]. They'll have a statement that comes direct from the *New York Times* to mix them up. . . .

PRESIDENT NIXON: Yeah. But the thing is what Fred is basically saying is that the big picture is to put this out and then put Krogh's statement near it and then put Walters' statement. Well, basically it doesn't really fit. I don't think the Walters thing or the Krogh [thing fit]. . . . I think there's a tendency to try to make this into a massive thing. I regret—I think it's better to keep it—keep it a little bit more confused.

Now that Krogh thing [psychiatrist's office break-in]. I don't think there's any reason for us to say to take the—on the Krogh thing. I'll tell you why. The Krogh thing, I am sure, is not apart of this. Do you see my point? This was a—the Krogh thing was a separate White House operation to handle leaks and Ehrlichman had said that Krogh exceeded his authority on that particular one, correct?

HAIG: Right.

PRESIDENT NIXON: Now we get into this thing. This presents problems because of what—it's a big paper saying it. We shall have a domestic intelligence program and we'll do this, that and the other thing. Do you know what I mean? And involving this, that and the other thing. Now the real question is not the paper. The real question is what the hell was done under the plan. . . . [I]f what was done was minuscule, hell, I would just stand on it.

HAIG: If I recollect, one day I saw Tom Huston in the dining room and he said, I'm leaving and I said why. He said, I'm working on a project and nothing is happening. I bet you a dollar that nothing was done on that operation.

PRESIDENT NIXON: . . . Well, Goddamnit, it wasn't terrible to have such a plan.

HAIG: A period when the Goddamn [cops?] were being killed in the streets.

PRESIDENT NIXON: And I'm not—I don't want you to reassure me on something you don't believe in. My own view is, I still say, looking at these papers, in other words, Goddamnit, these—what that is is a plan for the purpose of domestic security, domestic security involving and there were foreign operations and foreign support for these damn things. Right? . . .

HAIG: Goddamn, this was one helluva place to be along about May of 1970.

PRESIDENT NIXON: This was simply an action plan which was basically a contingency plan.

HAIG: And we had a situation in which there were students killed at a school. The city of Washington was tore up. There were—dear God.

PRESIDENT NIXON: . . . This will be the thing that they'll try to say this is grounds for impeachment of the President. . . . You're not coming around to the resignation-thinking rationale, are you? . . .

HAIG: Don't be afraid to stir this one. . . . I think every civil libertarian knows that the mass, the majority, of the people of this country do not want to tolerate this bullshit. That is what the election is all about. . . .

PRESIDENT NIXON: Basically, in my case I am stuck with and have to be stuck with knowing Krogh talked to [Ehrlichman], you know, which I did and ordering Bob and John to go in and talk to Walters, which I did and approving this plan, which I did. . . . I didn't check to see whether there were burglaries and all that. God to hell, we didn't even think of such things. . . .

I think—let me say something. I think Buzhardt's thing perhaps looks very good, but . . . Ervin's got this and now this is all going to come out and so forth and so on, and so let's be prepared for the President to go on national television and attack them. . . . And to sweep—and to sweep Walters into this and to sweep Krogh into this. I don't think so. I don't think we need to. . . .

MAY 16, 1973: THE PRESIDENT, HAIG, AND BUZHARDT, 4:55–5:22 P.M., OVAL OFFICE

The President and his aides rationalize and justify the Huston Plan further.

PRESIDENT NIXON: . . . Huston got pissed off and left. He said nothing was ever done under this Goddamn thing. He said Hoover wouldn't allow it. . . . And he screwed it, and Al said that Huston recalls that I rescinded and I think that's right. I don't remember it, but I think what happened was that it just wasn't working or something like that. . . .

BUZHARDT: Let me give you where we are right now. Huston says his best recollection is that it was recalled. I want to search his files. He may have a copy. He thinks not but I sent him home to look.

PRESIDENT NIXON: Is he here in Washington?

BUZHARDT: No, sir. He's in Indianapolis.

PRESIDENT NIXON: He took his files with him? . . . Jesus Christ.

BUZHARDT: But next, he said that in August of 1970 John Dean came into the White House. He was moved to Dean's office and Dean took over his responsibilities with respect to this type of activity.

PRESIDENT NIXON: That's how Dean got it.

BUZHARDT: He said at the same time Mardian came in as assistant to the Attorney General for internal security. . . . And he's aware that Dean and Mardian formed a federal agency committee. He doesn't know anything about what they did. . . . He originally said he thinks he sent out a memorandum implementing the plan, told them it's your decision. . . . He said that he . . . thinks Hoover went to Mitchell. Mitchell came to you and you turned it off.

PRESIDENT NIXON: I don't recall except that I know that Mitchell had been— Hoover didn't like it worth a damn and wasn't working on it. But, you know what I mean. You see how it is with these things. I sat in one meeting and I don't recall anything else. . . . If Huston was the activist, and I know he didn't do a damn—did he know of anything while he was here?

BUZHARDT: *He said nothing was done while he was here.* You see, he left just after the approval of the thing as the record shows it. He moved to Dean's office and out he went and he says Dean took it over. He left in frustration of Hoover. He was just furious. . . . Then maybe Dean did something. I think if anything was done, it was done between Dean and Mardian. There was some activity, Mr. President. I know they had a committee. I know they produced intelligence reports. Whether they got it from direct of tape, whether they did anything extra, I don't know. I suspect, quite frankly, that we'll find that there's a fair likelihood that the Ellsberg thing was justified on this.

I know Bob Mardian quite well. . . . Bob was extremely aggressive. It may be that that's what he'll hang his hat on if he was involved. He may not have been, but we'll find out when we get him. In the meanwhile, we've got the others looking to see if there are any documents turning it on, turning it off or whatnot. I've got Huston looking in his files.

PRESIDENT NIXON: I'll lay you a little bet on that that Ellsberg was not justified. They may try to.

BUZHARDT: I say they may try to justify it.

PRESIDENT NIXON: I'll tell you what. I think they're separable. The Ellsberg thing was something that we set up. Let me tell you. I know what happened here and Al knows what happens. We set up in the White House a independent group under Bud Krogh to cover the problems of leaks involving, at the time, of the Goddamn Pentagon papers; right? Remember we called it—they called—I remember they called it the plumbers operation. That was independent. It was not connected with these things at all, not at all. They had no connection whatever with dealing with those. . . .

And may I say I think that, looking at our earlier conversation, I think we should treat them separately, treat them separately. I think this idea of saying, well, that could have been this and maybe the reason that—the reason that we had to check the Watergate buggers was because of this thing. Huh-uh. I don't think so. You see, I think you're going to find that this thing was either dead because—either in limbo or was one of those things that was never implemented. . . .

[L]let me say what I think, Fred. I'd like for you to think in totally separable terms. I don't want to get Ellsberg involved. We've got that where it belongs. Let Ellsberg be where it was. I mean, I'm sorry it broke and somehow I hope that California law isn't too tough on breaking and entering. Have you found out yet?

BUZHARDT: No, sir, I haven't is the answer to that.

PRESIDENT NIXON: Goddamn, let's hope it's a misdemeanor.

BUZHARDT: I hope so.

PRESIDENT NIXON: It should be. Incidentally, have you even been in touch with Krogh? . . . Some day will you call and just tell him that I thinks he's a helluva guy, will you?

HAIG: All right. . . .

PRESIDENT NIXON: Good. Okay. As far as this thing again, as far the Ellsberg—now as far as this thing itself is concerned, I would have anticipated that the idea that we're going to get all up in a—our balls in an uproar because something like this is going to make it come out. . . .

. . . [W]hat jingled my mind is when you said Huston left because he was pissed off and I do remember he was. . . an activist kind of a guy. He got pissed off and just took off and said it didn't work. Now I don't know whether somebody else did something. I would doubt it. I would doubt it.

BUZHARDT: I would doubt it. . . .

PRESIDENT NIXON: . . . But basically the worse kind of thing is, frankly, the Plumbers operation.

BUZHARDT: Yes.

PRESIDENT NIXON: Because that looks like one of these Goddamn clowns hired a bunch of people here. But here you've got the CIA, the DIA, the FBI, all working together on something.

BUZHARDT: And Internal Revenue.

PRESIDENT NIXON: Huh?

BUZHARDT: And Internal Revenue.

PRESIDENT NIXON: They did, too?

BUZHARDT: Yes.

PRESIDENT NIXON: There you are, all working on something like this. Well, God-damnit, now what? They all get together and get together a paper for the President of the United States. That's something that's pretty Goddamn important, isn't it? That's what's involved here. And it involves groups that were engaging in violence, disruption, and unbelievable hell around this place. The trouble is we didn't do much good with it, did we? Had a riot the next year. Let's see. Cambodia was in '71 [1970]. Yeah. May Day. . . . But I don't think the country is going to get excited about a damn plan that was drawn up by agencies to control the Goddamn riots. . . .

HAIG: . . . In fact, most people will say *thank God*. Again, if we had done less, we would have been irresponsible. You know, this is the farce of the whole thing. *God-damn, we're doing what's right for the people in the country*. You develop these vulnera-bilities. It's just something. . . .

PRESIDENT NIXON: Well, that may be a separate issue. But don't let us start getting all upset about this thing. This will be another story. That's all, in my view. In my view when this busts, it will be another Goddamn story. The President authorized a super-duper activity in 1970 and so forth for the purpose of doing that which involves bur-glary, *et cetera*. And wiretapping and there's your story. And what we plan to say is just say you're Goddamn right, however, we rescinded. I mean, we—it did not prove op-erable and so forth and so on. It was to deal with the specific problem at a specific time and it's been discontinued and was discontinued at such and such a time. . . . You see, with Dean gone the sonofabitch wouldn't put that in his file. Oh, the in-credible treachery of that sonofabitch.

MAY 16, 1973: BUZHARDT AND ROBERT MARDIAN, 4:57–9:33 P.M., WHITE HOUSE TELEPHONE

Buzhardt calls Robert Mardian, former Assistant Attorney General, Internal Se-curity Division, to confirm that the Huston Plan never was operational.

BUZHARDT: Bob, there were some documents that were released by the court today.

MARDIAN: Yes.

BUZHARDT: Which consisted of a certain domestic intelligence plan. . . . Now, this was handled here by a fellow named Huston until about August of '70, at which time Dean came aboard and took over the responsibility. . . . Some time along about that time you came aboard and formed a committee, interagency. . . . On the committee you ran, Bob, was it an analysis group solely and simply, or were there any activities?

MARDIAN: No activities whatsoever.

BUZHARDT: No collections?

MARDIAN: What?

BUZHARDT: No collections?

MARDIAN: No. The only activities was an attempt to—I understood this was at the direction of Ehrlichman or *the President,* actually. That's what they told me. And the only purpose was to—originally, it was set up in the White House, and then it was moved over to internal security because everybody—the various members of the intelligence group were concerned about everybody seeing them coming in and going out together when they had meetings. . . . And the sole purpose was to attempt to bring the intelligence to coordinate the activities of various law enforcement intelligence agencies within the government. . . . Now, . . . it was a White House operation, and moved over to my shop. And what they would do would be to respond to requests. There's a—I don't know whether you'd call it a charter, but an agreement as to what they would do, what their scope would be. . . .

BUZHARDT: All right. Let me ask you this, Bob. I have to know some specifics here. To your knowledge—and I need to know this on the square—were any surreptitious entries made specifically for this purpose?

MARDIAN: *Absolutely not.* Hell, no. . . . All they were doing was making assessments. . . . There would be a request for information concerning whatever it was the White House wanted, and an assessment was made. Copies went to the constituent liaison agency as well as the White House, and that's all. . . . They weren't operating anything. . . .

BUZHARDT: . . . Okay. To the best of your knowledge, I know the problem while Hoover was there. I'm sure there weren't any. But thereafter, you know of no entries made by the Bureau?

MARDIAN: Hell, no. No, sirree. Here again, not as a result of that operation. What the hell did they come up with as far as in these papers that indicates what this group was doing?

BUZHARDT: Well, I don't want to talk too specific over the phone. . . .

MAY 16, 1973: THE PRESIDENT, HAIG, AND BUZHARDT, 8:45–9:33 P.M., OVAL OFFICE

On the eve of the Senate hearings, the sense of crisis heightens. The President hears that the Huston Plan never was operative.

PRESIDENT NIXON: . . . We have to realize they're not after Bob or John or Henry or Haig or Ziegler. They're after the President. *Shit.* That's what it's all about. You know that . . . They want to destroy us.

HAIG: Yeah. What they're hung up on. They're really in a dilemma up there. They want to get you and yet they don't and that's tough for them, too. . . .

PRESIDENT NIXON: . . . You know, it's ridiculous that the President of the United States has to spend his time for the last—almost two months—worried about this horse's-ass crap. Unbelievable. Come in. Hi, Fred.

BUZHARDT: Yes, sir.

PRESIDENT NIXON: I hope you got something to eat. . . .

BUZHARDT: I'll get something. It's confirming out very well. . . . There are no documents. Apparently Huston was wrong. There was no document turning it on in the first place.

PRESIDENT NIXON: What is this document you've got in the file there?

BUZHARDT: That was from Haldeman telling Huston that the answer was yes that you had made the decision. . . . There was no action memorandum, though, to tell the people to go into business.

PRESIDENT NIXON: I see. . . .

BUZHARDT: Then what I'm told is that [J. Edgar Hoover's deputy, Clyde] Tolson found out about it and got to Hoover.

PRESIDENT NIXON: Clyde Tolson; right?

BUZHARDT: Clyde Tolson said this will ruin your image. Hoover then took his copy, footnoted it, screamed at Mitchell, got the issue raised. I think he may even have seen you. There ought to be an impression he did.

PRESIDENT NIXON: I think he did. Yeah.

BUZHARDT: And you suspended the operation. That's the word that he used. You suspended it out.

PRESIDENT NIXON: When?

BUZHARDT: It was within two days of it being issued to the best of their recollection.

PRESIDENT NIXON: Jesus Christ. [*Laughs.*]

BUZHARDT: It just took Hoover a reaction time. Tolson got to him. He came right back. [William] Sullivan thinks he has notes that will give us the precise times. But the whole thing was suspended immediately. . . .

PRESIDENT NIXON: . . . Let's get it nailed down. Let's knock the shit out of this one. Knock the ball right out of the park. . . .

MAY 17, 1973: THE PRESIDENT AND BUZHARDT, 8:44–9:36 A.M., OVAL OFFICE

The conversation focuses on Buzhardt's estimate of difficult situations. The opening material indicates how Nixon dealt cautiously with his lawyers, and how much they remained in the dark. Much of the conversation focuses on handling the news of the Huston Plan. Buzhardt assesses Senator Sam Ervin, indicating that the President has little to worry about from the Senate hearings that are about to begin.

SEGMENT 1

BUZHARDT: . . . [CIA Director] Jim Schlesinger already knows. . . . He knows that it was not—never went forward.

PRESIDENT NIXON: Yeah. I want him to know. . . .

BUZHARDT: He had some misgivings and I had a long talk with him and explained, I think, the Walters memorandum. I explained and sit him on down. I personally called Henry [Kissinger] and made the appointment and reassured (unintelligible).

PRESIDENT NIXON: You called Henry about this thing?

BUZHARDT: No, sir. Jim was a little worried about the—

PRESIDENT NIXON: Walters memorandum.

BUZHARDT: —Walters thing.

PRESIDENT NIXON: Yeah.

BUZHARDT: And so I—

PRESIDENT NIXON: Was he worried about presidential involvement?

BUZHARDT: Yes. So I went over and personally had a talk with him. Jim and I are kind of long-time friends.

PRESIDENT NIXON: I just wanted Jim to know that, by God, I am totally innocent of all those things. . . .

BUZHARDT: I explained that to him and he thinks so. . . . Now, this morning's *Washington Post*—they've already played the business. . . . Interestingly, they say that the series of burglaries, . . . they allege that these were not done by the agencies but done by separate front groups and special groups working out of the White House. Now that's the worse point, Mr. President.

PRESIDENT NIXON: The worse point is true.

BUZHARDT: Well, I doubt if it's true. You know, outside of this one group and all the evidence indicated that they really didn't do any others, you know. Hunt was telling everything. I went back and read his testimony this morning. He swore under oath and laid it all out. But he said no. They did no others.

PRESIDENT NIXON: They did no wiretapping. They did no burglaries.

BUZHARDT: No wiretaps and no burglaries except the one of the psychiatrist. Krogh's affidavit says he knew of no other such activities. . . .

PRESIDENT NIXON: I know of no other group whatever.

BUZHARDT: I have never heard of another group. Of course, we hadn't heard of this one either. . . . Incidentally, we're doing our monitoring on that [Senate] Committee by television. So nobody representing the White House will be in that room. . . .

PRESIDENT NIXON: Could you get a plane to get Sullivan flown down or something?

BUZHARDT: We'll get him flown down somehow or another.

PRESIDENT NIXON: And get an affidavit from him.

BUZHARDT: Right.

PRESIDENT NIXON: He is the key in the sense that it was turned off.

BUZHARDT: I think so. I think we need to bring Huston back, too.

PRESIDENT NIXON: Yes. He in California?

BUZHARDT: He's in Minneapolis.

PRESIDENT NIXON: Minneapolis. And you bring Huston back and Huston comes back and recalls his purple language, doesn't he. What did he tell you?

BUZHARDT: He told me it didn't go. He told me that it didn't go.

PRESIDENT NIXON: And that's what he remembers.

BUZHARDT: The decision went against him and that's why—he said, you know, I was really teed off and I left. He didn't say precisely that was the reason.

PRESIDENT NIXON: I know.

BUZHARDT: I was real teed off and I left.

PRESIDENT NIXON: If you know Tom Huston, that sounds like him. I've only met him about three or four times, that he's an explosive (unintelligible).

BUZHARDT: I think I met him when he was a college freshman, Mr. President.

PRESIDENT NIXON: He's smart as hell, smart, tough, ruthless. He did well and a decent man. I tell he just wants to do something.

BUZHARDT: That's true.

PRESIDENT NIXON: But Huston could have a memorandum because he was here at the White House and—

BUZHARDT: He looked last night. He hadn't found the memorandum in the files. He said he would not have taken anything that was classified with him. . . . Let me say candidly, I do not think we should try to run an investigation out of the White House at this point.

PRESIDENT NIXON: And run an investigation with a newspaper leak. Christ, there's a story of my house, for example, and things like that. There are going to be more and more and more.

BUZHARDT: There's going to be more.

PRESIDENT NIXON: . . . And they want to believe that we have every Goddamn newspaperman in town. How much we did was so, so insignificant. It's unbelievable.

BUZHARDT: There may have been some even you didn't know about, Mr. President. We can't tell how many. Private people do it.

PRESIDENT NIXON: I know. . . .

SEGMENT 2

BUZHARDT: . . . Schlesinger knows what's in the Dean papers.

PRESIDENT NIXON: What?

BUZHARDT: Schlesinger knows what's in the Dean papers.

PRESIDENT NIXON: How do you know?

BUZHARDT: Because I've talked to him.

PRESIDENT NIXON: Oh.

BUZHARDT: You see, the intelligence community is up there now trying to keep this [Huston Plan] from being published hoping there will be clear understanding there are serious national security implications, the release of these papers.

PRESIDENT NIXON: Well, [Senator] Stuart Symington [D-MO] will never, never play that game while they try to keep them from being published. (Unintelligible.)

BUZHARDT: I doubt it very seriously.

PRESIDENT NIXON: What?

BUZHARDT: I doubt very seriously that he will assist in preventing their disclosure. . . .

PRESIDENT NIXON: Are they going to let him read the papers?

BUZHARDT: Yes.

PRESIDENT NIXON: They're going to let him read the papers.

BUZHARDT: Yes.

PRESIDENT NIXON: And they're going to say what and they're—have they—

BUZHARDT: They're going to point out the sensitivity of—you see—

PRESIDENT NIXON: Can they point out that it didn't go?

BUZHARDT: Yes, sir.

PRESIDENT NIXON: I think they should.

BUZHARDT: [Exasperated; impatient] Yes. Yes, they will!

PRESIDENT NIXON: Can I suggest—

BUZHARDT: They will. They will.

PRESIDENT NIXON: Can I suggest that that's important that they do that.

BUZHARDT: Yes.

PRESIDENT NIXON: I mean, let's just say to point out that this was a study that was made. It had been going on back to '67, '68. It was approved and then approved to within two days the order was rescinded and no action whatever was ever taken under this program.

BUZHARDT: Yes.

PRESIDENT NIXON: He must be assured of that so that he—then he can go with more assurance. Or do you think we should talk to him?

BUZHARDT: He won't—if we tell it, he won't believe us, Mr. President.

PRESIDENT NIXON: Okay, then. Don't tell him.

BUZHARDT: I think we should tell him.

PRESIDENT NIXON: All right.

BUZHARDT: I think we should tell him. We should be quite candid with him that it did not go. Shouldn't leave the inference with him that it didn't. We shouldn't be a party to that. . . .

PRESIDENT NIXON: Well, he's [Ervin] putting the small fry in today.

BUZHARDT: Yes. These are going to be very leisurely hearings. . . . He's going to stretch it out.

PRESIDENT NIXON: He wants to be in the public eye for a long time. This is not in his interest, let me tell you, to be leisurely, not for a reason because there's—I'm fair judge on the public relations side. If you run them too leisurely, people can get bored as hell with them—

BUZHARDT: They will bore. . . . He's our biggest asset. Ervin.

PRESIDENT NIXON: Why?

BUZHARDT: He conducts *terrible* hearings, Mr. President.

PRESIDENT NIXON: Terrible person to preside?

BUZHARDT: Yes. He stutters, stammers—you can't understand his questions. He garbles them up. It's—he is not, you know—he's the opposite of Senator McClellan who sits quietly. One of the next mistakes he's making is he's going to let the members of the committee only do the interrogation. He is not going to let his counsel interrogate—

PRESIDENT NIXON: Thank God.

BUZHARDT: I breathed a sigh of relief when I found this out. . . .

MAY 17, 1973: THE PRESIDENT, ZIEGLER, HAIG, AND BUZHARDT, 10:31–11:30 A.M., OVAL OFFICE

Rumors fly that the White House had authorized a burglary of Senator Thomas Eagleton's doctor's office in 1972. More agonizing over Walters's memcoms and the Huston Plan. Nixon expresses some misgivings about Buzhardt: "There's a lot of crap going around here and, Al, I cannot ever be in a position with any staffer of having to say, look, fellas, I didn't do it." Haig is quick to defend his friend. Finally, Haig suggests that Nixon defend his actions as being necessary to counter the excesses of the 1960s.

ZIEGLER: . . . [T]hat's in the story today, too, that John Ehrlichman had the [Thomas] Eagleton file two weeks before it broke.

PRESIDENT NIXON: Eagleton? Do you mean his getting off the ticket?

ZIEGLER: His medical.

HAIG: His medical file [in] Philadelphia.

PRESIDENT NIXON: Oh, that was in the campaign, for crying out loud. I'm not concerned about that. That was something that came out of newspaper sources or something like that. I know the story on that. I'll tell you who had that. Pat Buchanan had it if that's what you're talking about.

BUZHARDT: We have some indication the doctor's office was burglarized, Mr. President.

PRESIDENT NIXON: Eagleton's doctor's office? . . .

HAIG: We got a letter from his doctor. . . .

BUZHARDT: We got a letter that came in two days ago.

PRESIDENT NIXON: Well, let me say. I will be utterly shocked. . . . I really would on that. The doctor's office—Eagleton's [situation] was one we had the slightest interest in except to let it ride. . . .

HAIG: . . . [I]t's in the papers this morning that Ehrlichman knew this well before it was made public which he may have and which may be damn good. It shows—

PRESIDENT NIXON: —dead news.

HAIG: That's right. The other thing he had this very worrisome letter.

PRESIDENT NIXON: A letter from a doctor?

HAIG: From the doctor.

BUZHARDT: It says that he was approached by security people to do something. It's very carefully phrased. . . . He doesn't refer to Eagleton. He doesn't refer to anything.

HAIG: He doesn't refer to Eagleton or anybody else but there's a linkage there. . . .

BUZHARDT: He was approached by a couple of security people. And asked to do something. He refused and shortly thereafter his office was burglarized. Now that's what the letter says. . . .

PRESIDENT NIXON: Who did he give that to?

BUZHARDT: He wrote that to Al Haig. Now, I think the only thing we can do under the circumstance is to give that letter to Petersen. . . . Stand away from it.

PRESIDENT NIXON: Stand away—stand away totally. Don't get in that because we know nothing about whatever it is—

BUZHARDT: We don't know anything about it.

PRESIDENT NIXON: Good God almighty, but in fairness shouldn't Ehrlichman be informed?

BUZHARDT: I don't think so. There's no relationship in this evidence to Ehrlichman. I mean, there's no indication of the level that's connected.

HAIG: And we don't even know that it is Eagleton. . . .

PRESIDENT NIXON: Was this before Eagleton—the Eagleton story broke?

BUZHARDT: I don't know. He did not give dates in his letter.

PRESIDENT NIXON: For Christ sakes, I know when the story broke. The story about Eagleton's drinking and all that sort of thing was well-known at the time he was nominated. Pat Buchanan comes from St. Louis. He thought all about that and that he had, also, been under medical treatment. That was, also, printed. I don't know. But anything about—we didn't do a Goddamn thing. All we did was sat back because we could win either way. I know Ehrlichman didn't do a damn thing on this. I just know he didn't do anything. . . .

BUZHARDT: . . . We need to get back to Dean. . . .

PRESIDENT NIXON: How does he look on television, for instance?

BUZHARDT: Oh, he looks very pretty.

HAIG: I think he looks like what he is, he looks like a weasel.

BUZHARDT: But he's going to look weak and he's way off base. He's going to be way off base. It's a long time before he'll be before that committee. . . .

[Buzhardt leaves.]

PRESIDENT NIXON: You should have very confidence in Buzhardt now. I don't mean in his work and intelligence, but also in his confidence. . . .

HAIG: I think he's the best possible man you could have gotten.

PRESIDENT NIXON: Good. Because he sees all this crap and he knows, however. He misinterprets it. Do you know what I mean? There's a lot of crap going around here and, Al, I cannot ever be in a position with any staffer of having to say, look, fellas, I didn't do it.

HAIG: Oh, God—

PRESIDENT NIXON: Do you understand that?

HAIG: —no. You haven't got that problem with him at all.

PRESIDENT NIXON: Okay. . . .

[Ziegler enters.]

ZIEGLER: I just watched a few minutes of that [Senate] committee. I'll tell you, it is going to be a farce.

PRESIDENT NIXON: Why?

ZIEGLER: Sam Ervin is just a pompous, fat. . . . Rob Odle [Director of Administration, CREEP] is doing a beautiful job. He's a smooth, good-looking guy. . . . I'll get to the typical water service [UPI reporter] Helen Thomas question, you know, has the President had a battery of TV sets set up and so on. Here's what I'm going to do. I'm just going to state—I'm going to say the President has made it clear that—

PRESIDENT NIXON: . . . "He cannot, just as you know, ladies and gentlemen, he does not have the time to watch the television programs. We did not or can. But he gets a full summary of the hearings insofar as they might bear on anybody in the White House. . . ."

On this so-called Walters memo, . . . it isn't going to kill us. It's going to embarrass us. I mean, it's going to embarrass us, you must remember, but not kill us, because there's some good stuff in it as well as bad stuff. . . . [I]f the Walters thing is going to come out, I don't want it to become a capital case. Let the damn thing out. In other words, I could simply say, well, we don't—the only reason we held it here is because of the security problems, but if you all work out the security problems, we'll let it come out. But understand I'm not going to give on it yet. . . .

HAIG: [Regarding the Houston Plan] It might be necessary to have the spokesman for the intelligence community, maybe all of them, maybe the key guys that participated in that committee. And have it explained in detail. Hand out the White Paper at a press conference, maybe a congressional meeting. It's not your business to be there. Goddamnit, this is the intelligence community.

PRESIDENT NIXON: Well, it was their recommendation to me and it was their recommendation to me that I approved, and it involved a lot of things. It's an unfortunate thing. The bad thing is that the President approved burglaries as a tactic.

HAIG: Yes. But, you know—that's right. That's—

PRESIDENT NIXON: That's tough. Real wild. . . .

HAIG: Then there's a possibility that you would want to rally the country on that issue. Look what has happened. Now is the time to get this thing back out and you speak no more on this subject, but here's what the facts were: boom, boom, boom. . . . And it may be the time, you see, to wipe out the hearings on a wave of popular revulsion. You see, that's all these things that can hurt you to where this might be what you want to do. It is a PR game. There is no Goddamn question about that. And we want to be able to think along a number of contingency lines as to the best way to do it. . . .

PRESIDENT NIXON: There's a long-term scheme that started in '69; right?

HAIG: (Unintelligible.)

PRESIDENT NIXON: Didn't start in '69.

HAIG: . . . There are those who would like to trace it back in the earlier [Johnson] administration as building of civil liberties, the over-concentration of power in the presidency. That's what this is all about.

PRESIDENT NIXON: That's why we've got to throw it back to '67, too.

HAIG: Damn right. That's the way you talk about that. What these polices were. These weren't anything new. This was a return to the policies of '67. Then you get every President who's ever—any man who's ever supported a presidency on the issue. . . . It is so easy to handle. Every American lives with his television watching this stuff, and it's the good guys that do it. And if they do it successfully, they're better guys. We haven't done it. We're not going to have difficulty with anything in that neighborhood. . . .

PRESIDENT NIXON: I still feel, myself, Al—I don't care what you say. They're trying to slop this whole damn thing right on us. You see, Watergate now is getting—I don't know. I don't know. They're now getting the CIA involved and mixing it up with that and then, of course, they'll try to mix it up with this. Maybe that's bad—bad in the sense that the country looking at Watergate as a caper the paper is one thing, but the country looking at Watergate in the context of, sort of a repressive fascist—

HAIG: That's the great danger. That's the one we've got to be so sensitive to . . . .

MAY 17, 1973: THE PRESIDENT AND BUZHARDT, 3:11–3:16 P.M., WHITE HOUSE TELEPHONE

The Senate Select Committee opens its hearings and Buzhardt gives Nixon a report of the proceedings. The President attempts a light-hearted, cavalier response.

PRESIDENT NIXON: . . . What's the situation in—I guess the Ervin Committee grinds on today.

BUZHARDT: The Ervin Committee grinds on. They're down to the arresting officer now and going through the tedium of that.

PRESIDENT NIXON: Somebody told me it's a very dull show. I haven't looked at it.

BUZHARDT: It is a very dull show.

PRESIDENT NIXON: Is it?

BUZHARDT: And you know, the commentators are talking about the impact this will have on the trials, too. . . . [I]t helps the defense, because all of the networks are going gavel-to-gavel coverage nationwide, and you've got that preemption and that's I guess kind of historic. I don't know any other hearing that has been gavel to gavel with really a preemption, all networks.

PRESIDENT NIXON: All daytime television.

BUZHARDT: Yes.

PRESIDENT NIXON: Let me tell you, they're going to find that they're going to lose their audience with that stuff. People will be looking for late, late shows. That's a dull thing. A committee hearing is dull as hell. . . . Unless you've got a striking witness, like a Joe McCarthy. . . . I remember Joe McCarthy and Welch. That was good. But the rest of that hearing was dull as dishwater.

BUZHARDT: It really was. . . .

MAY 17, 1973: THE PRESIDENT AND ZIEGLER, 10:41–10:54 P.M., WHITE HOUSE TELEPHONE

Ziegler is refreshingly frank in an evening talk with the President, trying to keep him focused on making rational, effective counterattacks. Two hours later, the President calls Ziegler again, apparently distressed, and looking to Ziegler to boost his spirits. The youthful Press Secretary handles the President very carefully in this strange, sad conversation.

ZIEGLER: . . . What we're talking about, Mr. President, is the presidency.

PRESIDENT NIXON: I understand that.

ZIEGLER: And we're talking about being a very cold, not weak, but very cold, thorough, calculating analysis of what we're up against. . . . I don't say that out of a sense of concern or panic or—

PRESIDENT NIXON: Desperation.

ZIEGLER: —or desperation or feeling of (unintelligible), but just a sense of how you approach a battle.

PRESIDENT NIXON: Right. We're in a battle and we've got to fight it and fight it on our ground and not on theirs.

ZIEGLER: Yes, sir. And in order to fight it, we've got to really, quite frankly, cut through any sense of, on the part of those who are here, any sense of reaching for the false premise, reaching for the sense of false sense of the situation, and just deal absolutely with reality. . . . And in the coldest terms. And people don't matter. I don't mean—I'm not talking about people don't matter from the standpoint of a purge or anything of that sort, but—

PRESIDENT NIXON: But other people than the President.

ZIEGLER: *Nothing matters. Nothing matters.* And I don't say that out of—you know, I say that out of, of course, loyalty—

PRESIDENT NIXON: I understand what you mean. . . .

ZIEGLER: . . . My point is those around you cannot in any way look at their self-interest. There's only one thing involved here.

PRESIDENT NIXON: Yeah.

ZIEGLER: And that's the presidency. . . .

PRESIDENT NIXON: No, no, no, no. You're absolutely right, absolutely right. And I have reached that conclusion. You know, it's an interesting thing. Your attitudes sort of change, and my view is that in the last week, you know, since the sixth of May, let's face it, we've started fighting it. . . . It's taken us a little time to try to get in the mood and everything, and at the Cabinet tomorrow we're going to be strong and firm. Don't you agree? . . .

ZIEGLER: That's right. In other words, what I'm saying, we shouldn't dwell on the Dean problem.

PRESIDENT NIXON: I think we've probably over-dwelled on it, don't you think?

ZIEGLER: Oh, I don't know. We've thought it through well and put it in perspective . . . .

PRESIDENT NIXON: Well, the hell with it. I mean, we just cannot be in the position, Ron, of, you know, every day of simply getting all disturbed about some fact that a psychiatrist's office was broken into in New York [*sic:* Beverly Hills] or that Dean is going to have some papers or this or that.

ZIEGLER: That's right.

PRESIDENT NIXON: Goddamnit, that's what's wrong. The point is the President is involved here and we're going to fight to maintain the leadership of this office and of this country, Goddamnit. That's what we're around for, and we're not going to let this issue drag us down. . . . And, as a matter of fact, looking at this week and the next week and so forth, we are, from the standpoint of public presidential things, we're doing rather well. I mean, you know, you can't overdo that damn thing.

ZIEGLER: Sure, that's right.

PRESIDENT NIXON: But, on the other hand, in fighting this other battle, why it's—by God, we've got to do it. And also, Ron, we've got to—I mean, let's face it. Our fellows that are under attack, to wit, Haldeman, Ehrlichman, Colson, they've got to get into this damn battle. . . . I think their own interests require that.

ZIEGLER: Well, but also, as much as I love them, their interests—

PRESIDENT NIXON: If they conflict—

ZIEGLER: —is their interest [laughs]. I'm not saying we move away from anyone. . . .

PRESIDENT NIXON: Well, just like the terrible decision we had to make on the 30th of April. . . . We made it, and I—you still think that was right, do you [*chuckles*]?

ZIEGLER: Oh, absolutely, absolutely. . . .

PRESIDENT NIXON: Even though it didn't help us much, at least it avoided a hurt; is that it?

ZIEGLER: It helped us a great deal, helped us a great deal.

PRESIDENT NIXON: How?

ZIEGLER: Well, it helped us because we are not dealing at this moment with—you know, we're not talking about whether or not individuals leave or take a leave of absence. We're talking about whether or not they have access to White House cars.

PRESIDENT NIXON: Right. That's a hell of a lot different problem.

ZIEGLER: A lot different problem. And we're not talking about things that are breaking and impacting on the presidency. You know, we're talking about strong men involved in this, who are out there.

PRESIDENT NIXON: But let us not—I understand that, but let us not underestimate. These guys, without our doing a thing, are going to help us, in my opinion.

ZIEGLER: Oh, I think so, yes, sir.

PRESIDENT NIXON: I mean, good God, I mean, because—look, the best answer to Dean, Goddamnit, is not us but, frankly, it's Ehrlichman. Or you don't agree?

ZIEGLER: Well, I don't know if I agree with that. I don't disagree with it. But I think this is all part of that cold assessment we're talking about, and it's not important talking about tonight. . . .

MAY 18, 1973: THE PRESIDENT AND HALDEMAN, 12:49–1:52 P.M., EXECUTIVE OFFICE BUILDING

The President and Haldeman frankly admit that the purpose of inaugurating the cover-up was to protect the secrets of other White House operations, notably the Plumbers. They discuss their use of General Walters. The raising and using of hush money is rationalized in a unique way, with Nixon disavowing any contact with Thomas Pappas. Haldeman reports on the opening of the Ervin hearings. The two men engage in a surreal discussion of the strategy of forcing an impeachment vote, incorrectly believing the House of Representatives would vote merely because Congresswoman Bella Abzug [D-NY] offered a motion. Nixon raises the possibility of resignation, which Haldeman dutifully discourages. Haldeman remains a loyal, faithful retainer.

PRESIDENT NIXON: Robert?

HALDEMAN: Hi.

PRESIDENT NIXON: Come in. It's good to see your face.

HALDEMAN: Back at it, huh?

PRESIDENT NIXON: Always back at it. . . . Bob, . . . tell me the honest-to-God truth, were we trying to get Walters and Gray put together (unintelligible)? If we were, I need to know it. . . .

HALDEMAN: . . . [There] was that one meeting, and that's all. And I did not know that there were Dean meetings. John says he didn't know there were Dean meetings subsequently. And I don't ever recall, even in the—

PRESIDENT NIXON: As far as that meeting is concerned, . . . people get in here and say we don't want this to go further. Let's find out what the hell the score is. Walters go over and see Gray. Gray said there were CIA people involved, was

Mexican money involved? (Unintelligible) I'm more concerned about that—the Plumbers operation—

HALDEMAN: —the whole question of where this can lead outside the Watergate. We were not concerned about the investigation on Watergate.

PRESIDENT NIXON: Not at all.

HALDEMAN: We were concerned about the investigation expanding beyond, for reasons that now we have no problem saying, because all that stuff is out.

PRESIDENT NIXON: Is out. We'll say that that's exactly the reason.

HALDEMAN: And it is exactly the reason, is because we didn't want the Plumbers' operation out.

PRESIDENT NIXON: In other words, you don't think I should be impeached for that?

HALDEMAN: No. You were doing what you had to do to defend your own operations in here, your own—

PRESIDENT NIXON: . . . Well, now, I'm not going to go through impeachment (unintelligible).

HALDEMAN: The way—I think we've got to put it out. And this was Ehrlichman's view the other day. This is the point he was making to them, and I think they had a miss—from what Al tells me, we had a misreading of Ehrlichman's position on this, which I'd like to correct, because I know exactly what his position is. John feels very strongly, and he's talked to Buzhardt and to Ziegler and made the point that on the CIA thing you're making a mistake at the White House to let this be drawn out by the committee, that the White House should still get out ahead of it.

PRESIDENT NIXON: Get the memcom out this afternoon.

HALDEMAN: And say what happened, and say why it happened.

PRESIDENT NIXON: That's right. I agree.

HALDEMAN: And John, in impressing that on us, said inevitably someone's going to have to do that at some point. It's infinitely better for the White House to do it—

PRESIDENT NIXON: Better than (unintelligible).

HALDEMAN: —then for John Ehrlichman to do it, which, if they get it in the grand jury or if they get it at the trial or at the Senate or if [Senator] McClellan calls me up to his committee, which he said he's going to do. Then I've got to say it, and then it sounds like an Ehrlichman or Haldeman defense rather than an offensive of why the thing was really done, which—

PRESIDENT NIXON: I ordered the meeting. I directed that you get together, didn't I?

HALDEMAN: Yes, sir, you did.

PRESIDENT NIXON: You remember I said get Walters and Helms, remember?

HALDEMAN: I can't remember why we ended up or why it was to have Walters go over. That, you know, is a question they raised, why we bypassed Helms and sent Walters.

PRESIDENT NIXON: It might have been because Helms was busy with other things. . . .

HALDEMAN: I said it was the President's wish that Walters call on Gray and suggest to him that since the five burglars had been arrested this should be sufficient and was not (unintelligible) going to be (unintelligible), especially in Mexico, et cetera. . . . I raised that point, or John did, and that was one of the questions we were supposed to determine in that meeting—was the CIA involved in the Watergate or any of their people involved?

PRESIDENT NIXON: That's right.

HALDEMAN: And Helms said no. And the next point was that the investigation of the Watergate, they got these five suspects arrested who are related to CIA, and they're talking about Hunt. They hadn't arrested Hunt yet, but they were talking about it at that point, who we knew was involved in the plumbers thing. And we were concerned about the investigation going beyond Watergate. I think we've got to admit to that.

PRESIDENT NIXON: Absolutely.

HALDEMAN: Because it's true. We were. As a matter of fact, we were concerned and emphasized, and I think Dean probably emphasized to the Justice Department, to Silbert and everybody else, that this should be limited to the Watergate. And Kleindienst probably did too.

PRESIDENT NIXON: I did too.

HALDEMAN: And I don't think there's anything wrong with that, because we knew that these (unintelligible) incidents, these characters had been involved in another activity, and we also knew that they'd been involved in another activity much earlier, the Bay of Pigs. And there was concern, as I recounted, which he doesn't mention at all here, about the Bay of Pigs, and I specifically got into that point, or John did, at that meeting.

PRESIDENT NIXON: You had a memorandum on that?

HALDEMAN: No, but I sure as hell remember it, because I remember being interested in Helms's reaction to it, because I didn't quite understand what the interest was in the Bay of Pigs question, but I knew you had some interest in it. And Walters—I mean, Helms said, oh, no. He kind of jumped on that fast, too fast, too hastily, you know. He said, oh, we have no problem with the Bay of Pigs, of anything, and that surprised me, because I had gotten the impression from you that the CIA did have some concern about the Bay of Pigs.

And his impression was, oh, you know, we've not concerned about (unintelligible). We have nothing to hide on the Bay of Pigs. Well, now Ehrlichman tells me in just the last few days that that isn't true. CIA was very concerned about the Bay of Pigs, and in the investigation apparently he was doing on the Bay of Pigs stuff at some point there is a key memo missing that CIA or somebody has caused to disappear that impeded the effort to find out what really did happen on the Bay of Pigs.

In any event, we raised the concern about the investigation going too far, that (unintelligible) that CIA was involved, the question of the Bay of Pigs, and I guess—I don't remember it, but I have to (unintelligible) he says it—the point that we had heard there was some question of Mexican money involved in this and raised the question is the Mexico money CIA.

PRESIDENT NIXON: Yeah, that's right.

HALDEMAN: And does that get into covert sources. Now, we don't know what the Mexican money is.

PRESIDENT NIXON: I had no idea at that time.

HALDEMAN: And I don't think we did, because it hadn't come out in the paper yet about the Mexican money. It came out a couple days later. So we probably knew about the Mexican money from Dean. And, the fifth point—(unintelligible) the fourth point—the fifth point was that the FBI had indicated, I think through Dean, that they were concerned about the CIA, and even later than that they kept coming back that they thought there was CIA involvement, or at least Dean said so.

And this now goes back to, I think, you have a second case here, and this is somehow what has got to be gotten out, of Dean picking up a different line of inquiry than this, because if you look at the memcoms even, the line of inquiry that we laid out fits with the memcom that he writes.

PRESIDENT NIXON: Incidentally, with that, just thinking of the game plan, without those memcoms, shouldn't a statement by you and Ehrlichman be put out at the same time, or would that hurt you?

HALDEMAN: It doesn't hurt us.

PRESIDENT NIXON: It would help a great deal to add to your recollection of the meeting.

HALDEMAN: You know, it's interesting. I hadn't noticed this before, but it's interesting that Walters didn't write these memcoms until June 28, which was—he then went back after he had had three meetings with—

PRESIDENT NIXON: Dean.

HALDEMAN: —Dean.

PRESIDENT NIXON: I know, and then saw it all in that kind of context.

HALDEMAN: Then went back and wrote the things. The only connection between the Dean meetings is this thing of Dean saying you can check with Ehrlichman on the phone.

PRESIDENT NIXON: Dean told who?

HALDEMAN: Dean called Walters on June 26, three days later, said he wanted to see him about the matter that Ehrlichman and Haldeman had discussed with him on the 23rd, and I can check this out with them if I wish. I called Ehrlichman to find out if this was all right, and after some difficulty I reached him and he said I could probably (unintelligible). Well, that's possible, too, although Ehrlichman says that didn't happen. . . .

PRESIDENT NIXON: We've got to get back to the Dean memo.

HALDEMAN: And to the whole Tom Huston project and all that stuff.

PRESIDENT NIXON: Well, that's—we've got a good record on that. . . . I would put the whole Goddamn thing out and let the whole schmear sit there. . . .

HALDEMAN: But it's not Watergate. . . .

PRESIDENT NIXON: The wiretaps, the Plumbers operation (unintelligible), the unanimous recommendation of the intelligence agencies that this has to be developed, and then turned off.

HALDEMAN: I knew it had never started.

PRESIDENT NIXON: No. It was turned off, solid evidence, (unintelligible), affidavits from you three and statements from everybody that it was turned off (unintelligible). [William] Sullivan called them on the phone and said—Hoover objected to it.

HALDEMAN: Yeah, I remember that.

PRESIDENT NIXON: And so they turned it off.

HALDEMAN: Hoover refused to cooperate, so it must be specifically directed on each case by the Attorney General. . . .

PRESIDENT NIXON: So it was turned off, period, the whole policy paper was withdrawn.

HALDEMAN: Of course then they make the case that that being turned off led to doing illicit things in order to accomplish the same thing they were trying to accomplish.

PRESIDENT NIXON: Well, what did they do?

HALDEMAN: (Unintelligible) the Plumbers operation, another break-in involving the Plumbers operation. . . .

. . . You were aware, as everybody was, in a general sense that there were the Cuban defense fund and that sort of thing. You were aware of that.

PRESIDENT NIXON: I sure was.

HALDEMAN: And that, a perfectly logical thing, that funds were being raised to defend these people who had been caught doing something over there, and there was some sense of obligation by the Committee [CREEP] to take care of their legal needs and so on. That in itself there's nothing wrong with. Where it's wrong is if they tie that, if they can conclusively tie that to an effort to get them not to testify. . . . Then there was an effort to obstruct justice.

PRESIDENT NIXON: That's right.

HALDEMAN: And the problem is that it now appears after the fact that that was the case. Then, however, according to our attorneys, one must go back and establish the intent of the individual participating in such a conspiracy. In other words, the fact of his having, of my having moved the 350 [$350,000] over there or having approved Kalmbach raising money for over there is not in itself involvement in the conspiracy unless we intended that that be used for the purpose of—

PRESIDENT NIXON: Silencing them.

HALDEMAN: —causing them not to testify.

PRESIDENT NIXON: And, Bob, that was not—

HALDEMAN: And that was not our purpose.

PRESIDENT NIXON: No, sir. Wasn't John's purpose in launching Kalmbach.

HALDEMAN: But there was an interest in keeping them from getting off the reservation, as Dean put it, in terms of talking about their other activities. And there was a concern about that. That's why laying down this groundwork and this stuff could be helpful. . . . Dean is raising the point that there was a problem of a question of a conspiracy to obstruct.

PRESIDENT NIXON: That's right. I know.

HALDEMAN: But that's the first time we hear about that problem.

PRESIDENT NIXON: From our lawyer.

HALDEMAN: From our lawyer. And now we know that—well, we don't know, but now I suspect that he was an integral part of that conspiracy. . . .

PRESIDENT NIXON: Bob, he never mentioned . . . it on the 28th, the 29th, the 30th, the 31st. The first time he ever mentioned a Goddamn thing to me was on the 21st of March—I mean about the demand for money and so forth. Right?

HALDEMAN: I think so. That demand had just come in at that point.

PRESIDENT NIXON: . . . [T]homas Pappas was being helpful.

HALDEMAN: That's right.

PRESIDENT NIXON: But what in the hell he was being helpful on nobody told me, and I didn't discuss it with Pappas.

HALDEMAN: Well, there again it was the same effort to raise money that I was aware of that I had no knowledge was a problem.

PRESIDENT NIXON: . . . [Dean] brought up the Pappas thing and said—

HALDEMAN: (Unintelligible) knew Pappas was being helpful.

PRESIDENT NIXON: Yeah. I didn't know what the hell he was raising for. . . .

HALDEMAN: My position is that what you've got to do is put all this out, and I think it should not be the President going on television. It's not a television-type story. It should be a very careful document issued by the White House—

PRESIDENT NIXON: That's what they're working on now.

HALDEMAN: —which puts these matters into perspective and so on, and that—I think Buzhardt's idea of then demanding an impeachment vote is over-grandstanding it and also moving out—Haig seems to think maybe that's a good idea.

PRESIDENT NIXON: He's for it. . . .

HALDEMAN: They can vote every day on it if they want to.

PRESIDENT NIXON: On impeachment, let them go on impeachment. . . .

HALDEMAN: The House would never vote to impeach, so there would never be a trial. . . . You can't stop an impeachment vote, if any Member asks for it.

PRESIDENT NIXON: Only one?

HALDEMAN: As I understand it, it only takes one. If a Member moves to impeach and the motion is seconded, then all business of the House stops immediately and this becomes the privileged business, and the House must move to debate and vote on the matter of impeachment.

PRESIDENT NIXON: Well, that's probably what we're up against. . . .

HALDEMAN: I think you've got to face the possibility that you may, because you've got a Bella Abzug or somebody who, with one of her cohorts, is capable of the motion and second or whatever it is that's required. . . . I can see some appeal to that strategy that Buzhardt argues of having an impeachment vote and having it not carry. . . .

The people in this country are thinking, for God's sake, get this Goddamn mess cleared up so we can watch the soap operas on television. They've ruined their whole television thing. So you get the whole thing out, and you say there are the facts. . . . I tell you, Rob Odle [the first witness]—you probably didn't see any of it, but, Jesus Christ, this guy deserves to be Secretary of State when this thing's over.

PRESIDENT NIXON: I understand he handled himself very well.

HALDEMAN: He did a superb job, and he came on with an opening statement that was a real tearjerker and it came from this, you know, bespectacled, clerk-looking type, young, baby-faced young guy who just said, as strongly as he could, what great people he had worked with in this campaign, and they were dedicated to the service of the greatest President this country's had, and made his whole pitch and was one heck of a guy.

He did a hell of a job in answering the questions, and of showing the conviction of what needed to be done while not being ground down by anybody. And that's the attitude that we need to establish, I think, out of here and that then all of us have got to back up, which is that the things that were being done—you've got to separate the problems of the leaks and the internal security problems and all that sort of thing from the Watergate and the campaign. You've got to justify, and proudly so, and say we would have been, given the circumstances—

PRESIDENT NIXON: Derelict.

HALDEMAN: —derelict in our duty. In fact, we probably were derelict in not going further than we went. If we're subject to any criticism, it was in not pursuing the thing more vigorously and letting some things get away, like the Pentagon Papers. . . .

PRESIDENT NIXON: When you come down to it, Bob, I raise this as a devil's advocate. . . . Don't tell me this unless you believe it, Goddamnit, because I've got to have good advice now. . . . Maybe (unintelligible) [I should] resign on the basis you can't do your job because of all this (unintelligible), et cetera, et cetera, and you've got to resign in order to clear your name. Shit. I can't do it, Bob.

[Withdrawn item. Privacy.]

HALDEMAN: My resigning didn't clear my name. My resigning proved to everybody in the world except the few people that believe in me that I'm guilty.

PRESIDENT NIXON: The same as John.

HALDEMAN: And your resigning will prove it conclusively. It will prove that you're guilty and that I'm guilty and that everybody else in here is guilty.

PRESIDENT NIXON: So, therefore, your view is fight (unintelligible).

HALDEMAN: Because you aren't guilty.

PRESIDENT NIXON: I know I'm not.

HALDEMAN: You won't clear your name by resigning. . . . But, see my resigning doesn't shake the whole world; your resigning does. My resigning was necessary for other reasons. . . .

May 18, 1973: The President, Haig, and Ziegler, 1:55–2:55 p.m., Executive Office Building

Further talk of resignation and impeachment. Haig supplies a corrective to Haldeman's earlier misinformation. At this late date, Nixon brazenly says that he knew nothing about the Plumbers, Hunt, Liddy, or the surveillance of Senator Kennedy.

PRESIDENT NIXON: Shit. If I were to resign, I would admit the whole Goddamn thing. If I resign because they've made my job too hard, everybody will say the son-ofabitch is guilty. I'm not going to do that, damnit.

HAIG: That would be impossible.

PRESIDENT NIXON: I've got to fight it out.

HAIG: Of course you're going to fight it out.

PRESIDENT NIXON: Now, the idea of trying to trigger impeachment, it may come anyway.

ZIEGLER: That is the worst thing we could even consider.

PRESIDENT NIXON: Well, the point about that, according to Haldeman, he said impeachment required only one member moving it and one member seconding it, and we would have impeachment.

HAIG: It would go to a committee first. I've looked into it. . . .

PRESIDENT NIXON: It goes to a committee first? It might be a select committee? . . . Well, thank God. I don't want the impeachment.

ZIEGLER: No, sir.

PRESIDENT NIXON: I do not—look, going through an impeachment—you see, if it goes to impeachment, I would have to go through a trial, which I would have to do, because otherwise (unintelligible) it all. But if you have an impeachment fight down there in Congress and the President of the United States (unintelligible), shit. . . .

ZIEGLER: Now, we know, going back, that the President did not offer clemency. We also know that the only reference ever to that question was a compassionate statement in relation to Hunt. . . .

PRESIDENT NIXON: With Colson.

ZIEGLER: With Colson. . . .

PRESIDENT NIXON: Let me say I am sure there was talk of clemency. There was. There had to be, and Dean and maybe Ehrlichman participated in it. But I know that nobody offered a Goddamn thing. You know what I mean? Well, I mean—I never did, and I'm sure Ehrlichman never said the President says go ahead and do it, but not too much, or something like that. You know what I mean? . . .

ZIEGLER: Did those Plumbers take anything (unintelligible) that if not illegal could be embarrassing—the whole Kennedy Chappaquiddick thing or (unintelligible).

PRESIDENT NIXON: That's Colson, and I'll be Goddamned if I know, to be perfectly frank with you. Goddamned if I know. . . . Colson can answer that. I didn't tell you. I don't know anything. I had never even heard who Hunt, Liddy, et cetera, were—you know what I mean? The only people I ever talked to were Krogh and Young, and about national security. Colson talked to me about all kinds of political activities. You know what I mean? We ought to investigate Chappaquiddick and all that sort of thing, but he never talked about anything illegal—never, never, never, not to me. But Colson should be asked. . . .

MAY 18, 1973: THE PRESIDENT AND HAIG, 8:49–9:06 P.M., WHITE HOUSE TELEPHONE

Haig responds to the hearings, but with a harder edge. There is again talk of resignation, but unlike earlier references laced with sarcasm and irony, the remarks now have a more somber tone. Attorney General Richardson has indicated that Archibald Cox is his choice for Special Counsel. The President is resigned to accepting him as the best of a bad lot.

SEGMENT 1

PRESIDENT NIXON: . . . But, you see, getting the President out on national television saying there's a hell of a crisis and so forth I think has a tendency to overplay the Ervin hearings, overplay me, overplay that I'm guilty and I'm going to resign, and all that bullshit. Goddamnit, I'm not going to do that. . . . It'll get tougher, you see.

HAIG: Oh, it's going to get tougher. . . .

PRESIDENT NIXON: . . . Richardson [soon] will have his prosecutor and all that horseshit.

HAIG: I see he got a humdinger.

PRESIDENT NIXON: Who'd he get?

HAIG: A fellow named [Archibald] Cox that used to be Solicitor General for Kennedy.

[Withdrawn item. Privacy.]

PRESIDENT NIXON: But he's very well respected.

HAIG: Yes, conscientious.

PRESIDENT NIXON: I don't think he's too bad. Did he take him?

HAIG: Well, they haven't endorsed him yet, but he's out, and it would be hard for them not to.

PRESIDENT NIXON: Oh, Christ. If he asks Cox to do this, they can't turn Cox down, believe me.

HAIG: No. I don't see how they can.

PRESIDENT NIXON: Cox is not a mean man. He's a partisan, but not that mean.

HAIG: That's right. That's the description I got. He's not a zealot.

[Withdrawn item. Privacy.]

PRESIDENT NIXON: Believe me, if he'd get Cox, that'd be great. Fine. Fine.

MAY 20, 1973: THE PRESIDENT AND HALDEMAN, 12:26–12:54 P.M., CAMP DAVID TELEPHONE

The President decides to counterattack forcefully and deny any use of the CIA for the cover-up. He plans to invoke images of the turbulent days of protest and violence in the 1960s. The conversation centers on Nixon and Haldeman's coordinating their stories. They discuss the Huston plan, and again, the President expresses concern about keeping Ehrlichman on the reservation.

PRESIDENT NIXON: What did they [the media] get you there about?

HALDEMAN: . . . I don't pay much attention to the questions because I don't answer them.

PRESIDENT NIXON: Right. Good.

HALDEMAN: Same thing—I did get a chance—the raised—I made my usual pitch about, you know, that I'm cooperating fully and that I know when the truth is known, you know, it's all going to clear it up. And then they said something about, well, did the President know anything about the [Richard] Helms meeting or something like that. And I said, as I said before, I'm not going to comment in any specific questions. I can't tell you flatly and categorically that the President had absolutely no knowledge or involvement in any kind of cover-up or anything else related to the Watergate in any way, shape or form.

PRESIDENT NIXON: Good. . . . The general statements are the best to make.

HALDEMAN: And I just left it at that. I'm not going to get into—

PRESIDENT NIXON: That's right.

HALDEMAN: —the specifics at this point.

PRESIDENT NIXON: Yeah. We'll get into that. Look, I don't want to hold you if you were just going to have lunch or something. Do you have about a couple of minutes? I can go over three or four and nail them down.

HALDEMAN: Sure.

PRESIDENT NIXON: What we're planning to do, first, with regard to the—I'm planning probably to meet with the leaders including—bipartisan leaders—including Armed Services Committee. And I'm going to put out all of the national security kind of stuff which incidentally is going to be very helpful, not so far from your standpoint, but John's [Ehrlichman] standpoint because I'm going to take—say that I ordered the plumbers operation, that I ordered the meeting. I'm going to say that I directed that you and John meet with Helms and Walters for the purpose of seeing whether the CIA was involved and so forth and so on. I think this is a good idea. Don't you think so?

HALDEMAN: Absolutely. I think it's essential. . . .

PRESIDENT NIXON: And we put the issue out where it belongs, that you're Goddamn right we had a meeting and so forth.

HALDEMAN: Right.

PRESIDENT NIXON: And so forth. You see, the only difficulty—well, the difficulty with the so-called Helms, I mean, the memoran—I mean, Walters' memcoms is an indication that—is the follow-up of Dean's, you see, where he went and asked for cover because the implication there would be that you and John and, of course, then the President, that we set up this whole Goddamn thing for the purpose of getting the CIA to put a cover on this and so forth which is not the truth.

HALDEMAN: Right.

PRESIDENT NIXON: And John [Ehrlichman] flatly will testify to that effect or has, I assume. I just want to be sure you know that we don't put anything in this statement that is not—

HALDEMAN: Right.

PRESIDENT NIXON: —papers that is going to be at all contrary to what he says. Perhaps you and John have talked about it. You had your meeting, but the purpose of the meeting was the four things that you mentioned.

HALDEMAN: That's right. . . .

PRESIDENT NIXON: And the whole Plumbers operation, I'm going to take that. Also, I want you—I deliberately am only calling you because I don't want to talk to John. . . .

On the famous Dean papers, you'll be interested—pleased to know that we've got that nailed down on all four corners [news of the Huston Plan].

HALDEMAN: Good.

PRESIDENT NIXON: The go order was issued by you, I mean, you and carried out by Huston on one day and then 24–48 hours later a no order was issued, and everybody—and we have affidavits on that and some have notes on it that they have the no order. The other point is that nothing whatever was done by any of the agencies involved.

HALDEMAN: That's what I thought.

PRESIDENT NIXON: You know, what I mean is there were no break-ins. . . . Now it's a rough one. I mean, not rough on us so much, but it's rough in terms of these agencies recommending everything from surreptitious entry to—

HALDEMAN: Yeah.

PRESIDENT NIXON: —bugging to everything else. Yet the point is—

HALDEMAN: But it was signed by all of them.

PRESIDENT NIXON: They all recommended it.

HALDEMAN: Yeah.

PRESIDENT NIXON: It was unanimous.

HALDEMAN: Well, that's good because that shows the tenor of the times.

PRESIDENT NIXON: Yeah.

HALDEMAN: That needs to be done.

PRESIDENT NIXON: It needs to be done, Bob. Also, I'll point out the plumbers thing. Why we did it, that we had massive leaks and that I had given orders to all departments to do everything that they could and at the White House we developed the capability to do what we could there.

HALDEMAN: Yeah.

PRESIDENT NIXON: And that everything that we did there was on that. Now on the point, just a couple of things to nail down. I want to be sure because I don't want to do a damn thing that would be at all harmful or inconsistent with what you or John may have recalled and, therefore, have testified to. I have no recollection of John ever telling me about the unsuccessful break-in or whatever it was until after, I mean, until we got into the March period.

HALDEMAN: The psychiatrist?

PRESIDENT NIXON: Yes. And I don't know what his recollection is. Do you know?

HALDEMAN: That's what I recall, too, but I can check it with him.

PRESIDENT NIXON: The point is that he once said that he thought that I knew and I don't remember. I have no recollection of his coming in and saying, look, Krogh's or the group did this. Do you know what I mean? You see, John says that, you know, Krogh stood up like a man and took the blame for it. . . . But I don't remember, Bob, John ever telling me, look, there was an unsuccessful break-in to a psychiatrist's office and you should know it. Will you narrow that one down for me because I don't want to say it unless it's true.

HALDEMAN: Yeah. . . .

PRESIDENT NIXON: If I had to know, I had to know. But, I—what I meant is I don't want—I don't want John to get up and testify to the effect, well, I told the President something.

HALDEMAN: Okay.

PRESIDENT NIXON: I don't think he would because I don't think he did tell me. . . .

The other point is that I need some recollection on the part of John is on this issue of clemency. I have said, you know, that I, and Ziegler has said, that I never authorized anyone to offer clemency. Now that's a flat statement and that is true. I never did. The question is they said, well, whether or not anybody ever discussed it with me. The only recollection I have of any discussion was, which John reminded me of, was on the beach in June or July just before we went over to there and it was only for a minute. He said, you know, looking down the road, one of the problems we're going to have is that I imagine—he says I would imagine these fellas will want clemency and then I said, well, we'll have to face that when we come to it, or words to that effect. . . . Dean had made this preposterous statement to the effect that they talked about clemency and that John Ehrlichman walked into the Oval Office, then came back and said you can offer clemency but don't be too specific. The President says so.

HALDEMAN: John totally denies that. . . .

PRESIDENT NIXON: I think that Mitchell is the fellow that, you know, had the greatest stake there and he was telling them to promise the Goddamn clemency and Mitchell, believe me, never talked to me about it. What he will say, I don't know. But I never recall any conversation of Mitchell about it. None whatever. None whatever. In fact, Mitchell to his credit never discussed it.

HALDEMAN: Right.

PRESIDENT NIXON: I don't remember. . . .

HALDEMAN: I note one other thing in the paper that I assume your people are aware of that you ought to cover probably is there's a story that high officials in Pentagon, CIA and State Department suggested the lie-detector test during the White House investigation into leaks. That's true, you know.

PRESIDENT NIXON: I know. Sure.

HALDEMAN: And I think you ought to say so. . . .

PRESIDENT NIXON: That doesn't bother me a bit, the lie-detector thing, you'll see. You're damn right we did. Yes, sir.

HALDEMAN: It gives you one more chance to—

PRESIDENT NIXON: Get the national security.

HALDEMAN: Lead to something, yeah.

PRESIDENT NIXON: The national security thing.

HALDEMAN: Right.

PRESIDENT NIXON: Yeah. And let these people scream about it. The other point is that I wish you would get clarification from John on. I have no recollection of John or you ever asking me, and I mentioned this to you the other day, about whether you could call Kalmbach, you know, at that time.

HALDEMAN: No.

PRESIDENT NIXON: And I don't know where you've testified to that John has or so forth. Do you know?

HALDEMAN: I'm sure that he has not thought of that because we've gone over that in considerable detail and that point never came up. That wasn't even a factor, but I'll check it specifically. . . .

PRESIDENT NIXON: Well, apparently that's it. . . . Let's see. What were the other points?

HALDEMAN: There was talk. The basic question is, was the CIA involved?

PRESIDENT NIXON: Yes.

HALDEMAN: Had they been involved—

PRESIDENT NIXON: Yes.

HALDEMAN: —is one point. The next point was the question of the FBI concerned about asking for guidance on an investigation and we did say that they should limit the investigation to the Watergate involvement of these people because there was concern about other activities in the national security area that had been done in the past.

PRESIDENT NIXON: Right.

HALDEMAN: —carried out by these people totally unrelated to Watergate. . . .

PRESIDENT NIXON: I guess the two critical points are, one, what John, if anything, is going to say with regard to having discussed clemency. . . . [Two], whether I approved—

HALDEMAN: —psychiatrist break-in.

PRESIDENT NIXON: And the question of whether or not I was informed of the psychiatrist break-in.

HALDEMAN: Right.

PRESIDENT NIXON: You see, because if I was informed, then, frankly, I am derelict for—I mean, they can blame John but they've also got to blame me for not firing Hunt and that bunch right then, you see. You see, that's the real question there. But, Bob, I don't—

HALDEMAN: I don't think that—

PRESIDENT NIXON: I just can't imagine that I would have known of such a jackass thing without doing it, but I don't want—if John testifies to the fact that he told me—

HALDEMAN: Right.

PRESIDENT NIXON: I've got to know that, see.

HALDEMAN: We'll find out. I don't think he does but I'll check it.

PRESIDENT NIXON: Yeah. And I would—I'm sure it's not true. I'm sure it's not true. And if he hasn't testified, I would hope he wouldn't. But with all your other problems, if you could weigh into those. Those are the loose ends here and I can assure you the statement is going to be a humdinger.

HALDEMAN: Right. . . .

PRESIDENT NIXON: And it's going—it's going to lay it all out there. . . . On the national security thing, . . . I'm going to defend the bugging.

HALDEMAN: Yes.

PRESIDENT NIXON: I'm going to defend the bugging. I'm going to defend the Plumbers. I'm going to defend—not only defend, I'm going to say why we did it. And I'm going to say why we tried to keep this out of the—out of the Watergate. . . .

HALDEMAN: Henry's [Kissinger, regarding telephone taps on reporters and NSC staff] got to shift to a positive attitude on all this, too.

PRESIDENT NIXON: Henry?

HALDEMAN: Yeah.

PRESIDENT NIXON: Oh, he will.

HALDEMAN: And they're trying to make him out as being so deeply concerned about the morality of this and all that. That's a lot of baloney. And he's got to get off of that and get onto the thing of the—

PRESIDENT NIXON: Well, Haig is—

HALDEMAN: —with—with the question of leaking the stuff out.

PRESIDENT NIXON: Haig is being—going to be very tough on them when he gets back.

HALDEMAN: Yeah.

PRESIDENT NIXON: If Henry—Henry wants to be—talk about morality, I mean we've got him nailed six ways to one.

HALDEMAN: Right.

PRESIDENT NIXON: Because you remember, Bob?

HALDEMAN: Oh, yeah.

PRESIDENT NIXON: Who the hell was pushing for this stuff?

HALDEMAN: Absolutely.

PRESIDENT NIXON: Who was squealing the most about the leaks? You know, about these NM, NM—I mean the—

HALDEMAN: Yes.

PRESIDENT NIXON: —NSSMs [National Security Study Memoranda] and so forth.

HALDEMAN: Yes, right.

PRESIDENT NIXON: I didn't give a shit about the NSSMs.

HALDEMAN: But he was right.

PRESIDENT NIXON: Yeah, I know he was right.

HALDEMAN: He was right in squealing about it. . . .

PRESIDENT NIXON: How else you're going to get the leaks? And that's—that's what we were trying to do.

HALDEMAN: Yep.

MAY 20, 1973: THE PRESIDENT AND HAIG, 2:55–3:07 P.M., CAMP DAVID TELEPHONE

Nixon and Haig talk again about asserting the need to maintain national security, emphasizing "the big issue of the climate" at the time. A few days after Archibald Cox's appointment, the President reiterates his view of Cox as a "good" man. Meanwhile, Fred Buzhardt, Haig's lawyer of choice, is, according to Haig, a "tower."

SEGMENT 1

PRESIDENT NIXON: . . . [T]he major feeling I have about the whole thing is to really—to hone this down in terms of the national security thing, rather than being a great big apologia about Watergate. You know what I mean?

HAIG: That's right. No, we've—that's the—that's the core of this.

PRESIDENT NIXON: Watergate should be only incidental to it.

HAIG: That's right. We've got to—we've got to build a climate, the situation, what we were faced with.

PRESIDENT NIXON: And everything we've done, and say, you're damn right—for example, somebody told me about the fact that—somebody tried to—the fact that we had—that I ordered lie-detector tests—of course I did. Good God, you know, the—you know, in the—in the various departments—you remember that? And—

HAIG: Absolutely.

PRESIDENT NIXON: And, by God, they—in one event, they—they produced results which we can't talk about.

HAIG: That's right. But that's—you know, that is all—

PRESIDENT NIXON: Yeah.

HAIG: —peripheral stuff. We're—we've got to take on the big issue of the climate, . . . and just get that into the clearest kind of perspective.

PRESIDENT NIXON: And the things that we did. We did things at the FBI. We did things throughout the government. That the big memorandum. We did things in terms of a White House capability. And—and that's that.

HAIG: That's right. And that's what we'll do. I've—I've talked to Elliot today. And he's quite optimistic now [about confirmation].

PRESIDENT NIXON: Oh, hell, he'll go through like Flynn, I think, now.

HAIG: Right. Well that's going to be a big help to—

PRESIDENT NIXON: And he'll be—when does he think he'll get through, Al?

HAIG: Well, his—his man is going up tomorrow with Cox. And he's hopeful he'll get right through.

PRESIDENT NIXON: Mmm-hmm.

HAIG: And there'll be a little bit of squabbling more about his authority, but Cox has already come out supportive of it. The press has been picking on [Senator Edward] Kennedy, and what have you, over the weekend. And I told Elliot to—

PRESIDENT NIXON: Picking on Kennedy, what, to—

HAIG: Well, to be tougher on—on authority for Cox, you know, autonomy.

PRESIDENT NIXON: Kennedy has said that?

HAIG: No, Elliot told me that they have been working on—on Kennedy to—to stand firm against—

PRESIDENT NIXON: Yeah.

HAIG: —any Elliot authority at all.

PRESIDENT NIXON: Oh, boy. [*Laughs.*] . . . He's got a good man. He's got—he's giving him great authority. One thing, incidentally, that was mentioned—I think somebody was talking to me today about some stuff where Henry [Kissinger] had done some hand—hand-wringing about—you know, about he was—and he, Henry, was concerned about the morality of what was done.

HAIG: No, no.

PRESIDENT NIXON: Good God Almighty, he—he's got—when—when you—when he gets back, Al, you've got to tell him he's got to stand like a rock on this, because he is the guy that Ehrlichman, Haldeman, everybody is going to say that pushed for this, you know.

HAIG: Well, you don't have to be concerned about that. I talk to him twice a day now—

PRESIDENT NIXON: Oh, tell me about that.

HAIG: —and he's—he's fighting mad. He wants to get out and just fight. He wanted to give a press conference to say you're Goddamn right and—

PRESIDENT NIXON: Good. . . . I think it's very important for him to come out and say we had a massive problem and we couldn't have had our China initiative, our Russian initiative or our Vietnam successes without having some sort of control. And as it was, the leaks impaired those initiatives.

HAIG: That's right. Well, the *Post* is working on Henry, and they're trying to get to me now the same way, you know. . . .

PRESIDENT NIXON: Of course I did it, you know, and everybody else has done it. Every President and—and at the height of it, during, of course, the Bobby Kennedy administration [in the Justice Department].

HAIG: Damn right. There's nothing to be apologetic about in any of that, not a thing.

PRESIDENT NIXON: Also, because we're really standing up for our foreign policy, what we've accomplished. We've accomplished great things. And, Goddamnit, we can't accomplish them with having everything printed in the press.

HAIG: No. That's exactly right.

PRESIDENT NIXON: And that's the way it goes. Well, then, I won't bother you the rest of the day, then, Al.

HAIG: No, I don't think you should be bothered with the paper [a proposed "White Paper" in defense of the Administration]] until it's worth your time.

PRESIDENT NIXON: Yeah. And you just work on it and do your best. And what time do you want me to start looking, about 9 tomorrow morning or—would that be a good time?

HAIG: Yeah, I think we ought to have a draft for you at 9.

PRESIDENT NIXON: Right. I think the best thing is for just you and me to talk about the damn thing first, don't you think so? . . .

SEGMENT 2

PRESIDENT NIXON: . . . But we've got to hold—we've got to hold the Stennises and the Goldwaters and the others and so forth and so on. But I can't help believing when they hear me talk that they've got to be with us on this, don't you think so? I would even think—I don't know. I don't know.

HAIG: Well, I know—I have gotten word that Stennis is being very, very active, totally supportive, and has had a hell of an impact. . . .

PRESIDENT NIXON: Yeah. How's Buzhardt doing?

HAIG: Oh, great. He's—God, he's a tower.

PRESIDENT NIXON: You know, the way he—the way he nailed down that damned [Dean] memo we were so concerned about, that damned thing—we'll kill them with that. Do we think we should put that out, though? I just wonder if that thing isn't too sensitive to put out?

HAIG: Well, it might be. But we want—

PRESIDENT NIXON: We could tell the [congressional] leaders. . . .

MAY 20, 1973: THE PRESIDENT AND HALDEMAN, 4:11–4:21 P.M., CAMP DAVID TELEPHONE

The President remains close to Haldeman, but again indicates another attempt to distance himself from Ehrlichman. Haldeman acknowledges the cover-up, although hardly its real dimensions. Meanwhile, he is confident the nation will prefer its soap operas to the Senate hearings.

SEGMENT 1

PRESIDENT NIXON: Hello, Bob.

HALDEMAN: Yeah, I haven't been able to reach John [Ehrlichman]. He's left where he is to go down to L.A. . . . .

PRESIDENT NIXON: Oh, that's right. He's in the West.

HALDEMAN: He's—he'll be coming back—he—he's staying out at [businessman] Justin Dart's place in Carmel—

PRESIDENT NIXON: Good. Good.

HALDEMAN: —with his sons for the weekend. But he went down to L.A. today to meet with a lawyer on this—on the L.A. grand jury deal. So he is going to be back up to Carmel tonight. And I'll get him then.

PRESIDENT NIXON: Good. Good. . . . [T]he point that I make is that I didn't want—I—I think my recollections are correct on this.

HALDEMAN: Yep, I do, too.

PRESIDENT NIXON: You and I have discussed it previously, one—that I was not aware of the damned—you know, the psychiatrist business. . . . And that was late, you know.

HALDEMAN: Mmm-hmm.

PRESIDENT NIXON: Do you—I don't recall any discussion of it, do you?

HALDEMAN: Nope.

PRESIDENT NIXON: And I don't think John ever did, that I ever—I don't think he did. And, second—

HALDEMAN: I don't think so either. . . .

PRESIDENT NIXON: I don't recall a damn thing. And they, basically, too, are also privileged conversations as we know them.

HALDEMAN: Yep.

PRESIDENT NIXON: If anything is privileged. Right?

HALDEMAN: Yes, sir. . . .

PRESIDENT NIXON: Oh, I was going to ask you—tell—ask you another thing. You have given Larry [Higby] thorough instructions—to the whole damn staff—that when they're in there as notetakers, that those notes belong to the President and they're not theirs; is that—isn't that true?

HALDEMAN: Ab—absolutely.

PRESIDENT NIXON: And I was thinking, for example, that's true of John's notes and it's true of yours, right?

HALDEMAN: Yes, sir.

PRESIDENT NIXON: And they're are supposed to be in the President's custody. That's a point that, you see, we're going to stand like a rock on. We're never going to give up on those notes. . . .

HALDEMAN: Oh, of course. You've got to. And that—I don't think you're going to get a rational challenge on that.

PRESIDENT NIXON: Yeah. I don't know where the hell Colson's notes are, you know, what—what—was he told the same as everybody else?

HALDEMAN: Yeah, but I don't know what he did with his.

PRESIDENT NIXON: Mmm-hmm. Well, if he's got them, he can get them in here now. I mean, you know what I mean; there's no problem there. . . .

SEGMENT 2

PRESIDENT NIXON: Just let me say, by God, we're going to fight this sonofabitch to the—and win it, too. . . .

HALDEMAN: If we get—yep—get the—get away from any appearance of—of—

PRESIDENT NIXON: Apology about—

HALDEMAN: —of your trying to cover up, and the reasons—and explain why there was that appearance earlier, and be perfectly frank about it. You're darn right we weren't anxious to get all this stuff out, because it was a problem.

PRESIDENT NIXON: You mean the—

HALDEMAN: It's obvious that it is.

PRESIDENT NIXON: You mean the stuff on the national—

HALDEMAN: National security stuff.

PRESIDENT NIXON: Hell, yes. That's right. We can't put out that whole stuff. That's right. That's right. . . . I don't think that these hearings are going to be the TV smash hit that everybody thought they were going to be.

HALDEMAN: No, I don't either. They're—they're pretty dull.

PRESIDENT NIXON: [*Laughs.*] You know what I mean? A lot of people, I think, prefer their soap operas. And they'll be on and off and so forth and so on. But they—and the senators don't look all that good either.

HALDEMAN: Well, and it gets—you know, when it drags on—now, they've only had two days of it—when they get three solid days this coming week. . . .

PRESIDENT NIXON: . . . Well, you know, though, by that time, I would think the Grand Jury would have acted, wouldn't you? I don't know.

HALDEMAN: I would sure think so. Well, I don't know. It depends on what your prosecutor [Cox] does.

PRESIDENT NIXON: Oh, that's right. That's right. . . . He's going to to have himself a helluva lot of reading to do, isn't he?

HALDEMAN: I guess. It's just incredible, the—the volumes of stuff they must have on this now. . . .

MAY 20, 1973: THE PRESIDENT AND HALDEMAN, 5:30–5:41 P.M., CAMP DAVID TELEPHONE

Haldeman passes on Ehrlichman's version of when the President learned about the Plumbers. Ehrlichman wants Nixon to cover the Plumbers' operations with a national-security blanket defense to help with his testimony to a grand jury in Los Angeles. Nixon reports that Buzhardt believes that breaking and entering is only a misdemeanor in most states if no theft has occurred.

PRESIDENT NIXON: Hello.

HALDEMAN: Hi. I—John [Ehrlichman] called in. . . . He says on the [Ellsberg] psychiatrist thing that he doesn't believe you knew about that until February or March. And he suspects that the first thing you found out was—Dean told you about the picture [that Hunt and Liddy took of themselves burglarizing Dr. Fielding's office and which was in the CIA files].

PRESIDENT NIXON: No, but I think that was probably March 21st, then.

HALDEMAN: Okay. Well, that—he wasn't sure when, but he—

PRESIDENT NIXON: Because we never discussed anything, Bob, in Mar—in February or early March. . . . Well, Dean, you know, kept saying Krogh had a problem. . . .

HALDEMAN: But he [Ehrlichman] said that—that you had made the point very strongly to him that you wanted him to be sure that Young and Krogh maintained absolute secrecy on the Plumbers operation.

PRESIDENT NIXON: That's right.

HALDEMAN: And that was in late December of January of '72, long before the Watergate.

PRESIDENT NIXON: Oh, yes.

HALDEMAN: And so they had the right, he felt—Young and Krogh—

PRESIDENT NIXON: Yeah.

HALDEMAN: —to assume that the whole deal was impressed by—

PRESIDENT NIXON: National security.

HALDEMAN: —your national security.

PRESIDENT NIXON: Well, that's—that's right. That—

HALDEMAN: (Unintelligible)—

PRESIDENT NIXON: And that—and that, incidentally, has to be John's defense when he goes down to the grand jury.

HALDEMAN: Right. It will be. But he says anything that your statement or—or anything he can say in that regard would be very helpful—

PRESIDENT NIXON: Well, that's what I plan to do.

HALDEMAN: —in covering their groundwork. Because—

PRESIDENT NIXON: Yeah.

HALDEMAN: —he felt that all three of them were under total wraps on the Plumber thing, and they—they need—that's the line they're going to take. And—and they—any substantiation they can get on that will be—

PRESIDENT NIXON: Of course, I suppose that even under the Plumber thing, illegal activity is not—[laughs]—and not—not impressed with national security.

HALDEMAN: Well—

PRESIDENT NIXON: What's he think on that?

HALDEMAN: They thought it was. And of course you didn't know there was an illegal activity.

PRESIDENT NIXON: I did not. No, no, no, no, no

HALDEMAN: Yeah. And so you can get into an honest misunderstanding there. They knew there was an illegal activity—

PRESIDENT NIXON: And John knew it.

HALDEMAN: —but they had—well, John knew it last summer. He didn't know it before that apparently. . . .

PRESIDENT NIXON: I thought that Krogh had said that—that he had told him, and then he had dressed him down and said don't do it again, or something like that. But—

HALDEMAN: Oh, that's right. That's right. About the break-in, that's right. . . .

PRESIDENT NIXON: He didn't know the evidence story, that's right. See, the—the problem that I have is that knowing it in March, the question is whether or not I should have immediately gotten ahold of Petersen and told him, now, look here—

HALDEMAN: No, because he already knew about it.

PRESIDENT NIXON: Yeah.

HALDEMAN: See, at the time you found out about it, you also knew that Petersen knew.

PRESIDENT NIXON: That's true.

HALDEMAN: Because he had the picture.

PRESIDENT NIXON: That's right. Well, he had the picture, but, of course, Dean—

HALDEMAN: And Dean told you that Peterson knew about it.

PRESIDENT NIXON: Yeah—that he was aware of that there was a picture which indicated that there had been a break-in.

HALDEMAN: Yeah.

PRESIDENT NIXON: That he informed me of that in March, right. Right.

HALDEMAN: . . . On clemency, he says he—his recollection is better than—than yours really. He says the only discussions on clemency was July [1972] on the beach [in California].

PRESIDENT NIXON: That's right.

HALDEMAN: And he says that—that your recollection is correct, except that you didn't simply say that would have to—you know—

PRESIDENT NIXON: Yeah.

HALDEMAN: —that was down the road. He said you very strongly took the position that no one was—no one was to even infer or imply any offer of clemency.

PRESIDENT NIXON: Mmm-hmm.

HALDEMAN: That there—because that would be in—it would appear to be looking like we were trying to cover something up.

PRESIDENT NIXON: That's right.

HALDEMAN: And that was not to be done.

PRESIDENT NIXON: I told him that? . . .

HALDEMAN: That's what he would say. And he—he feels very strongly on that.

PRESIDENT NIXON: Yeah. Well, I—

HALDEMAN: The only problem that he has—and he can't testify to it and has no knowledge of it—is the impression of—that you did discuss clemency with Colson in some way.

PRESIDENT NIXON: I have no problem with that either.

HALDEMAN: And I told him that you didn't. . . .

PRESIDENT NIXON: The only problem is whether or not at that point somebody—some asshole might say, well, the President tried to keep the Justice Department from following up on, basically, a burglary. [*Laughs.*] There's your—

HALDEMAN: Oh, yeah. But, good night!

PRESIDENT NIXON: I don't know. They had the—they—what do you think on that? I guess the—I guess you get back to the point there, Bob, that just—just—every time you turn around here there's some damn thing. But—

HALDEMAN: Yeah.

PRESIDENT NIXON: —that was the farthest thing from my mind, though. I didn't give a shit about Hunt either or—

HALDEMAN: Covering up the burglary was covering up the national security operation. . . .

PRESIDENT NIXON: God, this Krogh is a terrific fellow.

HALDEMAN: He's solid on all these things. . . .

PRESIDENT NIXON: . . . I don't know whether—as a matter of fact, the very thing, even taking the breaking and entering, Krogh's—Krogh's deal, I suppose, with Ehrlichman, they could say he should have reported a crime, right?

HALDEMAN: I guess so. . . . But he's got a pretty good mitigating circumstance under the—

PRESIDENT NIXON: National security.

HALDEMAN: —national security question. . . .

PRESIDENT NIXON: That's right, yeah. A strong mitigating—and also, you got to remember this, Bob, the whole thing here is that this—I don't know what it is in the California Code, but Buzhardt was pointing out that, generally speaking, a breaking-and-entering, where—which involves no theft or anything—you know what I mean? I mean is in most states only a misdemeanor.

HALDEMAN: Hmm.

PRESIDENT NIXON: . . . I hope to Christ is the case, because it's just a crime to have Bud Krogh kicked around on this damn thing. . . . Okay, boy, thanks a lot. . . . Keep the faith.

MAY 20, 1973: THE PRESIDENT AND ZIEGLER, MAY 20, 1973, 7:09–7:14 P.M., CAMP DAVID TELEPHONE

The President, a long-time student of media behavior, exchanges thoughts with his press aide on the unfolding of Watergate during the past several weeks.

PRESIDENT NIXON: . . . I was just thinking today that since about eight weeks now we've had—virtually every Sunday has been a big deal, well, particularly since April 15th. The big deal has been Watergate. And, of course, that's always been a big deal in the press. But the really remarkable thing about the resiliency of this country is that even with this massive stuff, it has not yet destroyed us. Do you know what I mean?

ZIEGLER: Sure.

PRESIDENT NIXON: I mean, I—there's not some surprise you can extend—It must have surprised the press. They must—because when you really come down to it, there's never been such a massive attack on the presidency, you know. What I mean is there have been attacks, terrific attacks in other times, but, you see, they didn't have television before.

ZIEGLER: That's right.

PRESIDENT NIXON: And now they go night after night after night, and it is a son-ofabitch. . . . [Laughs] And we all know, too, that even though they shoot sometimes at Ehrlichman and Haldeman and so forth, they're really shooting at the President. That's their whole line, isn't it?

ZIEGLER: Uh—

PRESIDENT NIXON: You don't agree?

ZIEGLER: Do—you have to separate that out a little, Mr. President, before I make, you know, just a general response to that. My view is that it is not a correct assumption to assume that all of the Congress and all of the press have the objective of destroying the President. I think we would be making an incorrect assumption if we assumed that.

PRESIDENT NIXON: I didn't mean all. No.

ZIEGLER: No. I think many of our—I think this Watergate thing, those who are pursuing it, divides itself out. There are critics. They're the political critics. They obviously aim it to the, you know—

PRESIDENT NIXON: Right.

ZIEGLER: —the President of the White House.

PRESIDENT NIXON: Yeah. . . .

ZIEGLER: But I think more than attack against the President, a personal attack, it's an impact against the presidency which we're dealing with mixed, of course, with the political aspects of it, which is attack.

PRESIDENT NIXON: Okay. . . .

MAY 23, 1973: THE PRESIDENT AND HAIG, 10:20–10:53 A.M., OVAL OFFICE

In a May 22 statement, known as the "White Paper" within the White House, and largely prepared by Buzhardt, the President denied prior knowledge of the Watergate break-in or cover-up. But he admitted to ordering some aides to restrict the burglary probe because of national security considerations. Here, referring to that statement, Nixon again tells Haig that he did not know of the Watergate cover-up until his March 21 meeting with Dean. "We've got to hit him just right between the eyes on those things. But we must not become obsessed with him," the President remarks. From that, he spends considerable time perfecting his story for himself and his aides. He labors to incorporate new revelations into his basic story.

PRESIDENT NIXON: . . . [T]he sonofabitch Dean will say the President was warned of a cover-up in March, which is true; he warned me. But on that, we did something, didn't we?

HAIG: Did something? It's all out now.

PRESIDENT NIXON: . . . Dean, I'm now convinced, he did it probably because I rather think Mitchell must have guided him, rather than over here. I rather think so. I have this feeling in the back of my—but he did a helluva lot of things he never told me about, even when he came in on March 21st to say, basically to tell me that, look, there are problems, Mr. President. But he *didn't* tell me about his suborning perjury

to Magruder. He *didn't* tell me the fact that Liddy, as he later said, had told him everything on June 19th. He didn't tell me that. He *did* tell me about his attempt to get the
CIA involved in this. He *did* tell me about the fact that he had authorized the offers
of executive clemency, he.

HAIG: No, that's right.

PRESIDENT NIXON: . . . . You see my point. We have here a fellow who was deeply involved in this whole damn thing, who ironically now is trying to drag everybody else
down with him. But if he knew all of these things, why the hell—where in the hell was
he, where the hell was he? Even when I saw him early March he didn't tell me. It
wasn't until March 21st. And even when I saw him on March 21st he never told me
those things. In other words, there was a hell of a lot of things he was still keeping
back.

HAIG: That's right, that's right.

PRESIDENT NIXON: We've got to hit him just right between the eyes on those things.
But we must not become obsessed with him. . . . Another thing is, while we don't
want to blind ourselves to anything that comes up, as new, sensational charges and-or
developments occur, let's take them, but recognizing the fact that we expected them,
and let's say, Goddamn, we're here to fight, we're going to knock the ball right out of
the park. Don't you agree?

HAIG: That's the way you do it, and not go into panics and saying, gee, you have to
do this or that. You've laid your case out and it's there. The other things that have
come up, these charges, sure we'll have to respond promptly if they're that serious,
but we have now a base from which not to be rattled as time goes on.

PRESIDENT NIXON: . . . The only problem, the major problem you have, our image,
the major problem, is when you think of these damn Walters memcoms, other
memcoms people may have. Those are really very bad. But what the hell can you do
about it?

HAIG: You can't do anything about it.

PRESIDENT NIXON: Fortunately, I've had few meetings, very few meetings. I mean,
I had Krogh in on one occasion, only one, never another. I've met Ehrlichman many
times, Haldeman many times, Colson many times. Ehrlichman, Haldeman, and Colson (unintelligible), and their devotion to the presidency is going to be—that they are
not going to drag us down, I don't think. The point is that Dean will try. As far as anybody else is concerned, that's the beauty of not talking to too many people. . . .

HAIG: That's right, you could have an unmanageable problem. I think we're in a
much stronger position than we were two weeks ago, much, much stronger.

PRESIDENT NIXON: Do you think so?

HAIG: Yes, sir. . . .

PRESIDENT NIXON: And also, we have to bear in mind the fact that blackmail
didn't work, because Hunt has talked, correct?

HAIG: Right.

PRESIDENT NIXON: Now, we mustn't be concerned either about any leak from the
bureaucracy about it. Helms, we will remember, what a piss-ass performance that
was, but don't let him know that we're concerned.

HAIG: No, no. . . .

PRESIDENT NIXON: [Regarding the Huston Plan.] The language in the first draft, the one that came over to me, which said that I told them, I ordered that they use any means necessary, including illegal means, to accomplish this goal. The President of the United States can *never* admit that.

HAIG: Of course not.

PRESIDENT NIXON: And the way it was stated is that I ordered them, I impressed upon them the immense urgency, and highly motivated people may have gone on, but I never specifically authorized any illegal things, and I never did. . . . Well, I'll tell you, Al, from a political and managerial standpoint, that one phrase could have knocked this office right out of the park. Other people can go out and say the President told them this, but I can't go out and say that I ordered the use of illegal means or that I condoned it. You understand? . . .

HAIG: You can never admit illegality or authorization of illegality. You just can't.

PRESIDENT NIXON: Well, okay. Let's leave her go for today. Bring in any problems. In the meantime, don't let it wear you out.

MAY 23, 1973: THE PRESIDENT AND ROSE MARY WOODS, 10:55–11:12 A.M., OVAL OFFICE

The President is anxious for his secretary to contact Thomas Pappas to make sure he will tell the right story.

PRESIDENT NIXON: . . . Good old Tom Pappas, as you probably know or heard, if you haven't already heard, it is true, helped at Mitchell's request fund-raising for some of the defendants. . . .

WOODS: I hadn't heard that Mitchell bit.

PRESIDENT NIXON: Right. Well, he did. He did. And that's what we've learned. He came up to see me on March the 7th, Pappas did. Pappas came to see me about the Ambassador to Greece, that he wanted to—he wanted to keep [Henry] Tasca there. We did not discuss Watergate at that point. It's very important that he remember that.

I did thank him for all the help that he gave Mitchell in fund-raising activities. I just want to—I don't know how we can—I don't—I think he's smart enough to know that investigators might ask him, did the President know of your fundraising activities? You see, I learned of his fundraising activities in that period of time, but I didn't—but they were not illegal, understand. They wouldn't be illegal. Pappas would not get in trouble for doing it unless he—unless his purpose, any more than Kalmbach's purpose was, his purpose was, to keep the defendants shut. You've a right to raise, you know, contribute money for legal defense. Hell, they've given to Ellsberg and other people. I don't know whether—it's very important I not talk to him about it at all. . . .

WOODS: I think it's dangerous to talk on that kind of line.

PRESIDENT NIXON: Oh, no, no, no, no. I wouldn't. I was thinking if he were down some time.

WOODS: I can find out.

PRESIDENT NIXON: Find out when he's here, and simply say: Remember the brief meeting you had with the President? The President's recollection was that the subject was that and that there was no discussion of Watergate, and that his recollection and his statement was based on that; and it's very important that, if you were asked, that that is your recollection. We're not trying to—understand, Pappas can say anything he wants, but I don't want him, I'm not asking him to lie. This is the truth. But on the other hand, when I thanked him for his—I thanked him for all his fundraising activities, you know—

WOODS: Well, he worked over there almost alone.

PRESIDENT NIXON: Right. Just say that there was no discussion of Watergate or fundraising—of the Watergate issues. I think it's very important. That's my recollection and I want to be sure that his is the same. Well, just keep it in the back of your mind. . . .

WOODS: Well, I can call his office. He has an office in Boston I can call and I can find out.

PRESIDENT NIXON: See, Dean was aware of his fundraising activities. . . . Dean apparently worked directly with Mitchell on fundraising—I mean, with Pappas. Pappas raised the money and all, but Pappas did it discreetly. He just raised it, you know. He was just like Kalmbach, much earlier.

MAY 23, 1973: THE PRESIDENT, ROBERT J. DOLE, GEORGE H. W. BUSH, AND WILLIAM TIMMONS, 12:27–12:55 P.M., OVAL OFFICE

Nixon still commands broad support in the Republican party. The loyalty and the yearning for leadership from outgoing and incoming Republican party leaders, Bob Dole and George Bush, is touching.

SEGMENT 1

PRESIDENT NIXON: You know, thank God, as a matter of fact—we didn't plan it, but I was thinking about, but thank God you are not the chairman now.

DOLE: Right, right.

PRESIDENT NIXON: Because Bush has to take a lot of gas, even though he didn't have anything to do with it, and you have to. And thank God you're out of it. But I will appreciate anything you can say, you know, just say, without a doubt, the President didn't know, hell, you know, you've read that statement, and correct it all out there. It's just one of those things where well-intentioned people made some dumb, some bad mistakes.

DOLE: . . . We keep issuing statements and they're not picked up. But I've talked with Bebe [Rebozo], too, occasionally.

PRESIDENT NIXON: I have as well.

DOLE: And we've, I think, made the first statement—

PRESIDENT NIXON: You made one?

DOLE: Right, in Chicago weeks ago, about the President, and have since done it a number of times on the *Today* show, et cetera.

PRESIDENT NIXON: That's good.

DOLE: But you know, you make news, you make news by attacking your own family. If you attack the President—

PRESIDENT NIXON: Or your grandmother.

DOLE: Oh, sure. That's a headline. That's what they want to talk. . . . What we really need is, you know, somebody down here to give us a little guidance, so we're not only doing it, we're doing it—

PRESIDENT NIXON: Fred Buzhardt is here now and he's very good on this sort of thing.

DOLE: What, is Pat Buchanan available?

PRESIDENT NIXON: And Pat Buchanan, you're damn right. Buchanan, Buzhardt. They're all available. But Buzhardt I put on full time, and he's got every damn answer that there is. . . .

DOLE: I find, and I think I understand politics very well—[*Nixon laughs*]—that you have a great reservoir of strength. . . . It would seem to me that that would really make a great change so far as all this stuff they talk about, and I've said as much in my own statement. People agree with me and I got a standing ovation when I said that in Chicago. I talked about standing up, now's the time to stand up for the President and all this.

PRESIDENT NIXON: This was the Committee?

DOLE: No, I was speaking to the dairy and butter people. I think we've gotten a little money from them.

PRESIDENT NIXON: They gave a standing ovation?

DOLE: Yes. I think people want to believe—

PRESIDENT NIXON: We've had an enormous amount of mail to that effect. It's very curious, you know, that's always in politics, is action and counter-action in a situation. . . . For Christ sakes, they've got people up to accuse the President of everything from thievery to cover-up, lying. Jesus Christ.

DOLE: Well, of course, the Nixon-haters are having a field day now. . . . But there are all of those people in the middle out there, the great majority who are just waiting for something to latch onto, it seems to me. . . . I think there's a feeling that, you know, if the President isn't involved then he ought to come out here and tell us.

PRESIDENT NIXON: Oh, yeah.

DOLE: Instead of being a captive of the Oval Office and all this stuff. But I really believe it's there and that the strength is there. And as you know, these stories have a way of turning around, and there's been such a revulsion. My farmers have criticized, you know: Is that all they're doing back there, is talking this Goddamn Watergate? What about the farm bill, the REA bill? They're sick of it. . . .

PRESIDENT NIXON: But the point is, the main point is, you shouldn't comment on any of those specific issues. The main point is to say now all this Goddamn—using this to attack the President is wrong, hurts the cause of peace in the world, and everything else, and they ought to lay off that crap. . . .

SEGMENT 2

BUSH: Mr. President, after a meeting, I was telling Bill [Timmons] yesterday, a walk-down, a couple of press guys said: How'd the meeting go? Well, frankly, it was *damn good,* because the [Congressional] leadership felt very strong that this positive stuff was what we need now, the country needs. And I said, "And I know it's true from traveling around this country." And they looked at me, you know, with a sour look and said. "Well, wait a minute; how do you explain this?" . . . I said, "This is what the American people are going to understand if you present it at all fairly." But none of the stories got into the very positive statements by the President.

PRESIDENT NIXON: No.

BUSH: And Martin Schramm, I walked out of here with him, a *Newsday* guy, and I said: Marty, tell me now, what was the view? He said: It was unanimously hostile. I said, "Well, Goddamn it, that's simply not *fair* now; in terms of fairness it's simply not fair. You're entitled to your damn opinion, but that's not the way the country's going to look at it." And they're homing in on the CIA thing, you see, today with Ziegler, on kind of some technicality, instead of separating out the national security from Watergate.

PRESIDENT NIXON: As I've told Ziegler, our purpose with regard to the CIA was not to get it in Watergate, but to keep it out. That was the whole purpose of the thing. Let them talk a little about the CIA, though, instead of Watergate.

BUSH: Well, people are going to be, Mr. President, Bob, I think—I know they would in Kansas, I know they are in Texas, on protecting this national security, on government secrets, government procedures, government. They're bound to be with you on that, Mr. President.

DOLE: Right, and that's where I think some of us, including the chairman [Bush], could be helpful. If somebody could get that stuff together for us—we're still making speeches all over and so are other Senators—we could be making the points locally, in Kansas or Illinois, wherever we might be. . . . I think what may be interpreted as silence in some quarters—in fact, many of us, all we want is a signal, and you don't want to go off half-cocked and say something that's going to trap someone. . . .

I'd suggest, I think there are a lot of us, probably counting House members and Senators, you know, they get you off in a corner with the press people and they get—Barry Goldwater has some damn thing that came out in the paper—because we don't have any, we don't have any quarterback. And I don't see what's wrong with it if we believe in the President and we want to set the record straight, if somebody does—

PRESIDENT NIXON: Now, let's get the people guilty in Watergate brought to justice, but let's quit attacking the President with innuendo, et cetera, et cetera. That's wrong. And let's quit endangering the national security and the foreign policy of this country. What do you think, George?

BUSH: Because I think basically people are with the President. The presidency, this President, in spite of some of the crap you're reading. I think in terms of the national security, the American people understand that. They basically do not want Communists or anybody else looking at our mail. And I'm just convinced on national security that this whole sophisticated thing is a veneer. I just believe that when you can get it out, why, people are going to say, "Well, how could that make sense?" Of course not.

So I think it will be separated out. Right now they're in there trying to weld into one pot. I don't think they're going to succeed on that. . . . And indeed, if Dean did what he's alleged to do, he indeed is an individual who was trying to do that. . . . And that's the kind of thing that we've got to separate out from the presidency. . . .

DOLE: I think what we ought to do is have Gerry [Ford] or [Senator] Hugh Scott—we've never had a joint meeting of the members of Congress and Senators,

Republicans. We're going to back the President and the guys that aren't going to do it aren't going to show up anyway. I think it's a show of unity and determination to do something about it, instead of meeting in our own little groups all the time. We don't communicate that way. . . . [T]o just talk very frankly about how important it is that the Republicans, not for Richard Nixon, but for the presidency and the party, that we do something. The time is right, I think.

BUSH: I like that. I think it's a great idea.

PRESIDENT NIXON: But if you fellows would come up with something like that, I think it's a great idea. . . .

MAY 24, 1973: THE PRESIDENT AND ZIEGLER, 12:01–12:22 P.M., OVAL OFFICE

Nixon angrily assaults Kissinger's sanctimoniousness.

ZIEGLER: . . . I may misjudge him [Kissinger], but he was—I was very pleased with my conversation this morning with him. He's, of course, bitter against John and—and—

PRESIDENT NIXON: And Bob. Why?

ZIEGLER: Well, simply—and not strikingly—and he's not talking about it—

PRESIDENT NIXON: Because they wouldn't leave?

ZIEGLER: No, no. Just because of the—the activities of—you know, like the—some of the things that they did do. And not referring to the funds and so forth, but the—the Plumbers activity and so forth—what that did and—

PRESIDENT NIXON: Bullshit. He knew what was going on in the Plumbers activities. Don't let him give you that crap. He was—he was clear up to his ankles himself.

ZIEGLER: Oh, was he?

PRESIDENT NIXON: Look, I—I don't like those activities as much as Henry. Henry was the one that was, Christ, pounding the desks, squealing about it and so forth. But, anyway—but, forget it. There's no—no reason for him to do that. But I don't want to have people around here pissing on Bob and John. . . .

MAY 25, 1973: THE PRESIDENT AND HAIG, 12:58 A.M.–1:25 A.M., WHITE HOUSE TELEPHONE

The hour is late. Nixon is tired, and slurs his words a bit. Haig, too, sounds tired, but both men are quite lucid. They talk a good deal about a stirring speech the President had given to recently returned POWs earlier that evening, in which he affirmed the government's right to maintain secrecy in national security matters and denounced those "who steal secrets and publish them in the newspapers." He received a standing ovation. Yet the President is despondent. He suggests that the time has come "to just check out." Haig, of course, quickly dismisses the notion, but later in the conversation, Nixon returns to that theme. No one more realistically assessed his situation.

SEGMENT 1

PRESIDENT NIXON: Coming right down to it, Al, when you look at it, you know and all this crap we're taking, and the Congress being Democratic and the Republicans being weak and all the rest, wouldn't it really be better for the country, you know, to just check out?

HAIG: [*Laughter.*]

PRESIDENT NIXON: No, no, seriously. I mean that, because I—you see, I'm not at my best. I've got to be at my best, and that means fighting this damn battle, fighting it all-out. And I can't fight the damn battle, you know, with people running in with their little tidbits and their rumors and all that crap, and did the President, you know, make a deal you know to pay off this one and that and the other thing. Huh?

HAIG: I'll tell you, sir. If you ever even conceive of leaving, think what it would have done to those people who worked tonight.

PRESIDENT NIXON: But they are such a small group, Al.

HAIG: No, sir, they're not, not at all. I saw two groups, one at noon today and last night, and I tell you it's just not so. They're all with us and they're with you. It would be the greatest shock this country ever had. My God, look. You just put out that paper, the stock market's soaring.

PRESIDENT NIXON: Did the stock market go up?

HAIG: Twenty-nine points today, sir.

PRESIDENT NIXON: What was that? Oh, the balance of payments?

HAIG: No. The Wall Street Journal thinks it was a combination of your statement, which renewed confidence, the balance of payments, and the lousy show yesterday [the Senate hearings] on television which proved that these bastards don't even know what they're talking about.

PRESIDENT NIXON: Well, Al, we've got to take a hard look at it because I'm—you see, the thing is what really counts is the man. And Goddamn it, the man's got to be doing the job, and I'm not really doing the job because I'm so wound up in this son-ofabitching thing, you know. You know, people like Buzhardt comes in with this scare story, and this one and that and the other one, and so forth. You know, you've got Dean out there, you know, ready to scream about this and that. Huh?

HAIG: We'll have that, sir. But we're—

PRESIDENT NIXON: Richardson is sort of a weak reed.

HAIG: He's coming along. I spent about an hour and a half with him today. That's the worst and he's doing it and he's proud as hell he got through. I think the Cabinet's never been in better shape. I was worried about [Secretary of the Interior] Rogers Morton because of that fellow [Congressman William O. Mills, R-MD, who recently had been accused of taking an illegal $25,000 cash contribution from CREEP] shooting himself today. I called him tonight. . . .

PRESIDENT NIXON: What did you say, what fellow?

HAIG: The fellow who took his seat, you know—

PRESIDENT NIXON: Yeah.

HAIG: —committed suicide.

PRESIDENT NIXON: Committed suicide?

HAIG: Yeah.

PRESIDENT NIXON: Who did? What?

HAIG: The Representative that was Rogers Morton's replacement.

PRESIDENT NIXON: Why'd he commit suicide?

HAIG: Oh, he had a problem. I don't know what it was. . . . We've got to do a little work in the House now, but we had to do the other things first, you know, with our own little people.

PRESIDENT NIXON: You see, we don't have the big guns fighting, though, *Goddamn them.* Well, Scott maybe, yeah.

HAIG: Scott did, he did a superb job, he really did. Everything that I saw tonight told me that the Congress, the Republican Congress that you saw this week, he said they'd never been higher. That business [Nixon's speech to returning POWs] last night, he said those men left there, they could hardly even walk, they were so proud and pleased (unintelligible).

PRESIDENT NIXON: One thing that I would like you to do with Henry, you know, because Henry is under great pressures with all these jackasses. You've got to see that he doesn't come in emoting about this and that, because Henry is not capable of making this kind of decision. Hmm?

HAIG: Well, I tell you, sir, he's ready to go out there on Tuesday. I thought we were going to have a problem there. No, he said: "Hell, I'll go out and brief." And I loved it today. He had a question on wiretapping and national security. He'll take it on.

PRESIDENT NIXON: Well, he should take the line, that line that Henry ought to really read and assimilate that damn speech I made this afternoon, because that was a God—as I told (unintelligible), that was a *Goddamn effective* speech.

HAIG: That's the finest speech I've heard. (unintelligible) some good ones, but that was the best.

PRESIDENT NIXON: But how do we get it around? The press, they all said: "Ho-hum, the son of a bitch is defensive."

HAIG: No, no, it played beautifully tonight on the television.

PRESIDENT NIXON: You think so?

HAIG: Oh, boy. Everybody's been raving about it. And the line on Ellsberg, by God you drew the line. Just the—to hell with it. It needed to be said.

SEGMENT 2

PRESIDENT NIXON: Well, you know, one thing you got to figure, though. You got to say, let's assume that none of it's true, but all this crap's going to fly and this son of a bitch Cox and the rest will try to—I mean, they're all saying, oh, they're going to try the President and all that horseshit. It's going to be rough.

HAIG: I'm not so sure. It'll be rough for a while, but I think we've turned the corner. I think we've passed our low point. I think it's going to get better each day. We'll get a few jolts, but we've got momentum behind us now.

PRESIDENT NIXON: Well, we may have to do something that Ron, of course, is not too keen on, and that is to take on—believe me, Al, we may have to take the press on, because basically the press is going so far here. Hmmm?

HAIG: Henry told me he took one on today, the *Time* magazine guy, [Jerrold] Schecter. He said he's sick and tired of this Goddamn (unintelligible).

PRESIDENT NIXON: Who said? Henry said it or Schecter?

HAIG: Henry said it to Schecter.

PRESIDENT NIXON: But you see, Al, the Schecters and all the rest are desperately wanting us to lose. That's our problem.

HAIG: They want us to lose, but you know why, sir. It's a hell of a lot deeper than Watergate or the Republican Party or you. It goes even beyond that. They don't want the country—they don't want the right principles to survive in this country. You happen to represent that. That's just too much for them. They're not all that way.

SEGMENT 3

PRESIDENT NIXON: But got to take a hard look, you know, because basically they're too big stakes. I mean, good God, we cannot allow the Russian summit to fail. We cannot allow these great things that we're doing to go down the tube simply because of the fact that people lose confidence in the President, Al.

HAIG: Well, there's no loss of confidence in the President. I just don't believe that. In fact, I know it's not so. And I think what you did this week was just right to get this thing . . . and to go ahead. . . . So I think we've really turned a corner on that.

PRESIDENT NIXON: Yeah, but you see, we got so many weak people on our Cabinet, you see. . . .

HAIG: . . . We've got one, that guy in Transportation [Claude S. Brinegar]. The rest of them are just solid as a rock. Butz, Morton, Schlesinger.

PRESIDENT NIXON: Schlesinger's pretty good?

HAIG: Oh, he's just first class. He's just solid.

PRESIDENT NIXON: See, Richardson's in the spot where, as you know, he's going to have to prove that he's the white knight and all that bull, and so he's going to try to—he and Archie Cox will try to try the President, you know, well, and all that crap. How do you handle that?

HAIG: I don't think those people are going to—well, Richardson, what does he gain by that? He's going to have to keep that guy under control, that Cox. But Cox, he's not much.

PRESIDENT NIXON: You don't think so?

HAIG: No. No. I've checked on him. He's not an effective guy. In fact, I'm not sure those things will ever even come to trial. . . . He'll have these cases, these portfolios, so screwed up nobody'll be able to be brought to court.

PRESIDENT NIXON: Well, the stuff they're going to throw, you know, is rough, it's going to be rough.

HAIG: We didn't have an easy first four years, but look what we've done. It was uphill every inch of the way, as you know.

PRESIDENT NIXON: Well, okay, boy.

SEGMENT 4

PRESIDENT NIXON: You see, the real problem, though, is me, because the Goddamn thing has gotten to me, you see, you know, because of the personal factors. And you get to the point, you know that, well, if you can't do the Goddamn job you better put somebody in there that can.

HAIG: [*Laughs.*] *There's no one that can.* You're the one to do it.

PRESIDENT NIXON: Well, Agnew's just panting to get at it.

HAIG: [*Laughter.*] No, sir.

PRESIDENT NIXON: Huh?

HAIG: He might be, but that's out of the question. There's just no alternative. There couldn't be. I think just the very act of not doing what you're doing would tear the country apart.

PRESIDENT NIXON: What?

HAIG: I think that just the very *fact* that you didn't stay would tear the country apart. There's just no way.

PRESIDENT NIXON: But put yourself in the position of the other side. They control the Congress, they control the committees, and they're going to try to do everything to get the President to testify, to turn over his papers, and all that. How do you answer that?

HAIG: I don't think, I don't think they can do it. And I think there's too many—too many important things. We're going into a period now at the Iceland and the Soviet summit, the Vietnam problem. This other thing is going to slip out of most people's consciousness. Hell, they've dug up all they can dig. They've done all—

PRESIDENT NIXON: No, they've got more. You know, I mean, they've got Dean. He's going to have to come out to save his ass.

HAIG: Well, I think he said most of what he had to say. I really do believe that, sir. And it doesn't make any difference what they have. The power of the office is in there. The power of your accomplishments in the past and ahead are going to swamp any of these other difficulties.

MAY 25, 1973: THE PRESIDENT AND RICHARDSON, 12:09–12:31 P.M., OVAL OFFICE

Richardson reports on Archibald Cox's installation, and the two men have an interesting discussion on executive privilege. Nixon assures Richardson that he can talk in total confidence, another ironic reference to the tapes.

SEGMENT 1

PRESIDENT NIXON: Now, I don't know where—where you go in terms of your—the present time—you've got your miserable Watergate thing now—but you've got Cox in there. Will he be housed in the Justice Department or outside of the Justice Department. . . .

RICHARDSON: I think he ought to be in—in—not in the main building—

PRESIDENT NIXON: Good.

RICHARDSON: —but he could be on a floor of some place where they're operating in an office building. I think there's some advantages in that. I think he'll be good. He's—

PRESIDENT NIXON: I hope it moves along.

RICHARDSON: He's certainly fair, honorable, scrupulous, and so on. He—he—he's going to get a fellow who has had some experience in prosecution—the kind of fellow he'd like to have—I don't know whether he could get him—but the kind of guy he's looking for is somebody like Whitney North Seymour, Jr., who was U.S. Attorney [in New York]. . . .

SEGMENT 2

PRESIDENT NIXON: . . . And on this thing, though, you've got—I want you to know you've got a—you've got complete support here and you can talk in total confidence.

RICHARDSON: One of the best things you've done, I think, was the—the decision communicated in a statement the other day that executive privilege would not be invoked. . . .

PRESIDENT NIXON: Yeah. Now, one point that I think we should note is that there is one area here that we do—will not enter and have to stand firm on as far as executive privilege. Executive privilege is revoked as far as any individual's oral testimony is concerned and as far as—however, it cannot be revoked with regard to the President's papers. In other words, like when you're sitting here making a note for me or if you write a memcom, that's made for me and not for anybody else. . . . Even if we discuss whether or not I'm going to burglarize the 10-cent store. Now, you—but you can testify. Because, you see, the—the—if you ever break into the President's papers, Elliot, we'd have a hell of a problem here. . . .

MAY 29, 1973: THE PRESIDENT AND ROGERS, 9:59–11:06 A.M., OVAL OFFICE

Again, Nixon awkwardly jokes about resigning. Meanwhile, Rogers delivers a grim report on Mitchell, indicating that he might kill himself. The two men, who have a long history of working together on investigations, comment on the men investigating the Nixon White House—Senator Sam Ervin and Special Prosecutor Archibald Cox.

PRESIDENT NIXON: I was just thinking since you and I met on it, God, I'll tell you I haven't had no—you know, you sometimes wonder how you take this thing (unintelligible) responsibilities of the office and you try to do the best you can. I think of really how we sheltered Eisenhower, . . . I mean, even how on [Sherman] Adams (unintelligible) you and I both did it. . . . They've canned Presidents before, but never with the media, you see. We never had television before, did we. And so you had 15 minutes of nightfuls since the 15th of April, two solid months.

ROGERS: And it isn't—

PRESIDENT NIXON: . . . David [Eisenhower] did a very interesting comparison. He said, you know, he says the military is rigid. In politics the politician develops friendships and the military you really don't. People come and people go. Interesting statement, very interesting statement.

ROGERS: Yeah.

PRESIDENT NIXON: . . . What's your view of the whole thing?

ROGERS: . . . I think that it's beginning to turn. Of course, it depends a little bit on what Dean says, it seems to me. If Dean, if he tries—well, if he lies—you see, any time that he lies, the whole thing is going to come apart. . . .

PRESIDENT NIXON: . . . Dean's major problem is that he has lied under this point. He did not tell me, for example, he suborned Magruder to commit perjury ever. He did not tell me there were lies. He tried to get the CIA to hire these buggers. . . .

ROGERS: Of course, he's been dickering for clemency for so long and it casts doubt on his credibility. . . .

PRESIDENT NIXON: . . . I suppose that if Cox really wanted to play this politically, as he obviously does, versus anything at all on McGovern people.

ROGERS: I never figured out how did Elliot get him?

PRESIDENT NIXON: Couldn't get anybody else [*chuckles*]. He just had a helluva time getting anybody. Elliot—well, anyway. We had to keep hands off. So he's got him. That's that. The point is, though, that if he wants to fight politically, I suppose what they can do is, if they wanted to really embarrass the President, is to have the grand jury—can't the grand jury at the end, they can put out some sort of—what do they call it? Just a—what do they call those?

ROGERS: Presentment.

PRESIDENT NIXON: Huh?

ROGERS: Presentment.

PRESIDENT NIXON: . . . [T]hey could send the presentment down or send something down to the Congress and say we suggest you consider this for impeachment. That's the other thing they can do.

ROGERS: Basically, they don't have any evidence. Do you know what I mean? Not a Goddamn thing. They would only do that if it the Department [of Justice] recommended it. They're not that sophisticated. So it would have to be a recommendation about it.

PRESIDENT NIXON: We're getting now over into the political atmosphere. . . . Dash is obviously a partisan McGovernite. Dash. Old Ervin is (unintelligible). He's not going over well on television. He's an old fart. . . . The other point that we have to bear in mind, though, is that, you know, to really consider, is that, you know, we have some just ridiculous suggestion the President ought to resign and all this filthy—you couldn't resign, for Christ sakes, if you'd stole the whole Goddamn White House.

ROGERS: No.

PRESIDENT NIXON: You know. What the hell are you going to do? Turn the reigns over to Agnew? Huh? [*Chuckles.*] Is that what they want? What is your feeling at the present time? . . .

ROGERS: Yeah. I mean, yet it's going to be tough. It's going to continue to be tough for awhile. I think it's going to turn around. I don't—certainly as far as other leaders in the rest of the world are concerned, they just say, well, for Christ sakes, "The President has been a great President. Give my best regards and tell him not to worry." . . .

PRESIDENT NIXON: That's true in the world, but I guess it doesn't make much difference in the country. Well, anyway what you take here we can take, but I would think in the Congress, I would hope, that after a certain point they begin to realize that this is not in their interest to really to destroy the Presidency. . . . Goddamnit. There was a cover-up. We know that. And now it's very apparent. The whole Goddamn thing, frankly, was done because it involved Mitchell. The Goddamn thing—

ROGERS: Jesus. The poor fellow looks awful.

PRESIDENT NIXON: He'll never serve a day.

ROGERS: You don't think so?

PRESIDENT NIXON: [*Exhales.*] Well, I don't know about the legal thing. But I know his emotional state and so forth and so on but poor guy. He's got the crazy wife. He's got a nice little daughter. . . . John is a proud man and so forth. What the hell was he going to do?

ROGERS: I think there's a good chance he'll kill himself.

PRESIDENT NIXON: That's exactly right. I think the other point is that on the other hand you can never serve a day for another reason. How in the hell can anybody get a fair trial in the light of this kind of publicity? . . . I would think his attorneys could just raise holy hell about this. Wouldn't you agree?

ROGERS: I don't see how. . . .

PRESIDENT NIXON: I think they'll fight this until hell freezes over. Let's come back to the President. How does he get a fair trial here or does he just continue? Well, do what we're doing. Don't you think?

ROGERS: I think you have to do what you're doing and I think that, as time goes on, there will be weak spots developed. And when those weak spots develop, we have to figure out how to take advantage of them. In other words, there will be conflicting testimony. Dean will make some mistakes. The committee will make mistakes. And at that point, it seems to me, we ought to focus in and point out about what a ridiculous thing this is. . . .

PRESIDENT NIXON: . . . If it's a question of whether—maybe I'm wrong, then the President must go. But if it's a question of the attack on the President himself, others must defend him; right?

ROGERS: Right. Now it may well be—

PRESIDENT NIXON: See a Goldwater, Agnew and all the rest have got to step in there. . . . But when you really get down to it, this was basically a political assault of great magnitude where you've got opposition in Congress with almost total support from the press and for that's reason it's tough titty.

ROGERS: It sure is.

PRESIDENT NIXON: But it can be won. . . .

JUNE 1, 1973: THE PRESIDENT AND KISSINGER, 4:33 P.M.–7:01 P.M., CAMP DAVID TELEPHONE

The President taunts Kissinger about the wiretapping done by his "liberal" friends, particularly during the Kennedy Administration. Kissinger dutifully joins in the President's tirade.

SEGMENT 1

PRESIDENT NIXON: Uh, you told me that [former JFK aide and Kissinger's Harvard colleague] McGeorge Bundy had the effrontery to tell you that Bobby Kennedy and that period didn't have any taps on national security.

KISSINGER: Yeah, yeah.

PRESIDENT NIXON: Have you heard the figures?

KISSINGER: Uh, Al mentioned them to me.

PRESIDENT NIXON: Well, let me—let's get away from the bullshit. Bobby Kennedy was the greatest tapper. . . . I'm getting the names, I'm going to publish the names next Thursday. . . . So let your assholes know that they're going to get this, Henry. Right in the can.

KISSINGER: I think you should. Absolutely.

PRESIDENT NIXON: Because they have done us in on this thing. Now, the biggest tapper was Bobby Kennedy. Now, Johnson doesn't appear to be so big, but he had the Secret Service do it. And I've ordered [Secret Service head James] Rowley to give me the names of the Secret Service tap and I'm going to put those out too.

KISSINGER: I think—

PRESIDENT NIXON: We're gonna, they, they've started, they wanna have a gut fight, they're gonna get one, Henry. You understand? . . . And they think they know how to fight, but never they've never fought anybody before. . . . But you see, Bobby Kennedy was the biggest tapper of all. Now I want you—now this is not gonna come up for Monday, but leak it to somebody. Talk to one of your liberal friends and say we've got a, a blockbuster coming out. Now will you do that?

KISSINGER: Certainly, I can.

PRESIDENT NIXON: You can say, "Look, this whole business of tapping, they have, they have opened, they have really opened it up, because Bobby Kennedy—." Hoover had told me this, you see, and I knew this and I recollected. Remember, I told you that maybe McGeorge Bundy was lying. Well, Hoover told me, he said, "Bobby Kennedy had me tapping everybody." I think, incidentally, I'm on that list. And I—

KISSINGER: Wouldn't be surprised.

PRESIDENT NIXON: —and so, my point, I don't mind. But my point is, I don't want this Goddamned hypocrisy.

KISSINGER: Well, if we can get the names, Mr. President, we ought to put some of them out.

PRESIDENT NIXON: Not some—all of them. Everybody's going to go out. I'm going to put the whole damn bis —, uh, list out.

KISSINGER: But then (unintelligible) about that.

PRESIDENT NIXON: Well, I don't give a damn about that. I'll put ours out. But we're gonna, we're gonna, we're gonna force them right now—if they're gonna play this game. Ours will get out anyway, Henry. You understand?

KISSINGER: But what we should do in any event is to get this list out.

PRESIDENT NIXON: That's what I mean, yeah. Well, we're going to do that Monday, but just let one of your liberal friends know that there's a real blockbuster coming, that the most tapping was done in the Kennedy Administration, this study has shown, and the facts are going to come out.

[Withdrawn item. Agency policy, investigatory information.]

PRESIDENT NIXON: I know that, right. But I just, just want, for your reassurance, but don't let McGeorge Bundy give you any of that bullshit anymore, because it just gets beyond belief.

KISSINGER: Beyond belief.

PRESIDENT NIXON: Double standard.

SEGMENT 2

PRESIDENT NIXON: But remember on this tap business, it's gonna catch some of your friends, incidentally. Cause I know some of the names.

KISSINGER: Well, I wouldn't be a bit unhappy.

PRESIDENT NIXON: I know some of the names, and boy, I—they want a brutal fight, they're gonna get one. And they're gonna get it Goddamned soon.

KISSINGER: They've been asking for it for a long time.

PRESIDENT NIXON: Be sure McGeorge Bundy knows this is coming out. That'd be a very good one.

KISSINGER: All right.

JUNE 2, 1973: THE PRESIDENT AND HALDEMAN, 10:54–11:13 A.M., CAMP DAVID TELEPHONE

Haldeman has just testified to Senator John McClellan's [D-AR] Appropriations Subcommittee on Intelligence Operations, which was looking into charges that the CIA had been used to interfere with the FBI investigation of Watergate. The President and Haldeman again coordinate their stories. Suddenly, the President remembers the Helms–Walters meetings in June 1972; now, Nixon and Haldeman elaborate their contention that John Dean tried to influence the CIA.

PRESIDENT NIXON: Hello.

HALDEMAN: Hi.

PRESIDENT NIXON: I thought you'd be pleased to know that David [Eisenhower] said . . . that you just came through like gangbusters on television—

HALDEMAN: Oh, good.

PRESIDENT NIXON: —after you'd appeared, and Haig read the transcripts and said that yours was exceptionally good.

HALDEMAN: Well—

PRESIDENT NIXON: He was—he was rather sorry that John [Ehrlichman] got in a pissing match with [former CIA Deputy Director General Robert] Cushman, but otherwise—

HALDEMAN: Oh, we couldn't avoid it, though. That Goddamn Cushman is really screwing him, but—

PRESIDENT NIXON: What does Cushman do anyway?

HALDEMAN: I don't know. . . . John [Ehrlichman] did an awfully good job, which they didn't give any play to, of laying out the national security problem, and he—he does that well and he'll have a chance to do that again at this grand jury in Los Angeles. . . . Somewhere he's going to get through on that point, and he—

PRESIDENT NIXON: Because he knows it.

HALDEMAN: —is very good at that.

PRESIDENT NIXON: He knows it. He's very effective and I wish he would get it through publicly, too. . . .

HALDEMAN: . . . I've decided to just go the categorical denial thing which they play the hell out of for some reason. . . . I swamped the whole news thing after my day by simply going out and making a flat statement, and I said, I categorically deny that I had any—that I suggested, directed, or participated in any cover-up, and I brought the President in and said that any actions that were taken beyond the specific things that I outlined for that meeting were without my knowledge and without the President's knowledge, and you know.

PRESIDENT NIXON: You mean that basically was that—you mean the Dean actions, huh?

HALDEMAN: Yeah. I didn't say Dean. I haven't named anyone at all.

PRESIDENT NIXON: No. Don't ever do it.

HALDEMAN: I'm not about to. Now, John did.

PRESIDENT NIXON: Yeah. He shouldn't.

HALDEMAN: I don't think that's a good idea. . . .

PRESIDENT NIXON: John—John should not—all he's going to do—I know how strongly he feels about Dean and I feel the same way, but there's no reason for him to keep hacking Dean and then forcing Dean to hack him.

HALDEMAN: Yeah.

PRESIDENT NIXON: You know, Dean could be bad enough with him anyway. . . .

HALDEMAN: Well, my position on that is that I don't know what anybody else did, and that's the truth and I lit in very hard. I got a chance where [Senator John] Pastore [D-RI] was grinding on me in—in the hearing that will show in the transcript at some point when it comes out, but I just—I—finally—I did it on purpose and I had planned to do it, so it wasn't an accident at all. But I said, Senator, could I speak to a personal point for a minute? And—and [Senator John] McClellan [D-AR] looked kind of startled and he said, well, yes, go ahead. And so, I said, all the people who have appeared here and testified seemed to be drawing a conclusion, which appears in your transcripts, in the record of your committee hearings here, that I and John Ehrlichman committed some crime or did—participated in some way in the Watergate crime and therefore we're—we're motivated to try to cover it up afterwards. And Joe Alsop has said this and—and your witnesses have said this. *Goddamn Walters* said it directly.

PRESIDENT NIXON: Did he?

HALDEMAN: He said, it's now apparent to me that Ehrlichman and Haldeman were involved in this crime and were afraid the President would find out and we're trying to find a way to cover it up.

PRESIDENT NIXON: Oh, for Christ sakes.

HALDEMAN: Now, I said, some of the Senators have said the same thing, which they have. And I said, I have complete confidence in the American judicial system and I know that when this case is completed, it will be *totally* clear to you gentlemen, to the witnesses that have been before you, and to the American people that I had *absolutely* no involvement in the commission of the Watergate crime whatsoever in any way. And a lot of people are going to be very ashamed of themselves when the truth is known. And I looked right at Pastore and he wouldn't even look up at me.

PRESIDENT NIXON: Um-hmm. Good, good. Well, that's the way to do it. That's the way to do it.

HALDEMAN: We've got to, you know, get more categorical I think.

PRESIDENT NIXON: . . . You know, I can't understand what in the hell Walters did this for. He—

HALDEMAN: Well, he's got himself kind of trapped too, you know. He has this—he's a super-egotistical guy.

PRESIDENT NIXON: Yes, I know.

HALDEMAN: And he has this great pride in recollection and his recollection got crossed up.

PRESIDENT NIXON: Yeah.

HALDEMAN: And I think he just—it's the same kind of thing as Cushman did. They kind of got caught in the middle of their own web.

PRESIDENT NIXON: Yeah, but damn it. I'm sure Walters—Walters—Walters has got to know that you and John didn't have a Goddamn thing to do with—you know, with the Dean thing. You know what I mean?

HALDEMAN: Well, I would think so . . .

PRESIDENT NIXON: Why are they [the Senate Select Committee] pulling all these small fry in there?

HALDEMAN: Well, because they're trying to lay this whole base of what actually happened. . . .

PRESIDENT NIXON: Well, they're going to bore the country to death if they keep—if they—until they get—unless they get some big stars pretty soon. . . . What the hell. I mean, they want to get up—get up before a committee—you see, I suppose in—I suppose in Ervin's case, Bob, he's—despite his approaching senility—he and the others—they don't want to get this thing brought to a head and finished quickly. . . . They want it to hang over the public mind and the doubts to be out there.

HALDEMAN: Yeah.

PRESIDENT NIXON: . . . How's Baker handling himself?

HALDEMAN: Well, he hasn't—since they've been in recess, he hasn't been heard from really. . . .

PRESIDENT NIXON: Good God. Well, I'll tell you, nevertheless, I'm—I'm hopeful that I'm never—that this is not an accurate appraisal but I—I think that they're—with the *Times,* the *Post,* the networks, and so forth, and all this, they can get the God-damn country bored as hell with this thing if they just continue to whack it around there. Everybody is—you know, like we go out to Iceland and you see 4,000 or 5,000 Americans at the airport and so forth, and it's just not there. You know what I mean? It's—it is a—I'm sure it worries people and they wonder what the hell is it all about and so forth and so on and it gnaws away. But it's not a—as Bryce Harlow says, an issue that *has legs.* [*Chuckles.*] I don't know what he means by that, but . . . anyway, my own feeling is that—that there—there does come a time when the public—the people become, you know, just saturated with stuff, and when—they want to get on to other things. Don't you think that's true?

HALDEMAN: Yeah.

PRESIDENT NIXON: . . . Well, in the meantime, I think that our friends, Cox and Dash, are going to have themselves a good game because Cox—and this isn't [chuckles]—Cox is going to have one hell of a time getting anybody convicted if those hearings go on—anybody, including Mitchell.

HALDEMAN: Yeah.

PRESIDENT NIXON: And—don't you agree?

HALDEMAN: Yeah. . . .

JUNE 2, 1973: THE PRESIDENT AND HAIG, 11:56 A.M.–12:05 P.M., CAMP DAVID TELEPHONE

After a desultory conversation about the wiretaps of the Kennedy and Johnson Administrations, Nixon and Haig optimistically assess upcoming events. Haig gleefully reports on conflict within the Senate Committee and between Archibald Cox and the Committee over public testimony by potential defendants.

PRESIDENT NIXON: It's interesting that—that most of the people are, rather like Buzhardt, feel that—even—even the ones that know the facts feel that the psychology is starting to—has started to turn rather substantially.

HAIG: No question. . . . [W]hat is most important is that the whole Cox apparatus split, the Ervin apparatus split wide open on partisan lines now.

PRESIDENT NIXON: Is it really?

HAIG: Oh, yes. They're at each other's throats. Baker is fighting Ervin and refuses to go along with the release of that document. They're fighting tooth and nail about the whole character of the Senate investigation. We've really got the—

PRESIDENT NIXON: Incidentally, the release of that document [Huston Plan]—if it comes out, it comes out.

HAIG: It doesn't hurt us either way.

PRESIDENT NIXON: Yeah, in my view. Don't you agree?

HAIG: Yes.

PRESIDENT NIXON: Because mainly the point is it's signed by four—the four top people, including Brother [Richard] Helms.

HAIG: Exactly right. It doesn't hurt us either way. . . . That damage I think we can winter [?] because in many ways we—

PRESIDENT NIXON: . . . [B]ut Ervin—it shows you what a senile old shit he is too, and unpatriotic to want to release the document [Huston Plan].

HAIG: Exactly. They're split wide open on that issue. They're split wide open on the overall issue of recognizing what they're doing that it has become partisan.

PRESIDENT NIXON: They feel that, Al, do they?

HAIG: Over in the committee, yes, sir. . . . The staff is split out there.

PRESIDENT NIXON: What is the—why is the—the Cox shop —what are they splitting on?

HAIG: Well, they're split on the issue of the dilemma to move quickly with indict-

, ments or to try to get some indictments that are comprehensive or not to do that and to try to continue to get Bob, John, and Chuck indicted, and they have—they have a very weak case on them.

PRESIDENT NIXON: I don't think they've got a strong enough case for—they'll never convict the three of them. . . .

HAIG: Well, Buzhardt really thinks they'll never be brought to trial.

PRESIDENT NIXON: Because of what? The Ervin committee?

HAIG: Yes.

PRESIDENT NIXON: I personally think you're going to have—I called Bob this morning to run over a couple of things with him, not on this matter, but others. But I just told him that everybody thought he had done well before the [McClellan] Committee. And he said that his people were—his people were—felt that they had already—they had already ruined their case with him because they convicted him a hundred times in the press already. . . . Even Bob, you know, and Mitchell is convicted, of course. Mitchell and Bob—they've been convicted in the news magazines. They've been convicted in the newspapers. Worse, they've been convicted on television. Their pictures have been in. They look like felons. And Goddamn it, you know, how the hell can you get a fair trial with that sort of thing? . . .

HAIG: Yes, and he [Buzhardt] thinks that the longer these hearings go on, the more we gain from it. . . . He does. It's just building this terrible—now that it has become partisan and they're fighting each other, it's going to be more of a fiasco.

PRESIDENT NIXON: One thing I just wanted to touch base with you on, the—I noticed that McClellan mumbled something to the effect, well, the only one that could clear up the—this thing is the President or something. Well, McClellan is a fine one to be talking that way. Jesus Christ, I mean, we've done everything for him, and you know, not only that, but he knows that—he knows that the President is totally blameless in this thing. Is there anybody that could have a little talk with him?

HAIG: Yes, of course.

PRESIDENT NIXON: Who could? I mean, I don't mean you. Maybe Bryce [Harlow] or somebody because—you see what I mean?

HAIG: Bryce or—or even Buzhardt. I think Buzhardt knows him.

PRESIDENT NIXON: You got to have a responsible person go down there and say, look, have you read the President's statement. I mean, I covered that whole damned CIA thing in the statement and Bob and John's stuff backs it up a hundred percent. Right? . . . [W]e got to drive anybody off of this silly absolutely line that the President ought to appear before the committee and do that. If that is ever—you know, we can't even let that become a—if it does become an issue, then we'll just have to knock the hell out of it. . . .

JUNE 3, 1973: THE PRESIDENT AND ZIEGLER, 10:10–10:35 A.M., CAMP DAVID TELEPHONE

On June 2, John Dean revealed the numerous meetings he'd had with the President, contradicting previous White House figures. Nixon meets Ziegler to prepare a response. While Nixon remains in denial on the extent of his contacts with Dean,

including the September 15, 1972 meeting, he candidly admits to Ziegler that Dean was not in cover-up meetings, implying that such meetings took place.

ZIEGLER: . . . [Dean is] making reference to the meetings he had with you and—you know, since January. . . .

PRESIDENT NIXON: There weren't any.

ZIEGLER: Yeah, that's the point.

PRESIDENT NIXON: The first—the first meeting we had with him—we've checked that out—was February the 27th. . . . What is he saying in the meetings? That he informed me about things in the meetings, or what is the—what is—

ZIEGLER: Well, he's making—he's making reference to the fact that in meetings which he had, that the matter of—some aspects of the cover-up were discussed and that he's prepared to so testify. Now, he is not saying this directly. This is coming from various sources. And we put out a very stinging thing yesterday . . .

PRESIDENT NIXON: . . . [W]e don't know really, Ron, how much we can deny because—except that what our own records show, you know. February the 27th was the first time he came in, you know. . . . And he was in but not then on—on the cover-up stuff. . . .

February 27th is the first time he saw me, February—with—with Dick Moore. Now, he went to La Costa, you know. He was out there with Haldeman and Ehrlichman, but he did not see me.

ZIEGLER: That's right.

PRESIDENT NIXON: So, that's the only other time that that's—but he didn't see me, and they didn't talk to me about it either. So, they didn't talk to me, so there was no problem there. Actually my first knowledge of anything was in that period. . . .

JUNE 3, 1973: THE PRESIDENT AND COLSON, 10:48–11:07 A.M., CAMP DAVID TELEPHONE

This conversation has the two men denying unassailable facts and incidents. They recite a catalog of Dean's crimes, pretending ignorance and of course denying their own complicity. Colson's loyalty to the President was absolute and unquestioning, undoubtedly a welcome situation for Nixon. Throughout this period, however, Colson is not a White House visitor; the contacts are by telephone.

PRESIDENT NIXON: . . . And our day will come, though, Chuck, believe me. The *Times* and the *Post*—for them to—and not to mention the networks—but for them just to—just do such in a—in a totally irresponsible way to say that here's a guy [John Dean] that they know is asking for immunity, and they take leaks and so forth. And he—they say he is prepared to testify that, that he saw—and that the President was aware of something in this period. Well, now, for Christ sakes, I mean, suppose I was aware even.

COLSON: Yeah, that's right.

PRESIDENT NIXON: You know, the whole point is that we've indicated awareness as of March 21st in any event, but—

COLSON: Sure. So, all he is talking about is—

PRESIDENT NIXON: When. . . . Well, not only when, but he's—he—and there was nothing in January or February I know. Nothing at all.

COLSON: But not only that, but John Dean, of all people to believe—here was John Dean who had foreknowledge of the Watergate which we didn't know until January—John Dean had foreknowledge of the Watergate.

PRESIDENT NIXON: He suborned—he suborned—he suborned Magruder to perjury. . . . And he never told me that. . . . He promised the defendants clemency. He never told me that.

COLSON: That's right.

PRESIDENT NIXON: He—he—you know what I mean. Here was the fellow that was—and—and, of course, had worked very closely with Gray and so forth and so on. Well, all these things—all these things. Here was the fellow that was really doing it all, Chuck as far as the cover-up was concerned. How the hell was he—how could he— how could he—and then why didn't he walk in on the 28th or 29th and say so? Why did he wait till the 21st of March to come in and say, look, I think we're in a real spot here. I think that—that Hunt's attorney is blackmailing us and so forth. Well, why didn't he say so earlier?

COLSON: That's right.

PRESIDENT NIXON: I don't know. He never—never—never said the payments earlier were blackmail or anything or payoff or hush money or so forth and so on. Never implied as much. . . . He said the White House was clean, kept telling me that, kept implying that Mitchell was the one that was involved. You know what I mean. There was our problem, Chuck, you know. . . .

COLSON: Exactly. And I remember your saying to me many times, well, thank God this doesn't extend into the White House. John Dean was in a—is in a very hypocritical position because he has to—to make his case, to make his bargain for immunity, he has got to put himself in the position where he—he has to try to lay as much off on you as he can.

The problem with doing that is that he was—he was a participant and full of knowledge which he could have imparted to you at any time for ten months and did not and didn't—not did not to you, did not to me. I don't know what he did to anyone else, but—

PRESIDENT NIXON: He didn't to anybody. . . .

COLSON: That's exactly right. And every conversation I've had with him—although a couple of times I got little glimmers of evidence, and I've already told the U.S. Attorney this. I'd get little things that might be—might indicate a problem, and I would send them to Dean and he would tell me, forget it, don't do anything with it. . . . So, he really was actively suppressing. And, of course, in hindsight I realize now that I should have raised more ruckus than I did. This was, of course, towards the end of last year. You had a rather major, all-consuming problem.

PRESIDENT NIXON: No. I couldn't pay any attention to all this. Never—and didn't. . . .

COLSON: That's right. You couldn't—you had no way that you could be sitting around in strategy sessions with people in how you cover up the damn Watergate. It's preposterous.

PRESIDENT NIXON: Shit, I didn't. . . .

COLSON: . . . I can honestly say that in all the hours that I sat in your office, I never saw Dean come in once.

PRESIDENT NIXON: *Hell, no.* Let me—we know. We've got the figures on that and that's what kills them is that Dean saw me before February the 27th. He saw me only twice; once five minutes when we signed the will, and the 15th of October—September when he came in to report on the fact that the—they had indicted the seven burglars. That was all. That was the only time. We never had another conversation. I never saw him once. . . .

COLSON: There are those who are not—we can't be self-righteous about it, but there are those who are perfectly prepared to lay out of the facts and—

PRESIDENT NIXON: Take the consequences. That's right.

COLSON: —and be judged ultimately. I think it's important, however, that the principal thrust be from someone who was in daily contact with you.

PRESIDENT NIXON: Yeah. . . .

June 3, 1973: The President and Haldeman, 12:35–1:11 P.M., Camp David Telephone

The talk between Nixon and Haldeman is relaxed and knowing, with their exchanges often anticipating each other. Here, in almost comic manner, they consider the possibility that Dean had taped them.

PRESIDENT NIXON: . . . It's interesting. Apparently in this story, Dean's—or the source says that Dean does not have any documentary evidence. I wonder why he says that. He doesn't have, of course.

HALDEMAN: Well, they probably asked him and he—it's interesting though. Did you see they lobbed out that he had tape recordings?

PRESIDENT NIXON: No.

HALDEMAN: That's buried in one of the stories, that one of his sources lobbed out that everybody was making tape recordings of phone calls and that Dean did too.

PRESIDENT NIXON: Hmm.

HALDEMAN: I don't think that's true.

PRESIDENT NIXON: Let me say this. Tape recordings that he had. I mean, if—I don't believe that—he didn't have any at Camp David, Bob, when you called him here or I—when I called him at Camp David, you know. We—he was—you know what I mean. I don't know how the hell he could tape record at Camp David, do you?

HALDEMAN: No. Well, yeah, you can easily. I've got a little thing you just plug onto the phone and stick it on your tape recorder and it records the conversation just with a little—

PRESIDENT NIXON: Well, so be it.

HALDEMAN: —suction cup on the telephone and do it.

PRESIDENT NIXON: So, he does have. So, he does have. What the hell is the difference? Huh?

HALDEMAN: That doesn't bother me. They hurt him worse than anybody. At least his conversations with me do.

PRESIDENT NIXON: Yeah.

HALDEMAN: And he didn't have very many with you I don't think. . . . He's claiming that Easter phone call. He makes the claim that you said in that phone call that you were just kidding about that we could raise the million dollars if it was needed. . . .

PRESIDENT NIXON: We never even discussed it.

HALDEMAN: And he may have a recording of that that has something in it, but they're trying to make something out of that. But we can set that one to rest on the basis of investigations. I mean, hell, at that point you were trying to find out. In the first place, it was the question—

PRESIDENT NIXON: Now, let me tell you that in the Easter call—I remember that very well. That was a very brief call and we didn't discuss any damn—anything of that sort at all. . . . He talked about his—he wanted—said how he was going to plead and all that sort of thing and wanted to see me. And I said—and of course, we couldn't do that.

HALDEMAN: Yeah. . . .

JUNE 3, 1973: THE PRESIDENT AND HAIG, 3:12–3:27 P.M., CAMP DAVID TELEPHONE

The two believe that Watergate is a dying story; they also are convinced that a left-wing plot exists to sabotage the Administration. The prospect of Dean's public testimony sharpens the President's thinking. In his memoirs, Nixon acknowledged that it did not matter whether Dean's testimony was accurate; "it only mattered if *any* of his testimony was accurate." Then, admitting an emerging theme of his own later conversations: "Dean's account of the crucial March 21 meeting was more accurate than my own had been. . . . [I]n the end it would make less difference that I was not as involved as Dean had alleged than that I was not as uninvolved as I had claimed."

SEGMENT 1

PRESIDENT NIXON: You know, . . . they're going to try to crap on us about once a week. Don't you think so?

HAIG: Yes, and they—well, they've already started the pattern of late Saturday afternoon to get the Sunday press. But I don't think people give them a Goddamn anymore. They're not reading it and we shouldn't. . . .

PRESIDENT NIXON: . . . Yeah, you take—you take the—the Dean story, you know, and so forth. Well, it's full of the usual innuendos. So, you saw the President a lot of times, and he—and he says the President was—had to be—was aware of a cover-up in—in January, February, or March, and so forth. So—so what? What the hell does that prove? . . . Well, the point is, we have not denied that I was aware of a cover-up. I mean, the point is, though, it's a matter of a question of a date then, isn't it?

000HAIG: Exactly.

PRESIDENT NIXON: And we know damn well the date isn't March, but nevertheless the number of times he sees me, of course, he—he says forty. Actually it was 20 or whatever the hell. But it doesn't make any difference. I wouldn't argue about that. . . . But anyway, we—I guess we just have to—to live with these stories. I think we get too—we—I mean, I suppose I'm the worst offender. I tend to get more excited about it because I do—I know what they're up to. It's basically just a pattern to say, well, the President's lying or something like that. I just don't know how much it gets through. What do you think, Al?

HAIG: Well, I think it's time for—for advocates to be out, the Cabinet and other people, taking this stuff on, not the White House. All it does is—is focus more attention on what people are not paying any attention to anymore anyhow. . . . But I don't think . . . it pays any dividends to get out and give a detailed rebuttal from the White House. . . .

SEGMENT 3

PRESIDENT NIXON: Look, this kind of crap we just—I must say we're getting a little thicker skin. If they had hit us with this, say, about the 10th of May, it would really—it would have really knocked us over, wouldn't it?

HAIG: That's right.

PRESIDENT NIXON: Don't you think so?

HAIG: It would have been very bad.

PRESIDENT NIXON: Yeah.

HAIG: And you know, if he had come out with that on top of those memcoms and if we'd have set without an answer, we'd have been in bad shape. So, I think we played it just right.

PRESIDENT NIXON: But actually, we do have an answer out there. We've said, by God, I was not aware of a cover-up.

HAIG: That's right.

PRESIDENT NIXON: I mean, I did not, of course, participate in one.

HAIG: You know, we'll get a lot of nitpicking, but now it's the extremists who are doing it. The good guys have shut up.

PRESIDENT NIXON: You really think some of them have?

HAIG: Yes, sir. You know, you get a [Senator Charles] Percy [R-IL] who's popping off and you got a—one of these left-wing damn—he'll start screaming. But the fight is beginning within the committee. It's—it's now along partisan lines. We're just—we're just in a hell of a lot better shape. And we can—we can afford to ride these things without getting all exercised each time.

PRESIDENT NIXON: Yeah.

HAIG: It's calculated. There's no question—

PRESIDENT NIXON: Yeah, sure, on that part it is. Yeah.

HAIG: Yes, sir.

PRESIDENT NIXON: They're trying to hit it every week, keep the story going and bounce another one off of us, trying to knock us over.

HAIG: Well, it's just not going to happen now and I think we're all convinced of that. We've got to get some of our own people shored up a little bit and that comes from continuing accomplishments—

PRESIDENT NIXON: Yeah. Well, they've got to think that we're here to stay. That's really what it gets down to. . . . You see, for example, one of the reasons that none of our people would speak—some of our people wouldn't speak up when our enemies were hitting us so hard after April 30th—you know, that Bob and John announcement—is that they really thought seriously they might knock us over, knock me over. You know, they really—I think a lot of them thought there might be a resignation or impeachment or some damn thing.

HAIG: Well, they were in a state of shock and that wasn't discounted by some of them. But I think that we're well past that. . . . In fact, as good a bellwether as you can find is Henry. Henry is just—he's solid now. He said, Goddamn it, we've passed it. He's elated.

PRESIDENT NIXON: Of course, the Dean kind of thing will worry him because of its being in the *Times* and *Post*. [*Chuckles.*]

HAIG: No, no. I—I talked to him today. He—he's really not paying attention anymore to this stuff. . . .

JUNE 5, 1973: THE PRESIDENT, CONNALLY, AND HAIG, 3:07–5:18 P.M., OVAL OFFICE

Nixon and Connally had engaging conversations, particularly marked by Connally's blunt advice to the President. "[E]verybody thinks you knew about it anyway and you can't prove you didn't," Connally tells him at one point. He urges Nixon to get on with the business of governing, using the vast resources of his office to restore his standing. Of course, Connally does not appreciate all of Nixon's vulnerabilities, but his unabashed candor is a rare commodity in the Nixon White House.

SEGMENT 1

PRESIDENT NIXON: [Clark] Clifford came out for the President and Vice President to resign, resign and set up a coalition government. Governor [Patrick] Lucey [D-WI] says the President should resign and the Vice President should set up a coalition government. Well, all of that did not just happen last Sunday. I think it was all planned, starting weeks ago. I think if it had hit us three weeks ago, it could have been pretty, pretty damaging, or could've, well, wouldn't, probably might have been. I don't know, though. But what is your judgment as to where it stands now?

CONNALLY: Mr. President, you're beginning, you've talked out, um, I think frankly you ought not to say anything more about Watergate—

PRESIDENT NIXON: I don't intend to.

CONNALLY: —at all, under all, any circumstances. Under any circumstances. I think—

PRESIDENT NIXON: As you know, a lot of people want me to get up and answer questions about Watergate and all that sort of thing. Have a press conference on Watergate.

CONNALLY: . . . As for me, I wouldn't issue any more statements about it. For two reasons: first, I don't know that you have anything to add to the body of information, but be that as it may, uh, and secondly, I don't care what happens, I don't care if they really say that you knew about it—

PRESIDENT NIXON: Yup.

CONNALLY: Uh, either about the break-in or the cover-up. I don't think that, at this point, is important or critical to you, strange enough. I don't even know you can respond to it. Strangely, most of the people think you do know about it.

PRESIDENT NIXON: I know.

CONNALLY: So, and there's no way you can keep, there's no way we can prove you didn't know about it. . . . [F]rom this point on, I think, unless somebody is just absolutely crazy and just accuses you of all kinds of heinous crimes or something, I would just pay no more attention to it. Now you obviously have to have Len Garment or somebody keepin' up with it, workin' on it, trying to be sure that you do everything for Haldeman or Ehrlichman or whoever—

PRESIDENT NIXON: Oh, I'm doing that.

CONNALLY: —that you can. But as far as you are concerned, your policy and your position, I think that's already said. And now it seems to me that you just forget about it—and you can't run from the public—you go on about your other business, you create as much activity—

PRESIDENT NIXON: Right.

CONNALLY: —in the government. You do as many things as you can within the government. . . . Get out where people can see you, because this is part of the answer to this whole thing. This program, however limited it is, will give you an opportunity to do that, the mere crossing the country with [Soviet President Leonid] Brezhnev. But you oughtta make one or two trips, hopefully next week, before that. But the point I'm making . . . and then I'm going to make one other point, you have begun to top out at the hearings end. Don't try and don't let any of your people try to suppress them. . . . Your hope of salvation is the continuation of them ad nauseam because the people are already beginning to get sick of them.

PRESIDENT NIXON: You think so? . . .

CONNALLY: There's no way you can stop it so let it run. And even if somebody says you knew about it, everybody thinks you knew about it anyway. . . . And you can't prove you didn't, so you almost immune to any further damage. . . . [I]f you'll remember, Roosevelt used to give these "fireside chats" and he used to talk about their problems and . . . everybody thought he knew about them, he was concerned about them, he had great care about them. And this is really all the people expect; they don't expect miracles. But you have to be in this posture at a time when these guys are trying to persecute you. And if you are, you'll come out of it in very good shape.

PRESIDENT NIXON: Surviving, in other words.

CONNALLY: Oh, you're gonna do more than survive, hell, you're gonna be, you're gonna come out ahead of the game. . . .

PRESIDENT NIXON: The main thing is, John, gotta do the job for the country and if we've got big things to do in the world and big things to do at home—

CONNALLY: You'll come out of it with enough strength to carry on any program you want to carry on. But you're gonna have to come out in a, in a very aggressive, in a fighting mood. . . . The only thing, it seems to me, that you have to be concerned with is manifesting leadership. Now, how do you do that? You can't solve all the problems in the world, you manifest leadership and that's the only thing that you really ought to be concerned about.

Now, sometimes, particularly coming out of the dark days such as this Watergate thing, the best way to manifest leadership is through the espousal of an unpopular cause, not a popular one. Always use the reverse psychology: it's easier anyway, political leaders to come out and support a popular issue. But it takes a strong dedicated leader to come out with something that, at least on the face of it, might not be a popular cause. Now I'm not advocating anything, I don't have anything in mind, but uh, but whatever you do, it oughtta be done with an air of decisiveness and strength. . . .

[Connally leaves.]

SEGMENT 3

HAIG: . . . I do think getting out of Washington is a good idea. . . .
PRESIDENT NIXON: Getting into California's a good thing. . . .
HAIG: [Soviet President Leonid] Brezhnev will be a great watershed.
PRESIDENT NIXON: You think so? I think he has got to be. . . .

June 5, 1973: The President and Buzhardt, 5:29–7:14 P.M., Executive Office Building

Buzhardt emerges as the consummate staff man for Watergate containment. His reputation for loyalty is excellent as a longtime staffer and assistant to senators and Pentagon officials; moreover, Buzhardt, as a lawyer, occupies a special vantage point. He has precisely those qualities Nixon values and needs at the moment. Charles Alan Wright, the distinguished constitutional authority from the University of Texas, has joined the White House legal team and is advising Buzhardt. The President particularly is worried about Haldeman's and Ehrlichman's notes. He now remembers his September 15 meeting with John Dean, yet he minimizes its importance.

SEGMENT 1

PRESIDENT NIXON: . . . Well, I just wanted to say to you that I haven't seen much of you, but, as I told Al, I am very grateful for what you've been doing. You've worked night and day, you and Len. I know you've been the honcho.
BUZHARDT: Thank you, sir.
PRESIDENT NIXON: And I did have a long talk with John Connally. He thinks it's very important that I stay away from it. . . . And more and more I'm going to have to do that, you know what I mean. I had to be involved in it, you know, going through

that terrible experience with Bob and John for the weeks thereafter, you know. . . . [Connally] said don't comment . . . . Most people in the country think you probably did it anyway, and he said they don't care whether you did it or not. . . .

BUZHARDT: That's probably true. . . . I think there's no need, you know, for you to be involved, unless there's a basic policy decision. . . . Or something of that type, which we will bring to your attention.

PRESIDENT NIXON: Sure. With regard to papers and things of that kind.

BUZHARDT: On the papers, let me say, this is a procedural approach, and you read [White House Counsel] Charlie Wright's paper in there, we have one case, which is the [Aaron] Burr case, which [Chief Justice John] Marshall decided [in 1803?], and that case probably goes further than any test in history. And the questions there were the questions of the St. Clair expedition. The Court, of course, attempted to compel Jefferson's appearance. He declined or he said he wouldn't. After that, they said or Marshall ruled that he had the right to subpoena papers. Jefferson, I believe, gave the papers to his Attorney General to make the decision of whether it was in the national interest to release them. . . . And Marshall held that that was unsatisfactory, that was not a delegable function, and that the executive privilege only extended to those matters which the President, without delegation, where the President made the determination of whether or not it was in the national interest to make the disclosure.

Now that's the narrowest definition probably we have of executive privilege. But it's something to consider here if we reach close to the point of litigation, that instead of saying a blanket no in order to avoid any invocation of the holding of that case, we say okay, you ask for a specific document. We will make—the President will make— the determination of whether it's in the national interest.

That way you avoid the point, if a court now were to agree with that holding, we have . . . avoided by you making the decision—as with respect to each request for papers—rather than just saying no papers. You could make it for anything they ask for with respect to the national interest. Now, judging from John Dean's papers, 95 percent of them are totally irrelevant.

PRESIDENT NIXON: Yeah.

BUZHARDT: It's pretty hard to imagine anything in there that would be relevant that actually exists or that would be releasable in the national interest. . . . Chuck Colson brought me a file. Of course, I had a long talk with both Chuck and his counsel, and I said you cannot protect documents that you have in your possession. . . . And finally Chuck brought me in a rather big file. Now, there's nothing about [Watergate] in his files. There are some political matters which should never be disclosed. But after having read the entire set—and Chuck explained the background on most of them—I'm convinced there would be no problem of you making a pivotal determination that these documents, it's not in the national interest, because they do deal with national security matters.

PRESIDENT NIXON: Chuck's papers?

BUZHARDT: They deal with the Plumber operation. . . . You don't have any problem on that.

PRESIDENT NIXON: I'll tell you . . . the real problem is this. If, for example, they get Haldeman's notes or Ehrlichman's notes of conversations with me, that is a rough cut, because I discuss (unintelligible).

BUZHARDT: But the point is, I'm not suggesting that we ever give them the first one of those notes. I'm suggesting this as a matter of procedure. . . . No, sir. That we turn the papers down on an item by item basis rather than on a bundled basis, that we tell them—

PRESIDENT NIXON: You couldn't say, Fred, that it was not in the national—that Haldeman's notes where I talk and say very frankly that some judge was a clown. On Sirica, I might have said that.

SEGMENT 2

BUZHARDT: Well, I think from a procedural standpoint, this will give us no problem. We discussed this somewhat at length to see what would be best. And we discussed it on the assumption—to weigh the pros and cons. We discussed it on the assumption that if we went this route we would have to be able to turn down anything to do with Haldeman and Ehrlichman's notes.

PRESIDENT NIXON: On what ground?

BUZHARDT: On the interest it's not in the national interest.

PRESIDENT NIXON: National interest, huh?

BUZHARDT: It's not national security. It's not in the national interest. That's the decision you have to make.

PRESIDENT NIXON: Right.

BUZHARDT: But what we're saying is, to claim executive privilege would have to say in the first place, it's not in the national interest. . . . And we would be in a stronger legal position to say that with respect to specific requests than we would if we said it in a blanket fashion. . . .

They will have a great deal of difficulty getting specific about documents. And we have to understand that many of the relevant documents, memoranda written from here, that they consider relevant, ones written from here to the committee, they have already gotten most of the committee's records.

PRESIDENT NIXON: Oh, sure.

BUZHARDT: Bob and John have both turned over tapes of conversations with various people. . . .

PRESIDENT NIXON: Conversations they had with other people?

BUZHARDT: They had with other people. For your information, I found no record of where anybody has taped conversations with you that was ever questioned.

PRESIDENT NIXON: I think Colson has. He'd probably do that.

BUZHARDT: He says he has no tapes of conversations. If he ever made them, he says he does not now have them. Now, I know he made some. I've seen the record where he taped [television commentator] Howard Smith. . . .

PRESIDENT NIXON: . . . What is your feeling about him, Haldeman, and Ehrlichman going [to testify before Senator McClellan's Committee?]? . . .

BUZHARDT: They had different recollections of conversations and their conversations were apparently in conflict. Now, that's bad news. I talked to [Haldeman and Ehrlichman's lawyer] John Wilson about it. . . . I think John's [Ehrlichman's] statements have not had much work by his counsel, and that presents a problem because he raises questions by the way his statements are phrased that don't have to be raised. So that gives me a little caution—I'm speaking very candidly—about the type of statements he gives that can raise more problems for himself. And they're not questions as to you, except for the Mexican money (unintelligible) that John raises.

PRESIDENT NIXON: Yeah. Well, it's a problem to me only in this sense, only in this sense, though, Fred. There had been a newspaper story about the Mexican money.

BUZHARDT: John did straighten this out.

PRESIDENT NIXON: You know what I mean? That's the reason. Actually, they came in and told me about it.

BUZHARDT: John says he told you this five or six days after the meeting with Gray and Walters.

PRESIDENT NIXON: I don't know. I don't recall the whole thing.

BUZHARDT: That is his recollection, because he didn't see you prior to the meeting, he said. That was his testimony. Bob Haldeman saw you and then told John that you wanted to him to sit in on the meeting. So he (unintelligible). And Haldeman says he didn't tell him about that you were interested in the Mexican connection. He doesn't remember it being mentioned. But Ehrlichman testified that was your primary concern, and he then didn't say at what point in time. He later checked his notes and went back to the press and said that was about five or six days after the meeting that he talked with you about it, and there was no howl from the press. Well, it's one that he will correct before he testifies in another forum.

PRESIDENT NIXON: . . . Well, we're bound to have these. There is going to be more—there is already more conflict in this stuff up there. They're having a heck of a time.

BUZHARDT: They are.

PRESIDENT NIXON: They are. And you know, part of it is just conflict because of differences in recollection. They're not all lying.

BUZHARDT: If they had a pat story, why, I would get very suspicious

PRESIDENT NIXON: What?

BUZHARDT: If they all remembered exactly as the same thing, it would be very suspicious. . . .

[Sam] Dash, the counsel for the Ervin Committee, has just announced his intention, or the intention of the committee to subpoena the President's logs, and then says: our understanding is the subpoena will relate to the meetings with John Dean. The subpoena will issue tomorrow. . . . I frankly think that—I think we all agree that we don't ever give them the logs. I think at some point we should give them the dates, we should give them the information. . . . I think we should reject their subpoena to maintain the principle of the matter and make it clear that they never did ask for the information. We'll reject the subpoena and then give them the information.

PRESIDENT NIXON: What do you think Dash is up to with Dean? Does Dean aspire to immunity?

BUZHARDT: I think he hopes so. I think he hopes so. I think the committee at this point [has] not a single purpose by any means, as is [Archibald] Cox. They have to a kind of consensus, and I think Dash is trying to retain the confidence of the full committee. This requires us to separate out his individual motives. . . .

On the 21st you met with Dean, and I notice that on the 22nd that you called in Dean, Haldeman, Ehrlichman, and Mitchell for that conversation. I assume, I assume, at that point you did not have enough details. Was Mitchell still denying that he was involved? . . .

PRESIDENT NIXON: Oh, he's never. Still, he denies it today. Today. The purpose of my calling them in on the 22nd was to say, "Look, we've got to get this story out." I was the hang-out man, and so was Ehrlichman. Dean kept saying, no, we can't get it out because it would raise more questions than it would—you know what I mean. That's another thing. No, the purpose of that was to say, how can we get it out, how can we cooperate, and so forth. And then it was after that that I sent Dean off—

BUZHARDT: There are two telephone calls, one from Florida. One was to here in Washington at (unintelligible) in the afternoon, and he apparently right after that to Camp David because you talked to him later in the day at Camp David. So that day, apparently, the [March] 23rd, he came up to Camp David later in the day (unintelligible) on the 23rd. . . .

PRESIDENT NIXON: Oh God, no. There was never any discussion of a million dollars except on the 21st. Never, never, never. Good gosh, that was pure hypothetical crap, frankly. . . . Let me explain. The whole business about dollars is to me embarrassing because we were discussing it, but I was really—you know how (unintelligible) what in the world do you fellows think you're doing here? How much would it cost? Where would we get the money? How do you do it? What do you do about clemency? They're going to talk anyway.

BUZHARDT: You could have done it?

PRESIDENT NIXON: Oh, yes, yes. We could have always gotten the money. There are always people to contribute money. So, the next day when we met—and here you have to, we will have Haldeman's and Ehrlichman's recollection. And we said, how can we get this whole story out? It's getting bigger and bigger and bigger and bigger. . . . See, Dean on the 21st—this is an important thing—did not tell me about—I've already told you he didn't tell me about what he had done here. He didn't tell me that he had offered clemency. He didn't tell me that he had suborned Magruder's perjury. He didn't tell me that he, Dean, had handled the money. . . . The only thing that he really implied was a real problem, was a real problem, was that now there was blackmail. He used the term "blackmail" in the first conversation, with Bittman asking for $120,000 for Hunt for attorneys' fees and for expenses. I think it was all for Bittman, basically. Bittman said he wasn't paid, or he was going to reveal the very thing (unintelligible) to Ehrlichman. And that's when I began to cross-examine him as the day went on.

I mean, it's hard for anybody to believe that I would not have known about the money. But you see, the way we operated, both Haldeman and Ehrlichman thought it was perfectly proper. Second, they didn't want me to be diverted from dealing with the war and a lot of other things. . . . I paid no attention to the doggone thing until, until basically the Ervin Committee started. And then I got into it. And the Ervin Committee—we were worried as much about Watergate—we didn't get into Watergate conversations with Green—Dean—until the 7th, 8th, the hearing then. But mostly it was about the Ervin Committee, how do we make our appearances, what are the—who are the—et cetera, et cetera.

BUZHARDT: That is easy for those of us who have worked in the government to understand.

PRESIDENT NIXON: Outside, nobody's going to believe it. Well, I think what you have to have in mind is that from the 21st on . . . is what triggered my own investigation, first under Dean, and then second under Ehrlichman when Dean didn't come through. . . .

BUZHARDT: I frankly hope and think there's a good chance we'll never really have to deal with this in sworn testimony by Dean.

PRESIDENT NIXON: Really?

BUZHARDT: I do think there's a good chance we won't. We may have to.

PRESIDENT NIXON: Well, if we do, we have to. Let's face it.

BUZHARDT: If we do, there are several ways we can handle it with the testimony of—

PRESIDENT NIXON: Haldeman. . . . For me to have to answer, for me to have to answer a treacherous counsel to the President, "the President answers John Dean."

BUZHARDT: That's just not appropriate.

PRESIDENT NIXON: That's very bad. . . . Because the other thing they do, the minute you do that—the other thing you've got to watch out for is the committee and/or the grand jury, this jazz of asking the President to testify. . . . Why, it's absolutely ridiculous. Any President ever testify?

BUZHARDT: No, sir, no President.

PRESIDENT NIXON: Well, he shouldn't.

BUZHARDT: Interestingly, when Johnson was impeached by the House, he did not testify at his own impeachment. There is no precedent, not even close, under any circumstances, for a President testifying. I think at some point you may want one of us as your counsel, if it gets to that stage—and I'm sure hoping it won't, for the presidency. . . .

PRESIDENT NIXON: Actually, you see, part of the problem here, when I called Dean on Easter, actually it was basically just, I would say, an act of kindness. I called my staff (unintelligible), that poor son of a gun, here he is, scared and all that sort of thing. . . . Dean called him [Ziegler] right back and said it was such a nice thing to do. That's all it was. Dean did say, you know, I might have to come talk to you. . . and of course I didn't even say yes, no, or maybe. I mentioned it to [Henry] Petersen perhaps later, and he of course advised against it. . . .

. . . [F]rom the 15th of April to the 30th of April I had to go through the tortures of the damned. I had to work on Haldeman and Ehrlichman, and I had to do it alone. I had nobody here who could handle it for me. And between that and that, I could not move on the Dean problem.

BUZHARDT: We have—

PRESIDENT NIXON: Oh, another point that may be raised (unintelligible) the question, why was it that I let Haldeman and Ehrlichman, they resigned voluntarily and why was it I said I had requested and accepted the resignation of Dean. Simply, very simply, because he was asking for immunity. Anybody who asks for immunity naturally is automatically out. . . .

You see, Fred. The story his lawyer has put out is that from January to April he saw me 40 times or so. It gives the impression that before these guys pled and so on that he was sitting in there talking with me all the time. And the first time, the first time I saw him, was February 27. There was no telephone call before. And before that, the last time I had seen him was September the 15th, the day these guys were indicted. . . . So—and maybe his lawyers figured that their immunity thing is made stronger by making it appear that his contacts began earlier.

BUZHARDT: I think there are two stories that were read on this subject. One was written by Sy Hersh. It was very careless. He's the man who said he saw you about forty times. I don't think that's even what the lawyers would say. I think Woodward and Bernstein wrote it accurately.

PRESIDENT NIXON: Thirty-five. . . . Actually, there are fourteen telephone calls, twenty-one times he saw me. . . .

BUZHARDT: The September 15 meeting, do you remember what that was about?

PRESIDENT NIXON: Oh, sure, sure. He came in to tell us about the guys who were indicted. Haldeman has a record on that. I don't, but Haldeman has it. You know, he sat in the meeting and made a record. Oh, it involved a number of things. I said, when are we going to get the dope on [Larry] O'Brien's IRS investigation. We talked about that. Everything not related to Watergate at all—offensive tactics that we ought to be engaged in, when are we going to get information, counterattack information on the Democratic harassment of our campaign, and so forth and so on, things you would normally discuss in a campaign. . . . The only other time I saw him in 1972 was when he came in for my will signing. . . . Of course, he was the lawyer. That's the only other time he was ever in my office. I didn't see him in the planning stages of Watergate or right after that or anything like that. . . .

JUNE 6, 1973: THE PRESIDENT AND ROSE MARY WOODS, 8:25–8:53 A.M., OVAL OFFICE

Rose Mary Woods—often known as the "Fifth Nixon" —may have been privy to the President's secrets as much as anyone. After Dean met with Nixon on March 21, Nixon immediately spoke to Woods about raising some cash. Here, she talks about her contacts with Thomas Pappas, the Greek-American businessman who had provided hush money for the burglars. Ms. Woods also gives the President her views on Senator Baker and the Senate hearings.

SEGMENT 1

PRESIDENT NIXON: I want to check on one thing, is to, it's quite important—have you been able to get ahold of Pappas yet?

WOODS: He won't be back. I keep checking his girl, because the minute he gets back, she'll have him call. . . .

PRESIDENT NIXON: Things are very much in his interest, and it's very much in ours for his reason that uh, he brings money for Lenny Hall [the one-time Republican Chairman in the 1950s]. . . .

WOODS: For Lenny Hall?

PRESIDENT NIXON: I'm sorry, I said Len Hall—for John Mitchell and uh, when he came in to talk to me, you know, he came in to talk to me about this Hall—he wants just to have for Ambassador [sic: Henry Tasca, to Greece]. . . . On the 7th of March. On that occasion I thanked him for raising money. . . . But I just want to be damned sure that Pappas, Jesus, doesn't get implicated in this damn thing, see. And of course I don't want to have anything indicating that I was thanking him for raising money for the Watergate defendants. I think he's smart enough to know that, but you know, uh, you just never know.

WOODS: Well, I, I think he is too, but because of that fact, is it even safe for me to talk on the phone . . . ?

PRESIDENT NIXON: No, don't talk on the phone. . . .

WOODS: I'll call his girl today and say as soon as he gets back into town, say I need to see him.

PRESIDENT NIXON: Tell him it's a, tell him it's a personal thing. See, what they could do to him is if they went out, "Mr. Pappas, you raised this money. Did the President ask you to? Did you . . . ask him anything?" . . . I think somebody called down there and said Pappas is very helpful . . . [Y]ou know I never go behind these things. . . . But you know, we went through this whole period, as you well know, Rose, and uh, good God almighty, if I'd ever heard or ever known about this darn thing, I would've blown it right out of the water, it's so stupid.

WOODS: It's just unbelievable. . . .

PRESIDENT NIXON: You'd think that, you know, because they're not bad men, Rose.

WOODS: No.

PRESIDENT NIXON: Good God, they're not like the Teddy Kennedy outfit. . . .

SEGMENT 2

PRESIDENT NIXON: Well—but Pappas has raised money, see, the first Kalmbach apparently raised—I'm piecing this together now—and after that, Mitchell got Pappas into the act, you know, to help him raise money. Mitchell needed Pappas. . . .

WOODS: — . . . my heart aches for him [Mitchell]. He never wanted to come down here—

PRESIDENT NIXON: It is? Oh God—

WOODS: . . . He wouldn't have done anything—

PRESIDENT NIXON: And the thing that we've got to remember about him, too, as far as this case is concerned—[Long pause.]

WOODS: He would never knowingly have done anything. . . .

PRESIDENT NIXON: You know, Baker's problem was he won't work hard enough.

WOODS: Well, I think Baker's problem, frankly, is that Baker looked great on the television.

PRESIDENT NIXON: Sure.

WOODS: . . . Baker looked more handsome on television than he is, because of his size. He looks big sitting there, you know, tall. And he is apparently the idol of the soap opera people who watch. . . .

PRESIDENT NIXON: Well, he isn't gonna do it by running down the President. Well, he isn't doing that, I guess, he's just—

WOODS: He isn't running you down. But I keep saying to our friend, if you get a chance to talk to him, tell him to . . . keep repeating that this is hearsay. He does it occasionally . . .

JUNE 6, 1973: THE PRESIDENT AND HAIG, 9:01–10:03 A.M., OVAL OFFICE

The President adds former Republican congressman and Defense Secretary Melvin Laird to his staff. Laird is popular among Republicans, but Nixon thinks he will be useful "to leak and everything." John Connally's visit the previous day has lifted the spirits of Nixon and Haig. They are bent on a vigorous White House counterattack, but Nixon, ever the realist, recognizes the growing danger because of slippage in his congressional support. California Republican Congressman Pete McCloskey threatens an impeachment resolution. Nixon realizes that the Democrats will hesitate to support such a move, fearing the President's vast reservoir of public support at this time.

SEGMENT 4

HAIG: . . . We made a helluva move and I think [Melvin] Laird's gonna be a big asset around here. We need—

PRESIDENT NIXON: Somebody to go out and leak and everything.

HAIG: That's right.

PRESIDENT NIXON: He loves to do that.

HAIG: That's right. And at some point, (unintelligible) a tough political in-fighter and that's what he is. He knows where all the, all the monkeys are. And the same with Bryce [Harlow], although Bryce is a little less aggressive. . . .

SEGMENT 5

PRESIDENT NIXON: . . . [S]ome of the more partisan Democrats who didn't turn on us earlier because they didn't think it would be popular are starting to. They're laying back just a little now. Maybe—

HAIG: You wanna call Jerry Ford and see how his discussion with [Congressman Paul] McCloskey [R-CA]—

PRESIDENT NIXON: Oh, I got him yesterday.

HAIG: Did you get him?

PRESIDENT NIXON: He said uh, that McCloskey probably was not going to put in a [impeachment] resolution, he's just gonna make a speech about it. . . .

HAIG: Yeah, I think that's the best we could do.

PRESIDENT NIXON: So, if McCloskey makes a speech, that's all right. . . . [Speaker Carl] Albert [D-OK] doesn't want it, Jerry said. And the Democratic leadership doesn't want to put their guys on the spot. . . .

HAIG: It would be impossible at this time to, to visualize such a thing. . . .

JUNE 6, 1973: THE PRESIDENT AND CLARENCE M. KELLEY, 10:05–10:35 A.M., OVAL OFFICE

The President meets Kelley, his newly nominated Director of the FBI. He feigns horror that William Sullivan has turned over material to the Justice Department that implicates J. Edgar Hoover in illegal wiretaps, ignoring the fact that Sullivan is his man. Nevertheless, Nixon points to the "young Hoover" as a role model for Kelley. The conversation is poorly recorded, but it reveals Nixon's determination to have Kelley look to him for guidance.

SEGMENT 1

PRESIDENT NIXON: . . . That's why these taps—Hoover kept perfectly legitimate national-security taps, half of what was done in the Kennedy and Johnson period— were removed from the FBI files by [William] Sullivan, who did the tapping and brought them to the Justice Department, . . . because he said that Hoover might use them to blackmail us. . . . That an officer of the Bureau would suggest that Edgar Hoover would blackmail the Attorney General or the President of the United States. I just couldn't believe it. And I don't believe it today. Uh, I was going way back to the days of the Hiss days when I was a young Congressman. . . .

SEGMENT 2

PRESIDENT NIXON: But what is needed at the Bureau is not just a figurehead. . . . But what is needed is a fearless administrator who will go in there with the spirit of the young J. Edgar Hoover, . . . taking virtually the whole top echelon and [dismissing them?] and finding people you can bring up. Now this, this can't be done overnight, but you must get your team in there and get them in place.

I'm not ordering you to do this, but I'm telling you based on my, with the analysis I've had, everybody has studied it in Justice and here, the Bureau desperately needs this. And I think we should talk to some people about it, I think maybe Henry Petersen and others . . . But, but if you just go in and just sit on the Bureau the way Edgar left it, you won't have served him any. You will have the usual madness of the what the confirmation—they'll ask you how you stand on civil rights and how you stand on wiretapping and all the rest. But you can handle all that. And you'll be, you'll be approved. . . .

KELLEY: Yes, sir. Yes, sir. . . .

SEGMENT 4

KELLEY: Frankly, I look forward to it because, as you say, there are many things that can and should be done and uh, one of those things is that I don't think the Bureau has had quite the relationship with local law enforcement that they could have. Not that they wouldn't want, but that they actually could have and there has been somewhat of a, of an antagonism among the various other federal investigative agencies —

PRESIDENT NIXON: Yeah, for example, Edgar wouldn't even talk to [Richard] Helms because he didn't trust him. That was one of the reasons that we got into that fiasco with regard to the CIA and so forth and so on. The problem was that the, uh, that they just had to be sure that the two would talk to each other. . . .

SEGMENT 5

PRESIDENT NIXON: Now they'll probably ask a few questions over Watergate, but you can easily handle that.

KELLEY: I haven't seen a damn thing that they don't know. . . .

JUNE 6, 1973: THE PRESIDENT, HAIG, BUZHARDT, AND CHARLES ALAN WRIGHT, 11:44 A.M.–12:53 P.M., OVAL OFFICE

On this day, the White House announces what long had been fact: Haig succeeds to Haldeman's duties as Chief of Staff, and Melvin Laird takes Ehrlichman's place. Nixon also names Charles Alan Wright as White House Counsel on a consultancy basis. Nixon here educates Wright on why the President must maintain control over internal White House matters. He seems to hint that there might be a better record of conversations than just memoranda. This conversation, particularly when involving Nixon's dealings with Dean, indicates that he was withholding information from Buzhardt. The men also discuss Dean's forthcoming testimony and the question of his immunity. Finally, following in the vein of John Connally's comments the day before, Haig expresses total optimism, even if Nixon is culpable. The President briefly ponders the possibility of admitting everything, but quickly discards the thought.

SEGMENT 1

PRESIDENT NIXON: . . . [W]hat is the latest with regard to the uh, uh, the uh, the Dash's controversy with Cox? Is that still rolling along, or?

BUZHARDT: That's, they're still at odds. I mean, the Committee won't back off from the hearings.

PRESIDENT NIXON: You know, I don't know what you think—I don't see how a prosecutor can convict even Mitchell.

WRIGHT: I, I, neither do I.

PRESIDENT NIXON: But this, and they've convicted him already—

WRIGHT: 'Course they have.

PRESIDENT NIXON: —let alone Haldeman and Ehrlichman, whose relationship is almost totally tangential. But goodness, you know, even take on Mitchell where they have a lot more evidence, I don't see how in the world you could ever convict him. What do you think?

BUZHARDT: I think they're gonna have a very difficult time.

PRESIDENT NIXON: And that's what, don't you think Cox has studied the law and worried about that?

WRIGHT: I'm sure he would notice the [Sam] Sheppard case and the Billy Sol Estes case [and issues of pre-trial publicity], they are, they were—

PRESIDENT NIXON: The [Bobby] Seale case. . . .

WRIGHT: Yup. . . .

BUZHARDT: We're going down to see Cox this afternoon. . . .

PRESIDENT NIXON: Well, let me, let me explain to you why the, this paper thing is so sensitive. Fred was telling me and Al has. It's not only because of my conversations with Haldeman and Ehrlichman, and uh, (unintelligible) Dean. . . . Haldeman and Ehrlichman, inside men, took it upon themselves to (unintelligible) at the end of the day, to cover the items that they had talked about with the President. . . . They're subject to massive distortion and it depends on who the heck's reading them, through whose eyes. . . . The difficulty with papers, if you ever break into them, you are going to have—you could hang any president.

WRIGHT: Sure.

PRESIDENT NIXON: For just, what, sitting around talking about things. I was telling Al while he was trying to reconstruct my memory a little bit, my own memory, conversation I had, maybe I was talking with Ziegler, that Dean, as we were, we got into the whole matter of the courts, you know. I said we were gonna have to appoint some new people to the courts, and I said, "No, we've gotta have it stronger." I said, "when is that nut [D.C. Court of Appeals Chief Judge David] Bazelon going to get done," and uh, I don't what I said, but this is something that I recall, and I said, uh, it's kind of language we would use, and he's gotten worse. And "senile," and so forth.

Then we got into the Supreme Court appointment and I characterized some of the Supreme Court judges in very colorful language, I'm sure. I probably said two or three real boobs, which I believe, that Marshall was just there because he's black and I said "Now, if you, if you ever get that seat open," I said, "we've got a pretty good fellow in [first name unknown] Brown. I remembered that because I think Brown, a fellow at the office [U.S. Attorney's?] in Philadelphia, is a very fine, first-class lawyer. I said the best one is . . . Jewels [Jewel S. LaFontant]. I said, "there you get a woman and a black and that kills two birds with one stone." And I said, and then I said, "I'd like to see those bastards in the Senate vote against her." [Laughing] Now if that were out—

WRIGHT: [*Laughing.*] Of course.

PRESIDENT NIXON: That would be a *very embarrassing thing.* It'd ruin the chances to get Jewels . . . .

BUZHARDT: . . . [W]e've got pretty good rapport with Fred Thompson. . . .

PRESIDENT NIXON: He isn't—he isn't very smart, is he?

BUZHARDT: He squeezed Gurney. Not extremely so, but—

PRESIDENT NIXON: But he's friendly.

BUZHARDT: But he's friendly.

PRESIDENT NIXON: Good.

BUZHARDT: We're gonna work with him over the weekend. . . . We are hoping, though, to work with Thompson and prepare him, if Dean does appear next week, to do a very thorough cross-examination. . . .

PRESIDENT NIXON: . . . I don't know whether . . . the [March] 21st meeting [with Dean] is supposed to come in here. . . . [H]e did point out that, uh, he had been the subject of this blackmail threat. . . . Christ! not for ten months, he ran the thing and never said a word! . . . How much it would cost over four years—a million. I said, "Well, we can get it," I said, "How would you get it out?" So he puts out the story, President says "we'll pay a million dollars." . . . Now, how do I know the answer to such a thing? . . .

BUZHARDT: Oh. You can't, you can't answer it head-on, because you shouldn't ever be in the position of contesting with Dean. . . .

PRESIDENT NIXON: . . . [W]hat had really happened here is that decent men collected money in the beginning for the defense attorneys. Their motives were proper, right? And that's where Haldeman and Ehrlichman have a defense there. Later on, as the cheese got more binding, then uh, the uh, the defendants began to uh, began to talk, or a lot more money—this was blackmail, right? Okay? And, as, when the cheese got binding, uh, what was earlier a perfectly legitimate thing becomes obstruction of justice. . . .

And so they tied all of them together. Well, the whole thing was obstruction of justice. Right? . . . That's, that's what, uh, Haldeman was telling me that their, the way their counsel looks at it. You take Haldeman and Ehrlichman, neither of them had knowledge of the darn thing. Who the heck were they trying to protect? Huh? Not themselves. I don't know.

BUZHARDT: Can't conceive that either one of them would try and protect Mitchell. [*Laughing.*]

PRESIDENT NIXON: Their attitudes were rather negative towards him.

BUZHARDT: This shows in all of their statements, you know. That would be hard to make anybody believe. So they really did it. It's hard to figure how they would've had—

PRESIDENT NIXON: Well, in a sense. I think what you might say, in fairness, maybe they were trying to see that nothing blew before the election. That makes sense—

BUZHARDT: Mm-hmm.

PRESIDENT NIXON: —makes sense. But I don't think that it was obstruction of justice at that point. . . .

BUZHARDT: . . . [T]he only thing he [Archibald Cox] could want with the Dean conversations are the relationship of you to the case. There's no other pertinent purpose for them, you know. So this nails him right to the wall, that's what he's interested in, that's it. If he gives Dean immunity, it can be only for one thing, that's to get you. . . . It oughtta be made clear to him that we know that and we're gonna fight him right down to the wall. . . . His guidelines [from Richardson] are very unfortunate. . . . But unfortunately, those guidelines stating his jurisdiction, that he was given by the Attorney General, state that he'll have jurisdiction over all allegations against the President. . . . And that's about as stupid a thing as could be in there. The courts don't have any jurisdiction over you; how in heaven's name did he be given any? . . .

SEGMENT 4

HAIG: . . . Our position is in excellent shape. It will be some tough going for a while, but the ultimate truth is going to come out. The overriding fact is that Goddamnit, the monkey business was going on for months, for months. And if you— at best, you could be charged with not moving maybe quickly enough. That's all and uh—

PRESIDENT NIXON: That's a legitimate charge.

HAIG: There's just nothing—hell, that's, that's peanuts. The simple fact is, I think you could weather total, total culpability, quite frankly. You could win.

PRESIDENT NIXON: Probably could. . . . Laird will be of enormous assistance.

HAIG: . . . These guys on the Hill are just uniformly excited about it. . . . Well, I'll tell you, there isn't a guy on the Hill who doesn't know that a shrewd sonofabitch like Mel Laird would never have entered your staff if he wasn't very convinced that this was a viable option for him. . . .

PRESIDENT NIXON: I was thinking too, that they, like Mel said, well, we're, from now on we're gonna go up. . . .

JUNE 6, 1973: THE PRESIDENT AND BUZHARDT, 1:00–1:04 P.M., WHITE HOUSE TELEPHONE

The President pulls the gloves off and orders Buzhardt to make it clear to Archibald Cox that he is now an adversary. Only Nixon's voice is heard on this tape.

PRESIDENT NIXON: Hello, Fred. With regard to your meeting with Cox, . . . I want you to say, quite candidly, "Mr. Cox, it's all over town that you're out to get the President. Now, if that is the case we want you to know we're ready to fight." I think you should say that to him, yeah, that you're out to get the President. Several columnists have written this and so forth, that you and your staff are out to get the President. With your record and so forth, we can't believe that. We want you to know that some of the junior members of your staff, they have been saying that. Put it on them. If that's it, we're ready to fight." . . .

[[J]ust say, I base it on nothing you have said, but that apparently there have been a number of calls, apparently coming from some of the junior members of his staff, that have said—perhaps when they had too much to drink—"we're out to get the President." Say, "if that's what you're trying to do, we want you to know we're ready for the fight and you're not going to get him, because that's wrong. The President is cooperating and doing everything he can on this thing, and that the President is totally innocent and everybody knows it, including me. His testimony under oath will so prove." . . . Just say, you know, basically, you know more than he does, because you know everything. You understand? All right. Play a tough game.

JUNE 6, 1973: THE PRESIDENT AND HAIG, 3:48–3:59 P.M., WHITE HOUSE TELEPHONE

The President reacts with typical fury over what he views as a double standard toward wiretapping done by the Kennedy Administration versus his own. Nixon relishes raking over his predecessors' misdeeds.

SEGMENT 1

HAIG: . . . I got a very funny call here from Joe Califano [a member of Lyndon Johnson's White House staff]. . . . And he said that [Cyrus] Vance and [Kennedy's NSC Director McGeorge] Bundy and everyone is all upset about this tap information that was put out. . . . He said that Bundy insists it never happened when he was in the White House and that [Robert] McNamara's all upset about it and said it never happened. . . .

PRESIDENT NIXON: You think they're—what do you think did happen? I think Bobby [Kennedy] did it and maybe didn't tell them.

HAIG: Well, that's, yeah, that's very possible. That's very possible.

PRESIDENT NIXON: Nevertheless, we know it happened. Don't we, Al? . . .

SEGMENT 2

HAIG: It's quite interesting from Califano, though. . . .

PRESIDENT NIXON: We're not shooting an empty cannon on this one.

HAIG: Well, and some guys found some other things too. Like to keep them on edge, I said, "You oughtta know that J. Edgar Hoover would come to each President when he'd come in and tell him what he can do in this area," and I said, "don't, don't even kid yourself that there wasn't some political activity done in the past." I said I don't know the details but I know it was done. . . .

PRESIDENT NIXON: . . . Bundy had told, called Henry, and said he thought he ought to resign again, because of the taps. And then I told him, why don't you ask him about his taps and then Henry said, "Well, he told me they didn't do it." I said that he sure did and Henry didn't believe me and now we got the figures. . . . Why is it taking so long to get the names? What do you think they're doing? . . . I don't want the names going back to Roosevelt. I just want them for those three years. Can't they just work those three years? [19]61, '62, '63—

HAIG: Yeah. We told them to do that.

PRESIDENT NIXON: —and 64.

HAIG: Yes, sir. . . .

PRESIDENT NIXON: Oh boy. Well, they're gonna, they're trying to hang us with stuff that they did, too. And, incidentally, all perfectly legitimate. I don't criticize them for doing it, never did, you know what I mean. . . . But if—they're not gonna get away with hitting us, Al, for something for the national security when they did something for the national security. You know it's like on the war. Heck, when they were running the darn thing I didn't bust them on it. You know, not for the, uh, for getting us in and all that sort of thing. I criticized the conduct, which is perfectly proper. But here, they, when we were in, shucks, they turned around, the Bundys and the rest, and knocked our *brains* out. You know, it's just unconscionable; *that's just a double standard!* . . .

JUNE 6, 1973: THE PRESIDENT AND BUZHARDT, 5:43–6:00 P.M., EXECUTIVE OFFICE BUILDING

Buzhardt reports on his meeting with Archibald Cox and Charles Alan Wright. The session did not bode well for the Administration or for Cox. "I think we need to smoke the man out," Buzhardt tells Nixon. The White House lawyer has a rather low opinion of Cox. "It's hard to get a feeling for Cox," he says. "[H]e has a very superficial knowledge of the case." A confrontation between Nixon and the Special Prosecutor is inevitable, for the President has no intention of cooperating with Cox. Nixon carefully hedges on the existence of any tape of his meetings. Furthermore, he unnecessarily lies to Buzhardt about his ongoing relationship with Haldeman.

SEGMENT 1

BUZHARDT: . . . First, let me characterize the conversation. It was civil. Perhaps we had the—I had the impression that it was two people talking to themselves, if you will, me on one channel and him on another channel, with our statements obviously in conflict, our positions, but nobody wanting to precipitate a—

PRESIDENT NIXON: Confrontation.

BUZHARDT: —confrontation at this meeting. So we went in, sort of defining positions. . . . That's right, exploring positions. He made it clear early . . . that he was of the position, having been confirmed on the basis of his guidelines, that he would have the jurisdiction as set out in his guidelines, he would have access across the board, and trying to establish himself more or less as outside the constitutional structure. . . . He made it plain that he would like, well, he said in the meeting he would like to have access to all the documents, just rather plainly. At that point I told him . . . that that was impossible, that he would not have access to the files, and I explained what our position was on that. . . .

PRESIDENT NIXON: The law cannot go beyond the Constitution.

BUZHARDT: There's a plain separation of powers issue. . . . I made it perfectly clear also that there was a question about precisely what was his purpose. . . . I explained that it's clearly understandable (unintelligible) whose purpose was to get the President. He had no jurisdiction, as far as I was concerned, for getting the President. If that was his purpose, we would make it clear to start with we're perfectly prepared and ready, if that were his purpose or turned out to be his purpose, to engage in a conflict, no problem.

PRESIDENT NIXON: Did he state his position?

BUZHARDT: He said, well, he guessed there was some difference on the question of whether he was out to get the President or whether he was authorized to investigate allegations against the President; and the latter he was undertaking, the former was another matter and could only be determined after.

PRESIDENT NIXON: His answer was affirmative?

BUZHARDT: His answer was in the affirmative. . . .

SEGMENT 2

BUZHARDT: . . . Next, he said that Henry [Petersen] prepared a memo, a one-page memo, which he was led to believe was a summary of the evidence that they had at that time against Haldeman and Ehrlichman.

PRESIDENT NIXON: I have that. Do you want it? . . .

BUZHARDT: The third thing he mentioned was, he said Henry had told him that you had offered to permit him to hear or say—about this he was very vague—a tape of a conversation with Dean that you had on Sun—on the evening of Sunday, April the 15th. We did not comment on that.

PRESIDENT NIXON: I haven't got a tape. I don't have any tape.

BUZHARDT: So it was a misunderstanding on his part?

PRESIDENT NIXON: I have—in fact, I haven't any notes on that. . . .

BUZHARDT: You had a conversation. I haven't looked back at the log, but I remember.

PRESIDENT NIXON: I had a conversation with him that evening. . . . But I can assure you that there's nothing in the conversation that is of any particular interest, except there is one thing that Dean did throw into one of those conversations at that time about Henry. That is, that Henry had given him grand jury reports. Now, Henry vigorously denies, of course. I don't think it makes any difference.

BUZHARDT: The next thing he [Cox] said he wanted us to consider was conversations of Haldeman and Ehrlichman on dictabelts related to the matters under investigation or of conversations with the people under investigation.

PRESIDENT NIXON: There's no dictabelts.

BUZHARDT: You know, John has turned over quite a few dictabelts.

PRESIDENT NIXON: Oh, these are memorandums that he made?

BUZHARDT: These are tapes of conversations he made with other people. . . .

PRESIDENT NIXON: But that would not be of me. . . . I don't care about that.

BUZHARDT: . . . [H]e did want the information on the meetings you had with Dean, and this gave us no problem. . . . We told him we would give it to him, and we're now having it verified. I want to make sure it's accurate before we give it to him. . . . He also asked for the same information with respect to Ehrlichman, Haldeman, and Mitchell. Now, he asked for that from June the 17th, 1972, and on. . . . I explained, well, there's a problem. We're giving you this information on Dean and we're taking it under consideration, but I'm sure that certainly Haldeman was in very—

PRESIDENT NIXON: Very heavy.

BUZHARDT: —and it will take quite a while to compile this information.

PRESIDENT NIXON: Ehrlichman was in almost every day.

BUZHARDT: I said, those would take a lot of time to prepare. He said, then, . . . "I would like to have . . . [a record of meetings with Haldeman and Ehrlichman] from the present back to March the 15th." Now, this gives us a problem. It's not what you've said, what you've met or talked to between Haldeman and Ehrlichman since March 15th, the date, but it goes to his purpose. And we discussed this. The only conceivable reason he could have for wanting any conversations past April 30th between, the dates, with you and Haldeman and Ehrlichman, would relate to allegations against you. I do not think—I think we have to be very careful here, because I don't think we should cooperate with any investigation of you, and where that is the apparent motive I think we have to draw the line.

PRESIDENT NIXON: No, but they had left. As a matter of fact, I've had no conversations with Ehrlichman since April 30th. I have had with Haldeman about a half—maybe 10 to 15—not that many. But anyway, however many, but all on transition and things that we were having to do. But no concern about this case, I can assure you. . . .

BUZHARDT: . . . He proposed an inventory of all the files. And I already told him no way he could approach the files. He said, well, he wouldn't like for us to comment on this, he'd just like to suggest it. . . . That's about the size of where we ended. We told him that—we reiterated that we were very confident; I told him I did not think he had any jurisdiction to investigate the President, and if that appeared to be his motive, while cooperating with the Watergate investigation, he should be assured that he had a real fight on his hand, one he'd lose. And any evidence that he was going after the President—

PRESIDENT NIXON: You also indicated confidence that he couldn't get the President on the merits, didn't you?

BUZHARDT: Yes, sir, I told him he would not have you—I told him not only he couldn't get you on the merits, that we would win, but also I had no intention as a procedural matter of having you *treated as a defendant* when you responded to specific charges by anybody, that we weren't going to come back answering allegations, whether made by him or any witness he had, and he might as well understand that from the beginning, that we just weren't going to do that.

I think he clearly understands our position. I think we understand his. I think we can anticipate that at some point—

PRESIDENT NIXON: He'll make an issue of it.

BUZHARDT: —he'll want a confrontation. He will serve you with a subpoena at some point. He has not done his research.

PRESIDENT NIXON: When he serves a subpoena, then we'll realize it's a public relations game and we've just got to be ready then to kick him right in the teeth and say that he's trying to try the President and that's not his jurisdiction, that we have no problem on it, but we're not going to do it. . . . It's hard to get a feeling for Cox. Cox has, it's very evident, he has a very superficial knowledge of the case or whatever he has at this point in time. That's the trouble with the special prosecutor. . . .

BUZHARDT: He just has no feel at this point. . . . I let him go on forever. . . .

JUNE 7, 1973: THE PRESIDENT AND HAIG, 9:20–10:04 A.M., OVAL OFFICE

Nixon offers some ominous advice about Archibald Cox.

PRESIDENT NIXON: . . . Let me tell you this. I think that Cox, it might not be beyond the pale, Al, to think in terms of it maybe in our interest to get him out of there. You understand?

HAIG: (Unintelligible), he's a—sonofabitch.

PRESIDENT NIXON: And then let the U.S., and then let the Justice Department go ahead and choose your course and then delegate. See, this Cox is gonna delay and delay and delay; if he fools around—now, on the plus side—there are some pluses, I guess—you notice Cox . . . will slow Ervin just a bit. . . .

JUNE 7, 1973: THE PRESIDENT AND HAIG, 12:33–1:26 P.M., OVAL OFFICE

The President learns that Bebe Rebozo is under investigation by the IRS. Nixon attempts to persuade Haig to warn Rebozo, but Haig deflects the request.

SEGMENT 1

HAIG: I got another thing that I don't know what it is, but I've got a feeling you're going to be talking with Bebe [Rebozo] this weekend. I got this through the regular sources that he's in some tax problem—

PRESIDENT NIXON: Mm-hmm.

HAIG: Nobody knows this—I got it through the Treasury surreptitiously. And it could break in three, three, four, five months. . . .

PRESIDENT NIXON: What does it involve, do you know?

HAIG: I understand it has something to do with a campaign contribution of some kind—

PRESIDENT NIXON: I guess I know what then, the Hughes, Hughes' campaign contribution. I'll tell you what it is, basically, the Hughes people made a campaign contribution in 19—1970. And Rebozo, uh, they gave it to him for the purposes of uh, the congressional and senatorial committees which were visiting. He did not lose it—he had it, totally, all, had not spent a cent of it. He didn't do it because Hughes got into trouble, . . . and he did not turn it over. They had come down to see him and he said, "I've got the money here; I have not spent it and not intend to until we get further directions from Hughes, the Hughes people as to how they want to spend it." But that's where it stands at the moment. How did the Treasury people say they were going to go after it?

HAIG: Where I got this was through the audit shop, it was in the litigation shop over there. There is no way that you can turn it off. . . . I don't know whether you want him to talk to a lawyer about it. . . . We have that guy in Philadelphia who did such a very good job on the San Clemente—it might be worth, if he wanted to talk to somebody, just so that we know that there's no surprise coming. . . .

PRESIDENT NIXON: Yes, I sure wouldn't hurt him—good God almighty—because he, . . . if anything he's overly honest and overly cautious. He didn't report it and has not used it—the money's in the safe. . . . And, so therefore, he retained it for the '74 elections. . . .

HAIG: . . . I got this through the back door. But if Bebe feels that we have one helluva good lawyer who's totally reliable, trustworthy, this fellow in Philadelphia, if he were to come down, he'd have the best brain you could get to consult with him on how to proceed with this thing. We can't help him—you can't do a thing for him.

PRESIDENT NIXON: Unfortunately. . . .

SEGMENT 3

PRESIDENT NIXON: I wonder, Al, if . . . you wouldn't mind just calling him [Rebozo]? . . . I think you'd better. Not to alarm him so much, just say. . . .

HAIG: Well, I just thought we'd have him talk to—

PRESIDENT NIXON: Huh. Tell him, huh.

HAIG: I'm a little—he, he just oughtta talk to somebody. See, what I'm afraid of is that I didn't have anyone here who knew—

PRESIDENT NIXON: I see.

HAIG: —we knew about it. See, we can't know about it, legally, at all, without it looking—. . . . So I was hoping to just not even mention the subject to him, just get him the fella [lawyer]. You could do it, because you would (unintelligible) questions of him.

PRESIDENT NIXON: Okay, I'll do it.

HAIG: If he just comes to me, if you just tell him to come to me and I'll, I'll take care of it.

PRESIDENT NIXON: All right. [*Long pause*] . . . Incidentally, there wouldn't be any problem with my talking to him here on the phone?

HAIG: No. . . . Well, there'd be a problem if someone were conceivably listening—that could be a problem.

PRESIDENT NIXON: You mean listening to him?

HAIG: Or to the discussion between the two of you. It's not that urgent, it's—as I say, we have plenty of time.

PRESIDENT NIXON: Well, never plenty of time, never, never. . . .

JUNE 7, 1973: THE PRESIDENT AND BUZHARDT, 3:53–5:30 P.M., EXECUTIVE OFFICE BUILDING

Melvin Laird and Buzhardt had worked closely at Defense, and had an excellent relationship. Taking the new post, Laird claimed that the President had told him he was not criminally involved. Buzhardt similarly assures Laird. Nixon also expresses concern about the liability of Thomas Pappas.

SEGMENT 1

BUZHARDT: . . . [Y]ou know I had long talks with Mel.

PRESIDENT NIXON: Sure.

BUZHARDT: And I told him absolutely you weren't involved, and it would be a rocky road probably for a while, but when it all came out you'd be absolved. . . .

PRESIDENT NIXON: We have only this one clinker of a conversation of the [March] 21st, which is a clinker because I did raise questions. I can't get around it. I said, how much would it cost over four years? Da, da, da, da. But then I said: No, we can't go that route. . . .

BUZHARDT: It's a problem. . . . But it's not an insurmountable problem, at all. That's not a big problem. . . . And you can sense everybody is loosening up a little bit, going back and forth, not paying attention to that.

PRESIDENT NIXON: Early conclusion: The shit'll still fly around, but that's it. But the kind of stuff, believe me, that would have killed us three weeks ago won't today. We're a little stronger. We got a little stronger. . . . Tell me about Pappas. I don't want him to get hurt. I don't want anyone to get hurt. But that lovable guy, Tom Pappas— . . . . it's clear that the conversation of the 21st that Pappas was raising money for Mitchell. Now, that wouldn't make him guilty, would it?

BUZHARDT: No.

PRESIDENT NIXON: Are you sure?

BUZHARDT: Not unless he knew the money was to be used for an illegal purpose and he was part of a conspiracy.

PRESIDENT NIXON: Well, that would be his motive, wouldn't it? I mean, that's a question of his motive.

BUZHARDT: That's a question of what his motive was and what his knowledge was at this point. . . . And frankly, it will probably turn on John Mitchell's version.

PRESIDENT NIXON: I don't think Mitchell will ever testify.

BUZHARDT: I don't think so, either.

PRESIDENT NIXON: Do you think Mitchell would ever testify?

BUZHARDT: I don't think so. . . .

SEGMENT 2:

PRESIDENT NIXON: On Vesco, you think they've got him [Mitchell]?

BUZHARDT: I'm afraid so. I think it will be a long, difficult course to go. Well-represented—I understand. It might be a long time before they come to a final conclusion on this trial. I hate to think of. . . . Mitchell. I feel very highly toward him.

PRESIDENT NIXON: We all do. Well, he's a former Attorney General of the United States. . . . Wasn't there an Attorney General under Harding [Harry Daugherty]?

BUZHARDT: Yes.

PRESIDENT NIXON: What was he sent up for? Stealing?

BUZHARDT: He was convicted for—

PRESIDENT NIXON: John didn't take anything. Poor John, all he's got is a crazy wife.

BUZHARDT: He's been very patient. He's a very patient man. I will check on the Pappas thing and see what I can find out on that. . . .

PRESIDENT NIXON: Very encouraged. . . . Do you know Pappas? . . . Well, his wife raised money for the Republicans for years. He would never do anything wrong, for John Mitchell or anyone else. It's like Kalmbach. Kalmbach didn't take part in any cover-up. I know he didn't. I mean, I know. He hasn't told me. I never talked to him about it. Well, the Pappas thing is good. If you can't do it discreetly, don't do it at all. . . .

BUZHARDT: . . . They may come out with a story, and you can see them writing off the walls, of rumors of additional burglaries. I expect somebody's going to put together a story on this at some point.

PRESIDENT NIXON: Additional burglaries, you mean by the Plumbers?

BUZHARDT: Yes. Well, they won't know by whom, and I don't think they're going to try to lay it on the plumbers. I think they're going to try to lay it somewhere on the Justice Department.

PRESIDENT NIXON: Do you think there were?

BUZHARDT: That's what I think.

PRESIDENT NIXON: I don't think so.

BUZHARDT: No, sir, I don't believe there were.

PRESIDENT NIXON: As a matter of fact, I don't think there were even with the plumbers.

BUZHARDT: I don't think there were [additional burglaries?]. I don't think they did any wiretapping.

PRESIDENT NIXON: . . . Ehrlichman didn't tell me.

BUZHARDT: I don't believe there were any. I don't believe they did any wiretapping. They'll be working hard on this fellow whose name starts with a "U" [Anthony Ulasewicz] that worked for Ehrlichman. They are going around with a rumor that there was a super-spy, a man whose name hasn't surfaced yet. . . .

JUNE 7, 1973: THE PRESIDENT AND BUZHARDT, 5:37–5:52 P.M., OVAL OFFICE

The two again discuss fighting Cox and protecting presidential prerogatives.

PRESIDENT NIXON: . . . And your, our friend Cox, wants to know all meetings that I have had up to the present time? . . . What is the purpose of that?. . . .

BUZHARDT: It can be only one purpose. . . . If he goes after the documents, and he will put them up in writing to say that he is investigating the President, then we can also tell him on jurisdictional ground, because he has no jurisdiction. So—

PRESIDENT NIXON: . . . [A]lways make the case the President has nothing to hide, you've got to do that.

BUZHARDT: We will maintain the President has nothing to hide. . . .

PRESIDENT NIXON: Let me, let me tell you—nobody can serve in this office in the event that we broke this down further than we've al—we've gone very far on this. . . . [A]t the present time, we've got a situation where no President can sit and talk with anybody. He just couldn't. You know that? . . . [L]et me tell you, the next step is not gonna be easy. To talk about crime, the next step could be coming out and defend why we bombed [Cambodia] on December the 18th. They'll say that was illegal, excessive use of power, right? . . . Cambodia is beyond the power of the Congress [the President?], that we insist on the President's meetings da-da-da-da-da-da—get it?

JUNE 7, 1973: THE PRESIDENT AND CHARLES G. REBOZO, 7:27–7:29 P.M., WHITE HOUSE TELEPHONE

"Bebe" Rebozo relays a message from a supporter in Leavenworth, Kansas. Nixon does not mention the IRS's investigation of Rebozo.

REBOZO: I had a funny thing today.

PRESIDENT NIXON: Uh-huh.

REBOZO: My God, I got this, I got a, I got a letter from Leavenworth Prison—

PRESIDENT NIXON: Mm-hmm.

REBOZO: —from the former mayor of Jersey City, who got 15 years—

PRESIDENT NIXON: Oh boy.

REBOZO: —sympathizing with you—

PRESIDENT NIXON: I'll be darned.

REBOZO: —and, and gave the media the very devil, you know—

PRESIDENT NIXON: Yeah.

REBOZO: What a guy. I really felt sorry for him, but—

PRESIDENT NIXON: Well, you know, I think of all of our good people that are being involved in a way that, you know, they're all doing what they thought was right—

REBOZO: Sure.

PRESIDENT NIXON: It's just *terrible.* It's the media; they're doing it.

REBOZO: It's gonna work out. . . .

PRESIDENT NIXON: I think it's picking up, though, what do you think?

REBOZO: Oh, no question.

JUNE 10, 1973: THE PRESIDENT AND COLSON, 11:05–11:35 P.M., WHITE HOUSE TELEPHONE

Soviet President Leonid Brezhnev is about to arrive for a Washington summit. Nixon is anxious to have the meeting, apparently looking for some respite from Watergate and an opportunity to improve his popularity. Senator Henry Jackson [D-WA] and others want the visit canceled, fearing Nixon will concede too much to the Soviets in order to gain some agreement. Ultimately, Senate leaders Mike Mansfield [D-MT] and Hugh Scott [R-PA] manage a recess in the Senate hearings to avoid embarrassing the President. Nixon is unhappy with that compromise, believing public opinion will favorably contrast a successful summit with the Senate hearings.

COLSON: . . . [Senator Henry] Scoop Jackson coming on today, saying that the summit should be canceled, because while Brezhnev is here, it's likely that Mitchell and Haldeman and Ehrlichman and others will be testifying.

PRESIDENT NIXON: For Scoop to say that is totally irresponsible. The summit isn't going to be canceled.

COLSON: *Of course not!* But, but which comes first? [*Laughing.*] I mean, he should really be saying why don't we call off the Ervin Committee hearings while Brezhnev is here.

PRESIDENT NIXON: Mm-hmm. And it's really rather surprising he would say that because he's really a very responsible guy, but I guess he's running for President again, is that it? . . .

COLSON: . . . [I]f he's really worried about the impact of Watergate on Brezhnev, why don't they call off the damn witchhunt in the Senate, what's the point of that?

PRESIDENT NIXON: He said we should cancel the summit because Haldeman, Ehrlichman and Mitchell were gonna be before the Ervin Committee then and that'd be bad.

COLSON: While, while Brezhnev was here and therefore we should cancel Brezhnev, not cancel the Ervin Committee—and it's preposterous! . . .

PRESIDENT NIXON: . . . I guess you're right about Jackson; he's against dealing with the Soviet in any event because of the Jews [and Soviet emigration policies] and all that other thing, you know, the uh, you know—

COLSON: But he, but he sounds silly when he says it, but his reasons are, reasoning is very clear that he, he'd like that trip called off on any basis.

PRESIDENT NIXON: One week before? You, so you call up Brezhnev and say, "Look, let's not come now because we're having Watergate problems"? . . . Good heavens, and let the peace of the world suffer? . . .

COLSON: I think he puts himself in a terrible position—and any Democrat who takes that line, he's the only one who has. Others have taken it on the grounds that, uh, this isn't, you know, a good time—you're not, you're not in a strong position to bargain as the—

PRESIDENT NIXON: Aw, that's [Senator J. William] Fulbright [D-AR] and all those people. . . .

JUNE 11, 1973: THE PRESIDENT AND HAIG, 10:01–10:07 A.M., OVAL OFFICE

The President and Haig continue to grow disenchanted with Elliot Richardson.

HAIG: I had a good talk with Richardson and he said that uh, the charter that he gave to Cox on the Hill, uh, included a mandate to clean up unresolved investigations. . . . Then he said, you know, "I feel I can serve the President best by keeping a distance between the President and myself." And I said, "Elliot," I said, "not right now." I said, "You were selected for your reputation and your qualifications, and there's no one that can challenge that, that impeccable record that you have." I said, "I think you're overly sensitive." . . . I said, "The worst stage for you and for the President is the manifestation of any lack of confidence between you and the President."

PRESIDENT NIXON: Mm-hmm.

HAIG: And I did a helluva piece and he's one fast-stepping smoothie, and I'll be Goddamned if we have to put up with that crap. . . .

PRESIDENT NIXON: By God, the Attorney General of the United States is one of the President's top legal advisers, now doggone it, he can't do that and uh, or uh—

HAIG: Well, I fight a helluva shouting match—

PRESIDENT NIXON: Right, right, right, right—we can't go today, but boy, I'll remember. . . .

HAIG: . . . I said, "As far as your role as Attorney General," I said, "By God, the man picked you."

PRESIDENT NIXON: That's right.

HAIG: "With full recognition of your qualifications." I said, "You don't have to go out and contrive distance." I think he understood. . . .

JUNE 11, 1973: THE PRESIDENT AND KISSINGER, 12:18–12:36 P.M., OVAL OFFICE

Kissinger again denies any knowledge about the Plumbers.

KISSINGER: . . . But also what is it really, I mean, these guys did things that should not have been done.

PRESIDENT NIXON: Sure.

KISSINGER: But most of it was minor-league, uh, minor-league stuff. Colson has been going, has been saying that I found the Plumbers, which really he shouldn't say, because I didn't know a damn thing about the Plumbers. And it doesn't do any good to get me involved.

PRESIDENT NIXON: *Fuck it*—he doesn't know. They don't pay much attention to Colson, though, Henry, let's not believe. They will believe Bob and John when they come out and say that—

KISSINGER: I think the best course is to hang tight.

PRESIDENT NIXON: Darn right.

KISSINGER: And uh—

PRESIDENT NIXON: Well. I think that's the attitude, don't you uh, we'll hang tough. Look, we survived—look, we've been through very difficult situations. . . . Then came April 15th and [Henry] Petersen finally just came in and said Haldeman and Ehrlichman ought to go and it took me two weeks to get them to go, which was terrible for them and hard for me. I hated to turn these men out.

KISSINGER: It's hard for them and terrible for you.

PRESIDENT NIXON: But then April 30th, until now, they've just continued to bombard me with an arrest and leaks and source stories and it's almost unbelievable. . . .

KISSINGER: Oh, that's the most unbelievable character assassination. Any source, any sonofabitch can say anything, get the front page of the *Post* or of the *Times*—

PRESIDENT NIXON: Or of the networks.

KISSINGER: —or of the networks.

June 11, 1973: The President and Buzhardt, 2:13–2:55 p.m., Executive Office Building

After a lengthy review of legal and committee-hearing matters, and as his counsel prepares to leave the EOB office, Nixon again raises fears that Dean has tapes of their conversations.

PRESIDENT NIXON: . . . I think the fellow's shooting blanks with regard to his insinuation that he had any tapes.

BUZHARDT: Well, I just don't think he has any tapes. Now—we can live with them, but it's harder if he has the tapes.

PRESIDENT NIXON: You get down to the point if it's his word against the President's, we'll kill him. Right?

BUZHARDT: I hope it never comes to that.

PRESIDENT NIXON: No, it'd be a terrible thing.

BUZHARDT: Our best effort will be to prevent that from ever happening. . . .

June 11, 1973: The President and Buzhardt, 9:07–9:23 p.m., White House Telephone

Buzhardt is priming Fred Thompson for Dean's cross-examination. He also reports on Cox's growing conflicts with the Department of Justice. Finally, White House suspicions and hostility toward John Ehrlichman are rising.

PRESIDENT NIXON: Give me a brief report.

BUZHARDT: Well, it was a pretty good afternoon all in all, Mr. President. I found uh, uh, Thompson most cooperative, feeling more Republican every day.

PRESIDENT NIXON: Really?

BUZHARDT: So he tells me.

PRESIDENT NIXON: Yeah.

BUZHARDT: Uh, perfectly prepared to assist in really doing a cross-examination. He thinks, well, he knows the earliest they'll [Senate Committee] get Dean in a private session under oath is Friday.

PRESIDENT NIXON: A private session under oath?

BUZHARDT: They always put these witnesses in, they bring them in executive session and have one senator come in and swear 'em, and they cross-examine him under oath, uh, before they put him on the public session. . . . So that gives us until Thursday to get with Thompson. . . .

PRESIDENT NIXON: Does he realize that Dean has some problems?

BUZHARDT: Oh yes sir. Quite a few. He knows it's quite a few inconsistencies here, problems of his own, all the way across the board. . . . He is also now willing to work with us on shifting some folks that are Democrats. . . . I mentioned to him casually that while it wasn't our primary effort, I could be of some help to him. [*Nixon laughs.*]. . . .

PRESIDENT NIXON: Incidentally, you, did you, uh, probably heard about this, [U.S. Attorney Harold] Titus letter of the 22nd. Did you know about that?

BUZHARDT: No sir.

PRESIDENT NIXON: Well, Titus wrote Dean a letter on the 22nd, we, that he couldn't grant immunity because he was guilty of obstruction of justice. . . .

BUZHARDT: Then after finishing with Thompson, I went by and had a long talk with Henry Petersen. . . . Henry's extremely upset, uh, about Cox coming in there and having such a wide jurisdiction.

PRESIDENT NIXON: Right.

BUZHARDT: He says it's like turning the whole old Kennedy clan loose. Turning the Justice Department over to them.

PRESIDENT NIXON: That's right.

BUZHARDT: And he's *extremely* upset about that.

PRESIDENT NIXON: Good. . . .

BUZHARDT: Uh, his animosity's with Cox; that's showing very firmly. . . .

PRESIDENT NIXON: Henry Petersen is a guy that came to me on the 15th of April and said "You've gotta get rid of Haldeman and Ehrlichman." Good heavens, I mean, what more do you want?

BUZHARDT: But he is very indignant. Extremely so. . . . [Y]ou know, his relations with Cox are very poor. I think whatever information he gets, he gets likely through the prosecutors.

PRESIDENT NIXON: [Harold] Titus, oh yeah.

BUZHARDT: Um, to whom he's fairly close. Uh, they kind of feel like they're in the same position, Henry is. . . . And they feel almost as much animosity toward Cox as he does.

PRESIDENT NIXON: Good.

BUZHARDT: They take the attitude that Cox doesn't have any idea what the case is about; he doesn't know what evidence is there and what isn't. And uh, apparently Cox recognizes himself he doesn't have enough to really even deal at this point. . . . Henry did say that, on one occasion, he said that Dean never gave him a hard time. He said on one occasion John Ehrlichman gave him a hard time, uh, about sub-poenaing Stans last summer. . . .

PRESIDENT NIXON: I didn't know about that, of course, but that's all right.

BUZHARDT: Oh, there's very perceptible animosity toward John Ehrlichman among the prosecutors and Cox. [*Chuckles.*] Comes through loud and clear.

PRESIDENT NIXON: I see.

BUZHARDT: Oh, I'd say if they, if they were focalizing on one man, er, focusing on one man it would be John Ehrlichman. Much more so than Bob Haldeman. Or even Dean.

PRESIDENT NIXON: Good God! Even Dean? . . .

BUZHARDT: They all believe that he was doing it at Ehrlichman's instruction. . . .

PRESIDENT NIXON: Yeah, well, Ehrlichman's the only one that can answer that and he will. . . .

BUZHARDT: . . . Thompson . . . he was far more cooperative really than I expected him to be. He's willing to go, you know, pretty much the distance now. And he said he realized his responsibility was going to have to be as a Republican increasingly.

PRESIDENT NIXON: He realizes that Ervin, et al., and Dash are being totally politi-cal, does he?

BUZHARDT: Right. He said it's just getting to be a political dogfight. And um, he's gonna—

PRESIDENT NIXON: Does his, does his boss realize that, does Baker think that?

BUZHARDT: Oh, he says Baker's aware of it, but he was quite candid with us; he thinks Baker will move much more slowly than he will let Thompson move.

PRESIDENT NIXON: Right. . . .

JUNE 12: THE PRESIDENT AND ROSE MARY WOODS, 8:46–9:18 A.M., OVAL OFFICE

Rose Mary Woods, Nixon's long-time confidante, again hears about Thomas Pap-pas and the money she was holding, which the President mentioned following his March 21 meeting with Dean. The sound quality is poor, and the references are not always clear. But the two are knowing parties and their elliptical talk only under-lines the intrigue they discuss. Finally, they have a poignant exchange about Nixon's ability to survive. Nixon's voice betrays his stress and inner turmoil; talk-ing to such a faithful friend of such long standing probably made the conversation even more difficult.

SEGMENT 1

PRESIDENT NIXON: Never got hold of Tom Pappas, did you?

WOODS: Nope, and I don't want to ask his secretary again.

PRESIDENT NIXON: No.

WOODS: I got a wire . . . saying he'd be in touch with you, he'd be in touch.

PRESIDENT NIXON: He'll be all right. . . . When he came into the office all we talked about was [the campaign], which is true.

WOODS: Yeah.

PRESIDENT NIXON: But I meant to thank him for his campaign, for his help he was giving in the campaign. . . .

WOODS: He may (unintelligible) it because, in the first place, he'd worked about eight or nine or ten months over there. You know, he worked the whole period, so that you could thank him for that without [mentioning the money he gave to Mitchell?].

PRESIDENT NIXON: Yeah, I'll just say, I just wanna be sure that that's what I had said and that that's what my notes say, so it doesn't—I don't, I don't want him to lie or anything like that. Tom, Tom knows.

WOODS: He knows. . . . But you know, I think this week Pat [Nixon] has understood a little. . . .

SEGMENT 3

PRESIDENT NIXON: You know, Rose, . . . you know that money you got from that fellow? I would like to find a way to get that to the campaign committee; I don't know how it could be done. . . .

WOODS: . . . I'm concerned . . . who can hand it to them. Who do you hand it to who doesn't have to say he got it? . . . It's, it's safe and sound already.

PRESIDENT NIXON: Third parties. You just never know when he's [William Brock, Committee to Re-elect the President] going to be investigated. . . .

WOODS: But I think he won't need it, but if so, it's out of the safe in my home. . . .

PRESIDENT NIXON: But just discreetly ascertain if contributions still can be made. That's what we need to know. . . . Well, what I meant is the simple thing. Ask an innocent question, that we, some do wanna make cash contributions—can they do it? And—

WOODS: Well, I can ask that.

PRESIDENT NIXON: Ask . . . Brock. Say that we get inquiries from time to time from people that want to make substantial cash contributions. Is there any way it can be made? Make it to the Senate Campaign Committee? . . .

WOODS: I'm gonna tell him a lot of people have expressed that, you know, concern that this is gonna hurt the campaign coming up. . . .

PRESIDENT NIXON: It's not, it's not any harder. . . . [T]here is someone that contributes substantial amounts of cash—is there any way it can be done and if there is, add this on right now. And if so, he'd let you know. . . .

. . . It's almost a miracle that I've survived this, you know. 'Cause I came out of the year '72 terribly tired.

WOODS: I don't know how you've survived it.

PRESIDENT NIXON: And then to have this brutal assault, brutal, brutal, brutal assault—day after day after day after day—no let up. And I had to make that rough rough rough thing with Bob and John. And then to see, and then to have a friend like Mitchell you read about in the paper—

WOODS: I know.

PRESIDENT NIXON: But they're good men, Rose, they're *good men*— . . . and poor old Krogh, you know. Just breaks my heart every time I read about it because I know they're good men and they—

WOODS: I know, and I don't know either how you could have done it. 'Cause in the first place—

PRESIDENT NIXON: It hurts, but the other thing is the, to have an assault out to impeach the President, that impeachment crap. That's the saddest of all.

WOODS: That's [awful and look at] the people who, who were starting it, the Abzugs, the Ellsbergs, and the [Ellsberg's co-defendant] Tony Russos, and the Chicago Seven. The United States isn't ready for that kind of—

PRESIDENT NIXON: Well, I hope to survive it. . . . You don't let down all those people in the United States, let down the world.

WOODS: . . . [Y]ou're killing yourself with the job.

PRESIDENT NIXON: Well, I don't mind killing myself, what I mean is, but I would expect to kill myself and I would do it. . . .

WOODS: That's right, the whole world would lose.

PRESIDENT NIXON: And our, what we stand for in this country would lose.

WOODS: Exactly. That's right, and that's why, I think, most of the letters that come in are letters that all are hoping that . . . God will give you the strength to take this terrible thing. People do realize—they don't feel it—some of those people realize better than some of your close friends.

PRESIDENT NIXON: I know. . . .

WOODS: The burden of the presidency, the, the awful loneliness. You should read some of the letters—they just, they're gorgeous. And their prayers every day and every night. . . .

JUNE 12, 1973: THE PRESIDENT AND HAIG, 11:57 A.M.–12:36 P.M., OVAL OFFICE

The President has had only one brief contact with Ehrlichman since the April 30 dismissal. There is concern about Ehrlichman's loyalty, but Nixon, while privately blaming Ehrlichman for some things, believes he will not turn on the President. Later, Nixon said, Ehrlichman is not "out to hurt me, he'd die first." Meanwhile, Nixon and Haig continue to discuss Dean's forthcoming testimony—knowing for certain he is the one man who will turn on the President.

SEGMENT 2

HAIG: . . . He [Fred Thompson] thinks that we're in very, very good shape . . . with Dean, but he thinks the toughest one is going to be with John.

PRESIDENT NIXON: Ehrlichman? Why's that?

HAIG: Well, he said that . . . Mitchell's gonna to be in trouble, and he's [Ehrlichman] gonna be in trouble. . . .

PRESIDENT NIXON: Only he doesn't feel John is going to turn on me, does he? He might?

HAIG: No, but we can't ever discount that possibility. I don't think he will, but uh—John's really done an awful lot of talking, you know, in various forums where he's testified, and uh, he has got no flexibility to turn on you. There's no way he can really do it without opening himself to perjury.

PRESIDENT NIXON: Has he said that the President was not involved?

HAIG: No. See, he's got—

PRESIDENT NIXON: That I didn't know about the financial matters? That I didn't know about the uh, the break-in—

HAIG: It's all under oath.

PRESIDENT NIXON: Huh?

HAIG: It's all under oath.

PRESIDENT NIXON: Good heavens, I'll be—the only thing John could say is that well, geez, I don't what he'd say.

HAIG: . . . [H]e himself is very, very boxed in now, uh, on his testimony which is under oath, so I think that the pitfalls have been very, very well-produced. And that's what I like about Buzhardt; he just follows every *Goddamned thread,* every one of them, he works them all.

PRESIDENT NIXON: Well, I, I feel for John, because I think that Dean may have reported more to him and he may implied more than he told me.

HAIG: It's very possible. . . .

PRESIDENT NIXON: Well, Al, the way I feel about John Mitchell—John Mitchell, from a personal standpoint, but secondly, I had no contact with him whatever. . . .

HAIG: I just think he just really started drinking there at the end. . . .

PRESIDENT NIXON: That's right, right. The second point is Haldeman's gonna be like a rock. . . . [T]he third one is Colson, will be like a rock, about the President, you know, he'll knock everybody else. . . .

HAIG: Fred thinks that you're going to get through this very well. Well, you'll have a tough period, where there's a gap between when Dean talks, . . . that we have to be prepared for. . . .

PRESIDENT NIXON: [W]e hope to take leadership with Brezhnev.

HAIG: Oh no, that's going to be wild, that's going to be great. . . .

PRESIDENT NIXON: And about that time Dean's talking. So let's play it up like hell. . . . Well, I suppose the other argument is that Dean proves everything he said is true, is that right? You said as far as—

HAIG: I think he's the only witness they have.

PRESIDENT NIXON: Against the President?

HAIG: Yeah. . . .

JUNE 12, 1973: THE PRESIDENT AND BUZHARDT, 9:37–9:56 P.M., WHITE HOUSE TELEPHONE

The President and Buzhardt hope that Minority Counsel Fred Thompson is up to the task of cross-examining John Dean. Nixon also looks for help from an old friend, Senator Herman Talmadge [D-GA], a member of the Senate Committee.

BUZHARDT: . . . I'm hoping that guy [Senate Committee Minority Counsel Fred Thompson] will do a pretty good job, Mr. President, if we spend enough time with him and coach him on the questions and that sort of thing. He's, he's the only horse we've got running right now—

PRESIDENT NIXON: That's right.

BUZHARDT: Gotta make him a good one.

PRESIDENT NIXON: Well, I hope he's as good as, uh, the one that won, er, made, got the Triple Crown, huh.

BUZHARDT: Yeah. [*Chuckles.*]

PRESIDENT NIXON: Secretariat, huh?

BUZHARDT: Hell, I'd be satisfied if he could win one race. I hope he's a thoroughbred, . . . you know, if we do it well enough we don't need a outstanding cross-examiner, just a passingly good one.

PRESIDENT NIXON: Yeah, if we had Marlowe Cook in there he would do well.

BUZHARDT: Yes, sir. . . . Well, if we get [Senator Edward] Gurney [R-FL] to do it, you know, he would be very good at this. . . . He can be quite insistent. Yes, sir. Of course, the man I had rather have than any of them is Herman Talmadge.

PRESIDENT NIXON: Oh boy, Herman'd kill them.

BUZHARDT: Because he's good.

PRESIDENT NIXON: Oh boy, he's smart and, boy, he'd be great, but he—

BUZHARDT: I'm gonna explore that again.

PRESIDENT NIXON: Yeah.

BUZHARDT: I'm not sure that's a completely dead alley. If we get this going, and you know, make a dent in him the first day—

PRESIDENT NIXON: Yeah.

BUZHARDT: I'm gonna talk to (unintelligible) and see if, at that point, he might be willing to see if Herman's willing to participate a little bit. . . .

JUNE 13, 1973: THE PRESIDENT, ZIEGLER, AND HAIG, 9:22–10:20 A. M., OVAL OFFICE

Nixon receives a letter from John Ehrlichman, but it is directed at undermining the President's confidence in his present aides. Nixon questions his staff on dealing with the press.

PRESIDENT NIXON: . . . John Ehrlichman thinks that [Leonard] Garment is leaking very heavily to the press.

ZIEGLER: Mm-hmm, now there's no evidence of that. . . .

PRESIDENT NIXON: Well, he says, "I do not understand . . . when Garment refuses to defend you. . . . These fellows apparently don't care if you were fighting the fight of your life, personally. I gather their loyalty is only to the institution of the presidency." If that's Garment's attitude, I'll fire him today.

ZIEGLER: Well, it's not. It is not his attitude. This guy is, is active and, and—

PRESIDENT NIXON: He's working for a person, you understand, the President person.

ZIEGLER: The President, Mr. President, Len Garment is . . . loyal in his every discussion you had with him and I bet many, and I think Al has too, his loyalty very definitely goes to you the man. And uh, I think what this is—

PRESIDENT NIXON: Why does he refuse to defend the President?

ZIEGLER: He re—he defends the President.

PRESIDENT NIXON: Where is, where is Ehrlichman getting this?

ZIEGLER: I just don't know. . . . Len has been the toughest guy. Don't you think, Al? Haven't you observed it? . . .

PRESIDENT NIXON: He is not seeing [*Washington Post* reporter Robert U.] Woodward?

ZIEGLER: No, he's not. He is not seeing Woodward.

PRESIDENT NIXON: [*New York Times* reporter Seymour] Hersh?

ZIEGLER: He is not seeing Hersh either. Do you, do you have any indication of that, Al?

HAIG: I certainly don't. You're right, he's seen them, but he's seeing them so he knows what the bastards are up to.

ZIEGLER: Yeah, but I don't think he's seen Woodward or Hersh recently. . . .

JUNE 13, 1973: THE PRESIDENT AND COLSON, 9:41–9:53 P.M., WHITE HOUSE TELEPHONE

In two late-night telephone conversations, Nixon and Colson eagerly feed each other's anger and hostility. Colson never doubts or questions Nixon; he is the ever-loyal follower, ready to be more Nixon than his leader. The conversation is catty and nasty, whether talking about Dean, Richardson, or the prosecutors. Colson, though, has great admiration for Richardson, "a gut fighter," who ran the "dirtiest campaign in Massachusetts's political history." Media criticism is stinging the President badly. He sounds tired and weary, and occasionally slurs his words.

PRESIDENT NIXON: They tell me, incidentally, that Stans has been a good witness. I haven't heard, but—

COLSON: Stans has been a superb witness. . . .

PRESIDENT NIXON: I don't watch this crap, but I, you do.

COLSON: Oh, my God, you should—

PRESIDENT NIXON: Yeah, but you know, he's an honest man, Chuck. All of our people are honest. . . . Even Gurney, I understand, finally took on Ervin.

COLSON: Oh God, Gurney was tough today. Gurney was really tough. Now we're gonna get a little time—I don't know whether you saw that *Star* piece—

PRESIDENT NIXON: No, what is it.

COLSON: Well, it had a big piece that uh, Dean and I are now pitted against each other. . . .

PRESIDENT NIXON: Incidentally, though, on Dean, . . . apparently Cox has decided *not* to give him transactional immunity, is that true?

COLSON: That's right. Remember, I mentioned to you Sunday—the prosecutors *hate his guts.* . . .

PRESIDENT NIXON: Well, you don't want to be pitted against anybody, Chuck, doggone it, I don't want you hurt in this thing, you know that? I don't want you hurt.

COLSON: Doesn't matter, Mr. President.

PRESIDENT NIXON: Oh, the hell it doesn't. . . . You're our man and you and all, you know, I stand with all my people, Doggone it, you fought the battle and we know that you've had to do some things that were damned important for us and I'm not gonna let this little pipsqueak knock you down.

COLSON: But you pass this way once in this world and my great satisfaction is seeing what you're doing for the country and that's all I really care about.

PRESIDENT NIXON: Yeah.

COLSON: But the—the thing with Dean is that, uh, I've just—I've met him head-on and—

PRESIDENT NIXON: He'll say some terrible things, I imagine, when he goes up Friday and we've gotta be prepared, I've got Buzhardt and all prepared, put out a brief one-sentence disclaimer, but that's about all we're gonna do. I don't think we oughta get—I—the President oughta get in a fight with John Dean. What do you think?

COLSON: Absolutely, that'd be the worst thing you could do. . . . Dean is gonna be out there all by himself.

PRESIDENT NIXON: Really?

COLSON: Yes, sir. And when even *Newsweek* labels him as a turncoat, then you know he's in trouble.

PRESIDENT NIXON: A Judas. He's a Judas and a turncoat. . . .

COLSON: No, no, they can't rehabilitate him. And his pictures are terrible! The one in the *Times* on Sunday was—

PRESIDENT NIXON: You told me about that, yeah.

COLSON: The one in the *Star* tonight was terrible and, and they, the photo editors were helping us. They had two pictures—one of me and one of him and his looked, I, I thought, awful. He just looked a little deceitful.

PRESIDENT NIXON: Yeah.

COLSON: Then *Newsweek* had that thing of him—the preppie, you know, the boy-from-prep-school routine. They have not built him up and I don't think they can. . . .

PRESIDENT NIXON: You were telling me something else, what was it?

COLSON: Well, I've been in some communication with the prosecutors and they, they just aren't gonna let this guy get off. They're gonna go, they, they are gonna indict him.

PRESIDENT NIXON: Well, they've got to indict him. To let him off, they may not have many more to indict, if they let him off. . . . He was a central figure. Now, understand, we all know—he may have thought he was doing it for the cause—

COLSON: But he deceived a lot of people.

PRESIDENT NIXON: But he deceived all of us.

COLSON: He deceived me, he deceived you, I mean—

PRESIDENT NIXON: I was, I, I hadn't the slightest idea what had happened. I didn't know he'd been on to, I mean, particularly the CIA thing. *To ask Walters to put them on the CIA payroll is unbelievable!*

COLSON: Yeah.

PRESIDENT NIXON: Now you know you wouldn't've asked Ehrlichman, I wouldn't, that's the damnedest thing I ever heard of—it sounds like a *kid*. . . . I think he's sort of a pretty boy that had all the rest. Incidentally, I have not been pleased with Richardson. . . . Not at all. And I know you've been very high on him, but I thought his saying the President oughta himself be his own personal lawyer and all that, uh, his saying that he, uh, he's said two or three things that have been very disturbing to me and we have really—Haig has brought him on the carpet. He either, he either shapes up—he's either the Attorney General for the President of the United States or he's out. . . . And I'd put him out damn fast, too.

COLSON: The only thing about Elliot that—

PRESIDENT NIXON: We don't owe him a damned thing.

COLSON: No, Christ! The only thing I can say about Elliot is that he is a very, uh, tough politician.

PRESIDENT NIXON: Yeah, I know, you've always said that, but he hasn't acted that way lately, Chuck. . . .

COLSON: But he may be building up a, uh, he may be trying to build up a, a record, I don't know.

PRESIDENT NIXON: I don't know. Well, he can't build it up against the President.

COLSON: No.

PRESIDENT NIXON: He can't, you see, the idea that uh, that uh, he told Haig a couple days ago, that he keep a little distance between him and the President—

COLSON: No—

PRESIDENT NIXON: —and Haig, Haig just raised hell with him, says "Don't you kid yourself."

COLSON: I mean, it's good to have Al, because hell, Al's so tough, oh, he's great. [Chuckles]

PRESIDENT NIXON: But you know, Elliot can't do this, Chuck. He can't do this. . . . I mean, he can appoint this jackass Cox, but then, but Elliot Richardson is the Attorney General of the United States. And, uh, incidentally, we really rolled him on one thing—you know, he *violently* opposed the appointment of our FBI guy. Violently.

COLSON: Oh, is that right?

PRESIDENT NIXON: Oh, good God! Oh, god, yes. And uh, uh, because he, he wanted a Harvard or some Ivy League dean or criminologist. And I turned him down, and so we got this nice cop [Clarence Kelley] who was an FBI guy and a graduate of law school and he violently opposed it and Al Haig just rolled him.

COLSON: Well, that's, that's—

PRESIDENT NIXON: And . . . be sure you get that story out. That Elliot Richardson put it out and I rolled him. I rolled him.

COLSON: I think it's marvelous, Mr. President, because what you have is a guy [Kelley] who is, is, first of all, he's Irish, secondly, he's middle America—

PRESIDENT NIXON: That's right.

COLSON: —thirdly, he's got all the credentials.

PRESIDENT NIXON: He's FBI, cop.

COLSON: Yup.

PRESIDENT NIXON: We have 25 percent decrease in crime.

COLSON: And the blacks don't—

PRESIDENT NIXON: And the blacks don't like him—

COLSON: [*Laughing.*] Yeah.

PRESIDENT NIXON: —and finally, I don't know the guy, so there's no problem of influence.

COLSON: Oh, he's a perfect appointment. . . .

PRESIDENT NIXON: . . . Goddamnit, Elliot's over there with Jonathan Moore, what the hell do you think they've come up with? What in the name of God do you think they'd come up with?

COLSON: You know, Mr. President, that the dirtiest campaign in Massachusetts's political history was conducted in 1964 by Elliot Richardson. The *Boston Herald-Traveler,* the staunch—

PRESIDENT NIXON: Republican.

COLSON: —bastion of conservative Republicanism, blasted him on a front-page editorial. I mean, Elliot is a gut fighter, and uh—

PRESIDENT NIXON: Well, he better start fighting for me or he's gonna be out. . . . I want him to do right, but he must not cut the President. . . .

JUNE 13, 1973: THE PRESIDENT AND COLSON, 10:32–10:39 P.M., WHITE HOUSE TELEPHONE

PRESIDENT NIXON: . . . This business of attacking the President has gotta stop.

COLSON: The whole—

PRESIDENT NIXON: And as far as this press corps, they can go to hell.

COLSON: Oh sure. The hell with them, man, Mr. President, the great Silent Majority see right through them. My God, if you could, if you could see the mail that I've gotten in the last week. . . .

PRESIDENT NIXON: Yeah. We've been on the defensive for two months, because basically, you see, they were right, in a sense. There was a cover-up, let's face it. Uhh, but on the other hand, they have built up first the crime and the cover-up to unbelievable things and of course the fact that people had to leave, a number of them. Good God, I mean—

COLSON: That's right, that's right.

PRESIDENT NIXON: An undersecretary like Krogh—happens this is a tragedy. Not to mention Haldeman and Ehrlichman and the head of the FBI, you know, that poor stupid Gray. Good God, he shouldn't have to go—why the hell did he burn those papers?

COLSON: Terrible personal tragedy.

PRESIDENT NIXON: Good God, he should've—you know, he's an honest man, he just did a stupid thing.

COLSON: Yeah, bad judgment.

PRESIDENT NIXON: I know. But my point is that all of this indicates there's a widespread, as they say, the greatest, uh, you know, uh, corruption in history. That's baloney. Nobody stole anything. Take ITT—ITT didn't make any money out of this. Take Vesco—Vesco didn't make any money; we're *prosecuting* him. The whole point about this, nobody has made any money and I haven't seen one of our little boys make that point. . . .

JUNE 13: THE PRESIDENT AND HAIG, 10:43–10:49 P.M., WHITE HOUSE TELEPHONE

Haig offers the President an upbeat report on the Senate hearings, particularly on Maurice Stans's spirited defense of his reputation.

HAIG: And we're moving, that's the difference. They're going backwards and we're—

PRESIDENT NIXON: We're moving and when they come out with their little boy Dean and all of his jackass things, fine.

HAIG: Yeah.

PRESIDENT NIXON: We just, we just slap it with a wrist and let 'er go.

HAIG: Yeah, I'll tell you, ol' Maury [Stans] put them all to shame today. He really did.

PRESIDENT NIXON: Maury they said was great, huh.

HAIG: Yes, he was, he gave a closing statement that left them in shocked silence.

PRESIDENT NIXON: Wha'd he say?

HAIG: He said, "I want you people to know that you owe me something, and that's my good name." And Christ, they said, a pin could've dropped in that room. He said a lot of innocent people have been vilified in this thing.

PRESIDENT NIXON: Mm-hmm. Good.

HAIG: It was an open break in the Committee with one Congressman jumping on the Chairman for badgering Stans. . . .

PRESIDENT NIXON: Well, we're gonna turn it more, because one day I'm gonna attack that Committee and when I do, it's gonna be a blockbuster. I'm gonna take it apart like it's never been taken apart. . . . Not yet. I'm gonna wait 'til Dean's on.

HAIG: No, no let 'em get so ripe that they—

PRESIDENT NIXON: After they're on—

HAIG: —that they just have to fall.

PRESIDENT NIXON: . . . And they'll be destroyed like the McCarthy Committee was destroyed. Absolutely destroyed. . . .

HAIG: They don't realize what they're up against, this stupid Ervin. Drinking too much and pointing his finger. Hah! That's right, that's right. . . .

PRESIDENT NIXON: They'll run their things next week and they'll rest and then I'll take them on. You watch, it'll be awful rough, too. And very effective.

HAIG: That's what it should be. Now, I just think it's been a great week, and last week was a great week and we're, we're going.

JUNE 14: THE PRESIDENT AND HALDEMAN, 3:58–4:10 P.M., WHITE HOUSE TELEPHONE

Haldeman reports on the hearings and the danger represented by his former aide, Gordon Strachan. In a strange passage, Nixon concedes that logically Haldeman might have approved some sort of action, but not the Watergate bugging and

break-in. Haldeman still speaks easily and confidently with the President; for his part, the President is very much at ease with his ex-aide.

HALDEMAN: . . . Magruder's up and he's lobbing some very rough stuff. He's totally wiped Mitchell out and he's totally wiped Gordon Strachan out, which is gonna be tough to deal with. . . . And it's kind of interesting, because he's covered stuff with Strachan—if it's true—that I had *absolutely* no knowledge of. . . .

PRESIDENT NIXON: He's really hit Strachan, huh? . . .

HALDEMAN: Everything, that he knew all about everything, step by step. Knew the plan, knew when they broke in the first time, knew what the results were.

PRESIDENT NIXON: Mm-hmm. Damnit, if Strachan knew that, I think Strachan would've told you or something, you know what I mean. . . . [T]he reason you didn't know it is that you would've never approved the damn Democratic National Committee as a target! I suppose you might've approved something else which I doubt, but nevertheless. I mean, let's, let's, let's consider our venality. *We're not stupid!* . . .

HALDEMAN: Ervin is a real jackass.

PRESIDENT NIXON: Is he?

HALDEMAN: Oh yeah, he's just awful.

PRESIDENT NIXON: Mm-hmm.

HALDEMAN: He's so pleased with himself.

PRESIDENT NIXON: Pompous and, uh, oh yes. Yeah, pandering to the press.

HALDEMAN: Yeah, he's really—

PRESIDENT NIXON: Preening himself.

HALDEMAN: Yeah, that's exactly it.

PRESIDENT NIXON: Mm-hmm, mm-hmm.

JUNE 19, 1973: THE PRESIDENT AND KISSINGER, 9:18–9:34 A.M., OVAL OFFICE

Kissinger offers some advice on Cox, his former Harvard colleague. As the Senate hearings heat up, Nixon and Kissinger prepare to neutralize them with news from the forthcoming summit with Leonid Brezhnev, confident that the media will give undivided attention to the event. The President also realizes that he cannot depend on uncritical support from Republicans.

SEGMENT 1

KISSINGER: Cox will—Cox will come after you, I don't doubt it.

PRESIDENT NIXON: He's a liberal Democrat—

KISSINGER: Well, he's a *fanatic* liberal Democrat and all of his associates are fanatics. It's another one of the things—

PRESIDENT NIXON: Yeah.

KISSINGER: —that Richardson, uh, I mean, for this job, one should have picked somebody like [John J.] McCloy, I mean, not McCloy himself but somebody—

PRESIDENT NIXON: I—

KISSINGER: —who has a natural interest in us and who knows that you do not smear the President of the United States, uh, apart from his participation, you do not do this to the country.

PRESIDENT NIXON: Well, if Cox does it, we'll survive it. . . .

KISSINGER: But, but you shouldn't have to go through it. I think after the Dean testimony, uh, well, I think the summit will put you into a much different [position]—I mean, you just can't watch this television. . . . And after Dean is off, I thought maybe a press conference where you'd recognize the nastiest sonsofbitches and let them look as if they're harassing you.

PRESIDENT NIXON: That's what I plan. . . . I was planning to do it next Tuesday. . . . I mean, they've got Dean trying to save his ass. Everybody all, I mean, they all knew that the President wasn't involved in this damn thing. Hell, they'll plummet up there and it's just, it, disgusting, absolutely—

SEGMENT 2

KISSINGER: . . . What national interest is served by this?

PRESIDENT NIXON: Well, only if they're gonna try to say the President is trying to cover up or use Dean, who's a Goddamned liar to save his soul. And everybody, everybody—they get, when they get Haldeman on, he'll kill Dean. Colson'll kill him. Ehrlichman'll kill him. Moore will kill him. You know, but those will be on. . . . One of the most disgusting things, Henry, is the attitude of our Republican senators and Congressmen. . . .

KISSINGER: They never supported you when you needed them on anything else. . . . They only support you when they know you're going to win. They love to come to the White House for dinner.

PRESIDENT NIXON: Yeah, disgusting, disgusting, they come through to whine and whine and to bitch about everything. . . .

JUNE 19, 1973: THE PRESIDENT, HAIG, ZIEGLER, AND BUZHARDT, 9:37–11:00 A.M., OVAL OFFICE

Archibald Cox is replacing John Dean as the President's favorite demon. At a June 18 press conference, Cox said the question of whether a sitting President could be subpoenaed or indicted prior to impeachment was under further study. Nixon is outraged. "What the hell has Elliot done here," he complains to his aides. Dean's Senate testimony is approaching and the President's staff is worried. Buzhardt is optimistic, confident that the cross-examination questions he has prepared for Fred Thompson will force Dean "to admit every piece of chicanery . . . and it's going to be a real sordid record." Yet Nixon is the realist, and far more on target: "[I]sn't he going to cover all that [his wrongdoing] in his statement . . . ?"

SEGMENT 2

PRESIDENT NIXON: . . . What is your, uh—let's talk just a minute about the strategy and so forth. One thing I was, noted this morning was that, oh, that fucking shocking statement by Scott, I mean Cox . Good God, that, uh, now look here—I maybe you can write a brief little rejoinder there. Ziegler's gonna try to get [Congressional liaison William] Timmons to find somebody on the Hill. Maybe Stennis could say something, you know, I don't know. Is this the time to try? But that was an ugly shocking thing.

HAIG: It really was.

PRESIDENT NIXON: Because, first, it's wrong, as far as the Constitution; it's partisan . . . . [C]an the President be subpoenaed or indicted, Jesus Christ, he knows better than that. . . . Well, he's highly partisan.

BUZHARDT: He's a highly partisan fella and he's gonna play it political.

PRESIDENT NIXON: Yeah.

BUZHARDT: Because he knows he can't subpoena the President; he knows he can't indict the President, but he's gonna play this game quite opposite. . . . I think we— he said yesterday he had made no decision on whether to get into the San Clemente property thing or the gifts, and I'm gonna talk to Elliot Richardson.

PRESIDENT NIXON: What does "the gift" mean?

BUZHARDT: Uh, the gifts of presidential papers and the fact—

PRESIDENT NIXON: God Almighty.

BUZHARDT: —uh, but we'll handle that one. I'm gonna talk with Elliot. That is not within the jurisdiction he gave Cox; he's got to make it perfectly plain it's not.

PRESIDENT NIXON: The San Clemente property—what the hell is he getting into that for? . . . [W]hat Elliot's done? What the hell has Elliot done here, uh? . . .

BUZHARDT: Elliot has got to get him back to the middle ground. . . .

HAIG: And say that this man hasn't got a hunting license.

PRESIDENT NIXON: He has got to get into this now. We expect him to say something. . . .

BUZHARDT: . . . [H]e cannot allow this fella, for the sake of everybody in government, to think that this fella has a hunting license as a Kennedy advocate to go after Republicans any way he can, and the President in particular. . . . [After the Ervin hearings conclude], then we meet him [Cox] head-on. And we just blast the fire out of him. That's the only thing we can do. But if we come out of the hearings in good shape, and I believe we will, and the public's gonna be fed up with it at that point. I think, I think at that point, Mr. Cox is gonna reach the point where he's gonna have a very difficult time getting the press to attend his press conferences. It's just not gonna be that kind of news. It's all gonna be re-hash and by that time, I hope we'll have the Committee with enough information on Democrat financing. . . .

PRESIDENT NIXON: I wouldn't anticipate it that much. . . . [P]erhaps you can find out from [Fred] Thompson as to why did, they did postpone these hearings? . . . Dean was gonna be so embarrassing or what?

BUZHARDT: No sir, they postponed the hearings on [Senator Leaders Mike] Mansfield's and [Hugh] Scott's request [because of the visit of Leonid Brezhnev]. They acted solely on that. They had not started the cross—the examination of Dean in the Committee—

PRESIDENT NIXON: Mm-hmm.

BUZHARDT: —before they got the letter. The letter came in before they actually started.

PRESIDENT NIXON: Scott and Mansfield sent the letter [asking the Committee to postpone the hearings pending the conclusion of the summit meeting]?

BUZHARDT: Yes, sir. A very detailed letter asking—

PRESIDENT NIXON: How could Scott do such a damn dumb thing? Go ahead.

BUZHARDT: Mansfield called Scott at home, uh, called Scott in his office—they got together, drafted the letter they then carried over to Baker, with a copy to Ervin. It arrived in the Committee before they really got started. They sent Dean and his lawyer outside while they discussed it and then they voted six to one to [postpone]. . . . And they said there'd been a lot of pressure from some who thought they were acting unwisely to crash into this thing this week. . . .

Well, I don't think we're doing bad, Mr. President, I think we're coming up every day on this thing.

PRESIDENT NIXON: You do?

BUZHARDT: And, and I'm, I feel real confident about how these hearings are gonna go. If not, someone will cross-examine Dean. From what Dean says, he expects them to cross-examine him. Because he's got to admit every piece of chicanery he was ever involved in to prevent his prosecution. And it's gonna be a real sordid record. And that, politically, they can't sit there on the television and not interrogate him about it.

PRESIDENT NIXON: Yeah, well, but let's assume for that, isn't he going to cover all that in his statement, he doesn't have to wait for them to interrogate him, he can say, "I admit this, I admit that, I admit every dollar," in other words, the purpose of that is to get immunity in all those points, right?

BUZHARDT: Yes, sir. But it's gonna be a very sordid record and they're gonna have to go in and make him explain it in detail. They cannot just concentrate on his allegations about other people. He's gonna be in conflict with every witness practically that's testified, that's been involved.

PRESIDENT NIXON: Really?

BUZHARDT: Yes, sir. And they're gonna have to use the testimony they had publicly and the testimony that's been given to the staff to cross-examine him. . . . And I told them if they didn't ask the questions, I was gonna publicly blast them on it.

PRESIDENT NIXON: Good.

BUZHARDT: Because they weren't asking for it fairly. All we want is fairness in the cross-examination. . . .

PRESIDENT NIXON: Did you tell them we need to get Baker interested and wants to ask, ask a few questions?

BUZHARDT: I don't know. We can get Gurney. But whether or not Baker's gonna swing him around is still in the balance. . . . Wouldn't wanna mislead you. . . .

PRESIDENT NIXON: No, heavens, . . . he's been a weather vane a long time.

BUZHARDT: If he sees that Dean is beginning to crumble, if he sees that he's beginning to look bad, then yes, I anticipate he'll jump on with both feet. . . .

I'm convinced that [Dean will] . . . convict himself.

PRESIDENT NIXON: Really?

BUZHARDT: Yes, sir. As a liar, and we'll give him all the help we can.

PRESIDENT NIXON: As a liar, huh.

BUZHARDT: Yes, sir. Mr. President, he can't go through this whole place and tell a legitimate story and have it stand up under all circumstances. He doesn't know enough and he doesn't remember enough. He can't put it all together. . . . Yes, sir. I think we're gonna have a bad day of publicity the day he reads his opening statement, because the press won't play all of the admissions in it, they'll play the allegations.

PRESIDENT NIXON: Sure. Dean alleges the President was involved and the President knew and the President said "Pay a million dollars," right? They'll replay that all night—

BUZHARDT: They'll replay it, but it's all been in the press before. . . .

PRESIDENT NIXON: But we need to be on that day with some kind of disclaimer on. . . . Goldwater is a, a lost cause, I guess, huh.

BUZHARDT: . . . Barry [Goldwater] Jr. and Dean were roommates in college.

PRESIDENT NIXON: There's the problem, okay. . . .

JUNE 19, 1973: THE PRESIDENT, ROSE MARY WOODS, AND HAIG, 11:04–11:17 A.M., OVAL OFFICE

The President's secretary reports on the latest doings of Martha Mitchell. Haig briefs Nixon on Richardson's weaknesses and Archibald Cox's aggressiveness.

PRESIDENT NIXON: . . . I think you should call our friend Brother [Howard] Baker. . . . He's put out a story as we were going out there on a plane that he made it a point, he made it a point, never to be alone with the President. He was practically on us, all of us, with his camera, you know, taking pictures and the rest of it. For him to make such a point like that was utterly insulting.

WOODS: Well, it was insulting. What he's trying to do is protect himself, from the other people saying he's—

PRESIDENT NIXON: Well, yes. . . . [L]et me just say, we're watching him closely because he's not behaving well. . . .

PRESIDENT NIXON: [Senator Edward] Gurney's going to help some. . . .

WOODS: He is the only one left. I'll call him [John Mitchell] and see what he can do. . . .

PRESIDENT NIXON: . . . Look, it's got to be done with total discretion. . . .

[General Haig enters the room.]

PRESIDENT NIXON: . . . The one item that I don't remember talking about is [UPI reporter] Helen Thomas. For her to print another story on that poor sick Martha [Mitchell]. . . . And you know what she did by that story? She convicted John. She said that John told the Prez, Mr. President. Well, for God sakes, John's denied it.

WOODS: I know.

PRESIDENT NIXON: Denied his own involvement. Unbelievable.

WOODS: Well, she's [Martha Mitchell] a nut. She is a nut, you know, as far as I'm concerned. . . . Helen Thomas is bad. . . . Martha called other people. She called [*Washington Star* reporter] Betty Beale a lot of times. She doesn't call her because Betty won't print [that talk?]. . . .

PRESIDENT NIXON: No. Betty's a decent person.

WOODS: That's right. . . .

HAIG: I talked to Elliot [Richardson]. He was concerned about, see, he's meeting with [Archibald] Cox today to go over his charter. He said, Goddamn it, that was bad. And he said, the other thing's on the subpoena and what have you, that Cox has sort of taken out of context. I said, You go over that transcript; it is just blatant partisanship, and if that is what this man is going to perpetrate, we've lost a great deal in terms of objectivity and the kind of proceedings we want.

PRESIDENT NIXON: Elliot has got to—Buzhardt been over and reassured him, the dumb bastard. Elliot knows the President's not guilty of anything, doesn't he?

HAIG: He knows it. He knows it.

PRESIDENT NIXON: Well, why in the name of God can't he step up to this?

HAIG: Well, I'll say this for him. He was very responsive this morning.

PRESIDENT NIXON: Good.

HAIG: And he said, I've already requested an appointment with Cox and I'm going to have a talk to him and talk with him about it. . . .

PRESIDENT NIXON: Well, good enough. I guess we shouldn't get our balls in an uproar about him.

HAIG: No, no, we can't.

PRESIDENT NIXON: About the Committee and all that sort of thing. I must say that the crap just floats so much. I don't know. Maybe there just comes a point where people are going to say, well, the President's either guilty or not guilty. I don't know what we can do about that, I really don't.

JUNE 19, 1973: THE PRESIDENT AND JULIE NIXON EISENHOWER, 3:01–3:04 P.M., WHITE HOUSE TELEPHONE

Nixon assures his younger daughter that Dean cannot incriminate him.

PRESIDENT NIXON: Actually, let me tell you, the thing is on this, uh, uh, we'll, we're ready to strike back but uh we're, we've got a plan and I just want you to know that. I have very much in mind, but when we do, we want to just take the offensive and stay on it.

EISENHOWER: Right.

PRESIDENT NIXON: You know what I mean? And we're just gonna go all out, and uh—

EISENHOWER: Hey, Dean doesn't have any damning documents, does he? He's just talking?

PRESIDENT NIXON: No, no, no.

EISENHOWER: I don't think so.

PRESIDENT NIXON: Oh no, no, no, no—don't worry about that. . . . Dean is just going to make a lot of charges, you know, about this and that and the other thing, cause he was the master of the whole cover-up. He said the same thing himself.

EISENHOWER: Yeah.

PRESIDENT NIXON: He was the carry-outer of the thing. And uh, he led us for ten months—[*chuckles*] . . .

EISENHOWER: Boy. But it's, it's working out.

June 19, 1973, The President, Haig, and Buzhardt, 3:09–3:38 p.m., Oval Office

Fred Buzhardt tells Nixon that the former prosecutors had wanted to indict John Dean, implying some hesitation on Archibald Cox's part. U.S. Attorney Earl Silbert had always insisted that Dean not be given immunity, as he believed the case would lose credibility. Buzhardt discusses Dean's alleged misappropriation of CREEP funds for his personal use. Buzhardt and Nixon are convinced this will be Dean's undoing.

PRESIDENT NIXON: . . . Ziegler says that the prosecutors have given a sealed envelope to the Judge.

BUZHARDT: That's the evidence they have on Dean. . . . They want to go after Dean. Cox can't fight Silbert and Silbert thinks Dean is the central figure in the whole business and wants to put him in jail. So, you know, he can't very well be in the position of not putting somebody guilty in jail if the prosecutors say this is one of the guiltiest guys. Now, the Committee to Re-Elect is getting off a letter to Dean this afternoon demanding return of the $14,000 and an accounting.

PRESIDENT NIXON: Is it fourteen rather than four now?

BUZHARDT: Yes, yes, it's 14,000. . . . He said he used 4800 for his honeymoon, put an IOU in the safe, his wedding and honeymoon.

PRESIDENT NIXON: Put an IOU in the safe? . . . That's a nice way of operating.

BUZHARDT: Then he said that after he hired a lawyer, [Charles N.] Shaffer, in late March or early April of '73, he put an identical amount of money in a trust fund. That's exactly the way he phrased it: He put an identical amount of money. I suspect the reason he had to do this is because we could trace his finances and see if he had borrowed it. Now—

PRESIDENT NIXON: So he'll just claim he borrowed the money, is that right?

BUZHARDT: To put back, I guess. Borrowing from somebody else's money is—

PRESIDENT NIXON: Without telling anybody.

BUZHARDT: . . . [Seymour] Hersh has called us again. He's going to inform us now of what he finds, and he asked us did we know that Dean was quite a big spender. Hersh says that he will know before the afternoon is out how much he paid for the diamond ring and how much he paid the caterers at the wedding; did we know that he bought a brand-new car at the time he got married? Did we know all this from our investigation? No, we didn't investigate all this, you know. . . .

Well, if the newspapers will print enough to give the public the clear impression that this was quite a man about town who was a big spender, really threw his money around, bought very expensive diamond rings, automobiles, motorcycles.

PRESIDENT NIXON: A boat?

BUZHARDT: Yes. You know, he just bought things right and left. We get all of this in the paper and the public is ready to understand then why he would keep the money, and it's coming through. . . .

PRESIDENT NIXON: Does Hersh understand this?

BUZHARDT: Yes, sir. yes, sir. Hersh understands that very clearly, and we didn't tell him.

PRESIDENT NIXON: Oh, he got it?

BUZHARDT: He got it. We put it together, but he got it from somebody else.

PRESIDENT NIXON: Good.

BUZHARDT: And he called us to try to verify it and we said, well, you know, we can't verify this.

PRESIDENT NIXON: He got it.

BUZHARDT: But he got it elsewhere.

PRESIDENT NIXON: I see. Well, there's no question in my opinion that Dean probably filched the whole fourteen.

BUZHARDT: . . . And the letter has gone to Dean demanding an immediate response and return of the money. If by about Friday we don't have an answer on it we'll file suit, CREEP will file suit for the money.

PRESIDENT NIXON: Go ahead.

BUZHARDT: And that'll mean some more publicity.

PRESIDENT NIXON: Good.

JUNE 19, 1973: THE PRESIDENT AND KISSINGER, 4:40–4:41 P.M., OVAL OFFICE

Kissinger is pleased to hear the tales of Dean's appropriation of campaign funds for his personal use. He shares Nixon's optimism that this will finish Dean.

KISSINGER: Buzhardt thinks he's got Dean finished with this misappropriation of funds?

PRESIDENT NIXON: Well, when I see that, I just don't know whether the press will go after it, although this fellow [Seymour] Hersh has been digging.

KISSINGER: It's on the front page of the *Times* today.

PRESIDENT NIXON: On the *Times?* That's Hersh. It's his exclusive. Well, I've got to say, I think people will say—he's got a crazy story. He says, well, he took $14,000 from the Committee . . . and used it on his honeymoon and the rest and put an IOU in the safe, and then, however, he did not return the $14,000 until after he had consulted a lawyer in April.

KISSINGER: Right.

PRESIDENT NIXON: Now what the heck?

KISSINGER: But when you've got a common thief on top of a man who admits having run the cover-up—

JUNE 20, 1973: THE PRESIDENT AND ZIEGLER, 11:58 A.M.–12:02 P.M., CAMP DAVID TELEPHONE

The White House releases its "Golden Boy" memo to discredit Dean, accusing him of, among other things, taking White House funds for his honeymoon. Ziegler reports to the President on media reaction.

PRESIDENT NIXON: [*Chuckles.*] Fred [Buzhardt] must be just like a—just like a kid with a—with a new toy with this money thing. You know, he brought that up himself.

ZIEGLER: Right.

PRESIDENT NIXON: How did he find that out? Do you know? How the devil did he do it?

ZIEGLER: I don't know. I think he got a tip on it or—I just don't know. I haven't asked him that.

PRESIDENT NIXON: A curious—a curious thing here. You know, I didn't—did you ever hear about the—did you ever think that Dean was stealing money?

ZIEGLER: Never, never, never, never.

PRESIDENT NIXON: Good heavens. You know they can talk all they want about Haldeman and Colson and the rest, but they're honest men, Ron.

ZIEGLER: That's right.

PRESIDENT NIXON: You know what I mean. They wouldn't steal a penny.

ZIEGLER: That's right.

PRESIDENT NIXON: No. This has—this has got to—I would think that even *Time* magazine would have trouble with this one.

ZIEGLER: Yes, sir, absolutely.

PRESIDENT NIXON: The "Golden Boy" business. . . . Even the *Post* and Walter Cronkite [CBS] maybe, huh?

ZIEGLER: That's right.

PRESIDENT NIXON: The nets [networks] didn't pick it up yet, did they, or did they?

ZIEGLER: Yeah, the nets ran it. Yes, sir. . . .

PRESIDENT NIXON: But we stay miles away from it.

ZIEGLER: Yes, sir.

PRESIDENT NIXON: Just let her run.

ZIEGLER: Yes, sir.

PRESIDENT NIXON: Unless it starts to drop and then we'll—

ZIEGLER: Then we'll have to goose it.

PRESIDENT NIXON: Buzhardt is having a letter written to Dean asking for the return of the money, you know.

ZIEGLER: That's right from CREEP. . . .

PRESIDENT NIXON: He should return the money. It doesn't belong to him. . . .

JUNE 22, 1973: THE PRESIDENT, HAIG, AND ZIEGLER, 9:45–10:28 A.M., OVAL OFFICE

As Dean prepares to testify on June 25, the President meets regularly with his aides, almost obsessing on the forthcoming appearance. He worries, however, that Dean might emphasize "crap," such as Nixon's table talk about Supreme Court justices.

PRESIDENT NIXON: Well, anyway, what I was going to say, though, I want to be sure that there is a plan, to knock his [Dean's] brains out, other than just rely on little, old [Fred] Thompson to do the cross-examining. . . . You know what I mean?. . . .

HAIG: We're—I'm going to have a meeting, as a matter of fact, on this, this morning with Buzhardt. . . .

PRESIDENT NIXON: Buzhardt has got good ideas and so forth, but . . . Buzhardt thinks in terms of the outcome legally a great deal. This doesn't make any difference here. It doesn't make any difference legally.

ZIEGLER: No, Buzhardt is—

PRESIDENT NIXON: What makes an awful difference is how the darn people think about it.

HAIG: Huh—

ZIEGLER: Buzhardt is not playing a PR role. What he is doing is serving the PR objective. . . .

PRESIDENT NIXON: What does Dean say?

ZIEGLER: Dean is not saying much of anything. He's wallowing over there, behind his door. Dean is really quiet. It's—

HAIG: Yeah. He's probably scared—

ZIEGLER: I don't think he has anything more to say. He's scared to death now. . . .

PRESIDENT NIXON: . . . [H]e's going to have all sorts of crap. We'll be in trouble with the Supreme Court, because I made some very acid comments about some of Court Justices—said that some of them are jerks.

ZIEGLER: That doesn't matter. . . .

JULY 9, 1973: THE PRESIDENT AND CHARLES G. REBOZO, 6:50–6:58 P.M., WHITE HOUSE TELEPHONE

The Soviet summit meeting is over, and so is Dean's testimony. Sensational as it was, Dean still was in the unenviable position of having his word taken versus that of the President of the United States. Charles ("Bebe") Rebozo provides occasional uplift for the President. Nixon seems to sense that Rebozo, like Rose Mary Woods, offers him a compassionate, uncomplicated, dedicated relationship. Here, Rebozo talks about knocking down rumors of Nixon's Key Biscayne property improvements at public expense.

REBOZO: . . . I know you got to get sick of hearing me say it, because they get in, you know, in the good 'ol Washington and other places, but every place I go—now this weekend I went down to Ocean Reef and I was coming out of drugstore these people coming out a very fine looking family—

PRESIDENT NIXON: Um-hum.

REBOZO: —and one of them recognized me. She called back and she says, "would you deliver a message for me?" And I says, yes—"would you tell our President, we just love him." And this is the same—this is the typical story that I can—

PRESIDENT NIXON: We ran into an awful lot of that in Kansas City.

REBOZO: Over and over and over again. You know, you read these three newspapers and you wouldn't know it or look at the damn press.

PRESIDENT NIXON: Yeah. Well, you know—

REBOZO: The hell with it.

PRESIDENT NIXON: I understand John Mitchell apparently is going to testify tomorrow [to the Senate Committee].

REBOZO: It looks like it. It looks like it.

PRESIDENT NIXON: But boy, I just wish him the best.

REBOZO: Well, I do, too.

PRESIDENT NIXON: We've gotten the word to him in every way, haven't we?

REBOZO: I know it. He knows it. He knows it. No problem. But this one I might take a little time out to watch.

PRESIDENT NIXON: You're going to watch it?

REBOZO: I might watch—I'll watch as much of it as I can.

PRESIDENT NIXON: What's a shocking damn thing, now the former Attorney General of—

REBOZO: I know.

PRESIDENT NIXON: —the United States the best—a man that was a campaign manager for the President of '68—

REBOZO: Unbelievable.

PRESIDENT NIXON: —and then a campaign manager up through the primary—

REBOZO: Unbelievable.

PRESIDENT NIXON: —and they bring him before the stinking Committee on a stinking little crappy thing like this.

REBOZO: That's exactly right.

PRESIDENT NIXON: It's unbelievable.

REBOZO: Exactly right.

PRESIDENT NIXON: And the country just—but this press is just—

REBOZO: It ain't going to work.

PRESIDENT NIXON: Yeah.

REBOZO: It ain't going to work. And I'll tell you people will go out of their way to write letters. I got a letter from a little boy today, I sent it on to Rose. Just a very sweet, sweet letter, tell your friend he loves him. You know, it's just unbelievable that these things go on. . . .

PRESIDENT NIXON: . . . [W]ith all this business [of investigations] of going into the California property and the Florida property and all the rest—they'll say now how much of that has been held, which is none of their damn business. . . .

REBOZO: I know. And they know it.

PRESIDENT NIXON: And also we've all handled it in a way that's perfectly above board.

REBOZO: Without any problem. There's no problem on that.

PRESIDENT NIXON: And I'll tell you—I'm telling you just as soon as that Haldeman is finished, I'm going to take them on, believe me, and finish it off.

REBOZO: That's right. If there's any answering done, somebody else can answer the little, nitpicking stuff. . . .

PRESIDENT NIXON: . . . [P]oor 'ol [Nixon's and Rebozo's friend, Robert] Abplanalp, the only reason these Jews brought this thing against him was because he had the best [valve product] and they couldn't get in the market.

REBOZO: Well, that's—the amazing thing is that really kills them, they just surmise. See [*Washington Post* columnist Maxine] Cheshire did a despicable thing. . . .

PRESIDENT NIXON: Did she talk to Abplanalp?

REBOZO: Oh, no, no, no, no. No, no but she called his office and talked to his PR man and lied to him. She told him that the Secret Service had told her things that were absolute lies. But anyway we got it all—we got her hung.

PRESIDENT NIXON: About what? About the—

REBOZO: About this relation—do you know that Abplanalp not only paid [at Nixon's Key Biscayne residence] for the—all the buildings, the Secret Service quarters, . . . he paid for the heli[copter]pad, the roads. He even paid for the security devices in the main house, and the smoke devices and everything.

PRESIDENT NIXON: Yeah.

REBOZO: Everything, everything. And he insisted on it. They wanted to do it. He insisted on it.

PRESIDENT NIXON: And so she [Cheshire] wrote that he didn't pay it though, huh?

REBOZO: . . . See she lied. She told Abplanalp's man that the Secret Service had told them that they had paid for this.

PRESIDENT NIXON: Well, why don't we do something about it?

REBOZO: And Abplanalp and I were together when we got the word, so we nailed it right down. We nailed it right down.

PRESIDENT NIXON: What can we do about her though about that?

REBOZO: There's no problem. That'll be good. I think the Lord will take care of her. . . .

PRESIDENT NIXON: . . . It shows you how the *Post* works.

REBOZO: I think [Frank] Sinatra was too kind. [*Laughter.*] [Sinatra once had thrown money at Cheshire, saying she worked a profession other than journalism.]

PRESIDENT NIXON: Oh yeah.

REBOZO: He was too kind.

PRESIDENT NIXON: Two bits, not two dollars.

REBOZO: But she's taken care of. She's taken care of. The whole thing is taken care of. It was a nothing—you know, nothing thing. But she just tried to making something of it. . . .

PRESIDENT NIXON: . . . Well, they're not going to get Bob on something like that. . . . I think actually—well, wherever the hell—heck, we're moving up [in the Senate hearings] and everyone else knows it.

REBOZO: Exactly.

PRESIDENT NIXON: And this fellow Dean —listen by the time these other guys get through, we'll have some rough knocks—

REBOZO: That's right.

PRESIDENT NIXON: —and poor 'ol Kalmbach, they'll work him over, too. But by the time we get through—

REBOZO: Yes.

PRESIDENT NIXON: —every other witness is going to knock Dean's brains out.

REBOZO: That's right.

PRESIDENT NIXON: He's going to be discredited. Huh?

REBOZO: No problem. No problem. We just, you know, that's the way it goes. . . .

JULY 11, 1973: THE PRESIDENT AND ZIEGLER, 2:28-2:34 P.M., WHITE HOUSE TELEPHONE

With the rest of the country, the White House watches the Senate hearings. Nixon and Ziegler assess John Mitchell's appearance, apparently pleased at Mitchell's stonewalling and defiance. Still, Mitchell had acknowledged the "White House horrors" of the first term, providing linkage between Watergate and the Administration's past behavior, and inadvertently implying a justification for the post-Watergate cover-up.

PRESIDENT NIXON: Ron, it occurred to me that one of our boys probably—just thought of this, but probably nothing would be done—but you didn't mention the fact, I just learned it that they—you know, they carried Dean on three networks for five days straight.

ZIEGLER: Absolutely.

PRESIDENT NIXON: And they carried Mitchell on one.

ZIEGLER: Sure.

PRESIDENT NIXON: I understand the reason for that was that when they met with him, they determined that his testimony was not going to be damaging enough to the President. Has anybody thought to do anything to suggest something to one of the networks that we're aware of the screwing we're getting or we just forget that sort of thing?

ZIEGLER: No, no, we don't forget that, and I've done that already.

PRESIDENT NIXON: Who did you do it to?

ZIEGLER: Well, I talked to the people here about it, and I've also been mentioning that to press guys which I did with just [syndicated columnist] William S. White.

PRESIDENT NIXON: Yeah. Yeah. They didn't realize that's a little queer that all we hear is the major—the major one, so forth and so on and so on. Well, it just shows you what we're up against [chuckles], I guess. But this is one time when I put [Kenneth] Clawson and the bomb throwers to work on the things like that —let them bitch a little.

ZIEGLER: Well, yeah, Ken was in the meeting here with White with me. And these are things we're thinking about and—

PRESIDENT NIXON: I know that you can't be, you know, you can't be obvious and mean and rough and so forth. But there are ways, Ron, to—not to let them think that we just aren't aware of being totally screwed, you know. You know, I just—listen, it's a matter of pride. I just don't want them to feel like. We're not going to change them. They aren't going to change a thing. We just let them know, you know.

ZIEGLER: Well, as I say, we have done that. I have done it with the people here. I've done it with [news president William] Small at CBS and, you know, just a shot across a bow type of thing.

PRESIDENT NIXON: You might say we're getting scores of calls in here about this, protesting the wires.

ZIEGLER: . . . [T]his this thing is passing quickly. [columnist William S.] White was very complimentary of Mitchell. . . .

PRESIDENT NIXON: . . . White [is] probably worried . . . about that [his friend, Lyndon Johnson's] bugging and so forth. Hell, I was the one who stopped from putting that out, yeah. . . . We didn't want to embarrass the FBI or Johnson.

ZIEGLER: White also mentioned that you were under great pressure and growing pressure to put out the information you had on the bugging in the Kennedy and Johnson Administrations. So we fired that out there a little bit more.

PRESIDENT NIXON: Good.

ZIEGLER: Mitchell continues to do a good job.

PRESIDENT NIXON: Good.

ZIEGLER: Dick Moore is the first witness tomorrow, as I mentioned to you earlier. . . . Who's after him [Mitchell] now? Weicker?

ZIEGLER: No, no. It's—Inouye is questioning him now.

PRESIDENT NIXON: Oh, yeah, he can—

ZIEGLER: I just was told that Ervin is beginning to question him now.

PRESIDENT NIXON: Yeah, yeah. That will be a nice battle.

ZIEGLER: He will do all right with Ervin.

PRESIDENT NIXON: With Ervin? He'll kill him. And Ervin is not that smart. I mean he's a—I mean he may have in his younger years but he's 77, forgetful and, you know—goes into those poses and all that sort of thing. . . . But Mitchell will do very well with Ervin.

ZIEGLER: I think so.

PRESIDENT NIXON: They may finish with Mitchell today, won't they?

ZIEGLER: Yes, sir.

PRESIDENT NIXON: They don't want him on there very long, do they? That's what it seems to me.

ZIEGLER: Well, two days, right?

PRESIDENT NIXON: No, but for God's sake they had Dean five days.

ZIEGLER: That's right.

PRESIDENT NIXON: Now, why don't they want Mitchell on? You know why. [*Laughter.*] They don't want a good witness on that long. They're trying to get him the hell off of there.

ZIEGLER: Well, sure—I'm sure of that. That's a political move—that would be the political move. . . . [T]hey will probably move to Kalmbach or someone like that, and wrap up the week in that fashion or something.

PRESIDENT NIXON: Yeah. Yeah. And you still have the reports to the effect that they may get Haldeman and Ehrlichman on before the end of the month, huh?

ZIEGLER: That's—that's the report we have, yes. . . .

JULY 11, 1973: THE PRESIDENT AND CONNALLY, 3:03–4:22 P.M., OVAL OFFICE

Press attacks mount because of Nixon's alleged public expenditures for his private use and for his links to several wealthy friends, including Robert Abplanalp and Charles Rebozo. With the widening Watergate inquiry, the besieged President lashes out at his critics. John Connally again is a refreshing Oval Office visitor, offering spirited advice to Nixon.

SEGMENT 1

PRESIDENT NIXON: But you saw, there was a little story—

CONNALLY: Yes, sir. It's a long story.

PRESIDENT NIXON: And we'll handle it in our own way and so forth and so on. First of all, they put out a story with regard to the property, the property at San Clemente, to the fact that the President had a million dollars in campaign funds in that property. He, of course, did not—it's a total lie. . . . I had to come up with that (unintelligible) money to pay the mortgage myself, but the people who owned the property—it was about an acre and a half, the whole piece—wanted only one mortgage, so Abplanalp loaned the money to me. He paid for it all. . . .

CONNALLY: Right.

PRESIDENT NIXON: Now, Abplanalp at the present time, I tell you, just to show you how vicious the press is—Abplanalp at the present time, . . . Abplanalp does no business with the government and I was gonna pay 8 percent interest. . . [N]othing's higher than 8 percent. . . .

CONNALLY: And who are the other ones in the trust?

PRESIDENT NIXON: It's Rebozo. Rebozo, . . . he says, "Well, I'll take a piece of it." So two friends, neither of whom does a damn bit of business with the government, own the title to that property. There isn't a nickel of campaign funds in it—never— and the *Los Angeles Times* had a story to the effect that there's Teamster money in there.

CONNALLY: [*Laughs.*] How in the name of God would I get Teamster money? Aren't they cruel.

SEGMENT 2

PRESIDENT NIXON: . . . [T]he GSA spent all the money [for improvements of Nixon's San Clemente estate.]. . . . [T]he Secret Service insisted. You saw the fence around it—

CONNALLY: No.

PRESIDENT NIXON: They put a big fence up around it afterwards and they put in all sorts of communications equipment and they put up a, you know, the, the spotlight over the—they put up things around the house, in it, and so forth; . . . watchtowers and so forth and so on. It cost them a lot of money. . . . Now our good friend [Congressman] Tom Steed, to his great credit, came forward yesterday and said, "I approved [the appropriation]," and said, "one president has been shot, a candidate for president has been killed, and we need this kind of protection." . . . [T]hey say that if we don't have that damn fence, they would have to have at least a hundred Secret Service [agents], providing protection there. . . . I didn't have a damn thing to do with it. . . . I prefer not to have a fence, you know. So there's the problem. . . .

. . . I don't know how to, how to stop it—

CONNALLY: The best way you can do it is probably attack them, but you can't do that—

PRESIDENT NIXON: —but not now.

CONNALLY: You can't do that now. You—

PRESIDENT NIXON: Well, I know, but let me—here's what I intend. I intend not to say a damn thing about Watergate until I finish, until Haldeman's been on.

CONNALLY: Right. . . .

PRESIDENT NIXON: But then, from then again, the point is, John—how the hell will we handle this, this frankly persecution of our friends. . . . You know, you know where this is leading is, don't you, Precision Valve. He [Abplanalp] makes the best valves in the world. What happened is that in 1970, there are some Jews, that you, that you might, as you might have guessed, doesn't mean that if there were some Gentiles it might not be this bad. There are some Jews in New York [who wanted an anti-trust suit], because Abplanalp . . . makes the best valve at the cheapest price.

To try to bring an anti-trust suit against him, because he was committed, basically, in other words, he had the market, uh, the Justice Department just threw it out. I never heard about it; Abplanalp never told me. I imagine his lawyer didn't bother him with it too much. And then a Jewish Congressman the other day in the House gets up and says the Nixon Administration killed an anti-trust case against Abplanalp. What in the name of God do you do? . . . Abplanalp or Rebozo, they'll never, in all the time I've known both, have never asked for one thing—they even refuse to ride the damn plane unless I insist.

CONNALLY: Sure.

PRESIDENT NIXON: You know, there are men like that. . . . And there are others who are not that way. I don't mean all are not that way, Vesco is a crook. I never met the man. . . .

CONNALLY: Let me tell what advantage, Mr. President, you could get out of it. . . . [S]ee, the one thing that we're gonna have to do in this country, we're gonna have to openly talk about these contributions and you're gonna have, you're gonna have to find humor, cajolity, uh, sarcasm, you know how take this press on, dig into all these people. . . . Congress is gonna magnify it by drying up contributions from anybody with a little money, and they're gonna try to run everybody out of public life that has any sense of decency or honesty about him or anybody who's got ten cents.

PRESIDENT NIXON: That's right.

CONNALLY: . . . [T]hey'll make it so miserable and so unpleasant—

PRESIDENT NIXON: As a matter of fact, John, . . . I don't know who it was—they want their money back, and I said, "Give it back."

CONNALLY: Why, I would too.

PRESIDENT NIXON: I said, "hell with them," give it back, I don't want the damn money. . . .

CONNALLY: Some of the fellows who were fairly unsophisticated gave you some money, God almighty, they've been down there hounding them and checking on them and wanting their records, oh hell. . . .

CONNALLY: The [Senate Select] Committee.

PRESIDENT NIXON: The Committee. The Committee has seventy-nine lawyers and we've got three. . . .

CONNALLY: [I]t's got them just shaken. They don't know what the hell, but I said, "For God's sake, don't worry about it. Just go on, admit you gave him money and say I wish I could've given twice as much." . . . The press knows this and Cox knows this and the Committee knows this and they're trying to hound everybody and make them look like they're a bunch of crooks.

PRESIDENT NIXON: We're gonna hang Cox at the proper time. . . . If he continues this harassment. . . . He hasn't been brought down there to conduct an investigation. . . . He's down there for the purpose of conducting this prosecution. . . .

SEGMENT 3

CONNALLY: . . . Watergate is going to become increasingly less important.

PRESIDENT NIXON: You feel so?

CONNALLY: No question about it, and, and—

PRESIDENT NIXON: Is it because people are just sick with it? . . .

CONNALLY: I know, but the minute that's over, then people will have had that emotional experience and they don't want it anymore. You asked if people are interested in all these contributions, you know, you can satiate people, you can get so much chocolate cake, or ice cream—

PRESIDENT NIXON: You can only give them so much champagne.

CONNALLY: —or champagne, or sex, or anything else, you know, you can get enough. And they'll have enough. They're already at that point.

JULY 11, 1973: THE PRESIDENT AND HAIG, 4:24–5:05 P.M., OVAL OFFICE

Fred Buzhardt's questions for John Dean's cross-examination had failed badly to discredit or shake the witness, and there is growing dissatisfaction with the White House legal team. Haig also speaks to Richardson about Cox, and warns Nixon that he does not trust either of them.

HAIG: I had a good talk with [Chicago lawyer Morris] Liebman last night.

PRESIDENT NIXON: Yeah, how'd that go? . . .

HAIG: . . . [H]e thinks we should have a strategy group, uh, which he'd be willing to chair, participating with [former Nixon law partner [H. Chapman] Chappie Rose and somebody else to just come in pretty regularly and make an assessment on, on Fred, how he's handling the issues, how to handle that.

PRESIDENT NIXON: Not bad.

HAIG: And I think, I think it's pretty good.

PRESIDENT NIXON: Get us a broader, get us basically a consulting group.

HAIG: That's right and that whole time they could come in and spend a couple days and look at where we are and then we'll go into that, this issue or that angle. Then he thinks we need more lawyers on the staff. . . working for Fred.

PRESIDENT NIXON: We find any honest lawyers we can trust? . . .

HAIG: I talked to, to Elliot. Elliot's going on leave tomorrow for a week; he said he got tired of this stuff.

PRESIDENT NIXON: Good.

HAIG: He had a meeting with Cox yesterday; Cox is agreeing that they'll, that Elliot will investigate everything. . . . [E]ven though Cox may be referred to in the charge, Elliot will, will do the [investigating?]. In other words, all the substance, uh. I'm not convinced—I just don't trust either of them—

PRESIDENT NIXON: Yeah.

HAIG: We need to watch them like a hawk. . . .

JULY 11, 1973: THE PRESIDENT AND ZIEGLER, 5:16–5:41 P.M., OVAL OFFICE

The President reports on Connally's visit. He sharpens his attack on Cox, and Ziegler dutifully suggests firing the Special Prosecutor.

PRESIDENT NIXON: I talked to Connally. . . . He said there comes a time when people get tired, they get tired out, of too much ice cream, too much champagne, they get tired of anything, too much sex, anything. You get too (unintelligible), you get too tired of the damn thing.

ZIEGLER: I've agreed with Connally on everything. . . .

PRESIDENT NIXON: And, he feels too, that after September I should go out and attack.

ZIEGLER: He's right.

PRESIDENT NIXON: . . . I should give them a kick in the ass now and then. . . . [T]hat sonofabitch Cox. . . . We gotta get a case on him, that's the point. . . .

ZIEGLER: I think the case on Cox would be based on the fact that, look, we've had it with him, we're not going to allow the institution of this government to be destroyed by distortion of this type, and therefore these activities, these investigations, these inquiries are being placed by the President of the United States, which is your authority to do, into the framework of the Department of Justice, where they belong. Mr. Cox, I'm relieving you of your responsibilities. Period. And let him squeal. Archibald Cox will not be remembered.

PRESIDENT NIXON: Hmm. What are our major stories today?

ZIEGLER: Well, sir, nothing major breaking today. . . .

JULY 12, 1973: THE PRESIDENT, HAIG, AND KISSINGER, 2:29–2:50 P.M., OVAL OFFICE

Kissinger reports that author Norman Mailer is a convert to the President. Nixon and Haig discuss the hearings and Senator Ervin. The President again promises a full-scale assault against the Committee. In the meantime, he instructs Haig to pass the word to Colson: no finger-pointing against others. Finally, Nixon refers to his September 15, 1972 meeting with Dean. He may have heard the tape of that conversation for he has a good sense of the opening lines; in any event, he tells the others that he can "check in my own way" for what was said.

SEGMENT 1

PRESIDENT NIXON: I read a news summary on Ervin and so forth and I'm glad I read it and saw it. I'm glad I was so tough on him, hard, what he and Weicker asked is disgraceful.

HAIG:: Disgraceful.

PRESIDENT NIXON: Disgraceful. And they say they're not out to get anybody. [Senator Ervin:] "We wish there was nobody; the best thing I could do is to find out nobody is involved." The old incredible bastard. . . .

KISSINGER: I, I just had a call from Dr. Norman Mailer, who is doing an article on Watergate.

PRESIDENT NIXON: (Unintelligible).

KISSINGER: Well, he says . . . for the first time in his life, he's beginning to like you. He says Mitchell [in his testimony] turned it around as far as he was concerned.

PRESIDENT NIXON: (Unintelligible).

KISSINGER: I said, you know, I just want you to know what a radical leftist is thinking. If he's—

PRESIDENT NIXON: Mitchell, huh, turned it around?

KISSINGER: Because he said any man who can inspire such loyalty and he said now he's beginning to believe maybe the President didn't know about it and he said—

PRESIDENT NIXON: I did not know.

KISSINGER: —he said it doesn't make any difference. I just thought it might interest you to hear the man who's pathologically almost—

PRESIDENT NIXON: What we're what we're talking about is that, Ervin is—I just had to give him a call. . . . Ervin wants [Sam] Dash to come down and look over the [presidential] papers and determine which ones could come out. I said, "Not on your life, there ain't gonna be no papers come out."

KISSINGER: I wouldn't give them. . . .

PRESIDENT NIXON: Let him sue. Christ, they—If the Supreme Court wanna decide in its wisdom to help destroy the presidency, the Supreme Court destroys it. I'm not gonna destroy it. I'll just be a second—let me finish this one thing.

[Nixon prepares to leave the Oval Office.]

KISSINGER: . . . I think they shouldn't make anybody (unintelligible)—

PRESIDENT NIXON: That's you, you're our best spy.

KISSINGER: . . . [Mailer] said it's serious, you know, he said, he thinks you're going to come out of this eventually stronger. That the public is beginning to identify with you and somebody gets kicked so much and endures and overcomes it; that's what a lot of people have experienced in their own lives.

PRESIDENT NIXON: They do, don't they?

KISSINGER: That's what he says. And—

PRESIDENT NIXON: And Mitchell impressed him?

KISSINGER: Yeah, I found it fascinating. [I called] so that I could give him a few arguments and I find that I had to pull him off, you know. He wants to write that it's all a CIA conspiracy against you because you were on detente. [*Short pause, then laughter from all.*]

HAIG: [*Laughing.*] *That's a little weird!*

PRESIDENT NIXON: Thank you, that's nice to hear. . . . I'm not going to allow this slick Southern asshole [Senator Ervin] to pull that old crap on me. He pretends he's gentle and he's trying to work things out—bullshit. . . .

HAIG: They . . . let that Goddamned Dean have his day and he looked like a slick merchant, a dishonest guy, let them have their unobjective (unintelligible) Goddamned orgies up there. Put a quiet, gentle older man like Mitchell on there and Goddamnit, he just ripped them apart. From this point onward, we're going uphill. There isn't a question about it.

PRESIDENT NIXON: Oh, there's other problems. Haldeman's gonna have a rough day, a rough day and Colson's probably gonna have the roughest. But I made one note to myself last night—you have talk to Colson or have Buzhardt talk to him and tell him he's gonna be the last witness, above everything else he must do nothing to screw the others. *Nothing, nothing, nothing.* . . . Goddamn him, he mustn't say, "Well, I thought Mitchell was involved," or "I think there was a veil around the White House." You knows what I mean. Very important, Al, very important to do this.

HAIG: We're gonna come out of this Committee in good shape.

PRESIDENT NIXON: As Connally says, in the fall we'll attack the Committee, you know, we'll do it. If I thought the President ought to—I mean, this whole idea that I should sit here like a little chump and take this carload of shit—I'm not gonna do it. Not personally and not for this office. . . . [The President is discussing his September 15, 1972 meeting with Dean.] . . . I have a little secret for you. . . . I'm so curious about what really was said. I oughtta check in my own way [the tape, undoubtedly]. . . . I never questioned it and Haldeman did not question it. Did not start off, "Hi, John, Bob tells me you've been doing a great job." The conversation began thus. "John, I understand you've had a lot of hard work over the last two weeks. Had a lot of work over the last two weeks." That's the way it started. . . . [S]ee, all these little lies. Haldeman will kill him on that.

HAIG: By the time Haldeman gets to him, he'll be nervous. He got—I think Mitchell just destroyed him. He heard—we know what [Richard] Moore is gonna do to him. . . .

PRESIDENT NIXON: What's Moore doing?

HAIG: —on the, the March 21st. My God, Moore is the one who told him—

PRESIDENT NIXON: Come see the President.

HAIG: —"My God, you've got to see the President."

PRESIDENT NIXON: . . . I asked him [Dean], I said, "Now, John, is anybody in the White House involved?" He said there's not a scintilla of evidence involving anybody in the White House." And sitting right in that chair, Goddamn him, on the 21st he didn't say anything about it. He says "Ehrlichman's got a problem," I said "What the hell," I said and he said, "That's because of the break-in. Haldeman's got a problem because of the 350,000 dollars." That's all. Nothing new about that. Mitchell *might* be involved. Never mentioned that Dean was involved.

HAIG: No, but you see, the difference between Mitchell and that little shit is—

PRESIDENT NIXON: —their tone. . . .

JULY 12, 1973: THE PRESIDENT AND HAIG, 3:26–4:00 P.M., OVAL OFFICE

Nixon and Haig discuss the proposed meeting with Ervin, which Nixon intends as a snub to Baker and the other Republicans on the Committee. The President is enraged by his lack of support, lashing out at all the Republican members. Haig is frustrated by an inability to negotiate an end to the affair. "It's just like Vietnam," he says, "a strange place." Finally, on this the last day of tape recordings, Nixon and Haig discuss taping the meeting with Senator Ervin.

SEGMENT 1

HAIG: . . . Ervin has . . . read his letter to you on television.

PRESIDENT NIXON: Sure.

HAIG: He's stated that he had a conversation with you on the phone, that you had agreed, had agreed to meet with the chairman privately.

PRESIDENT NIXON: Mm-hmm.

HAIG: It seems as though other important business, uh, you could work on was taken care of. And as I came in the door he was then reading the unanimous resolution of the Committee that they were entitled, uh, to documents—

PRESIDENT NIXON: All documents?

HAIG: —of the White House.

PRESIDENT NIXON: Even [Senator] Gurney? . . .

HAIG: Gurney called Mel Laird. And he said that this morning, he and [Senator Daniel] Inouye are trying to prevent a subpoena action. And he said, "Why don't we talk to the President before we do this?" And he said, "I've got no one here I can talk to, uh, Dan Inouye is trying to be helpful, couldn't I come down, come over and have a drink with you and Bryce Harlow and bring Inouye?"

PRESIDENT NIXON: No problem. . . . I don't know if there's a problem.

HAIG: Now Len [Garment], oddly enough, is against this. He said . . . this will be interpreted as a negotiating effort. . . .

PRESIDENT NIXON: He's right, he's right, he's right.

HAIG: And I think he's right. Even though Bryce [Harlow], Mel [Laird], Buzhardt are of the other view. . . . Inouye and Gurney are trying to make this call; we can't just turn them off. I think we, we should find another way, so that it doesn't look like Bryce and Mel are negotiating a compromise—

PRESIDENT NIXON: The trouble is you can't get Mel in it at all and, uh—

HAIG: It'll only come out one way and that's—

PRESIDENT NIXON: They can't negotiate. I mean, these people are trying to—

HAIG: It's just like Vietnam, a strange place—

PRESIDENT NIXON: Does Bryce know, realize how hard I feel about this thing?

HAIG: Well, I've told him that you felt very hard about it and I'd like to go back and tell him that there'll be no Goddamned meeting and we wanna tell Gurney that we're with him, and God bless him, he's the only friend we've had up there.

PRESIDENT NIXON: But that I—that, in view of my conversation with Ervin, I think it would be in derogation of Ervin for us to do it, put it that way.

HAIG: Right.

PRESIDENT NIXON: And that I want to talk to Ervin alone. . . .

SEGMENT 2

PRESIDENT NIXON: . . . I said I would talk to him alone. . . . Otherwise, we'll get that simpering asshole [Senator Howard] Baker down here wanting to talk to [William] Timmons. I'm not gonna let him come in. What have you told these guys about what I'd said about Baker? Did you give them the rundown to Congress?

HAIG: Yes, I did, and the way they played it here on television, Ervin, when he was talking about the letter, he said [*mimicking Ervin's southern drawl*], "My great friend, the vice-chair, dictated most of this letter, to his credit. He is the reliable man who's looking for a compromise." Just a sonofabitch.

PRESIDENT NIXON: He's compromised us right into the trouble. And he ain't gonna come down to see me. Baker will not be in this office again—do you understand that?

HAIG: Yes sir.

PRESIDENT NIXON: Weicker will not be in this office again.

HAIG: Why don't we put it into the press and say that you had a discussion, you received a letter, you had a discussion. Uh, you had agreed that there be a meeting sometime next week with you and the Chairman, privately—

PRESIDENT NIXON: That's right.

HAIG: —and uh, that there is no change in your position outlined in your letter to the Committee.

PRESIDENT NIXON: Good.

HAIG: And that's exactly the way we should handle this. . . .

PRESIDENT NIXON: In all this crap, I was saying, "Well, now Sam, maybe you can work this out"—bullshit, there ain't nothing to work out. He put this out in the press.

HAIG: It's quite—and then he said "private eyes only letter to the President, which I read"—everybody laughed. The sonofabitch.

PRESIDENT NIXON: Well, I told him, I said, "Christ, why in the heck leaks all over the place? We don't want this." . . . You see, what I could come up is a—now, Buzhardt now makes a big study as to what, if anything, we can give the sonofabitch. But I mean, you know, now we allowed these clowns to go and make notes, right? But I'm not gonna allow them to go in and make copies. Do you agree?

HAIG: Totally. . . .

PRESIDENT NIXON: Let me say that as far as the presidency is concerned, I am so disgusted with Cox in the press that I'm about to let him go next, next week anyway. I don't know if it's right or if it's wrong, but believe me here, we're fighting a desperate battle against a bunch of damn partisans and, and Elliot will come back in his flabby face and so forth, da, da, da, da, da. . . .

But, by God, Buzhardt or somebody . . . gotta get off their ass and get up to chapter and verse on what Cox and his colleagues have said, which indicate, you know, "We're out to get the President" and all that stuff. Gotta do that. Also, how they leak. How many leaks they had. Look—Goddamnit, if I had the time now I could do this. Do these fellows think of this sort of thing? . . .

SEGMENT 3

PRESIDENT NIXON: . . . Well, the best putdown for Baker, and our Republicans who lost the ball on this. I said see Ervin alone—that's a helluva put down for them.

HAIG: It is.

PRESIDENT NIXON: . . . Gurney's got a problem because of the way he questioned Dean. So the hell with him. He's not coming in. . . . Goldwater has no brains at all in terms of this—Goddamnit, I can't, I can't—Look, Al, if you have any doc—papers issued, let me know. I don't think we have selective release without releasing everything. . . . Buzhardt's feeling is that we may have to turn over papers to Cox.

HAIG: Well, he thinks that, uh, we may have to, we may *want* to in order to not precipitate any constitutional issue. . . .

PRESIDENT NIXON: Maybe by that time we, uh, fire him. . . .

HAIG: That's a good issue to fire him on. But I don't think it's a good issue to try to buy off the Committee on. We're not buying those bastards off; they're television hounds, that's what they are. . . .

PRESIDENT NIXON: The main impression, though, I nailed him [Senator Ervin] hard on that. I said, "You're not gonna cross me, the President?" "No, that's not the issue." "They're talking only about papers." "All right, fine. If we can, we'll talk. . . ."

HAIG: . . . So, you defused that, and we're now in a position where we can fight and you're not being charged with being unreasonable. They may charge you with being principled—that's fine.

PRESIDENT NIXON: What I will do when I meet with him, of course, is to record the conversation. I think this will make it clear, for what it's worth. This phone is [tapped], I don't know whether that one over there is, no, I'm sure it is.

HAIG: I'm sure both of them; I assumed it was.

PRESIDENT NIXON: Nice little conversation. Historical, isn't it?

HAIG: Yes, sir.

PRESIDENT NIXON: What I'll do is to meet with him and record it. Think I should tell him to—no. In advance, that I'll record it, no. Would you? I'll just do it. . . .

HAIG: If you told him that, I don't think you'd have any meeting at all. . . .

JULY 12, 1973: THE PRESIDENT AND WILLIAM TIMMONS, 4:01–4:22 P.M., OVAL OFFICE

Here and in the next conversation. with Rose Mary Woods, Nixon is furious with Senator Baker. The President thinks that Baker was easy on Dean, not appreciat-

ing that Baker's pointed question about what Nixon knew or when he knew it really was designed to pit Dean's word against that of the President of the United States, and thus protect Nixon.

SEGMENT 1

PRESIDENT NIXON: . . . Now Howard Baker . . . never be in the White House again—never, never, never.

TIMMONS: I understand.

PRESIDENT NIXON: He will never be on a presidential plane again. I don't care what he does, the softballs he threw up to Dean. But what he did to John Mitchell was unforgivable.

TIMMONS: Yes, sir, I agree.

PRESIDENT NIXON: Unforgivable. And he's now playing that, that game. Now I screwed him today. . . . Ervin . . . said he and Baker he wanted to come, I said, "Oh, no," I said, "I'll see you alone. Baker is not going to be here again." Is that clear?

TIMMONS: Yes, sir.

PRESIDENT NIXON: I think, I think it's despicable conduct and I just don't understand how, out of Tennessee or something. . . . [John Mitchell's] helped all these guys, including Howard Baker—

TIMMONS: That's right.

PRESIDENT NIXON: —he's held their hands, he's appointed their nominees and the rest, and for him to treat him like a common criminal was inexcusable. He's finished. Absolutely totally finished. . . .

TIMMONS: I understand, yes, Mr. President. He's never been one of my favorites, as you know, 'cause I've been identified with a broad [different] faction down there, but it, it's kind of difficult for us out of here to go up and put the squeeze on him—if we get caught at it—

PRESIDENT NIXON: Oh, oh, I realize that. . . . Now, you see, he's turning out to be the television star, all the rest—he's gonna lose. He thinks he's gonna be President. He's finished. . . .

TIMMONS: . . . Gurney's coming out pretty good, uh generally. He's uh, although, he votes with him [Baker] all the time, they come up with unanimous things. They say, but he's the only guy that halfway stood up on that damn Committee. Uh, the rest of them are so damn—and Ervin, for Christ's sake, he's terrible.

[Withdrawn item. Privacy.]

PRESIDENT NIXON: And uh, Howard has no excuse, Howard's smart enough to know better. He also owes a great deal to all of us. I've campaigned for the son-ofabitch time and time again. He's been in here; we've done favors for him. He's not gonna get away with this now. I don't know what you're gonna do, but—What's [Senator William] Brock [R-TN] think? Let him go because he's part of the club?

TIMMONS: Bill [Brock] is uh, madder than hell at him, and Bill says that his Tennessee mail is running strongly against the Committee and so I've asked him to stimulate some more and to try to lean on Howard a little bit because of the Tennessee reaction that Bill's getting. He said he would. Now I can go talk to Howard; I know him well, if you think—

PRESIDENT NIXON: No.

TIMMONS: —want me to lay it out to him.

PRESIDENT NIXON: Never, never. No, never. No, I don't want anybody in the White House to ever have any contact with him again. Ever. And another thing is this: cut him off. Give him a deep freeze. . . . We've got to get the campaign stuff of McGovern. But Baker—what's he doing. He thinks this is the way to be president. He loves the adulation of the Georgetown set.

TIMMONS: He's got the stars in his eyes, all that camera and he's been floating stories, backgrounders, you know, on, uh his own career and the Dirksen tie-in and all that stuff. And uh, he's trying to—

PRESIDENT NIXON: . . . [H]e is totally finished. . . .

JULY 12, 1973: THE PRESIDENT AND ROSE MARY WOODS, 4:30–4:36 P.M., OVAL OFFICE

PRESIDENT NIXON: Howard Baker, Rose, I have no hatred at this time, I have no hatred here. . . . But I remember loyalty. Howard Baker will never be in the White House again, as long as I am in this office. Never, never, never—I won't say that about Inouye, I won't say that even about Montoya, and I didn't say it about Weicker, I didn't—

WOODS: Weicker, you don't wanna see him—

PRESIDENT NIXON: Weicker . . . was mean to Mitchell. . . . Ervin phoned today, though I didn't expect him to call. I said, "Look, everything leaks from your Committee, Senator, I'm sorry." . . . [He] said "Senator Baker and I would like to come out and talk to you about it." I say, "No, Senator, I won't do that." I said, "I'll see you alone." So I put Baker down that way too.

WOODS: Yeah.

PRESIDENT NIXON: Baker will never be in this office again. He'll never be in the White House again. I mean it, Rose.

WOODS: I, I agree with that, too.

PRESIDENT NIXON: His name will not be on the Christmas list; there will never, never ever be Baker in the White House as long as I'm here. . . .

JULY 12, 1973: THE PRESIDENT AND KISSINGER, 4:48-5:09 P.M., OVAL OFFICE

Nixon reports on his conversation with Ervin, boasting to Kissinger on his toughness during the telephone call. At the close, Kissinger lashes out with his frustrations on the war, referring back to the Pentagon Papers—unknowingly bringing the tapes full circle. In this poignant close to the tapes, Nixon tells Kissinger not to worry, and employs his life's metaphor—fight.

SEGMENT 1

PRESIDENT NIXON: [T]he hell with them. I'll sit on those papers, if I have to burn them, I'll burn every Goddamned paper in this house. You realize that? Every paper in this house before I hand them over to that Committee. . . .

SEGMENT 2

PRESIDENT NIXON: . . . I spoke to Ervin today. I said, uh, "What's your goal, Senator? Who you out to get?"

KISSINGER: Did you talk to him?

PRESIDENT NIXON: Hell, yes. No, because I had to, because he had written a letter demanding documents and said I'd like to call you about it. And I knew I would've been, I wanted to put off so that I didn't see him. Why, it was a hairy conversation. Al sat there next to me. . . .

[Withdrawn item. Privacy.]

KISSINGER: Good, you always do it in a very pleasant manner. You do it tough. . . .

PRESIDENT NIXON: I was not this too damn pleasant with him, though. . . . [H]e wondered about the documents, . . . and I said, "Why don't you tell us what you want." He said, "Look, we want any activities that have to do with Watergate." . . . He said, "Well, we'd have our counsel come down and go through the documents." I said, "No, Senator, that is not happening." I said, "Everything from your Committee leaks and you know it." . . . [H]e wanted himself and the members of his staff to come down and have a talk with me about it, this document thing. I said, "Senator, no, I won't do that." I was really tough. . . . [A]s for Senator Baker, if he could come, I said, "No," I said, "Baker is no constitutional lawyer." I said, "I'll see you alone if you wanna come, but I can't do it this week," I said, "I'm busy with economic matters. Gotta work on that." . . . [W]e were talking about Haldeman and Ehrlichman, yeah, and I said, "When are you gonna hear them?" He says "Next week." . . . And he was sitting there, of course, the old ass and of course, I was right. Oh, boy, he got it too, though. . . . I was decent but I was very tough.

KISSINGER: I think the press has had it, and they know it. I think they have had it.

PRESIDENT NIXON: . . . As far as I'm concerned, so we'll have a Constitutional crisis. If we do, it'll be a Goddamn ding-dong battle and we might, if we lose, I'll burn the papers. 'Cause I got them. That's the point, 'cause I would never turn these papers over to a court. Never give them over to the Committee, you know that. . . . I said, oh no, your counsel isn't gonna paw through my papers. I just used that word. He got the message.

No, after the way Baker . . . [was] too soft, first, he threw softballs to Dean and then manhandled Mitchell. Howard Baker's just never gonna be in the White House again.

KISSINGER: That's bad, he threw softballs. . . . But actually, it's working out pretty well. Mitchell came across as a mature, tough guy.

PRESIDENT NIXON: Really?

KISSINGER: Yes, I admit I didn't see much of him, but what I saw, he impressed me. And compared to these selfish little bastards like Magruder and Dean, at least you could see why Mitchell was in a top job. . . . It is irrelevant what you do. . . . I, of course, believe what you say, but it's irrelevant. Ninety percent of this stuff they are talking about goes on all the time. We just—in this place it was shot in a stupid bureaucratic—

PRESIDENT NIXON: . . . I mean, I cut off two arms [Haldeman and Ehrlichman]. Who the hell else would've done such a thing—who ever has done that before? I cut off two arms and then they went after the body.

KISSINGER: Then you consider the meritorious things you have done for the country, the treasonable actions that these people condoned—

PRESIDENT NIXON: They are treason.

KISSINGER: Well, taking 10,000 government documents in the middle of the war [Pentagon Papers], attacking the military, attack, having riots, attacking, I mean, on January 3rd, knowing I was going over for negotiations and [Senator Mike] Mansfield passed [legislation], that cut off funds [for] the war. *That is immoral.* . . .

PRESIDENT NIXON: Well, don't you worry.

KISSINGER: Oh, I don't worry.

PRESIDENT NIXON: Keep, keep fighting.

EPILOGUE

THE FINAL YEAR:
THE FALL OF THE
PRESIDENT

JULY 1973 – AUGUST 1974

The last taped conversations apparently occurred on Thursday, July 12, 1973. That night, President Nixon was rushed to Bethesda Naval Hospital and diagnosed with viral pneumonia. The next seventy-two hours were momentous for his presidency.

On Friday, Senate Select Committee staff investigators interviewed Alexander Butterfield, a former White House aide. Butterfield's task was to ensure "the smooth running of the President's day." Ushering visitors in and out of the Oval Office, providing talking papers for the President, and often overseeing White House operations during Haldeman's absence, Butterfield was one of the few aware of the taping system. In the early stages of the investigation, Assistant U.S. Attorney Earl Silbert occasionally requested "electronically gathered" data in his subpoenas. But after John Dean suggested in his testimony that his conversations might have been taped, Senate investigators routinely queried White House personnel about a taping system.

Butterfield, believing he was corroborating what Haldeman already had told the Committee, and naturally fearful of perjuring himself, acknowledged that "there is tape in the Oval Office." Butterfield had overseen the installation of the system, located in various White House rooms, telephones, and Camp David. "*Everything* was taped . . . as long as the President was in attendance. There was not so much as a hint that something should *not be taped*," he told the Committee staff.

J. Fred Buzhardt confirmed the existence of the system on July 16. He promptly invoked that most familiar Nixon defense: everybody did it. But the Secret Service noted that the Nixon Administration was unique in using a voice-activated system. On July 23, the President rejected requests for copies of the tapes from both the Senate Select Committee and the Special Prosecutor, and the next day, Assistant Press Secretary Gerald Warren announced that the taping had been discontinued. Meanwhile, the President left the hospital on July 20, returned to a warm reception at the White House, and said that plans for his resignation "are just plain poppycock." "Let others wallow in Watergate," he added, "we are going to do our job."

Three months earlier, Nixon had warned Haldeman that the tapes had to be kept secret. "Have we got people that are trustworthy on that?" Nixon asked. "I guess we have," as he answered his own question. With the tapes now public knowledge, Howard Baker's famous question to John Dean took on a new thrust. For now, the President himself could reveal what he knew and when he knew it.

For the next thirteen months, the story of Watergate is a struggle for control of the President's tapes, one that both focused on and heightened the furious political struggle between Nixon and his adversaries. The President consistently asserted constitutional principles in his defense; his opponents, however, insisted that the Constitution could not protect criminal behavior. Special Prosecutor Archibald Cox launched an effort in the courts to gain access, one that resulted in the Saturday Night Massacre in October and his dismissal, along with resignations by Attorney General Elliot Richardson and his deputy, William Ruckelshaus. That event heightened Republican skepticism toward the President, convincing many that indeed he had something to hide. The ensuing "firestorm," as Alexander Haig described it, prevented Nixon from achieving his avowed goal of abolishing the Special Prosecutor's office. Instead, he was forced to name a new prosecutor, this time choosing Leon Jaworski. A former president of the American Bar Association, Jaworski was a conservative Texan and headed the Texas Democrats for Nixon movement in 1972. With those credentials, Jaworski proved a much more formidable political force than Cox. After a month on the job, Jaworski visited Haig and suggested that the President should hire a criminal lawyer.

Later in October, the President's attorneys went to court and agreed to surrender the tapes to Judge Sirica. Dramatically and firmly, Nixon's lawyer, Charles Alan Wright, said "this President does not defy the law." On October 10, Vice President Spiro Agnew resigned and made a *nolo contendere* plea to income tax evasion. Within a month, Nixon reluctantly chose Gerald Ford as his Vice President. If Agnew had been Nixon's insurance policy against impeachment, Ford now gave the nation's political leaders a viable alternative to the President. October competed with April for Nixon's cruelest month.

The new year began what the President called "the campaign of my life." He vowed not to resign; instead, he would "fight"—"to use the full power of the President to fight overwhelming forces arrayed against us." Resignation, he knew, "admits guilt." But the President was in full retreat. The first tapes appeared in April 1974, and the reaction was devastating, as diverse forces around the nation denounced the low level of White House conversations or, like Billy Graham, expressed dismay at the dominance of "situational ethics." In July, two devastating blows fell upon the President. On July 24, the Supreme Court ruled in *U.S. v. Nixon* that "executive privilege" was no protection for the subpoenaed tapes. That night, the House Impeachment Inquiry, launched in October following Cox's dismissal, assembled for a nationally televised debate that resulted in three articles of impeachment against the President on July 26.

On August 6, following the Supreme Court's directive, the White House released new tapes, including the famous "smoking gun" conversations of June 23, 1972, that described Nixon's and Haldeman's plans to use the CIA to thwart the FBI investigation. That tape had worried Nixon "ceaselessly"; by his own admission, it could not be "excerpted properly." The revelation stunned Nixon's remaining supporters. Charles Wiggins, his chief defender on the House Judiciary Committee, sadly announced that "the magnificent public career of Richard Nixon must be terminated involuntarily." Conservative columnist James Kilpatrick lamented, "My President is a liar. I wish he were a crook instead."

Nixon's last word to Kissinger on these tapes—fight—sums up his political career and, above all, his desperate battle to retain his office. In his final address to the nation, he said he was not a quitter. But for more than a year, Richard Nixon had envisioned the inevitable. Still, he fought, with diminishing congressional and public support, with his resources spent and exhausted and his emotions frayed and worn, until he had to choose the option he had derided with scorn and ridicule for two years: he resigned.

ACKNOWLEDGMENTS

In 1974, Congress mandated the release of Watergate-related tapes "at the earliest possible" time. The National Archives began processing the material in 1977. When the tapes were ready for release in 1987, the leadership of the Archives chose to cooperate with Richard Nixon's continual efforts to prevent their release. After five years of such tactics, Public Citizen and I filed suit against the Archives, and Richard Nixon joined the case as Intervenor. At first, the Archives insisted that all Watergate-related materials had been released (mainly the tapes used in the criminal trials), but I proved the existence of several hundred more hours of conversations regarding the Watergate affair. The Archives finally acknowledged the existence of 201 additional hours. Following Nixon's death, we negotiated a mediated settlement, announced in April 1996, providing a firm schedule of release for approximately 3,700 hours of Nixon tapes. The first materials, required under law, are the Abuse of Power segments included in this volume.

My lawyers, Alan Morrison and Patti Goldman of Public Citizen, made the release of the tapes possible. They recognized the bedrock truth: the National Archives was not in compliance with the law, and their successful litigation has greatly enhanced the historical record. We all are in their debt.

Historians and the American people also owe a huge debt to the archivists who toiled for ten years preparing the tapes for public use. Current Archives and Nixon Project staff extended numerous courtesies to me during my work. I am particularly indebted to Karl Weissenbach, as well as Pat Andersen, Calvin Jefferson, Richard McNeil, and Miriam Nesbit.

Alderson Reporting, of Washington, led by its happy band of Garrett Williams, Jessica Ledet, and Brooke Marcus, and an excellent group of transcribers, provided a basic, rough draft of the conversations. President Stephen Joel Trachtenberg and Professor Edward Berkowitz of George Washington University kindly provided housing for me during my extended stays in Washington when I listened to the tapes. The late Willard Hurst, Stanley N. Katz, Thomas McCormick, and Richard Sewell offered sound advice and encouragement, as always. Elias P. Demetracopoulos has never wavered in his steadfast support of my work. Bruce Nichols and his staff at the Free Press have generously given their help and enthusiasm to the project. John W. Wright, dear friend, who doubles as my agent, pushed this project from the start, and he is a true virtuoso of the carrot and the stick. At the end, he had to practice daily acts of psychology. Finally, Adam Land was indispensable. He shared the burden (and some of the pleasure) of listening to the tapes with me. He also provided an invaluable reading of the manuscript, insisting on clarity, coverage and, above all, fairness.

Sandy, as always, has coped with her management problem with skill and love, ably reinforced by Jeff, Nikki, David, Susan, Andy, and now Jay. Alex and Kates have my love and gratitude for sharing ComPeter time.

Stanley I. Kutler
August 10, 1997

INDEX